Understanding Mass Media

Fifth Edition

Understanding Mass Media

Fifth Edition

William Jawitz

National Textbook Company
a division of *NTC Publishing Group* • Lincolnwood, Illinois USA

Cover Design: Design Associates, Paul C. Uhl
Cover Illustration: Wendy Grossman
Executive Editor: John T. Nolan
Project Manager: Sue Schumer
Interior design: Ophelia M. Chambliss
Production Manager: Rosemary Dolinski

Published by National Textbook Company, a division of NTC Publishing Group
© 1996, 1991, 1986, 1981, 1975 by NTC Publishing Group,
4255 West Touhy Avenue,
Lincolnwood (Chicago), Illinois 60646-1975 U.S.A.
Library of Congress Catalog Card Number: 94-68800
Manufactured in the United States of America.

5 6 7 8 9 0 QB 9 8 7 6 5 4 3 2 1

CONTENTS

FOREWORD

Some forty years ago at Wayne State University, I began teaching a new course on the topic of mass media with the help of a colleague at the University of Toronto, the visionary Marshall McLuhan. In his groundbreaking book *Understanding Media: The Extensions of Man*, McLuhan argued that "the medium is the message." He also claimed that mass media were creating a "global village."

Today, the world lives surrounded by a Niagara Falls of sight, sound, and motion. Thanks to satellites, 70 percent of the world's population—three and one-half billion people—saw all or part of the 1992 Summer Olympic Games. With the advent of the Internet, fiber optics, and a host of new communications technologies, global interactivity is just around the corner. McLuhan was right.

And because he was right, we need to respond critically to the fury of mass-mediated images and sounds that crash around us daily. This textbook, and the media literacy it fosters, provides a much needed resource in the struggle to help us truly understand the ever-growing power of mass media.

—Lee Sherman Dreyfus

Lee Sherman Dreyfus has taught at the University of Wisconsin, Madison, and was Chancellor at the University of Wisconsin, Stevens Point. He is also a former governor of Wisconsin. Dr. Dreyfus is a member of the National Advisory Board of the National Telemedia Council in Madison.

PREFACE

As you read these words, you are probably sitting at home or in a classroom wondering what this course you have just started will be like. Will you relate to it? Will it be interesting? Will you learn anything useful?

These are fair questions. No doubt you are expecting me, as the author of *Understanding Mass Media,* to answer them "Yes, yes, yes." You are also probably wondering what the subject of mass media is all about and whether it is worth studying. You may already know that the term *media* refers to different systems of communication; the term *medium* refers to a single system. The term *mass media* refers to those communication systems that carry information to huge audiences. These systems—these mass media—have become almost as important in our world as the air we breathe. Just as we take air for granted, we often take our dependence on mass media for granted.

Before you begin your media studies course, before you read Part One of this textbook, take the time to assess how big a role media play in your life. Consider all that time and money you devote to media. If you're anything like "the average American," *you spend more time using communications media than you spend doing anything else during your waking hours!* Whether you are in school, at work, or enjoying leisure time, you are constantly using some kind of communications medium and spending considerable amounts of money in the process.

To what degree do your values reflect the values portrayed on prime-time TV shows or in your favorite magazines? How do the thousands of advertisements or commercials you see and hear every month influence you? How do your listening and viewing habits influence what radio stations play and what films get made? Who profits when you use these media, and how much money is at stake? When you can answer these kinds of questions, you are on your way to becoming **media literate.**

It used to be enough to be literate in the traditional sense (to be able to read and write the printed word). However, as our rapidly changing *information society* relies more and more on sophisticated mass media, being media literate becomes increasingly important. When you are media literate, you don't just passively consume the mass media; you understand how and why they're directed at you, you analyze their impact, and you use media to create your own communication.

Features of This Book and How to Use Them

Throughout this new edition of *Understanding Mass Media,* you will find a variety of information, readings from a wide array of publications, illustrations of media products, information on future trends, profiles of professionals in media industries, and "Student Close-Ups," sketches of students like you who have produced their own media communications. In addition, each chapter offers you the following features:

- **Learning Targets** and **Checking In.** Scan these lists for a preview of the information and skills you will focus on in the chapter. "Checking In" will ask you to think about what you already know and your experiences with media.
- **Media Labs.** Use these activities and project ideas as a class or as an individual to critically think, write, and talk about issues and media products covered in the chapter. You will apply what you learn to your real life.
- **Reflections.** Keep a notebook or journal and build a portfolio of your ideas and thoughts—your responses to the media messages, issues, ideas, and questions raised in the chapter.
- **Practice.** Use this exercise with each reading to apply new skills and techniques. Analyze the media product and what the message of the particular article is in terms of the media literacy framework, the paradigm introduced in Chapter Three.
- **Career Bank.** Research one or more of the careers listed in the chapter by reading about a specific media industry career, interviewing a local professional, or "trying out" that career as a project in school, at home, or in your community.

- **Building a Media Archive.** Collect and analyze one sample of the mass medium discussed in the chapter, applying your new knowledge and skills.
- **Create Your Own Media.** Produce your own media communication for the chapter—a magazine or newspaper article, a recording, a videotape, an advertisement, and so on.
- **Recap.** Review the major highlights of the chapter using this summary.
- **Resources for Further Reading.** Refer to this list for books, periodicals, audiovisual materials, and suggested topics for further exploration of the mass medium or subject in the chapter.
- **Segue.** Prepare for the next chapter by reading the *segue* (pronounced "seg-way"), a feature that concludes each chapter and makes connections between the territory you just explored and the territory you will explore next. *Segue* means transition.

As you begin your course using *Understanding Mass Media*, I hope you will find this textbook interesting and informative about the communications environment that engulfs all of us. I believe this book will challenge you to think deeply and creatively and to view media and your information environment differently for the rest of your life.

ACKNOWLEDGMENTS

I have many people to thank for helping with this book, but first thanks go to my students at Manchester High School, Connecticut, who helped develop many of the ideas and activities found in these pages. I am continually inspired by their curiosity and encouragement. I am indebted to the many committed educators and organizations who are blazing the trail in media literacy. Grateful acknowledgment is extended to Jeffrey Schrank, the author of the first four editions of this book. I am especially grateful to these important teachers in my life: LeRoy Hay, John Gourlie, David Greenfield, my parents, David and Elaine Jawitz, and finally my wife, Lia, and my daughter, Laura.

Special thanks go to the following educators who reviewed material or provided support for writing this new edition: Julia Robinson, Media Specialist, Indianapolis Schools, Indiana; John D'Anieri, Sheboygan Falls High School, Wisconsin; Chuck Lewis, Jim Spafford, Rich Gagliardi, and Jenn Therian, Manchester High School, Manchester, Connecticut; Marieli Rowe and Laura Bucuzzo, National Telemedia Council, Madison, Wisconsin; Gary Clites, Northern High School, Maryland; Lori Schlabach, Franklin Central High School, Indiana; Tim Comolli, South Burlington High School, Vermont; Betsy Fair, Larkin High School, Elgin, Illinois; and Steve Goodman and Zoya Kocur, Educational Video Center, New York City.

The following industry folks were most generous with their time and support: Colleen Doran, Roger Fidler, Knight-Ridder, Inc., Colorado; Steve Nelson, Brilliant Media, San Francisco; Jeff Greenwald, Oakland, California; John Long and Scott Johnson, *The Hartford Courant*, Connecticut; Sarah Baisley, Twentieth-Century Fox; Jay Nilson; Mick Duffek and Scott Nierendorf, Round Trip Productions.

Finally, I would like to thank the following students and former students from around the nation who are featured in the "Student Close-Up" readings: Dawn Wilson, Miguel Castillo, Jason Hawkins, David Eastwood, James Martin, Brooke Willmes, Amanda Johnson, Antoinette Bennett, Mark Brodie, and Clark Baker. I appreciate their contributions to this book and their commitment to media literacy.

William Jawitz

The Nature of Communication

COM·MU·NI·CATE

To make known, to display, to spread to others,
to have an interchange, to express an experience,
to be connected.

Adapted from *The American Heritage Dictionary, Second College Edition*

You probably have a general idea of what the term *communication* means. You can picture yourself talking with a friend on the phone, taking notes in class, or silently gesturing to a friend to meet after class. These are clear examples of communication. How conscious are you of the rest of the communicating you do in your waking hours? Are you aware of how your body language changes depending on the situation you are in? Do you realize that people read your body language loud and clear (even though they may not be conscious of doing so)? Have you ever really examined all the things that are happening—both on-screen and inside your head—when you watch a television special such as the *MTV Music Awards*?

Whether you are engaged in **interpersonal communication** (where you experience direct, back-and-forth communication with someone) or **mass communication** (where you receive communication from a **mass medium** such as radio), you are engaged in a distinctly human activity.

Anthropologists, scientists who study the human race, believe that one of the most important differences between humans and other animals is humans' highly developed ability to communicate. Though other species do transmit simple messages, only human beings share with each other the mind-boggling range of life's experiences in a thousand different ways. We constantly send messages back and forth to our fellow humans. We seem to *need* to communicate with each other.

Here are the "Five Ws and an H" of human communication:

Who communicates? Everyone.
What do we communicate about? Every kind of idea, experience, and emotion.
Where do we communicate? Wherever we are.
When do we communicate? Almost the entire time we are awake.
Why do we communicate? For reasons ranging from the practical to the spiritual.
How do we communicate? By creating and using symbols and by harnessing technology.

For most of human history, interpersonal communication—"live and in person"—was the name of the game; you could communicate only with someone who was close enough to hear you or see you. It was not that long ago that we harnessed technology to create the mass media which transport our messages for us—much faster and farther than we could transport them ourselves. Yet we're still only at the beginning of the digital revolution, which many believe will truly bring about a "global village."

Part One of *Understanding Mass Media* focuses on two aspects of the nature of communication: communication behavior and the explosion of communications technologies.

CHAPTER ONE

The Communication Process

Learning Targets

After working through the introduction to Part One and this chapter, you will be able to

- Explain key terms used to describe the communication process;
- Describe the main elements of your communication behavior;
- Use the Shannon-Weaver model to analyze specific acts of communication; and
- Identify different kinds of symbols as they relate to the communication process.

Checking In

- List the many different ways that you communicate with other people.
- Depict what it would be like to spend a week of your life without one of these abilities: speaking, seeing, or hearing.
- Observe a brief act of communication between two people (for example, two students walking into a room together) and record every single detail you notice.
- Explain in your own words what a symbol is.

Your Communication Environment

Along with every human being on earth, you live in a sea of information. The individual drops of information that make up the water in this sea surround you moment by moment, just as water completely surrounds each fish living in a real sea. Like the fish that swims around in its sea, you swim around in yours by communicating. You continually receive information contained in the sounds, images, smells, tastes, and physical sensations of your everyday life—the quick, encouraging smile of a coach, the aroma coming from a pizzeria, the click of drumsticks counting the beat to start a song at a concert.

You also transmit your own information for others to receive— that slight change of posture when you walk past someone you're attracted to, the high-five you offer to a friend, the sarcastic tone of voice you use with a little brother or sister. All of this receiving and transmitting makes up your sea of information, or your **communication environment**.

A philosophical question involving fish fits here: Is a fish aware of the water that surrounds it? What do you think? Maybe when it is caught and is flopping around on the deck of a boat it senses that something is strangely different. Obviously, no one can get inside the consciousness of a fish, but the question prompts us to think about just how conscious we are (or aren't) of the communication environment that surrounds us.

Indeed, people who have recovered from brain injuries often mention the incredible frustration of not being able to communicate effortlessly the way they did before. Often they cannot come up with the names of their loved ones even through they recognize their faces. Their injuries cause them to become intensely conscious of their communication environment.

It is very difficult to become conscious of your own communication environment unless you focus on it. One way to focus on it is to specifically change or limit your **communication behavior** in a given situation.

Your Communication Behavior

Imagine going through a full school day in total silence—no verbal response when your friends talk to you in the hall or when a teacher calls on you in class. How about spending an entire day at school with headphones on so you cannot hear anything anyone says? In the first case you might annoy a lot of people and get in trouble (if they didn't know about your experiment), but at least you would be able to hear what other people were saying. In the second case you'd get in trouble too, but you would also miss a lot of what was going on around you, because much of your communication environment is made up of sound. When you make sounds for others to hear or hear the sounds around you, you are communicating **acoustically**.

Now imagine being without your sight for a certain portion of each day—say, from 2:00 to 6:00 P.M. How would your life change for those four hours? How would you get home or get to work? How would you catch your friend in the hallway on your way to the student parking lot? (She would have to look for you, because *she's* driving.) What would you *not* be able to do until 6:00 that you otherwise would if you were able to see? When you do anything for others to see or when you take in information with your eyes, you are communicating **visually**.

 # Reflections

Describe what you would miss most if you were not able to see, and then describe what you would miss most if you were not able to hear.

The point is that minute by minute, every time you receive information with your eyes and ears or do or say anything that someone else sees or hears, you engage in communication behavior. *Through your visual and acoustic communication behavior, you experience your communication environment.* Though you also communicate through your other senses—tasting, touching, and smelling—these senses are used much less frequently throughout the day, even less when you use communications media.

A Life of Communicating

From the very moment we are born, we participate in our communication environment. Let's look at the life of a girl named Rosa. Within a few moments of her birth, Rosa exercises her lungs and begins to cry. Why is she crying? Maybe she's cold; or maybe the light is too bright for her eyes. After she eats and warms up, she either sleeps or just lies there, taking it all in . . . until she gets hungry or gets uncomfortable in any other way. When Rosa is uncomfortable, she communicates that discomfort to everyone very effectively.

Six months later, Rosa is sitting up in her crib giggling at her father's silly faces and stuffing into her mouth any object she can get her hands on. She still cries when she's hungry or her diaper needs changing, but now she follows her father's eyes when he walks around the room playing peek-a-boo, and she experiments with making the sounds that she will soon form into words.

On her first birthday, Rosa uses about a dozen words to communicate with her parents, who marvel over the amazing sound of "mama." Her proud parents ask her to practice her tiny vocabulary every time company comes over. Now that Rosa can walk, she has much more control over what she can see up close. She can't stand being held when she has the urge to explore, so she masters the "I want to get down" squirm. Rosa has definite opinions on meals and baths and begins her lifelong use of the short but powerful word *no*.

Over the next few years, Rosa's vocabulary grows and she begins to express herself by arranging words into short sentences. These sentences grow more complex until she can recognize letters of the alphabet and begin reading. Rosa continues to learn that people use different tones of voice to express different ideas and feelings. She becomes more comfortable interacting with the people in her world.

By first grade, Rosa's communication skills are in high gear. She whispers with a friend so her teacher won't hear her. She listens in on her parents' conversations from the top of the stairs. She draws recognizable pictures of people and dogs and sends them to relatives with the words "I love you" scrawled on the page. Rosa has learned all the basics of acoustic and visual communication behavior, and she is quite comfortable in her communication environment. She's used to speaking, listening, and looking at pictures; the rest of her education will mostly involve reinforcing and developing skills based on her communication behavior. What actually happens when Rosa communicates? What process do we all experience when we communicate?

A Communication Model

Whether the actual communication lasts one second or three hours, it has a basic pattern. First, a **sender** begins the communication. Then the sender decides what **information** she wants to communicate and picks a **medium** to transmit her information.

Sender ☞   Info ☞   Medium ☞   Receiver ☞   Feedback

The **receiver** then gets the information. Finally, the receiver responds with some kind of **feedback** to the sender. This pattern can be shown as a model, known as the *Shannon-Weaver Model*, named after the two engineers who created it in the 1940s.

Let's fill in the model with a simple act of communication between two people: Tahira (the SENDER) is zipping along on her rollerblades when a little boy steps into the street ten feet in front of her. She screams "Move!" (the INFORMATION) with her voice (the MEDIUM). The boy (the RECEIVER) hears her and jumps out of the way (the FEEDBACK).

Here is another familiar act of communication: Victor sits five seats away from Justin in class. Victor silently mouths "Meet me after class" and points his head toward the clock. Justin nods quickly and then returns his attention to the video the class is watching.

Practice

A. Apply the above act of communication to the model by duplicating the blank model on a sheet of paper and filling it in.
B. Describe in writing an act of communication between yourself and another person, then apply that situation to the model.

You Communicate a Thousand Times a Day

You communicate in this way every day, though you're hardly aware of it. Think of the individual acts of communication you take part in every hour! Quick verbal interactions and quick glances, each exchanging acoustic and visual information through your ears and eyes, each following that basic pattern—almost all of it done without your even thinking about it! The "head fake" athletes put on each other is a great example of this lightning-fast, unconscious communication pattern: As the guard is racing to the basket on a fast break, she *sends information* ("I'm cutting left") through the *medium* of body language to the defender, who *receives* it and provides *feedback* by either falling for the fake or not. And all of this happens in a split second!

You only become aware of your communication when something goes wrong with the pattern—when the communication just doesn't go right. There are many reasons for communication problems. Communication can break down anywhere along the way, and when it does, you know it (although you may not know why it breaks down). For example, in the model on page 11, what if Tahira had laryngitis and couldn't yell? She would not have been able to send acoustic information; that is, she would not have been able to begin the act of communication. Or what if Tahira's voice was fine, but the boy had headphones on? He probably would not have received her information because the sound from his headphones would have blocked it out. In both cases, something would have interfered with the communication between Tahira and the boy.

Where Is That Noise Coming from?

Let's look at the situation where the boy is wearing headphones. It is easy to pinpoint the sound—the noise—coming from the boy's headphones as the place where the communication breakdown occurred. And while we usually think of noise only in terms of sound, the term *noise* is also used in a broader sense. In the field of communication, **noise** refers to anything that interferes with the communication between the sender and receiver. Tahira's inability to shout (in terms of analyzing an act of communication) would be considered noise. By adding the concept of noise, we complete the communication model. For Tahira's situation, a completed model might look like the one at the top of page 13.

You are already familiar with this idea of noise. Think about the occasional fuzzy reception on your TV, the hiss on an old cassette tape, the wavy, slanted picture you occasionally have to correct by adjusting the tracking on your VCR, or your friend's

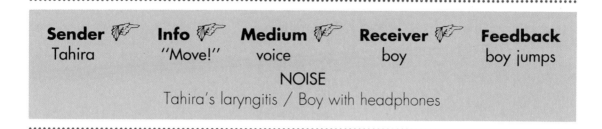

Sender ☞	Info ☞	Medium ☞	Receiver ☞	Feedback
Tahira	"Move!"	voice	boy	boy jumps

NOISE
Tahira's laryngitis / Boy with headphones

illegible handwriting. Now go back to the situation where Victor is trying to get Justin to meet him after class. What are some examples of noise that might interfere with their successful communication?

Practice

A. Describe three examples of noise that could interfere with Victor and Justin's communication.

B. Go back to the situation you described in the first practice example and describe one example of noise that could interfere with your communication.

Symbols: The Raw Material of Communication

So far you have looked at two of the key elements of the communication process. First, you explored the fact that humans are constantly engaged in communication behavior. To use a phrase made famous in Nike ads, we just do it—all the time! You next looked at a model of the communication process which explains how we communicate; we follow a basic pattern when sending and receiving information, and when something goes wrong with the pattern, the communication breaks down. This last section of Chapter One explores the symbol systems we use to do all of this communicating.

Though an explanation of just what a symbol is can get quite complicated, a basic definition is: A **symbol** is something which

MEDIA LAB   Communication Events Log

Keep a communication events log throughout the course in which you observe actual acts of communication (communication events) between people and record them in a log based on the Shannon-Weaver model. For each entry, identify the sender, the information sent, the medium used, the receiver, the feedback provided, and any noise that interfered with the communication. Write a paragraph describing the **context** of the event, clearly indicating the date, time, exact location of the observation, and length of the event. Finally, explain the role you played in the event (neutral observer, indirect participant, and so on).

stands for, or represents, something else; the thing the symbol stands for is called its **referent**.

For example:

Symbol		Referent
The written word "Doberman"	represents	a breed of dog
A photograph of Queen Latifah	represents	the actual person
A recording of a train whistle	represents	an actual train whistle blowing
A painting of a sun	represents	the actual sun setting
The spoken word "Pepsi"	represents	a brand of soft drink

Our Dependence on Symbols

When most people think about symbols, they usually think about well-recognized images and signs, such as religious symbols (the

Cross or the Star of David), or cultural symbols, such as a peace sign or a No Smoking sign. Remember, in the context of communication, a symbol can be anything—including any sound or image—that represents something else. While there are almost an infinite number of individual symbols, any symbol can be placed into a handful of categories. These categories are known as **symbol systems**: written words, spoken words, music, art (such as drawings and cartoons), and photo-realistic pictures.

Understanding the idea of symbols and how we use them is important because so much of our communication depends on them. We couldn't live without using symbols. Think about what you do during one day of your life—what you experience directly. Now think about all of the information in your daily communication environment that you either receive or transmit in that day. You obviously get information about many more things than you actually experience. For example, your best friend may leave a note in your locker telling you that she overslept and missed the bus. You may watch a local morning news story about a severe hailstorm that passed through the next county. You might listen to a cut from your favorite band's newest live recording in your car on the way to school.

Were you present for any of the actual events—the referents—that these three acts of communication expressed? Did you experience them directly? No. But they were *represented* to you using symbols. Your friend used written words to refer to her oversleeping. Spoken words and visual images on the TV referred to what happened during and after the storm. Your car stereo pumped out music which referred to—which represented—what the band originally performed live.

 Practice

  A. Make a list of ten symbols and the referents for which they stand.

  B. Describe five separate acts of communication you engaged in yesterday, as either sender or receiver, which used symbols to refer to an event or idea you did not experience.

Symbols and Your Brain

You're swimming in a sea of symbols and adding to that sea all the time. So what? Well, your mind deals with different kinds of symbols in different ways; that is, your brain actually does different things depending on the symbol it is working with. For example, look at the following three visual symbols:

The Bettmann Archive.

They all represent the same **referent**—the same thing—yet they give you different amounts of information, and, as a result, your brain reacts to each of them a little differently. The first symbol communicates using letters, in other words, written language. You have no difficulty understanding it, but only because you speak English. (What if it were written in Vietnamese, or Arabic? Chances are, you wouldn't understand it.) You also have no difficulty understanding the second symbol because it looks a lot like the thing it represents; you do not need to speak a particular language to understand it. However, it does not give you as much detailed information as the third symbol, which looks even more like its referent.

Now imagine someone saying the word *jet* aloud to you. The spoken word jet is also a symbol of an actual thing we all agree to call a jet. But the same fact applies to the spoken word *jet* as to the written word *jet;* that is, if the word *jet* was spoken to you in Vietnamese or Arabic, you would still not understand.

High-correspondence and Low-correspondence Symbols

Which of the following symbols seems to be closest to an actual jet: the written word *jet,* the spoken word *jet,* the drawing of a jet, or the photograph of a jet? The photo does. You do not have to know how to read a particular language, or even to read at all, to understand it because the photo looks like the thing it represents. Another way to say this is that the photo is a **high-correspondence symbol**—there is a clear correspondence between the symbol (the photo) and the thing it represents, its referent. The word *jet* on the other hand, whether written or spoken, is a **low-correspondence symbol**—there is no clear correspondence between the symbol (the letters J E T, or the sound J E T) and its referent, an actual jet.

All words are low-correspondence symbols. A word only means something if people agree on its meaning. If we all agreed that the word *elevator* was the written and spoken symbol for what we now refer to as a "dress," then we would look forward to seeing all the beautiful elevators at the senior prom and anticipate seeing the captain of the football team all elevatored up in his tuxedo. Fortunately, no matter what language we speak, how old we are, or whether we're literate, when we see a photograph of a dress, we instantly recognize it as a dress.

Think about the amount of information contained in low-correspondence symbols (low-C symbols) versus the amount of information contained in high-correspondence symbols (high-C symbols). With the low-C symbol "dress," you have to supply a lot of your own imagination. What kind of dress do you see in your mind? What style? What length? What color? How do you see it—hanging on a store rack or being worn by a model in an ad? We all see a different dress in our own minds. With a high-C symbol, such as a watercolor painting of a dress, your imagination is much less involved; the symbol has given you much more information. The dress is a certain color and style and is presented in a certain situation, in a certain context. It's more definite, more concrete.

Sound can also be represented in high-C or low-C symbols. Again, think about the jet and the sound it makes during takeoff. To represent that sound, written language would use low-C symbols such as "loud," "rumbling," or "whooshing." Spoken language would use the same words, though you might also make a sound effect to imitate the jet. An actual recording of the jet taking off would be a high-C symbol of the noise and, obviously, the most realistic.

It is important to note that there is a progression between high-correspondence and low-correspondence symbols. In the previous example, the graphic of the jet is clearly a higher correspondence symbol that the word *jet,* but it is not as high as the photo of the jet. Between the word and the graphic we could place a four-year-old's stick figure drawing of a jet, then a cartoonist's sketch of a plane. These last two symbols could be called **mid-correspondence symbols.**

Practice

A. List three referents and then describe a low-C, mid-C, and high-C symbol for each.
B. Conduct a visual survey of your bedroom and list the low-C and high-C symbols and their referents.

Symbols and Your Emotions

Not only do different kinds of symbols require different brain responses, they also evoke different emotional reactions in us. Take, for example, the famous Jessica McClure story. In 1987, a one-year-old child fell into a well in Midland, Texas, and was trapped for several days. The entire nation received daily accounts of the rescue effort. Which medium do you think conveyed the strongest sense of emotion: newspapers, radio, or TV? You could get emotional by reading about the story and seeing a photo of the tired parents in the paper. The radio reports, with the sounds of Jessica's

MEDIA LAB   Symbol System Posters

Design a series of seven posters that illustrate the symbol systems used by each of the following mass media: books, comics and animation, film, musical recordings, newspapers, magazines, radio, and television. Since several of the media use more than one symbol system, focus on the ones that are most important to the medium you are illustrating. Include both low-C and high-C symbols in your posters.

faint screams, machines drilling, and people shouting, let you feel closer to the actual event. TV, though, clearly conveyed the strongest sense of emotion because of its ability to present two kinds of high-C symbols. Hearing the cheers as Jessica finally was lifted from the well and seeing her parent's tears of relief brought us as close to experiencing the actual events as we could get without being there. (While it is true that the low-C symbol system of written words can be wonderfully descriptive and evoke strong emotions in us, the higher-C the symbol system, the more realistic our experience of it will be.)

The reason understanding symbols is so important to understanding mass media is that so much of what we know and experience in our communication environment comes to us through mass media, and *all of it is presented using symbols—symbols which influence how we experience the reality being represented to us.*

Recap

We live in a **communication environment**, and we are constantly engaged in **communication behavior**. We communicate acoustically and visually with those around us (**interpersonal communication**) and with the mass media (**mass communication**). Communication is a central part of our very nature as human beings.

The process of communication follows a basic pattern (called the *Shannon-Weaver model*) in which a **sender** begins the act of communicating by transmitting **information** through a **medium** which is aimed at a **receiver**, who then provides some kind of **feedback** to the sender. Most of the time, we're unaware of the process until the communication breaks down somewhere along the way when **noise** interferes.

Humans use **symbols** to communicate their ideas, feelings, and experiences. In any given act of communication, the symbols we use refer to, or represent, **referents**. The words, sounds, and images (that is, the symbol systems) in our communication environment have different effects on us depending on whether they are **low-correspondence** or **high-correspondence** symbols.

Resources for Further Reading

Galvin, Kathleen. *Person to Person: An Introduction to Speech Communication*, Fifth Ed. (Lincolnwood, Ill.: National Textbook Co., 1994).

Hayakawa, S. I. *Language in Thought and Action*, 5th Ed. (New York: Harcourt Brace, 1989).

McLuhan, Marshall. *The Medium Is the Message, Understanding Media—The Extensions of Man* (New York: Signet, 1967).

Severin, Werner J. *Communication Theories*, 2nd Ed. (New York: Longman, 1988).

Psychology Today magazine

SEGUE

The Nature of Communication

You've just explored an area of your life you probably hadn't thought much about before. You're far more aware of how much of your daily life involves communication. Information is buzzing around you all the time, but where does it come from? Sure, you send and receive plenty of information during interpersonal communication, but you're also constantly being bombarded by huge amounts of information, thanks to technology.

Refer to your Media Use Inventory, which was completed as a Preface activity.

What do you think society was like before these media were invented? What would your life have been like if you had lived before these communications technologies? What kinds of information that you now rely on and take for granted simply would not have been in your consciousness?

The next chapter will give you a sense of the information explosion that took place only recently in the course of human history and where the next level of that explosion is likely to take our communication environment.

CHAPTER TWO

The Information Explosion

Learning Targets

After working through this chapter, you will be able to

- Identify key developments in the history of communications technology;
- Project how the digital revolution is likely to affect our communications environment;
- Explain and evaluate the concept of the "global village"; and
- Apply new background knowledge to your understanding of the Future Watch sections in Part Two of this book.

Checking In

- Estimate the year you think each medium became available to the public.
- Write a four- or five-sentence paragraph explaining the reasons why technology evolves.
- List ten aspects of current American life that would not be possible without computer technology.
- Draw a bar graph or pie chart to illustrate the percentage of information you get from different sources: friends or family, school, TV, magazines, radio and so on.

A Communications Technology Chronology

In his popular book *Future Shock*, Alvin Toffler discussed an idea that is both simple and profound at the same time—the idea of *change*. On the one hand, it is easy to see that things change in our daily lives all the time: We get new clothes, sports seasons come and go, MTV airs new videos. But on the other hand, it is difficult to notice the technological changes that take place in society over the course of, say, a decade. You have to stop and think about it.

How many of the communications technologies which you use now were not around when you were born? If you were born somewhere between the late 1970s and mid-1980s, CDs, CD-I, DAT (digital audiotape), DBS (direct broadcast satellites), and MiniDiscs came into being only since your birth. Having been born in 1958, I spent my high school spent with vinyl records and 8-track tapes. Getting my first cassette player was very exciting; getting my first

Walkman at age 22 was absolutely amazing! And I had never noticed the constant hiss and pops on my albums until I got my first CD player in 1988 when I was 30 years old.

What communications technologies will you be using when you are in your thirties? You'll probably be using some kind of technology related to what is currently referred to as **virtual reality**. What other technologies have yet to be invented that will become commonplace in our lifetime? Though it is hard to predict, one thing is certain: The rate of change is changing, and it's accelerating.

This means that the amount of technological change that takes place in a set number of years almost doubles. For example, from 1850 to 1950 the United States experienced tremendous growth in the areas of communications, factory production, medicine, and almost all other technology-based industries. Since 1950, we have matched that amount of technological growth in less than half as many years! And predictions are that the 20-year period from 1990 to 2010 will bring another doubling of technological change!

Clearly, we live in an era of human history where huge changes take place from one generation to the next. We take for granted the fact that we use technologies our grandparents didn't have, and that our children will use technologies that don't even exist yet. Yet the pace of change was not always this fast. It was often hundreds of years and many generations between technological advancements. The following time line presents some of the highlights in the development of communications technologies.*

Tens of thousands
of years B.C.*   Speech
   4000 B.C.   Pictographic writing (hieroglyphics)
   1500 B.C.   Alphabetic writing
   1450 A.D.   Printing press
      1835   Photography
      1844   Telegraph

*Note: Many of the dates in this time line are approximate. Historians disagree as to when several of these technologies were actually invented. Some dates reflect when the technology finally became available after years of development.

1876   Telephone, phonograph
1894   Wireless telegraph
1895   Silent movies
1922   Radio broadcasts
1927   Sound movies
1930   Magnetic recording tape, full-color printing
1935   Color movies
1939   Pocket paperback books
1940   Black-and-white TV broadcasts
1945   Modern computers
1947   LP (long-playing) records
1954   Transistor radios
1960   Color TV broadcasts, photocopiers
1962   Satellite communications, cassette tapes
1965   Local cable TV
1972   VCRs
1973   Fax (facsimile) machines
1977   Apple II home computers
1978   Laser disks
1979   Personal stereos (Walkman)
1980   Home laser printers
1983   CDs (compact discs), fiber optics, camcord-
       ers, cellular phones
1988   Digital audiotapes
1990   High definition TV, digital photography
1991   CD-ROM, CD-I
1993   Videophones, digital radio, MiniDiscs
1994   On-line services, PCS (Personal Communica-
       tions Services)

Major Milestones
Hieroglyphics

While all of these technologies are important, a few were true milestones in the history of human communication. Speech, though not a mechanical technology in the modern sense, was the first major way we communicated. We've been speaking to each other for a very long time—since our origin as a species. Only 6000 years ago did people figure out that they could record their communication by carving symbols (**hieroglyphics,** Greek for

A high priest in ancient Egypt stands before a wall of ideographs, pictographs, and hieroglyphics. *The Bettmann Archive.*

sacred carving) in stone, as illustrated above. Humans could now leave messages for each other without having to be there in person; for the first time, communication became semipermanent. Because the symbol system was limited, however, what got recorded on cave walls and on stone tablets was also relatively limited.

The Alphabet

Another 2500 years passed before humans devised a more precise way to communicate in writing: the alphabet. If you were among the powerful in your society, you now could write down laws about government and religion, and you could preserve accurate economic and historical records of what life was like. Advancements in the production of paper and inks made writing a more portable and durable medium over the next 3000 years. Unless you were a person of power in the government or the church, however, you were locked out of the writing game, and you certainly did not know how to read. Few books existed because

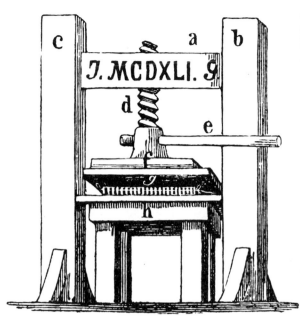

A centuries-old diagram of the Gutenberg printing press. *The Bettmann Archive.*

a single copy of a book such as the Bible could take years to reproduce by hand.

The Printing Press

Communications technology made little progress until the fifteenth century when, around 1450, Johannes Gutenberg perfected the printing press, shown above, in Germany. Within fifty years of Gutenberg's first book, *The Gutenberg Bible,* a total of 20 million copies of 35,000 different books had been printed! The age of mass media had been born. And with the medium of books came some very big changes, such as the Protestant Reformation and, a century later, the Age of Discovery (the Enlightenment). Now that people could have their own Bibles, they learned how to read. Once people learned how to read, they began to think for themselves and make their own decisions such as how they should practice their faith. Eventually, the widespread publishing of scientific knowledge had a snowball effect: By 1800, magazines, journals, newspapers, and books were all available for scientists, authors, and the common person. The information explosion had begun.

A diagram of an early camera and photographer's supplies.

Photography

The dominant symbol system was still low-C; that is, printed communication took place primarily with *words*. Books and newspapers contained some drawings and illustrations, but it wasn't until the mid-1830s that Englishman William Talbot developed the basic process for photography. Reality, as humans saw it with their eyes, finally could be reproduced. Even though the visual quality, or **resolution** of early photos was not great, the **graphic revolution** had begun. Imagine the excitement: you could capture a lasting visual record of any event you wanted, from a birthday celebration to a U.S. Civil War battle. Think of it! You could know exactly what your deceased grandparents looked like. You could see a photo of the President in the newspaper. Through the new business of advertising, you could see what a product looked like before you went to the store to buy it. Remember, it was only 150 years ago (a blink of an eye, in terms of human history) that we became used to experiencing the visual representation of the world as realistically as we now take for granted.

The Telegraph

There are several more milestones in the technology chronology to emphasize at this point, each of which added a crucial element to our modern communications environment. In the mid-1800s, a given media product could be transported anywhere, and, if well maintained, could last a long time. But it could only be transported as fast as a human could physically get it there, either by foot, horse, boat, or train. From the dawn of human civilization until about 150 years ago, the speed of human communication topped out at about 35 miles per hour (with the exception of smoke signals); that is, until the invention of the telegraph. In 1844, Samuel B. Morse perfected the technology that others had been experimenting with for a decade. He sent a famous telegraph signal over wires from Washington, D.C., to Baltimore in which he asked, "What hath God wrought?" Morse understood the significance of his success. By harnessing electricity, human communication could now travel at close to the speed of light—a mind boggling 186,000 miles per *second*. Physical barriers of distance were shattered. Time was compressed to near-instantaneousness. With his question, Morse acknowledged that the world was going to change in many ways and very quickly, and it did. Go back to the time line on pages 24–25 and look at the rate of technological evolution since electricity entered the communications picture.

The Telephone and the Phonograph

The next element of modern communications to be developed was sound reproduction. Until 1875, if you *heard* an act of communication, you were hearing it live. Alexander Graham Bell changed that in 1876 with his invention of the telephone. Once again, electricity was used, not to carry beeps, but to carry any and all sound that passed from end to end along the telephone wire. You no longer had to be physically near the act of communication to hear it, but you did need to be near the telephone receiver when it happened. In 1877 Thomas Edison invented the phonograph, which reliably recorded **low-fidelity** (one tone) sound and allowed its playback for the first time in human history. Edison's phonograph, like many of the new communications technologies, was considered a miracle machine. Not only could you own a photo-

Edison and his first phonograph. *The Bettmann
Archive.*

ever you wanted! Reality was getting more reproducible all the
time.

Motion Pictures

The last hurdle to jump was capturing the *movement* of real life
through a communications medium. In 1893, Edison exhibited
the first commercial motion-picture machine, the *kinetoscope*. In
1896, two French brothers, Auguste and Louis Lumière invented
the first projected motion pictures (which eventually became
known as "movies" in English because they simulated movement).* Even though their first movies were black and white,
silent, and only 20 seconds long, they seemed amazingly real to
the audiences who had never seen moving reality recreated before.
One film, *Train Arriving at a Station*, showed just that. The
camera was about 15 feet away from the track as an arriving train
approached the camera. It is well documented that many people

*Within a month, Thomas Edison, working independently of the Lumières, developed an almost
identical system of filming and projection.

A kinetoscope. *Courtesy of Edison Museum, Fort Meyers, Florida.*

in the audience fled in terror as the train approached, thinking that they were about to be run over. When we imagine that audience now, we laugh; but the point is that those first audiences were experiencing a brand new representation of reality. Given the level of media people in 1896 were used to, moving pictures seemed astonishing.

It is not that hard to imagine us having a similar reaction today. Let's say you walk through the front door of your house tomorrow night and you sense that something is different. You greet your mom in the kitchen and stop to pet your cat. Then, as you turn the corner into the hallway, you bump into your mom and cat again, even though you just left them in the other room. Completely confused, you race back to the kitchen where your holographically projected mom and cat are standing, as your real mom and cat enter the kitchen. It is quite possible that if you were among the first humans on earth to experience such a realistic representation (virtual reality), you might react with the same sense of panic and disorientation those first film audiences felt.

The Era of Television and Telecommunications

Look back at the rest of the communications developments listed on page 25; clearly it has really only been one century—a tiny fraction

The invention of the micro-chip or integrated circuit ushered in the digital age. A micro-chip, or integrated circuit, is made up of transistors on a chip of silicon. The one shown, enlarged from its actual size of a half-dollar coin, contains 3.6 million transistors and is the heart of the Macintosh Power PC computer. *Photo courtesy of Motorola.*

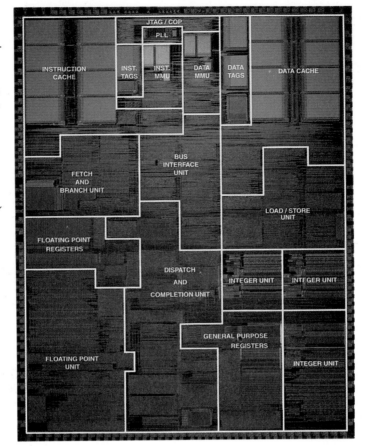

of a percentage of human history—that we have been living in the modern **telecommunications** era; an era of television and computer technology where lifelike information can be transmitted anytime, anywhere, and at the speed of light. It was only in 1962 that TelStar, the first communications satellite, broadcast a transatlantic TV show. The current world would have been unimaginable to all but the last three or four generations of human beings.

One of the difficulties in writing a book that deals with technology is keeping the information in it up-to-date. Between the time this book was published (July, 1995) and the time you're reading it, there will have been changes in the communications technology landscape. As the rate of change keeps accelerating, new technologies often become obsolete within a few years or even a few months; that is, they become out-of-date and unusable. In fact, **obsolescence** is a direct result of the acceleration of communications technology; the faster members of a society can share information,

MEDIA LAB — Communications Technology

- Create a time line illustrating your predictions for the next 50 years of communications technology.
- Watch a film set in an earlier time and do a technology assessment of that era; then describe how the plot would change if you inserted a current communications technology into the story.
- Create a time line illustrating the evolution of a particular electronic industry, such as video games.
- Write and perform a sketch depicting a current experience comparable to the reaction of the audience at the first projected movies.
- Interview someone over 50 years old and present a profile of what his or her media environment was like as a teenager.

the faster scientific and social changes occur. And the lightning-fast evolution of computer technology is further speeding up the changes under way.

The Digital Age

It is almost mind-boggling how fast the computer revolution is moving. The first generation of modern computers in the late 1940s were often as large as an average living room and required huge amounts of electricity to run. However, they were only as powerful as today's five-dollar calculators. Two inventions, the transistor in the 1940s and the integrated circuit in the 1960s, dramatically reduced the size of computers and increased their power. It is widely known that computers now lie at the heart of everyday American life. Banks, public transportation, retail stores, and almost every other industry in this country rely on computers to function. Tiny computers are also found in your watch, your coffee maker, and your car stereo. What makes the computer such a powerful tool is how it uses **digitized** information. In the article beginning on page 35, writer Ron Goldberg explores the role of digital technology.

The two most important changes brought about by digital technology will be that previously separate communications devices will be combined into some form of universal information device and that this device will be **interactive**. The second reading, "An Interactive Life" (page 40) explains this development.

The Global Information Village

The communications time line on page 24–25 illustrates the technological explosion that began accelerating 150 years ago. The growth of technology is only half the story. The other half of the story is the information explosion sparked by that growth. New telecommunications technologies dramatically increase the flow of information wherever they're in widespread use. An important question, then, becomes: What information is flowing through all these media?

Self-generated Information

You know how easy it is to pick up the phone and dial a neighbor two houses away, a friend on the other side of town, or a relative in another part of the country. Though you may not have had a chance to do so yet, it is just as easy to call someone on the other side of the globe. Via the telephone, you can send and receive information to and from almost any place on earth. You can also use a fax machine for the same purpose. If time is not crucial, you can use regular "snail mail" via the U.S. Postal Service [so named because it's so much slower than e-mail (electronic mail), which is sent instantly by computer].

Predictions are that we will see a truly global phone network early in the next century. Phone companies are devising a system using personal identification numbers in which you are assigned a permanent phone number (similar to your social security number) so you'll never have to change phone numbers if you move.

Turning On to Digital

Ron Goldberg

Some day, an ad executive with a sense of humor will write a best-selling lexicon of meaningless marketing terms. You know the type—catchy, blathery phrases that vaguely signify something good, like "vitamin fortified," "computer designed," or the all-time favorite, "professional quality." Think about it and you'll probably come up with a few more.

Without a doubt, one of today's most popular (and misunderstood) catchwords is "digital." And while the term is far from meaningless, it's commonly used to describe everything from big-screen TVs to cappuccino makers. Lately, it seems almost anything you can plug into a wall touts some kind of digital feature. What difference does this make?

Let's start at the beginning. Digital, unlike "advanced formula," actually does mean something, at least most of the time. But calling something "digital" is as ambiguous as saying it's "electrical." It's a description of sorts, but it doesn't tell you much. That's because digital isn't an end in itself. Rather, it's a way of doing things. Regardless of its technology and no matter the product, digital simply means that some aspect of that product's operation is under a simple form of computer control.

And while that might sound like a big so-what, the implications are actually quite profound. Though it might be as tiny as a single chip the size of your pinky nail, the computer in your digital whatever can make a drastic difference in the way it operates.

A digital circuit does two things. First, it breaks down incoming electronic information (like audio or video signals, for example) into the basic language of ones and zeros that computers understand. This is called "digitizing." Then, simply put, it does something else with this digitized information. It can duplicate it, like the picture-in-picture effects on a television. It can lock it into certain settings, like the thermal limiters on a digitally controlled cooking range. Or it can manipulate it in unusual ways, like the special effects settings on camcorders.

Once information has been digitized by the appliance, it's often stored in computer memory so you can recall it later. Telephones that remember your favorite numbers are an obvious example. You program them by setting a switch and punching in the phone number. While you're doing that, a digital circuit records the tones of the buttons and stores them in a reserved space in its memory. When you later press the appropriate memory number to make your call, the circuit goes to that reserved spot, finds the stored combination of tones you entered, and plays them back. *Voilà,* a call to your relatives in half the time.

For a lot of appliances, this is as "digital" as it gets. A digitally controlled toaster is nothing more than a plain old toaster that can accurately memorize the precise amount of heat to turn your brand of English muffin golden brown. A digital coffeepot is only slightly more sophisticated—the thermostat is digitally regulated to maintain the optimum temperatures for brewing and serving. Sometimes, the digital circuitry on an appliance is simpler yet. A digital clock radio, for example, is often considered digital because it displays the time numerically. The alarm is triggered by a circuit that monitors the current time—easy stuff. A digitally controlled microwave works the same way. You enter the amount of cook time on a digital keypad, much like a calculator. When you press "enter," the machine starts working until it finishes counting backwards from your chosen time down to zero. Obviously, you could get the same results with a nondigital microwave (or clock, or coffeepot, etc.)

ARMCHAIR RECITAL
Of course, depending on the amount of computer power, digital wizardry can be much more exciting than remembering a few phone numbers or keeping

the coffee hot. Some appliances use techniques to dramatically alter digitized information. The "ambience" settings you find on newer stereos are a good example. Using a deft combination of cutting-edge technology and psychoacoustics, these settings are designed to fool your ears into perceiving a larger listening space than you're actually in, like a stadium or a concert hall. For your stereo to perform these exotic tricks, your music goes through an extensive treatment of digital signal processing, sometimes called DSP.

To achieve the desired effect, certain information has to be preprogrammed into the stereo's digital memory at the factory. In this case, it's data such as the amount of reverberation a large concert hall might add to the music, and the distance from the stage your imaginary seat might be. After all, it takes a few milliseconds of time before the direct sound of an orchestra reaches the good seats—never mind the cheaper ones. Time delay, as well as other acoustic qualities of the re-created space, can often be adjusted by the user. When you run your favorite CD through these DSP circuits, the musical information is digitized and flavored with the information programmed into memory. On more elaborate audio gear, the digital control is so precise that you can literally dial in your favorite seats, like two on the left aisle in the back of a smoky jazz club—minus the smoke.

Stereo playback has been an excep-

Turning On to Digital *(continued)*

tionally fertile ground for digital signal processing ideas. One of the most interesting and useful applications is now in final development and expected to hit the market at the end of this year. The device, designed by a new company called MusicSoft, will tailor the sound of your speakers to their environment. For the uninitiated, the makeup of your room is just as important to sound quality as your equipment. Depending on the room's shape and how it's furnished, the sound can be bass heavy, trebly, muffled, or overly reverberant—even with the best gear. This new device, called the Music Operating System, digitally evaluates the sound of a room while a disc is playing, and corrects any anomalies before they come out of the speakers. If a heavy carpet is soaking up the treble, for example, the unit fills in the appropriate information. Or, on the other hand, if certain tones are unduly emphasized, the unit will cut them back accordingly.

FUZZY LOGIC

One liability of these new digital technologies, and of computers in general, is that strictly speaking, they're stupid. They can only do what they're told to do, and even that has to be explained to them in the same ones-and-zeros language that was previously mentioned. Obviously, human beings don't work that way; we change our minds, we improvise, we act in nonlinear (and often, nonlogical) ways. But as computer chips become more powerful, they creep ever closer to mimicking human thinking. One of the best examples is a digital technique called "fuzzy logic."

Despite its indecisive name, fuzzy logic is actually a "smart" circuit. This means that its actions can be flexible, depending on what it's asked to do and under which circumstances. A fuzzy logic circuit is designed to make qualitative "decisions" before performing its appointed tasks at any given time. These actions, of course, are based on information that's been preprogrammed at the factory, so the possibilities are finite. But even this rudimentary version of artificial intelligence is an impressive breakthrough.

One particularly clever use of fuzzy logic comes courtesy of your camcorder. Camcorders are designed for a primary goal: to record pictures and sounds as accurately as possible. But as anyone who's ever shot a video knows, the machine is rarely as creative as the user. Take the auto-focus feature, for example. What should the camcorder focus on? How does it know the difference between the subject and background, especially when capturing fast-moving action? Several electronic answers to these questions have become standard. Focus on the largest object in the viewfinder, or on the biggest object in the frame, or the brightest. Yet none of the camera's automatic decisions give you the desired result ten times out of ten.

Turning On to Digital *(continued)*

Enter fuzzy logic. By dividing the viewfinder up into several areas of priority, the auto-focus tries to keep up with your more creative compositions. It often assumes that you want the center of your shot in focus, so it looks for the subject there first. If it doesn't find it, the circuit hunts the various zones, one by one, until it comes up with an object to focus on. More often than not, and certainly more often than with previous techniques, the auto-focus does what you want. The same goes for exposure. Whereas typical automatic exposure systems accurately react to any change in light, this isn't always a good thing. For instance, if you're shooting indoors and your subject steps in front of a daylight-flooded window, you can expect a dark silhouette. But a fuzzy-logic circuit is smart enough to follow your subject and calculate the correct exposure, even under tricky conditions.

ON THE HORIZON

It's easy to see how smart circuits like these can make your appliances work better. Imagine an oven that can determine the difference between a tenderloin of beef and a turkey, adjusting cooking time accordingly. Or a dishwasher that automatically works harder on pots and pans than it does on glassware. In fact, digital technology will soon be found throughout your home, with smart wall outlets that know the difference between an AC plug and a toddler's finger and security systems that recognize your voice.

Of course, there's little denying that the digital age does have its low points. It's no fun having unruly machines flashing "12:00" all through your house. And teaching your kids about a clock's big hand and little hand now seems like charming nostalgia. But all in all, the digital domain, as it's called, is doing its best to make your work go faster, your play more interesting, and your home more livable. Not bad for a tiny piece of silicon, no? ■

Reprinted courtesy of *Home* magazine, © March 1993.

[As the previous article points out, communications media use a great deal of digital technology, with CD players probably being the most familiar. Within the next few years though, the digital revolution will make its way into every corner of your communications environment. Until now, the basic technologies used to transmit different media have been distinct from each other. Telephone lines carry sound in a unique way. Television signals are only understandable by a certain kind of receiver built into each TV. AM and FM signals travel through the air in a similar way to TV signals but can only be picked up by radio receivers. Home computers can only work with the digitized information they are designed to understand.

Turning On to Digital *(continued)*

As all communications media begin transmitting their information in digital form, the way we receive and use mass media is going to change. Signs of this change began cropping up everywhere in 1994, especially in TV commercials. Beverage, automobile, and telephone companies aired ads depicting the near future with people using their TVs in all sorts of new ways: to purchase groceries, to test drive a sports car, and to videochat with ten friends simultaneously. These ads tend to exaggerate—to *hype*—how quickly these changes will happen, but they will happen.]

The future offers phone-users great mobility. Using a combination of satellite and cellular technology, you will be able to use a portable phone from any location to call someone else wherever they are, as long as they have their phone with them. Wherever you travel, you'll just bring your phone and always be reachable.

The old-fashioned concept of a village, with its sense of community, implied that all the people in the village were within reach of each other; you could communicate interpersonally with anyone you needed to. In the early 1960s, Canadian philosopher Marshall McLuhan coined the phrase "the global village" to describe how electronic communications technologies were allowing the entire world to experience the kind of connectedness that used to belong only to small villages.

Millions of Americans are already cruising the information highway via **on-line services** such as Prodigy, CompuServe, and America Online. These computer networks allow users with the right equipment to communicate with a massive central computer so they can interact with each other, browse through electronic libraries, and purchase thousands of products. A "screen capture" from an online travel guide, serving as a "map" for America Online, is shown on page 49.

Another development that is bringing about the global village is called the **Internet**. This worldwide computer network, made up of thousands of other computer networks and online services, allows computer users to connect with each other from any part of the globe. In many ways, the Internet was the first stretch of information highway to be paved in the early 1970s. Back then, "the net" was used mostly by scientists and universities to exchange

An Interactive Life

Barbara Kantrowitz with Joshua Cooper Ramo

To get an idea of what the future might bring, step into the past. At the Edison National Historical Site in West Orange, N.J., there's a room full of a dozen old phonograph machines. Some were built by Thomas Edison, who invented recorded sounds in 1877, and others were produced by competitors. In the decades represented by the display, the concept and purpose of sound recording changed dramatically. Edison conceived of his phonograph as a business machine that would help people in distant places communicate. He intended to record voices—nothing more. His competitors envisioned the greater potential for entertainment and art. Where he saw internal memos, someone else saw Beethoven.

Someday, there may well be a similar memorial to the unfulfilled prophecies of the creators of the latest breakthrough—interactivity. Will it really change the world? With so much big money and so many big dreams pinned to an idea that is still largely on the drawing boards, there's no limit to the hype. Simply put, the ultimate promise is this: a huge amount of information available to anyone at the touch of a button, everything from airline schedules to esoteric scientific journals to video versions of off-off-off Broadway.

Watching a movie won't be a passive experience. At various points, you'll click on alternative story lines and create your individualized version of "Terminator XII." Consumers will send as well as receive all kinds of data. Say you shoot a video that you think is particularly artsy. Beam it out and make a small fortune by charging an untold number of viewers a fee for watching. Peter Jennings would be obsolete. Video-camera owners could record news they see and put it on the universal network. On the receiving end, the era of the no-brainer will have finally arrived. An electronic device called an "intelligent agent" would be programmed to know each viewer's preferences and make selections from the endless stream of data. Viewers could select whatever they wanted just by pushing a button.

Sounds great in theory, but even the truest believers have a hard time when it comes to nailing down specifics about how it will actually work. Will we control the data via the telephone, the TV, the personal computer or a combination of all of the above? When will it be available? Will it be cheap enough for everyone? How will we negotiate such a mass of images, facts and figures and still find time to sleep? Will government regulate messages sent out on this

An Interactive Life *(continued)*

vast data highway? And, frankly, what do we need all this stuff for anyway?

The quick answer is: no one knows. "We're a long way from 'Wild Palms'," says Diana Hawkins, who runs an interactive TV consulting firm in Portola Valley, Calif. But even if the techno-chaos of that recent mini-series is far off, some consumers may indeed notice that their personal relationships with their TVs, telephones and computers will be entering a new and deeper phase within a year or two. Instead of playing rented tapes on their VCRs, they may be able to call up a movie from a library of thousands through a menu displayed on the TV. Game fanatics may be able to do the same from another electronic library filled with realistic video versions of arcade shoot-'em-ups. Instead of flipping through the pages of J. Crew or Victoria's Secret, at-home shoppers may watch video catalogs with models demonstrating front and rear views of the latest gear. Some cable companies are also testing other interactive models that allow viewers to choose their own news or select camera angles for sporting events.

While these developments are clever, fun and even convenient, they're not quite revolutionary. Denise Caruso, editor of Digital Media, a San Francisco-based industry newsletter, calls this "fake interactive," just one step past passive viewing, pure couch-potato mode. In the most common version of this scheme, consumers will communicate with the TV through the combination of a control box and their remote control, or, perhaps, the telephone. To some degree, viewers already have accepted a certain amount of fake interactivity by channel-surfing with their remotes, ordering pay-for-view movies and running up their credit-card bills on the Home Shopping Network.

Moving beyond phase one, into what Caruso calls "true interactive," will require major changes in the technological and regulatory infrastructure. Today's television cables will likely be replaced by fiber-optic cables, which are capable of transmitting much more data at higher speeds. Either a government agency or the communications industry itself will have to set a performance standard so that different networks can connect with each other. At home, viewers may have to learn to use a TV monitor that functions more like a computer screen fronting for a gigantic hard disc full of all kinds of data, everything from games and movies to specially created programs.

The shows of the future may be the technological great-grandchildren of current CD-ROM titles. These are compact discs that store data instead of music and can play on either television or computer screens. To play CD-ROMs today, you need a special machine. There are at least four models on the market, and titles produced for one format won't play on another. CD-ROMs do provide a glimpse of what

An Interactive Life *(continued)*

the future might hold, however. A number of companies, including Newsweek, are developing multimedia products that combine text, video, sound and still photographs. The result is what may someday be a powerful new medium with no set story line as in a book or magazine. Users pick and choose information that interests them. Philips Interactive, for example, has dozens of titles, among them a tour of the Smithsonian, in which the viewer selects which corridor to enter by clicking on the screen. Other titles: "Jazz Giants," a musical history, and "Escape from CyberCity," an animated adventure game.

Many investors are betting on entertainment as the most lucrative interactive market. But some industry observers predict the development of two parallel home markets, one catering to leisure activities and the other to businesses. Hawkins says the work-at-home market could be computer based and provide an outlet for teleconferencing and portable computing devices, like the Newton touted by Apple chairman John Sculley that can be carried in a pocket and runs on handwritten commands scribbled on a small screen. The entertainment market, primarily games and movies, would be centered on some kind of monitor.

If all this comes to pass—still a very big if—the next step could be what Digital Media's Caruso calls "complete viewer control." She says consumers would be a little like information "cowboys," rounding up data from computer-based archives and information services. There will be thousands of "channels" delivered, Caruso thinks, through some combination of cable, telephone, satellite and cellular networks. To prevent getting trampled by a stampede of data, viewers will rely on programmed electronic selectors that could go out into the info corral and rope in the subjects the viewer wants.

Caruso's "final frontier" is what she calls video telephony, a complete two-way link of video, audio and data. A user might stand in front of a monitor/receiver and just talk and listen, communicating with whatever or whomever is Out There. Images and voices would be beamed back and forth. (At the very least, it would probably mean the end of anonymous obscene phone calls.) "There is no exact analogy to any technology we've seen before," says Red Burns, chair of the Interactive Telecommunications Program at New York University. "Interactive means we are all involved. There is no viewer. Interactive is like a conversation."

"Interactivity" may be the biggest buzzword of the moment, but "convergence" is a close second. It means different things to different people. To the moneymen, it means that everything will come together and they'll clean up. To scientists, it means that the technology has reached a critical point where fantasy could now become reality. Nicholas Negroponte, director of MIT's Media Lab, a leading think tank in this new world, remembers that back

An Interactive Life *(continued)*

in the 1970s, a government agency gave him a grant on the condition that he remove the word multimedia from his proposal. "They were afraid we would get one of Proxmire's Golden Fleece awards," he says. Now, politicians, from President Clinton on down, are falling over themselves to proclaim support for the new medium.

These dreams are possible because researchers have made vast leaps in both the quality and quantity of data transmittal. In the past decade, the amount of data that could be put on a silicon chip has doubled every year while the price has been cut in half. In 1960, a high-quality transistor cost several dollars. Today a chip with the capacity of 4 million transistors costs about a tenth of a cent per transistor.

Transmission—putting the information into the hands of everyone who wants it—is also much more efficient. Until now, data have been sent as a series of electrical signals along wires or cables or through the air as radio waves. But as the amount of data and the demand for them have increased, these electronic highways have become clogged. The solution: fiber optics.

Both of these developments are possible because of digitalization, a mathematical scheme that translates data into the simplest form. Called binary formatting, the system expresses numbers and letters in a code using only 1 and 0. The letter "A," for example, could be 00000. "Z" would be 11001. Originally, this code was stored as on-or-off

electrical charges along the standard wires and cables; now it can be transmitted as pulses of light on the fiber-optic cables. Bringing high-speed computers into the loop means that much more complicated information can be digitized: combinations of sound, still images, video and text. "Multimedia" is the wrong word, says MIT's Negroponte. "Everything has now become digitized," he says. "We have created a unimedia, really. Bits are bits."

At the Media Lab, Negroponte and other scientists are experimenting with the future. Pattie Maes, an expert in artificial intelligence, is trying to build some working "intelligent agents." (At a recent Media Lab conference, an actor dressed as a butler took the stage, playing the part of an agent. That's interactive humor.) In one program, Maes has created four "icons" on the computer screen representing agents with specific marching orders. For example, one dressed in a business suit seeks out business news. Although the agents are initially programmed, they actually learn by watching their masters' preferences. She thinks that one day, agents may even communicate with agents from other users: "Let's say both you and I like the same movie reviews. Our agents could get together and determine that we also had other interests in common." (Imagine the conversation: "Have I got a compatible user for you!")

Maes and others concede that there's a dark side to all these bright dreams. Who will protect the privacy of consumers

An Interactive Life *(continued)*

whose shopping, viewing and recreational habits are all fed into one cable-phone company data bank? And where there are agents, can counteragents be far behind: spies who might like to keep tabs on the activities of your electronic butlers? "Advertising companies see my presentations and get very excited," says Maes. Indeed, intelligent agents could be a gold mine of information. Advertisers aren't the only ones who could abuse the network if they were able to tap into it. The government could electronically spy on individuals; bosses could track employees.

If the tolls for using the information highway are too high, interactivity may widen the gap between the haves and the have-nots, the rich and wired vs. the poor and unplugged. Some plans call for charging hundreds of dollars for the "black box" in the first phase of interactivity. Other plans are cheaper, but would still levy a fee for services used. One suggestion is to make much of the data free to all users, similar to the way public libraries lend out books. If that happens, some experts think that the new technology may eventually have a democratizing effect. Access to a universal information library could equalize opportunity. "It's a shift from elitism to populism," says Bernard Luskin, president of Philips Interactive Media of America.

In the next few years there's likely to be considerable debate over the realistic presentation of violence in the new generation of video games, which will include viewer-directed movies. It's one thing to zap a cartoon in an arcade, quite another when clicking on the screen means shooting bullets and spilling blood from a human. Would you want your child—or any child—to play that game?

At this point, so much is still speculation. While the big players and major thinkers spin predictions, it's quite possible that some entrepreneur in a garage is coming up with a really new idea that will forever alter the best-laid plans. "What we are looking at now is just the first generation," says Stephen Benton of MIT's Media Lab. In that case, the best advice is: hang on for the ride. ■

[The interactive media described in the *Newsweek* article are based on our current understanding of computer technology. Keeping in mind that the rate of technological advancement continually increases, what do you think computers might be capable of in 20 years? The following article from the *New York Times* describes a 1993 experiment that could lead to computer chips that are 1000 times more powerful than the most powerful chips we have today. Imagine the virtual reality games those chips will allow! As the old saying goes, "We ain't seen nothin' yet!"]

Just One Electron

Andrew Pollack

TOKYO—Hitachi Ltd. said today that it had overcome a major hurdle blocking development of a computer chip that is fantastically tiny and powerful, even by today's standards. It has demonstrated what it says is the world's first electronic memory that uses only a single electron to store a bit of information.

Scientists have known and previously demonstrated the principles of single-electron memory devices, but such demonstrations required extremely low temperatures. The Hitachi technique can operate at room temperature.

In memory chips, the presence or absence of electrons represents a one or a zero in computer code. Current devices require more than 10,000 electrons to represent one bit of information. Hitachi said the single-electron technology could be the basis for the development of a memory chip that stores 16 billion bits, about 1,000 times the capacity of the most advanced chips sold today.

Promise of Efficiency
Chips based on single-electron devices would require very little power, making possible hand-held computers that could store reams of data and moving images, as well as operate far longer on batteries than computers do today.

Previous experimental devices have had to operate at temperatures near absolute zero, or almost 460 degrees below zero Fahrenheit, to reduce atomic vibrations that could obscure the presence or absence of the electron. The need for extreme cold has been one of the biggest obstacles to developing such devices for practical use.

But Hitachi's achievement of a room-temperature operation should encourage development efforts. "From now on, single-electron devices should not be the research topic, only of physicists," scientists from Hitachi's Central Research Laboratory in Kokubunji, Japan, wrote in a paper that is being presented this week at the International Electron Devices meeting in Washington.

Still, single-electron devices are not expected to be practical until the next century and many other problems must be overcome.

Beyond Tiny
According to Hitachi, achieving room temperature operation requires confining an electron to an area with a diameter of only about 10-billionths of a meter. By contrast a human hair has a diameter 10,000 times that. Such minuscule structures cannot be made using existing semiconductor fabrication techniques.

Just One Electron *(continued)*

Hitachi's scientists developed a technique in which grains of silicon of the required size form naturally, without the need for making patterns on silicon using a conventional technique known as lithography.

In the memory, an electron can be trapped on a tiny silicon island because of the principles of quantum mechanics. A trapped electron will impede the flow of other electrons through the circuit because electrons repel one another. This reduction in the electron flow can be detected, allowing the memory to be read. ■

[In many ways, it is a fascinating and historic time to be studying mass media because we are experiencing firsthand the end of an era in human communications. The days of simply consuming media products sent to us via one-way media technologies are fading. We are quickly approaching a time when you will be able to broadcast your own digital movies and CDs from your home over a computer network to as many people as want to receive your work. You'll be able to play multiuser video games with each player participating from their own location anywhere on earth. No one knows exactly all the ways we'll be connected to the digital **information highway** in ten or twenty years, but construction of the highway is swinging into high gear. Computer, telephone, software, cable, electronics, and entertainment companies are investing billions of dollars to make it happen. And as it happens, more information than ever will be blanketing our lives.]

Reprinted by permission from the *New York Times*, December 8, 1993.

data. Today, over 20 million people from every continent regularly "hop on the net" to exchange every type of information imaginable. Before long, you will be able to participate in the global village, either through on-line services or directly through the Internet.

Media-generated Information

As you now know, it is only recently in the scope of history that humans could communicate with anyone beyond their immediate location. Your village was pretty much it. Until 100 years ago you probably did not know a lot about what life was like in distant villages, much less in distant countries. Even if you knew someone in a far-off place, you couldn't communicate with them—at least

MEDIA LAB   Computer-based Technologies

- Analyze an episode of "Star Trek: Voyager" or "Deep Space Nine" (or another high-tech show) and catalog the computer-based communications technologies.
- Research newspaper and magazine articles to determine when experts believe the information highway will actually happen. (Key words: "Information Super highway," "Infobahn," "Information Highway," "Internet," "Bit Stream")

not easily. Today, via mass media, you receive mass information about everything. You, your friends, your family—just about everyone—has access to the same information. When you hear about a movie star's latest marriage from your local morning radio personality, thousands of other people are hearing about it too. When you read about your favorite band in *Rolling Stone*, tens of thousands of people are reading along. When you watch an event on television, such as the Olympics, hundreds of millions of people are watching with you, getting the same information and experiencing the same emotions.

 Reflections

Why is all this mass information transmitted to you? Why is the information you get through media so often the subject of your conversation? How do you use all this information in your daily life? What is its value to you? Where does its value come from?

© 1995 Ewin Sanchez.

The "Internet," a global network of computer networks, is an integral part of today's information explosion.

Because you're so used to information coming at you so quickly from all directions, it seems like no big deal. Like every other American, you are used to local television news shows which bring you dramatic pictures of a volcanic mudslide killing thousands of Asian farmers, immediately followed by a story on the misadventures of a little boy whose lost pet boa constrictor terrorized residents of the nursing home near his house. The stories you consume in this global information village can get pretty strange.

Imagine for a moment that you lived in a society with only two television stations run by the government. You had no access to cable TV, VCRs, home computers, CDs, cordless telephones, and so on. How would you react to the avalanche of information that these technologies would bring if your society suddenly had access to all of them within a one-year period? In the reading by Jeff Greenwald on page 50 describes how Indians are reacting to the lightning-fast growth of satellite TV in their country.

Greenwald's article hints at how information changes a society. Will the values of India's teenagers change now that they are watching MTV? Probably. It is hard for us, though, to see the impact of new information because we are already swimming in it. One more drop in our own information ocean doesn't seem like much. As you'll discover in later chapters, America's strongest export in the next century is likely to be information—entertain-

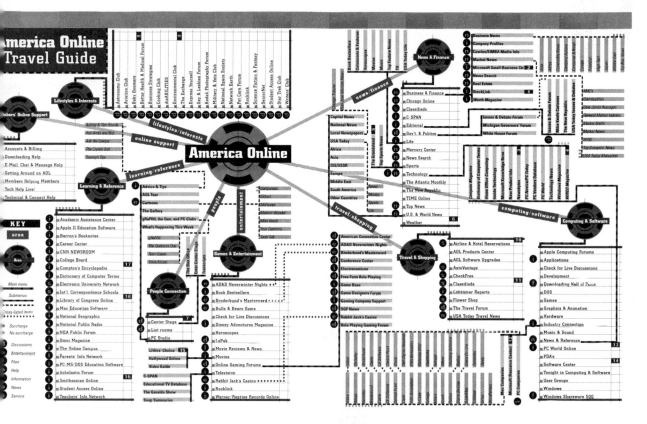

ment-based information. The world already sees more American
films and TV shows and listens to more American music than
any other nation's, and that trend is growing. We are the largest
contributor to the global information village. Part Two of this
book will examine what we contribute.

Dish-Wallahs

Jeff Greenwald

Just beyond the shadow of South Delhi's ancient Red Fort lies the Lajpat-Rai market, a sprawling maze of dusty passageways and tin-roofed stalls that at first glance looks like any other Indian bazaar. Carts piled with boxes weave between cattle and pedestrians, oily smoke rises from fast-food booths, jets of crimson beetle-nut spittle sail through the air, briefly catching the sunlight before splattering anonymously into dusty corners.

But Lajpat-Rai is not a typical Indian market. Within this musty labyrinth, littered with trash and dung and spittle, you'll find not saris, spices, or sandals, but the raw ingredients of India's current television revolution. In a mad atmosphere reminiscent of *Blade Runner*'s futuristic funk and William Gibson's orbiting ghettos, turbaned hawkers sell the latest in satellite dishes and signal splitters. Shoppers sift through bins of transistors, men haggle over the prices of LED displays, and rolls of fresh video cable hang on crooked nails, framing lush paintings of the Hindu gods.

Alone with a few similar electronics bazaars across the Indian subcontinent, Lajpat-Rai is a crucial link in this vast republic's exploding market for satellite television—and a central supply port for a new generation of opportunistic entrepreneurs called "dish-wallahs"—*wallah* being a common Hindi phrase which translates to something between "hack" and "specialist." Using no-frills satellite dishes, simple modulators, and hundreds of meters of cable, these inventive television hackers are affecting a transformation that many locals feared would never come: propelling Mother India out of information limbo by hard-wiring its living rooms directly into the global jet stream of satellite news, live sports, and the geosynchronous gyrations of MTV.

Although it's touted as the world's largest democracy, India has managed to remain one of the most culturally prudish countries in Asia. The news that flesh-filled MTV and violent, sexy American shows are now being watched in Hindu and Muslim homes may shock people who have long viewed this country—quite accurately—as a stronghold of ascetic spirituality, religious tradition, and deeply rooted taboos against public displays of affection. But thanks to an ever-increasing cadre of dish-wallahs, satellite television—with its enticing western immorality and materialism—is here to stay.

Dish-Wallahs *(continued)*

Meet the Wallah

Deepak Vishnui resembles an Indian Spike Lee: wide-eyed yet vaguely bored looking, with a rough black mustache and his thick round glasses. A 31-year-old New Delhi electrician, he's also the president (and entire staff) of Channel Vision—a company he founded in July 1992.

"The World Cup cricket games were beginning," he said, "but the Indian government wasn't broadcasting all the matches." Sensing a classic case of demand outstripping supply, Vishnui borrowed 60,000 rupees (about $2,000) from his brother, bought a dish, and started his business. "I began with households," he said. "Each one paid 500 rupees (about $10) for installation, and pays a regular monthly fee of 100 rupees." With 60 apartments hand-wired to his rooftop dish, Vishnui may be one of the smallest dish-wallahs in Delhi, but his operation is completely typical. With subscriber bases ranging from 50 to 1,500, all of Delhi's 200 to 500 cable networks (a fraction of an estimated 20,000 scattered across India) are privately owned, bare-bones businesses with tiny overheads.

The initial investment, of course, is the dish itself. Prices have plunged from $6,000 in 1990 to less than $500 today. The dish-wallah's "control room" is usually a corner of a living room. There you'll find a simple modulator, amplifier, and VCR stacked on wobbly shelves above the family TV. Beyond this, the only remaining costs are for cable, connectors, and dirt-cheap signal amplifiers.

"There is no doubt," said a salesman for a New Delhi dish-wallah, "that anyone with 25,000 rupees (less than $1,000) can walk into the Lajpat-Rai market and walk out with everything they need to build their own cable television station."

A Speedy Revolution

Rooftop dish antennas and the dish-wallahs who pipe their signals through India's urban sprawl have become a fixture of contemporary Indian life. Yet just three years ago, India was still wallowing in an information backwater—cut off from the rest of the world by government apathy, xenophobic censorship, and limited access to even the most rudimentary hardware. Not that the hardware alone would have done any good. Back then there were precious few signals to receive.

Before the satellite boom there was one dull and unwelcoming channel. *Doordashan,* or Indian National Television, featured saccharine soaps, official exhortations, and numbing cultural documentaries, all carefully engineered to offend (or inspire) no one. Videocassettes reached India in the early 1980s; but VCRs were well beyond the means of most people in this underdeveloped country. It was in the mid-1980s (and mainly in the high-rises of Bombay, India's equivalent of Hollywood), that

Dish-Wallahs *(continued)*

the first real video entrepreneurs appeared. Their strategy was simple: Wire up willing neighbors to a single VCR, then show rented films for a monthly subscription charge.

For countless Indian city dwellers, January 1990 will be remembered as the month when the world at large—long an impenetrable nut—was finally cracked open. As U.S. troops assaulted Iraq, the satellite revolution struck India with equal force. Anyone with a 12-foot dish antennae could receive CNN. Among the educated but news-starved classes of the subcontinent, linked to the Middle East by decades of oil dependency and a millennium-old Islamic heritage, the market for up-to-the-minute broadcasts was immediate and enormous. Government officials made no attempt to limit or control the profusion of dish antennas that bloomed over the city skylines. Kilometers of cable snaked through apartment buildings, over trees and across roads, bringing the world's first real-time spectator war into hundreds of thousands of living rooms from Bombay to Calcutta.

CNN remained a fixture in many Indian homes for well over a year; but in April 1991 a new company called STAR TV, broadcasting out of Hong Kong, began offering a near-irresistible alternative. In contrast to CNN's single channel, STAR's satellite broadcasts four: BBC Asia, MTV, Prime Sports, and Star Plus—a channel featuring con-

temporary western programs and soap operas (*Santa Barbara* has become the most popular show in India). Best of all, though, STAR requires a much smaller dish than CNN; even a 3-foot-wide model can easily capture its powerful signal.

Within weeks, nearly all of India's satellite antennas had been reoriented. STAR became the new standard; and its strong, accessible beam inspired thousands of would-be dish-wallahs to leap into the fray. In the first six months of 1992, the number of households receiving STAR TV jumped a staggering 211 percent—from 720,000 viewers to 1.6 million viewers, according to the Indian Market Research Bureau. For a network that relies on international advertisers, the figures were ambrosia—and the end is nowhere in sight. In early December, the BBC's immediate and even-handed coverage of India's Hindu-Muslim riots ignited yet another mad scramble for hookups. And the boom continues; in New Delhi alone, dish-wallahs are still wiring up more than 250 new subscribers every day.

Regulation? What Regulation?
Aside from the sheer speed of the process, the most astonishing thing about India's video revolution is that it remains totally unregulated. India's bureaucracy is one of the most sluggish on earth, and only now is there any talk (so far it's just gossip) of imposing taxes and/or licensing fees on dish-wallahs.

Dish-Wallahs *(continued)*

Any attempt to limit broadcasts or impose official censorship would be utterly impossible: There are tens of thousands of satellite antennas, and nearly all of them could be folded up and hidden within a matter of minutes. The only recourse—one that the Indian government is rather unlikely to take—would be to shoot the offending sputnik out of the sky.

The Indian government may find a way to squeeze a few rupees out of the dish-wallahs, but they will never be able to control the revolution that began in those first tense months of 1990. India is wired in, and nothing can turn back the clock. Meanwhile, *Doordashun* is bravely attempting to compete: It added a second channel, and even took the huge ethical risk of broadcasting the Miss World Beauty Pageant. But it seems unlikely that it will be able to hold its own against STAR, much less the new ATN (Asia Television Network), which will begin broadcasting an all-Hindi channel later this year.

What, one has to wonder, are India's teenagers making of this stuff? Are they glued to their TV sets, or repelled by the godless depravity beaming down at them from the stars?

The answer, so far, seems to be neither. While western fashions, hairdos, and country music are experiencing a surge in popularity, and some wild outfits are surfacing in the trendier districts of Bombay, all of the teenagers I spoke with had similar reactions. Their favorite programs, far and away, are the BBC documentaries. Asked about MTV and the ultra-suggestive content of western rock videos, they simply smile and shrug.

"A few of the songs are good, but we still feel ashamed seeming some things," admitted Geeta, whose older brother is a dish-wallah in new Delhi. "When we're alone, okay, we'll watch; but if another family member comes in we must change the channel."

Their Indian parents, however, have different ideas. A recent documentary abut the impact of western television on Indian society soberly warned of headaches, blindness, and epileptic fits. Even the dish-wallahs themselves have expressed mixed feelings about the new world they are helping to create.

"There is a problem," admits Vinod Tailang, president of the 120-member Cable Television and Dish Antenna Operators Association of Uttar Pradesh, and father of two teenagers. "Much of what we show is totally against Indian culture. It is definitely changing the way Indian boys and girls react to each other. I see them dancing and moving all the time. Jumping, jumping. They have become action-packed." ∎

Reprinted from *WIRED*, May/June 1993. © Jeff Greenwald and *WIRED*.

A couple stands before their apartment in India, now equipped with "dish-wallah-installed" satellite dishes.
Photo © Jeff Greenwald/WIRED.

Recap

Though humans have been around for a very long time, our ability to communicate was extremely limited until about 500 years ago when the printing press enabled the first mass media—books. The rate of technological change has steadily accelerated since then, with new media allowing us to represent reality with increasing accuracy.

We are living at the beginning of a revolution in technology as important as the revolution brought on by printing press. The ability to **digitize** acoustic and visual information, combined with the rapid evolution of **computers**, is leading to the development of an **interactive information highway** which will change many aspects of how we communicate with each other.

Even before the information highway, humans had conquered the communications globe. We can now exchange information with someone in China as easily as we can with someone two towns away. The distance between societies is shrinking as media and the information highway connect the world into a **global village**. As we become more and more connected, it becomes increasingly important to examine the information we are consuming.

MEDIA LAB   Information Overload

- List all the news articles in one edition of your local newspaper and categorize them by their geographic origins. Chart the percentage of stories which originated locally, nationally, and internationally (globally).
- Construct a chart projecting how American society will have changed by the year 2010 as a result of the information highway. Place the information highway at the center of your chart and cluster outward from there.
- Research the Internet and present a graphic representation of it.
- The amount of information crisscrossing the globe is enormous and growing. Is all this information good for us, as individuals and as a society? Author Bill McKibben explores this question in his book *The Age of Missing Information*. In 1990, McKibben taped all 24 hours of every channel his cable system offered and then spent months watching the more than 1000 hours of TV. A few weeks later, he spent one day camping alone in the woods. His book contrasts the information he encountered during the two experiences and raises questions about the effect on society of too much exposure to media and too little exposure to nature. Organize a similar experiment and record your findings. Even if you can't arrange a camping experience, try abstaining from all electronic media for one weekend, and then immersing yourself in those media the following weekend.

Resources for Further Reading

Bunch, B., and A. Hellermans. *The Timetables of Technology* (New York: Simon and Schuster, 1993).

Clarke, Arthur C., *How the World Was One* (New York: Bantam, 1992).

Cotton, R., and R. Oliver. *Understanding Hypermedia* (London: Phaidon, 1993).

Lubar, Steven. *InfoCulture* (Boston: Houghton Mifflin, 1993).

Macaulay, David. *The Way Things Work* (Boston: Houghton Mifflin, 1988).

Internet World magazine, 11 Ferry Lane West, Westport, CT 06880.

Mondo 2000 magazine, Box 10171, Berkeley, CA 94709-0171.

NewMedia Magazine, 901 Mariner's Island Blvd., Suite 365, San Mateo, CA 94404.

Online Access, 920 North Franklin, Suite 203, Chicago, IL 60610.

Wired magazine, 520 Third Street, 4th Floor, San Francisco, CA 94107.

SEGUE

The Information Explosion

You have now looked at the two key prerequisites for studying mass media. You have seen, in Chapter One, that we humans, by our very nature, *must* communicate, and that we do so according to a basic pattern. You know that we use various types of symbols to do our communicating and that we employ technology to send and receive those symbols. Finally, you looked at how that technology has blanketed the earth with information. And while more and more of that information is sent back and forth between individuals hooked up to the information highway, the majority of information in our environment still flows from the mass media. Taken as a whole, what mass media give us is known as *pop culture*. The individual media and the pop culture they both create and reflect will be put under the microscope in Part Two.

Mass Media–
The Agents of
Popular Culture

The Content of Mass Media

What exactly are you consuming when you consume all that mass media? You are consuming **popular (pop) culture**: "popular" because so many of us share the experience, and "culture" because these experiences help shape our identity as a society and as individuals. Pop culture refers to the endless stream of name-brand products, entertainment celebrities, live-coverage events, and advertisements you swim in every day. Nike is pop culture. En Vogue is pop culture. Dan Rather reporting live from wherever the latest world event happens to take place is pop culture. You guessed it. Today's pop culture is brought to you by . . . the mass media. Pop culture is the first thing you'd notice was missing if you suddenly found yourself on a remote primitive island.

The Impact Debate

Given the sheer volume of pop culture the mass media disseminate, it is not surprising that they are a constant topic of intense debate. Some argue that modern mass media are the most powerful democratic tools known to humankind. Through the media, we learn the truth about our government leaders and right the wrongs of our system when momentous events (such as the Rodney King beating) are broadcast for all to see. Even the end of the Cold War has been attributed largely to the growth of mass media; it has been argued that the philosophy of totalitarianism could not handle the increasingly open flow of information that outpaced the government's ability to suppress it. Western pop culture is brimming with the values of individualism and capitalism, and once people in the former Soviet bloc experienced ads for Levi's and Pepsi, their move toward freedom was not far behind.

On the other side are people who believe that American mass media have been corrupted precisely because of their economic dependence on advertising. To charge advertisers the maximum amount of money to run their ads, media companies need to promise their advertisers a big audience—the bigger, the better. To attract the biggest possible audience for their TV shows, newspapers, and so on, the media hook us with whatever they think will entertain us the most—the pop culture of drama, sex, violence, comedy, sports, fantasy—so that we will absorb the advertising that, according to some critics, brainwashes us into a state of mindless consumerism.

61

In addition to these opposite views on the broad social effects of media, debates also rage regarding the effects media have on us as individuals. Depending on whose opinion you listen to, media help to make us educated, empowered, and compassionate or ignorant, lazy, and violent. On the one hand, think of all we learn through mass media; we become educated about environmentalism and change our recycling habits. We see entire midwestern towns ravaged by floods and contribute money to help the relief effort. On the other hand, we absorb the cultural stereotypes presented on television which reinforce our personal prejudices. We waste hours and hours of time surfing the channels just to fend off boredom. We even, on occasion, mirror the aggression we see on TV (for example, it is claimed that reports of domestic violence rise dramatically every Superbowl Sunday).

Media and Society: Partners in Pop Culture

The rest of this book argues that there is truth in all of the above points of view. As the agents of popular culture, however, the media are only half of the equation. We, the individuals who consume the specific media products that convey pop culture, are the other half of the equation. Mass media do influence us. However, we also influence the mass media. To borrow an idea from biology, there is a *symbiotic relationship* between society and the media; that is, both institutions depend on each other. The media give us what we want, and we want what the media give us.

To better understand exactly what the mass media give us and why we want it, Chapter Three presents a **Media Literacy Paradigm**, which is a system for analyzing the mass media and the effects they have on us. Chapters Four, Five, Six, and Seven focus on the four mass media that do not depend primarily on advertising revenues: books, comics, film, and recordings. Chapter Eight presents an introduction to the economics and regulations which guide the various media industries. Chapters Nine, Ten, Eleven, and Twelve examine the mass media that do depend primarily on advertising for their money: newspapers, magazines, radio, and television.

CHAPTER THREE

A Media Literacy Paradigm

Learning Targets

After working through this chapter, you will be able to

- Explain the meaning of the term "paradigm";
- Identify several of your personal paradigms;
- Explain the key idea in each stage of the Media Literacy Paradigm; and
- Apply the Media Literacy Paradigm to specific media products.

Checking In

- Describe, in general terms, how people come to hold opinions about things.
- Consider your basic view of a topic such as commitment to schoolwork or participating in school sports and then explain how you came to hold that view.
- Select a media product, such as a film, TV program, or CD, to analyze in this chapter.

What Is a Paradigm?

A **paradigm** (pronounced *par-a-dīm*) is a way of seeing something. It is a combination of your beliefs and attitudes that influence how you respond to the world around you. It encompasses your previous experiences and expectations that come into play when you encounter new people and events. A paradigm is like a camera lens; the image that comes into the camera first passes through—and is affected by—the lens. The final picture is determined by the particular lens on the camera. Two cameras photographing the same object with different lenses will produce two different pictures. Just as all cameras have lenses, all people have paradigms. An interesting thing about paradigms is that people are usually unaware of them. Imagine that you were born with a thin purple film covering the pupils of your eyes. You wouldn't walk around thinking how interesting it was that everything looked purple. You would just think that was how reality looked.

Most of your paradigms were formed at an early age. Your opinions on everything from racial and financial issues to recreation and religion were molded by what you experienced when you were young. You grew up seeing the world through your paradigms, and, as a result, they are a very important part of who you are—even though you are hardly aware of them or how you got them. You have a musical paradigm that guides what music you like to listen to. You have an academic paradigm that shapes what kind of student you are. You have a social paradigm that influences how you spend free time.

Most Americans have several media paradigms. For example, we accept the role of television as an ever-present source of entertainment. Most of us accept that news media present a basically honest picture of the world in their magazines, newspapers, and news broadcasts. We accept that advertisements are almost everywhere we turn. We believe that all of these situations are normal. This is why the Media Literacy Paradigm is so valuable—it is a way of looking at media in a much deeper way so that you don't automatically accept as "normal" the media experiences that you take for granted every day.

The Media Literacy Paradigm, shown on page 67, is a series of questions you ask about the media products in your communication environment. When you use the Media Literacy Paradigm to understand the media you consume, you are putting a filter on the lens of your mind. Whereas otherwise you would have just read, watched, or listened to your magazines, TV, or CDs, when you are media literate, you begin to question them, think about them, and become more aware of their effects. You become a more discriminating consumer of media products and the popular culture they carry.

One of the key ideas behind the Media Literacy Paradigm is that our overall communications environment is made up of hundreds of thousands of individual media products. Refer to your Media Use Inventory. When you spend X number of hours a year watching TV, you are watching hundreds of individual shows. Likewise, the time you spend with any medium is made up of time spent with *specific media products*—specific CDs, specific magazines, specific films. Tens of thousands of separate ads are targeted at you every year. And the news you consume in the course of a year, whether on TV or in a paper or magazine, is made up of thousands of individual media products.

A Media Literacy Paradigm
Five Stages to Media Literacy

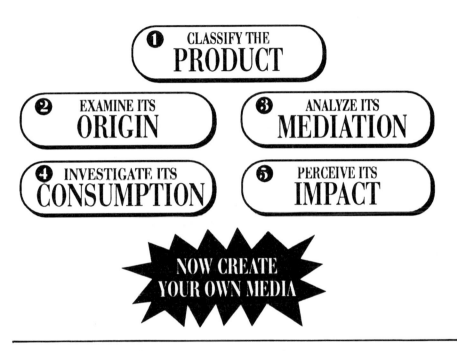

❶ CLASSIFY THE PRODUCT

❷ EXAMINE ITS ORIGIN

❸ ANALYZE ITS MEDIATION

❹ INVESTIGATE ITS CONSUMPTION

❺ PERCEIVE ITS IMPACT

NOW CREATE YOUR OWN MEDIA

Using the Media Literacy Paradigm

The Media Literacy Paradigm can be applied to many of the readings in this book. For example, in the chapter on film a Hollywood director describes what her job is; a lot of what she writes relates to the third stage of the paradigm, *mediation*. A reading in the chapter on recordings addresses the debate as to whether the current pop music scene is better or worse than it was 20 years ago. You will probably consider stage four of the paradigm, *consumption*, in your response to that reading. Many of the **Media Lab, Reflections,** and **Practice** exercises will ask you to focus on one or more of the paradigm stages.

Throughout the text, you will be asked to build a collection or portfolio of media products and messages, a Media Archive. On occasion you will be prompted to analyze a product—for example, a magazine—using questions such as the following: What can you find out about the editors of your magazine? How many people read it? What impact does it have on its readers? Why does it have the "look" it does? As another example of how you will be using the Media Literacy Paradigm, you will be analying a TV show in Chapter Twelve, asking such questions as: What is the show's genre and purpose? Who is it targeted to? How is it scripted? How does it use sound and music? What are the effects of watching that show?

After each stage of the paradigm is presented, it will be applied to *Understanding Mass Media*—the media product you are holding in your hands right now. You'll see how the paradigm is a tool for generating information about the media products you consume.

Stage One: Classifying the Product

1. The first stage in applying the paradigm to a media product is to *classify* it by answering some basic questions.

    *   What is the product's medium?
        Book • Comic • Film • Video • Recording (tape, CD) • Film • Newspaper • Magazine • Radio • TV
    *   What is the product's identifying information?
        What is the product's official, **copyrighted** name? • What is its copyright date? • How much does it cost? • Where was it obtained? • When was it obtained?
    *   Is the product you are analyzing part of a larger one or complete in itself?
        Magazine or article? Textbook or chapter? TV miniseries or episode? Film or series? Video or segment? CD or single cut? Radio show or programming block? Newspaper or section? Comic book or single cartoon?
    *   What is the product's **genre**?
        Books: science fiction, mystery, textbook, etc.?
        Comics: superhero, humor, fantasy, etc.?
        Film: comedy, documentary, Western, horror, etc.?
        Video: music/concert, training, promotional, etc.?
        Recordings: jazz, rap, rock, R&B, etc.?
        Newspapers: daily, tabloid, alternative, etc.?
        Magazines: fashion, current events, sports, music, etc.?

Radio: news/talk, top 40, urban, classic rock, etc.?
TV: sitcom, drama, reality-based, soap opera, etc.?
Advertisements: infomercial, political, PSA, product
information, product identification, etc.?
- What is the surface-level content of the product?
What is the product basically about? • What are the
surface-level messages that are obvious in the product?
• If the product is an advertisement, what is being
advertised?

Classifying the Product: *Understanding Mass Media*
- What is the product's medium?
It is a paper-based book (as distinct from a book on
tape, or CD-based book).
- What is the product's official identifying information?
The copyright information for this book is located on
the third page. The book was obtained from the
publisher, National Textbook Company, which is
located near Chicago. Check with your teacher to
find out when your school purchased it.
- Is the product part of a larger one or complete in itself?
The book is complete in itself, not part of a series of
books, and for the purposes of this example, we'll
consider the whole book, not just a specific chapter.
A teacher's manual and workbook were written to
accompany the book.
- What is the product's genre?
Understanding Mass Media is a textbook.
- What is the surface-level content of the product?
The book is basically about the study of human com-
munication and mass media.

Stage Two: Examining the Origin

2. The second stage of digging into a media product
involves examining its origin—what the product is
based on and the people who created it.

- What is the *content* of the product based on?
Is it based on an **actual event** (for example, coverage
of an earthquake)? • A **pseudo event** (for example,

a televised award ceremony)? • An original creative work (for example, a novel or musical CD)? • A political or philosophical belief (for example, a government propaganda film)? • A social issue or trend (for example, a news magazine)? • A field of study (for example, a textbook)? • A desire to sell something (for example, a radio or magazine ad)?

- If it is based on an event, who decides to turn it into a media product?

  Does an entertainment conglomerate, a news corporation, a freelance writer, or a filmmaker decide? • What are the decision-makers' attitudes, values, goals, and motivations? • How do these factors influence their work?

- If the product is based on a creative work, who is its originator?

  What is the personal background of the originator (for example, gender, ethnicity, age, race, religion, amount of formal education, family condition, career, economic status, and peer group? • What are the originator's attitudes, values, goals, and motivations? • How do these factors influence his or her work?

- Who are the actual mediators of the product, and who funds these mediators?

  Who is involved in turning the idea or event into a media product (for example, editors, agents, journalists, writers, producers, directors, actors, technicians, executives, lawyers, politicians, public interest groups, and advertisers)? • What are their personal backgrounds, attitudes, values, goals, and motivations? • In what way do these factors influence how they mediate the original idea or event? • Do the mediators acknowledge or hide their role in the mediation process? • Who pays for the creation of the media product?

- What are the messages the mediators intend to convey?

  What messages do the mediators of a given product hope the consumer will remember? • Are the meanings and purposes the mediators intend to convey clear or ambiguous, open or hidden?

Examining the Origin: *Understanding Mass Media*
- What is the *content* of the product based on?

  Understanding Mass Media is based on a field of study,

that is, media. It is also based on the idea—the philosophy—that it is important for people to understand their communication environment. The first edition of this media product appeared in 1975.

- If the product is based on an idea, who is the originator of the idea?

    The originator of this book is an author and former teacher named Jeffrey Schrank (who wrote the first four editions). As the author of this edition, I am now its main originator. The aspects of my background I'll share with you are that I was born in 1958 and I have a Bachelor's and a Master's degree in communications. I'm a high school teacher and a writer. I'm married and have one daughter.

- If it is based on an event, who decides to turn it into a media product?

    Understanding Mass Media is not based on an event that happened somewhere; it was planned in advance to be produced as a media product.

- If the product is based on a creative work, who is its originator?

    As the author, my values and motivations are reflected on almost every page of this book. I have been in love with media as far back as I can remember. My father traveled to Japan often while I was very young and always brought home the newest electronic gadgets he could find. We always had newspapers and magazines around the house, so I read them. I watched way too much TV as a kid. During high school, I had music going 24 hours a day. From my first rock concert at age 16 to my most recent one, I have been fascinated with musical acoustics and amplification. My thoughts about media and mass communication have been influenced by several teachers I had in college and by many authors who have written about the subject. I wrote this book so I could share with as many students (readers) as possible the subject I care so much about.

- Who are the mediators of the product, and who funds them?

    After I decided what to put in the book, there were many people involved in mediating the final product that you are reading right now. Editors at National Text-

book Company gave me feedback about my writing
and suggested certain changes. Artists and designers
created the book's layout, typesetters, and printers
put the book together, and marketing professionals
promoted and sold it.

The values and motivations of the rest of the origina-
tors of this media product were similar to mine.
The editors and designers I worked with personally
were interested in publishing the best book possible. But they, along with the businesspeople at the
company, knew that no matter how great a book
they produced, if it didn't sell, it wouldn't help them
earn a profit. In the case of this book, you/your
parent, your school district, or a state or federal agency
bought it.

- What are the messages the mediators intend to convey?
  In the case of a textbook, it's usually clear up front
  what the book is about. National Textbook Company and I hope you come to appreciate the central
  role media play in society. We hope you learn to
  think critically about the mass media you consume.
  We also hope you will apply what you learn from
  this course to the creation of your own media products.

Stage Three: Analyzing the Media of the Product

3. The third stage in the process of digging into a media
   product is analyzing how it was constructed—how
   it was *mediated*—into its final form.

- What are the visual and acoustic properties of the
  product?
  Does the product use low-C or high-C symbols or
  both? How does the final media product communicate?
  What graphic elements does it contain? What is the
  visual resolution of the product? Does the final
  media product communicate acoustically? Does it contain spoken words, music, or other sounds?
- What are the physical properties of the product's
  medium?
  How portable is it? Does it require electricity? How
  durable is it?

- What are the main production techniques of the medium? How flexible is the medium in displaying visual and acoustic information? Do the visuals move? Does the volume change dramatically? How are the images and sounds presented? How are they assembled? What equipment is used to create the product? How expensive are the production techniques? How time-consuming are they?

- What are the **conventions** of presentation—the routines, patterns, and traditions—within the product's genre, and how are they applied to the specific product? What narrative formulas are used to build storylines? How are stereotypes used? How is shot distance manipulated? How are camera angles and movements used? How is sound used? What information is typically left out or emphasized? How is time compressed or expanded? What lyrical patterns are used in songwriting? What are the patterns of timing and length for the genre? How are items within the product separated? How are elements such as music or headlines used to identify parts of the product?

- From the entire range of information that was possible to present, what was included and how was it included? What was excluded and why?

Analyzing the Mediation: *Understanding Mass Media*
- What are the visual and acoustic properties of the product?

    Understanding Mass Media, like all paper-based books, communicates visually (as opposed to a book on audiotape which communicates acoustically). This textbook primarily uses the low-C symbol system of written words (text), although it contains many high-C symbols, such as illustrations and photographs as well as charts and graphs. Many of the photos are in full-color, though they obviously do not move. As you'll learn more about in Chapter Six (on recordings), the digital technologies of **CD-ROM** and **CD-I** combine written words (text), moving visuals, and stereo sound. In the not-too-distant future, some textbooks—including, undoubtedly at least one on mass media—will come in digitized form, which will provide a very different experience. You will be able to watch the film or TV show, see the ad, or listen to the recording in addition to reading about those products and looking at photos of them.

- What are the physical properties of the product's medium?

    Understanding Mass Media is quite portable and fairly rugged; you can plop it down without it breaking. It is a paper based media product and does not require electricity to use.

- What are the main production techniques of the medium?

    I composed the text on a computer using word processing software. Many of the photos were provided to the publisher in the form of 35mm slides, which were then enlarged. The text, photos, and other graphics were assembled using a variety of manual and computer-aided design techniques. The final pages were printed on large, color printing presses and then covered, stitched, and bound. The entire production process—from the time the publisher received my **manuscript** (which I wrote in about a year) to the time the book was ready to be shipped for purchase—took a little less than a year.

- What are the conventions of presentation within the product's genre and how are they applied to the specific product?

    This book illustrates many standard textbook conventions; for example, chapters are divided by topic (whereas chapters in novels are usually divided by a flow of events or other organizing idea). Textbooks, almost by definition, are educational, so *Understanding Mass Media* contains Media Labs and Practice activities. (Imagine a best-selling paperback presenting quizzes and activities to help you determine what you got out of it.) It includes photos and other graphic elements. Important terms and phrases are highlighted by **boldface type** and are explained separately in a glossary. To help you find specific information, there is an index of topics and names in the back.

    The paper *Understanding Mass Media* is printed on has a certain weight and feel to it; compare it to paper found in your other textbooks. The main text is printed

in a certain **font** (called Galliard Roman) in a standard size, while chapter headings are printed in another
font (called Galliard Bold) and at various sizes.

   Two relatively new elements found in this book are
the *Learning Targets* and *Checking In* features at the
beginning of each chapter. Only in the last ten years
or so have most textbooks told their readers what
they can expect to learn, or asked them to think about
what they already know before they dig into a chapter. These approaches, however, are quickly becoming
textbook conventions.

- From the entire range of information that was possible
  to present, what was included and how was it included?
  What was excluded and why?

   The purpose of *Understanding Mass Media* is to provide an introduction to the topic of mass media,
   so each of the major areas are covered. Many important
   areas of mass media (such as ownership of media
   companies) are only touched upon because so many
   changes take place so quickly. For example, the first
   half of 1994 saw literally dozens of multimillion-dollar
   deals between communications companies. Companies merged or simply bought each other in a frenzy
   to secure a place on the information highway. Other
   companies announced plans to merge and then
   retracted those plans. That kind of specific information would be out-of-date within a year of this book's
   publication and so is not included.

Stage Four: Investigating the Consumption of the Product

4. The fourth stage in applying the Media Literacy Para-
    digm is to investigate how you *consume* the prod-
    uct—how you experience and interpret it—and how the
    unique characteristics of the product's medium influ-
    ence the way you consume it.

- Who is the intended audience for the product?
  Who is the target market for the product? What do
  people in that market—that demographic group—have

The Media Literacy Paradigm can be used to analyze any media product.
Photo: Bradley Wilson.

in common? Why did the originator of the product target that group?

- How does your background influence how you consume the product?

  In what ways do these paradigm lenses affect how you experience and interpret the product: gender, ethnicity, age, race, religion, amount of formal education, family background, personal value system, career, economic status, peer group, prior experience with the medium, prior knowledge of the product's subject?

- What is your motivation for consuming the product?

  To kill time? To become educated? To be entertained? To become informed? To meet a requirement? How does your motivation influence the way you consume the product?

- How might other people consume the same product differently given their unique motivations, back-grounds, and experiences?
- What are the particular requirements for consuming the product based on its medium?

    What kinds of skills are required—for example, reading, sustained concentration, or computer skills? What physical senses, such as sight, hearing, or touch, are used when consuming a particular media product? What are the immediate environmental requirements of consumption—for example, lighting, absence of noise, solitude, group experience, or a large or small space? Who controls the timing of the presentation? How interactive is the product?

- Who has access to the media products in a given category?

    How do the cost of the product and the equipment needed to use it determine who consumes it? To what degree is equal access to the product guaranteed by the government?

Investigating the Consumption: *Understanding Mass Media*

- Who is the intended audience for the product?

    Identifying the target market for textbooks is fairly easy. You are a member of the demographic group for this textbook—high school and college students. You share many things in common with the millions of other students, but in terms of this media product, you share real-life experience with media: you watch TV, read magazines, listen to the radio, and so on. As the author of this media product, I targeted you because you are the age student I like to work with. I also believe it is critical for people to become aware of their communication environment as early in life as is practical. The issues addressed in this book are presented at an academic level too complex for younger students.

- How does your background influence how you consume the product?

    No matter how good or interesting or boring you think this book is, someone else will have a different opinion. Why? Because people are different. You may have noticed the use of African-American and Hispanic names in Part One, or you may not have, depending on your race or ethnicity. Your family's values may influence how hard you are willing to work for a good grade in this class; or you may not care too much about the subject. These variables and more help explain how and why we sometimes react differently to media products, including textbooks.

- What is your motivation for consuming the product?
  Your first motivation for consuming *Understanding Mass Media* is probably to meet a requirement so that you can pass the class and eventually graduate. My hope is that your first motivation will give way to a more self-directed motivation and you consume this product in a more meaningful way. In either case, your reasons for consuming this product affect what you get out of it.

- How might other people consume the same product differently given their unique motivations, backgrounds, and experiences?
  Some of your classmates may read the book less carefully than you; some may have a tougher (or easier) time with some of the vocabulary. Some of your classmates may have substantial prior knowledge of certain topics if they are on the staff of your school newspaper or TV station.

- What are the unique requirements for consuming the product based on its medium?
  First, you need to know how to read fairly well, which, incidentally, means you need to be able to *see* the book (since it's a visual medium). You need to touch it, and you need a relatively quiet environment in which to use it. It's portable, so you can use it in a variety of settings. Since each copy of this media product is designed to be used by one person at a time, you have control over the pace at which you move through the information it presents. Unlike new **multimedia** products (such as CD-ROMs), traditional textbooks are not very interactive. *Understanding Mass Media*, however, does attempt to engage you by presenting models such as this Media Literacy Paradigm, which you'll refer to and then apply to your own learning activities.

- Who has access to the media products in a given category? Books are the most economically accessible medium in this country; public libraries do not require you to own a piece of communications technology and (in most places) do not charge a fee. Textbooks, however, are not as widely available to the public. You have access to *Understanding Mass Media* by virtue of your being a student and are allowed to use it regardless of your economic status.

Stage Five: Perceiving the Impact of the Product

5. The fifth stage of the Media Literacy Paradigm is to perceive how you are affected by specific media products and by the overall media you consume. How do media products influence who you are? How does the overall media environment influence society's attitudes, beliefs, and behaviors?

- How do the production techniques and conventions of genre influence the way you respond to the product? How does your mind respond differently to printed words, visual images, spoken words, music, and sounds? How do you respond emotionally to these? How do particular camera angles and movements, visual layouts, and manipulated sounds affect you?
- What are the personal effects of the media you consume? How are your personal attitudes, tastes, goals, and behaviors shaped by specific media products and by your overall media consumption?
- What are the local, national, and global effects of the media we consume as a society? How do media isolate people? How do media provide shared experiences? How are our views of the world beyond our own lives framed by the media we consume? How do media contribute to globalization?
- What are the effects of spending time and money on media? How much time and money do we spend consuming media products individually, as a nation, and throughout the world? How does our consumption influence the

creation of media products? Who benefits from the money spent on media products?

- How will our current consumption of media influence the media we will create and consume in the future?
  How are media evolving? How will they be similar to or different from the media we consume now? How will we use them?

Perceiving the Impact: *Understanding Mass Media*

- What is the personal and social impact of the product?
  Only you can explain your reaction to this book. As the author, I hope your attitudes toward media and their messages change for the better. Perhaps you will consider a career in one of the various media industries explored in this textbook.

- How do production techniques and conventions of genre influence the way you respond to the product?
  As you learned in Chapter One, your brain works a little differently when it encounters words, pictures, and sounds. The absence of sound and moving images makes reading a book a more **cognitive** experience than watching a film or a TV show (both of which provoke emotional responses more easily because of the high-C symbol they use). *Understanding Mass Media* does not present itself to you the way a radio show does; you have to work a little harder for it to be meaningful to you. There are no thunderous sound effects to startle you into paying attention. You have to supply a dose of imagination each time I use words to refer to a situation or event. You may well have flipped through *Understanding Mass Media* the day you received it and said to yourself, "Just another textbook." You probably have a number of feelings about the genre of textbooks. However, you might have stopped at some of the photos and reading titles and thought, "Hmmm . . . what's this about?" If you did, the text design and the photos worked. They had the impact the mediators of this product wanted them to have.

- What are the personal effects of the media you consume overall?
  It is unfortunate but true that you, as an American

teenager, often see textbooks as not being relevant to your life—at least not compared with the music, films, and other pop culture which surround you. Yet the textbooks you used in elementary school played an important role in the formation of your social paradigms, and the textbooks you use now and in college will play an equally important role in building up your knowledge of yourself and the world.

- What are the local, national and global effects of the media we consume as a society?

    By definition, a *mass* medium provides large numbers of people with the experience of watching, reading, or listening to the same product. Will *Understanding Mass Media* have a local or national impact? Thousands of students throughout the country will use it, and maybe some of them will devise projects which involve their communities. However, as you'll discover in Chapter Twelve, thousands of people is a miniscule number compared to the billions of humans who can now receive either CNN or CNN International. Though the media product in your hands right now will not have a global impact, it will shed light on the ones that do.

- What are the effects of spending time and money on media?

    Whenever you watch a show, buy a CD, or go to a film, you influence the creation of new media products. In America, if it "sells," more of it will be produced; if it doesn't sell, it will disappear. This holds true for all media products, including textbooks.

    The direct economic effect of your school's having purchased *Understanding Mass Media* is that its publisher can earn a profit and continue in business. So too, the billions of dollars Americans spend annually on media products filter down to millions of people who either work in media-related industries or own stock in those industries.

- How will our current consumption of media influence the media we will create and consume in the future?

    As mentioned earlier, some textbooks in the near future (along with other genres—books, magazines) will be interactive and come in a digital medium such as CD-I. The mediators (producers) of these textbooks will be people who are already comfortable with computer technology and who can envision presenting information in the new ways such technology will allow. Change evolves from generation to generation.

The people who create the shows on MTV were the first generation of human beings to truly grow up with TV. The TV they watched was produced—mediated—by people who grew up listening to radio. It's amazing to compare a show such as "Bewitched" from the 1960s to MTV's "Liquid Television" from the 1990s; you can see how far the mediation of TV products has come in one generation. You are the first generation to have grown up with MTV, the cable jungle, and rapid-action video games. What will you produce 10 or 15 years from now when you are populating the control rooms of the interactive entertainment companies? What will you create to keep consumers interested?

No one really knows how the next era of human communications (**global, point-to-point interactivity**) will change society. But if we are going to try to forecast the impact of these changes, we must start by examining the impact of our current media consumption.

 Reflections

Some students feel a little apprehensive about becoming media literate because they think they won't enjoy a given media product as much once they know how it was put together. Do you feel that way? If so, why? If you don't, why do you think some people do? What do you think will happen to your tastes in media as a result of becoming media literate? Will you change what you watch, read, or listen to? Why? How? How do you think American society would change if everyone were media literate?

Part of media literacy involves producing your own media. Students shown here are shooting a video about gangs. *Photo courtesy of the Educational Video Center, New York City.*

Create Your Own Media

Using the Media Literacy Paradigm to dig into media products and to really understand them is important. However, there is one more crucial step involved in becoming truly *media literate:* creating your own media products. It is one thing to analyze someone else's media product; it's another to work through the creative process yourself. Throughout the rest of the book, you'll find lists of project ideas and suggestions on how to produce them.

What you create depends on the resources available. Even if your school does not have many resources, however, there are a variety of things you can do. For example, many large video stores rent camcorders; your class may "chip in" toward the rental fee or you (your instructor) may ask the video store if an education-related arrangement can be made. You can call your local AM or FM radio station, or local cable TV station, and ask them whether they would air a class-produced Public Service Announcement (PSA) on, for example, drunk driving. If you don't have the basic recording equipment needed, you may investigate equipment available through public libraries or communicating centers, asking whether they would lend you what you need. If you prepare your proposal well and offer some form of public recognition in return, you can usually find someone in your community who will help out. Whether you produce media products for each other in the class, for your school via posters, the school paper, radio, or TV station, for your community via cable TV or radio, or for the world-wide online community via computers (Internet), the point is to get out there and apply the paradigm!

Recap

All human beings have a collection of **paradigms** that influence how we see the world around us. These paradigms form early in life and help determine our opinions and values. They are a result of the experiences we accept as being normal. Even though our paradigms are a fundamental part of who we are as individuals, we are often unaware of them.

We all have different paradigms which shape our personal philosophies and tastes, but we also share many paradigms because we have many experiences in common. Among these common paradigms is our acceptance of the central role media play in our lives. It is almost impossible to imagine life without telephones, television, recorded music, or paper-based media. We rely on media for our education, work, and leisure, yet we rarely stop to think about these media—where they come from, how they operate, and the impact they have on us.

The **Media Literacy Paradigm** presents a way of seeing and understanding the media around us. It serves as a lens through which to study the media products you consume in the course of everyday life. First, you pick a media product to run through the paradigm, then examine its **origin** and analyze how it was **mediated**. Finally, you investigate its **consumption** and perceive its **impact**.

MEDIA LAB   Media Products

- **Product:** Create a profile or description for a fictional media product by applying each question from the first stage of the Media Literacy Paradigm to it. Make up a title and a copyright date, select a medium and genre for your product, and so on.

- **Origin:** Find out who produced an ad (for example, a local restaurant or car dealership) on your cable TV system (usually a local ad agency or the cable system itself). With the merchant's permission, interview the mediators of the ad and ask them the questions found in the second stage of the Media Literacy Paradigm.

- **Mediation:** Design a CD-ROM based on a chapter of one of your textbooks. Decide how much of the printed material will stay as text to be read off the screen and how much will be recorded so the user can hear it being read. What kind of voice will read it? Will you include music or sound effects in the background? What kind? What portions will you include as film? Will you present the material in a fixed sequence or let the user browse the information in any order? Why?

- **Consumption:** Create three fictional media products, each targeted at one of the following demographic groups: (1) single men in their mid-forties; (2) upper-income retired couples; (3) female high school students. Think about each target group as they relate to the questions in the third *(Consumption)* stage of the Media Literacy Paradigm and then write your product profiles as you did in the first activity.

- **Impact:** Conduct a survey to determine media impact. Ask respondents to rank the mass media presented in Part Two according to the impact each medium has on their lives, from greatest to least. Also ask for an example of a specific product from each medium that the respondent remembers had an impact on him or her. Try distributing the survey to two different age groups (for example, 50 surveys to fellow students and 50 to a group of parents over 45 years old). What conclusions can you draw from the results?

The media product you are reading right now serves as an example of how the paradigm can be used. *Understanding Mass media* had a particular origin and was mediated in a way consistent with its genre. As the main consumer of this media product, you are responsible for the impact it has on your life.

Resources for Further Reading

Considine, David. *Visual Messages* (Englewood, N.J.: Teacher Ideas Press, 1992).

Lusted, David. *The Media Studies Book* (New York: Routledge, 1991).

Adbusters magazine, The Media Foundation, 1243 West 7th Avenue, Vancouver, B.C. V6H 1B7 Canada.

Media Culture Review magazine, The Institute for Alternative Journalism, 77 Federal Street, San Francisco, CA 94107.

SEGUE

A Media Literacy Paradigm

Armed with the Media Literacy Paradigm, it is time to examine each mass medium in greater detail. The first four media (books, comics, recordings, and film) do not depend on advertising as much as the next four (radio, magazines, television, and newspapers), though all are powerful channels of pop culture. We start with the first mass medium, books.

CHAPTER FOUR

Books–The First Mass Medium

Learning Targets

After working through this chapter, you will be able to

- Understand the linear structure of books as a medium;
- Find your way around a local bookstore;
- Identify basic elements of book design;
- Discuss how books contribute to popular culture; and
- Explain how and why censorship of books typically occurs.

Checking In

- List five books you have read recently, whether assigned or by choice.
- Draw a flowchart of how you think books are categorized in a typical bookstore.
- Identify a book you think has had an important impact on American society and briefly describe that impact.
- Define the word *censorship*.

Books As a Medium
How We Read

Though the significance of this concept is tough to grasp, one of the most important qualities of written language is that it presents information in a *linear* fashion. This means that words and sentences follow each other in line, or in sequence. Our eyes move along a line of print, reading each word and building words into sentences. We then build the meaning of sentences into thoughts which flow together in sequence and (usually) make some kind of sense. We read individual paragraphs and chapters, and, for that matter, entire books, in linear order. As you read this page right now, you are not jumping around reading random words. At first you may have scanned the page until something caught your eye, but eventually you settled into a linear pattern of reading the words in sequence, because that is the only way they make sense. This is so obvious that you may ask yourself, "So what?"

The linear quality of written language provides a much more controlled communication experience than the language we use inside our own minds. Take stock of all the thoughts in your head at this exact moment. You'll become aware of thoughts such as "I'm kinda tired," or "It's pretty quiet in here," or "I wonder if I'm going to be tested on this." As I write these words at 11:15 P.M. on July 27, 1994, sitting at my computer, I'm aware of other thoughts floating around in my head, such as "I'm running out of hard drive space—bummer," and "I'm sick of this 95-degree weather."

Except for this one occasion to illustrate my point, I do not write down any of those other thoughts. I stick to a very linear, sequential presentation of my ideas by w iting linear sentences, in carefully sequenced paragraphs, sections and chapters. And you read them that way! This would be a b zarre book if I merely collected my thoughts about media into random sentences and then chopped up those sentences into a random word order. It would be equally bizarre if you randomly skipped around the book reading it as a hodge-podge of unconnected words. In either case, it would not mean anything, and that's the crucial point! Written language causes the mind to think in a linear, sequential, controlled way. It forces you to focus your attention in order for its communication to be successful. As you'll discover in later chapters, not all media require or foster this kind of mental activity.

Uniform Communication

You know the telephone game where someone starts a message and whispers it into the ear of the next person, who in turn whispers it to the next and so on, until the last person says the original message aloud. Most of the time the message ends up changed at least a little bit.* Imagine if the same thing happened with books. Every time an original **manuscript** was printed, each copy was changed a little bit. After a few hundred copies, you'd have many slightly different books. Such a lack of uniformity would certainly render books less effective as educational tools and as vehicles of

---

*How would this communication event fit the Shannon-Weaver model presented in Chapter 1?

pop culture. It would be quite strange indeed if each member of your class were reading a different version of *Understanding Mass Media*—a word left out here and there, a different chapter order, different page numbers, different definitions of key terms. (Now *that* would cause more than a few teacher headaches!) The whole value of books as a system of storing and distributing knowledge is based on their ability to present that knowledge in a standardized and uniform way.

One of your many paradigms is that the particular version of the media product you consume is the same as everyone else's version. The episode of "Northern Exposure" you watched last night in your living room was the same one your friend watched at his house. The novel you're reading, recommended by a friend, is the same one she read. However, this paradigm did not exist among human beings until the printing press, invented in the 15th century, turned books into the first mass medium.

Permanent Communication

Not only did the printing press make possible the quick and reliable copying of information, it allowed people to store information permanently, or at least for many generations. Imagine all of the wonderful ideas which, until 500 years ago, just passed away along with the people who thought them. Prior to the printing press, the ideas and knowledge you wanted to share with others had to be transmitted either orally or by handwritten manuscript. If you died or your manuscript was lost, your idea was lost too. Your family or friends could pass on your work orally, but it would change a little with each telling. Once your work was published in a book, however, and hundreds of copies of it were available, it had a much better chance of being available for a long time.

It is no wonder that the Age of Enlightenment followed on the heels of the invention of the printing press. Knowledge became permanent and accessible, and, as it built up in libraries, more and more people could educate themselves. Those people in turn made new scientific discoveries and published their knowledge for even more people to read, and the expanding storehouse of knowledge continues to grow at an increasing rate. We don't think twice about borrowing from a library books written 30, 60, or 100 years ago. Books are still the major medium by which knowledge is cataloged and stored. I used books more than any other medium to prepare for writing *Understanding Mass Media*—books I read in high school and still have, books I've researched in my public library, and books I've purchased over the last ten years as I've studied the field of mass media.

One of the downsides of permanence is that while the information in a book stays the same, the world around it changes. While this does not pose a problem for many novels (fiction), which don't depend on being current, it does affect nonfiction books. New knowledge is developed all the time, yet the knowledge in a given book remains frozen in time—at least until it is revised and republished. For example, this is the fifth edition of *Understanding Mass Media*; the first edition first came out in 1975. A lot has changed since then, even since the last edition appeared in 1990. (To prevent this book from being out-of-date as you're reading it now, I have tried to present ideas about how to think about media such as the Media Literary Paradigm, rather than just facts and figures about the media in 1994, which, though interesting, will remain frozen on these pages.)

Portable Communication

Another quality of books that made them so important as a mass medium is that they were portable. Though we now take such portability for granted, being able to transport books easily made the widespread distribution of knowledge possible even before the discovery of electricity. We don't think twice about bringing paperbacks to the beach, on airplanes, or just about anywhere; you have no doubt lugged this book around with you. Magazines, newspapers, and comics share a similar degree of portability, though books are the most permanent of the print-based media. While this next observation may strike you as amusingly obvious, it is still an important one: Books do not require batteries. This simple fact makes them technologically immune to the ravages of obsolescence; that is, unlike computers (or any other electronic technology on which written words are stored), you do not have to constantly purchase new equipment to read a book. You don't need any equipment to read a book. (In the future, there may come a time when new books are only published electronically and paper-based books are entrusted to museum libraries. Many people point to the trees we would save if paper-based media became a thing of the past.)

Books are a popular and portable communication medium. *Photo of book-signing courtesy of author Alzina Stone Dale. Photographer: B. Nicholas.*

A Brief History of Books

The history of books contains a few interesting stories. The first books go back about 5000 years. Etched on clay tablets, these collections of legal, religious, and mythic writings were relatively permanent but not very portable. The invention of **papyrus** by the ancient Egyptians changed the basic technique of writing from etching to writing with ink. Papyrus could also be strung together into scrolls, which allowed longer, portable documents. Improvements in writing surfaces (such as animal-skin parchment) and inks made steady progress, and books finally moved from scroll form to the form we are familiar with: folded sheets of paper bound in the center and protected with a strong cover. Still, books were quite rare until about 500 years ago; historians claim that England's Cambridge University, one of the finest in Europe, had only 22 books in its entire library in the early 1400s. Then Gutenberg came along.

Though Johannes Gutenberg is generally credited with inventing the mechanical printing press, the key to his success, **mov-**

able type, probably was invented by the Chinese a few centuries earlier. Gutenberg worked out many of the problems of movable type and took advantage of a flourishing European economy in the late 1400s to print Bibles on his modified wine press for the growing numbers of clergy and businessmen. His basic design was copied all over Europe by the early 1500s.

One of the interesting things about those 22 books in the Cambridge University library of the 1400s is that none of them had page numbers, which meant that none of them had a table of contents or an index in the back—how could they without page numbers? Not until after the invention of the printing press, when the printing and binding processes made folios (page numbers) a reality and books became widely used as sources of knowledge, did **pagination** become important to readers. Some historians even argue that the *idea* of numbering pages is what really made the Enlightenment possible. With page numbers, information within a book could be *organized* and *categorized* for easy reference; and that notion of categorized knowledge helped pave the way for the development of organized scientific disciplines, such as biology, physics, chemistry, and astronomy.

The technology of printing did not change much until the 1800s, when continuous-roll paper was invented and metal presses replaced wooden ones. In America, as more and more people learned to read, the publishing industry took off. Magazines, newspapers, and books thrived in a political environment which guaranteed freedom of the press. The early 1900s gave birth to many of today's largest publishing companies, such as Prentice-Hall and Random House. Finally, with the huge success of the pocket paperback in the 1940s, books became the mass medium they are today.

Industry Snapshot: Publishing
The Two Main Markets for Books

The largest segment of the book business is not directly available to the general public. This segment is made up of the two largest categories of books: textbooks, which account for about 30 percent of all books sold, and professional reference books (including technical, medical, and scientific books) which account for another 25 percent. The remaining 45 percent of books are the ones we see

> **The 1990s: Publishing in the United States**
>
> - Approximately 20 billion dollars worth of books are bought each year.
> - Roughly 50,000 new books are published each year.
> - More than 20,000 book publishers exist, but only about a dozen of them publish over 80 percent of all new books. (The vast majority of publishers release fewer than four new books a year.)
> - Americans buy over one million mass market paperbacks every day.

in bookstores, which come in three basic formats: hardcover, mass market paperbacks (any book in the familiar 7-x-4-inch size), and trade paperbacks (paperbacks of any other size).

Book Genres

Bookstores usually categorize their stock by fiction and nonfiction. In the area of fiction, you'll find classic and current, literature including a group of genres such as science fiction, romance, mystery, horror, and young adult. Nonfiction books are divided into sections such as art, sports, sociology, business, and travel.

Best-sellers

Only a small fraction of all books published annually make what most of us would consider a lot of money. Most authors toil long hours for thousands or sometimes only hundreds of dollars, but those who make it big make it really big. Getting a book on the best-sellers list means huge revenues for the author and its publisher. Well-known authors like Danielle Steele and Stephen King frequently earn millions of dollars per book. Other best-selling authors, such as Tom Clancy and John Grisham, whose books make good movies, can earn additional millions by selling to a Hollywood studio the film rights to a book they have not yet written. Even certain first-time authors can make it big in the publishing world if they have a story enough people are interested

MARCH 6, 1995

PublishersWeekly

PAPERBACK BESTSELLERS

MASS MARKET

	Title	Last Week	Weeks on List
1	**Tom Clancy's Op-Center.** *Tom Clancy.* Berkley, $6.99 ISBN 0-425-14736-3	1	7
2	**The Day After Tomorrow.** *Allan Folsom.* Warner Vision, $6.99 ISBN 0-446-60041-5	3	7
3	**Accident.** *Danielle Steel.* Dell, $6.99 ISBN 0-440-21754-7	2	4
4	**Inca Gold.** *Clive Cussler.* Pocket Books, $6.99 ISBN 0-671-51981-6	4	2
5	**The Cat Who Came to Breakfast.** *Lilian Jackson Braun.* Jove, $5.99 ISBN 0-515-11564-9	5	3
6	**The Robber Bride.** *Margaret Atwood.* Bantam, $6.50 ISBN 0-553-56905-8	10	4
7	**Icebound.** *Dean Koontz.* Ballantine, $6.99 ISBN 0-345-38435-0	6	8
8	**Embraced by the Light.** *Betty J. Eadie.* Bantam, $5.99 ISBN 0-553-56591-5	9	24
9	**Star Wars: Ambush at Corellia.** *Roger MacBride Allen.* Bantam, $5.99 ISBN 0-553-29803-8	8	4
10	**Night Prey.** *John Sandford.* Berkley, $6.99 ISBN 0-425-14641-3	11	2
11	**Fatal Cure.** *Robin Cook.* Berkley, $6.99 ISBN 0-425-14563-8	7	7
12	**Sisters and Lovers.** *Connie Briscoe.* Ivy, $6.99 ISBN 0-8041-1334-3	14	2
13	**Heartstone.** *Phillip Margolin.* Bantam, $6.50 ISBN 0-553-56978-3	13	4
14	**Smilla's Sense of Snow.** *Peter Hoeg.* Dell, $6.50 ISBN 0-440-21853-5	15	28
15	**Family Blessings.** *LaVyrle Spencer.* Jove, $6.50 ISBN 0-515-11563-0	12	6

TRADE

	Title	Last Week	Weeks on List
1	**Chicken Soup for the Soul.** *Jack Canfield & Mark Hansen, eds.* Health Communications, $12 ISBN 1-55874-262-X	1	32
2	**The Shipping News.** *E. Annie Proulx.* S & S/Touchstone, $12 ISBN 0-671-51005-3	2	40
3	**The Celestine Prophecy: Experiential Guide.** *James Redfield and Carol Adrienne.* Warner, $8.99 ISBN 0-446-67122-3	5	9
4	**7 Habits of Highly Effective People.** *Stephen R. Covey.* S & S/Fireside, $12 ISBN 0-671-70863-5	3	214
5	**What to Expect the Toddler Years.** *A. Eisenberg, H. Murkoff & S. Hathaway.* Workman, $15.95 ISBN 0-89480-994-6	4	15
6	**Driven to Distraction.** *Edward Hallowell and John J. Ratey.* S & S/Touchstone, $12 ISBN 0-684-80128-0	7	4
7	**What to Expect When You're Expecting.** *A. Eisenberg, H. Murkoff & S. Hathaway.* Workman, $10.95 ISBN 0-89480-829-X	6	91
8	**How We Die.** *Sherwin Nuland, M.D.* Vintage, $13 ISBN 0-679-74244-1	9	7
9	**Care of the Soul.** *Thomas Moore.* HarperPerennial, $12 ISBN 0-06-092224-9	12	60
10	**Makes Me Wanna Holler.** *Nathan McCall.* Vintage, $12 ISBN 0-679-74070-8	10	2
11	**Ten Stupid Things Women Do to Mess Up Their Lives.** *Laura Schlessinger.* HarperPerennial, $10 ISBN 0-06-097649-7	8	4
12	**Soul Mates.** *Thomas Moore.* HarperPerennial, $13 ISBN 0-06-092575-2	11	9
13	**The Artist's Way.** *Julia Cameron with Mark Bryan.* Jeremy Tarcher, $13.95 ISBN 0-87477-694-5	–	2
14	**Tightwad Gazette II.** *Amy Dacyczyn.* Villard, $11.99 ISBN 0-679-75078-9	14	2
15	**Bingo Palace.** *Louise Erdrich.* HarperPerennial, $13 ISBN 0-06-092585-X	–	1

Publishers Weekly (ISSN 0000-0019) RPUSA 123397457 is published weekly, with the exception of the last week in December. Published by the Cahners Publishing Company, 249 W. 17th Street New York, NY 10011-5300, a Division of Reed Publishing USA, 275 Washington St., Newton MA 02158-1630. Robert L. Krakoff, Chairman and Chief Executive Officer; Timothy C. O'Brien, Executive Vice President/Finance and Administration; John Beni, Senior Vice President/General Manager, New York Division; Fred Ciporen, Vice President/Publishing Director. Circulation records are maintained at ESP Computer Services, INC., 19110 Van Ness Ave., Torrance, CA 90501-1170. Phone (800) 278-2991. Second Class postage paid at New York, N.Y. and additional mailing offices. Canada Post International Publications Mail Product (Canadian Distribution) Sales Agreement No. 0607509. POSTMASTER: Send address changes to PUBLISHERS WEEKLY, P.O. Box 6457, Torrance, CA 90504. PUBLISHERS WEEKLY copyright 1995 by Reed Publishing USA. Rates for non-qualified subscriptions including all issues: U.S.A., $139; Canada, $187 (includes 7% GST, GST #123397457); Foreign, $270. Except for special issues where price changes are indicated, single copies are available for $5.00 US and foreign; $10.00 for Announcement issues. Please address all subscription mail to Publishers Weekly, P.O. Box 6457, Torrance, CA 90504. PUBLISHERS WEEKLY is a (registered) trademark of Reed Properties, Inc., used under license. PRINTED IN THE USA.

Reprinted by permission from the March 6, 1995 issue of *Publishers Weekly*, published by Cahners Publishing Company, a division of Reed Publishing USA. Copyright © 1995 by Reed Publishing.

in reading. General Norman Schwarzkopf, who commanded Coalition troops in the Persian Gulf war, was given a five-million-dollar advance for his autobiography.

The Look and Feel of Books
Typography and Design

Though you are quite aware that books have unique cover designs, you are probably less aware of how varied the inside pages of books can be. The **typography** of the pages in a book—that is, the style, size, and spacing of letters—helps determine the book's "feel." Mass market paperbacks are usually printed in a **serif** font of about 9 or 10 **points**. A serif font, or typeface, has curlicues at its edges like the letters you're reading now. (By contrast, this is a sans-serif font, with no curlicues.) Points refer to a unit of size; this is an 11 point font called Galliard.

This is 14 point type.

And this is 18 point type. Large-print books for the visually impaired are often printed in 18 point type or even larger.

The last element to consider when placing words on a page is **leading**. Leading refers to the amount of space between lines of type, and is measured in points from the baseline of one line of type to the baseline of the next line. Leading is proportional to the point size of the text. This text is printed with 13 points of leading.

This sample of text is printed with 9 point leading. You can see that it looks more crowded and is tougher to read.

This sample of text is printed with 16 point leading. You can see that it looks more spacious and is easier to read.

This book uses a different font for some of its **headings** and photo/illustration **captions**. Books (and magazines, as you'll see in Chapter Ten) increasingly are being designed with a less traditional, more creative typography.

Picture Books

Not all books are based on written language. Books for preschoolers, though they may have some text, are primarily picture books. Though the term *picture book* is usually associated with children, there are hundreds of thousands of books which present high-correspondence (high-C) symbols (pictures). Books are a fantastic medium for capturing the entire range of visual arts. Collections of drawings, paintings, computer art, photography, and three dimensional images make up a sizable chunk of the nonfiction market. In fact, books featuring three-dimensional (3-D) graphic images, such as *Magic Eye 3D Illusions by N.E. Thing Enterprises* have been a national best-sellers. (Going back to Chapter One for a moment, that 3-D image is interesting because it starts out as a very low-C symbol when you look at just the seemingly random colors, and then it changes into a higher-C symbol when the hidden 3-D picture appears.) Other types of picture books include high school and college yearbooks.

Judging Books by Their Covers

From the preceding Industry Snapshot you know that a majority of books (at least in this country) are purchased for academic or professional reasons. When it comes to reading by choice, what makes a person select a particular book? If you are talking about nonfiction, people usually select books to *learn* something; for example, how to repair a motorcycle, why Communism collapsed, or where to find an entertainment agent to promote your musical group. When you are talking about fiction, people usually select books in order to be entertained in some way. Once you've been drawn to a certain genre (let's say you're a horror buff), what makes you pick up a particular book? A recommendation from a friend? The author's reputation? Maybe. Book publishers think they know why you'll finally settle on a particular book: It's not how good the book is, it's whether its cover grabs you. The reading on page 100 from *Publishers Weekly* discusses the impact of cover design.

Books and Popular Culture

Books have contained the world's scholarly knowledge for centuries, and, in one form or another, will continue to serve educational purposes. New research in areas such as medicine, computers, and

Park Avenue Script
Aa Bb Cc Dd Ee Ff Gg Hh Ii Jj Kk Ll Mm
Nn Oo Pp Qq Rr Ss Tt Uu Vv Ww Xx Yy Zz
1234567890 .,;:"&!?$

Parliament
abcdefghijklmnopqrstuvwxyz
ABCDEFGHIJKLMNOPQRSTUVWXYZ
1234567890 .,:;"&!?$

Parsons
abcdefghijklmnopqrstuvwxyz
ABCDEFGHIJKLMNOPQRSTUVWXYZ
1234567890 .,;:"&!?$

Parsons Italic
abcdefghijklmnopqrstuvwxyz
ABCDEFGHIJKLMNOPQRSTUVWXYZ
1234567890 .,;:"&!?$

Parsons Bold
abcdefghijklmnopqrstuvwxyz
ABCDEFGHIJKLMNOPQRSTUVW
XYZ1234567890 .,;:"&!?$

Pascal
abcdefghijklmnopqrstuvwxyz
ABCDEFGHIJKLMNOPQRSTUVWXYZ
1234567890 .,;:"&!?$

Pegasus™
abcdefghijklmnopqrstuvwxyz
ABCDEFGHIJKLMNOPQRSTUVWXYZ
1234567890 .,;:"&!?$

Pegasus™ Italic
abcdefghijklmnopqrstuvwxyz
ABCDEFGHIJKLMNOPQRSTUVWXYZ
1234567890 .,;:"&!?$

Pegasus™ Bold
abcdefghijklmnopqrstuvwxyz
ABCDEFGHIJKLMNOPQRSTUVWXYZ
1234567890 .,;:"&!?$

Peignot® Light
abcdefghijklmnopqrstuvwxyz
ABCDEFGHIJKLMNOPQRSTUVWXYZ
1234567890 .,;:"&!?$

Peignot® Demi
abcdefghijklmnopqrstuvwxyz
ABCDEFGHIJKLMNOPQRSTUVWXYZ
1234567890 .,;:"&!?$

Peignot® Bold
abcdefghijklmnopqrstuvwxyz
ABCDEFGHIJKLMNOPQRSTUVWXYZ
1234567890 .,;:"&!?S

Perpetua
abcdefghijklmnopqrstuvwxyz
ABCDEFGHIJKLMNOPQRSTUVWXYZ
1234567890 .,;:"&!?S .

Perpetua Italic
abcdefghijklmnopqrstuvwxyz
ABCDEFGHIJKLMNOPQRSTUVWXYZ
1234567890 .,;:"&!?S

Perpetua Bold
abcdefghijklmnopqrstuvwxyz
ABCDEFGHIJKLMNOPQRSTUVWXYZ
1234567890 .,;:"&!?S

Perpetua Bold Italic
abcdefghijklmnopqrstuvwxyz
ABCDEFGHIJKLMNOPQRSTUVWXYZ
1234567890 .,;:"&!?S

Perpetua Black
abcdefghijklmnopqrstuvwxyz
ABCDEFGHIJKLMNOPQRSTUVWXYZ
1234567890 .,;:"&!?$

Pierrot
abcdefghijklmnopqrstuvwxyz
ABCDEFGHIJKLMNOPQRSTUVWXYZ
1234567890 .,;:"&!?$

politics will continue to be published and read by people involved in those and other fields. However, the role of books in creating and reflecting pop culture is important because of their sheer numbers as a mass medium. Deeply rooted American cultural icons such as the cowboy and the detective were—and still are—born in books. They reappear in new media.

Just a few of the many typography choices the book designer has.

Covers That Catch the Eye

Beth Feldman

What is it exactly that prompts a bookstore browser or a library patron to choose a book from the shelf? Though many people believe the axiom "You can't judge a book by its cover," this doesn't necessarily apply when one is actually selecting something to read. Above all else, visitors to bookstores and libraries are apt to reach for a book with a jacket or cover that appeals to them, for any number of reasons. They may be attracted to an author's name, to a familiar series format, to the characters, action, theme, or mood presented in the jacket's artwork, even—especially in the case of small children looking at picture books—to the colors used. According to children's booksellers and librarians, a book's jacket or cover can solely determine whether or not a potential reader will ever pick it up.

Publishers recognize the power of the jacket. Betsy Groban, v-p and associate publisher of children's books at Little, Brown, declares that a book's cover is "absolutely the single most important thing about the physical object that is a book." Barbara Marcus, executive v-p and publisher of the Scholastic Book Group, says, "We look at the jacket as advertising. It is the first invitation to the reader to pick up the book."

Having acknowledged that a book's first impression is essential, what can publishers do to ensure that that impression is favorable?

Conceptualizing book jackets or covers—even in these days of increased input from sales and marketing departments—is a largely unscientific process. Much is left to the instinct and experience of editors and art directors, and to an artist's own interpretation of a manuscript. At most houses, a book's eventual "look" begins with a meeting between the book's editor and an art director. They discuss the book's theme, characters and overall "spirit." The art director then sends the manuscript to an artist whose style strikes him or her as appropriate. Most art directors expect an artist to read an entire manuscript; others are willing to let jacket artists work from plot summaries or synopses.

Cecilia Yung, art director for Viking Children's Books, says, "I deal with illustrators who don't balk at having to spend the time to read the book. Occasionally I use favorite illustrators who, because of the time element, can only take on a project if I tell them what to do. But I prefer not to do that." The majority of art directors believe that if they allow an artist free creative reign at this point, they receive the best result

Covers That Catch the Eye *(continued)*

in the end. "I want the illustration to be a personal experience for the artist," says Michael Farmer, art director for the children's book division of Harcourt Brace Jovanovich.

Some publishers, however, establish an idea *before* contacting an artist. Disney Press art director Ellen Friedman, drawing on her years of experience at HBJ, Harper and Macmillan, comments, "I find that fewer and fewer illustrators have the time to sit down and read a long manuscript. It saves time later on in the sketch stage if we say, 'This is the feeling we want; this is the character we want; this is the background information we want.' ". . . .

[Publisher] Little, Brown has an actual "jacket committee." It includes the publisher, editor-in-chief, marketing director, sales director, president of the trade division and director of trade production, and it confers on every jacket. Betsy Groban says that these meetings are helpful because an art director might not recognize, for example, that a particular book's author is its selling "handle" and his or her name should be more prominent. Librarians and booksellers comment that readers often do seek out particular authors (Beverly Cleary, Robert Cormier, Gary Paulsen and Katherine Paterson were a few of those mentioned) and, in those cases where an author's name carries more weight than a book's title, it should be the focal point of the spine or front.

Authors, often to their disappointment, usually don't have a say in their book's final appearance. Though most editors and art directors agree that they would like to include authors, they have concluded from experience that this can complicate matters almost impossibly. Authors may be too "close" to their books to be objective about what might be the best jacket, unaware of sales and marketing considerations. . . .

Deciding What Works

Almost without exception, booksellers and librarians polled cite a jacket's "honesty" as its most important feature: in the words of Terri Schmitz, owner of the Children's Book Shop in Brookline, Mass., covers must "show some respect for the content of the book. If a character is described in one way within the book and shown in a completely different way on the cover, I find it offensive. Some covers feature contemporary looking kids, no matter what the time setting of the book is." Barbara Marcus comments that at Scholastic they may take "a period piece, a book that is set in the '40s, for instance," and "make the costume or clothing innocuous. If it's a good read, why put off someone who thinks that it's not going to speak to them because the girl on the cover is wearing saddle shoes?"

A trend toward jackets and covers that are "of the moment" is, in some cases, an effort by publishers to compete

Covers That Catch the Eye *(continued)*

with the slick images vying for kids' and teenagers' attention in other media—TV, videos, movies, and magazines. Lauren Wohl, marketing director for Disney Press and Hyperion Books for Children, remarks that publishing people need to recognize that "we're in that same world; we're not separated from it. Increasingly, we're even sold in that same world: booksellers are carrying audio tapes, videos, games. We need to be able to win a child's attention, and looking good is part of that."

Some publishers have responded by producing photorealistic jackets that feature glamorous kids in fashionable clothes and hairstyles. But others, like Orchard Brooks, reject this notion. "We want a book to look like a book and not like a record album," says Norma Jean Sawicki, president and publisher. "We want the book to work for the kid, but it is a *book*, not a magazine or a video. We also try hard not to have particularly good-looking boys or beautiful girls—we want the characters to look like *kids*. Many of our artists do use models, but they go to a park, or into schools, and they just look for the kids that they think reflect the spirit of the novel." . . . Publishers, booksellers and librarians agree that a book jacket doesn't have to depict a scene from the book: in fact, some of the most powerful jackets present an abstract or isolated image that conveys a mood. Several booksellers mention the jacket of Jerry Spinelli's *Maniac Magee* (Little, Brown) as an example of outstanding jacket design. Rosemary Stimola, owner of A Child's Story in Teaneck, N.J., called it her "very favorite" cover from last year. "That cover said so much in the very little that it actually showed. All you saw were feet, running. There was no face; the character is there but he's not in a detailed portrait. You want the cover to provoke the reader visually: 'What is that book about?' It doesn't have to say everything—sometime it's kind of nice to leave the questions there." ▪

One cultural icon, the rugged, individualist cowboy still fills our screens and advertisements (the Marlboro Man). Detective shows, such as "Murder She Wrote," are constant TV favorites. All of these were first implanted in the **psyche** of American pop culture through books.

Just because a genre or a particular book is widely popular doesn't mean that there is widespread agreement regarding its

Practice

Identify a passage from the reading on covers and state which of the five stages of the Media Literacy Paradigm (presented in Chapter Three) is covered. For example, the first paragraph talks about reaching for a book with a cover that appeals to you; this act involves motivation, which is one of the elements of media products consumption.

impact. For example, the cowboy image reflected in books and films called Westerns has been criticized for portraying Native Americans in stereotypical and racist ways. Another example of disagreement regarding the impact of books is the increasing attention being paid to violence in books read by teenagers (which the publishing industry broadly labels as young adult novels). See the article on page 104.

Instant Books: A Response to Instant Interest

Tragedies and scandals, and the mass curiosity they evoke, provide just the right factors to encourage a relatively recent development in the publishing industry: instant books. John Lennon, David Koresh, Jeffrey Dahmer, Nancy Kerrigan, O. J. Simpson—the list is long and will certainly grow. All of these people had books published about them within weeks—or even days—of the tragic events which brought them into the national media spotlight. Whereas most books, including simple children's books, take about a year to publish, instant books take only days.

Many trends explain the success of instant books, but two stand out. First, the intensity of media coverage given to certain events both *reflects* and *fuels* the public's thirst for information about them. Second, the flexibility of new communications technologies, such as **desktop publishing,** make it technologically possible to satisfy that hunger in record time. One of the curious things about many of these books is that they are often advertised as "the definitive story of" this or that person or "the true behind-the-scenes tale" of so-and-so. "Definitive" and "behind-the-scenes,"

Carnage: An Open Book

Paul Gray

When the era of network TV violence advisories dawns in September, some such scene will play itself out in millions of U.S. households. Warned that an upcoming program contains material unsuitable for young people, parents order their children away from the set and then brace themselves for whines and grumbling. Oddly, the exiles disappear without complaint and go off to their rooms . . . to read books. Sis, 13, picks up her copy of R.L. Stine's *The Babysitter III:* "His expression was blank, as blank as death. And with a quick, simple motion, he grabbed the baby's head with one hand, twisted it, and pulled it off." Across the hall, Junior, 11, turns the pages of Christopher Pike's *Monster:* "Mary pointed her shotgun at Kathy's face and pulled the trigger. The blast caught Kathy in the forehead and took off the top of her skull, plastering a good portion of her brains over the railings of the nearby staircase."

Downstairs, Mom and Dad are snoring in front of a flickering car chase.

Books like *The Babysitter III* or *Monster*—and there are suddenly a remarkable number of books very much like them—do not reach such underage readers by subterfuge or stealth. Adolescents now constitute a booming niche market for the peddling of published gore and violence. "Teens' inter-ests go in cycles," says Patricia MacDonald, editorial director of Archway Paperbacks, an imprint of Pocket Books and a major player in the teen-horror field. "In the '70s it was problem novels, the disease of the week. Then it was romance novels, soap operas like *Sweet Valley High* and *Sweet Dreams.* In the '90s it's the thrillers." Hardly a blip on publishers' sales charts a few years ago, such thrillers claimed three of the top four spots on the *Publishers Weekly* poll of the best-selling children's paperbacks in 1992.

Like all genre fiction—gothics, romances, police procedurals—teen tinglers follow a fairly consistent set of formulas. The heroes or heroines are invariably adolescents whose lives fall mysteriously into jeopardy; adults are either the source of the menace or remote, almost inanimate objects. The dialogue comes laced with teenspeak—*gnarly, totally awesome*—and the plot steamrolls over lesser details like setting and characterization. Chapters are short and end in suspense, luring readers with short attention spans to forge onward. The level of violence ranges from the implied to the horrific, and the bloodier bits are sometimes mitigated by context: it was all a dream, the demonic villain got what was coming to him, etc. Explicit sex is largely forbidden.

Carnage: An Open Book *(continued)*

Still, these hair-raising books are being tailored for and energetically hawked to children. Is that frightening? The two most successful writers of teen thrillers, understandably, think not. Says Christopher Pike, 37, who stumbled into his calling in 1985 and now has 8 million copies of his books in print: "They want to be scared or they would not pick up the book and read it. The kids have fair warning and know it's all good fun."

R.L. Stine, 49, who turns out a thriller a month and has 7.5 million copies of his 27-part *Fear Street* series in print, agrees that such books mean no harm. "Part of the appeal is that they're safe scares. You're home in your room and reading. The books are not half as scary as the real world." At the same time, Stine also implies that the real world needs embellishment; his challenge, he says, is "to find new cheap thrills" for his young readers. "I mean disgusting, gross things to put in the book that they'll like: the cat is boiled in the spaghetti, a girl pours honey over a boy and sets ants on him. They like the gross stuff." Surely his young readers have some taboos? Furry animals? "The pets are dead meat," Stine replies. "If the kid has a pet, he's going to find it dead on the floor."

Such calculated shock tactics seem qualitatively different from the methods of *Alice's Adventures in Wonderland,* *Treasure Island* or even the horror stories of Edgar Allan Poe. Classical children's literature is full of overt and implicit terrors because some gifted authors could remember and portray a child's view, those feelings of awe, uncertainty and fear inspired by the world outside. Fright requires no invention; conquering it through language does.

Some educators believe teenagers' reading these lurid thrillers, as opposed to playing Nintendo or watching *Beavis and Butt-head* on MTV, is a good thing. Viviane Lampach, a librarian at a Bronx high school in New York City, notes that her young patrons check out new paperback novels in this genre and never return them: "You hope to wean them from horror to something deeper and more meaningful." Roderick McGillis, a professor of English at the University of Calgary and author of a book on children's literature, takes a darker view. "What disturbs me is that we're developing in our culture, in our cities, a kind of siege mentality. A lot of these books reinforce this, make it sort of normal to think that the world is a place in which violence can erupt at any moment."

Maybe the youngsters will move upward in their tastes, through Stephen King and V.C. Andrews to Hemingway, Joyce and Shakespeare. Or maybe they will boil the cat in the spaghetti. ∎

Reprinted by permission from the August 2, 1993 issue of *TIME*. © 1993 TIME INC.

however, imply a sense of detail and completeness. How complete can these books be? The reading on page 107 from an article in *Entertainment Weekly* gives you an idea of the lightning-fast pace of instant book production.

Practice

Identify examples of concepts from the Media Literacy Paradigm in the article on page 104 and state which of the five paradigm stages each example relates to.

Censorship

Perhaps no other word is as controversial when it comes to mass media as the word *censorship*. Limiting the information people have access to and the right of people to express themselves have been thorny issues for all of recorded history. Few would argue that absolute freedom of expression at all times in all circumstances is the way to go. All societies have limits on expression, a classic example of which is the prohibition against falsely yelling "Fire!" in a crowded theater. In America we have walked the fine line between free expression and government censorship fairly well for over two centuries. Indeed, there is very little direct government censorship of the publishing industry, thanks largely to the First Amendment to the Constitution. Debates do rage though, involving issues of *personal* expression, such as whether burning the American flag should be considered a constitutionally protected form of free speech (it is, in specific circumstances).

Most censorship of books today occurs within the context of local libraries and public schools. There are two closely connected reasons for this. First, many people in America hold widely varying views regarding right and wrong. As a result, there is often disagreement within a given community as to what *ideas* should and should not be promoted by libraries and schools. Second, since libraries and public schools are financially supported by local taxes, people with strong opinions on right and wrong want to make sure that their money is not spent on books which oppose their point of view.

Pulp Nonfiction

Albert Kim

Only two hours after the bodies of O.J. Simpson's ex-wife Nicole Brown Simpson and her friend Ronald Lyle Goldman were discovered lying in a sea of blood in a posh Los Angeles enclave, Tom Colbert was on the phone to Bill Birnes, an L.A. book packager. Colbert, the president of Industry R&D, a research company that seeks out hot stories before they get hot, told Birnes, "There's a really big story breaking in Brentwood. It hasn't even hit the wires yet." By six the next morning, Birnes was talking to New York publishers about doing an instant book on the grisly murders.

Is the Simpson case too tragic to commercialize à la Tonya and Nancy? Not when you consider that 95 million people watched spellbound as Simpson made his last dash across the L.A. freeways on June 17. That number is just too hard to ignore for the loose conglomeration of agents, movie producers, and book publishers who turn today's tragedies into tomorrow's entertainment.

"The true-life drama in this is so sensational," says Howard Braunstein, who produced NBC's Amy Fisher movie. "How much more can be done?" Plenty. The Simpson story has already spawned its own cottage industry. Three instant books are being written, two TV movies are in development, and countless hours of network time have already been devoted to what's turning out to be one of the most sensational crimes of the century. . . .

Instant Books: Soon after Birnes' first calls to publishers, he sold his book to supermarket-tabloid publisher Globe Communications. The volume is set to hit shelves July 6. Such breathtaking rapidity is nothing new in the world of quickie publishing. "In this business," says Sarah Gallick, executive editor at Pinnacle Books, whose 328-page Simpson bio was the first to reach stores (on June 27), "if you're not the lead horse, the view is always the same." But even before the first pages of this book could be thumbed, the second Simpson publishing wave had started. Best-selling writer Joe McGinnis (*Fatal Vision*) was reportedly closing in on a $1 million deal last week for the "definitive" book on the case. ■

Practice

Analyze the "Pulp Nonfiction" reading in terms of book production (mediation), the fourth stage of the Media Literacy Paradigm.

It is important to understand the two levels to book censorship. The first level is when a book is challenged as inappropriate by an individual or group. At this point the library or local school board will hold meetings to discuss the book in question and decide what to do. When this first level of pressure is successful, it leads to the second level: the actual removal of a particular book from a public library, classroom, or school library.

While most challenges do not result in removal, they do have a direct impact on future book selections and on what publishers will publish. If a school or library thinks it is going to meet resistance if they select a particular book, they may reject it even though it is the book they really want to use. Likewise, publishers may ask authors to stay away from certain controversial topics to make sure their books get bought. The American Library Association publishes an annual report describing attempts at censorship around the country. Some of the most frequently attacked books may surprise you: Mark Twain's *The Adventures of Huckleberry Finn*; J. D. Salinger's *Catcher in the Rye*; Judy Blume's *Forever*. One of the most frequently attacked contemporary writers is Robert Cormier, author of *The Chocolate War* and *I Am the Cheese*. In the following excerpt from a 1992 essay, Cormier discusses censorship from an author's vantage point.

Practice

Analyze the following reading on censorship in terms of the fourth and fifth stages of the Media Literacy Paradigm: consumption and impact of the product (books).

A Book Is Not a House

Robert Cormier

Whenever the subject of censorship comes up, I don't think first of headlines or heated debates or Letters to the Editor or angry voices. I think instead of a girl in a school on Cape Cod in Massachusetts. She sat every day in the school library while the other members of her class were discussing *The Chocolate War*. Her parents had protested the use of the novel in the classroom and a hearing had been scheduled. Meanwhile, the novel continued to be studied by the students, pending an official hearing. (In some schools, a book is automatically removed from the classroom prior to a hearing.) I think about that girl. Sitting in the library alone while her classmates were back in the classroom. Was she lonely, embarrassed? Did she feel isolated, ostracized? Did some of her classmates pass remarks about her? I don't know if any of this happened, although I suspect it did. I have this suspicion because a classmate of hers wrote to me about her predicament and his letter showed sympathy and concern. It struck me then as it strikes me now that in a tender time of blossoming adolescence, when a teenager wants to belong, to be part of the crowd, part of *something*, this girl sat alone in the library, sentenced there by her parents. I wonder which was more harmful—her isolation or reading the novel. Which brings us to the ironic P.S. in her classmate's letter to me: the girl had read *The Chocolate War* a year before the controversy and "liked it." . . .

Writing a novel is a subjective occupation, in contrast to, say, building a house, which is completely objective. The builder follows an architect's blueprint, erects walls, installs a ceiling and floor, cabinets and bookshelves. At the end of the day's work, the builder looks at what has been accomplished and pronounces it a room. At the end of the day, the writer isn't sure about what has been accomplished. Words on paper, yes, but not in response to a blueprint. All the choices that were made. What to put in and what to leave out. This adjective or that. Or no adjective at all. Did this metaphor go askew, calling attention to itself? And the characters: did they come alive? Even when the writer is satisfied with the work and pronounces it, somewhat tentatively, a chapter, there is always the judgment of the reader, the beholder waiting.

This is what writing is all about—the sweaty work of creation, the frustrating and sometimes painful putting down of words on paper to move and excite the reader.

A Book Is Not a House *(continued)*

And into all of this stomps censorship, flexing its muscles.

Censorship tells us what to write and how to write it. Or what not to write. Does not trust the motives of the writer. Does not acknowledge the toil that goes into the writing of a book. Blunts the sharp thrust of creativity and, in fact, is afraid of it. Wants everything simple. Wants everyone in a book to live happily ever after.

Censorship goes beyond the writer, of course, to the reader, particularly children. Doesn't want children to read a paragraph that may make them pause and think. Doesn't want children to be challenged.

Censorship sees danger everywhere:

- *Goldilocks* was banned because Goldilocks was not punished for breaking into the house of the three bears.
- Anne Frank's *Diary Of A Young Girl* was removed from schools because a passage in the book suggested that all religions are equal.
- *The Chocolate War* is banned because of teenage attitudes and because the good guy loses in the end.

Censors wish to hand out blueprints for the writer to follow, blueprints that include designs that are safe and secure, that contain no concealed passages, no corners around which surprises or challenges wait. A house, in which every room is furnished with the bare necessities, with no shadows, no closets, no hidden corners. And no light.

But a book is not a house.

My writing has always been a learning experience, and each time that I sit down at the typewriter I learn something about my craft and also about myself.

I have learned, astonishingly, that not all censorship is bad and that, in fact, censorship for the writer begins at home. At the typewriter or the word processor.

This is what angers me most about censorship, the fact that I have already been censored—and willingly—before my manuscripts leave my house.

I am that censor.

And I've learned my lessons well. . . .

Fifteen years after *The Chocolate War* was written, I sat at the typewriter as usual. Another novel. Another cast of characters. I had embarked on a novel that would eventually be published with the title, *Fade*. Some things never change and among these things are the daily demands of creating characters on the page and setting them in motion.

In this particular novel, a sensitive teenage boy whose name is Paul is the recipient of the gift—or is it a curse?—of becoming invisible. Which, of course, is impossible. Or is it? This kind of enigma intrigues me and made the novel fascinating but difficult to write.

For the purpose of this article, let's suspend disbelief and accept invisibility as entirely possible so that we can focus

A Book Is Not a House *(continued)*

on one demanding aspect of the novel. The aspect is this: it is necessary for Paul to be shocked by what he sees when he's invisible.

Paul witnesses two unsavory events as he lurks unseen by others: One involves a sordid act between a middle-aged man and a teenage girl. The other involves an act of incest between two young people Paul admires.

Paul must be shocked by what he witnesses, so shocked that he begins to question whether invisibility is indeed the marvelous gift he had envisioned or a terrible burden that he must assume. The scenes must also shock the reader because the reader must share Paul's horror, must feel the revulsion Paul feels.

I wrote the scenes carefully with all the craft I could supply, rewriting as usual, trying to strike the right notes, to convey what was going on in order to make it all seem real. There was also the need to stop short of titillating the reader or sensationalizing the situations.

After the chapters were finished I was left with the eternal questions: Do they work? Would they be convincing to the reader?

Two people whose opinions I value highly read the novel before it was submitted for publication. Both were enthusiastic about it, indicating that the novel had accomplished what I had set out to accomplish. But these two readers also were upset by those two vital scenes. They wondered whether the scenes were written too graphically. "Is it necessary to go into all those details?" one of them asked.

Here again, the writer faces the agony of choice and selection, a question of degree, and delicate balance that must be struck between verisimilitude and exploitation. Was I exploiting the situations, so set on shocking Paul that I had gone overboard? Where do you draw the line?

Rewriting was clearly in order and that is exactly what I did. The younger of the two readers was especially disturbed by the description of incest as witnessed by Paul. I rewrote the scene so that Paul turns away—he can't close his eyes to cut off his view because his eyelids, too, are invisible—and *hears* what is going on rather than sees what is going on. I felt this made the scene less offensive.

In the scene involving the man and the girl, I emphasized the squalidness of the situation, kept the act itself to a minimum. Yet, the act had to be graphically portrayed to justify its purpose in the novel.

The younger reader agreed that I modified the description of the incest but was still bothered by it. Yet, I knew that if she weren't bothered by it, then the scene probably wasn't working. The older reader accepted the scenes as rewritten but without enthusiasm. "I know they're necessary," she said, "but I wish they weren't."

A Book Is Not a House *(continued)*

There followed some days of agonizing over the chapters. Some more rewriting and then reaching the point where I felt I could do no more without losing all perspective and compromising myself. . . . those scenes in *Fade* remain troublesome for me even to this day. The choices that are really agonizing are those involving *degrees*—how much and how little? And there are no clear-cut guidelines. I have, finally, to be guided by my own instincts.

I have gone into detail about those writing problems to point out that the words that go into books are not chosen gratuitously or casually, that a writer does not press a button and have the words magically appear, that writing is a demanding, exacting occupation. Ah, but when the words sing and dance on the page, when characters leap to life and behave or misbehave, when people read your books and shake their heads and say, yes, this is how life is and how it must be—that is beautiful. . . .

Every writer I know whose books are challenged enters that battle, flies across the country, makes the speeches, debates opponents, offers encouragement to educators who find themselves targets of the book-banners.

I believe, however, that the greatest thing writers can do is simply to keep writing. Writing honestly with all the craft that can be summoned. Writing to illuminate as well as entertain. Writing to challenge the intellect and engage the heart. To make the reader, in Robert Daley's words, laugh and cry and suffer and triumph and understand.

This is what I try to do each day when I sit at the typewriter. This is my best answer to those who would ban my books. ■

Excerpts from "A Book Is Not a House: The Human Side of Censorship" reprinted courtesy of Robert Cormier. The essay appears in *Authors' Insights* edited by Donald R. Gallo (1992, Boynton Cook Publishers).

Future Watch: Books in the Digital Age

The near future is already here when it comes to books. Audio books (on cassette) are increasingly popular; they even have their own best-selling list. Obviously, there are important differences between print-based and audio books. Most importantly, you don't have to *read* an audio book, which opens up the experience of books to the millions of Americans who are illiterate. On the one hand, you can do other things while *listening to* your book; for example, audio books are advertised as perfect for long car rides. On the other hand, the experience is not as personal, not as *solitary*. You don't contribute as much of yourself to the experience, because

Reflections

- How do best-sellers create or reflect pop culture?

- Are there any ideas so wrong or bad that people should not be able to read about them? What are they? Why should these ideas be censored? Who decides what ideas are inappropriate or too dangerous for people to hear? What happens when people with whom you disagree gain the authority to impose limits on expression? What is the relationship between society's changing values and censorship?

- Why do so many teenagers (and adults, for that matter) dislike reading? How did this situation come about? How might people begin to enjoy reading?

you are provided with a voice and all of its particular qualities: its tone, its **inflection**, its pace. The reader's voice may evoke an image in your mind that you wouldn't have if you were reading the words yourself.

As digital media continue to evolve, products such as Sony's Data Discman (shown on page 14) will provide new ways to experience books. About the size of a handheld calculator, these **electronic books** can hold thousands of pages of text and graphics on a 3-inch floppy disc, and some include sound as well. The screens, though, are quite small, and so far these devices have not caught on. They just do not enhance the reading experience in practical ways. CD-ROM-based books, however, are getting sophisticated enough to provide users with a multimedia reading experience. Played on a computer, **CD books** present written text, spoken text, and still and moving graphic images. The market for CD books is growing rapidly as more people get the needed equipment and as evolving technology allows more and more information to be stored on a disc.

Three other factors will shape the future of books and publishing. The first is **on-line publishing**. Entire books can be entered on computer networks and made accessible to millions of users

The Sony Data Discman allows you to read books with CD-ROM technology. *Photo courtesy of Sony Electronic Inc.*

via the Internet. Book clubs will someday transmit your monthly selection via computer; you will read it on any number of digital devices you have around your house, or, if you want, you'll be able to print out a paper version of the book on your printer.

Which brings us to the second factor. As copying machines become faster and smarter, the existing system of book distribution is changing. Instead of a publisher printing 50,000 copies of a book and then paying money to have them stored until they're shipped around the country or the globe, publishers will be able to send books electronically to local printing-on-demand services, which will print out a copy of the book you want in two or three minutes. Known as **digital document preparation**, the publishing industry hopes this development will save money and be more flexible. No more wasting thousands of copies of a book that didn't sell as well as the publisher predicted, or waiting weeks for special orders of books currently not in print.

Finally, the entire field of **desktop publishing** is dramatically changing the way books are produced and distributed. Combined with the previously mentioned high speed copy machines, individuals can now write, design, and distribute their own books without the assistance of big publishing companies. There are already thousands of books—especially computer books—that were completely desktop published.

Building Your Media Archive
Applying the Media Literacy Paradigm

It is sometimes difficult to uncover the details of how a particular media product came into being or who is responsible for it being the way it is. Some media, however, provide more information than others (film credits), and some products receive more attention than others (an Ice T recording).

Archive Analysis: Books

Make sure you have read the book you will analyze. Refer to the Media Literacy Paradigm in Chapter Three and answer the questions for each stage. The Product stage will be the easiest to do. The Origin stage will require a little outside research. Depending on the type of book, you may be able to locate a biography to give you insights into the author's background, and so on. You may have to go the extra mile to determine who mediated the book, since books often do not provide that information (for example, who edited the book or who designed its layout). Write the publisher of the book if you have questions. If you prepare carefully, you may be surprised at the responses you'll receive; few media companies receive communication from high school students, and when they do, they usually take them very seriously.

As you work through the Mediation-stage questions about your book, remember the unique characteristics of books in general and of your book in particular (for example, typography and conventions of genre). For the Consumption and Impact stages of your analysis, you consider your personal responses to the book.

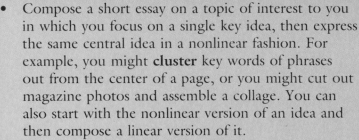

MEDIA LAB   Books

- Compose a short essay on a topic of interest to you in which you focus on a single key idea, then express the same central idea in a nonlinear fashion. For example, you might **cluster** key words of phrases out from the center of a page, or you might cut out magazine photos and assemble a collage. You can also start with the nonlinear version of an idea and then compose a linear version of it.

- You own a new printing press in the year 1500. Create a poster advertising your services. Before you produce your ad, determine these facts: your location, population of the area, social conditions, and target audience.

- Take a tour of a local bookstore and draw a poster-sized map of its layout for display in your school. Indicate main sections and other pertinent information, such as a recommended selection from each section.

- Research the latest instant books available in your area. Check your bookstore for this starting information: when it arrived, what incident it is based on, and how many copies the store purchased. Determine the length of time between the actual incident and book publication. Follow the subsequent developments in the story and track new information that was not in the book.

- Use your school library or public library to research the history of book challenges by individuals or groups. What books have been challenged? When? Upon what grounds were they challenged? What were the results?

- What are the key issues students in your school should understand regarding censorship? Design a series of posters outlining those issues.

Create Your Own Media

Although it may be difficult to imagine publishing your own book, there are many ways you can break into the publishing business. If your school has a literary magazine or newspaper, you can write for them. Your local newspaper may be willing to give you space for an occasional column about teen or school life. Check with your English teacher and friends to locate student-written essays you could edit and publish as an anthology. If you market your request well, you might get a local printer or copying service to print a few hundred copies of your book. If you can't actually get a book or booklet produced yourself, many organizations publish student writing, some of which are listed under **Resources for Further Reading** on page 120. Remember that S. E. Hinton was in high school when she wrote *The Outsiders*.

With an interest in books and reading often comes an interest in creative writing and the desire to be published. The following reading profiles a student who pursued that desire.

Career Bank

Following are just a few of the many careers available in the book publishing industry:

- literary agent
- author
- editor
- publisher
- proofreader
- researcher/fact checker
- typesetter
- designer/graphic artist
- publicist/promoter

Recap

Books, like all forms of media, have a unique history and unique characteristics. Because books present written language in a **linear** fashion, they organize information in a tightly structured, precise sequence. The **printing press** allowed the accurate reproduction

Student Close-Up

Dawn Wilson—North Carolina

Dawn Wilson in her junior year at Buncombe High School.

For Dawn Wilson, writing started as a game when she was 5 years old: writing down all the imaginary adventures of her toys. It was a game that hasn't ended.

Wilson, from Weaverville, North Carolina, had several short stories and poems published while she attended North Buncombe High School. In tenth grade, she appeared on "CBS Morning News" during a segment on young authors. Her stories and poems have appeared in *Young Author's Mag-* *azine, Prism, Event,* and the *National Beta Club Journal.* In addition, she was a state finalist for the 1988 North Carolina Writing Award and received an achievement award from the National Council of Teachers of English.

Dawn graduated in 1993 from the University of North Carolina at Chapel Hill, where she worked on the school newspaper and studied creative writing under authors Doris Betts and Bland Simpson. While at college, her play *Satan in the Shower* was performed as a part of the Student Writer's Showcase. Currently, she is a newspaper reporter and working on a play.

According to Wilson, when she was in high school, writing meant essays on Charles Dickens, not creative adventures about another universe. One of the most frustrating things for her as a writer was that there were few people to help her improve her stories or help get them published. Creative writing classes for her age group were not offered at the time in her area. However, she said, "If you want to be a writer, you need to take the initiative. . . . you write because you love it."

She loved it enough to seek out her own opportunities to get her writing published. She bought a *Writer's Market*, a reference book that lists all the

Student Close-Up *(continued)*

magazines in the country that accept work by writers for possible publication. She sent off stories, poems, anything she could.

As her teachers learned of her love of writing and interest in getting published, they started sending her information about contests. She recalled, "I was in eighth grade when I had my first piece of creative writing published. I sent a poem to this national poetry magazine that was based in Washington state. It wasn't a very big magazine. It only had yellow construction paper for the cover. It looked as if someone had printed it in his basement. But the poem, the poem was MINE. And that was my name in print below the title. Seeing your name in print like that—even if it's only once—makes up for all the rewriting and rejections that you get from other magazines. It's like finishing first in a track meet or winning the Homecoming football game."

Wilson added, "Appearing on 'CBS Morning News' was great, overwhelming, in fact. But still, there is nothing quite like seeing your name in print after your first story or poem is published . . . the bottom line is, whether or not you get anything published, you write stories because you like writing them."

Writing skills will not only help you in the classroom, they will help you in the job market. Wilson advises students: "Write all you can, even if you can't find a place to get your work published, keep writing—that way, when the opportunity does arrive, you will be ready to meet it." ■

of books, which captured ideas in a more permanent and portable form than previously handwritten **manuscripts**.

Books are available in two main markets: The larger of the two markets is made up of educational and professional books which are not readily available to the public; the second market comprises the trade and mass market books available in bookstores.

Books come in a large variety of designs, the most important feature of which is their **typography** (how the print looks on the page). The look of a book's **cover** is an important factor in getting people to buy it.

Books contribute to pop culture in many ways. **Genres**, such as Westerns, reinforce long-held literary images. **Instant books** satisfy the mass curiosity that arises from highly publicized, dramatic current events.

The issue of **censorship** is extremely complex because there is legitimate disagreement in a free society as to what is right and wrong. Censorship of books rarely comes directly from the government; rather, individual books are attacked as inappropriate for school and local libraries and sometimes removed from the shelves.

Resources for Further Reading

Biographies or autobiographies of famous authors which provide insight into the Origin stage of the Media Literacy Paradigm for a given book

Henderson, Kathy. *Market Guide for Young Writers*. (annual). Whitehall, VA: Shoe Tree Press.

Local bookstores

Publisher's Weekly magazine

Rising Voices magazine, Poets and Writers, 72 Spring Street, New York, NY 10012.

SEGUE

Books—The First Mass Medium

Much of what you learned in this chapter applies to other media. For instance, since all mass media contribute to the vast sea of pop culture, all have been subject to censorship in one form or another. Most written language is presented in linear form whether in books, magazines, newspapers, or comics, yet all print-based media have their own conventions of typography and design. Comics, more than any other medium, combine text and pictures (that is, low-C and high-C symbols) as their most defining characteristic. Though they are hard to define, you know a comic when you see one. The next chapter sheds some light on this often underappreciated medium.

CHAPTER FIVE

Comics and Animation

Learning Targets

After working through this chapter, you will be able to

- Explain the unique characteristics of comics as a
  medium;
- Identify the main presentational conventions of
  comics;
- Create your own comic
  strip;
- Explain the essential stages
  of the animation production process; and
- Apply the Media Literacy
  Paradigm to the comic
  book in your Media
  Archive.

Checking In

- Chart all the similarities
  and differences you can
  think of between comic
  strips, comic books, and
  animated film (cartoons).
- Interview a couple of your
  peers about their favorite
  comic strips or comic books,
  what they like about them,
  and how long they have
  been reading them, and
  what they change about
  them, if anything.
- On a small pad of self-stick
  removable notes, create a
  stick-figure flip book "animation" (Hint: draw on
  the half of each page opposite the glued binding of
  the pad.)

Comics As a Medium

To most people—at least to most adults—the word *comics* means children's reading material, a simple medium not meant to be taken seriously, superheroes whooshing around fighting evil villains bent on world destruction.

While a large part of the comic book universe is made up of whooshing superheroes, it also includes a surprisingly wide range of categories, genres, and artistic styles. Likewise, the readers of comics are more diverse than many people believe. White males aged 10 to 17 still make up the majority of readers, but a growing number of females, people of color, and older readers are buying comic books. When you take into account the number of people who read newspaper comic strips, the audience is even larger and more diverse. Part of the reason comics are popular is that, far from being simple, comics are quite sophisticated. More than any other medium, comics combine multiple elements of several media in a unique way.

Combining Text and Illustrations

Comics are unique in two primary ways. The first is that they combine text (written words) and illustrated artwork to communicate with the reader. Unlike books, which rely overwhelmingly on text, and even magazines (which include graphics to enhance communication), comics blend text and illustrations in a single integrated system. The text gives meaning to the illustrations they are part of, and the illustrations give meaning to the text with which they are joined. Scott McCloud, in the excerpts from his book *Understanding Comics* on pages 126 and 127, describes several ways this is done.

The Reader's Contribution: Closure

The second distinguishing feature of comics is the format in which they are presented. Comics communicate by presenting a sequence of snapshot moments—a series of freeze-frames laid out in a logical order. These "snapshots," usually contained in boxes called **panels**, lead you along a storyline which, when well-crafted, involve your imagination more than any other form of visual storytelling. Film and TV (the other visual storytelling media) capture the appearance of fluid motion so that, for example, when someone is walking from the refrigerator to the sink, you see the entire four seconds of action. In comics, you see a person at the refrigerator in one panel and the same person at the sink in the next panel. Your mind has subconsciously filled in the action between what the artist has provided in the panels. In other cases, hours can pass between the action taking place in two panels, yet your mind accepts this passage of time, referred to as **closure** by Scott McCloud.

Based on your prior knowledge and experiences, you make connections between specific events all the time, both in real life and in media products. For example, you are walking in the hallway between classes and you see your friend putting books in his locker. You notice him and keep walking. Ten seconds later, you stop at your locker to pick up some books and then head to your class. When you arrive in the room, the friend you had passed in the hall is already seated. You instantly fill in the gap between the two "snapshots" of your friend at his locker and in his seat by engaging in closure. Experience tells you that your friend walked from his locker to the classroom, even though you didn't see him do so.

Likewise, whenever you watch a film or TV drama, you engage

in closure. For instance, when the shot on the screen switches from a close-up of the face of a crazed man sitting in an airplane seat to a close-up of a briefcase sitting on an empty seat four rows away, you probably think "bomb." Furthermore, you probably think the briefcase (bomb) belongs to the man. In this type of closure, you make an **inference** about the relationship of the two images. You contribute your imagination to link the images in a meaningful way. Back to comics, it is this *constant* reliance on reader involvement—the reader supplying closure and linking every panel—that helps to make comics a unique medium.

Categories and Genres
Strips

The first of the three major categories of comics is the comic strip, which first appeared in newspapers in the early 1900s. Due to newspapers' vast audiences, strips have always been the most widely read category of comics. Typically two to four panels long during the week and six to ten panels long on Sundays, most strips are either of the slice-of-life or serial variety. "Peanuts" and "B.C." are examples of the slice-of-life variety in which a new point or situation is presented each day. "Doonesbury" and "Apartment 3-G," on the other hand, are serialized (meaning that they often stick to a theme or storyline for a week or more).

Graphic Novels

The second main category of comics is the graphic novel. Though growing in popularity, it accounts for only a small percentage of the comics industry. A graphic novel is a full-length story illustrated in traditional comic book style. It is bound like a trade paperback book and is usually printed on higher quality paper than standard comics, which allows for richer color and explains its higher cost. Graphic novel titles range from adaptations of classic literature, such as *The Hobbit* (as shown on page 128) to brand-new superhero adventures such as *Double Dangerous* (see page 129).

Comic Books

The third and best-known category of comics is the traditional comic book, which, in its current familiar form, dates to 1930.

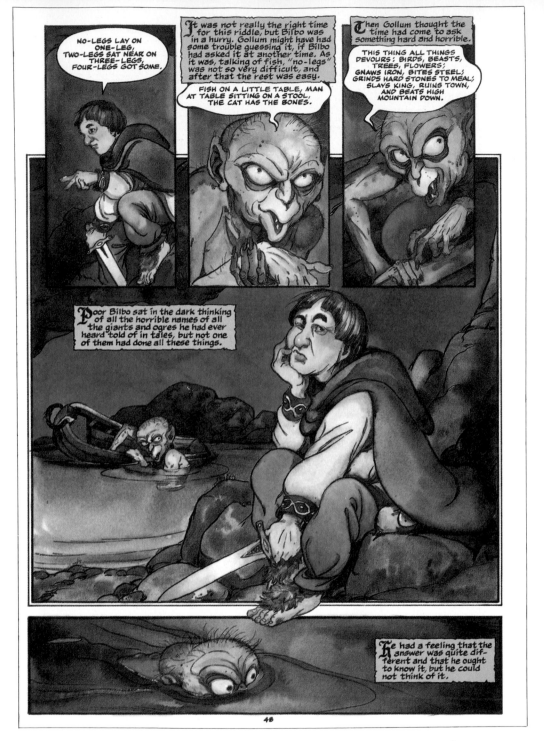

A page from a graphic novel, *The Hobbit* © 1965 by J. R. R. Tolkien, adaptation © Chuck Dixon and Sean Deming. Art © David Wenzel. Reprinted by permission of Eclipse Books.

Adventure comics such as *Double Dangerous* are of the *superhero* genre.
Reprinted courtesy of Malibu Comics Entertainment Group, Inc.

The first comic books were simply bound collections of strips which had previously run in newspapers (the same way popular strips today are published in book form). The 1930s saw the publication of *Funnies on Parade*, the first collection of original, previously unpublished comics. In 1938, the modern comic book was born with the publication of the first issue of "Superman," the father of the *superhero* genre.

Genres

Some of the other major genres of comics that developed over the next 30 years continue to dominate both strips and books today. Superheroes take up the most shelf space in comic-book stores, though the traditional heroes, such as Flash and Spider-Man, have been joined by newer superheroes, such as Prime. After superheroes, the most popular genres in the comic-book category are *fantasy/horror*, such as "ElfQuest" and "Tales From the Crypt"; *action/adventure*, such as "Star Trek" and several titles from Valiant comics; and *general humor*, such as "Beavis and Butthead" and "Archie." ("Mad Magazine" was first published in 1952 in comic-book format but changed to a magazine three years later; it did, however, retain standard comic conventions.) In the strip category, the *animal* genre is represented by the likes of "Garfield" and "Outland." Other genres include *general humor*, such as "Cathy" and "Funky Winkerbean," and *drama*, such as "Judge Parker" and "Rex Morgan, M.D." Finally, graphic novels are dominated by the superhero and fantasy genres.

Conventions of Presentation

Some Tricks of the Trade: Balloons, Motion Lines, and Sound Effects

The use of panels is *the* basic presentational convention in comics, but you can easily identify many others. The most recognizable convention is the text balloon in which the words, thoughts, and feelings of characters are displayed. By convention—that is, by tradition—smooth-line balloons with a "tail" toward a character indicate the words that character is speaking aloud. A tail of decreasingly small circles indicates the character's unspoken thoughts or feelings. A jagged-edge balloon often is used to emphasize a scream, while a jagged-edge tail is used to indicate dialogue coming from a phone or other piece of technology. Other text-related conventions include the enclosed rectangle for narration and the wavy-line balloon to indicate dreams. While these are the most common balloon conventions, comics artists experiment all the time with balloon lines and shapes. Conventions related to text are also found inside the balloon. Bold and italicized printing are used for emphasis, while a more stylized print can be used to indicate anger, fear, or uncertainty.

As mentioned earlier, superheroes are constantly whooshing around. How do you know that? How does the artist clearly communicate a sense of action? She uses motion lines and textual sound effects. Motion lines range from the little lines that indicate a hand waving to the long, bold curves that amplify a superhero's punch. Lines are also used to indicate odor and heat, as in the wavy vertical lines seen coming from a garbage dump or a vat of boiling oil. The "KABOOM" or "SLAM," leaping from the pages of action stories, illustrates another convention of comics: the textual sound effect. This convention was made recognizable to millions of noncomic-book reading fans through the TV show "Batman."

A Brief History of Comics in America
The Glory Years

From the turn of the century to the late 1930s, newspaper comic strips grew in popularity while comic books struggled to find a

"Captain America" created by Joe Simon and Jack Kirby. © Marvel Comics Group.

unique identity as a medium. Two events provided the spark: the publication in June 1938 of Action Comics' "Superman #1" and America's entrance into World War II. The superhero genre clicked almost instantly with millions of young Americans who, having lived through the Great Depression, were finally feeling optimistic about their future and about America's strength as a nation. The appeal of an ordinary guy who used supernatural powers to do good played well with America's developing self-image. When Captain America urged you to become a Sentinel of Liberty and to "wear the badge that proves you are a loyal believer in American-ism," chances are, you did. During the war, American comics reflected and reinforced themes of patriotism and industriousness.

The Unsettled 1950s

After WWII and throughout the 1950s, however, comic books suffered a second identity crisis. Without the war as a motivating theme, superhero and adventure comics seemed to lose their appeal. Comic-book writers turned to crime and horror themes to interest young readers but were met with the criticism that their gory storylines and graphics were corrupting America's youth. In response to a government investigation into the comics industry, publishers banded together in 1954 to form the Comics Code Authority, which established guidelines for acceptable content. While this move satisfied critics, many saw it as hindering comic-book publishers from experimenting with new characters and storylines. As a result of the somewhat unimaginative uniformity of comics in the 1950s, readership continued to decline. Newspaper strips, with their increasingly dramatic themes that paralleled the boom in TV soap operas, fared a little better during this decade.

The Comeback of Comics

A rebirth of comic books occurred in the 1960s, with "Spider-Man" and "The Fantastic Four" leading the way. These were superheroes whose characters faced real human problems such as loneliness and had to make morally complicated decisions. Readership in the 1970s and 1980s remained stable, while the comic-book market was dominated by DC and Marvel. The late 1980s and early 1990s have seen the emergence of new publishers such as Valiant, Dark Horse, Image, and Malibu; these four companies, as of 1994, published about 30 percent of the comic books available in the United States. Marvel and DC still dominate the market with about 57 percent of comics sold, and literally dozens of very small publishers produce the remaining 13 percent (although many of these publishers have followings of very devoted fans). Only about 30 percent of new comic books have the Comics Code Authority seal of approval.

Comics and Popular Culture
Two Universal Human Connections

When "Superman" turned 50 in 1988, it was big news—big enough that the Man of Steel even appeared on the cover of *Time*—and when he died in November 1992, articles appeared in *Newsweek* and *The New York Times* speculating about how long he would remain dead (which turned out to be only nine months). Millions of Americans have consumed "Superman" media products, all of which originated from the comic-book character created in the 1930s by teenagers Jerry Siegel and Joe Shuster. From 1940s radio dramas to the black-and-white TV series of the 1950s to Hollywood films and back to TV with the 1990s show "The Adventures of Lois and Clark," "Superman" continues to resonate deep within the American psyche. Why do millions of us still seek out "Wonder Woman," "Batman," "Dick Tracy," and "The Incredible Hulk"? Why is "Spider-Man" still recognizable to so many children? What about "Cathy," "Peanuts," "B.C." and "Calvin and Hobbes"? Tens of millions of Americans read them every day! What is it about comic strips, such as the one on the next page, and comic-book heroes that is so powerful?

On various levels, strips help us see the humor in our daily existence. We enjoy laughing at ourselves and at our fellow human beings. It brings us a sense of security to know that countless others also relate to the funny events our favorite characters present. We have all embarrassed ourselves in front of our friends, or at least we have seen other people embarrass themselves in ways the strips illustrate. The humor in comics is universal.

Another universal human quality can explain our attraction to comic-book superheroes. We humans need to create myths and legends to help us deal with the big mysteries of life. All cultures, both native and modern, have traditional stories about how we came into being and how we should behave. Whether secular or religious, these stories often present main characters as role models. The traditional literary genre of mythology, with its heroes and gods, is filled with half-human, half-divine beings who conquer evil and set standards of bravery and wisdom, just like Superman. Comics are so popular because of the deep commonality of human experience they communicate.

Future Watch: Comics in the Digital Age

Perhaps the biggest question facing the creators of comics as we enter the next century is how the medium will change as result of interactive technologies. If one of the central qualities of comics as a medium is that they combine still images and written text, how will the addition of sound and motion change their basic format? Will comics turn into animated cartoons? How will the

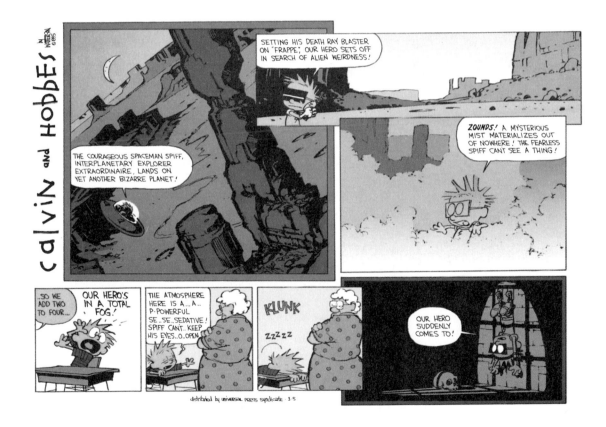

Reflections

- What needs do comics fulfill for the millions who read them so faithfully?
- Who are America's most worshiped heroes today? In what ways are they similar to comic-book superheroes?
- What are your favorite comic strips and why? If you do not read comics regularly, read a page of strips from your local newspaper and reflect on these questions: Which strip stuck out in your mind and why? What recurring themes can you identify in the strips? How do these themes relate to the "laughing at oneself" or "hero myth" theories of comics popularity?

development of CD-ROM comics influence their evolution? One of the exciting capabilities of the new technologies is that a storyline can contain many branches, allowing the reader to choose from several turns in the plot of a comic. Another possibility is the nonlinear plot, in which the user jumps into the plot at any point and builds the story by selecting random plot events.

America Online (an online computer service) has an area sponsored by DC Comics in which comics fans can get information on upcoming releases, new characters, and other issues relating to the DC line of comics. Users can chat with each other and **download** graphic files of comic-book covers which they can then view on their computers. Several publishers are experimenting with similar on-line distribution systems which eventually will make entire issues available for viewing.

Industry Snapshot: Comics
Comic-Book Careers and Breaking into the Business

Aspiring comic-book artists/writers should develop their portfolios carefully and prepare to send in submissions to comic-book publishers in acceptable format. DC Comics publishes submission guidelines, which describe how artists and writers may submit their

Current Facts and Stats

(*Sources: Comics Buyer's Guide 1994 Annual, Internal Correspondence Magazine*, August 1994.)

- There are roughly one million regular comic-book readers in the United States.
- Retail sales of comic books in 1993 were approximately 750 million dollars.
- There are about 6000 comic-book stores in the U.S.
- Approximately 100 comic-book publishers exist, though only six of them control about 85 percent of the market.
- Over 86 million Americans read the Sunday newspaper comics every month.

work for consideration. Following are excerpts from DC Comics' guidelines:

. . . PENCILS:

Pencillers should submit 4–6 COMIC BOOK PAGES in order, showing the progression of a story through a series of pictures. Don't send pinups and paintings. They don't tell us you can tell a comics story.

You can make up your own story sequence, visually advancing it from panel to panel and from page to page. Or you can work with a writer friend or rework an existing comics story (without copying the art). Your story should be easy to follow, moving along clearly and dynamically. It's better to draw a story well in traditional block panels than to try to impress us with sexy pin-ups, overly complex layouts or artistic gimmicks.

Your samples should also show basic drawing abilities. In addition to knowing how to draw heroic action figures and expressive faces, you must be able to draw the average guy on the street, buildings, cars, animals, aliens—ANYTHING you may find in a comic book. Your art should display an understanding of perspective and anatomy. You should be able to draw people in different types of clothing and in a variety of poses, from an old woman hunched in a chair to a muscular super-hero punching through a wall. It's best not to limit yourself only to comics as your reference and inspiration. Life-drawing and other general art classes and books are important parts of your education. The dedicated artist draws everything he sees, all the time.

Professional comics pencillers work in a $10" \times 15"$ image area on a sheet of Strathmore bristol board that measures $11" \times 17"$. They usually lay out their pages with a lead pencil or a non-repro blue pencil, and finish their art with a regular pencil. Don't use too hard a pencil (3H or harder) or bear down too hard on the page. This will leave grooves in the paper.

INKS:

Inkers should submit photocopies of both your inks and the pencils you have inked, so that we can compare the two. We would prefer to see your inks over more than one penciller. If you have no access to pencil samples from a friend or professional, write DC's Submissions Editor for photocopies but you must include a self-addressed $9" \times 12"$ envelope with about one dollar in postage. Inking on vellum over the photocopies or on bristol board with a lightbox is probably the easiest way for you to work.

A comic-book inker's job is to add DEPTH and CLARITY to the pencils without obscuring the penciller's work. This is done by spotting blacks and varying line weight to give the page variety and each panel a threedimensional feel, not by adding unnecessary detail. Objects in the foreground must look and weigh differently from objects in the background. You must also know which pencil lines should be omitted in the inking. Storytelling is an important part of the inker's job, and knowing how to draw separates the best inkers from the rest.

Professional comics inkers use artist's waterproof india ink, applied with a variety of brushes and pens. Corrections can be made by using one of several types of white paint. Remember, your ink line comes from your brain as much as from the tools you use.

LETTERING:

Comic-book letterers are responsible for captions, word and thought balloons, balloon shapes, panel borders, title lettering, credits and sound effects. Caption and balloon lettering have to be uniform and easy to read, with slight "breathing room" between letters, words and lines. Too tight letter spacing is hard to read. Story titles and sound effects are usually lettered in a bold, open style.

You can letter your samples onto full-size photocopies of pencilled pages (to secure copies of pencils, see the inking section above), or you may submit 3–4 pages of lettering without art, on a $8\frac{1}{2}" \times 11"$ paper. The first method is preferable, since it will show us how your lettering will look on an actual page. Show us all types of lettering, from word, thought, electric (jagged edge) and whisper (dotted line) balloons to sound effects.

Comics letterers use an AMES LETTERING GUIDE (set from 3 to $3\frac{1}{2}$ on the bottom scale), available at many art supply stores, for spacing and guidelines, and one of a variety of pens—ranging from technical pens to filed-down calligraphy pens—for words. Balloons and ruled panel borders are usually done with a technical or ruling pen.

COLORING:

Coloring is an essential part of comics storytelling. The colorist must interpret the art and tell the story through color, adding depth, dramatic effect, mood and, most important, CLARITY.

The most important characters and objects in each scene and page must be clearly visible to the reader. This often requires coloring people and things differently than they would appear in real life. For example, if a panel features Guy Gardner standing amidst a crowd of dozens of people, Guy could be colored normally, while the others could be colored in a monotone (or a series of related muted tones) to ensure that Guy is clearly seen in the panel.

Colorists can create MOOD by taking further liberties with realism. For example, if an artist has drawn a sequence of panels in which Lobo gets angry, a variety of reds—a color often used to convey anger—could be used on both Lobo himself and in the background. Blue and green, conversely, establish a placid feel.

Standard comics color guides are coded to match a chart of 124 colors available to us. Marking up your guides is an essential part of coloring.

Colorists should submit 4–6 pages of fully colored and coded comic-art photocopies. Colorists work on reduced photocopies (art reduced 64% onto 8½" × 11" paper). If you need photocopies to color, or a copy of the DC coloring chart showing the available colors, send a self-addressed stamped 9" × 12" envelope to DC's Submissions Editor with your request.

Professional comics colorists use DR. MARTIN'S DYES, although colored pencils or markers are also acceptable. . . .

CONTENTS OF YOUR SUBMISSION:

If you can't convince us that your story idea is something we have to publish, there's no point in going any further. No one has time to read a full script to see if there's something of merit there. With this in mind, you should submit a story SPRINGBOARD—a one-page, double spaced typed story concept. Despite what some novice writers think, literally any story we would be interested in can be described in this format. We will not review written submissions in any other form.

NEVER submit a full plot or script. Many prospective writers spend hours on full scripts. While we appreciate this enthusiasm, we don't have time to read complete scripts. Start simply and work your way up.

When constructing your springboard, think of the back-cover copy of a paperback novel. If it's well written, the customer is eager to buy the book and to read what's inside. Your goal is to make the editor ask for more from you.

There are five elements you absolutely must include in any springboard. They are:

1. A BEGINNING.
2. A MIDDLE.
3. AN END.

Do not underestimate the importance of these three things. This is the foundation upon which your story is built, and if any one of these is missing or lacking, your tale will not hold up. Here is where you introduce the characters and situations, develop conflicts, and indicate their resolution.

Conflict need not be hero versus villain. Man against himself, or nature, or a problem that must be solved, are all valid conflicts. Your opening should be compelling enough to grab our interest in the first sentence.

4. A HOOK (Also called The High Concept or theme). This is the essence of what makes your story unique and nifty. When you boil your story down to one sentence, if that sentence is compelling, that's the hook.

5. READER IDENTIFICATION. The events you describe must affect a character that we care about in some way. (This doesn't necessarily have to be the hero.) If no one in the story cares about what happens, why should the reader? We all share common emotions and experiences. Tap into these feelings and use them in your stories.

Continuity is very important in today's comic-book market. A comics writer has to be familiar with a character's history before trying to write that character. Make sure you've read enough to fully understand any series' current continuity—and the personalities of the cast.

STORY FORMATS:

Full length stories in DC regular monthly titles range from 22 to 25 pages, depending on format. But we strongly recommend you think in terms of our new anthology title, SHOWCASE. We buy 10-page stories using virtually all of our characters. This is the best place for a writer not currently working at DC to make a sale.

Our Superman, Batman, Star Trek and Sandman editors do not review unsolicited material, so don't send us anything using those characters or their mythologies.

Be aware that no novice writer will be allowed to make major changes in continuity. Don't rely on new powers, death of an existing character or personality changes to make your story compelling.

If you are writing a springboard for a new character you've created, you should also include a brief paragraph describing who the character is and what he's about. If you're creating a new world, what's the most interesting thing about it? Remember, like the rest of the springboard, you should keep this brief.

If your idea interests an editor, he or she will work with you on developing the idea further, either to plot or full script.

STYLISTIC REQUIREMENTS:
Professional work looks professional. Bad spelling, punctuation, and grammar are signs of the amateur. Editor will not be interested in proposals filled with errors.

All writing submissions must be TYPED double-spaced on one side of the paper. Hand-written submissions will not be considered.

Comic-book writing is about telling a story in pictures, with words supplementing the visual storytelling. No matter what story genre you want to work in, comic books convey, through pictures and words, action, movement, and urgency, a sense of drama and grandeur and "larger than life" excitement.

You should learn comic-book techniques and terminology and use them. "Comics and Sequential Art" by Will Eisner is an excellent bible for conventions of the medium. . . . ■

The preceding excerpts from *DC Comics Artists' Submissions Guidelines* are reprinted with permission of DC Comics, © 1993.

Building Your Media Archive
Archive Analysis: Comics

Make sure you have read the comic book you will analyze. Refer to the Media Literacy Paradigm in Chapter Three and answer the questions for each stage. First, list the Product stage information. The Origin stage will require varying amounts of outside research depending on the publisher (some comics list the mediators on the first page, others do not). Depending on the popularity of the comic, you may be able to locate a biography to give you insights about the author's background, the history of the main character,

Profile of a Comic Book Artist/Publisher

Colleen Doran, Illustrator and Animator, Virginia

Colleen Doran developed an interest in comics and animation at a very early age. She won her first prize at the age of five in a contest sponsored by Disney and picked up her first work as a professional artist at the age of 15, when she brought her portfolio to a science fiction/comics convention and was scouted by an advertising agency.

Doran received her first commission to work in comics at the age of 16, but turned the contract away because the contents of the comic book were objectionable to her. Less than a year later, she was approached by another publisher to illustrate a graphic novel series, but the publisher was nervous about hiring such a young artist, so they showed her work to WARP Graphics (a comic-book publisher). WARP became interested in Colleen's art and asked her about the storyline of some development drawings she had done. They eventually decided to publish Colleen Doran's creation *A Distant Soil*. Colleen had been working on the characters in *A Distant Soil* since she was 10, and came up with the storyline for the comic book at the age of 12.

Four things stand out as real landmarks in her career, according to Doran.

First, "when Disney called and asked me to do the book version of the movie *Beauty and the Beast*. . . . I'd wanted to work with Disney since I was a kid, but I didn't want to be an animator, so I got my big job on "B & B." It sold like crazy. . . ."

Second, "getting to work on an Anne Rice project [a graphic novel] was very exciting. She is one of my favorite authors. Originally, I was asked to do [illustrate] *Interview with the Vampire*, but that would require some 275 paintings and three years to complete, and I didn't have the time. So I chose *The Master of Rampling Gate*, a little known Anne Rice short story, the only one she ever wrote, which took about 5 months to complete and took 64 paintings. It's extremely gratifying to work on projects by your favorite authors. I've also worked on books by Clive Barker, and he was gracious enough to autograph one of my illustrations, which now hangs in my studio.

Third, "I've worked on many superhero comics, which is unusual for the comics industry. [As a woman] I've broken down a few barriers. When I worked on *Amazing Spider-Man*, we broke a 10-year sales record, which was a great surprise to everyone. I've drawn [comic] books no women creators had ever drawn before, and I think that

Profile of a Comic Book Artist/Publisher (*continued*)

makes it a little easier for other women to get ahead when someone else has already helped lay a trail."

Fourth, "starting my own company (Aria Press) and self-publishing my work *A Distant Soil* [see page 146] has been my greatest accomplishment. No one thought I would succeed. I don't think any woman had done it solo before, so everyone was surprised that it worked out. I am most proud of the work that I create and publish entirely myself. I like being boss. . . ."

Speaking to young aspiring artists seeking to have their work published, Doran advises them to know their legal and professional rights and do what is in their best interest. ▪

and so on. Several of the organizations and publications listed in Resources for Further Reading are very helpful. Remember, *you* are their target market and the source of their income. In most cases, they will receive a well-written inquiry enthusiastically.

As you apply the Media Literacy Paradigm (introduced in Chapter Three) and work through the third (Mediation) stage questions about your comic book, remember the unique characteristics of comics in general and of your comic book in particular (for example, dominant word/picture combinations). As you examine the product in terms of how it is "consumed" and what the product's impact is, consider your personal responses to the product.

Create Your Own Media

Create your own cut-and-paste comic strip by cutting out images from magazines and writing text balloons for them. Here's a sample procedure to follow: After you assemble a stock of images, decide on a story line or situation. Then decide on the number of panels you want to use and draw the panel boxes on an appropriately sized piece of heavy paper. Lay out your images; you may want to trim them so that you have room to draw or color backgrounds in the panels. Next determine the text, sound effects, and balloon styles to accompany each panel. Cut out and arrange the filled-in text balloons and effects in the panels. Once you are satisfied, secure the elements in place. You can add motion, odor, and heat lines if desired.

MEDIA LAB   Comics

- Find examples of varying passages of time between any two panels of a comic strip or comic book. Find an example of the passage of a few seconds, a few hours, and a day or longer.
- Create a poster illustrating the concept of closure. One possibility is to take two hand-drawn or magazine images (either related or not) and place them at the left and right edges of a piece of posterboard. Leave room between the images so viewers of the poster can write a sentence explaining what they think the connection is between the images. The poster might also include a definition of closure.
- Find as many examples as you can of the word/picture combinations described by Scott McCloud.
- Using a comic book or comic strips from your local newspaper, find examples of varying text balloon styles, including various motion, odor, and heat lines.
- Find examples of textual sound effects from both comic strips and books. You can also create a poster with textual sound effects (SFX) pertaining to different situations and environments (for example, a classroom, a concert, a basketball game, or a party).
- Make a copy of several comic strips from a Sunday newspaper, then cut up the originals between the panels. Give each strip (with its separated panels) to a classmate who has not seen it before and have him or her reassemble the strip.

A Distant Soil #7, February 1994. All rights reserved. Reprinted by permission of Colleen Doran, profiled on page 143.

Animation
Hybrid Entertainment

Animation is not a mass medium in itself. Technically speaking, animation is a category of filmmaking. Because TV is its main medium of distribution, animated cartoons are often thought of as a category of TV. The subject of animation is addressed in this chapter because it combines the fine arts of drawing and painting found in comics with the production techniques of film, which is the subject of the next chapter.

The Golden Age of Movie House Animation

Though animation dates back to the early twentieth century, not until the 1930s (when sound and color came to movies) did cartoons become part of American pop culture. The birth of Mickey Mouse in 1928 ushered in a 15-year parade of animated characters who still command worldwide audiences. In the 1930s alone, Disney studios added Donald Duck, Goofy, and Pluto, and Paramount created Popeye and Betty Boop. Warner Brothers rolled

Student Close-Up

Miguel Castillo, Illinois

A high school student describes how he got involved in cartooning.

As long as I can remember I have always had a deep love for cartooning. From about the age of six I could always be found within a three-foot radius of a set of crayons and notebook paper. I would draw anything. I was constantly making my family members sit and pose for my drawings. Another thing I especially enjoyed was trying to copy cartoon characters that I found in the newspaper comic strips.

It wasn't until I joined my high-school newspaper, however, that I was fully able to explore my talents. When I first joined the staff, they already had a cartoonist with much more experience. I mostly wrote articles that year, but I didn't care because I knew I had a lot to learn. By watching this cartoonist, I was able to see the techniques that I would need. I also have been able to attend journalism conventions where I have met other student cartoonists from all over the country. There I was able to learn new skills and even listen to professional cartoonists.

Now I draw almost all the cartoons for the paper. It's a hard job, but a fun one. I have to think fast because the writers basically just hand me their articles and say, "Draw something." Sometimes it's difficult to come up with ideas, but my fellow staff members are always there to help me if I get stuck.

All in all, I have thoroughly enjoyed being on my high-school newspaper and plan on being a member for my next two years of high school. Although it can be tedious at times, it can also be very rewarding. It has given me a chance to broaden my horizons and also given me a way in which I have been able to expose my work to a larger audience. ■

Miguel Castillo. *Photo and newspaper courtesy of Larkin High School, Elgin, Illinois.*

out Porky Pig in 1935, Elmer Fudd and Daffy Duck in 1937, and Bugs Bunny in 1938.

You represent the second generation of Americans to become familiar with classic cartoons through TV. Your parents also grew up knowing these animated folk heroes as Saturday morning and after-school television playmates. Your grandparents or great-grandparents, however, met these same characters in theaters as part of a very different experience from today's moviegoing. First, the six- to eight-minute-long cartoons were part of an entire package of film entertainment. Audiences in the 1930s and 1940s typically saw a short film (such as a mini-documentary about another country), a newsreel about a major current event, a new cartoon, and then the full-length feature film. (City theaters often included a live stage show as well.) The new cartoons were advertised and promoted the way new films are today. Mickey, Betty, and Bugs were stars whose next cartoons were eagerly anticipated. The second major difference in the presentation of cartoons at that time was that they were not thought of as only children's entertainment. After all, they were sandwiched between serious newsreels about WW II and Hollywood's newest dramas. This explains the often adult-themed humor found in so many of those early cartoons, as well as the spoofs on Hollywood stars of the 1940s, such as Humphrey Bogart, Jack Benny, and Bette Davis.

Animated Cartoons in the Television Era

During the 1930s and 1940s, Bill Hanna and Joseph Barbera worked as animators at MGM movie studios for Friz Freleng, who created Yosemite Sam, the Pink Panther, and other famous characters. There they developed Tom and Jerry, popular characters at movie theaters, and carved out a distinctive artistic style. They teamed up to form their own production company and throughout the 1950s and 1960s dominated the new direct-for-television cartoon market. Spanning the historical time line from "The Flintstones" to "The Jetsons," Hanna-Barbera depicted the typical American family. Their shows taught the same family values as their live-action situation comedy counterparts of the time, such as "Leave It to Beaver" and "Dennis the Menace." Another example of how media products both reflect and reinforce the attitudes of a given era can be seen in the popular 1960s cartoon series "The Rocky and Bullwinkle Show." One character, Boris

Badinov, Rocky and Bullwinkle's archenemy, was a product of the Cold War between the United States and the Soviet Union. Much of the country was gripped by a fear of spies, and Boris's fate served to let viewers know that the forces of "evil" would never prevail.

Continued Popularity

Thanks to cable TV, the Saturday morning time slot of the 1960s has expanded to become 24 hours long. Nickelodeon, the Cartoon Network, and an increasing number of cable channels are broadcasting more reruns and new animated series than ever. For the first time since the golden era of animation, the audience for cartoons spans the range from child to adult in significant numbers. From kids and their new cartoons such as "The Rug Rats" and the MTV-watching fans of "Beavis and Butthead" all the way to middle-aged fans of "The Simpsons" (see pages 152–153), more Americans are enjoying animation than ever before.

What's Next?

Computers are changing every medium of communication, including animation. The blending of live action and animation is increasingly sophisticated, and animated special effects, such as those in Steven Spielberg's film *Jurassic Park*, are expanding the definition of animation. Most animated film festivals have a separate category for computer-generated productions, and the impact is being felt outside Hollywood. Affordable software programs make animation tools available to the public. You no longer need the same drawing skills as are required for traditional animation, though you do still need some artistic vision to use the software creatively.

The Nuts and Bolts of Traditional Animation
A Condensed Look at Cartoon Production

Like any comic strip or book, a cartoon begins as a story in someone's mind. A plot is worked out and turned into a script, which is then revised and finalized. The script shows character dialogue, explains the action, and indicates basic sound effects. The dialogue

Reflections

- Cartoon violence is one of the big subissues in the larger debate over television violence. Some researchers claim that small children who watch a lot of violent cartoons, such as "The Road Runner," are more likely to be physically aggressive when playing with peers than children who watch fewer such cartoons. Start your own inquiry into this controversy. Do you think cartoon violence influences children? Why or why not? How does it affect them? Were you affected by the cartoon violence you consumed as a younger child? Observe a child or group of children watching a violent cartoon. How do they react? What do you think they are thinking as they watch? How do stages four and five of the Media Literacy Paradigm (Consumption and Impact) enter into the debate?

is recorded by the actors and placed onto a preliminary **soundtrack**, onto which sound effects and music will be added later.

Meanwhile, the artists draw **storyboards** which show the main points of action in the cartoon. The action between these storyboards is filled in with thousands of pencil sketches. These sketches are filmed, one frame of movie film at a time, and then played back. This very rough version of the cartoon is used to make sure the action is what the director wants and that the timing of the visuals are matched up with previously recorded dialogue. This rough version can change hundreds of times before it is finalized. At that point, artists use ink to redraw cleaned-up versions of each sketch. Each inked drawing is then transferred to a clear sheet of acetate, called a **cel**, where it is hand painted. The completed cels are checked for color consistency. Each one is placed on a translucent table, lit from underneath, while a special camera, mounted on top of the table, exposes one frame of movie film. The cel is removed, and the next cel is placed on the table and exposed for one frame. This process is repeated for all the cels in the cartoon.

A computer graphics artist is shown here creating special effects for use in an animated film. *Photo courtesy of Corplex Systems Group, Lincolnwood, Illinois.*

The Magic Formula: 24 Frames per Second

The early pioneers of film eventually figured out that to reproduce the illusion of smooth, natural motion, they had to make their cameras record events at a speed of 24 frames per second (24 fps). This means that you are actually looking at 24 individual photographs flashing on the screen of a movie theater every second. When filming live action, the film rolls through the camera at that speed and captures whatever it's pointing at. In animation, however, each frame—24 per second—is individually filmed. That means that a seven-minute "Bugs Bunny" cartoon requires 10,080 cels. A 22-minute animated show, such as "The Simpsons" or *Duckman* (30 minutes minus eight minutes of commercials), requires 31,680 cels (24 frames × 60 seconds × 22 minutes). A two-hour animated film, such as *The Lion King*, can require an amazing 172,800 handpainted cels!

Putting It All Together

During the production and filming of the cels, the audio portion
of the cartoon is developed. Music is composed and recorded,
sound effects are determined and recorded, and any new or
changed dialogue is also recorded. Once the cartoon is set visually,
the soundtrack is finished. The music and sound effects are added
to the dialogue and the entire soundtrack is added to the cartoon.
After any final edits or changes are made, copies (called **prints**)
are made of the original master film and sent on film to movie
theaters or on videotape to TV stations.

Here an ink and paint artist applies color to a cel for "THE SIMPSONS."
Photographer: Hal Fisher. Courtesy of Film Roman, Inc., and Fox Broadcasting.

Career Bank

Following are just a few of the many careers available in the comics and animated film industry:

- comic strip or book artist/illustrator/writer
- comic strip syndicate assistant/manager
- comic book publisher/distributor
- animator/computer graphic artist
- video/sound technician

- film/videotape engineer
- animation studio assistant/manager

Recap

Two prominent features distinguish comics from other media. First, their form is based on an interdependent blending of text and illustrated images. Second, they require a high level of involvement because the reader must constantly provide **closure** between every panel to interpret the comic's meaning.

There are a variety of categories and **genres** in both comic strips and comic books. Because of their presence in newspapers, strips are the most popular category of comics. The humor genre dominates the strips, while the superhero genre still dominates the comic-book market.

Comics were—and still are—an important part of American pop culture. They helped create support among youth for the U.S. role in World War II, and they rely on the universal themes of human fallibility and hero worship. Though the future of comics in an interactive, multimedia world is uncertain, for the near future, the standard jobs of writer, penciller, inker, letterer, and colorist will dominate comics production.

The classic Warner Brothers cartoons, as well as others such as "Popeye" and "Woody Woodpecker," were first shown in movie theaters in the 1930s and 1940s along with newsreels and a feature film. Hanna-Barbera was the first major producer of made-for-TV cartoons in the 1950s and 1960s. Animation is a form of filmmaking which requires the drawing, painting, and filming of 1440 separate **cels** for each minute of a cartoon.

Resources for Further Reading
Comics
Books

Benton, Mike. *Superhero Comics of the Golden Age: The Illustrated History*. Dallas: Taylor Publishing, 1992.

———. *The Comic Book in America: An Illustrated History*. Dallas: Taylor Publishing, 1993.

Eisner, Will. *Comics and Sequential Art*. Tamarac, Fla.: Poorhouse Press, 1985.

Horn, Maurice, ed. *The World Encyclopedia of Comics.* New York: Chelsea House, 1976.

Kane, Bob. *Batman and Me: An Autobiography.* Forrestville, N.Y.: Eclipse Books, 1989.

McCloud, Scott. *Understanding Comics: The Invisible Art.* Northampton, Mass.: Kitchen Sink Press, Inc., 1993.

McKenzie, Alan. *How to Draw and Sell Comic Strips for Newspaper and Comic Books.* Cincinnati: North Light Books, 1987.

Schoell, William. *Comic Book Heroes of the Screen.* New York: Citadel Press, 1991.

Wiater, Stanley, and Stephen R. Bissette. *Comic Book Rebels: Conversations with the Creators of the New Comics.* New York: Donald Fine, Inc., 1993.

Industry Publications

Note: Most of these organizations will send you an issue of their publication if you request it for educational or classroom use.

The Comics Journal: The Magazine of Comics News and Criticism
7563 Lake City Way N.E.
Seattle, WA 98115

Entertainment Retailing
151 Wells Ave.
Congers, NY 10920-2064

Internal Correspondence: The Newsmagazine for Specialty Retailing
2537 Daniels Street
Madison, WI 73704

Comic Buyers Guide
Krause Publications Inc.
700 East State Street
Iola, WI 54990

Animation
Books

Jones, Chuck. *Chuck Amuck: The Life and Times of an Animated Cartoonist.* New York: Avon Books, 1989.

Lenburg, Jeff. *The Great Cartoon Directors.* New York: De Capo Press, 1983.

Schneider, Steve. *That's All Folks: The Art of Warner Brothers Animation.* New York: Henry Holt, 1988.

Thomas, Bob. *Disney's Art of Animation: From Mickey Mouse to Beauty and the Beast.* New York: Hyperion, 1991.

White, Tony. *The Animator's Workbook.* New York: Watson-Gupte, 1988.

Industry Publications

Animato!
17 Spruce Street
Springfield, MA 01105

Animation Magazine
5889 Kanan Road, #317
Agoura Hills, CA 91301

Key word database searches for library research on comics and animation:

Comics, Comic Books, Comic Strips, Animation, Animators, Cartoons, Cartoonists

SEGUE

Comics and Animation

Like comics, the medium of film has distinct storytelling conventions, and like animation, feature films involve elaborate production techniques. As comics were attacked in the 1950s for being too violent for children, the film industry today is wrestling with how far it should go in portraying violence. Though film offers a wider variety of genres than comics, Hollywood is still basically about one thing: *entertainment*. And how we're entertained when we go to the movies is what Chapter Six is about.

Film

Learning Targets

After working through this chapter, you will be able to

- Explain the stages of film-making: preproduction, production, and postproduction;
- Identify examples of specific techniques of cinematography;
- Create a script for a three-minute film sequence;
- Write a review of the film in your Media Archive; and
- Apply the Media Literacy Paradigm to the film in your Media Archive.

Checking In

- List three films you have seen recently and briefly describe why you liked them.
- Name as many different movie studios and directors as you can.
- List as many criteria of film evaluation as you can.
- Which statement do you think is more realistic: Film imitates life, or life imitates film.
- Write three film-related topics you would like to learn about.

The Unique Qualities of Film

Unlike all other mass media, film requires you to be in a particular place to experience it—a movie theater. Because of this *requirement of consumption*, film is the only mass medium which gets you out of the house and puts you in a big dark room with other people, a room where your emotions are more easily manipulated than by any other medium you experience at home. You may watch films on your VCR, but that is a very different experience from seeing them in a theater.

First of all, the size of the movie screen in a theater takes up most of your **field of vision**. Unlike watching TV (unless you're sitting very close to it), you are not distracted by other visual information when you watch a film in a theater. The sheer size of the visual experience engulfs you. Add to that the volume and spaciousness of the sound in theaters, and you have a unique media environment. Even state-of-the-art wide-screen TVs with surround-sound home audio do not provide the same experience as watching a film in a theater. The 1994 action-thriller *Speed* (about a hijacked bus that must maintain a certain speed to avoid exploding) does not feel the same on a 25-inch TV screen as it does in the theater. It is not only how a film is *consumed* in a theater that gives it its emotional impact; it is also how the film is put together—how it is *mediated*. As you'll soon find out, film is an amazingly flexible medium. A director, along with dozens of other support personnel, can bring to the screen almost anything her imagination comes up with.

Reflections

- List as many words or phrases as you can that you associate with watching a film in a theater (for example, popcorn, dark, surprise, group of people, and so on).
- Describe the reaction someone from a nonelectronic native culture would have upon seeing a film in a theater for the first time.

The Life of a Film
Preproduction: Obtaining the Material

There are three stages in the life of a film: preproduction, production, and postproduction. **Preproduction** is usually thought of as the planning stage and covers all preparations up until filming actually begins. Preproduction on a film starts with the **development** phase, when a person or company **buys the rights** to a literary work, an original **screenplay**, or even a story outline. Once the rights to such a work are owned, no one else can turn that work into a film. The owner of the work usually hires **scriptwriters** to improve the work and turn it into a workable screenplay. After the owner of the revised work feels it has the potential to become a successful film, he will either keep the project or sell it to an interested movie studio or another producer. (The project may never get turned into a film, however. The studio may not be able to interest any big stars in it, or it may find out that a competing studio is already producing a film like it. If the owner of a project does not think it will make money, it will never show up on the big screen.)

Despite the intense efforts of movie studios to figure out what kind of movie we will go see, and despite the billions of dollars they spend making films (an average of about 20 million dollars per film), the executives in Hollywood still miss the boat fairly often. The article from *Variety* magazine that starts on page 162 describes how the script for 1994's summer hit *Speed* was dumped by Paramount Studios because executives thought it would bomb at the box office. Fox Studios bought the script, produced the film, and is still making money on it. You may be surprised to learn that a few other famous films were junked by one studio, and picked up by another—only to become smash hits.

Practice

As you read the article from *Variety*, analyze it in terms of the five stages of the Media Literacy Paradigm: Product Classification, Origin, Mediation, Consumption, and Impact. (For example, the article refers to the studio executives who decide whether to produce a film. Studio executives are among the many people who are responsible for turning creative ideas into movies, which is part of the Origin stage of the Media Literacy Paradigm.)

Preproduction: Developing the Material

Once the owner of a project decides to go ahead with it, preproduction activity kicks into high gear. The owner hires the key personnel for the project: a director, a business manager, the key **talent**, and any other people he wants to select personally. These people in turn hire the people they want to work with: talent agents, lighting designers, sound engineers, accountants, special effects coordinators, and hundreds of other people with specific tasks. Feature films require months of planning before the cameras ever roll. For example, entire teams of location managers search for places where particular scenes can be shot.

Rivals Reap Rewards from Turnaround

John Brodie and Jay Greene

The two biggest surprise hits of the summer—Paramount's "Forrest Gump" and Fox's "Speed"—have more in common than sub-verbal heroes who spend a lot of time around buses.

Both "Gump" and "Speed" are movies that were put into turnaround by major studios.

Turnaround is studio-speak for the development purgatory where scripts go when studios want to dump them. At some point in their development lives, "Gump" and "Speed" were given up for dead by studio execs who did not believe either film was commercially viable.

Putting into turnaround a film that becomes someone else's hit is an easy way to make a fool of yourself in Hollywood, and studios keep vowing to avoid the trap. "Everybody is living in fear of being the executive who put 'E.T.' in turnaround," says Barry Beckerman, a Warner Bros. executive.

But even though studios spend hundreds of millions of dollars nurturing scripts through the development process, several factors trigger the decision to throw in the towel.

A reshuffling of top production executives may spur the desire to start with a clean slate. A script may come in at too high a budget, or a top actor or director may decide to back out of the pic. And so-called genre gridlock can doom westerns or family pictures.

Hollywood history is rife with turnaround miscues. In addition to "Gump" and "Speed," studio execs have tossed such blockbusters as "E.T. The Extra-Terrestrial" and "Home Alone" onto the turnaround heap.

Missed opportunities like that explain why execs are terrified of being known as the idiot who passed on a blockbuster. After the success of "Speed," execs at Paramount Pictures, which spurned the Keanu Reeves starrer, are said to have put a hold on placing any projects in turnaround, despite top executive changes at the studio.

"We consider it to be inventory and assets of the company," says an exec at another studio that has become increasingly worried about putting projects in turnaround.

"People are always hesitant to look bad," says United Talent Agency's Jeremy Zimmer. "I don't think it's just 'Speed' or 'Gump,' but everyone seems to be looking a little harder at material before they will put it in turnaround."

There is no weekly tip sheet of projects in turnaround. And though studios ostensibly want to unload any project

Rivals Reap Rewards from Turnaround *(continued)*

they put in turnaround, they are loathe to advertise their failures.

The idea then is to find a buyer for the material, who, in turn, may wind up making the project. Typically, the buyer pays all the costs the studio has incurred to purchase and develop the material, plus a percentage for overhead and interest.

Right now the largest block of turnaround projects are the Hollywood Pictures slate assembled by its former studio head, Ricardo Mestres. When Mestres ankled in April and Hyperion exec Michael Lynton took the reins of the studio, the old Hollywood Pictures slate started looking like a garage sale.

Hawn project
A zany Goldie Hawn comedy called "College Mom," the Damon Wayans project "Good News, Bad News" and a bigscreen adaptation of "Hawaii 5-0" were all Mestres-era projects at Hollywood Pictures that are now in turnaround.

Aside from management changes, turnaround may also result when a key star drops out in pre-production—or a studio sours on a particular star. Don Simpson and Jerry Bruckheimer were slated to produce "Bad Boys" for Disney, with a cast including Dana Carvey and Jon Lovitz.

Sources say script problems arose and those stars fell out; Disney cooled on the project and put it into turnaround. Columbia then picked up the project, commissioned a rewrite and signed Will Smith and Martin Lawrence. The pic is currently in production.

Dangerous demands
Sometimes a project will come to a studio with a unique set of demands that make it problematic. Interscope recently put a project called "Shockwave" into turnaround simply because the screenwriter also wanted to direct the film.

THE ONES THAT GOT AWAY

A few blockbusters that were picked up in turnaround, and the studios that dumped them.

FILM	FROM	TO	DOMESTIC B.O.
E.T. The Extra-Terrestrial	Columbia	Universal	$399,804,539
Star Wars	Universal	Fox	322,000,000
Home Alone	Warner Bros.	Fox	285,761,243
Pretty Woman	Vestron	Disney	178,406,268
The Addams Family	Orion	Paramount	113,502,246
A League of Their Own	Fox	Columbia	107,404,544

Rivals Reap Rewards from Turnaround *(continued)*

David Twohy, whose credits include "The Fugitive," wrote what several development execs around town describe as an excellent action pic—but the screenwriter is anxious to make his directorial debut and will not let "Shockwave" go forward without himself attached as helmer.

Interscope, per sources, liked the script but refused to roll the dice on Twohy as a director. "Shockwave" is running into similar snags at other studios as it makes the rounds. Fox looked at the project but was also spooked by Twohy's enthusiasm for helming.

Projects also fall into the turnaround miasma because of genre burnout. Early last year, when studios were prepping a herd of Westerns—including "Tombstone," "Wyatt Earp," "Maverick," "Geronimo," "The Quick and the Dead," "Posse" and "Frank and Jesse"—a number of oaters moseyed into the turnaround corral.

Passing fancies

As in every other aspect of the movie business, passing fancy plays a pivotal role in deciding what gets put in turnaround. And just as genres are perceived as trending down, studios may perceive producers or stars coolly and put their projects into turnaround simply because of one less-than-stellar outing.

After comedian Dennis Leary failed to draw auds in "The Ref," another Simpson-Bruckheimer project at Disney, the studio brass soured on "Two if by Sea," a costly film from the producing pair that was also to topline Leary. New Line Cinema is currently flirting with the film.

Body heat is no defense against turnaround. Even screenwriters with cracker-jack track records have no guarantee against turnaround. Jeff Maguire, who wrote "In the Line of Fire," hasn't had the same success yet with "Counterfeit." It was put into turnaround by Fox before "In the Line of Fire" and landed with producer Arnold Kopelson. The project has yet to be set up at a rival studio.

'Bully' denied

At Warner Bros., a Mark Steven Johnson script called "Big Bully," which was with producer Lee Rich, has fallen into the turnaround heap. Johnson wrote the surprise hit "Grumpy Old Men" for WB and is penning its sequel.

"Bully" tells the story of a writer who returns to his Minnesota home town to teach at the local high school and discovers that his childhood tormentor is the carpentry teacher. Wags are already calling the script "Grumpy Middle-Aged Men."

"They just didn't like it," Rich said. ■

From *Variety: The International Entertainment Weekly*, Aug. 1–7, 1994. Reprinted by permission.

Preproduction: Organization and Script Development

Once the filming locations are determined, the team arranges for use of the location in conjunction with the film's transportation, scheduling, and financial managers in order to get the needed production crew to the location at the right time and within the designated travel budget. Plans also have to be made for catering the food, acquiring the props, and housing the crew, among many other details. Think how many films require dozens of locations.

Meanwhile, the director and her key assistants are constantly revising the script's dialogue and action, order of scenes, and so on. The director works with artists who draw storyboards in which the director begins to visualize the film. Storyboards are pinned on office walls to help the director, set designer, stunt coordinators, and others turn the written words of the script into visual images. To find out how storyboards actually work, look at the ones on page 166—actual storyboards from the production of the film *Terminator 2: Judgement Day*.

Production

The quality of the planning and work done in preproduction is tested once the **production** gets under way. Ideally, the crew and **talent** arrive on the set ready to **shoot**. The actors and actresses have studied their lines and directions and know where they are supposed to be. The sound, set, and lighting technicians have their equipment ready to go, and it's now up to the director to direct and the camera operator to shoot the talent. Of course, thousands of big and little problems crop up to prevent an ideal day of shooting—bad weather, talent forgetting their lines, and innumerable technical glitches (such as uncontrollable outside noise or equipment malfunction). Even without these hassles, a director may choose to have a single scene reshot dozens of times until the actor produces the exact facial expression or tone of voice she wants.

After the day's (or night's) shooting is done, the director assembles her key people to review the film that was shot. From these **dailies**, the crew gets a feel for how the filming is going and whether any scenes need to be reshot. Shooting and watching dailies is the basic routine of filmmaking, though the day-to-day activities vary significantly. If the scheduled scene calls for two

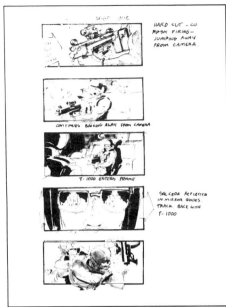

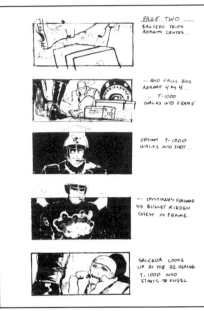

people talking on a park bench to be shot without fancy camera movements, you might get 15 minutes of usable film. Conversely, a complex special effects shot, such as a tornado slamming into a house, can take a week to shoot, even if it winds up being only two seconds worth of the final film.

During shooting, other people work away from the set on other aspects of the film. Music is composed and recorded. Computer-generated special effects are designed. Publicity strategies are mapped out—press releases announce the film, stars appear in print and TV interviews, advertising campaigns take shape. Back on the set, after months of shooting, the director has hundreds of hours of film from which the final two-hour movie will be pieced together.

Postproduction: Editing

When production on a film ends (or as they say in the industry, when shooting is **wrapped**) most of the actors and production personnel are done; they go on to another project. This is when the postproduction crew starts to feel the pressure. The director, her film editor, sound editor, and their assistants are now working against a studio-established deadline to get the film finished for distribution by a certain date.

The most important phase of postproduction is **editing**, where the miles of film on dozens of reels is cut up and **spliced** together to tell the story the way the director wants. First, the director selects the exact take she wants to use for every scene (during dailies, the director may have decided to keep takes 3, 4, and 9 of a particular scene). Once all the footage is picked, the director and editor decide on the order of the **shots**. In many cases, the director will rearrange shots after experimenting with their order. Perhaps she likes the shot of the child looking up from the table toward the door before the shot of the man walking through the door, instead of vice versa as was called for in the script. The Russian film pioneer Sergei Eisenstein was one of the first filmmakers to argue that the placement of shots back-to-back—what he called the *juxtaposition* of shots—is what gives films its unique power to communicate. When you see a woman in one shot look up and to the left, and in the next shot you see a man look up and to the right, you assume that they are looking at each other. Remember the discussion of closure from the previous chapter? That's what happens as you view those two shots; you provide closure to the two juxtaposed shots.

State-of-the-art film editing involves digital technology. Pictured above is the Media Composer 8000, Avid Technologies' digital online editing system, used by thousands of film/videotape editors worldwide. The Film Composer offers digitizing, editing, and playback capabilities at a true 24 frames-per-second. *Courtesy of Avid Technologies, Inc., Tewksbury, Massachusetts.*

After the shots are selected and their order determined, the next task is to join them with a **transition technique**. The most common transition technique for joining shots is called the **cut**, in which a piece of film is literally cut and spliced to another piece of film. A cut results in an instant change of image on the screen. Another transition technique is the **dissolve**, in which the shot currently on the screen gets lighter and fades away as the next shot simultaneously appears very lightly and gradually takes over on the screen. When to put shots together is as important as how to put them together. Let's say the shot on the screen is a person on the phone telling someone great news. As the director, you know that you're going to cut to the person on the other end of the phone for a **reaction shot**. At what exact moment do you cut? Is there a particular word at which you go from one person to the other? You could show most of the conversation with the news-giver on screen, or you could show just a few seconds of him and continue the rest of the conversation with the news-receiver on-screen.

Postproduction: Adding Sound

The importance of sound in films is often unappreciated. Yet all it takes is one viewing of a film with the sound off and you experience how important it really is. Though much of the sound in a movie is recorded as it is filmed, as much and often more is inserted during postproduction. If the studio is quiet enough, the dialogue spoken by the talent during shooting is what you hear when you see the film in the theater. Sounds that occur naturally in the course of a scene's action are called **ambient sounds** (such as silverware clinks, background crowd noise, or footsteps). Ideal recording conditions often are unavailable (as with almost any outdoor set), so the sound has to be rerecorded separately during postproduction. Dialogue that needs to be recorded again is done in a process called **looping**, where the actors watch themselves on a small screen in a recording studio and speak their lines; they're lipsyncing with themselves. The film's music—its **score**—is recorded and added to the film at the right spots and at the right volume. Vast libraries of sound effects provide every sound from intergalactic alien lasers to chirping birds. Finally, whatever ambient sounds could not be recorded at the time of shooting are performed in a sound studio and added to the film in postproduction. This process is the work of the **foley artist,** described in the reading "Foleys" beginning on the next page. It has been claimed that the moist slurps of some of Hollywood's best kisses are actually the sounds of a veteran foley artist kissing the back of his hand while a microphone captures each juicy acoustic moment.

••

Practice

As you read "Foleys," be prepared to cite a passage that can be analyzed in terms of the Mediation (production) stage of the Media Literacy Paradigm.

••

Promotion and Distribution

The last phase of postproduction involves selling the film. Coming attractions (known in the industry as **trailers**) are edited and sent to selected theaters. Posters are produced. Pre-release (test) screenings are often held for randomly-selected audiences.

Foleys, from *The New Yorker*

Most foley artists hate to work in water. Or mud. Tell a foley artist that he's going to be spending the morning on "Swamp Thing Three," or else stomping around in a tub of water, snarling and snapping pieces of wood together in order to duplicate a crocodile feeding frenzy for the soundtrack of a Jacques Cousteau film, while a rep from the oceanographer watches and after each take says, "I don't sink zat's good enough, let's try wance more," and—well, you better buy him a good lunch if you want his best work. Foley artists supply the sounds for many of the actions that take place in movies, on television, and in commercials. The sets on which those actions are filmed are all but dead quiet, because the sound engineers are trying to record what the actors are saying. What sounds can't be later supplied by sound-effects records and tapes—the slight clink, perhaps, of the beer bottle knocking against the ketchup when the refrigerator door is opened, the telephone receiver being picked up and put back, the rustle and scrape of fabric when a couple embrace, are re-created by the foley artist.

In New York City, there are five studios equipped with what are called foley stages. (Jack Foley, from whose name the term derives, worked at Universal Pictures during the thirties and forties and was responsible for solving a number of technical problems involving sound re-creation.) Most foley work involves the duplication of footsteps, which is why foley stages are built with what are called foley pits. There are six foley pits in a studio at Sync Sound, on Tenth Avenue between Fifty-fifth and Fifty-sixth Streets. Four of the pits have surfaces flush with the floor, which is carpeted, and two are a foot deep; one of these at the moment is filled with leaves and branches, and one is filled with dirt. The four flush surfaces are concrete, for duplicating the sound of footsteps on a sidewalk; marble, for courthouse steps and museums; sand; and gravel. By means of covers that fit over the pits it is possible to re-create the sound of footsteps on wood, on linoleum, on a metal grate like the ones over subway vents, and on a steel plate like the ones over the steps leading from sidewalks into the basements of buildings, and the squeak of sneakers on a gym floor.

The foley-artist-in-residence at Sync Sound is Rick Wessler. He is in his mid-forties. He is constantly picking up things and banging them to hear what sound they make. He has been an actor

Foleys, from *The New Yorker* (continued)

both on and off Broadway, in films, on television, and in commercials. He began his career in show business as a mime; he is fond of saying that he started out seen but not heard and now is heard but not seen.

Except for the foley pits, the studio Mr. Wessler works in looks like a suburban garage or an attic or a basement storeroom. It is, of course, full of shoes. Mr. Wessler buys them a size large, so that he can slip in and out of them easily. (He had difficulty finding size-11 high heels.) Elsewhere, on shelves or in corners, are a basketball; a tambourine; a shovel; a hoe; a grocery cart, for squeaks and rattles; two pieces of an old fire escape, to bank or scrape together to reproduce the sound of train couplings or falling elevators; a sledgehammer; a tire; a bicycle; a shoebox of broken glass; a piece of wood, for creaking; suitcases, for the sound of their snaps; a rubberized flight bag, to be picked up and squeezed for the sound of a leather jacket being taken off; a liquor bottle; a tray of dishes and glasses, for kitchen and restaurant scenes; and a tall canvas bag filled with sand—what boxers call a heavy bag—for punches and for those times when Mr. Wessler just doesn't feel like throwing himself on the floor to duplicate the sound of a falling body.

Mr. Wessler works mainly in darkness. On the far wall of the studio is a screen onto which the film is projected. If he is matching the steps of a person on a sidewalk, he walks in place on the concrete foley pit. He tries to duplicate the actions of the person on the screen as closely as possible: when the actor turns, Mr. Wessler turns. If it is a woman on the screen, Mr. Wessler walks as lightly as possible—unless, of course, it is a heavy woman. If the actor is walking on a rainy night, Mr. Wessler pours water he keeps in a Clorox bottle onto the concrete.

The other day, Mr. Wessler was working on an episode of a police series for NBC. To create the sound of a police dog's footsteps he wore a pair of leather gloves to the fingers of which he had taped Popsicle sticks. The episode featured a circus lion escaping from a carpeted office and running down a corridor. To duplicate its padding footsteps Mr. Wessler wore sheepskin gloves. He knelt on the carpet beside a foley pit that had a linoleum cover. He drew the back of his hand across the carpet to simulate the sound of the lion rising from the carpet on the screen, and when the lion came into the corridor Mr. Wessler transferred his hands to the linoleum. The reason he was foleying the lion's steps is that on the set a trainer had been shouting to the lion "Look over here!" and banging pots and pans to get its attention and calling out "You're a good lion, yes . . . you . . . *are!*"

Unless a foley is particularly elaborate or demanding, Mr. Wessler does no rehearsing. He reviews a tape of the

Foleys, from *The New Yorker* (continued)

film or commercial or television show beforehand and notes exactly where the effects he is to supply occur, and decides how he will reproduce them. Most are straightforward. For a difficult effect, you can spend a few hours coming up with a solution. The most contrived foley he has had lately involved duplicating the sound of an electric fan. The director had set up a scene in the sheriff's office in a small Southern town. In the background he had placed a fan with slowly turning blades, which threw a shadow across the room. Although Mr. Wessler pointed out that a fan with blades turning that slowly would make no sound at all, the director insisted on hearing the fan. Mr. Wessler built the sound from three components, recorded on separate tracks and later put together. For the sound of the fan's motor, he put the bicycle upside down and recorded the sound of its chain as he turned the pedals while pressing on the back tire to slow it up. For the sound of the breeze, he slowly passed a piece of paper back and forth in front of the microphone. To suggest an out-of-kilter fan blade striking the housing, he ran the point of a pocketknife around the inside rim of a hubcap.

Producers of movies and commercials and television shows usually want everything done yesterday, or the day before. Mr. Wessler must often work late into the night to complete a show by its deadline. The studio is down a long, windowless corridor, behind heavy, soundproofed doors, and is exceptionally quiet. When he leaves it early in the morning and steps outdoors, the first few moments are disorienting. Tenth Avenue, he says, sounds as loud as a drag race. ■

Test audiences are asked for their reactions to the film before it is released. This way, last-minute changes can be made, such as adding or cutting out a scene. Previews are arranged for film critics and industry executives, while behind the scenes, lawyers finish negotiations regarding domestic and international distribution schedules and copies of the film are shipped to theaters for opening day.

Film Terms and Techniques
Cinematography

Most people talk about the plot and the acting after they see a film, but they rarely talk about how the film was photographed—its

cinematography. Yet the conventions of camera technique are the foundations upon which film is built. Despite the crucial role of sound in film, it is still primarily a visual medium.

There are four levels of building blocks from which films are assembled:

Frame:	An individual picture, or exposure, on a strip of film. While shooting, film passes through the camera at 24 frames per second (fps); it is also played back by the theater projector at 24 fps.
Shot:	The basic unit of film. A shot is any continuous piece of unedited film, which can be as short as a split-second (a few fps) or as long as an entire reel of film. Most feature films contain shots *averaging* 20 to 30 seconds (taking into account two-second chase scene shots and two-minute dinner conversation scene shots).
Scene:	A group of interrelated shots taking place in the same location. For example, you might refer to a 20-second elevator scene.
Sequence:	A group of interrelated scenes that form a natural unit in the story. For example, the above elevator scene may be part of a two-minute escape sequence.

There are three ways to describe the form of a shot: distance, angle, and movement.

Distance

Long shot (LS):	A shot that shows the main visual subject of the shot in its entire surroundings; for example, a swimmer in an outdoor Olympic pool showing the entire pool and

surrounding bleachers. A long shot is also known as an **establishing shot** because it is often used at the beginning of a sequence to establish where the action is taking place. An **extreme long shot** (ELS), such as from a helicopter, is a form of long shot.

Medium Shot (MS): A shot showing the main subject in its immediate surroundings, such as the swimmer seen with a smaller portion of the pool visible.

Close-up (CU): A shot showing just the main subject; for example, if only the swimmer were visible with no indication of how big the pool is. An **extreme close-up** (ECU), such as of the swimmer's face, is a form of close-up.

Angle

Low angle (LA): A shot where the camera is lower than the subject and looks up at the subject. Low-angle shots can make the subject look powerful and important and are used to convey a sense of authority or strength. An **extreme low angle** (ELA) shot is where the camera is directly below the subject looking straight up at it.

Flat angle (FA): A shot where the camera is at the same level as the subject, also known as an **eye-level shot**. Flat-angle shots are neutral—they don't convey any particular sense about the strength or weakness of the subject.

High angle (HA): A shot where the camera is higher than the subject and looks down at the subject. High-angle shots can make the subject look inferior and insignificant and are used to convey a sense of defeat or weakness. An **extreme high angle** (EHA) shot is where the camera is directly above the subject looking straight down at it.

Movement

Pan: A shot in which the camera remains in place but swivels from side to side. Panning is used to survey a scene or to capture horizontal motion. For example, with the camera located in the middle bleacher section, you might pan left to right as the swimmer passed from one side of the pool to the other.

Track: A tracking shot also captures horizontal movement, but does so by actually moving the entire camera to the left or right. In a tracking shot, you would begin the shot with the camera at the left end of the bleachers and move parallel to the swimmer down the length of the pool.

Zoom: A shot in which the camera remains in place but the lens of the camera is manipulated to create the appearance of moving closer or farther away from the subject. Zooms in or out are used for dramatic effect.

Dolly: A shot in which the camera itself moves toward or away from the subject. The dolly shot differs from a zoom by leaving more of the background visible than a zoom.

You can contrast the visual effects of a zoom and a dolly by holding your hands vertically alongside your eyes (like horse blinders). Now walk (dolly) slowly toward an object 15 feet away and notice how much of the background remains visible. Return to your starting point. Move (zoom) your hands away from your face and toward each other until the object is between your hands, and notice what happens to the background.

Tilt: A shot in which the camera remains in place but pivots up or down. A tilt shot gives the viewer a trip up or down a building, person, or other vertical object.

Boom: A shot in which the camera, usually mounted on a crane or hydraulic arm, moves up or down. Booms can also move sideways while moving vertically.

Subjective: A shot in which the camera shows what the character sees. The camera is meant to take the place of the character's eyes. Subjective shots often are not perfectly smooth; they might bounce up and down a little to show that the character whom we're seeing through is walking. Also known as a **point of view** (POV).

Composition

A director not only has to decide what angle, distance, and movement to use in each shot, he also has to think about **composition**. Composition refers to the inclusion and arrangement of objects in the shot. The objects he includes and how he chooses to arrange

Practice

Turn a plain sheet of paper sideways and draw 4-x-2$\frac{1}{2}$-inch boxes as shown in the example on page 178. Number the boxes 1 through 4. In each box, draw a simple scene, paying close attention to how the objects in the scene are composed. What meaning does the composition of each box convey? When you are finished with your four drawings, record your intended meanings on the back of the paper. Ask a classmate to interpret the composition of each box, then let him or her read your intended meanings. How successful were you at conveying meaning through composition?

them (that is, how he **frames** them) are key creative decisions. For example, if the script calls for two people arguing in the front seat of a car, the director has many choices for filming this. He can include both of them in the frame at the same time, or he can film the two actresses separately and then cut back and forth between them as they're arguing, never showing them in the same frame together. The latter is a convention of filmmaking for this kind of plot situation. By composing the frame so that the characters are separated, the director communicates a sense of separation between them. If the characters "make up" at the end of the scene, he may decide to compose the last shot showing the two of them in the same frame, thereby communicating to the viewer that they are emotionally together again.

Here are two more examples of composition. In the 1954 film *On the Waterfront*, the main character, Terry Malloy, is a young mob member who feels increasingly confused about his mob involvement. Terry also raises pigeons and is frequently filmed behind the chicken-wire cage of his pigeon coop. It becomes clear that Terry feels increasingly "caged in" by his predicament, and director Elia Kazan composed Terry behind fences and cages in many shots to communicate his sense of being trapped. In the 1994 film *Forrest Gump*, Forrest's childhood girlfriend Jenny grows up into a life of drugs and loneliness. In the darker moments of her life, she is shown in many shots crowded off to the edge of the

A storyboard can start as a simple "thumbnail sketch."

frame with no room to move. She too feels trapped, and director Robert Zemeckis composed her in the frame to communicate her state of mind to us.

Evaluating Film

Film Statements vs. I Statements

Though it seems technically unimpressive by today's standards, the first *Star Wars* was a groundbreaking film when it was released in 1977. George Lucas created new film technologies to achieve the film's special effects, and his characters remain popular almost 20 years later. When *Star Wars* first came out, however, film critics were divided in their reviews. Here are some comments from several film reviews published at the time.

> . . . warmed-over 'Wizard of Oz,' Flash Gordon, Jack Armstrong, and World War II dogfights all rolled into one.—P. Rule (*America* magazine)

> Lucas has rather left his audience out in the cold, with only regularly administered shots of special effects to keep them warm. . . .—R. Bombs (*Monthly Film Bulletin*, a British magazine)

. . . so strong and so refreshing that it takes a crusty person indeed to resist its charms.—K. Turan (*The Progressive*)

This is the trippiest, most convincingly technological science-fiction film ever made.—D. Robbeloth (*Audience* magazine)

. . . fundamentally dull and misconceived . . . an empty thing . . .—*The New Statesman*

This is the kind of film in which an audience, first entertained, can later walk out feeling good all over.—*Variety*

You might expect six professional critics to agree if a major film is a crashing bore or an exciting masterpiece. As these excerpts show, opinions on *Star Wars* were quite divided, yet it turned out to be an immensely popular film. Six jewelers would not disagree on whether a necklace was made of diamonds or glass, but six film critics can look at the same film and judge it anywhere between "dull" and "extraordinary."

Critical opinion of almost any film, whether by professional critics or the weekend filmgoer, will vary from those who consider it the best film they have ever seen to those who find it puts them to sleep. Often a film widely praised by critics will play only to the projectionist and empty seats, while another film generally considered to be junk will break box office records.

One explanation for this wide range of opinions about film is that no two people "see" the same film. Each viewer enters into the world of the film and becomes part of that world. Comments made about films are often not comments about the film at all—they are comments we make about ourselves.

To help explain the special problem of discussing film, first take a quick look at the drawing on page 180. What do you see?

You may say the picture is an old woman, while someone else sees a fashionable young woman. The problem is not that you are disagreeing about age. If you look at the picture long enough, you will see it change from young woman to old woman and back again. To see the gnarled old woman, focus on the neck band of the young woman—this is the old woman's mouth. The young woman's chin is the nose of the old woman.

Drawn by cartoonist W. E. Hill in 1915, the following picture is actually no more an optical illusion than any other image. When looking at objects, we see selectively and are often surprised to find

that others looking at the same picture or situation see something completely different.

You cannot accurately say the picture is of an old woman any more than you can say it is of a young woman. You *can* say, "I see an old woman," or "I see a young woman," or "First I saw the young woman, then I saw the older one." In other words, you can make a statement about yourself that is accurate. The same is true in film.

Try listening to an audience as it leaves the theater after watching a film. Some will say the film was terrific, some, meaningless or simply bad. Some will leave the theater and have a long discussion, perhaps an argument, about whether the film was good or bad. Such a discussion is similar to an argument about whether the picture above is of an old or a young woman.

Most likely the participants in such a discussion aren't talking about the film at all; they are making statements about themselves but disguising the remarks as film criticism. In other words, most people do not distinguish between revealing personal reactions to film and criticizing the film itself. Let's say you see a film and later tell someone, "It was a bore." What you really mean is, "I was bored." There is a big difference between the two. Your comment is about *yourself*, not the film. Probably there were some people in the audience who weren't the least bit bored. There is no commonly agreed-upon standard by which to judge whether a film is boring, but you can easily recognize your own feeling of boredom.

When you talk about films, distinguish between comments about the film and comments about your reactions to the film. When talking with friends, you will probably stay on the level of speaking in terms of yourself—unless you want to impress someone with your knowledge of film. When attempting film criticism, especially to an audience who does not know you, making statements about yourself is of limited value. If someone tells you that a certain film is "sickening," that does not mean that you will find it "sickening"; you might enjoy the film. If you know the person well, however, you may say, "If that person found it sickening, I wouldn't like it either." A common error in film discussion is to confuse statements about the film with statements about oneself.

Criteria for Judging a Film

You are aware of the difference between making statements about a film and making statements about yourself. Why do you like some films and dislike others? Here are some categories—some *criteria*—by which to judge a film. If you still like a film after analyzing it according to the following 12 criteria, your appreciation of it will grow substantially. On the other hand, if you dislike a film after such an analysis, at least you'll have a better understanding of why you dislike it.

Subject:	What is the film about? What is its plot? Its storyline? What genre does it fall into? What is the value of the subject? How important is it to you? (An

example of a film's subject might be "Secret science experiment goes wrong, wreaks havoc on country, and is finally controlled by shy but brilliant college student.")

Theme: What are the big underlying messages and ideas of the film? Are they important messages to society? To you? (Two themes of the science experiment film might be "Don't be seduced by technology," and "An individual with faith in himself can make a difference.")

Acting: How believable are the actors and actresses? Do they express a wide range of experience and emotion? A depth of realism? Does their timing seem natural? Are the characters they portray believable relative to the situations they're in?

Dialogue: Are the lines spoken by the characters appropriate and natural for the time, place, and situations they're in? (A phrase like "gee whiz" might strike you as corny but would be completely appropriate in a film taking place in 1950.) Are lines spoken convincingly? Are they spoken to give the viewer clues about what is happening; that is, would they be spoken if the situation portrayed were happening in real life?

Settings: How are the locations, props, and costumes used to create atmosphere? Are they appropriate to the era in which the film is set? To what level of detail are the settings realistic? How are settings used as devices of character development? (In literary terms, how are settings used as an "extension of character?")

Lighting:	How is lighting used to set the tone and atmosphere of a scene? Are shadows and intense contrasts of light and dark used to communicate plot and character development? (For example, a dramatically side-lit face causes one-half of the face to be brightly lit while the other half is hidden in shadow. This often communicates that the character is lying or is deeply confused.) Are such lighting devices overused?
Sound:	Does the film's soundtrack rely on sound effects to create drama and emotion, or does it use sound to enhance the drama and emotion created by other means, such as acting and editing? Are the different parts of the soundtrack (dialogue, ambient sound, special effects, and music) **mixed** at effective volumes so you can hear what you're supposed to hear? How creatively are ambient sound and sound effects used to foreshadow a turn of events or establish the mood of a scene?
Music:	How much of a film's **score** is original, and how much is taken from other sources? Is the music used as a crutch to generate excitement or tension, such as the classic four-note refrain from *Jaws*, or is it used to complement the feel of a scene? How well-matched is the music to the action or mood on-screen?
Cinematography:	Are camera techniques used only in conventional ways or does the film include any unique visual style? Do shot lengths and angles vary? Is camera movement relied on to create excitement? Is composition used creatively to convey meaning?

Special effects: What purpose do special effects serve in the scene(s) where they're used? If the effects are supposed to be spectacular, are they? If the effects are supposed to be subtle, are they natural and convincing? Are they consistently believable or of uneven quality?

Editing: How does the pace of editing establish the rhythm and momentum of the film? Is it appropriate to the action taking place? (For example, chase scenes typically use fast-paced edits, while calm conversations use longer shots between edits.) Are creative transitions between shots, such as dissolves, used or overused?

Overall direction: Has the film's director skillfully blended all the visual and acoustic elements together? Is she clearly more comfortable with one element, such as dialogue, at the expense of another, such as creative camera work? Does the technical form of each shot—the distance, angle, and movement—bring out the inner nature of the subject matter she is filming? (For example, many directors slowly zoom in to the face of a character who has just gotten some horrible news; this movement would serve as a metaphor of the character's state of inner shock. The director might also fade away all ambient sound to further indicate the character's momentary mental isolation.) How well did the film achieve its objectives—to be funny, exciting, frightening, sad? Did any of the talent rise above their usual abilities?

Practice

The following statements were taken from overheard remarks or from written film criticism. Each statement is presented in terms of talking about the film. Imagine you are the person who made each statement, and change each comment into a personal statement about a film, using "I" (first person). Do not do this by adding "I think" to the beginning of the statement. For example, the statement, "It was good but too long" could be changed to "I enjoyed the film but was bored toward the end."

"This flick is really fantastic; you just have to see it."

"It was a confused movie with a stupid and complicated plot."

"A dumb, idiotic film that didn't make any sense."

"A moving work of art that will drive you to tears."

Thumbs Up or Thumbs Down: Film Criticism

The reading on page 187 is a movie review. Notice how the critic uses the criteria of film evaluation as the basis of his judgment; also note the use of the "star" rating system. After you read the *Roommates* review, complete this Practice activity.

Practice

Obtain several reviews about one film from your local newspaper, national news magazine, or other sources. Identify specific statements in each review that tell you about the film and about the reviewer. How do the reviewers use the criteria of film evaluation?

The 1995 film *Roommates* stars Peter Falk as a man who will not give up on his grandson, played by D. B. Sweeney. *Photo: Shooting Star.*

Film and Popular Culture
The Imitation Question

One of the oldest questions is: Does art imitate life, or does life imitate art? Countless debates on this topic have raged throughout history, and, like all philosophical questions, this one does not have one correct answer. Since the beginning of film, artists and social critics have approached the imitation question from all directions. On the one hand, it is fairly easy to see how films imitate life. For example, the settings of most films which take place in the present depict everyday life quite realistically: the cars, crowd scenes, food, and clothing all reflect—that is, imitate—life. On a deeper level, it seems clear that the broad social issues and specific human relationships which show up on-screen often resemble our own concerns and relationships. It has been argued that all art is a reflection of the era in which it's produced. Life is the way it is, and films reflect life.

On the other hand, there have always been those who believe that people (and societies in general) are influenced by the films they watch. This view is often the root of censorship. The 1920s and 1950s saw official government commissions established to

A Review of *Roommates*

Malcolm Johnson, film critic

Peter Yates, Peter Falk and Elmer Bernstein are old pros when it comes to directing, acting and composing, so "Roommates" initially proves much better than might be expected.

Yet though some observers will be profoundly moved by this tale of a crochety old Polish-American and his caring physician grandson, others will feel that it is a long haul from 1963, when the film begins, to 1993, when it finally breathes its last sentimental gasp.

Perhaps the most winning aspect of this film, co-written by Max Apple and Stephen Metcalfe, is its principal setting: many-bridged Pittsburgh. After the now-familiar aerial view of the river snaking through the city (Pittsburgh has become hot with filmmakers), Yates cuts to an atmospheric long shot of the Polish Hill district, and Bernstein's score stirs up a poignant mood as the film jumps to a cemetery.

Inspired by Apple's relationship with his own grandfather, "Roommates" begins with a funeral that leaves 7-year-old Michael Holeczek an orphan—even as the old boy whistles "Roll Out the Barrel" over the grave. At home in his dark apartment, Granddad, the rough-edged, loud-mouthed Rocky Holeczek, hotly declares he will raise the boy after his own surviving children decline to take him in. At this point, Rocky is 75 but strong as a bull and still working long hours at his bakery on Polish Hill.

Though his heavy makeup makes him look like a rubberoid movie monster at some angles and like Marlon Brando in the last moments of "The Godfather" in happier moments, Falk delivers his most watchable and sharply individualized performance in years as Rocky. To his credit, he even manages to vary his usually Falk persona.

For a time, during Michael's boyhood and teen years, Falk's outspoken, brash characterization totally dominates the film. Later, after a final transition, the teenager turns into someone who looks very like D.B. Sweeney, and Falk at least has some kind of rival up there on the screen.

By this point, however, Rocky and Michael are no longer roommates—the grandson having removed to Columbus, where he is interning as a surgeon. But the patriarch and his protégé are not to be separated for long. Michael gets an urgent call informing him that the old boy has barricaded himself in the apartment where he has lived all his life, refusing to budge, even though his building is being demolished. This time it is the kid who must race to the rescue,

A review of *Roommates* (continued)

talking the old boy (now in his mid-90s but as hard and crusty as ever) out of a confrontation with the cops.

Rocky reluctantly accompanies Michael back to Ohio, and the new phase of their life as roommates begins. Now the nonagenarian finds himself in a basement apartment, with comic relief provided by Asian students at Ohio State University who live upstairs in the large and comfortable old house.

Soon, though, trouble begins to brew in the young-old male bonding world as Michael strikes up a friendship with a stunning, ultra-liberal hospital social worker named Beth, acted with independence and quirky intelligence by Julianne Moore.

As their courtship progresses, Rocky takes a dislike to Beth, and Michael is taken aback by Beth's mom, the rich and spoiled suburbanite Judith, endowed with crisp arrogance by Ellen Burstyn. But love conquers all things, and in time, a Polish-WASP wedding ensues, with an amusing gaffe for silly Judith.

At last, "Roommates" takes another leap in time, proceeding to its lessons of tragedy and understanding. Burstyn gets a chance to become cold and nasty, and Falk plays his 100-year-old pillar of strength and folk wisdom to the hilt —right to the weepy but upbeat fade-out with "Roll Out the Barrel" in the air. ■

★★

★★★★Excellent; ★★★Very Good;
★★Good; ★Fair; ☆Poor

[**ROOMMATES**, directed by Peter Yates; written by Max Apple and Stephen Metcalfe, from a story by Apple; director of photography, Mike Southon, music composed by Elmer Bernstein; production designer, Dan Bishop; edited by John Tintori; produced by Ted Field, Scott Kroopf and Robert W. Cort; executive producers, Adam Liepzig and Ira Halberstadt. A Buena Vista Distribution, Inc. release of a Hollywood Pictures presentation of an Interscope Communications/Polygram Filmed Entertainment production in association with Nomura Babcock & Brown, opening today at Showcase Cinemas, East Hartford, East Windsor and Berlin. Running time: 112 minutes.

Rocky .... Peter Falk
Michael .... D. B. Sweeney
Beth .... Julianna Moore
Judith .... Ellen Burstyn
Bolek Krups .... Jan Rubes
Barbara .... Joyce Reahling
Stash .... Ernie Sabella
Burt Shook .... John Cunningham]

examine whether moviegoing was dangerous. There was concern that people—especially children—would imitate what they saw on the big screen. More recently the genre of urban films such as *Colors* and *Boyz N the Hood* have been criticized for encouraging gang violence. The directors of these films, however, argue that they are accurately representing life as it is lived by millions of inner-city youth.

The answer to the imitation question can often be found in the Consumption stage of the Media Literacy Paradigm, and the answer is this: You will answer the imitation question based on your personal background and experiences. If your life resembles the life portrayed in a given film, you'll probably view that film as imitating life, while if your life is very different from that shown in the film, you probably won't.

Americanization of Global Popular Culture

Films produced in the United States consistently dominate movie screens all over the world. During the last week of August, 1994, for example, the top three money-making films in each of the following countries were of the United States: Brazil, Germany, Australia, Spain, Sweden, South Africa, Taipei, and Canada. (The top three in each country were from among this group of films: *Speed, The Lion King, The Flintstones, Maverick, Naked Gun 33⅓, Forrest Gump,* and *When a Man Loves a Woman.* *

What does the rest of the world learn about the United States when they watch our films? Many people think that international audiences simply learn that our country is a land of extremes—either excessively violent or hilariously comic. They point out that only occasionally does a serious U.S. drama, such as *Schindler's List*, become an overseas blockbuster. On the other hand, some critics argue that even action films convey the traditional American values of perseverance and right winning over wrong.

Whatever critics in this country say about the image of the United States being shipped overseas, politicians in other countries are concerned about the number of U.S. films watched by their citizens. In 1994, the government of France tried to limit

Source: *Variety,* August 31, 1994.

the number of U.S. films it would import per year because it said the success of the American films was hurting the French filmmaking industry. Though France's effort was not successful, it has not been the only country to raise the issue of its people preferring U.S. entertainment. After all, much of the television programming seen throughout the world is also from the United States.

 # Reflections

- Adopt the point of view of Pakistan's Minister of Culture and Education. You are concerned about the increasing number of U.S. films your citizens are watching. Write a letter to the Minister of Trade explaining your concern and making a recommendation about what should be done about the importing of U.S. films into Pakistan. (*Note:* you may want to review the Dish-Wallahs article in Chapter Two.)
- Explore possible reasons violent American films are among the most successful internationally. What is it about violence, violent films, and how they are produced that makes them so appealing?
- What qualities make a movie star? Why are top stars worshiped with almost religious intensity?

Film and Videotape

Movies on videotape and the use of videotape in the film-making and television industries are important factors to consider in the study of film. In the following chart, the technical differences between these two media are presented.

Contrasting Film and Videotape

Film	Videotape
Images can be seen when film is held to the light because film is transparent.	No images can be seen on videotape; used and unused tape appear identical. Tape is opaque.
Unprocessed film is easily damaged by light but not affected by magnetic waves.	Unused videotape is not damaged by light but can be ruined by magnetism.
Film needs to be chemically treated (developed) before viewing.	Tape can be viewed immediately after shooting.
Film can be used only once and is not erasable.	Tape can be erased and reused.
Because film is transparent, it can be easily enlarged by a projector for viewing in large groups.	Video loses quality with enlargement. Large video images lack detail when compared to film projected on a movie screen.
Film can be copied onto another film only through an elaborate chemical process in a film laboratory.	A videotape can be easily copied onto another tape.
Film must be physically edited by cutting and splicing.	Videotape can be edited and manipulated electronically without physically cutting the tape.
Shooting movie film requires technical knowledge of lighting, angle, camera operation, and so on.	Videotaping has been made easy for the amateur with the invention of the camcorder.
A movie film camera produces refined images with a higher degree of resolution.	The quality of the videotape image is limited by the quality of the monitor. Even the most advanced monitors lag far behind the resolution (clarity) of a projected film.

Student Close-Up

Jason Hawkins, Connecticut

Now in college studying film and television production, Jason Hawkins reflects on his interest and first experience in film-making in this first-person account. Currently, Hawkins is working as a production assistant on a CBS television movie.

My interest in film-making began when I was around eleven years old. I would take empty tissue boxes and cut out the sides, so that when I looked through, it was like looking through a camera lens. I would practice panning, tilting, and following action as if I were a "real" cinematographer. When I was thirteen, I got my first movie camera—and my film-making days had officially begun. In the beginning, I would film just about everything in sight. Since I spent a great deal of time with my grandparents, they would often become the subject of my films. (Even if they were doing something as simple as eating breakfast!) I soon, however, began making films that actually had direction—and a plot. These films usually starred my friends and family, and had goofy names like "The Unlucky Painter," "The Killer Hair Dryer," "Attack of the Vacuum," "The Stupid Electrician," and so on. On Sunday afternoons I would hold screenings at my grandparents' house. My grandmother would make popcorn, my friends would come over, and for a few hours the basement was transformed into a movie theater.

At sixteen, I made a $4\frac{1}{2}$-minute film called "The Effects of Obnoxious Children on Parents." In the film, a mother becomes enraged at her two preteen sons for making her the victim of a prank, and chases them through the house with a hatchet. (Actually, from a non-literal perspective, the film is an exploration of subconscious thoughts and drives.) It took many hours of work, both shooting and editing, but in the end I was very pleased with the final cut. I can't explain it, but I knew right away that this film had something special.

Two years later, in 1990, that work paid off, when one of my high school teachers told me about a new film and video competition for high school students called "The Penny Awards." I immediately submitted "Effects," and two weeks later I got a phone call saying I was chosen as a finalist. The big screening ceremony was held a week later, and my film, despite being somewhat controversial, was a success there, winning third prize. After my film was shown, I received a loud ovation from the crowd, made up largely of local media heavies. Within the next week, I appeared in two television interviews and was written about in the local papers. In addition, my twisted little movie caught the eye of one MTV producer who called me a "budding Hitchcock," displaying great interest in showing it on MTV.

As I look back, that film award becomes more and more important to me. It represents the very reason why I make films: to communicate. The recognition I received was the proof that I so badly needed, that somebody cared about what I as an artist had to say—

that somebody really was watching and listening. For 4½ minutes the audience was in my world, seeing it exactly as I wanted them to—and in the end I had made a connection. The medium of film had allowed me to do this, and with a certain power. Most importantly, I finally felt as though I was being accepted as an artistic communicator; I had waited so long for that feeling. I can honestly say that even if I never find big success in the film industry, I will always know that for a fleeting moment, somewhere in the scope of media, my work as a film-maker really mattered. ■

Jason Hawkins, 1995.

Future Watch: Film in the Digital Age

The sale of VCRs in America has started to flatten out. This means that most homes now have them, so sales of new VCRs are starting to slow down—at least compared with the late 1980s. As a result, most experts think that the number of people who go out to movies will remain fairly stable (unlike the 1950s, when movie attendance dropped dramatically because of television).

What will change, though, is the way films are made. As in so many industries, the computer is revolutionizing the production process. First, the evolution of computerized special effects will continue. The famous dinosaurs in *Jurassic Park* provided a glimpse of the graphic sophistication computers allow. Second, editing and soundtrack production soon may yield completely to computers, such as the digital film editing system shown on page 168. Instead of physically cutting strips of film and then joining them together, all the film footage will be digitized and stored on a computer. Once on computer, the editor can experiment with each edit without having to touch the actual film. Special effects can be implemented as part of the editing process. The recording and mixing of the soundtrack will also be made easier and more flexible by computerization. When the final version of the film is just right, it will then be **downloaded** onto film.

Two Takes on the Film Industry
The Job of the Director

Although the stars get the attention, the most important person on the creative side of the film industry is the director. In the following interview, director Amy Heckerling (*Look Who's Talking* and *Look Who's Talking Too*) provides a sense of what it's like to be the person with the overall responsibility for the final product.

Amy Heckerling. *Photo courtesy of Janis Cole.*

An Interview with Amy Heckerling, Director

Janis Cole and Holly Dale

The blockbuster hit of 1989 *Look Who's Talking*, a contemporary comedy told from the point of view of baby Mikey, was penned and directed by native New Yorker Amy Heckerling. She grew up in Queens and the Bronx, and decided to become a film director while attending Manhattan's School of Art and Design. She graduated from New York University with two successful shorts to her credit, and relocated to Los Angeles in 1975 where she attended the American Film Institute. Her half hour short made there, *Getting It Over With*, starred Glynnis O'Connor as a nineteen-year-old virgin who did not want to be a virgin at twenty. Considered for an Academy Award nomination, it was her calling card to the industry.

A producer friend, Art Linson, offered Heckerling her first feature, *Fast Times at Ridgemount High*. The teen comedy, written by Cameron Crowe and starring a then unknown Sean Penn, had an affecting charm that was hard to resist. A huge success both artistically and commercially, it thrust the first time director into the limelight. On the heels of *Fast Times*, she directed Michael Keaton in the gangster spoof comedy *Johnny Dangerously*. Before that film was released, she took the

helm on her third feature, *National Lampoon's European Vacation*, starring Chevy Chase and Beverly D'Angelo. The slapstick comedy became one of the top grossers of 1986.

Formerly married to director, writer, producer Neal Israel, it was their daughter, born in 1987, who inspired Heckerling to write *Look Who's Talking*. She remembers looking at her daughter in her baby seat and wondering what thoughts were going on in her head. This prompted her to create a voice over to express the inner thoughts of baby Mikey which were brought to life by the voice of Bruce Willis. A huge box office success, she promptly started work on the sequel, *Look Who's Talking Too*. A director and screenwriter known for her comedic flair, Heckerling is one of the few female directors who has worked regularly within Hollywood's motion picture machinery.

Q: How did the original idea for *Look Who's Talking* come about?

A: I'd had a baby. And I spent some time developing a TV series based on *Fast Times at Ridgemount High*, but it didn't get picked up. I thought, now what am I going to do? I was having a lot of fun with the baby, so I got the idea and I got the script together and

An Interview with Amy Heckerling, Director *(continued)*

went around to pitch it. I don't like pitching, but TriStar picked it up.

Q.   Two women claimed to have given you their script with the concept of *Look Who's Talking*. What happened there?
A: They say that every movie that makes over one hundred million has its law suit, so we had ours. I'd never been through anything like that. It was a very Kafkaesque experience. I don't know if you ever read *The Trial*: a guy wakes up in the morning and people say you're guilty and now you have to go and deal with all this legal stuff. Well, that's what it was like. And when I did the sequel we started a deposition of discovery. It took forever. I went off to do the movie and when I got back it was settled out of court, apparently amicably.

Q: Tell me about the financing of your first project.
A: The first thing I ever wrote, in my life, I did when I got out of film school. Warner Brothers picked it up and they were going to make it. They were very excited, but by the time I handed it in, there were new executives there, and these new executives didn't like it. Now by that time, I had sort of established a relationship with executives at Universal. So I showed it to them and they picked it up. But again by the time I handed it in, there were also new people, and again they decided not to make it. And then it went to MGM, and they were definitely going to make it. So,

they said, "Just shorten it." So I shortened it and then we're finally making the film. We're two weeks away from shooting. I have an entire cast. I have a crew. I have the locations picked. The sets are all built. They were making costumes, and props, and the actors go on strike. So they told me to just keep working because as soon as the strike ended, we'd be making the film. The producer and I worked all summer. It got down to me knowing every single color everybody was going to wear, and which color every wall was going to be. I knew in my head how every line of dialogue was going to be said. I knew too much about how to make this movie. So, the strike kept going on and on and they said, "Don't worry, as soon as it's over." Then one day they said, "Oh-oh, the strike's been going on a long time and we're going to drop some of our films." And me being the sort of new kid, with this little budget film, they told me, "Well, it looks like we're not going to make this film."

Then a number of people came in and said, "We're going to make the movie. We'll put in half the money." So I had a number of halves of the money, but no two halves equaled a whole. Then I went off and I did *Fast Times*, and *Johnny Dangerously*. Periodically, in between those other films, new places would crop up. At one point, Orion tried. So I kept having meetings on the script. Then I did *Vacation* and I had a baby. Meanwhile, somebody

An Interview with Amy Heckerling, Director *(continued)*

else comes and says, "We raised money for that script. Now rewrite it." By this time I have eight drafts, so I said, "What do we do with it?" Because I have eight drafts. They said, "Just do what you think is best." So now I'm in a position of rewriting it again not knowing which way to go with it, but knowing that there's money there waiting for it to be made. And this has been a process that started as soon as I got out of film school. So it's been eight years of this one movie that never dies and never gets made. And some day maybe it'll get made, but it'll be very weird to see what it looks like.

I'm currently doing another rewrite. Columbia Pictures is paying me to write it again. It's like a perpetual motion machine. It's called *My Kind of Guy*. I was going through the old drafts and was surprised to see how much my point of view has changed over the years. You know, it's about relationships and one year it's completely negative, and the next year it's like this is the answer. Now two studios later there's even yet another point of view. One year it's about lowering your standards, and another year it's stick to your dreams. So it's hard to say what it will finally be about.

Q: How did you discover the script for *Fast Times at Ridgemount High*?
A: I knew Art Linson who was also at Universal. He had an office right above my office and we knew a lot of similar

people. He had shown me other scripts that he was working on. I would tell him what I thought of the different scripts and he would tell me what he thought of what I was doing. Then one day he showed me *Fast Times*, which I think was called *Stairway to Heaven* then. I would tell him what I thought about it, and then he surprised me by asking if I wanted to do it. That was a very big shock because I had absolutely no idea that he was thinking of me in those terms. Of hiring me to direct a movie. I was going, "Oh my God. Do I want to do this?" I was writing something that I really loved, and I thought, "If I do that, then I won't finish this. If I drop it now, it'll go away forever." I kept thinking about *Fast Times* and I thought, "If I don't do it, somebody else will, and if somebody else does it, I'll just be miserable." I loved Cameron's script, and I also loved Cameron's book. When I read that material, I thought this is very real. It just knocks you over compared to the other scripts that are floating around. And so my decision became clear. I knew I had to make the movie.

Q: What did you like about the script when you read it?
A: Cameron Crowe went to a high school and very accurately recorded and got to know all these kids. He put down this absolutely real account, non-judgmental, and with a lot of love for all these people and what they were going

An Interview with Amy Heckerling, Director *(continued)*

through. Surprisingly enough it all works as a story. We all tried to stay true to the spirit.

Q: Tell me about your first day on the set of a studio picture.
A: So there I was, making the movie. It was my first day, and I had to do a drive-by. It was my very first shot. There's a car, and it had to go from left to right. And I'm thinking, "How am I going to do that?" It's like, how big is the car? Should I start with the car and pan with it? Should I just let the car pass through the frame? Or should I pan all the way with the car? All of a sudden the possiblilities were far too endless. I didn't know how anyone had ever shot a car going by. Then we did it and it was over. And all of a sudden it was okay, and I thought, "Now I can shoot the girl standing looking at the car, the close-up of the girl looking at the car and the guy." All the other shots just came because I had gotten rid of this car.

Q: What is your approach to working with large crews?
A: Everybody always says, "How do you deal with these crew people?" As though crews were wild gorillas, and teamsters, and scary, and they're going to yell at you, and they're not going to listen. But the reality is that you interview a lot of people, and you hire the ones that you like the best. You have many meetings before you're actually on a set and you've already established relationships with your key people. On the set you meet the people that they're working with and you're all working together. You have your job to do and you do it. You've decided to work with these people because you've liked what they've done, and you like how you get along with them, and then there's no problem.

Q: Because of its popularity, what happened to your career after *Fast Times at Ridgemount High* came out?
A: After *Fast Times* came out, I had a lot of scripts offered to me that had to do with preppies, because they thought, "You did high school. You could do school." And they thought there was going to be this preppy trend, that everybody would think it was adorable to be rich and young and wear madras shorts. I couldn't relate to that. I didn't go to prep school, obviously. I didn't see what so cute about being young and rich. And my mother had said, "Don't do another high school movie and don't do a girl movie, and don't let them piegonhole you." So I was turning down all these preppie movies. Then I read *Johnny Dangerously*, which was a comedy about gangsters. It was guys and guns, and was very rowdy and dirty. I thought, "This is different. They're not going to think of me as 'the-girl-loses-virginity' if they see this."

An Interview with Amy Heckerling, Director *(continued)*

Q: How did that turn out?

A: Well, here we are working on this film, and we all think it's very funny because we know the references for the humor, which are the 1930s Warner Brothers films. I was also hoping that all these other gangster movies coming out before it would do well—*Once Upon a Time in America, Scarface,* and *City Heat.* I thought all these things would bring back the gangsters. But it didn't quite work out that way. So when we brought it out, here was this satire based on things that nobody remembered. So I thought, "Now what?" and before it came out I knew I had to do something fast, so I did *European Vacation.* And that came out and did well. So when people were saying, "Uh-oh, *Johnny Dangerously* didn't do well," I already had something else in the can. I remained this question mark. So I like to stay away from what they think you should do. And try to stay away from pigeonholes.

Q: Do you find that you get typecast because you are a woman?

A: Every time you do something people would like to say, "Oh, you do that, so let's put you in that slot." If they think you can do films with people against their lockers and the girls losing their virginity, then you can't do a thing with guns. Or if you can do something with people pulling their pants down, then you can't do something where people cry. You can do this, but you can't do that. So I feel this desperation to hop away from where they want you to go.

Q: Do you think there are certain problems that are specific to being a woman in the film industry, in Hollywood?

A: Just to keep my sanity, I have to not think about that. Because if I'm going to say "I am a woman, with women, in the women's group, on the women's list," then I'm in deep trouble. I just have to think of what I want to do, what I want to express, and not think about what this town thinks of me as a woman. I don't think about what's hot, and what's not. As soon as you start with that, you're dead. That's not to say you don't see the realities of the situation, but as soon as you start thinking in terms of I'm a woman, I'm a Jew, I'm a New Yorker, I grew up poor, or I grew up rich, I'm this, or I'm that, then I think you're pigeonholing yourself.

Q: What are the qualities that make a good director?

A: There's a pamphlet that Elia Kazan wrote about what makes a good director. And if you read it you'd say, yeah well, everything. You have to know about lenses, you have to know about dance, you have to know about diseases, you have to know about the world, you have to know about cars, you have to know about everything. I mean it lists

An Interview with Amy Heckerling, Director *(continued)*

everything you could ever know about. So if you know about all of this stuff, that's what makes a good director.

But basically, if you love the characters that you're portraying, and you have some sense of how to tell a story, how to amuse people, how to make people cry, how to scare people, whatever you want to do, if you can get that across, you're okay.

Q: How do you manage your time between a film career and a family?
A: If you're really worried about any career, you're going to push a lot of things back. You're not going to get married at the age of twenty, or have your first kid then. You're going to change your time schedule. And that's not to say it's a sacrifice. I think it helps.

Q: Has the situation for woman directors changed since you started?
A: When I was going to film school, my father would always say, "Yeah right, a woman director." He'd never heard of such a thing. And when I'd try to say, "Well what about Elaine May?" he's say, "Who else?" And I couldn't think of anyone else. If I was in film school now, I assume that I could say, "What about Claudia Weill? What about Lisa Gottlieb? What about Martha Coolidge? What about Donna Deitch? What about Joyce Chopra? What about several people?" I think that's a big difference.

But as far as the situation that there

is still X amount of women who would like to direct who haven't had the opportunity, or the fact that the Directors Guild only has one-millionth of a percentage that are women, then it's still fairly depressing. But still, there are a lot more women directing now than when I started.

Q: Do you consider *Fast Times at Ridgemount High* to be a film with a definite female perspective?
A: Well what happened on *Fast Times* was a good cross-sampling of male and female perspectives. There were two girls and four boys who were primary characters. Cameron and I went through what really happens to everybody in the story, and what would be good dramatically to wrap the people up. Because it was a slice of life film, a year in the life of all these kids, we both had to start pulling things in. We combined a few characters, and then we had to start pulling things out of our own lives. We had a wonderful couple of weeks where we went through all the information that was in the book, that was in Cameron's research notes from the book, and that was in our own lives. We took these characters that were real and kept giving them everything that we could find that we thought would work for them. So there's a lot of real girls that he knew, and there's a lot of me, and a lot of him. I think that is clear in the movie, the male and female points-of-view. We're both in there, both coming up with the stuff.

An Interview with Amy Heckerling, Director *(continued)*

Q: What are you going to do next? Are you looking for any particular type of material?

A: I think just to be true to myself. And I don't want to do anything like what I've done before. I'm writing a couple of things that I really want to do. I want to do more things that I've written. I feel like I got real anxious to be in the business, for people to say, "There's Amy Heckerling. She's making this movie." There's this rush to find material that will get made rather than asking yourself, "Does this express how I feel?" And it's hard to sit with blank pieces of paper wondering, "What is she going to say next?" And if you run into one of these agents floating around in restaurants and they say, "What're you doing?" and you go, "Well, I'm writing," they say, "Uh huh, so are the waiters." It's harder, and you don't feel that big shock, but that's what I want to do next.

Q: What type of films do you hope to make?

A: I don't want to do a movie that a bunch of critics say is great, but it makes no money. And I don't want people to go to the Beverly Center and see it and go, "That stunk." I want to make movies that people stand in line for, and they go back again. And I don't work independently. I go out and pitch things. I always seem to land at some studio, where I'm pitching a project within the big studio machinery.

Q: What is your latest project?

A: I've got a script in at Disney, and we have a green light on it, but there are a few things that are still up in the air, so we're going to see what will happen. And there's a sequel being mounted for *Look Who's Talking* [three], but I'm not writing or directing it. I'll be supervising it with the other producer. I'm trying to move away from movies with kids because having a kid, every moment is all encompassing. It really consumes you. At least on a movie you can take a break between shots if everything is going okay, but every second with a baby you're wondering, "Are they okay? What are they doing?"

Q: Any advice for aspiring filmmakers?

A: It's different for everybody. It's hard to describe how one person can end up making certain things for them work while another person will make completely different things work for them. There are a lot of things about Hollywood show business that I block out so I can stay in my own dream world, because I don't like that stuff. For other people, they might survive on the game, the aggression and all of that. So what works for me is not necessarily something I could recommend for anyone else. ■

Reprinted by permission of the publisher from *Calling the Shots: Profiles of Women Filmmakers*, Janis Cole and Holly Dale. © 1993 Quarry Press, Ontario, Canada.

What Makes an American Film American?

As the trend toward economic globalization grows, more and more U.S. businesses are purchased by international companies. In fact, three of America's top six movie studios were foreign-owned as of 1995. The Japanese company Matsushita (parent firm of Panasonic) owns MCA/Universal studios; Sony owns TriStar and what used to be Columbia Pictures (now called Sony Pictures Entertainment); and the Australian-based News Corporation owns 20th Century Fox.

Building Your Media Archive
Archive Analysis: Film

After you're familiar with your archive film, analyze it using the Media Literacy Paradigm. Classifying the product will be fairly straightforward. Most of the information is available on the video cover or in the film's credits. The film's genre and surface-level content should also be fairly clear after you've watched it. Examining the film's origin will take a little more work. Fortunately, many popular movies have books written about them and their directors. Magazines and journals, such as *Film Quarterly*, are excellent sources of information on the origin of films, directors, and studios. Articles about directors such as Spike Lee, Oliver Stone, and Kathy Bigelow provide insight regarding how and why they select their topics and how their backgrounds influence their political views—which in turn influence how they make their films.

The mediation stage of your analysis will probably be the most fun. Simply by answering the questions you will deepen your understanding of film in general—and of your archive film in particular. Dig further into your film. See if you can identify an example of each type of cinematography (for example, a favorite sequence, a long shot, or a low-angle shot. Find an example of how creative composition contributes to meaning or mood. How does a story that takes place over weeks, months, or even years get told in two hours? What routine aspects of life are left out of the film in order to tell the story? The final two stages of your film archive analysis, Consumption and Impact, can be addressed as straightforward questions which you can answer based on your analysis of the film.

MEDIA LAB   Scripting a Film

- On a blank piece of paper, list the script sheet column heads below. Plan the first three minutes of a film from your imagination by describing exactly what visuals and audio (sound) are in each shot. Label the number of each shot, starting with "Shot No. 1," and so on. Under Visual, describe the content of the shot. What exactly will be shown? Make sure you identify the angle, distance, and movement of each shot, as well as its composition in the frame. Likewise, under Audio, describe in detail whatever music, dialogue, ambient sound, and sound effects you want in each shot. Decide what Transition technique you'll use to join each shot. Finally, determine the Shot Time—how many seconds each shot will last—and then keep a Running Time total so you know when you've reached your three minutes. Draw a line horizontally between shots.

  Here's how to evaluate the success of your script: It should be clear and complete enough that a classmate would be able to shoot the three minutes the way you saw it in your imagination.

SCRIPT SHEET COLUMN HEADS:

Shot No.	Visual	Audio	Transition	Shot Time	Running Time

Create Your Own Media

Though you probably will not be able to make your own movie with actual film, you can follow the same film production steps using a camcorder. First, know what equipment you have available and plan from there. If you do not have access to an editing machine, you will have to plan your movie a bit differently. If you will be able to edit your tape, you'll have more room for experimentation. These general guidelines fit either case.

After you have decided on a basic topic and story line, divide your project into the three stages of preproduction, production, and postproduction. Limit your script to five minutes. As a rule of thumb, plan on having about five shots per each minute of final film. Use a script sheet like the one you used for your Media Lab to plan out each shot. Make sure you write out all dialogue completely. Once your script sheet is complete, draw out simple storyboards of each shot to help you visualize the scenes you've described in your script sheet. You can create storyboards by drawing nine 3-×-3-inch boxes on a sheet of paper and making several copies. Number them "Page 1, shots 1–9; page 2, shots 10–18"; and so on.

If you do not have an editing machine, you will essentially edit your film inside your camera. This means that you have only one take for each shot; that is, one chance to get your shot right. *Plan it out carefully, and rehearse it well.* In general, plan to shoot in locations in which you have control of the lighting and sound. (For example, unless you're using an external microphone, shoot in a quiet place, otherwise the dialogue will not be picked up well by the camera's internal microphone.)

If you have access to an editing machine, you can shoot several takes of each shot and edit them later. This brief introduction is intended only to start you thinking about your production. Consult one of the many how-to video production books available in any library or bookstore for further information.

Career Bank

Following are just a few of the many careers available in the film and video (movie) industry:

- actor
- talent agent
- screenwriter
- director/producer
- production assistant
- make-up artist
- costume designer

- camera operator
- computer graphic artist
- film/sound/videotape editor
- recording engineer
- sound technician

Recap

The life of any film can be divided into three stages: **preproduction,** when the majority of planning and up-front organization takes place; **production**, during which the film footage is actually shot; and **postproduction**, when the separate visual and acoustic elements are joined together and the film is packaged, advertised, and distributed.

There are generally 12 main **criteria** by which films are evaluated, whether you're an occasional moviegoer or a professional critic. Being conscious of these criteria can help you talk about films in a clearer way. You can distinguish between statements which say something about you and your tastes, and statements which say something about the film you're discussing.

As part of the larger debate about the function of art in society, much has been written about the role of film in the mix of American pop culture. Do films merely reflect (imitate) life in the United States, or is American life changing because the moviegoing public is influenced by (imitates) the films they see? Your answer depends on how you view the questions of consumption and impact. Because the United States exports so many films, the governments of many other countries are wrestling with how their populations are consuming U.S. films.

Resources for Further Reading
Books

Barnouw, Erik. *Documentary: A History of the Non-fiction Film*. New York: Oxford University Press, 1974.

Bouzereau, Laurent. *Cutting Room Floor: Movie Scenes Which Never Made It to the Screen*. New York: Citadel Press, 1994.

Brouwer, Alexander. *Working in Hollywood*. New York: Crown Publishers, 1990.

Cameron, James. *Terminator 2 Judgement Day: The Book of the Film, An Illustrated Screenplay*. New York: Applause Books, 1991.

Cole, Janis, and Holly Dale. *Calling the Shots: Profiles of Women Filmmakers*. Kingston, Ontario: Quarry Press, 1993.

Forlenza, Jeff. *Sound for Picture: An Inside Look at Audio Production for Film and TV*. Emoryville, N.Y.: Mix Books, 1993.

Lee, Spike. *By Any Means Necessary: The Trials and Tribulations of Making Malcolm X*. New York: Hyperion, 1992.

Medved, Michael. *Hollywood vs. America*. New York: HarperCollins, 1992.

Null, Gary. *Black Hollywood from 1970 to Today*. New York: Citadel Press, 1993.

O'Brien, Tom. *The Screen of America: Movies and Values from Rocky to Rainman*. New York: Continuum, 1990.

Schill, Robert J. *Single Camera Video*. Stoneham, Mass.: Butterworth Publishers, 1989.

Industry Publications and Magazines

American Cinematographer, Box 2230, Hollywood, CA 90078
Cinefex: The Journal of Cinematic Illusions, Box 20027, Riverside, CA 92516
Entertainment Weekly, 1675 Broadway, New York, NY 10019.
Films in Review, Box 589, New York, NY 10021
Film Quarterly, 2120 Berkeley Way, Berkeley, CA 94720
The Independent Film and Video Monthly, 625 Broadway, New York, NY 10012
Premiere Magazine, 2 Park Ave., New York, NY 10016

Key word database searches for library research on film and video:

Films, reviews, cinematography, special effects, Hollywood

TV Programs, Videotapes, and Films about Filmmaking

America at the Movies (1975 film about the portrayal of American life in American movies)

The Big Picture (1989 film about the struggles of a young film director)

Hollywood FX Masters (a videotape)

Movie Magic (Discovery Channel Series)

Movies of the 20's, 30's and 40's (Survey of films from these decades)

The Purple Rose of Cairo (1985 film by Woody Allen about the lure of the classic Hollywood fantasy film)

The Secret Life of Machines (Discovery Channel Series with episodes on film and video)

SEGUE

Film

Though the acoustic element of a film is extremely important, the visual component of film gets most of the attention from viewers and critics alike. The work that goes into the production of the soundtrack in all its dimensions is rarely noticed. In most cases, when people use the phrase "film soundtrack," they are referring to the music used in a film. Yet the production of strictly acoustic media, such as musical recordings, is as demanding and complex a process as filmmaking. The impact of recorded music on society is often as fiercely debated as the impact of film. The next chapter looks at the recording industry and some of the technological and social issues it faces.

CHAPTER SEVEN

Music and Recordings

Learning Targets

After working through this chapter, you will be able to

- Describe major developments in the history of sound recording technology;
- Debate the pros and cons of placing warning labels on music products;
- Write a review of a CD using musical criteria of evaluation; and
- Apply the Media Literacy Paradigm to the recording in your Media Archive.

Checking In

- Explain why you think so much contemporary pop music is controversial.
- Describe what you know about the process of producing a new CD.
- List three of your favorite CDs or songs, and describe why you like them.
- Describe how computers, television, and home stereos might be combined in the future to change the way we experience music.
- Write three topics you would like to learn about recordings.

A History of Recording

The First 50 Years

In 1876 Thomas Edison built a machine that recorded and played back sound. The phonograph (from the Greek words meaning *sound* and *writer*) was hand cranked and played a cylinder of tin foil. Sound quality was crude, but the machine drew crowds at vaudeville shows. At that point there were no practical uses for the machines, so Edison stopped making them.

Ten years later Emile Berliner patented a system using flat discs instead of cylinders. Although not a household name, Berliner laid the foundation for today's record industry. His flat disc could be mass produced from a master, whereas Edison's cylinders were necessarily one-of-a-kind originals. The shellac-coated disc also produced better quality sound compared to the original cylinder.

Berliner created a machine to play his new flat discs and called it the gramophone, a name still heard today on occasion. Berliner founded the Victor Talking Machine Company and began selling "Red Seal" recordings.

In 1917 Americans bought 25 million discs, spurred by the first recording superstar, opera singer Enrico Caruso. To most Americans, music before 1920 meant classical music. There was no rock music or top-40 radio, so opera singers who provided many listeners with a link to the "old country" became mega-stars. The 78 rpm (revolutions per minute) discs broke easily and lasted less than 10 minutes a side, so to record an entire symphony or opera took a series of discs packaged in an album. Although today's CDs are not in "albums," the term remains to describe a larger collection of songs from which a single or, hopefully, hit single is culled.

Radio and Technology Push Recordings Along

The history of any mass medium is one of conflict between technologies competing for public favor. In the late 1920s, the rise of radio threatened the recording industry. Radio sound was clearer than the record and its music was live. Radio stations broadcast big band music from live pick-ups and the quality was vastly superior to the still thin and raspy sound of records. The recording industry saw radio as a fatal threat. Since radio was used much like television today, record companies feared the public would have less time to play recordings. Remember, car and portable radios were still far in the future. Radio did hurt record sales, but some salvation arrived in 1948, when Columbia records introduced the $33\frac{1}{3}$ rpm long-play record (the LP), developed by Peter Goldmark. The improved record could hold over 20 minutes of music per side, was not as fragile as the 78s, and featured much-improved sound. Goldmark invented the LP because he was a music lover unwilling to put up with listening to a Brahms concerto while changing and flipping the six records in the album. Goldmark stated, "There was no doubt in my mind that the photograph . . . was murdering Brahms, and I felt somehow impelled to stop this killer in its shellac tracks." Stereophonic sound was first marketed in 1958 and quickly made "mono" obsolete.

Around 1950, television emerged as the leading mass entertainment medium. Radio had to change in order to survive. Early television simply "stole" programming from radio. Westerns, soap operas, crime and detective shows, and quiz shows began on radio. To survive, radio switched to music programming. Where did the music come from? Records, of course. Radio, a medium that was originally seen as fatal competition to recordings, embraced records as its content. Even today, recordings are the main content of radio.

The recording industry quickly learned that radio was an excellent way to promote its records. Young people as well as old listened to radio. A record that was played often on radio sold more copies than other releases, so the radio and recording industries became partners instead of enemies and teenagers of the 1950s started collections of 45's (45 rpm. recordings—plastic or vinyl).

Tape Recording

Before 1950, recordings were made by producing a master disc directly from the live performance. The method did not permit editing. If a musician hit a wrong note, the only alternative was to start over. In other words, recordings before 1950 had to be what are called real-time performances. A three-minute song was just that—a recording of a song that took three minutes to sing.

Magnetic (tape) recording first was introduced to the record industry in 1947 with a German invention called the magnetophone. What we call tape recording is a newer medium than the photograph that revolutionized music and the recording business. Tape recording made editing possible for the recording industry.

During the fifties and early sixties, tape recorders for consumers were of the reel-to-reel variety and were expensive and inconvenient. In 1964 the cassette was introduced, revolutionizing the recording industry. Cassettes meant that anyone could make tapes easily. Tape changed the recording industry in two ways: First, it made possible a new kind of multitrack music, and second, cassettes became to recordings what the photocopy machine was to the printed page.

Before the 1950s popular music on record meant mainly one of four types of music—classical, which was by far the largest-selling category; recordings from Broadway musicals; popular music by crooners, such as Perry Como, Bing Crosby, Kate Smith, Louis Armstrong, and Dinah Shore; and big band jazz by the Glenn Miller band, Tommy Dorsey, Benny Goodman, and many others.

A common feature of recording artists before 1950 was the need for real-time talent. To make a record required the ability to play an instrument or sing without error—it required technical ability with voice or an instrument. Tape recording, with its ability to erase mistakes and manipulate sound, made it possible for stars with less than extraordinary musical ability to record hit songs. Editors (called **sound mixers**) and record producers could take a live performance and alter it drastically to produce a sound that would sell on records. Record producers combined editing with newly electrified instruments to effectively record a new kind of music, labeled rock 'n' roll by Cleveland disc jockey Alan Freed in the early 1950s.

The second contribution of tape recording was in its role as an audio copy machine. When music was distributed only on flat discs, copying was not a problem. No machine existed for consumers to make their own duplicate discs. Cassettes made copying as easy as pushing a few buttons. Today, estimates are that over 80 percent of blank tape sold is used to make duplicates of copyrighted music. Record companies estimate losses of as much as two billion dollars a year to copying. One offsetting effect of copyable music is that it makes popular music part of our electronic environment. Music is democratic, available to everyone, instead of being limited to those fortunate enough to buy expensive equipment or hire professional musicians. The Supreme Court ruled in 1984 that home taping does not violate the copyright law, and the recording industry still seeks ways to recover income lost to taping.

The Era of Compact Discs and MTV

More than any other medium, recording has a history of new technological developments that seem to save the medium whenever sales lag. The invention of the compact disc (CD) by Sony in 1982 again saved lagging sales. A mere six years after its introduction, sales of CDs surpassed those of LPs. A compact disc consists of music converted to a digital code which is then read by a laser beam. A compact disc stores information in the form of 16-bit digital "words." "1010101011110011" is a bit of information that can be run through a digital-to-analog (D/A) converter to make a sound. A compact disc stores 44,100 of these 16-bit words to make just one second of music for one channel. The optical

Abbey Road Studio, London, where the Beatles recorded in the 1960s and 70s. *Photo Courtesy of AMS Neve, a Siemens company, London.*

pickup of a CD player reads data from the disc at the rate of over 4.32 million bits per second!

These discs were far more convenient than the LP, did not require turning over to hear the other side, and were quieter than vinyl records when played on inexpensive equipment. Early CDs were quite expensive because few processing plants existed to create the new medium. Even when supplies loosened, record companies found that consumers viewed the silvery discs as a premium product for which they willingly paid premium prices. In a relatively short time, compact discs virtually replaced the LP because of their convenience to consumers and their profitability to record makers, and because Japanese manufacturers sold CD players at reasonably low prices.

Recording companies also liked the fact that consumers could not create their own CDs—they were a "read only" medium. Innovations in technology in the 1980s, however, led to the introduction of CDs that could be erased and rerecorded.

As of the mid-1990s, interest is being rekindled in "vinyl" as

Sony's new recording (digital) technology. *Courtesy of Sony Corporation of America.*

a growing number of consumers seek out LPs and 7-inch records developed for select listening markets.

As CD technology is further developed, CD-ROM and interactive music CDs are being introduced as recording artists experiment with new media.

Music Videos

Music videos began in European dance clubs. They were produced by record companies to give both new and established groups added exposure—in other words, to help sell more records. Some were sent to the United States, where they were used as fillers between movies on cable-television outlets. In 1981, Music Television (MTV) was launched into cable homes. The 24-hour cable service introduced new music (much of it new wave European) via music videos.

Radio stations found their listeners demanding the music already seen and heard on MTV. Record companies quickly discovered that MTV sells records. A 1983 survey showed MTV as the most influential factor in determining record purchases.

Early videos were low-budget productions, but artists such as Billy Joel, Paul McCartney, and Michael Jackson quickly produced high-budget minimovies. Michael Jackson's "Thriller" generated nearly 20 million dollars in revenue, and music videos became a product themselves. Music videos became a testing ground for new film techniques and were on the cutting edge of special effects. Techniques perfected in music videos soon became part of television commercials and later influenced movies, TV shows, and political advertising.

So far, music videos on videocassettes or later videodiscs do not compete with sound-only CDs or tapes. The next technical advance that will "save" the recording industry will be a disc that combines high-quality sound with video. Such discs exist now, but are not yet available at a mass-market price.

Pop Culture and Pop Music
Warning: This Music Is Dangerous to Your Health

"Love Me Tender" and "All You Need Is Love": these two songs were sung by two of rock and roll's most popular artists—Elvis Presley and the Beatles. While they hardly seem radical today, both were attacked by critics in the early 1960s as dangerous. Their rebellious messages were destroying the youth of America (at least according to some concerned adults), and their records were sometimes burned in protest. That was over 30 years ago, so what's the connection to today?

Since the late 1980s, almost half of the states in the United States either had or were trying to pass laws that would require records, CDs, and tapes with "offensive" content to be stickered with warning labels. In some states, you have to be 18 before you can buy stickered recordings. Part of a typical label says this: "WARNING: MAY CONTAIN EXPLICIT LYRICS DESCRIBING OR ADVOCATING ONE OR MORE OF THE FOLLOWING: NUDITY, SATANISM, SUICIDE, SEXUAL VIOLENCE, MURDER, ILLEGAL USE OF DRUGS. PARENTAL ADVISORY."

It is true that many rock lyrics talk about extreme violence and other behavior that society usually thinks of as bad. Because of this, many people believe that recording companies should warn adults so they can either prevent children from buying the music or at least know what their kids are listening to. People who support warning stickers suggest that music warning labels are similar to other warning labels which are already accepted by society. For example, cigarettes contain warning labels (and in most states, you have to be 18 to buy cigarettes). Sticker supporters also point out that movie ratings are a type of warning label that society accepts, and you have to be 18 to see or rent a "NC-17" rated adult movie.

Those who disagree with stickering believe that labeling is a form of censorship. They believe that warning labels reduce our freedom to read, watch, or listen to whatever we choose. Opponents of stickering argue that once people in power begin deciding what is okay to listen to, they might censor anything they don't like. These opponents argue that a person's right to freedom of speech and expression always must be protected.

Reflections

What is your opinion about music warning labels? How about voluntary vs. mandatory labeling? If you support the idea of labeling, how would you decide which recordings should be labeled if you were in charge of the process? If you oppose labeling, how do you respond to the argument that labeling is merely a means to warn parents and does not prohibit the sale of the product—as is true with cigarettes and films?

Pop Music Is More Diverse than Ever

While the verbal content—the **lyrics**—of contemporary music are often the focus of controversy, many music watchers believe that the music scene in the 1990s is more varied and creative than ever. In the next reading, starting on page 218, Lee Ballinger of the *Rock and Rap Confidential* newsletter, reviews the state of current pop music. The title of his article clearly indicates where he is coming from.

Practice

Be prepared to analyze the next reading (by Lee Ballinger) in terms
of the origin and impact of rock and rap music, the recording
industry, and new technology such as **sampling,** the incorporation
of previously-recorded music in new recordings. Then discuss
the messages presented in the reading and the author's views. How
have music, performing artists, and the recording industry changed
in the 1990s?

It's in the Mix
Production

Though producing a CD may not seem nearly as complicated a
process as producing a feature film, it often takes as long. Many
of the same preproduction concerns have to be ironed out before
the first note is every played in the recording studio—booking
studio time, hiring technical support personnel, arranging transportation, negotiating financial agreements and international royalty payments to the artist—these are only a few of the behind-
the-scene activities which are part of the origin of any recorded
music product.

The actual recording of the music—the production phase—is
under the supervision of a few key people. The producer heads
the project. Unlike the film industry, where the producer is
strictly a management and money person and is not directly
involved in the artistic process, a **music producer** is the creative
leader. The producer is responsible for the overall artistic quality
of the product (in the same way the director is the main creative
person on a film). Two key people work under the supervision
of the producer: the **recording engineer** and the **mixing engineer.** The recording engineer is responsible for the technicalities
of recording the music, whether it's in a studio or at a "live"
location. Usually each instrument and voice is individually
recorded on a separate track of either magnetic audiotape or
digital computer memory.

Rock and Rap Have Never Been Better

Lee Ballinger

Amid the din of complaint created by the whining of nostalgists and the growling of censors, it's sometimes hard to hear the obvious truth: Music in the '90s is more diverse, interesting, and inspiring than at any other time in American history.

It all begins with rap. Rap has expanded from the spartan sound of drum machines and voice 15 years ago to become the only art form other than the blues that can incorporate (or be incorporated by) any style of music. For example, at last year's Ojai Arts Festival, director Peter Sellars staged a version of Stravinsky's opera *Histoire du soldat* that not only was inspired by rap (it ended with the audience encircled by smoke and blue and red flashing lights meant to invoke the police) but also was narrated by a female rap group that shared the stage with the Los Angeles Philharmonic. At the other extreme, the rappers in Arrested Development effortlessly blend in elements of blues and even country to create a distinctly Southern brand of hip-hop music.

Rap has been the primary vehicle for reggae's long-delayed conquest of North America, as the '90s have seen the raplike tongue-twisting toasting of Jamaican "dance-hall" musicians become part of the U.S. mainstream.

Rap has sparked experiments in jazz by the likes of Miles Davis; pushed the development of traditional R&B into "new jack swing"; and created the basic instrumental sound that has enabled the likes of Boyz II Men to restore black vocal group harmonies to the limelight. Rap has provided a new voice not only for young black men but also for women (Queen Latifah, MC Lyte), Latinos (Cypress Hill, A Lighter Shade of Brown), and whites (not just the cartoonish Vanilla Ice and Marky Mark, but important artists such as House of Pain and the Beastie Boys).

New musical technology has made possible sampling, which opens up the entire history of recorded music to fresh new uses and makes new generations aware of legends ranging from James Brown to Junior Wells. High tech has also spawned entire new genres of music such as house and industrial.

None of this means that the guitar has become extinct. What *has* happened is that we are seeing the full flowering of the seeds sown in the late '70s by the punk rebels, a harvest now bountiful enough that it has clearly ended the dominance of classic blues-rock. Freed of the conventions of that style, new forms of guitar-based music have rapidly emerged. There's speed met-

Rock and Rap Have Never Been Better *(continued)*

al—which bands like Metallica continue to take to new heights of complex artistry. Various "alternative" guitar-based bands ranging from the funky Red Hot Chili Peppers to the folky R.E.M. are enormously popular even though they're outside the conventions of rock. As for blues-rock itself, it still proves the bedrock for excellent music (Black Crowes, Aerosmith), while Seattle bands like Nirvana and Pearl Jam have kept it recognizable even as they refashion it into grunge.

Current pop music has brought women and poets to the fore. While the modern music scene remains a minefield for women, they have made considerable inroads musically (9 of the top 20 singles in late August were by women, and 6 of the top 20 albums). Women are even numerous in the male-dominated field of hard rock, whether it's in the mainstream (L7, 4 Non-Blondes) or in the underground of the "riot grrrl" movement. Outside the studios women have made real progress in punching holes in the corporate glass ceiling of the music business—rap labels, for instance, have allowed women an unprecedented degree of power, and Madonna owns her own record company.

Poetry is now undergoing a tremendous upsurge in popularity, and Bob Holman, a producer of poetry events in New York City, says it's because "rap is now making poetry cool." This revolution was televised on a July 28 MTV show in which several poets, including punk musician Henry Rollins, read over the backing of a rock band.

Even in this noisy age, music fans are eager for softer sounds, too. *MTV Unplugged*, a weekly show in which musicians of almost every style perform without amplification, has been a smashing success. Country music, still a haven for acoustic pickers and fiddlers, is more popular that ever before.

The U.S. music scene of the '90s is more open to the world around it. Latino artists ranging from El Tri ("the Rolling Stones of Mexico") to Beatles-influenced Dominican singing star Juan Luis Guerra are well known in many parts of the United States. African, Middle Eastern, and even Balkan music have finally become widely available in North America.

As the musicians of the '90s not only listen to each other but also work together, the lines between genres often blur. Speed metal guys in Anthrax record and tour with rappers Public Enemy; *Tonight Show* bandleader Branford Marsalis with Sting; R.E.M. with hardcore rapper KRS-1; reggae star Barrington Levy with Vernon Reid of Living Colour and Puerto Rican acoustic guitar legend Yomo Toro. In 1991, Little Richard made a video with Israel's Ofra Haza and hard rock heartthrob Sebastian Bach of Skid Row.

Finally, musicians are forming political alliances with each other and their fans on a scale never even dreamed of in the '60s. With the 1987 maxi-single

Rock and Rap Have Never Been Better *(continued)*

Stop the Violence, two dozen rappers set the stage for the gang truce now moving across the country, and it was rap that popularized the truce as it actually emerged in Watts in the wake of the Los Angeles rebellion. Musicians registered a million new voters last year under the banner of Rock the Vote and Rap the Vote, musicians were the first to raise money for Midwest flood victims, and musicians have carried the discussion of AIDS, homelessness, police brutality, the environment, and abortion into every corner of America.

We live in a time when Axl Rose, the bad boy lead singer of Guns N' Roses who once wrote a song about "niggers," now tours with rapper Ice-T. Last year, Rose stood on a stage in Phoenix and blasted the state of Arizona for refusing to honor Martin Luther King's birthday. That alone should make you want to open your ears and stop, look, and listen to the wealth of sounds that are changing the world we live in. ■

Reprinted by permission from the *Utne Reader*, November/December 1993 issue, *Rock and Rap Confidential*. Lee Ballinger is Associate Editor of *Rock and Rap Confidential* (Box 341305, Los Angeles, CA 90034).

The Structure of Contemporary Music

Though the styles of American recorded music are extremely diverse, many similarities exist among them. A major similarity has to do with the structural conventions upon which most contemporary songs are built. From metal to top 40, from rap to classic rock, they have standard patterns which are instantly recognizable once you become aware of them. For example, many songs begin with rhythm instruments playing the basic chord pattern or melody once. The second time the melody is repeated, the lead vocals sing the first verse of lyrics and a few more background elements are added. The full drum tracks are usually added with the second verse of lyrics. After the second or third verse comes the chorus, the part of the song you keep in your head and hum throughout the day. An instrumental break—a **bridge**—usually follows the chorus, and then the third or fourth verse is sung. The song usually ends with the chorus being repeated two or three times (which is why it sticks in your head). While this basic pattern has many variations, the structure of contemporary pop music—even music labeled as "alternative"—is extremely consistent.

A Word about Fidelity

Viewers can recognize the difference between watching a new videotape on high-quality equipment and watching a worn-out tape on an inexpensive VCR. One looks crisp and sharp, while the other looks a little jumpy and fuzzy. You also know the difference between a glossy color photo and a newspaper photograph. Again, the former looks crisp, while the latter looks a bit softer. The difference in these two examples is in the **resolution** of the visual information—the ability of the medium to reproduce the image. New videotapes on expensive machines and glossy photos have a higher resolution than old tapes on inexpensive machines and newspaper photos.

The parallel idea in the world of sound is that of **fidelity**. Different media allow for various levels of fidelity when reproducing sound. CDs on almost any CD player sound more crisp than vinyl records. Both CDs and digital audiotape (DAT) reproduce sound without the hiss and pops found on vinyl and traditional analog cassette tapes. Just as there is a difference between the resolution of images displayed by a $200 VCR and a $2000 VCR, there is also a big difference in the fidelity of the sound produced by varying levels of fidelity—low-fi, mid-fi, and high-fi—equipment. (The term *hi-fi* was used in the early 1960s when stereo came to vinyl LPs.) These days, equipment that is often referred to as "high-fi" is actually mid-fi at best. Most individual components at a typical stereo store (in the $200 to $700 range) are mid-fi. You have to get to a specialty store to hear high-fidelity audio equipment. Hi-fi components can range from $1500 to $8000. That's for one power amp, or one set of speakers, or one DAT machine!

Clearly, most of the music in our lives comes from low-fi equipment, such as a car radio, television speaker, or all-in-one portable system. As is the trend with all communications media, both visual resolution and acoustic fidelity are evolving quickly. What does the future hold? Engineers in the field of psychoacoustics are investigating ways to use technology to fool our ears (and minds) into hearing sound as "three dimensional," so that music coming from two small speakers sounds like it is surrounding us. Remember, we are at the very beginning of the digital age; you can be sure that how you experience music on a daily basis 10 years from now will be very different from today.

Evaluation

You frequently hear people refer to the film they just saw; you probably hear just as many people talk about their favorite new CD or song. Just as there is a big difference between making "I statements" and "film statements," there is a big difference between making "I statements" and "music statements." Is that new CD that you think is trash really trash? If it is, why do so many people love it? Why do other people refer to it as "cutting edge" or "powerful"? The answer is probably comes down to the key idea of consumption, the fourth stage of the Media Literacy Paradigm: Our personal backgrounds and experiences cause us to develop different values, tastes, and, in this case, musical paradigms.

Here are several criteria you can apply to make informed "music statements" when evaluating recorded music.

Genre: What is the genre—classical, jazz, urban, techno, punk, crossover, and so on—of the music? What is the origin of the genre? To whom does it appeal and why?

Lyrics: What do the lyrics say? What is the artist's purpose in writing particular lyrics? Do the lyrics convey a substantive message? (Whether you agree with the message is your personal value judgment—an "I statement.")

Musicality: This criterion deals with the four main areas of music theory, and, as a result, may be challenging for the nonmusician.

Rhythm essentially refers to the beat of the song. Most pop songs have a fairly strong and consistent beat to which you can tap your foot (unlike much jazz and classical music, in which the rhythm is often more subtle and varied).

The *tempo* of a song is determined by the speed of the beat. Romantic ballads tend to have a slow tempo, while (as its name implies) songs in the speed metal genre tend to have an extremely fast tempo.

In music, *harmony* refers to the chords—the collection of notes—that form the basis of the song. Songs written in a major key feel different than songs written in a minor key. Music which conveys an emotion of sadness is often written in minor keys. The entire genre of blues (out of which most modern rock and roll evolved) is based on a pattern of chords known by musicians as the 1–4–5.

Timbre has to do with the overall sound of the instruments used to make a particular piece of music. Because of their different physical characteristics, each instrument has a particular sound. A violin clearly sounds quite different from a trumpet, which sounds different from an electric guitar, and so on. In talking about a piece of music, you might describe its timbre as earthy and soft, or hard-edged and electronic. The difference between the sounds of an electric and acoustic guitar illustrates the basic idea of an instrument's timbre.

Convention: As described above, most songs follow various conventions, that is, basic structural patterns (for example: verse, verse, chorus, bridge, verse, chorus, chorus).

Artistry: How expressive are the artist's lyrics? Do the moods and styles of the songs vary? Does the artist use a wide range of instruments? Are there creative variations of convention? How well would the artist's natural musical talent stand up if you removed all the technical effects which were added later? How original are the artist's melodies, harmonies, rhythms, and so on?

Production: Is the overall sound and feel of the music pleasurable? Can you hear all of the instruments clearly? Is the mix of instrument and vocal volume effective? When you listen to the song carefully with headphones, do you hear clear stereo placement of the many musical elements or do they all seem to melt together? Is there an overreliance on effects such as echo (reverb), fuzz, and other electronic enhancements?

Industry Snapshot: Where Your Recorded Music Dollars Go

The graph on the next page breaks down the average costs of producing and selling a recording. As you can see, an average of 22 cents of every dollar you spend on a CD, for example, goes toward recording costs and royalties, which include the following: Studio costs, musician fees, tape or digital editing expenses, and arranging costs, as well as royalties. **Royalties** include payments to the copyright owners of the lyrics or music as well as payments to the performing artists when a recording is sold. The artist or group typically receives between 5 to 15 percent of 90 percent of the retail price of each recording sold. Recording costs are often charged against the performing artist's or group's royalties.

Future Watch: Music in the Digital Age

The rise of music videos in the 1980s had a big impact on the marketing of popular music all around the world. Success was

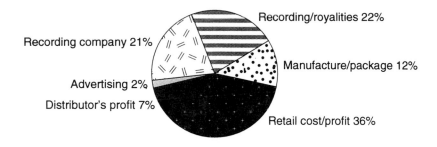

Recording/royalties 22%

Recording company 21%

Advertising 2%

Distributor's profit 7%

Manufacture/package 12%

Retail cost/profit 36%

Source: Recording Industry Association of America, Washington, D.C.

Practice

As you read "Rock and Riches," the reading starting on the next page, consider the reality of being a performer in a rock group or a rock star, and the "image" of such a life we listeners have. (Those guys *have* to be rich, right?) Analyze the article in terms of the mediation or production of the media product: a recording.

previously based almost solely on getting radio airplay, so record company strategies were aimed at maximizing radio exposure for their artists. Now, MTV (and emerging music channel competitors to MTV, such as The Box) are part of a company's marketing plans from the start. We have become used to seeing new videos accompanying the release of new CDs. What will we become used to in the future? According to Fred Davis, who writes about music, computers, and culture, the next big change in how we experience popular music will be the growth in CD-ROM and interactive media, as he explains in a reading later in this chapter.

Rock & Riches

Allan Parachini

The houselights dim; the clamor of the crowd falls to a low buzz—low enough that the anticipatory coughing can be heard amid the hum of the PA system. In a moment the show will begin. It makes no difference what band is about to play, and it doesn't matter where. What is about to be unleashed, like a genie out of a bottle, is an IMAGE—magical, mysterious, and glamorous—one of many raised up by that energetic cultural force known as Rock, swathed in clouds of sumptuous glory, lauded in hymns of hyperbolic praise, and flattered by the proliferation of those smaller-scale imitations known as Lifestyle. This pantheon of heros and heroines has no parallel in contemporary culture, and we must go back to the early days of the silver screen—of Valentino, Pickford, and Garbo—to find anything like it. What it is is *myth*, a highly selective metaphor about life, of which both performers and their audiences, romanticized and romanticizing, are at once creators and consumers.

But myths are like Chinese boxes, one nestling inside the other on into infinity. The myth immediately inside the myth of the Rock Star is that of Untold Riches, and there is just enough truth (though not much) to it to make it an effective magnet, drawing young people to New York, Los Angeles, Nashville, or wherever else music is made and recorded to declare themselves in on a piece of the action, a slice of the fabulous take.

They arrive in Los Angeles, for instance, by battered car or bus, check into the YMCA, and hit the street. They walk up to Yucca Street, or Vine near Hollywood Boulevard, look in the Yellow Pages under "Records," and start feeding change into a payphone. Then they wait, lounging on the sidewalk outside a liquor store, having given the payphone as "a number where I can be reached," for the return call that never comes. They have a common desire—a career in the music business—and a host of very uncommon, often highly original, misconceptions about just what that business is. They are, in short, as much prisoners or victims of their myth as any Forty-niner ever was, feeding their hopes on the good news of occasional rich strikes and ignoring the multitudinous evidence of failure all around them.

Rod Stewart, who once slept on a Spanish beach because he couldn't afford a hotel room, who used to play professional soccer to support his music habit, now earns millions. At the top,

Rock & Riches *(continued)*

the money piles up like winter snow in Donner Pass, and the bulldog tenacity that keeps so many musicians struggling up the lower slopes is fueled by the expectation that they too will eventually, if only they hang on, get to frolic in it. What are their chances?

Record companies sell almost two *billion* units in the United States each year. There are about 200 releases certified "gold" (meaning they sold 500,000 copies for an album, 1,000,000 copies for a single). Such figures translate very readily into Big Money, of course, and the myth has it that the musician is first in line to collect. And myth it is, for there are very few performers indeed in the most favored position.

The performer derives revenue primarily from two sources: live performances and record royalties. He may also earn something from song-publishing royalties (if he writes his own material), since there will then be royalty income from others who perform his songs and from radio stations that play them on the air as well. But before the musician realizes any income whatsoever, he must normally commit a percentage of all his earnings "up front" to a manager, unless he is clever enough to handle his own business affairs—including negotiating complicated contracts with record companies and booking agents; insuring that the provisions of those contracts are fulfilled; securing the most favorable possible terms for such seemingly incidental arrangements as production, promotion, and marketing of records, travel provisions for performance tours, and even the reservation of recording-studio time. . . .

For most musicians, a professional personal manager is an absolute necessity. Managers normally retain between 10 and 15 percent of the musician's entire gross income and can in some cases get as much as 20 or even 50 percent. Accountants (more and more indispensable the higher the sales figures get) are another accoutrement, and they get $300 to $800 a month. Such people are necessary not only to help the performer retain a reasonable part of his initial gross, but also to interpret the complex financial systems that appear to be peculiar to record companies; they are needed to make certain the musician does not, plainly and simply, get ripped off. . . .

Managers are not a race of white knights, of course. Their ranks are heavily populated by the shady and by the inept, either of whom can leave a client musician, in the manner of one of those bilked innocents in an old prize-fight movie, with no return whatever for his efforts, gold record sales or no. Selection of a good (honest, capable) manager is therefore one of the music business' biggest risks.

But to return to the question of income. Record royalties, unlike the fees paid for live performances, are

Rock & Riches *(continued)*

established contractually between record companies and musicians for periods of between one and five years. Gross royalties are computed on a base of 90 percent of the wholesale . . . price of each record actually sold. Retail discount prices do not bear on royalties. The performer gets between 5 and 18 percent of 90 percent of retail, say (depending on the terms of his contract), and though there are several ways to compute the amount, they generally work out to about [$.70–$2.00] per album. The record producer gets a 3 or 5 percent royalty, which may in some cases be deducted from the musician's share, and the a-&-r (for "artists and repertoire") man who signed the artist to a record contract in the first place frequently gets 2 or 3 percent, normally from the record company's gross.

Under the royalty system, the *potential* for income from a record that sells well is actually not bad (more than $250,000 for a gold album for example), and if a musician has written his own songs, he receives an additional gross of $1\frac{1}{2}$ cents per song, per record, in song publishing royalties. Normally, the manager has unobtrusively procured for himself some of the publishing proceeds; if he is honest, he has also done as much for his client. Otherwise, the naive musician may likely find that he has unknowingly signed away some or even all of the potential publishing income as part of a cash "advance" in an innocent-looking contract with a music-publishing firm or even his own record company.

Record companies have established what seems to be a unique sort of company-store relationship with their artists, one that tends to cut handsomely into the income potential of royalties. First, the record companies normally try to charge back to the artist as much of the actual cost of recording and marketing a record as possible. Such costs can amount to about $20,000 (for the most modestly produced album) to as much as $100,000 (for an over-produced spectacular). They include studio time, union pay for extra musicians, and other expenses too numerous and too unimaginable to mention—even the cost of the recording tape is levied against royalties. The record companies also charge their artists for some of the expenses of promoting and publicizing the resulting recording, including, for example, press parties and the cost (from $750 to $1,500 per month) of retaining a private publicist. A modest tour may also be underwritten by the record company—and charged against the royalty gross; even a short introductory series of engagements in small clubs can run to as much as $50,000.

What results is in many cases an arrangement that would be bitterly familiar to any old-time Appalachian coal miner. Some recording acts owe so much of their soul to the company store that they never overcome their indebtedness; they can only watch helplessly

Rock & Riches *(continued)*

as the royalties of their successful later records are eaten up in mid-career by early advances. Then too, determining the number of copies of a record actually sold is a task of no little difficulty. Records are distributed on consignment, meaning that unsold goods may be returned—for full credit—by individual record stores to small distributors, by small distributors to large, and large distributors to the original record company. The consignment arrangement is a necessary one, since without it distributors and their clients would probably never gamble on a first release by an artist they had never heard of, or even on a great second release by someone who had bombed with his first. The problem with this system is that it can take at least several months, and at times as much as several years, to determine accurately the exact number of copies of a recording sold. Record companies manage this situation to their advantage, often withholding a portion of royalties against the possibility of such returns. . . .

Though it is true that there is a comfortable living to be made in music (from $50,000 to $100,000 a year) for a small number of anonymous, unglamorous studio musicians (usually older, always highly skilled), the performing musician whose name appears on recordings and concert billings is usually not nearly so well off. Musicians are, in general, people of fragile egos and are often afflicted with a profound naivete. Those who can learn to adapt to the *business* of music survive—sometimes—and a few, very few, can move beyond that to the Big Money. But, for the most part, what the uninitiated see when they look up from the orchestra or down from the balcony is an illusion. Those are not dollar signs, but just the beam of a Super Trouper spotlight reflecting off a guitar purchased through an advance against royalties. ■

Adapted from an article published in 1974 in *Stereo Magazine*, Ziff-Davis Publishing.

The development of the Internet as a distribution system for recorded music began in 1994. Songs are being digitized and stored on this massive computer network for anyone to download and listen to. These digital transfers pose several questions. Do they violate copyright law? How will that affect music sales and recording artists?

A more encouraging possibility opened up by transferring digital sound via the Internet is that anyone with a computer and modem can make their digital music available for others to hear. Given the high cost of promoting a new band, very few are signed by

Practice

Identify examples of concepts from the Media Literacy Paradigm in the article that starts on page 231; state which of the five stages of the Paradigm each example relates to.

record companies. On the Internet, however, a band can place a demo (demonstration recording) of its music in hundreds of places where music lovers worldwide hang out electronically.

The music recording companies are fully aware of the threat the information superhighway poses, so, as of late 1994, they began establishing a presence on the Internet. For example, Warner Brothers Records has its own area of America Online, where it offers samples of new releases and promotes other Warner Brothers merchandise. Almost all big entertainment companies are trying to figure out how they will be a part of the information highway.

New technology poses many questions. Performing artists themselves are getting more involved with new media and technology, as you will see in the next reading.

Building Your Media Archive
Archive Analysis

Select a recording for your analysis. If you are not sure under what music classification your recording falls, check with a local music store. They should be able to tell you both how the record company classifies it and how the store itself classifies recording, if differently. As with the film in your media archive, your CD or tape provides extensive information on the personnel involved in its production (Origin). You'll have to do research to get additional biographical and background information, but there are hundreds of books about contemporary artists. The history of your artist's recording company might also prove interesting.

I Want My (Desktop) MTV!

Fred Davis

You're Peter Gabriel. You've been at the cutting edge of everything. You were in a supergroup. You left to go solo and earned superstar status on your own. Your videos made MTV worth watching. Your mantelpiece is crammed with Grammys and other awards. So, what's next?

When Gabriel began learning about CD-ROM*, the answer became obvious: interactive music. Gabriel's *Explora* CD-ROM, includes music and videos from Gabriel's latest album *Us;* an interactive tour of his recording studio, situated on the grounds of a beautiful estate somewhere in the English countryside; and a visit to a World Organization of Music and Dance (WOMAD) festival, all with Gabriel acting as your interactive tour guide.

By letting people look at the artistic process from the inside, Gabriel hopes his work will help blur the distinction between artist and non-artist. "I hope this technology will empower people who have a sense that they have as much right and ability for self-expression as anyone who goes under the officially approved category [of artist]," he says. "In some societies, the idea that anyone alive would not be an artist is ridiculous. I think that often the first generation

*Compact disk read-only memory.

of new technology can be dehumanizing; but the second generation can be super-humanizing."

Interactive technology could change both the public's conception of musician as well as the economics of the music world. Gabriel isn't alone in grasping the importance of music's newest medium: Every major Hollywood studio and media conglomerate is jockeying for a stake in the latest digital opportunity. Time-Warner, Viacom, Sony, MCA, Paramount, Fox, Philips—you name it—they've all got an interactive strategy. In fact, refusing to acknowledge interactive music nowadays would be about as smart as pretending video didn't matter during the ascendency of MTV.

Not everyone is so sanguine, however. "There are real questions in my mind as to whether even talented musicians can make a compelling interactive experience," comments Jac Holzman, founder of Elektra Records, now chief technologist at Warner Music.

Indeed, a cynic might argue that interactive music is yet another marketing trick foisted upon the consuming masses by aging rock stars eager to extend their popular lifespan. "MTV was essentially a new marketing methodology," Holzman says.

I Want My (Desktop) MTV! *(continued)*

"The life of a rock-and-roll musician used to be short," he adds. "Now it can be 20 to 25 years."

Holzman sees more renowned stars like Gabriel, Bowie, and others raising awareness of interactive medium's potential. But the artists who will truly define this new form have yet to be discovered.

"It's like the growth of the record industry as it came out of the '50s and '60s," says Holzman, who began his career when records still spun at 78 rpm. "The energy was with the independent labels." Inexpensive tools like Apple's QuickTime and Adobe Premiere will enable a whole new generation of artists to explore this medium, he adds.

Until then, veteran stars like Peter Gabriel, Billy Idol, David Bowie, and scores of others are working with computer technologists to add an interactive dimension to the music they've already written. Others, including Todd Rundgren, Thomas Dolby, and Cindy Baron, are creating music from the ground up using the new interactive technologies. Whether they create interactive music by integrating old tunes into new formats or by writing new music, both approaches yield what can only be described as an altered listening experience.

New releases from artists like Gabriel will let you do more than merely listen to your music. You'll be able to play along with the band, even if you're a tone-deaf klutz. You'll have the chance to create your own music videos, identify your emotional responses to certain kinds of music, and even explore a virtual musical world. And we're not talking some distant future—interactive rock and roll is happening right now.

Technologists and Artists

Today, creating interactive CD-ROMs requires both musical and technical knowledge. Some CD-ROMs, like *The Freak Show*, under development by the San Francisco-based performance-rock group The Residents, consume the talents of computer programmers, artists, designers, and computer-literate musicians. Musicians like Bowie, whose demo CD-ROM was produced by interactive wizard Ty Roberts, and Gabriel, whose . . . *Explora* CD was designed by Steve Nelson's Brilliant Media, are working with the best technologists around. . . .

There's even a non-musician, Tony Bové, an interactive chronicler and historian, whose CD-ROM-based documentary-in-progress about the Haight-Ashbury days is based on recorded music, art, poetry, and news footage.

Make Your Own Music

The first wave of interactive music falls into three main categories: interactive musical compositions, which let you make your own music out of preconstructed parts or let you jam along with the music; interactive rockumentaries,

I Want My (Desktop) MTV! *(continued)*

which bring you into the history of the creative musical process; and interactive experiences, which combine music, art, and even a sense of gameplay.

Interactive musical compositions include works with the primary focus on audio. The visual interfaces to these products let you set the mood of the music that's playing, remix or rearrange the various musical parts in the composition, or let you play along as one of the band members. "Any musical performance is actually a script of musical events, verses, choruses, solo sections, and other subjectively named musical events," says Todd Rundgren. "A traditional CD is essentially a list of these musical events.

"On my interactive CD, there will be three pre-defined scripts of musical events available. At the simplest level, it's like getting three albums in one, and you can choose the one you like best. If you want more, you can have the system create a custom script for you. You can control the tempo or mood. Or maybe you want to hear a certain kind of mix, like a very thick mix or a thin mix or a mix with no vocals."

Experimentation with mood and emotion is a major theme in the interactive music scene. Thomas Dolby describes how he designed a sound installation for a sculpture exhibit in an art gallery: "The nice thing about music is that when you add an element to a piece of music, your whole perception of it changes. You take a chord sequence played with a mellow choir sound in C major, and then somewhere else in the room you place a low throb or drone in A minor. As you move toward it, your mood goes from a happy major one to a more sinister, melancholy minor one. If you assign a different element to each event or character that the player can interact with, then he kind of creates his own mix."

What About Couch Tubers?
The obvious problem with this approach is that it makes demands of the listener. "The number of people who want to get inside the music and reconstruct it is relatively small," Warner's Holzman says. "Someone may want to pull out a guitar track, but that's a guy who is a guitar freak."

What if you're tone-deaf? You may not make "music" as we know it, but it still might be fun. At least, that's Rundgren's contention. "Music in people's lives is not an intellectual experience; it's a transcendental experience. The first major step is trying to convey to people that interactive is an expanded way of listening to music. They should not think that it changes their responsibilities in terms of music. People buy music because it brings them pleasure and enjoyment. It's not a job.

"For interactive music to become a popular concept," he adds, "it would have to be really simple to use. I think one of the most common ways that people will use interactive music is to set

I Want My (Desktop) MTV! *(continued)*

up a listening circumstance and let the CD-I player—or whatever—do the rest. Essentially, it will invent a record tailored to the listening circumstance. For example, tell the system that you're having a party and you'd like some fast upbeat songs."

Rundgren is practicing what he preaches. *No World Order*, due out this summer, will run on CD-I and Macintosh systems. The composition—performed entirely by Rundgren—contains a database of more than 1,500 musical segments and phrases, which you can rearrange to create your own composition.

Thomas Dolby holds a clear vision of the potential synergies between music, technology, and entertainment. In fact, he's already started his own Los Angeles-based company, Headspace, which he rather immodestly hopes will do for audio special effects what George Lucas's Industrial Light & Magic has done for visual special effects. At the moment, Dolby's doing the musical score for an interactive game on CD-ROM in which the music changes according to the dramas that take place.

Dolby agrees that for people to want to participate in making their own interactive music, technology must make the choices simple. "It's not a big leap when you have a graphic program that allows the user choices to create a sound score complete with music and special effects and even dialog that is generated

and even modulated by the specific choices the player makes. But," he warns, "don't burn your hi-fi systems."

The Electric Arranger

So what is it like for a musician to produce an interactive music CD-ROM designed to let the listener mix and match? Liberating, says Edgar Winter, a rock and blues composer who got fed up with traditional ways of composing music. "Doing a traditional album is creative up to a certain point, because you're building. But then you get to where you have to decide what can stay on the album and what has to go—I always hate that. Sometimes I'll do a couple different solos on several different instruments and often I like all of them—it's hard to decide what to throw out in the final mix for the album."

Winter wasn't quite ready to put a name to his first title when I spoke to him at his in-home studio in Los Angeles, where he's producing his latest album using a Macintosh-based desktop recording studio. But he did say that computers have changed the way he sees music. "With the power of computers," he said, "there's no reason why you can't let the listener select among the different musical ideas and use them to create their own arrangements. I feel like computers will help people experience the album's creative possibilities more the way that I did when I was working on it."

I Want My (Desktop) MTV! *(continued)*

Interactive Karaoke

Some people may want to do more than just rearrange someone else's music. They may actually want to play along with the band. Several companies, including Holzman's Warner, are working on products that teach music through interactive media. Others are working on titles along the lines of karaoke and Music Minus One—tapes of popular hits minus a key instrument.

Interactive Records's *So You Want To Be a Rock and Roll Star*, an interactive music title for the Macintosh, lets you pick a popular rock song and replace one of the musicians; you even get some instruction on how to improve your licks. Interactive Records is producing other titles, including *Country Goes Interactive*, which applies the combination karaoke and instructional approach to popular country tunes.

According to Steven Rappaport, the company's president, "The point of these products is to truly empower users so they can have a participatory musical experience, even if they're not musicians."

A fan of Thomas Dolby, Rappaport is in the midst of an imaginative project based on Dolby's music called *Astronauts and Heretics in the Land of the Pirate Twins: A Thomas Dolby Interactive Record*. This project is an interactive adventure game based on Dolby's first four albums. Although Dolby is immersed in the technology himself, this project was conceived and is being produced by Rappaport under license from Dolby.

MTV with Buttons

Although music still provides the *raison d'etre*, interactive rockumentaries tend to make greater use of visuals and text to explore how the music was created. In an almost educational fashion, they impart information as you explore a terrain of songs and pictures and text via the computer screen.

So far, the interactive rockumentary has attracted the most commercial interest among the three types of this *avant-garde* musical genre. According to Michele DiLorenzo, senior vice president of Viacom New Media (corporate sibling of MTV), "Most so-called interactive music titles are really reference material about music, and shouldn't really be considered interactive music." In some cases, such as Compton's *The Compleat Beatles* on CD-ROM, the original artist had zero involvement with the project—the result is mostly re-purposed from existing documentary materials.

Exploring the World

. . . Gabriel wants to see the new technology gain a stronghold in the Third World. "It's clear that some countries have the capacity to jump from an agricultural economy to an information economy without [passing through] an industrial economy. If you could get a

I Want My (Desktop) MTV! *(continued)*

very reliable, low-budget, self-sufficient information mode with computers, solar power, and satellite up and down links that could be dropped on any point on the planet's surface and kids there could be trained within three to five years in how to use all this stuff, they could then become information creators and processors able to compete equally with any other point on the globe."

Sound + Vision + Interactivity
The David Bowie CD-ROM, developed for Apple's Power CD player by interactive wizard Ty Roberts's company ION, shares some conceptual turf with the Gabriel production. Roberts, who has been a Bowie fan since his teens, projects his hero worship but skillfully combines it with a special effects culled from his years as a music and video programmer.

Based on the song, *Jump, They Say* from Bowie's new album *Black Tie, White Noise*, the CD-ROM allows the user to explore Bowie's creative process. Brewed from nine hours of outtakes and alternate scenes, the disc lets you see the behind-the-scenes creation of the album; view the *Jump, They Say* video; and then enter an interactive video studio and mix your own version of Bowie's video.

U2's *ZOO TV*
Supergroup U2 has been using interactive media technology in its live per-

formances, where giant screens depict synthetic drummers, replicas of band member Bono, and another band thousands of miles away. They're now making the move to CD-ROM.

U2 sees its forte in video. "What we're trying to create is television, except it's interactive MTV or beyond," says U2's producer Philip Van Allen. "The aesthetic for us is not computers. It's much more akin to the visual and audio aesthetic that's on MTV."

The project—*ZOO TV Interactive*—is still under development by Van Allen's Commotion New Media. Van Allen estimates production time will take one year. "Our approach is to create something that is not about the artist, but an expression of the artist. If all the music products are rehashing old material, we don't have an art form and we don't have a business." . . .

Exploring the '60s in the '90s
"I'm not interested in the fads, the backstage, and the groupies, but in why they decided how to write a song, how they used the studio to produce," says Tony Bové, who is producing a Macintosh CD-ROM rockumentary on the Haight-Ashbury era. "I'm interested in a more detailed examination of the creative process."

In its best form, the interactive rockumentary experience draws you into both the musical and documentary process to give you a much better feel for the subject, Bové says.

I Want My (Desktop) MTV! *(continued)*

"By interacting with the multidimensional artistic and cultural spectrum of information on the disc, people will learn more about the Haight-Ashbury than they could by any other method in the same amount of time. I'm not just recording a traditional film documentary onto digital media," Bové asserts, "I'm actually trying to create a new form of documentary."

Bové's not a professional musician, although he does play a mean blues harmonica and has an ear for what sounds good. But he definitely has a mission: "The key thing for me is to explore the creativity that went into making the rock music and exploring the roots and the influences for the musicians. What was the cultural context for the music, and how did the music itself influence our culture?

"The project contains a lot of different material that's never been brought together before. It crosses boundaries and mixes media. The music for this disc will be from lots of bands: the Grateful Dead, Jefferson Airplane, and others. There'll even be a special digitally simulated enlightenment at the end—Eastern philosophies merged with Western."

Bové plans to produce and distribute the CD-ROM himself, together with his partner and wife Cheryl Rhodes. *The Rise and Fall of the Haight-Ashbury* is scheduled for an early 1994 release.

The Interactive Revolutionaries

A few dream of venturing beyond interactive music, beyond the simple rockumentary, into a completely different realm. Devo founder Gerry Cosalis wants to produce a CD-ROM that could be a potent social force—maybe even a good one.

"In years past there have been a lot of examples of how a band could turn an audience into a mutinous angry mob, by pushing certain emotions," Cosalis explains. "That's what happened in the 1960s and 1970s with rock and punk. With computer technology and this new kind of complete interaction with the listener, you can be truly cyberpunk in a subversive manner that's potentially positive."

Cosalis is interested in reviving Devo as a virtual band, one that exists electronically as an interactive concept, returning to the band's roots of integrating theater, poetry, and music. To get at least a partial start, Cosalis has teamed up with the Voyager Company to produce a laserdisc, *The Complete Truth About De-Volution*, which is an artistically rich but technically simple rockumentary about Devo with rudimentary interactivity—limited by the constraints of the laserdisc medium.

A glimpse of *The Complete Truth* video gives one an idea what the potential CD-ROM might look like: mindbending. Culling strands from their Dadaist and German Expressionist roots, the video mixes music, murder,

I Want My (Desktop) MTV! (continued)

mayhem, mime, and sheer mirth, all in what appears to be a chaotic format. It isn't. But the total effect is shocking and at the same time compelling.

Artificial Emotion

Like Devo did before her, alternative musician Cindy Baron is definitely marching to the beat of a different drum machine. Baron was exposed to both technology and music at an early age. At three, she started the Suzuki method, and her childhood pastimes included playing math games with dad, who was one of the founders of Mead Data Central, the online providers of Lexis and Nexis. "My father taught me binary code, set theory, symbolic logic, and as a result I became a budding young geek," Baron says. "One of my clearest childhood memories was sitting on the playground—all the other little girls had their Barbies and stuffed animals—but I was happily sitting there playing with my slide rule and logarithm tables."

Baron grew up to lead a double life as a software engineer and rock-and-roll musician—she's played with The Card Game and is now with the New York-based rock band 2.5D. "The way one thinks about music and music structures is very similar to the way one thinks about programming and programming structures," she says. "I really believe that programming and music are very closely matched."

How is Baron applying her creative and technical talents in the interactive music arena? Baron has taken what she calls a "completely different approach"—using music and graphics to create what she describes as artificial emotion. She is working on a CD-ROM—which will be re-purposed as a traditional audio CD and a music video—that will help people "learn about their own emotional styles. People who listen and look at my product will get more of a sense of why my art is created than how it is created. Also, they are going to get a sense of why they respond to certain music the way they do."

Cyberpunk Rock?

A couple of years ago, rock star Billy Idol thought computers were only for geeks. Then he read William Gibson's classic science-fiction novel *Neuromancer* and realized that computers might be the hippest thing around. Idol's subsequent discussions with Gibson opened doors to high-tech enlightenment that "drove me wild," he says.

Idol's computer explorations quickly drew him to the WELL, an online service started by the *Whole Earth* folks (he's idol@well.sf.ca.us). So if you take Billy Idol, William Gibson, *Neuromancer*, a Macintosh, and the WELL, and stir them together in a big creative pot, you wind up with *Cyberpunk*, Idol's upcoming audio CD with accompanying software for the Macintosh. The product, published by EMI subsidiary Chrysalis, is due out early this summer. The album itself is a "musical manifestation of my explorations on the WELL," says Idol. The *Cyberpunk* software describes an underground science fiction movement that incorporates technology and art.

The Eyes Have It

Perhaps the most fully developed interactive experience is *The Freak Show* CD-ROM, based on a 1990 album and comic book of the same name, all created by The Residents, a San Francisco based rock/performance group, with the help of well-known interactive artist, Jim Ludtke. The Residents are an off-beat experimental music band—some of their music/video work is in the permanent collection of the Museum of Modern Art. The band performs only in disguise—the best-known being their giant eyeball masks with top-hats and tuxes. From our sneak preview, their disc resembles nothing so much as a modern-day morality tale—albeit at a low resolution. It is to be launched on the Macintosh later this year.

Homer Flynn, the band's manager, describes the disc: "The CD-ROM can be seen as an interactive book that's illustrated with graphics, text, and music. The interface is a tent containing an audience and stage. Some of the audience members will be interactive, as will the freaks performing on the stage. By moving through a door at one side of the stage, you can get behind the tent and explore the trailers of the individual freaks."

Ludtke's 3-D drawings are so surrealistic—a Dali sketchbook was lying open on the worktable when I visited —that you feel as if you are actually encountering Wanda the Worm Woman, formerly a nun. You explore her trailer, plush with baroque ornaments, and read her old love letters, which she received from a priest. Then you can click-wander your way into Harry the Head's trailer: He's a freak with just a head—no body—so you have to enter his *mind* to understand him.

Of course, there's a message. "In some way we are all freaks, and all freaks are really just people," Flynn says. "But it's not a completely serious project; it's an escapist fantasy as well."

What also distinguishes this CD-ROM from many of the others is that the concept came from the musicians—not from an outside technologist or programmer. And, as with Gabriel's *Explora* project, the musicians worked closely with the artist (and a programmer) to carefully develop the vision projected by their music.

Free To Roam, for Now

The market is so disorganized in these formative days of interactive music, it's hard to even figure out what discs play on what machines. . . . In this new medium, there are no real mega-hits

I Want My (Desktop) MTV! *(continued)*

and there are no real superstars. Creative freedom and artistic quality might flourish.

But the Hollywood sharks are already starting to circle. Madonna has launched an interactive company, Prince has announced that he will be doing interactive media and virtual reality projects, and two notorious Michaels—Milken and Jackson—are working on a massive interactive TV project that is under close wraps. Rumor has it that Milken will use his fortune to start an interactive cable TV venture that will use Jackson's vast media holdings—which includes much of the Beatles' work—as a content base.

Because interactive music is still in its exploratory and experimental stages, it is free from most of the constraints, oppression, and perversion of big-scale commercial interests. "Because the corporate presence is still fairly minimal on the cutting edge," says Peter Gabriel, "many explorers and artists have been left fairly free to follow their instincts and their hearts."

Some media executives feel this is as it should be. Viacom's DiLorenzo, who is in charge of developing her company's substantial content inventory (including MTV, Nickelodeon, and Showtime), prefers to train her producers and directors, and allow her developers to play for a while, in anticipation of the day when offline interactive (CD-ROM) becomes online interactive.

"Right now, we're not really deciding what our strategy will be," she said. "Instead, we're doing a lot of creative R&D. If you shortchange the creative R&D, you'll end up shortchanging your ultimate business opportunities."

Although the ultimate forms and formats are still emerging, one thing is sure. No matter how the art is produced, it still will be judged by the standards we have developed in the past. Or, as Todd Rundgren said when I asked his advice to artists venturing in this still uncharted interactive territory: "It's the content, stupid. It's not the dazzling technique."

So will interactive media be significant? "Absolutely," says Jac Holzman of Warner Music. "When someone does something miraculous with it." ■

Adapted from the original article by Fred Davis from the July/August 1993 issue of *WIRED*.

Photos of Peter Gabriel's Explora CD-ROM *courtesy of Interplay Productions, Inc.*

There are several methods you may use to analyze the recording in your Media Archive. You can use the Consumption stage of your archive analysis to further investigate the idea of audience. Find classmates whose archive selection is in the same music genre (alternative, country, etc.) as yours. Compile a list of facts about yourselves that you have in common which you think help explain why you like the same music. Compare your findings with another group of students who share a different musical interest. What

Student Close-Up

David Eastwood, Connecticut

A high school student describes how he got started as a member of a band and involved in the recording business.

Before there was anything even remotely resembling a structured, organized band, there was only the infrequent practicing of Jon Christopher and Ryan Price, who played the guitar and drums, respectively, and who both attend high school with me. Jon and Ryan were both enthusiastic adherents of the underground punk rock music scene with its defiantly independent streak and its loud, abrasive music. Both Jon and Ryan wanted to form a band like several other local kids, but back then they were only just getting in on the ground floor.

After several months of just messing around in Ryan's garage, they asked me to play bass with them, even though I had only been playing the instrument for about a month, since joining another local punk outfit, Shrike. We looked forward to the day when we would finally be able to play in punk shows alongside our favorite local bands, and began a hectic practice schedule to fine-tune our skills as a band.

We wrote seven songs, mostly about girls and the trials of day-to-day life, and learned to play a song by one of our favorite bands, Crimpshrine. It was with this set list that we played our first show at a local club, having been put on the bill because the promoter was a friend of ours. The show went pretty well, even though we were still a little rough around the edges, but we got the chance to hone our live act in the upcoming weeks, as we played show after show at this local club.

Finally, we (calling ourselves *Steadfast*) earned enough money to record a *demo* or demonstration tape at a local studio. The tape was recorded on an eight-track machine, meaning that there were eight microphones hooked up to the band to record us as we played (one microphone for lead vocals, one for the guitar, one for the bass, etc.). The recording was relatively cheap, and we sold the demos for two dollars.

After the demo, we were looking forward to putting out a record. Records, especially the 33 revolutions per minute, 7 inches in diameter kind, are the dominant medium of the underground punk scene because they are so inexpensive, and your band is said to have "arrived" when you put out your first record. Unfortunately, we had no money.

This problem was solved when another local high school student by the name of Phil Deslippe joined our band—playing the trumpet. Phil runs his own "DIY," or "do it yourself" recording business, the predominant business philosophy in the punk scene, recording under the label Youth Power Records. Phil had expressed interest in producing our 7-inch record, and so we had a new batch of songs with trumpet parts as well as a record in the works.

We recorded at a local studio, The Music Factory, on a sixteen-track recorder, a much more complex piece of equipment that the eight track used for the demo. We had some trouble recording Phil's parts, but overall the nine songs, which took nine hours to record, came out sounding okay. The recording, which was on a reel-to-reel tape, had to have the various parts (the instruments and vocals) mixed on a high-tech mixing machine at Master-works studio, another local business. The mixed tape was put on a DAT (digital audiotape) cassette and sent to a record-pressing plant in Connecticut called United. The labels that were affixed to the record and the sleeve which the record came in had to be printed separately—at Hamlett Printing and Sir Speedy Printing, respectively. Beginning with the mixing, Phil handled all this business, and paid for it as well. Some of our friends gave us money to help out with recording costs, and we raised $200 of the approximate $1200 total cost at a benefit show in Phil's basement.

After the record was finished, we began selling it for 3 dollars. We got some airplay on the University of Connecticut's radio station, WHUS, and the 7-incher was reviewed in such nation-wide punk publications as *Maximum Rock 'n' Roll* and *Heart Attack*. Unfortunately, there were some disputes over creative differences and Phil left the band in August.

Since then, we have made plans to co-release another record with a band called Highway 66, and we have hopes of touring the country in the summer of 1995. ■

This "Close-Up" was written by David Eastwood in collaboration with Tom Breen, Manchester High School.

impact does your recording have on you as an individual and on society in general?

Create Your Own Media

Even if you don't have access to multiple cassette machines and CD players, you can create original recordings. One possibility is

MEDIA LAB

Recordings

- Collect a few album and concert reviews from your local newspaper and identify "I statements" and "recording statements" from each review. Which of the criteria of evaluation discussed in this chapter did the reviewer use? If you have a student newspaper, write a review of a new CD and submit it for publication.

- Research the current state of warning label stickering in your area. What percentage of the CDs at your local music store are stickered? How do the store managers feel about stickering? What effect do they think stickering has on their sales?

- Conduct an analysis of conventions by genre. Locate and study representative songs from four or five major genres of popular music and identify conventions common to all and any unconventional patterns unique to each.

- Research the influences of an artist of your choice. With what genre is the artist most closely associated? Who were the influential artists in that genre 20 years ago? What musicians did your artist listen to during his or her early period of musical development?

- Research the current status of musical recordings on the Internet and on-line services.

to record a musical **montage** in which you combine many segments from a variety of songs into one new song. For example, you might find 10 songs from several genres which deal with a particular theme in their lyrics, or take songs with two contrasting themes (love and violence) and interweave them. Another idea for organizing a recording can be to illustrate the origins of a song—or even an entire genre of music. For example, many classic blues tunes made popular in the 1970s by bands such as The Allman Brothers were originally written and recorded in the 1930s, and guitar "greats" such as Eric Clapton still record them today.

You can edit together recordings of different versions of the same song. If you have access to multitrack recording or even dual tape decks, you can experiment with overdubbing and fading. You may want to refer to some of the many books on basic recording techniques to help you get started.

left to right: ryan price (drums), dave eastwood (bass, backing vocals, lead vocals on *), phil deslippe (trumpet), and jon christopher (guitar, lead vocals)

side one:
everyday life.
plum blossom fists.

side two:
empty cupboards.
scattered.*

youth power records number one
printed on recycled paper
This record was sold to distributers for a low wholesale rate. If you are paying more than three dollars for this record you are being ripped off.

YOUTH POWER Records
c/o Philip Deslippe
Post Office Box 3923
Manchester, Connecticut
06045-3923

Shown above is the record sleeve for *everyday life,* recorded by steadfast. *Courtesy of David Eastwood.*

Career Bank

Following are just a few of the many careers available in the recording (music) industry:

- recording artist (singer, musician)
- production assistant/studio worker
- recording engineer
- audio control technician
- field technician (portable set-up)
- business manager/agent
- sound mixer
- music publisher/distributor

Recap

The popularity of recorded music grew steadily through the twentieth century as new technologies improved the **fidelity** of the music and made using recorded music easier.

The **lyrics** of pop music have always raised the eyebrows of older generations. However, the lyrical content of metal, rap, punk, and other genres has caused enough concern since the mid-1980s that states have considered laws urging or even requiring recordings with particularly explicit lyrics to be labeled with a parental advisory.

The process of producing a professional musical recording is quite similar to the process of producing a film. There are distinct phases of **preproduction, production,** and **postproduction**.

Many conventions are followed by artists and producers. Artists usually write according to familiar patterns of songwriting, while producers usually **mix** the musical elements according to industry standards.

It is as tempting to make "I statements" about music as about movies. There are criteria, however, that you can apply in evaluating why you like or dislike a musical recording.

The recording industry is one of the most competitive media industries because so many young artists are trying to break in. Even dedicated artists wind up making little or no money most of the time.

Understanding how a recording is produced—being media literate—can make the consumer a better, more critical listener. *Photo: Bradley Wilson,*

Interactive CD-ROM, also known as CD-I, is where many see the future of recorded music heading. In addition to listening to the recording, you'll be able to customize variations of each cut and experience a coordinated visual experience along with the music.

Resources for Further Reading
Books

Everest, F. Alton. *The New Stereo Handbook.* Blue Ridge, Penn.: TAB Books, 1992.

Gaar, Gillian G. *She's a Rebel: The History of Women in Rock & Roll.* Seattle, Wash.: Seal Press, 1982.

Musician magazine. *The Rock Musician: 15 Years of Interviews—The Best of Musician Magazine.* New York: St. Martins Press, 1994.

Nelson, Havelock. *Bring the Noise: A Guide to Rap Music and Hip Hop Culture.* New York: Harmony Books, 1991.

Owens, Joe. *Welcome to the Jungle: A Practical Guide to Today's Music Business.* New York: Harper Perennial, 1992.

Rapaport, Diane. *How to Make and Sell Your Own Recordings: A Guide for the '90s.* Englewood Cliffs, N.J.: Prentice Hall, 1992.

Ross, Andrew, ed. *Microphone Friends: Youth Music, Youth Culture.* New York: Routledge, 1994.

White, Timothy. *Rock Lives: Profiles and Interviews.* New York: Henry Holt, 1990.

Industry Publications and Magazines

AXcess, Box 9309, San Diego, CA 92169

Billboard Magazine, One Astor Plaza, 1515 Broadway, New York, NY 10036

EQ: The Project Recording and Sound Magazine, 2 Park Ave., New York, NY 10036

Mix Magazine, 6400 Holis St. #12, Emoryville, CA 94608

Rolling Stone Magazine, 1290 Avenue of the Americas, New York, NY 10104

The Source: The Magazine of Hiphop Music, Culture and Politics, 594 Broadway, Suite 510, New York, NY 10012

SPIN, Box 420193, Palm Coast, FL 32142

Urb: Music, Clubs and Modern Primitive Culture, 1680 N. Vine St., Suite 1012, Los Angeles, CA 90028

Vibe, Box 59580, Boulder, CO 80323

Key word database searches for library research on musical recordings:

Rock and roll, hiphop, rap, fusion, house, dance, metal, punk, classic rock, recording studios, CD-ROM, PMRC (Parent's Music Resource Council), CD, DAT, sampling, charts

SEGUE

Music and Recordings

The first four mass media you have looked at so far have not relied directly on advertising for their funding. The money you pay for your books, comics, movie tickets, and musical recordings covers most of the cost of producing these media products. The rest of the media you will look at do rely on the advertising. Though many of the same Media Literacy concepts apply to understanding these media, the presence of advertising in the product changes how we experience them. It also changes how those media businesses operate. The next chapter takes a break from examining a specific medium, and instead looks at the economics and politics of mass media. Who owns the major media companies? Who regulates what they can do? You may be surprised.

CHAPTER EIGHT

Media Power: Economics, Regulation, and Ownership

Learning Targets

After working through this chapter, you will be able to

- Explain the basic economic structure of mass media in the United States;
- Explain how mass media are regulated by the government and by consumers;
- Explain the trend toward concentration of ownership in media industries; and
- Research the ownership of media products in your Media Archive.

Checking In

- Where do media companies get the money to produce their products?
- Who do you think decides what can be printed or broadcast in mass media?
- In the United States, we prevent the government from owning and controlling the content of mass media. Why?
- Which is better for society: many independently owned media companies expressing multiple points of view or a few media conglomerates expressing similar views?

The Economics of Mass Media
The Bottom Line: Profits

The eight mass media discussed in this book, as well as the two media-based industries—the news media and advertising, share one common goal: to make money. Because our economic system is based on free enterprise—**capitalism**—if a privately owned company does not make a profit, it will eventually go out of business. (Government-owned businesses, such as the postal service, can continue operating whether they make a profit or not.) As a result, media companies, like all companies, try to earn maximum profit; they do this by seeking the widest possible audience for their media products. What will make you want to buy one CD, newspaper, or book over another? Why do you watch a particular TV show or go to a certain movie? Media companies are locked in a never-ending pursuit of answers to these questions, and in their

251

pursuit they spend mind-boggling amounts of money. They engage in fierce competition with each other—often buying each other in order to reduce competition.

No Ads Needed

With the exception of some comic books, the media you have looked at so far do not contain advertisements *directly* in their products. (You'll discover, though, in Chapter Fourteen, that product placement in films is becoming more common: A company pays the film's producer to use its product in the film. Also, an increasing number of books and CDs contain advertising material on their inside covers or liner notes.) Books, comics, recordings, and films make most of their money through direct sales to the public. Companies make additional money when they sell or license the rights to their products to other media companies. For example, a comics publisher might license the rights to one of its characters to a movie company for a flat fee or, more likely, for a percentage of the profit the movie earns. In the case of recordings, record companies usually make a small amount of money each time a song is played on the air. Likewise, a film company makes money every time it sells the rights to air one of its films on television.

"Ads R Us": The American Way

The media you will examine in the rest of this book depend on advertising as their primary source of money. The importance of this fact is almost impossible to overestimate. Why? Because in our economic system, the media-advertising formula goes like this: The more people who see an ad in a particular media product, such as a newspaper or TV show, the more the media company can charge the advertiser to run its ad in that media product. Therefore, media companies try to produce media products with the widest possible appeal to obtain the largest possible audience, so they can charge advertisers the most money. The more people who watch your network, read your magazine or newspaper, or listen to your radio station, the more money in your pocket. The profit motive is the American way, but what is the effect of this formula?

The Power of Advertising Dollars

If your economic life depended on 20 companies that paid you to run ads for their products in your magazine, would you say those companies had some influence over you?

Consider how the following scenario illustrates the economic influence of advertising in newspapers: The AutoPrice Company attempts to buy ads in major newspapers and magazines. AutoPrice supplies customers with a computer printout of dealer costs, including options, on any new car. The company also supplies the name of a local automobile dealer who, through a special arrangement, will sell the customer the car for about $150 above dealer cost. The company charges the consumer $5 for this service, which is legitimate and helpful to consumers. However, when AutoPrice attempts to run a small ad, they are refused by most newspapers as well as by some magazines. The ads are refused without a detailed explanation. The newspapers claim they have a right to turn down any advertising—which is true. The reason for the refusal most certainly is related to the fact that automotive ads are an important source of income for newspapers and magazines. The AutoPrice Company would not be approved by other auto advertisers.

As another example, advertisers are not likely to buy time for programs that attack business or address a volatile topic. Eastman Kodak previews all scripts before the airing of a program; their policy is, "If we find a script is offensive, we will withdraw our commercials from the program." Although advertisers have no formal censorship power, they can exert great influence on the kinds of programs that networks offer the viewers. A TV network would think twice before showing a documentary exposing the faults of the over-the-counter drug industry because so much of the network's advertising revenue comes from painkillers and headache remedies. A central question asked at networks is, "Will the show bring in advertisers?"

Newspapers and magazines vary widely in the amount of control they allow advertisers to exert. Some keep news and advertisements completely separate and report the problems and failings of local food chains or auto dealers even though these provide the paper with thousands of dollars yearly in advertising revenue. Some newspapers, however, still have a policy of "not biting the hand that feeds them." If the health department closes or issues a warning to a local food store or restaurant, such papers will ignore the story for fear of hurting the advertiser's reputation. A story about a shady car dealer or home builder might go unreported if that

Nielsen Media Research uses "people meters" to measure TV viewership habits, placing them in randomly-selected homes to monitor television usage by household members. *Photo © Nielsen Media Research.*

company is a large advertiser in the newspaper. Such control is less frequent now than it used to be, but it still exists, especially among smaller newspapers struggling to stay in business.

The Public's Role in the Economic Life of Media

The most common kind of economic control over mass media is the one most often overlooked—control by the audience. If not enough people consume a media product dependent on advertising, the advertisers take their ads elsewhere. If few people watch a TV show, it dies. If only a few hundred people subscribe to a city newspaper, it stops publishing. The media consumer influences the content of all media by selecting which programs to watch, which magazines to subscribe to, which books or records to buy, which newspapers to read, and which radio stations to listen to. Even in the non-ad-dependent media, consumer choice has a major impact. Each decision to use a media product can be thought of as a vote approving that product's content. The owners of any media outlet keep a constant record of the size and type of audience they attract. The number of units sold is the main measurement for magazines, books, comics, newspapers, records, and films. The television and radio inducstries must rely on estimates of audience numbers called **ratings,** determined by media research companies such as Nielsen.

Government Regulation of Mass Media
Freedom of Speech and of the Press

In one sentence of the Bill of Rights is found the most significant statement about the U.S. government and the media. The First Amendment to the U.S. Constitution says: "Congress shall make no law . . . abridging the freedom of speech, or of the press; or the right of the people peaceably to assemble. . . ."

The First Amendment does not say that anyone can say anything. It simply says that Congress shall make no law that prevents—abridges—a person's freedom to speak. One reason for the First Amendment's existence is that a democracy needs an informed electorate who can vote and make decisions. Freedom of speech and freedom of the press exist not only for the speaker or the owner of the press, but also for the audience. In other words, part of freedom of speech is the right of the people to have access to a variety of viewpoints and opinions.

Freedom of speech, like any freedom, is not absolute. No modern society has ever existed without imposing some restrictions on the press, on free speech, and on the right of the public to have information. If a newspaper owner writes and publishes a scathing attack on someone, calling him or her "a crook without morals and a danger to our society," that person could take legal actions against the publisher. An attack on another person in print (or pictures or speech) that damages his or her character or reputation and is without truth is called **libel**. A person so attacked can sue the source of the libel for damages.

Freedom of the press is a long-established tradition for newspapers in the United States and remains today a carefully guarded right. In recent years one of the questions raised concerning newspaper freedom is the right of reporters to conceal their sources of information. In several cases reporters have gone to jail rather than reveal their sources. The reporters contended that if they were forced to reveal sources, they would be less able to report the news in the future. People who would talk to reporters if they could remain unknown might remain silent if courts could force reporters to tell who they were. Such a law would hamper the flow of news to the people and would, in effect, be a restriction on the public's "right to know." On the other hand, such a privilege might place the reporters above the law and interfere with the judicial process. Some groups advocate a shield law that would protect reporters from court orders to reveal their sources; such laws exist in some places.

Freedom of Student Press Is Limited

Another issue regarding newspaper freedom concerns school papers. In the 1960s students at some colleges and high schools claimed they were being denied the constitutional right to freedom of speech and a free press. School officials argued that the school newspaper was an extension of the school and that administrators had the right of control, just as they had control over rules of discipline.

In 1969 the U.S. Supreme Court made it clear that the Bill of Rights is not for adults only. The Court clarified the First Amendment rights of students in its ruling in Tinker v. Des Moines Independent School District. The case involved three Iowa high school students, aged 13 to 16, who wore black armbands to school to protest the war in Vietnam. They were asked by school authorities to remove the armbands, but they refused and were suspended from school. The Supreme Court sided with the students and observed that wearing an armband is symbolic speech and is thereby protected by the First Amendment. More important, the court held that students are indeed persons under the Constitution and have fundamental rights that school authorities must respect. According to the ruling, the freedom of speech and freedom of the press applied to students and student publications.

In 1988, however, the Hazelwood School District v. Kuhlmeier case came before the Supreme Court. In this landmark decision, the Supreme Court ruled that administrators may exercise "editorial control over the style and content of student speech in school activities, so long as their actions are reasonably related to legitimate pedagogical concerns." This latest decision has, therefore, somewhat restricted the freedom of the press as far as student speech and school-associated student newspapers are concerned. The chart on page 258 describes how a court would determine whether a particular act of censorship by school officials is legally permissible.

Government Regulation of Broadcast Media

Electronic communications media are still relatively young. Many people alive today remember the very first radios, and the early days of television are part of the memories of many adults. Because of their relative newness, radio and television have no long tradition of First Amendment rights. The subject of broadcasting freedom is still complicated and controversial. The complications exist because the airwaves, unlike printing presses, are a limited resource. There are a limited number of television channels in each city (although the technology now exists to expand this number considerably), and even the number of radio frequencies is severely limited. In any city, the people who control the radio and TV stations could assemble easily in an average classroom. Because both television and radio are one-way communication devices, great care must be taken to assure the "free exchange of information and opinions" that so concerned Thomas Jefferson. How can the government act to ensure this free exchange without setting itself up as a dictator of what people may hear and see? This problem remains unsolved.

In many countries the government owns and completely controls all radio and TV stations. These outlets are privately owned in the United States. Anyone with a few hundred thousand dollars can own a small radio station; TV stations cost more, often in the millions. If there were no central control over broadcasting, the result would be chaos. So many broadcasters would fight for the limited amount of airspace (a handful of TV channels, 97 AM frequencies, and about 120 FM channels) that stations would interfere with each other and few people would get clear reception from any station. In the early days of radio this is precisely what did happen, as many amateurs and basement scientists set up their

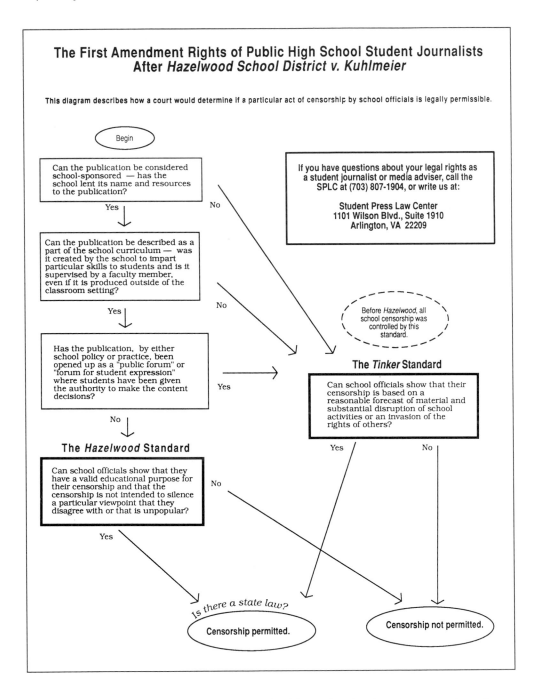

The First Amendment Rights of Public High School Student Journalists after *Hazelwood School District v. Kuhlmeier* © 1994 Student Press Law Center, 1101 Wilson Blvd., Suite 1910, Arlington, VA 22209. Reprinted by permission.

own radio stations. Confusion finally grew so great that in 1934 the Federal Communications Commission was established to regulate broadcasting.

The Federal Communications Commission (FCC)

According to U.S. law, the airwaves are owned by the people. They are a natural resource like air and water and cannot be bought or sold by individuals or corporations. The Federal Communications Commission (FCC) grants licenses to qualified groups or individuals to use the airwaves for the purpose of "serving the public good." Licenses are granted for a limited number of years and are renewed if the station can prove it has indeed served the public interest. Radio and television stations are required to ask the people in their broadcast areas for criticisms and suggestions for improvement of their programming.

The FCC has no clear laws about the broadcasting of obscenity or profanity, but the U.S. Criminal Code does. The code imposes a fine or imprisonment for material that is clearly "offensive to community standards." The FCC also requires commercials to be broadcast at the same level of sound as the surrounding program. Some TV stations have been known to turn up the volume for commercials, especially during programs shown late at night. This practice is illegal and TV stations argue that it is not done, yet many viewers report that commercials are often louder than the shows.

The Public Health Cigarette Smoking Act of 1970 forbids radio or television advertising for cigarettes and small cigars; even before Congress acted, the FCC required stations to carry commercials about the dangers of smoking. No laws exist to prevent the advertising of alcohol on television, but broadcasters limit commercials to beer and wine and do not advertise hard liquor such as whiskey. Advertisers and broadcast stations themselves control the number of commercials per hour and their content.

Deregulation: A Legacy of the 1980s

A major trend of the 1980s was **deregulation**, a loosening of media control. Ronald Reagan's presidency brought a general wave of decreased government control. The concept behind broadcast regulation in the United States before the Reagan presidency was that broadcasters were public servants entrusted with the airwaves. The airwaves were considered to be owned by the people. The government regulated television and radio stations to be sure they served the public good. Stations were required to devote time to public service programs and to serve local communities. Station owners were required to own a station for at least three years before selling it; this rule was intended to discourage quick buying and selling simply for fast profit.

Since deregulation, rules still exist, but they are far less demanding of station owners. The marketplace now exerts its own controls. Government during the Reagan years followed a hands-off policy toward broadcasters. The Fairness Doctrine, instituted in 1959 by the FCC to ensure that radio and television programs present all sides of an issue and avoid slanted news, was dismantled in 1987. In 1988, the U.S. Congress passed a bill to limit advertising during children's programming to 10.5 minutes an hour on weekends and 12 minutes on weekdays. The bill also required broadcasters to provide educational programming for kids in order to ensure license renewal. However, the bill was vetoed by President Reagan at the end of his second term and did not become law. During the 1990s, the media have been encouraged to regulate themselves, especially in terms of children's programming.

Government Regulation of Advertising

Advertising in the United States is not as strictly controlled by the government as it is in other countries. In some European countries an unfair competition law prohibits advertisers from using the "water is wet" technique in which a product boasts of a quality common to all similar products, such as "our hand lotion moisturizes your skin." Some laws also forbid acts that might lead to a wrong conclusion. Even "so what" techniques, such as the claim that "our margarine is packed by hand," are forbidden under these laws, because packing margarine by hand gives it no extra advantage. In Sweden the "truth-and-nothing-but-the-truth" Market Practices Act gives the government strict control to ensure that ads are scrupulously honest.

In the United States the federal agency charged with some degree of advertising regulation is the Federal Trade Commission (FTC). The FTC has limited power but reserves the right to take court action and order advertisers to stop what it considers deceptive advertising. The advertiser usually agrees to "sin no more"; if violations continue, the FTC can assess a civil penalty of up to $10,000 per day. In recent years, the FTC has become less strict with advertisers, but has levied penalties and has even required a few advertisers to run corrective ads to make up for misleading claims made in their past advertising.

The FCC forbids **subliminal advertising**. *Subliminal* means "below the level of consciousness." The most common subliminal technique is to flash one or two frames of film on a screen during a movie. The frame might say something like "Drink Fizzle." It would pass so fast that no one in the audience would be aware of having seen the message. Some psychologists believe that such a message still registers in the brain in spite of its invisibility. Even though no evidence exists to show that so-called subliminal advertising works, it is banned by the FCC.

Industry Self-Regulation

All mass media regulate themselves in some way. Newspapers can print only the news delivered to them or that their reporters cover. Television programs and films are controlled by their producers and directors; magazine articles are subject to the complete control of editors, writers, and publishers. As media content passes through these hands, it is influenced by normal human biases and perceptions.

Each medium has within it people who act as censors, although the word *censor* is rarely used. No magazine or book publisher has an official censor as an employee, yet the gatekeepers—all those who pass judgment on the suitability of printed material and photos—act in their own way as censors. Motion picture production is subject to several levels of censorship. The scriptwriter, the director, and the producer of a film control its contents so as not to produce a film that too many people will find offensive. Their consideration in censorship is not so much to protect the public morals as it is to foster a good box office performance.

Film Ratings

In the 1960s, the National Association of Theatre Owners found that many parents were hesitant to allow their children to go to movies because they had no way of knowing whether the film was suitable, so in 1968 the association's Rating Board established a rating system.

This system is voluntary and does not in itself carry the force of law; it is designed so that the parents or guardians bear the decision-making. However, many theaters interpret these ratings strictly, and many require proof of age for admission. The ratings are G, all ages admitted; PG, parental guidance suggested; PG-13, all ages admitted, but parents are urged to give special guidance to children under age 13; R, restricted, persons under age 17 not admitted unless accompanied by a parent or adult guardian; and NC-17, no children under 17 admitted. The former X rating, dropped in 1990, meant no persons under 18 admitted. Many theaters interpret these ratings very strictly and demand proof of age for admission to R- or NC-17-rated films. The rating system is referred to as the motion picture Code of Self-Regulation.

Broadcast Standards

Each of the major television networks has a standards department that watches commercials and programs for scenes or words that might offend viewers. Feature films are often edited for television to remove some of the violence, sex, or foul language in the original version. Local television stations also have the right to refuse network programs, although they rarely do. The reason for television's self-censorship is that the medium is public, open to anyone who turns on a TV set, including young children.

Radio stations often refuse to play songs the station director believes have double meanings, encourage drug use, are unpatriotic, or are in bad taste in some way. During listener call-in shows, many radio stations use a seven-second delay system. With such a system, callers speak to a tape recorder that plays their calls over the air several seconds later. This delay is introduced so the program director can "bleep" out offensive words or cut off possibly libelous remarks.

The Recording Industry's Approach

The recording industry has responded to pressure from parent groups, record retailers, and state legislators by instituting a voluntary uniform parental warning label program (see Chapter Seven). Labels are affixed to records, cassettes, and compact discs containing possibly objectional lyrics. The voluntary use of the label is at the discretion of the record companies and individual artists. The Recording Industry Association of America (RIAA), a trade association whose members produce 90 percent of the records sold in the United States, hopes this voluntary control measure will eliminate the possibility of government action—that is, legislation requiring such labeling.

The Owners of Mass Media

Freedom of speech and of the press exists to promote a free exchange of information and opinions. According to Thomas Jefferson, one of the writers of the U.S. Constitution, the public interest would be best served by a society in which there were numerous newspapers free to express themselves without fear of government censorship. The citizens would have to make up their own minds and would be able to do so because they were able to consider the various viewpoints on important public issues. Citizens could also use these newspapers and pamphlets to make known their own views.

In 1787, however, Thomas Jefferson and the others at the Constitutional Convention could not foresee the invention of electronic and mass media. They could not realize that today major cities would have a free press controlled financially by only a handful of individuals. They could not foresee that printing a newspaper would become a multimillion-dollar industry or that there would be a device such as television that gives citizens very little opportunity to talk back.

The number of independently owned newspapers in the United States has dropped dramatically in the last 50 years. Small and medium-sized papers have either been bought by large newspaper chains or have gone out of business—often because they cannot compete with the larger papers. The newspaper business is not the only media industry affected by this kind of competition.

Media Monopolies

In the 1993 edition of *The Media Monopoly*, journalist Ben Bagdikian describes a disturbing trend: Fewer media companies are controlling more of the media products produced in the United States than ever before; because U.S. media companies control the majority of globally distributed entertainment, these few corporations are actually global companies. Bagdikian rightly points out that Americans would scorn the idea of their government controlling newspapers, television, and other media. Such government control of the media may be acceptable in China and other totalitarian countries, but not in the United States. Why? Because with government control of the media, everything we saw or listened to or read would pass through a filter of governmental approval. The chance to hear and see alternative points of view on fundamental issues would be greatly reduced—if not eliminated altogether.

Yet this tightening of control over media—and the restriction of perspectives such control brings about—is happening in front of our eyes. A handful of global media companies is doing the controlling, and it is their perspective of corporate values through which the media we consume are filtered. Here is how Bagdikian describes this new era of media ownership in *The Media Monopoly:*

> Today, the chief executive officers of the twenty-three corporations that control most of what Americans read and see can fit into an ordinary living room. They can, if they wish, use control of their newspapers, broadcast stations, magazines, books and movies to promote their own corporate values to the exclusion of others. . . .
> It is possible that large corporations are gaining control of the American media because the public wants it that way. But there is another possibility: the public, almost totally dependent on the media for such things, has seldom seen in their newspapers, magazines, or broadcasts anything to suggest the political and economic dangers of concentrated corporate control. . . .
> The new global giants are doing more than expanding their control over the technological instruments that issue news, information and entertainment. They and their subsidiaries are also gathering up world copyrights of earlier information and popular culture: archives of news magazines, books, television programs, film libraries, and musical compositions. Much of what used to be free in libraries or inexpensive for the average consumer is rapidly growing in cost, thanks to exclusive corporate own-

ership. Examples include important statistics now in data banks available only for a fee or scholarly journals with greatly increased subscription costs.

The big firms describe their goals in terms that sound benign but, in the hands of monopolists, conceal a threat to freedom and diversity of information. For example, the giants aim for "market share," which every business wishes to increase. But once one or a few companies dominate a substantial part of any market, whether it is in detergents or news, they have wide latitude in setting prices and altering the product without fear of significant competition. In this case, "market" is the world, and "product" is the news, information, and popular culture for much of the human race.

They aim for maximum "synergism," a popular word in the corporate world. In biology this term describes two entities whose interactions produce something greater than the sum of their two parts. In the mass media it describes how one medium can be used to promote the same idea, product, celebrity, or politician in another medium, both owned by the same corporation. Each of the new global giants aims for control of as many different media as possible: news, magazines, radio, television, books, motion pictures, cable systems, satellite channels, recordings, videocassettes, and chains of movie theaters.

In their fondest scenario, a magazine owned by the company selects or commissions an article that is suitable for later transformation into a television series on a network owned by the company; then it becomes a screenplay for a movie studio owned by the company, with the movie sound track sung by a vocalist made popular by feature articles in the company-owned magazines and by constant playing of the sound track by company-owned radio stations, after which the songs become popular on a record label owned by the company and so on, with reruns on company cable systems and rentals of its videocassettes all over the world.

Contrary to the diversity that comes with a large number of small, separate media competitors under true free enterprise, dominant giant firms that command the nature of

the business produce an increasingly similar output.
The greater the dominance of a few firms, the more uniformity in what each of them produces. . . . Independent
and smaller voices will always exist and continue to be
important, but the growing power of the major voices
makes small voices even smaller. If small media firms
should grow large enough to be a threat, it is the easy
and common practice of the giants to use their economic
power to buy up the new voices or undercut them
economically.

Corporate Coziness

Bagdikian also describes a very common practice in the world of
high-powered corporate America: the **interlocking** of key personnel between companies. All major corporations have a board of
directors which usually includes the chief executive officer (CEO)
and about 15 to 20 directors. These directors are responsible for
overseeing the major philosophy and economic health of their
companies. Interlocking refers to the common practice of having
members of a company's board of directors also serving on the
board of directors of another company. In recent years, for example, the *New York Times*—considered to be the most influential
newspaper in America—has had on its board of directors men who
were also serving at the same time on the boards of Bristol Myers,
Johns Manville, American Express, IBM, Scott Paper, and First
Boston Corporation.

What is the result of this insider network of mutual influence?
According to Bagdikian, it becomes that much easier for corporations "to influence the news, to avoid embarrassing publicity,
and to maximize sympathetic public opinion and government
policies."

Time Warner: The Biggest of All

Time Warner came into being in 1990 when Time, Inc. and Warner
Brothers Entertainment merged. Time Warner's 1993 Annual
Report indicates that Time Warner, within five divisions, owns the
following mass media:

PUBLISHING DIVISION

Time, Inc.

Magazines:

Time, Life, Fortune, Sports Illustrated, Money, People, Entertainment Weekly, Parenting, Martha Stewart Living, Vibe, and 14 other magazines

Publishing

Book-of-the-Month Club; Time Life, Inc.; Little Brown; Warner Books; Oxmoor House Publishing; Sunset Books

DC Comics

Licensed titles include "Superman," "Flash," and "Batman"; second largest comics publisher, with about 22 percent of the U.S. comics market

Warner Brothers Worldwide Publishing

Licensed the rights to Warner Brothers films to other publishers who create "movie tie-ins"—the paperback books published in conjunction with a big-budget movie release

MUSIC DIVISION

Warner Brothers Records

Warner Bros., Reprise, Giant, Maverick, Qwest, Sire, Warner Nashville, American Recordings, Slash, Tommy Boy

Atlantic Recording Group

Atlantic, EastWest America, Interscope, A*Vision, Rhino, Select, Big Beat, Mammoth, Matador

Elektra Entertainment

Elektra, Asylum, Nonesuch, Mute

Warner Music International

16 international recording companies around the world

FILM ENTERTAINMENT DIVISION

Warner Brothers Studio

1993 Films (partial list): *Dave, Free Willy, Dennis the Menace, The Fugitive, Demolition Man, The Pelican Brief, Grumpy Old Men*
1994 Films (partial list): *Ace Ventura, Major League II, Maverick, Wyatt Earp, The Client, Natural Born Killers, The Specialist, Interview with the Vampire*

Warner Home Video

World's largest library of new and old Warner-produced and purchased films

Warner Brothers Television Production

Some of the shows produced by WBTP include "Family Matters," "Full House," "Lois and Clark: The New Adventures of Superman," "Murphy Brown," "Animaniacs," "Love Connection," "Jane Whitney," "Jenny Jones," and "The John Larroquette Show"

Home Box Office and Cinemax

Cable and satellite-distributed channels to 25 million subscribers offering theatrical and original films, sports and comedy programming, and special event programming

CABLE TELEVISION

Time Warner Cable

The second largest owner and operator of cable TV systems in the country, with 7.5 million subscribers

THEME PARKS

Six Flags Theme Parks

With seven parks, Six Flags is the largest regional theme park company in the country. Time Warner's 1993 Annual Reports states that Six Flags "... provides a unique, family-oriented venue to market and merchandise Time Warner's many familiar brands and franchises."

In addition to owning the media companies just described, Time Warner, as of 1993, holds stock in the following:

Turner Broadcasting System (owner of CNN, Superstation TBS, and the Cartoon network)

Courtroom Television Network (Court TV), which is managed by a Time Warner company called American Lawyer Media

Comedy Central

E! Entertainment TV

The Sega Channel, a video game pay-television channel

Black Entertainment Television (BET)
3DO Company, maker of interactive multimedia technology
Atari Corporation, video game manufacturer

Reflections

In his classic novel *1984*, George Orwell described a society in which
the government controlled the actions of its citizens with the help
of ever-present mass media. Even the society's collective thoughts were
controlled by the government, which had the power of mass media at its
disposal. In response to the novel (or the film if you haven't read the
book), draw up a list of similarities and differences between the government's use of media in the novel and corporate America's use of media
in contemporary society.

Future Watch: Profit and Privacy in the Interactive Age

Among the many issues facing the world in the coming era of the
interactive information superhighway, two stand out as crucial:
regulation and privacy. How should the information highway be
regulated? Who will create the regulations? Who will enforce them?
How will advertising be implemented on the highway? Will limits
be placed on advertising? Will there be regulations on who can
own territory and equipment on the information highway?

How will privacy be guaranteed? The electronic theft of cellular
phone numbers is already a huge criminal enterprise. If we will be
doing our banking, mail, and catalog purchasing over this giant
network of computers called the information highway, how will
the privacy of our communications be protected? Who will want
access to our communication? Many organizations already are
researching these issues and making recommendations to the federal government. However, giant media monopolies are also spending billions of dollars to get an ownership foothold in this new
era and have extensive designs on how to use the information
highway for profit.

Regulation and privacy are two concerns that society and travelers on the information highway cannot ignore. *Photo: Bradley Wilson.*

Should government set aside at least a portion of the information highway as nonprofit, for educational and medical institutions to exchange information freely? Will there be universal access to the information highway, so everyone can benefit from its potential to enhance communication? Will it be just the latest megamedium for existing media monopolies to conquer? This is one debate about which you should definitely stay informed.

Building Your Media Archive

Pick two or three of the media products in your archive and research who owns the companies that produced them. Are they independently owned? Are they part of a larger company? If so, what company? Where do most of the profits of each company come from? Write for the annual report of the company (and any parent company that may own it).

MEDIA LAB   Free Speech

- Research the government's 1970 decision to ban cigarette advertising from radio and TV. How did proponents of the ban defend against claims that the law infringed on the free speech rights of cigarette companies? What was the economic impact on TV stations?
- Research the Freedom of Information Act (FOIA) and its relationship to the First Amendment guaranteeing freedom of the press and freedom of speech.
- Conduct a debate on the following proposition: Even though they are blamed for producing "trash" (such as movie bloodfests and tabloid TV shows), the media are only giving people what they want; if people didn't want trash, they wouldn't watch it, and thus the media wouldn't produce it.

Recap

Mass media, like most industries in the United States, are based on **capitalism**. This means that to stay in business, media companies need to earn profits, and they do so in two ways. Books, comics, movies, and recordings earn most of their money when purchased by the consumer. Newspapers, magazines, and radio and television stations rely on the money they earn when advertisers place ads in their pages or programs.

Other than broadcasting and advertising regulations, the federal government exercises little control over mass media. Newspaper, magazine, and book publishers are subject to U.S. laws, but there are few specific regulations or controls limiting what they can print.

The trend in all media industries is for fewer and fewer giant companies to control the production and distribution of more and more media products. Many observers see this as dangerous because fewer owners means the public will be exposed to fewer points of view. Independent and alternative perspectives in the arts and in public policy debates are less and less available to the general public.

Resources for Further Reading

Books

Bagdikian, Ben. *The Media Monopoly*, 4th Edition. Boston: Beacon Press, 1993.

Jamieson, Kathleen Hall. *The Interplay of Influence: News, Advertising, Politics, and the Mass Media*. Belmont, Calif.: Wadsworth, 1992.

Marsh, Dave. *Fifty Ways to Fight Censorship*. New York: Thunder's Mouth Press, 1991.

Publications and Magazines

Center for the Study of Commercialism Newsletter, 1875 Connecticut Ave. N.W., Suite 300, Washington, DC 20009

Media Culture Review, 77 Federal St., San Francisco, CA 94107

Utne Reader, 1624 Harmon Pl., Minneapolis, MN 55403

Wired Magazine, 520 Third Ave., 4th Fl., San Francisco, CA 94107

Key word database searches for library research on the economics, regulation, and ownership of mass media:

Advertising, FCC, FTC, media ownership

Films about the Economics, Regulation, and Ownership of Mass Media

Broadcast News
Citizen Kane
The Paper

SEGUE

Media Power: Economics, Regulation, and Ownership

The next four media you will examine rely on advertising dollars to stay in business. As a result they are more closely tied to our consumer culture. These are the media through which we hear about new CD releases, get information on clothing bargains, and shop for new brands of pain relievers. Through these media we are targeted by advertisers who manufacture just about everything we own— or want to own. In our economic system of capitalism, these media are used as tools to sell us everything from toothpaste (and sex appeal) to tires (and peace of mind). If a media product is entertaining enough, we will consume it—and advertisers will pay its producer well for delivering our ears and eyes.

In addition to being entertaining, newspapers also have a more serious purpose. A newspaper serves as a kind of community archive where the life of a town is explored and documented. Besides all those ads, what is in a newspaper anyway?

CHAPTER NINE

Newspapers

Learning Targets

After working through this chapter, you will be able to

- Conduct a content analysis of a local newspaper by categorizing advertising and editorial content;
- Present an overview of the newspaper industry;
- Chart the basic organizational structure of a mid-sized daily newspaper; and
- Apply the Media Literacy Paradigm to the newspaper in your Media Archive.

Checking In

- How much of your community's daily newspaper do you think is taken up by advertisements?
- How does your local paper get the news it reports?
- What is your favorite section of the newspaper and why?
- What qualities do you think it takes to be a good reporter?
- Write three topics you would like to learn about newspapers.

What's in a Newspaper?

Advertising

Two basic types of content form an American newspaper: advertising and editorial. The advertising portion is made up of **display ads** for stores, products, and services, and **classified ads**, such as job openings, personals, and real estate listings. Of all the mass media that rely on advertising, newspapers present the most ads providing straight information. Where and when something is on sale and how much it costs are the most common kinds of information provided.

According to the May 1994 Standard and Poor's *Industry Survey*, ads take up 60 percent of the space in a typical American daily newspaper; in 1994, advertisers spent an estimated 33.7 billion dollars filling that space. By comparison, newspapers brought in about 9 billion dollars from the cost of subscriptions and single-copy purchases. Advertising keeps newspapers in business. When newspapers are produced each night, the ads are the first items to be placed on the pages. Whatever room remains on a page is filled with editorial content. This 40 percent left over is often called the news hole.

Editorial Content

The 40 percent of space left after ads are placed is filled with a variety of writing, photos, and graphics, all of which are referred to as editorial content because the editors of the paper have control over them. The editorial content is divided into sections or departments. All dailies have a section for national, local, and state news. The events and issues covered in this section constitute what is called **hard news,** and it makes up less than half of the editorial content. Almost every daily paper has a sports section. Most have a "living" section in which the comics and advice columns are found, and a business or money section as well. Some larger papers include sections on food, travel, science, and other interest areas, though these sections usually appear once a week. These sections present **soft news.**

In addition to the sections just listed, all daily newspapers have at least one page for editorials, opinion pieces, and letters. The **editorial** is the place where the editors of the paper take a position on a national or local issue of the day. For example, this is where newspapers endorse particular candidates for political office or argue against a proposed law. **Opinion pieces** are usually written by local or national experts or by **syndicated columnists** who appear in the paper regularly. Publishing letters from readers is an important tradition dating back to the beginning of newspapers about 200 years ago. Born in the context of the American Revolution, the newspaper industry has long served as a forum for public expression. Although newspaper ownership is far more centralized now than ever before, publishing letters to the editor is still a major function.

Photographs: Capturing the Moment

The importance of photographs to newspapers is often overlooked. However, photos often decide whether a story gets read or not. An interesting photograph will hook a reader into the story—a reader who otherwise might not have responded to its headline.

Beyond bringing the reader to the article, a good photo tells its own story. Because a photo is a high-correspondence (high-C) symbol, it affects the reader differently than the words of the article. Photos instantly convey the emotion of an event, whereas the writer's words tend to fill out the context of the event.

Interesting photographs may be used by themselves with a brief **caption** below explaining the gist of the photo. These photos are often of the human interest variety, such as an ice cream-splattered toddler on a 105-degree day. Photos present serious subjects as well. Serious photos frequently evoke the strongest reactions from readers. In October 1994 hundreds of newspapers ran a wire service photo of a Haitian man at the moment he was being shot. The photo showed an extended arm with a gun pointing at the man lying in a corner of a building. The photo caption described how the man who was being shot had been chased and cornered, just prior to the reinstatement of Haiti's exiled President Aristide on October 15, 1994. Many newspapers received complaints for running a photo that was *too* dramatic. However, the newsphoto worked: it got readers' attention and conveyed the visual truth about a tragic situation.

Sources of Editorial Content

Wire or news/newsphoto services, such as The Associated Press, Reuters, and Copley News Service, are large companies that employ reporters, editors, and photographers to cover national and international news. The services then send their reports (wire service bulletins) and photos to daily newspapers that do not have their own news/newsphoto agencies. The term **wire service** refers to transmission by telegraph or telephone wire; today, transmission is often done via satellite.

Local News

Each newspaper needs its own reporters, especially to handle local events that the national news services will not cover. Reporters are either part of a general reporters pool assigned to stories as they break, or are given regular beats, such as city hall, high school sports, the police, or the state legislature. A small paper, of course, has only a few reporters to cover everything.

Newspapers generally use their own photographers to supply photos for local stories. *Hartford Courant* photographer Stephen Dunn is seen here writing a caption for one of his photos. He scanned it on a Kodak RFS2035 film scanner and used Adobe Photoshop™ to process the photo for future publication. At the *Courant* office, all black-and-white photos are scanned and filed. Later, an editor will size the photo. Computers and scanners are replacing darkrooms in newspaper offices all over the world. *Photo by John Long,* The Hartford Courant, *Hartford, Connecticut. Reprinted by permission.*

Reporters write their own stories, which are then subject to rewrite by various editors. For a last-minute important story, a reporter may phone the information directly to the paper, where a rewrite editor takes it down and hurries it into an acceptable form for the paper.

A reporter covering a story never knows whether the event will be considered newsworthy enough to make the paper or how much space it will be given. For this reason, news reporters often write in what is called the "inverted pyramid style." They arrange the news item so that the essential details are all in the opening paragraph. Each paragraph thereafter is more general and less important. A good reporter writing in the pyramid style answers the questions *who, what, where, when, how,* and *why* in the first

Weather forces the space shuttle Endeavour and its astronauts to land Saturday in California instead of Florida.   Associated Press Photo

Weather reroutes shuttle to California landing

Reuters

CAPE CANAVERAL, Fla. — Dismal weather forced seven astronauts to make a detour to California Saturday after postponing their scheduled landing in Florida and establishing a record time of nearly 17 days in space.

Chased from the Kennedy Space Center by thunderstorms for the second day in a row, Endeavour swooped out of mostly sunny skies to touch down on a breeze-swept runway at Edwards Air Force Base at 3:47 p.m. Chicago time. The shuttle landed in the Mojave Desert, some 3,000 miles west of where ground crews had planned to receive it and its crew at the conclu-

sion of a marathon science journey.

"Welcome home, Endeavour, after a fantastic record-setting mission. It will be a tough one to beat, and it sure is nice to have y'all home," shuttle communicator Curt Brown radioed the crew from Mission Control in Houston.

"It's nice to be here, Curt," shuttle commander Steve Oswald radioed back from the cockpit.

The landing capped a flight of in-depth astrophysics research with the Astro Observatory, a $195 million suite of three ultraviolet telescopes tucked in the shuttle cargo bay.

Endeavour spent 16 days, 15 hours and eight minutes aloft. It circled the planet 263 times during

the mission, traveling 6.9 million miles.

The longest of all 68 shuttle missions was to have concluded Friday, but foul weather kept the crew of five men and two women in Earth orbit an extra day. The postponement pushed the flight well beyond the previous duration record of 14 days, 17 hours and 55 minutes.

Soon after touchdown, ground crews helped the astronauts out of the cockpit and began preparing the shuttle for transport back to Florida in about a week. Endeavour's cross-country trip atop a jumbo jet will cost as much as $3 million, according to National Aeronautics and Space Administration officials.

A news service, Reuters, supplied this article published on March 19, 1995. The photo was supplied by The Associated Press © 1995. Reprinted by permission.

paragraph. With this done, the news editor can fit the story into any available amount of space. A reporter might write 1,000 words on a story and have only 100 used in the paper. You can see the difference between the pyramid style and other writing styles by reading a front-page newspaper story and stopping after any paragraph—the story still seems complete. If you try this with a magazine article, the item seems incomplete and very likely lacks some essential information.

A bylined story carries the reporter's name. Most reporters are unknown to the general public and receive few bylines. The reporter's job is sometimes exciting but involves many long hours of boring meetings, writing and rewriting, and simply waiting.

Syndicated Material

Syndicates are another source of material for newspapers. Feature syndicates supply comic strips, cartoons, columns on topics from cooking to politics, and longer feature stories. Syndicates do not supply hard news. The material arrives by mail (or electronically) at the newspaper ready for printing or typesetting. Papers pay for what they use on the basis of circulation—the larger the paper's readership, or circulation, the higher the fee for using the item. Some of the larger syndicates include King Features, Universal Press Syndicate, Newspaper Enterprise Association, and United Feature Syndicate. Most syndicated material is marked with the name of the syndicate for copyright purposes.

What Fills the News Hole?

Many people read newspapers for the comics, advice columns, recipes, sports statistics, and pet tips. People also read the news for big international and national stories, such as presidential election results and outbreaks of war. However, we still think of local news when we think of a newspaper. What is covered by the reporters who work for local papers?

Newsmakers

One common reporting assignment for a local newspaper is to cover a speech, airport arrival, dedication, or whatever by a famous person—a newsmaker. This is more common in large cities than in small towns where few newsmakers appear.

Newsmakers are people who make news when they talk, marry, divorce, date, write, or do almost anything. They are celebrities—media heroes, people in the public eye. What they do may not be terribly important or newsworthy, yet it somehow ranks as news. Some newsmakers, such as the president, do things that are really news. They can also make news by doing ordinary things, such as jogging, talking to people on a street corner, or playing golf. "Pseudo" events, manufactured by an agent or public relations person, can be staged to generate news coverage of celebrities or aspiring newsmakers.

Crime and Disaster

Another common kind of local reporting covers the disaster or crime story. The story of a deadly accident, a fire, or a crime is the staple of the newspaper. Why these tragedies are so important as news is hard to understand, but they remain important to newspapers because people like to read them. The same subjects—crimes, fires, disasters—are important in novels, movies, and television programs as well as in news reporting.

Some sociologists claim that people like to read about the tragedies of other people to gain assurance that their own lives aren't so bad after all—things could be worse. Others guess that people like to read about crime and tragedy because they are exciting, something to break the ordinary and sometimes dull routine of daily life.

Investigative Reporting

There are many newspapers whose pages rarely see an investigative news report. Even the best papers can manage only a few a year. An investigative report is one that looks deeply into some situation and reveals facts not previously known. Investigative reports often reveal corruption in government or business. A newspaper might investigate the local ambulance services, for example, to look for corrupt practices, kickbacks, or hidden charges. It can check on city workers to see if the taxpayers are receiving a full day's work for a day's pay from those employees paid by tax money. A paper can investigate short-weighting and other dishonest practices in grocery stores; unsanitary conditions at restaurants and fast-food chains; housing conditions among the poor of the city; or political influences in the city school system. Such reporting takes time, money, and courage.

Investigative reporting in the early 1900s eventually resulted in the passage of the Pure Food and Drug Act when reformers and writers like Upton Sinclair described unsanitary packing houses and meats filled with waste and dirt. Ida Tarbell's investigative reporting on the Standard Oil Company in 1904 led to its breakup into smaller companies. Such reporting was once called muckraking and is still called that by some newspeople today.

Investigative reporting takes a great deal of time to do well and, unfortunately, many papers consider it a luxury. It sometimes leads to lawsuits, political pressure, threats, and loss of advertising revenues. However, investigative reporting if done *right,* represents journalism at its finest.

Practice

The reading on the next page is about a syndicated columnist. As you read, focus on how this writer's columns originate. Also, consider the impact of her columns on the readers.

Human Interest Stories

A newspaper that reported only the facts, only the world's most important events, only the actions and ploys of world leaders and criminals, might soon find itself without the large number of readers it needs to stay in business. Most newspapers include what are called human interest stories. Sometimes these are local stories written by staff reporters; other times they are provided by the wire services. Human interest stories are about non-newsmakers, about the troubles or heroics of the ordinary person. Whether tragic or humorous, they are often moving and dramatic.

Newspaper Giants As Their Own News Services

As larger papers have bought smaller ones and become newspaper giants, their parent companies have, in effect, created their own wire services. For example, as of 1993, the Gannett Company, which owns over 80 newspapers around the country, has its own news service.

An Interview with Donna Britt, Columnist, *The Washington Post*

Christopher Scanlan

In a city where politics and power brokers dominate the news, columnist Donna Britt covers a different beat. She is an investigative reporter whose assignment is the emotional landscape of modern life. "It is Donna Britt's great strength," says *Washington Post* executive editor Leonard Downie, "that she pays such careful attention to the background music of our lives. Britt hears the themes that accompany common events, and through uncommonly skillful writing entices readers to listen, too."

Britt joined the *Post* in 1989 and quickly established herself as a writer of special vision and voice with a gripping memoir about her brother who was killed by two policemen in her hometown of Gary, Ind.

She writes her twice-weekly syndicated column from the comfortable, African art-filled home in suburban Maryland that she shares with her young sons, Hamani and Darrell, and her husband, Kevin Merida, a *Washington Post* reporter. She usually types her columns on a laptop in a second-floor study where she can watch squirrels play in the trees outside. Her thinking goes on everywhere.

"I really do believe," Britt says, "that if you present any idea with enough grace and thought and sensitivity and chutzpah, that it will get printed."

CHRISTOPHER SCANLAN: In an interview with your paper after the ASNE awards were announced, you said that when you were growing up the possibility of column writing seemed so far out of reach it was not a concrete goal. Why was that?

DONNA BRITT: It's funny how much what you want is shaped by what you see, and what you can conceive as being possible for you. When I was growing up in Gary, Indiana, in the '60s and '70s, newspapers described lives that had no discernible connection to my own. I didn't see columnizing as a concrete goal, because I didn't know that was something I could do. And because the newspaper felt like such a foreign entity, I didn't identify with it. So to be in the newspaper talking about my concerns, and my life, and how I envisioned things, was out of the realm of possibility.

What was it about the paper that made it seem so foreign?

The sections that I was most interested in—the women's pages, the comics,

An Interview with Donna Britt, Columnist, *The Washington Post* (continued)

then on to news and sports—had almost no black people in them. The only time I ever saw anything about us was on crime pages or maybe in politics, because at that point, black people were becoming very powerful politically in Gary. But there was no reflection of our real, everyday lives. It was almost as if real life happened to white people, but problems happened to black people and Hispanic people and Asian people. One of the things that so impressed me about *USA Today*, my former employer, was that it made a concerted and conscious effort to be inclusive. If they ran a story about a toy fair, there was a good chance there was going to be a black kid interviewed. Or if there was a story about something that had no color, like TV show preferences, they were just as likely to show an Asian or a black person.

How do you describe what you do?

I'm a columnist at *The Washington Post*, but it's a column unlike any that you've probably read. It veers in all kinds of strange and unpredictable directions, and it's very reflective of my life and of me. I use my life and my kids and my husband and my friendships, my fears and likes and wants as being representative of those of many, many people.

Your column in today's *Post* is about black hairdos. In a column like that one, are you conscious of redressing an imbalance in coverage about the ordinary lives of black people?

I guess what I do is humanize black people. And I get lots and lots of letters from black people who appreciate seeing their plain, ordinary, everyday lives explored in much the way that white people's lives have been explored forever.

What are the wellsprings of your columns?

At some point along the way, I decided that the things that vitally interest me must vitally interest other people. Because I used to read the paper and not see anybody talking about the stuff that my friends were talking about, or that I was obsessing about. I guess it wasn't really until I got to the *Post* that I decided, "Well, I'd better start saying these things."

I will write about stuff that nobody writes about, and I don't think it's because I have any great vision, it's just those are the things that are the most interesting to me.

Maybe there really are people who care more about NAFTA than how their husband is looking at them on a certain day, or that their kid is turning 12. I'm just not one of those people.

An Interview with Donna Britt, Columnist, *The Washington Post* (continued)

I'm much more interested in the human connections. And so I write about those things. And I'm one of the only columns that I know about who will write regularly and frankly about God, because I was always sort of stunned that people can talk much more openly about their sex lives than about their spiritual lives. Lots of columns come from life. Not necessarily my life, but they come from feeling.

Why focus so much on feeling?

Feeling is at the basis of everything. When I was asked to consider becoming a full-time columnist, part of my hesitation was that I knew I could not pretend to be this dispassionate, all-knowing, authoritarian voice on high. I couldn't do that. That would be a lie.

And it is a lie, for the people who adopt that voice—and we know who they are. Their name is Legion. For me, it's like *The Godfather*. Everything is personal.

How do you report your column?

It depends. I have a column coming up on a piece that ran in the paper that talked about black kids' self-esteem. This guy wrote it based on discussions he had in his classroom. I interviewed a kid that was in the class. I interviewed teachers who taught with him. I interviewed him. So a column like that is going to be very much like any column in which you do the leg work.

If I did a column on beauty, and women feeling entrapped by the whole notion of that, I would probably talk to women I know, because it doesn't matter. You know, I don't have to call Naomi Wolfe, who wrote *The Beauty Myth*.

It's more interesting to stop some woman at my kid's day care, or someone at a mall, and just have them talk about their feelings than go to, quote, *experts*. And then there are columns on which I'm relying on me. Those are the ones where you're interviewing yourself. And I am trying to be as frank and as candid and as open as I can be. And it's a pretty scary act.

Your columns are rich in detail and they're clearly the product of great reflection and deep investigation of your feelings. Do you carry a notebook?

I need to do it all the time, but I don't. When I see something that I want to remember, I will repeat it to myself. My husband was trying to get me to do something the other day and he said, "Oh, come on, honey." And my 8-year-old looked at me and said, "You know, honey is 'please' in love language." And I said, I must remember that. In Gabriel Garcia Marquez's book, *One Hundred Years of Solitude*, he said that things were so new that they had not yet been given names. As a writer, part of the adventure is trying to see things as new, with that sort of childlike vision.

An Interview with Donna Britt, Columnist, *The Washington Post* (continued)

If you had to pick a metaphor that expressed your view of yourself, what metaphor would you use?

Alchemist. Because I try to take the small, the overlooked, the ordinary—be that an emotion, a person, an idea—and transform it.

What is the alchemist's role?

I guess I picked that because I'm just fascinated by the notion of transformation. Alchemists take a certain type of matter and transform it into something else. And you couldn't do that if the properties weren't already there.

Otherwise, you are a magician. So my hope is to let people see, through my craft, what's already there that they may not have noticed.

You were saying before that it's difficult to talk about how you produce your column. Why is that?

Because there doesn't seem to be any rhyme or reason to it. Sometimes it's like having a child. You know, you have all these assumptions. It's going to be this or that. And it comes out and it's your Uncle Harold. I don't know what it's like for other people, but I almost never write a column that turns out exactly the way I would have predicted.

Well, what if a camera were trained on you while you're writing your column? What would it show?

It would show me writing really fast, getting stuff down, and stopping and looking at it, and thinking, Can I say this better? Can I be more direct? Can I make this tighter? Can I clarify this point? Is this insensitive? Is this funny? What can I do to make it jump off the page? What's going to make somebody go with it to the end? You know, ride with me the whole way.

So it's lots of activity and then lots of silence in which I question everything. I will call the desk at midnight to change a word. It's crazy. Maybe you have to be nuts.

Why do you work so hard at it?

I really want it to be wonderful, so I work really hard at the craft of it. I work not to do the obvious, or to choose the easy word. I work to look at things the way my kids look at things, and to see things with a fresh eye, so that I can make people feel the image. Making yourself do that twice a week is no small task.

Writing is the constant challenge of making people see. It's the details. And what I hate about it is that I feel like I don't do it as well as I would like to. Sometimes there's just not enough time. Sometimes I'm too distracted. Sometimes the words don't come as fluidly as I would like them to come.

An Interview with Donna Britt, Columnist, *The Washington Post* (continued)

Most of the time sitting down to that challenge is not fun, because there's a big possibility that you're not going to live up to your own ideal.

What constitutes a lead in a Donna Britt column? Is it the first paragraph? Is it the first several paragraphs?

It's the first several paragraphs. At the very least, it's three paragraphs. It's usually three-quarters of a screen on my laptop, if you wanted to be that specific.

It's always hard to figure out where to start. You never know what you're going to land on. You never know if it's going to work. You know how you'll just say, "Oh, well, I'll just start out this way"? That always ends up being your lead. It always ends up being what you go with.

In your column, "A Life of Grace and Strength Offers One Last Precious Gift," you open with the startling image of the drool pooled on your grandmother's face. Why?

When I walked in that room, the thing that was most wrong was that this very stylish and manicured and consciously lovely woman had drool in the corner of her mouth. How could this be? So to take an ugly image and to bring people around to the beauty in it, as I was brought around to the beauty in it, seemed like something worth trying.

Did you set a goal for yourself when you decided to write that?

My goal for that piece was to write something that would help me remember the amazing thing that happened in that room. I never wanted to forget, and I knew if I didn't write it for the column, it would never get written. So that one was for me. But I think we live in a culture that doesn't want to acknowledge the lasting import of a death.

In your column about Mom-Mommy and many of your other columns, you display a special gift for capturing the universal in the specific.

It's never about Mom-Mommy. It's about all our grandmothers who meant so much in ways they could not possibly know.

Your column is so personal, intimate even. Do you ever worry, "Who cares about another column starring my kids?"

That's why it has to be good. I try not to use them unless I really have something to say.

And there really are people who aren't going to appreciate it, and who are going to feel like it's a "me, me, me," kind of thing—and certainly, in a way, it is.

But I feel like there's always a point. When I talk about my engagement ring

An Interview with Donna Britt, Columnist, *The Washington Post* (continued)

and my wedding, I'm validating the romance that lives in every woman that I know. And I get calls from them saying, "You give me hope," or "I'm so glad that you wrote that." Or when I write about my little macho 7-year-old throwing a fit because he's getting on a plane to go visit his father, if I do that column right, everybody who's a mother will feel it. And I think all that small stuff needs to be explored and celebrated. I really do.

It's the most pointedly beautiful part of life, the everyday wonderful stuff, that we notice. And that stuff has to be validated. So much ugliness is validated.

Do newspapers need more personal writing like yours?

Certainly the popularity of my column would suggest that. I think newspapers are much better at giving people the real now than they were when I was coming up. They're much more likely to deal with close-to-the-bone issues. I still think we have a long way to go when it comes to honesty, and acceptance of other people's honesty. Your hope is that people will appreciate what they see. And that doesn't always happen. A lot of people don't want to do that and I understand that. But if you want to connect to people, it takes risk.

How did you get into journalism?

Because I could write.

What was your first writing?

The first story I remember was called "White Milk, Chocolate Milk," and it was about discrimination among dairy products. And that's the truth. I think I was in the third grade. Civil rights was very much in the forefront of what was happening on television and in *Life* magazine. I was actually seeing people who looked like me, and it was pretty disturbing that they were getting hoses turned on them, and dogs sicced on them. And this piece was sort of about the madness of that. I don't remember the details. I just remember there were these two bottles of milk. And back then, people would bring you your milk and, you know, put it on your stoop. And I guess the white milk didn't think he should be subjected to being next to the chocolate milk. That's all I remember. But I always remember being told that I could write.

Who told you?

Teachers. I was never without a book. I just loved to read and hear other people's stories. And so many of the books that I read were books that my mother had read. I had these old lovely, beautifully bound copies of Louisa May Alcott books, and things like *The Little Princess*, and very romantic, fanciful moral books—the books that my mother had read when she was a little girl. And getting into pulpy novels and all. I must have read *Gone With the Wind* 14 times.

Teachers were important to your development as a writer. What roles does your editor play now that you're a professional?

She's not like me, so I like that. She's basically not as emotional. And she's white. Having someone who does have some differences in those surface kind of ways is good, because I want everyone to understand it.

Then my copy editor is a black woman whose background doesn't seem to have been all that different from mine, and that's good, because any column I write, I'm going to have a huge readership of white people and a huge readership of black people. And having the two people who first respond to it be representative of smart and caring people of both those groups is ideal for me. I trust their vision.

How much of an impact do they have?

Marcia Davis, my copy editor, is very specific. "Well, maybe if we moved this word here, that will be a bit smoother." Or, "I didn't quite understand what you meant here." I try to write conversationally, so I will break grammatical rules, and sometimes she'll challenge that, but lots of times she'll just let it go. She knows it's how I am. With Jo-Ann Armao, my editor, it's more of a visceral thing. Trying to hear how much

she likes it and to get her to talk about what she does or doesn't like about it, or what's missing. So it's more specific with Marcia. With Jo-Ann, it's more the big picture.

I knew a columnist once and everything to him was a column. Conversations were studded with moments where his eyebrow would lift and you'd realize he was thinking, "This could be a column." Is that a columnist's natural reflex?

Oh, yeah, because it's always there. George Bernard Shaw described it as living underneath a windmill, and every time you put your head up, you know, your head gets smacked.

I'm told that a regular topic at the National Association of Black Journalists Convention is the complaint, "I can't tell my story." You've overcome whatever obstacle it is that is keeping other people from telling their stories. Can black journalists not tell their stories and why not?

Most people get their ideas from editors. Editors usually draw on their own experience and what's already been done when they give assignments. In a mostly white press, most editors are going to conceive of and assign stories that they know about. Our stories are often stories that a white person may not even know about. So it becomes a

An Interview with Donna Britt, Columnist, *The Washington Post* (continued)

black journalist's special sort of duty to introduce his editors to areas that he or she may not know exist. And some people aren't comfortable with that. I mean there are reporters who like to get assignments, good assignments, and just do the work.

In telling your story, you have to introduce the idea of the story and convince an editor, who may not have any sense of it and no visceral sort of connection to it, that it's valid, which isn't always an easy thing. And if you do that once, twice, a dozen times, and there's very little interest or follow up, it can be really frustrating.

At the same time, I know of black reporters who have told themselves, "I can't do my story and I won't even try." So they won't even introduce the idea of a story.

Or sometimes you can suggest a story, and it will get twisted into something completely different because of the very different sort of vision that your editors might have.

I think it's a valid complaint. I think that it's one you have to push against a lot, and some people are uncomfortable pushing.

Do newspapers need a chorus of different voices?

They really do. And they don't even know how much they do.

It was always short-sighted and a little mean to be limited in your voices. Now, it's just plain stupid. Because you need every single subscription you can get.

You're enormously open about your feelings, your flaws, and yet many reporters find personal writing difficult. Why do you do it?

And there's not that much respect for it, either. When I first started doing it, I got the sense that people dismissed it and thought it was pure ego, and that it was too easy. But I felt driven to write that way, without really knowing why. I knew that what I wanted to do in the paper, more than anything, was to illuminate different, often unheard, people's humanity, and that I could often use myself, my experiences, my insecurities, my strengths, all that stuff, to let people know about people like me.

What do you wish you had known when you started out?

One of the hardest things to learn to do is to trust that your story, your vision, your focus, is valid. And to risk it by putting it out there, I think it's a very scary thing, and the inclination is to let someone else do it, to wait for someone else to say it. What I've learned is that once you do it, once you do step out on faith and explore whatever that is, there are people who will not get it, who will not feel it, who will not see it, who will not understand it. But there will be enough that do all

An Interview with Donna Britt, Columnist, *The Washington Post* (continued)

those things that it will be worth the trip. I wish I had known that earlier, to trust that inner voice that said, "This is important. This matters. That's wrong. That should be challenged." I think I let a lot of stuff go by because I didn't trust myself to be the person to challenge it.

Where do you get your ideas?

Everywhere. Conversations. Newspaper stories. Crocuses in my front yard.

How does an image, an idea, translate into a column?

It's like your mind is this field of daisies, and every daisy is a little bit different. And it's column time, and you sort of walk through the field and you decide which daisy to pick. So there's just this field of daisies, and you saunter through and pick whichever one nods at you.

When it's column time?

Twice a week, without fail. ■

Originally published as "Donna Britt: Alchemist, Transforming the Ordinary." Reprinted with permission from Christopher Scanlan, editor, *Best Newspaper Writing 1994,* published in 1994 by Bonus Books, Inc., 160 East Illinois Street, Chicago, IL 60611, and The Poynter Institute for Media Studies, 801 Third Street South, St. Petersburg, FL 33701.

Donna Britt. *Photo © Washington Post Writer's Group. Reprinted with permission.*

Weekly Newspapers

Many cities and towns have another kind of newspaper, the weekly, which is more often independently owned than a daily. Many weekly papers, such as New York's *Village Voice*, take a more politically liberal perspective on social issues than their daily counterparts, and therefore make room for minority viewpoints. Because of their schedules, weeklies tend to go into greater depth on a few issues, and they often focus on the arts in their communities. These weeklies often publish comics not carried by the more middle-of-the-road newspapers. The syndicated comic strip "This Modern World," for example, is found in more weeklies than dailies. (See Part Three, page 411, for an example of this issues-oriented comic strip.)

There are other kinds of weekly newspapers. Some actually look and feel like dailies, with an emphasis on old-fashioned local news coverage. Many are little more than a large classified section where anything and everything used can be bought or sold. Altogether, weeklies far outnumber dailies in the United States.

Pop Goes the Culture
USA Today Makes Its Mark

When *USA Today* was launched in 1982, many media observers pointed out that the street corner vending machines created by Gannett to sell the paper looked suspiciously like television sets. Whether or not Gannett intended people to make a subconscious connection, the TV metaphor cuts to the heart of how *USA Today* changed the American daily newspaper: It made newspapers more like TV. Lots of bright photos, shorter stories, colorful graphics, humorous headlines, and more space devoted to pop culture all helped bring newspapers out of the dark ages of black and white and into the fast-paced, image-dominated era.

Because *USA Today* does not offer coverage of local news, it needs to hook you somehow; that hook is an entertaining format. The rest of Gannett's 82 newspapers were quick to understand the success of the new look, and they soon updated their formats to the flashier look. So did the rest of the industry.

Tabloid Journalism

"Two-headed Alien Baby Discovered": Many readers ("inquiring minds") want to know how tabloid newspapers, commonly found in supermarkets near the check-out area, can publish such outrageous headlines and articles. The answer is that tabloids such as *The National Enquirer, The Globe,* and *The Star* are classified by the publishing industry as magazines. The usual standards of journalism do not apply to these newspapers. Their reporters are more like freelance short story writers than newswriters. Many make relatively high, sometimes even huge salaries for writing stories that boost the paper's sales. In addition to the obvious difference between the tone and purpose of tabloid newspapers and daily newspapers, there is another important difference: Tabloids routinely pay people to tell their stories. Tabloids pay to create the "news" they report.

Editors of tabloids openly describe what they do as providing gossip and entertainment, and they argue that most Americans know that what they print is not true. Maybe so, but 45 to 50 million Americans read them every week. Why? Because readers generally like to be entertained! While stories on the personal lives of pop culture heroes—celebrities—dominate the tabloids, the advertising in these papers is also worth studying from a pop culture, media literacy viewpoint.

 **Reflections**

Why do you think so many people are embarrassed to admit that they enjoy reading tabloid magazines? As a form of entertainment, are tabloids different from the comedy shows we watch or from the ads that regularly mix humor and fantasy to get our attention? What is it about tabloids that appeals to so many people?

Inside the Industry

Newspaper Chain of Command

As you can tell from the chart on page 295, a typical newspaper has many editors. The people most associated in the public mind with a newspaper are the reporters, yet their job is at the bottom of the totem pole of the news process.

Each person along the line of the news process makes decisions about the news, and each decision is subject to possible veto by the boss. The owner of a paper is the most removed from the paper's daily operation, perhaps visiting the paper only occasionally. Yet the owner influences the kind of news the paper prints by making the basic policies it follows.

Industry Snapshot: American Newspapers—the Statistics

Daily newspapers:	1714
Readers of dailies:	63 million
Weekly newspapers:	8131
Readers of weeklies:	55 million
Advertising revenues (dailies):	33.7 billion dollars
Circulation revenues (dailies):	10.6 billion dollars
Metric tons of newsprint per year:	11.5 million

(continued)

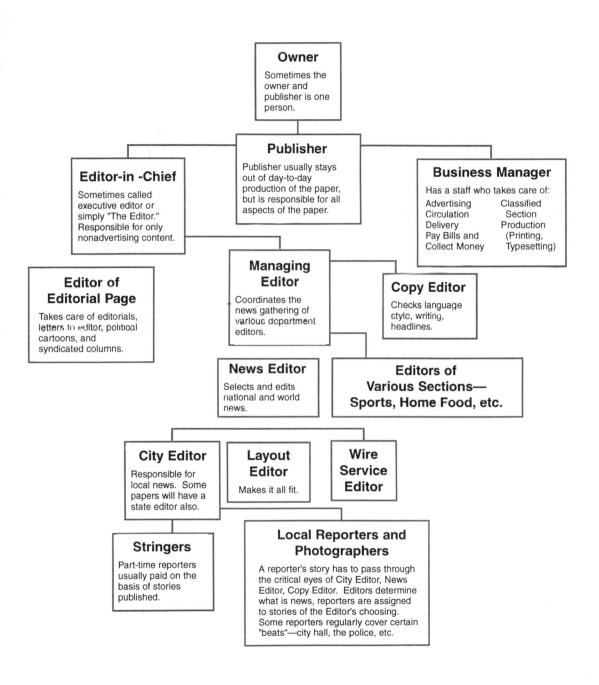

Owner

Sometimes the owner and publisher is one person.

Publisher

Publisher usually stays out of day-to-day production of the paper, but is responsible for all aspects of the paper.

Business Manager

Has a staff who takes care of:

Advertising	Classified
Circulation	Section
Delivery	Production
Pay Bills and	(Printing,
Collect Money	Typesetting)

Editor-in -Chief

Sometimes called executive editor or simply "The Editor." Responsible for only nonadvertising content.

Editor of Editorial Page

Takes care of editorials, letters to editor, political cartoons, and syndicated columns.

Managing Editor

Coordinates the news gathering of various department editors.

Copy Editor

Checks language style, writing, headlines.

News Editor

Selects and edits national and world news.

Editors of Various Sections— Sports, Home Food, etc.

City Editor

Responsible for local news. Some papers will have a state editor also.

Layout Editor

Makes it all fit.

Wire Service Editor

Stringers

Part-time reporters usually paid on the basis of stories published.

Local Reporters and Photographers

A reporter's story has to pass through the critical eyes of City Editor, News Editor, Copy Editor. Editors determine what is news, reporters are assigned to stories of the Editor's choosing. Some reporters regularly cover certain "beats"—city hall, the police, etc.

5 Largest U.S. Newspaper Companies as of 1993

Company	Daily circulation	No. of dailies
1. Gannett Company	6,101,961	83
2. Knight-Ridder	3,765,010	28
3. Newhouse	3,047,596	26
4. Times-Mirror	2,759,633	9
5. Dow Jones	2,404,361	22

*1993 statistics. *Source:* Standard and Poor's *Industry Survey*, published May 1994.

Future Watch: Newspapers in the Digital Age

The advent of the information superhighway has led many observers of media to speculate that newspapers will become a thing of the past—boring, industrial-age dinosaurs that can't compete with the interactive sizzle of new digital media. What are newspaper companies doing about these predictions? Read the article on page 297 to find out.

Practice

As you read "The Future Is Now," keep the Mediation stage of the Media Literacy Paradigm in mind. How will the digital delivery of information influence the production or mediation of newspapers?

From Darkrooms to Digital Photography

The future of newspapers is already here when it comes to photography. Digital photography is becoming more common and will eventually replace most of the traditional photographic techniques used in newsrooms for over a century. Rather than capturing images on film, digital cameras record images as digital information. The digitizing of images makes them much more flexible. For example, while still at her field location the photographer can preview her shots on a tiny monitor and make selections.

The Future Is Now

Kate McKenna

The last time newspapers were this interested in new technology, they were looking for ways to keep the ink from rubbing off on their readers' hands. Now they're exploring how a newspaper can survive, even thrive, without ink—and maybe without paper.

After decades of fearing that new information technology would put them out of business, newspapers are realizing that embracing technology is good business. Voice services, fax supplements and timely electronic news updates are options readers might want—and can increasingly get elsewhere. Although newspapers in their present form will be around for the foreseeable future, news managers now see the new information technology as a way to broaden their reach.

Somewhere between the May 1992 launching of the Tribune Co.'s Chicago Online, which was the first local service available nationwide, and the May 1993 debut of Knight-Ridder's San Jose "Mercury Center," the second nationally available local service, the industry entered a new era. Suddenly newspapers are doing the kinds of things they had always been wary of: investigating new methods and media, spending big money on research and development, and cooperating with the competition.

In the few months since the *Mercury News* went electronic—making it the first company to create a truly integrated newspaper and online product—a pack of new converts is lining up:

- Last summer 19 news companies, including Gannett, the Globe Newspaper Co., Hearst, Knight-Ridder, Newhouse Newspapers, Times Mirror and the Tribune Co., invested as much as $100,000 each to finance the development of the world's fist "personalized" newspaper at the Massachusetts Institute of Technology.
- Sometime this fall, Cox Newspapers' *Atlanta Journal* and *Constitution* and *Palm Beach Post* will unveil online editions, providing readers with complete versions of the dailies—plus police logs, community sports scores, school menus and other information that can't be squeezed into a normal daily news hole. The Atlanta service will augment Access Atlanta, which was started two years ago and currently has 1,000 subscribers. Cox-owned newspapers in Dayton and Austin may be next.
- The Times Mirror Co. is working to create online versions of three of

The Future Is Now *(continued)*

its papers, the *Los Angeles Times, Newsday* and *New York Newsday,* not coincidentally located in the nation's two biggest markets.

- Gannett Newspapers will launch electronic editions of its suburban New York City papers this fall, adopting its NewsLink online formula, which has worked well at Florida Today, at its Westchester, Rockland and Putnam county papers.

It's not a revolution, but an evolution—an industry-wide growth spurt that has hit newspapers, first one by one, then in groups, now in waves. From the *Los Angeles Times* to the *New York Times,* from the mega-chain to the small news group, newspapers are exploring new programs and finding nontraditional ways to give their readers all the news that's fit to print, fax and download. . . .

Much of the new activity within the print industry is fired by the same fuel propelling computer, telephone, cable and entertainment companies: fear. Technology is breaking down the barriers between these once-distinct industries, allowing unforeseen competitors into the new markets. This same technology could render any one of these industries obsolete.

"The potential arrival of interactive TV has opened the eyes and served as a wake up call to newspapers," says Victor A. Perry III, director of new business development at the *Los Angeles Times.* "The possibility of 500 channels in the home has shaken up the industry. We are at risk of being disenfranchised; they could take our advertising—and all we'd have left is an editorial product with no advertising to support it. So we've really got to insinuate ourselves in[to] these new worlds." . . .

One of the more enthusiastic high-tech converts, Cox Newspapers President David Easterly, points out another reason for news organizations to embrace this technology: "Greed. Because we're going to make some nice money on this." . . .

To launch its project, Cox has licensed software from the White Plains, New York-based Prodigy Services Co., a national home computer network owned by IBM and Sears. Consumers will be able to access online versions of the Atlanta papers and the *Palm Beach Post* through the Prodigy network. Easterly doesn't see the experiment stopping with newspapers, though. "Eventually Prodigy will be able to move this service [of providing Cox newspapers online] on to cable and off we go," he says. "We're not going to wait until cable operators define the world of journalism." . . .

Moreover, younger generations, and a growing number of older people, are more computer literate. More personal computers with modems in homes, more CD-ROM users, greater speed

The Future Is Now (*continued*)

and ease of usage have combined to create a viable market. Suspecting this, the *San Jose Mercury News* conducted a survey on local computer ownership and found that nearly 17 percent of adults in Santa Clara County own computers with modems—almost twice the national figure.

"We always think the new media is going to replace the old," says Bob Ingle, the *Mercury News'* executive editor. "Radio had us quaking; television, the same thing. With the possible exception of the telegraph, each new entry modifies the old media." The *Mercury News* launched Mercury Center, a 24-hour electronic newspaper, providing its Silicon Valley subscribers with the articles du jour, direct communication with editors and reporters, access to newspaper archives and wire copy, downloadable files and continually updated news. It's available for both Macintosh and IBM-compatible computers.

Mercury Center is similar to the Tribune Co.'s Chicago Online. Both are available through America Online, a nationwide computer network based in Vienna, Virginia. The Mercury News project is the first in a series of high-tech steps for the paper, which will soon launch fax and voice services. Many other companies, like Times Mirror and the Washington Post, took the opposite tack by inaugurating fax and voice programs before testing interactive projects.

Riding the Wave

As these and similar experiments continue, the fear that technology will supplant newspapers is receding; in its place stands an industry coming to terms with the inevitable high-tech future.

As Roger Fidler, director of Knight-Ridder's design lab in Boulder, Colorado, works on his "flat panel," a computer tablet that can display a specialized digital newspaper, he sees a significant change in attitudes among readers and news managers: They're getting ready for new news. "People are beginning to expect many changes to take place and I think . . . [that] will help make it a reality." . . .

What Is a Newspaper?

The question today is not simply the future of newspapers, but their essence—raising queries straight out of a communications theory class. What is a newspaper? Ink on paper? Or more? But, for once, there are as many answers as questions. And as many concrete examples of where news is headed as there are nebulous theories.

"It's helpful to think of the newspaper as more than a newspaper, a magazine as more than a magazine," says [Newhouse Newspaper's James] Willse. "What you have now in a newspaper is people who produce . . . advertising [and] editorial content, and then it goes on down to the printing plant. But this

The Future Is Now *(continued)*

huge news organization exists to provide more than just a printed thing in the morning.

"The thinking is that this organization could be at the center of spokes of a wheel. The information could be on television, computer, newspaper or Roger Fidler's flat panel. You've got multi-uses of what had been a fairly straightforward process. And in an era where newspaper penetration and readership is down, do we really care if people are getting their information from a newspaper or on a screen?"

The answer, says Wilse, is simply, "No, we don't."

Randy Bennett, who assisted on Knight-Ridder's now defunct videotex project and has worked at America Online, agrees. "Newspapers will become news companies, information companies," he says. "And one of the products they will offer is a paper product, as well as CD-ROM, news channels, online services, etc."

The philosophical debate also involves readers, whose needs and inclinations can get lost in the quest for high-tech news gadgets. "There are a lot of possibilities, but what's practical, what's cost-effective, what can be easily used—that's the $64,000 question," says the *Boston Globe*'s Jack Driscoll. "A lot of people talk about exotic things that can be done, but who really wants it?"

The New York Times' Henry Scott believes one can't assume too much about what readers want, especially when it comes to computers, which operate under a different set of rules. "There's a lot of things out there that look interesting," he says. "But the question is, do these [news] applications make sense on computers? Would I ever use it? I always argue that people won't read words off a screen unless they're paid to." . . .

Willse also sounds a note of caution for journalists who may be worshipping what he calls the "digital god" too enthusiastically. "It's wonderful that we are able to supply our readers with sports scores on demand, and stats going back to 1938," he says. "But the real reason we are protected by the First Amendment—and the Home Shopping Network isn't—is that we have to do good. We shine light in dark places, find out things people don't want us to find out. I would hate to see people get too seduced by the technology and forget that."

Certainly, there's a bit of the "millennium syndrome" afoot, as the approaching turn of the century makes people feel they're on the brink of a new age, with a Task Force 2000 forming in almost every industry. The problem is that no one really knows how newspapers will be read and distributed in the next 10 or 15 years, or even five years. Nobody knows if fax and audio services and online networks will prove successful, much less permanent. But the industry is in hot pursuit of the answer.

The Future Is Now *(continued)*

In any event, newspapers will continue to have a strong presence in the next century, according to those laboring to turn their visions of the future into their own Newspaper 2000. "The newspaper's future is absolutely vital," says Cox Newspapers President David Easterly. "The only newspaper companies that are going to get murdered on this are the ones that stand back." ■

Excerpts from "The Future Is Now" by Kate McKenna, originally published in the October 1993 *American Journalism Review*, are reprinted here by permission of *American Journalism Review*, College Park, Maryland.

How Newspapers Will Receive Digital Images

New technology now enables photographers to transmit photos by cellular modem back to the newspaper. Once received by the newspaper, the photos can be digitally manipulated using image processing software, then placed directly into the page layout using the newspaper's desktop publishing system—as shown on page 278.

No more film. No more darkrooms or chemicals. No more waiting. From the 50-yard line to the newspaper's computer in one minute. Digital camera setups are quite expensive (ranging from 7000 to 10000 dollars), though they are expected to come down in price dramatically in the next decade—at which time they will likely become a common method of photography for everyday consumers.

Building Your Media Archive
Archive Analysis

Here are a few questions to start your analysis. How does your archive newspaper communicate visually? Cut out the most dramatic photograph in your paper and ask class members to write a caption for it without reading the story it accompanied. What percentage of editorial content is written by reporters from the paper and what percentage comes from wire services? How much does your paper pay for its wire service subscriptions?

MEDIA LAB   Newspapers

- Make a collage of dramatic or interesting newspaper photographs. Decide on a point or idea you want to express as you collect your photographs.
- Invite a reporter, editor, and photographer from your local daily to your class to discuss their jobs. What have their most interesting assignments been? Why?
- Study an editorial about an issue of interest from your local paper, then conduct a class debate on the issue and on the position taken by the editorial.
- Tape the first 15 minutes of a local TV news program and compare it to the next day's newspaper. What stories do the two media products have in common? How did the newspaper's coverage of the story differ from the TV coverage?

In what way does your paper reflect the values of your community? Does it oppose any of your personal values? How so? Is your paper owned by a larger company? If so, who? If not, has its independence been threatened in recent years?

Find out how much your paper charges for advertising space. What are the most effective ads in your newspaper? What section are they in?

If a field trip can be arranged to a local newspaper office, you may wish to raise the questions suggested above, as well as examining the newspaper business in terms of the Origin and Mediation stages of the Media Literacy Paradigm (Chapter 3).

Create Your Own Media

If your school has a student newspaper, write an article or submit a photo for it. Contact a staff member or the adviser to get guidelines or a book on journalistic writing.

DOONESBURY   **COMMENTARY BY GARRY TRUDEAU**

Most papers gladly accept articles from **freelance** writers. If your school doesn't have a student newspaper, start one. That may seem like an overwhelming task, but look at it this way: You have no competition, you have a captive audience, and your school has a real need that is not being met.

Articulate student expression is one of the foundations of authentic student empowerment. Start small. Practice in your class. Journalistic writing is not difficult stylistically, but it requires that you be curious, determined, and organized. You may enroll in a journalism class or express interest in joining your school newspaper. Also, you may refer to the Resources list for further reading suggestions.

You need surprisingly little equipment to publish a student newspaper. Granted, your final media product may be stapled together on 8.5 × 11 sheets of paper, but the passion of your written expression does not depend on the size of the paper it's printed on. You can cover events and issues, write opinion columns, and take photographs that shed light on your lives as students and teenagers. Here are 27 ideas for articles you can tackle. These ideas will get you started. The following ideas come from among the 200 listed in *The Adviser's Companion* by Robert Greenman.

1. What does your principal believe are the greatest problems facing your school?
2. How is integration working at your school?
3. What interesting reasons for absence or tardiness have students given teachers lately?
4. What progress is the student government making in living up to its campaign promises?
5. Collect students' and teachers' comments on a controversial book, movie, or television program and weave them into an article.
6. What can the guidance counselors tell you about the kinds of problems students have been bringing to them lately? How have these problems changed from past types of problems, and how do the counselors help students to deal with them?
7. How are student teachers adjusting to being on the other side of the desk? What do they see now that they never saw when they were students?
8. How are newly instituted courses working out?

Student Close-Up

Jason Martin, Maryland

In 1993, senior Jason Martin was the sports editor of the Northern High School Patriot Press *in Calvert County, Maryland. In addition to writing for his student newspaper, he worked evenings and weekends covering sports for a local paper,* The Calvert Independent. *Here he describes his experience as a high school journalist.*

At the time I entered high school, I didn't have a clue what I wanted to do with my life. In my sophomore year, I decided to take Journalism One, a class you complete to move on to either the school newspaper or yearbook. We learned how newspapers are put together and also about the world of journalism, doing projects on everything from television to advertising.

During that year, I went on two field trips to WUSA-TV Channel Nine, the CBS affiliate in Washington, D.C. My journalism instructor, Mr. Gary Clites, has known the people at Channel Nine for a few years and they are really great about helping students learn about the world of professional journalism. We were part of tapings of a teen talk show they were doing at that time, got to meet and talk with the news staff and were sometimes allowed to sit in the news studio while they did the noon news. Soon after my first field trip, I

knew that journalism (probably broadcasting) was the field I wanted to go into.

How do you get started in a field like journalism? For me, the answer was to dive into newspaper work. Face it, when you are fifteen or sixteen, it's not always easy to get onto a TV station like WUSA. The interns there are all graduate students from major universities. However, getting started in print really only requires a notebook and a little aggressiveness on the part of a student trying to break in. My first step was moving on to the school newspaper in my junior year.

Through newspaper work, I have accomplished more than I ever thought I could. In my first year on the staff, I applied for the job of sports editor and was passed over. I didn't give up. On our school newspaper, the editors choose the stories that will be covered, then staff writers research and write the stories. After they are edited, we make up all the layout elements (copy, headlines, page headers, ads, etc.) in the computers and then lay out camera-ready paste-ups of all the pages for the school newspaper by hand. When we send them to the printer, we've completely created the finished newspaper. Therefore, I quickly learned everything about the newspaper business, from selling ads to bulk mailing copies to subscribers. In addition, I interviewed a lot of interesting people and tried to make a name for myself as a writer.

I also looked farther than the school newspaper. I called our friends at Channel Nine, and got to spend a day shadowing one of their sports reporters, Ken Mease, to learn about his job. Mr. Clites got me into the Washington Bullets Media program, in which I got to meet our local team and their coaches and to hang out with the reporters covering them for a game. Near the end of my junior year, I called a county newspaper and volunteered to write for their sports department. The editors were very generous and willing to help a beginning journalist. After printing my first few stories, *The Calvert Independent* hired me as a paid staff writer. So, at sixteen years old, I'd started my career as a professional journalist—getting paid to do something I enjoyed.

Writing for the local paper has earned me recognition from people in my school and from across the country. I know it will look good on my college applications and, hopefully, will help me get started in my adult career in the journalism field.

In my senior year on the school newspaper, I once again applied for sports editor on *The Patriot Press* and, this time, I got the job. Now I'm teaching the new staff how to write sports.

It may sound odd that, although I think I want to go into broadcasting, I am currently concentrating so hard on newspaper work. But I know that the skills and experience I'm gaining in print are exactly what my future employers will be looking for no matter what part of the journalism field I enter. As the professionals I've met have told me, they look for good interviewers, writers and editors first. Those are exactly the skills you have to develop to succeed in print.

My advice for young journalists is simple. Be aggressive and get out there into the field as soon as you can. Write for the school newspaper. And as soon as you know what you're doing, start submitting things to a local paper. They're often looking for copy, and if yours is any good, odds are they'll give you a chance. Journalism is one of the few careers where you can be judged on your talent, not your age. So don't ever be afraid to take your shot. ∎

9.   How well have students been handling independent study courses?
10.   Interview the proprietor of a well-known local pizza shop, pool hall, video game arcade, or other student hangout.

Jason Martin at work.

11. How helpful have students found private S.A.T. prepara-
     tion courses?
12. How prevalent is the use of study guides, such as *Cliff
     Notes* and *Monarch Notes*, among students? Why do
     they buy them? Do teachers think they are useful?
13. Interview custodial staff members and get their views on
     the school.
14. What tutorial help is available to students in school? What
     kinds of tutorial help are students paying for outside
     of school?
15. How much teacher absenteeism is there? Are more teach-
     ers absent on Fridays and Mondays, or just before or
     after holidays, than on midweek school days? What does
     the administration think about this?
16. Are your student government elections run so that there
     is no chance of ballot stuffing or other irregularities?
     Have staff members monitor the next student election.
17. Are various school groups, such as the cheerleaders or
     twirlers, free of favoritism when it comes to choosing
     new members?

18. How has the parents' association helped the school? What are its current priorities? What school problems is it dealing with?

19. What warnings do students who have held summer jobs have for those considering the same jobs next summer?

20. How many students have their own savings accounts? What are they saving their money for?

21. What can elderly residents of your school's area tell you about the way the neighborhood has changed through the years?

22. What are the frustrations and complaints of the school librarian? How can the library be better used? What can the librarian tell you about the reading habits of students at your school? How does the librarian select the library's books?

23. What are the problems of substitute teachers, as seen by both the students and the substitutes themselves? Which substitutes in your school are successful with students and why?

24. Why are certain teachers known as "high" or "low" or "easy" or "hard" graders?

25. Are diplomas held back from students who haven't returned library books or textbooks, or is that an empty threat?

26. Why do students cheat on tests? Why do they copy homework? Why do they plagiarize term papers?

27. What political and social causes are students involved in outside of school?

Career Bank

Following are just a few of the many careers available in the newspaper publishing/journalism field:

- copy editor
- layout editor
- reporter/stringer
- managing editor
- photographer/photojournalist
- business manager
- wire service editor
- newspaper publisher

Recap

The average daily newspaper in the United States contains about 60 percent advertising. The remaining 40 percent is editorial content, which is divided into sections and comes from a variety of sources.

Photography plays an important role in newspapers by attracting reader attention to the accompanying articles.

The job of a columnist is to reflect what he or she sees in life and connect it to readers' lives.

Newspaper companies are experimenting with electronic delivery systems to avoid becoming obsolete.

Resources for Further Reading

Books

Bates, Stephen. *If No News, Send Rumors: Anecdotes of American Journalism.* New York: Henry Holt, 1989.

Greenman, Robert. *The Adviser's Companion.* New York: Columbia Scholastic Press, 1991.

Ferguson, Donald L. and Jim Patten. *Journalism Today,* 4th ed. Lincolnwood, Ill.: National Textbook Company, 1993.

Smith, Helen. *Scholastic Newspaper Fundamentals.* New York: Columbia Scholastic Press Association, 1989.

Squires, James. *Read All About It.* New York: Random House, 1993.

The Best of Photojournalism: The Year in Pictures [annual] published by the National Press Photographers and University of Missouri School of Journalism staff: Running Press Book Publishers, Philadelphia, Pa.

Industry Publications, Magazines, and Organizations

American Journalism Review, 9701 Adelphi Rd., Adelphi, MD 20783

Columbia Scholastic Press Association, Box 11, Central Mail Room, Columbia University, New York, NY 10027-6969

National Press Photographer's Association, 3200 Croasdale Dr., Suite 306, Durham, NC 27705

Newspaper Association of America, 11600 Sunrise Valley Drive, Reston, VA 22091

Key word database searches for library research on newspapers:

Print journalism, newspapers, freedom of the press, tabloids

TV, Videotapes, and Films about Newspapers

Citizen Kane, 1941
All the President's Men, 1976
The Paper, 1993

SEGUE

Newspapers

Like newspapers, magazines rely heavily on advertising. Unlike daily newspapers, most magazines are targeted at a narrower audience. You can find a magazine about almost any topic you can think of, and magazines range in style almost as widely as the topics they cover—from scholarly scientific journals with few photos or art to fashion magazines with all photos and no articles. As is true for all the media addressed by this book, magazines can be classified by genres; they have origins which can be examined; they are mediated in particular ways to reach particular audiences; and they have an impact on us as individuals and as a society.

CHAPTER TEN

Magazines

Learning Targets

After working through this chapter, you will be able to

- Discuss how the variety of U.S. magazines reflect pop culture;
- Diagram a flowchart of how magazines obtain editorial content;
- Discuss the role of advertising in the magazine industry;
- Describe the key features of a zine; and
- Apply the Media Literacy Paradigm to the magazine in your Media Archive.

Checking In

- List as many magazines as you can.
- Recount highlights in the history of magazine publishing.
- Describe how you might go about getting an article published in a magazine.
- If you were going to start a magazine, what would it be about?
- Write three magazine-related topics you would like to research.

A Magazine for You

Probably the most amazing thing about the magazine industry is its diversity. The *1994 Gale Directory of Publications and Broadcast Media* lists 11,153 different magazine titles published in the United States. Whatever your interest, there is probably a magazine about it. Finding it may take some research, but it's there. Tattoos? There are dozens of magazines on the subject. Music? There are hundreds. New magazines are launched all the time. According to the 1994 annual *Guide to New Consumer Magazines*, 789 new American magazines were started in 1993 alone. Here is a sampling: *The Comedy Magazine, Dinosaur Times, Elvis International Forum, Healthy Woman, Indian Motorcycle Illustrated, Muscle and Health, Quake, Senior Golfer, Wake Boarding, WIRED.* Our culture—especially our pop culture—is on display at your local bookstore in the magazine section.

The variety of magazine offerings was always large, but recent advancements in desktop publishing and laser printing have fueled the explosion. Now it is possible for almost anyone to publish a magazine if they are so motivated. Of course, whether a magazine is successful is another story. Some magazines appeal to a relatively small number of people but earn a profit through the high subscription charge their dedicated readers are willing to pay. On the other hand, hundreds of magazines go out of business every year because of financial roadblocks. After all, like every mass medium in this book, magazines are a business.

A Short History of the American Magazine
Colonial Beginnings

Benjamin Franklin is credited with starting the first American magazine, a monthly with the ponderous title of *The General Magazine and Historical Chronicle for all the British Plantations in America.* His first issue in February 1741 made media history and gave many others the idea of publishing a magazine. Franklin's magazine and its early competitors were almost solid print and would be unlikely to receive a second glance from today's reader, who is accustomed to attractive magazines that depend heavily on the modern inventions of photography and four-color printing.

Within 50 years of Franklin's venture, almost 100 magazines existed in the United States, including *The American Magazine* published by Noah Webster (who is better known today for his dictionary than his magazine). Webster, Franklin, and their colleagues were among the early magazine publishers in the United States.

Industrialization Spurs Growth

In the mid-nineteenth century, magazines were read mainly by the educated elite. During this time magazines such as *Atlantic Monthly* and *Harper's* were started as intellectual journals. Even as early as 1840, however, there were signs of what we today would call mass-circulation magazines. One of the most popular, *Godey's Lady's Book*, edited by Sarah Hale, instructed women about manners, proper housekeeping, and fashion. Even during the Civil

War, *Godey's Lady's Book* distributed 100,000 copies and was probably read by four times that many people. Included in its pages were stories and poetry by writers now found in today's textbooks of American literature—Edgar Allan Poe, Nathaniel Hawthorne, and Henry Wadsworth Longfellow.

Many new magazines were started around 1880, after Congress passed a bill granting magazines special mailing privileges. Magazines were given a kind of government subsidy because they were "published for the dissemination of information . . . or devoted to literature, the sciences, arts or some special industry." This mailing privilege still exists, in modified form. A magazine can be mailed at a special second-class rate for approximately twenty to fifty cents, depending on size and weight.

The completion in 1869 of the first railroad line across the entire United States made the national magazine practical. Also, as education spread, more and more Americans were able to read, and the potential audience for magazines greatly increased. In the 1880s and 1890s, *Ladies' Home Journal, Good Housekeeping, McCall's,* and *Cosmopolitan* began. The *Saturday Evening Post,* founded in 1821, became the most influential and powerful magazine in the nation after it was bought by Cyrus Curtis, who also published *Ladies' Home Journal.* Curtis made the *Post* a reflection of American life and presented in it a probusiness image of "America for Americans." The *Post* published writers such as P. G. Wodehouse, Sinclair Lewis, F. Scott Fitzgerald, William Faulkner, and Ring Lardner.

1900 to the Present

The *Saturday Evening Post* had no serious competition as the largest magazine until 1932, when a small black-and-white magazine was issued from a Greenwich Village basement. It was the *Reader's Digest.* The *Digest* promised an article for every day of the month and caught the public's fancy almost immediately. Today the *Digest*, founded by Lila and DeWitt Wallace, has the second largest circulation in the world with over 18 million readers in dozens of different languages.

In 1923 Henry Luce published the first issue of a weekly newsmagazine called *Time.* The magazine helped the news make sense; it provided clear summaries of the succession of confusing events called news. *Time* was a success and gave rise to later successful imitators, such as *Newsweek* and *U.S. News and World Report.* In 1936 Luce started *Life* magazine, which brought vivid pictures of World War II into the homes of Americans in the pretelevision era. *Look*, with a similar slant, began publication the next year, and both thrived on superb, vivid photography.

From the end of World War II until the late 1960s, magazines attempted to be a truly mass medium, appealing to everyone. Then well-known and successful general-circulation magazines, such as *Saturday Evening Post, Life,* and *Look,* shocked their readers by announcing they were going out of business. (Later, all three had revivals; *Life* and *Saturday Evening Post* have survived as monthlies with limited circulations.) In general, by the seventies magazines that attempted to appeal to everyone found it increasingly difficult to compete with television as a general entertainment medium. By the eighties, the great circulation race slackened to a slow walk. Instead of a few gigantic magazines reaching tens of millions, the current trend is the specialized magazine for a small but interested audience. Increases in the cost of paper, printing, and postage have made magazines too expensive for advertisers who want to reach most of the nation with their sales message.

The Origins of Magazine Content

The **publisher** is the person who starts the magazine—the person (or group of people) with the idea and the money needed to make the magazine work. The publisher hires an **editor**, who finds articles for the magazine and has the general responsibility for the content of the magazine. The actual writing in the magazine is not usually done by the publisher or by the editor but by writers, both freelancers, who write for a number of publications, and full-time staff writers, who are employees of the magazine.

The editorial content of magazines is created by their own full-time staff, by freelance writers, or by both. Some publications written by a full-time staff are *Time* and *Newsweek.*

However, a completely staff-written mass-circulation magazine is the exception. Most magazine articles are written by freelance writers. Publications receive thousands of unsolicited manuscripts through the mail; their writers range from professional, often-published authors to students who submit school assignments that a teacher considers worthy of publication. The odds are against the freelancer who sends out unsolicited manuscripts, yet thousands of freelance articles are published each year. (**Unsolicited** means that no one at the magazine asked for the article—it simply arrived in the mail. On many occasions a magazine will originate an article idea and solicit an author to write it. **Unagented** means that no literary agent was involved. Professional writers often use a literary agent, a person who knows the best markets for articles. Agents sell manuscripts to publishers and receive for their services an agreed-upon percentage [often 10 percent] of whatever the author is paid.)

The best way for freelance writers to get their work published on their own is to read their targeted publication frequently to familiarize themselves with the types of articles it publishes. *Writer's Market,* a reference book revised yearly and available at most public libraries, is another helpful guide. *Writer's Market* lists magazines and their addresses along with a description of each publication's article needs and payment policies.

Once the writer has selected a magazine, he or she can send the typed manuscript along with a cover letter explaining that the article is being submitted for publication. (If the writer wants

Today you can find a magazine on just about any topic. *Photo courtesy of City Newsstand, Chicago, Illinois.*

the article returned, a self-addressed, stamped envelope should be enclosed.) Another approach is to send a query letter explaining the article idea, providing an outline of its content, and perhaps including an excerpt from the article. If the magazine responds positively, the writer submits the article to the editor, who may suggest minor or major changes before accepting the article for publication. Once accepted, the article will probably be published anywhere from one to eight months later.

Magazines and the Marketplace

Most magazines are sold by subscription and/or through news-stands. Neither the subscription rate nor the newsstand price alone is sufficient to enable a magazine to survive and show a fair profit. Magazines make much more money from advertising than they do from what the readers pay for each copy. A few publications, usually intended for very specialized audiences such as doctors or teachers, are actually given away. These controlled-circulation magazines assure potential advertisers that their message will be delivered to a guaranteed number of doctors or history teachers in the country. At the other extreme are specialized magazines and newsletters that contain no advertising and are supported completely by subscription prices that run to more than $100 yearly.

Demographics at Work

Advertisers often choose magazines rather than other media because of the specific demographics that magazines can provide. **Demographics** is the measurement of the kinds of people who read the publication—their age, income, interests, and the like.

If, for example, you wanted to sell a kit to chrome-plate an automobile engine, the best place to advertise would probably be in a special-interest magazine. You could select from the many magazines read by people interested in cars—for example, *Hot Rod, Motor Trend,* or *Car and Driver.*

If you advertised on television or radio or even in a general magazine such as *Time* or *Reader's Digest,* your money would be spent to reach millions of people who wouldn't want to chrome-plate their engines even if you supplied the kit free. Magazines, by limiting their audiences to specialized interests, create the best possible market segments for advertisers.

Mass-circulation magazines used to engage in circulation wars to obtain as many readers as possible. The more readers a magazine had, the more it could charge for each advertising page. However, magazines with millions of readers, such as *Look*, went out of business because, with their general appeal, they couldn't offer advertisers the specific kind of audience they wanted. On the other hand, magazines could not compete with television in the numbers game—the millions of viewers who might see one commercial. These magazines, then, did not stop publication for lack of readers or because of poor quality in the editorial content, but because of too little income from advertising. While mass-circulation magazines aimed at everybody have been going out of business or struggling to survive, specialized publications have prospered.

In order to fill as many pages as practical with advertising, magazines themselves advertise to the business community. Some of these ads give an idea of the aims of magazines that relate to both the editorial content and the advertising.

The purpose of a magazine is to deliver readers to advertisers; but those readers have to be potential buyers. Magazines survey readers to study their purchasing habits. For example, *Reader's Digest* knows that its male readers influence 49 percent of all salad dressing purchases. *Architectural Record* magazine knows its readers account for 90 percent of all money spent on architect-planned buildings.

In recent years the city-specific magazine has regained popularity. Most of the nation's largest cities have a magazine bearing the city's name. The magazines deliver a unique audience of usually upscale readers for local advertisers.

The number and circulation of magazines are currently at an all-time high. One reason for the newfound success of magazines is that they can deliver an audience not well reached by television. Magazines can target better educated, more affluent readers who prefer reading to watching television.

To further serve their demographic needs, large magazines use sophisticated computer modeling and printing plants to customize both editorial and advertising content. For example, each issue of *Time* is really over 50 different magazines. Some of the editorial and ad content appears in each edition, but other ads and articles are limited to editions targeted to specific geographic areas, such as the Midwest or the West Coast, or to readers who fit carefully defined demographic profiles, such as corporate executives.

Some Statistics

Time Warner's Time Inc. is the largest magazine publisher in the world. Over twice the size of its nearest competitor, Hearst Magazines, Time Inc. reported 1993 revenues of $3.27 billion. In addition to its 24 main magazines for the United States, Time Inc. is a major player in the world magazine-publishing market. For example, the Chinese language edition of *People Magazine* helps account for the 30 million people world-wide who read it every week.

American magazines displayed $7.63 billion worth of advertising in 1993. Automobile and auto accessory companies were the largest buyers of ad space, spending $1.053 billion. The second largest category of advertising was toiletries and cosmetics, with $800 million spent on ads. Cigarettes and tobacco companies ranked fifth among industries that advertise in magazines, spending $210 million. That's a little over $4 million a week to sell tobacco in magazines alone.

 **Reflections**

Respond to this admittedly one-sided argument against cigarette and alcohol advertising in magazines:

Set aside the question of the First Amendment protection of free speech for a moment and consider the effects of cigarette and alcohol advertising. Given the billions of dollars in medical costs society pays for the illness and death caused by these products, magazines should refuse to accept their advertising dollars. Television networks did not go out of business when cigarette ads were banned in 1970; in fact, TV ad revenues have steadily increased since then. Likewise, magazines—as an industry—will not be hurt either, although some individual magazines might not survive the lost revenue.

Zines: The Do-It-Yourself Magazines

This chapter so far has dealt with the traditional magazine industry. There is, however, another realm of magazines called zines, where the phrase "Do It Yourself" (DIY) is the rallying cry of its very independent publishers. Mike Gunderloy and Cari Goldberg Janice describe this realm in the reading beginning on page 322.

Future Watch: Magazines
in the Digital Age

Most people think of the standard $8\frac{1}{2}$-x-11-inch, paper-based format when they think of a magazine. It won't be long, though, before we think of magazines very differently. Already, dozens of magazines are distributed through on-line services and on CD-ROM. As of early 1995, on-line versions of magazines presented just the text of the articles found in the printed versions; the technology was not yet fast enough to transmit photos and graphics. Depending on what year you are reading this book and how the technology has evolved since then, on-line magazines may still present only text—or they may include full-motion video and sound as well. On-line magazines offer readers the ability to send electronic mail to the writers and editors of the magazine and to give and get more direct feedback. Most of the magazines also present on-line discussions about the articles in each issue where readers can share opinions and ideas.

CD-ROM magazines are further along in their ability to present audio and graphics along with text. Because they are still very expensive and time-consuming to create, they do not come out weekly (or even monthly—yet), and they are fairly expensive compared with the cost of the paper versions with which they compete.

Most predictions about the future of magazines indicate that paper magazines will be around for a long time, but that electronic (on-line) magazines will make up a fair share of the traffic on the information highway. The illustration on page 328 is an on-line screen capture of the *Omni* magazine, an "on-line" magazine available on America Online and the World Wide Web (WWW) on the Internet.

The World of Zines

Mike Gunderloy and Cari Goldberg Janice

A revolution in technology has inspired an amazing surge of free expression and cultural ferment creating the world of zines: thousands of small publications which are produced primarily for love rather than money. Individuals pursuing their passions by publishing and reading zines have created geographically sprawling communities of people networked together by common interests. There are at least ten thousand zines being published in the United States today, and hundreds more will begin publishing while this book is being prepared, as hundreds of others publish their last issue and quietly vanish. Even though most zines reach only a few hundred readers, their total audience is in the millions. What this book will do is help you find the zines you are interested in, and show you how to join the ranks of zine publishers yourself. Self-expression is addictive, and once you've discovered the pleasures of publishing your own words, you'll never go back.

Zine pleasures come in many different flavors. Consider a few of the various publications you'll find in the zine world:

- A newsletter produced by an author between assignments, ruminating on interesting things in his life and inviting publishers to get interested too.

- A zine for people who collect Pez candy dispensers, tying together an otherwise scattered community who once met only through mail auctions . . . .

Why do people spend their time and money producing a zine which, at best, probably fewer than a thousand people will ever see? Lloyd Dunn, a long-time denizen of the experimental small press, once said, "One publishes because one must; which is to say that *I* publish because I don't know what *else* to do to make my voice heard outside of the narrow confines of my home turf." This is a common theme for many zine people; we're somehow driven to publish, and fortunate enough to have something to say.

But there are other reasons for doing zines, perhaps as many as there are zines. Some people do it just to have fun, or to explore an area of the world which the mainstream media doesn't adequately cover. Some are in it to cause trouble, or bring about social change. Some find it more congenial than a soapbox in the park for spreading views, while others use a zine to keep in touch with family and friends. A few brave souls even try to make a living at zine publishing, though they usually fail.

There are many reasons for publishing various kinds of zines, but there is an

The World of Zines (continued)

overall purpose: people are building networks independent of big business, big government, and big media. The zine world is in fact a network of networks. Some groups, such as music fans or SubGenii, have their own relatively closed network of zines, acting as a sort of social glue between farflung people and groups. Yet gradually these small networks are joining up into what some have called The Network, an overarching collection of mini publications which fill mailboxes around the world, generally unnoticed by most people.

The terminology of the small press world is a confusing tangle. In this book we've chosen to use the generic term "zine" for the publications we write about, but there are lots of other choices. Investigating these will help us define somewhat the boundaries of our subject.

Underground Press was a term of the Sixties, a way to refer to the newspapers of the time which aggressively challenged authority. Though some of the big underground papers grew, changed and survived, many more vanished in waves of police repression and activist burnout. Today's small press is for the most part anything but underground: many publishers go so far as to print their phone numbers inviting readers to call in.

The **Alternative Press** is another question-begging term: alternative to what? For the most part it conjures up images of slick magazines with slightly different slants than the most estab-

lished major media. *Mother Jones* and *The Nation* are alternative press, but they're too big and respectable themselves to fall within the scope of this book.

Small Press would be an ideal name for our subject, but it's such a perfect term that it's already been appropriated for different purposes at least three times. The literary crowd grabbed it first: if you say "the small press" around most college English departments they will assume that you are talking about the thousands of small literary and poetry magazines. Both the comics fans and the wrestling fans seized the term "the small press" to describe their own networks of publications. And independent book publishers are also "the small press" movement, with *their* own magazine to prove it.

Fanzines hits closer to the mark. It's a contraction of "fan magazines," first applied by science fiction enthusiasts to the publications they were producing (in contrast to the "prozines," which actually paid for work). From there, "fanzines" expanded to apply to several other fields, notably music. Some of the first music fanzines were produced by expatriate SF fans. Independently produced magazines of cartoons and comic art have also been called fanzines for some time. Although the term has been applied widely (mostly through the efforts of *Factsheet Five*) there are those who rail against its "dilution" and insist that it should

The World of Zines *(continued)*

probably refer only to the SF variant.

And so we come to **Zine**, an all-purpose contraction. It's hard to say what defines a zine, though we think all of the publications described and excerpted in this book fit. Generally they're created by one person, for love rather than money, and focus on a particular subject.

No one know how many zines there are. We at *Factsheet Five* have seen about five thousand different titles over the past decade, but we're sure we haven't seen them all. One clue lies in the review columns in various zines, which list other zines in their field. For example, there are about 40 different zines for fans of professional wrestling. Yet we only know this because they're all mentioned in the half-dozen or so wrestling zines we actually get on a regular basis. Apply this same ratio to our list of 2,000 or so zines, and it seems likely that there must be tens of thousands of them out there. It's even more difficult to assign a definitive number since the boundaries of the zine field are fluid; by the broadest definition, every church bulletin and college litmag in the country would be a zine.

And how many active zine readers might there be? Some zines have five readers, some have five thousand. If there were an average of fifty per zine, our estimate of 20,000 zines would indicate a million readers, scattered across the country. Maybe the guy in the next cubicle at work reads a zine.

Maybe your IRS auditor publishes one in her/his spare time.

The zine field is in the middle of a boom that's been going on at least since the Seventies, and there is no end in sight. Cheap photocopying, cheap computers and cheap postage (at least compared to other industrialized countries), have made it easier than ever to publish a zine. And the Reagan years, with their legacy of a tattered safety net, have encouraged people to depend more on their own talents and abilities for everything from survival to entertainment. In some subcultures, like punk rock or wrestling, everyone knows about zines. They're epidemic there, by now an accepted way to participate in the scene. Other areas may have only one or two pioneer zine publishers—or still are ripe for the picking.

Over the centuries, as we've gone from the hired scribe to the first printing press to the photocopy machine (and now on to the computer networks), the print media have become more democratized. While a few mass media continue to dominate the communication channels, there are plenty of holes between their coverage where the dedicated and passionate small publisher can make a difference. Most zines start out with the realization that one need no longer be merely a passive consumer of media. Everyone can be a producer! That's the underlying message of the zine world, and the greatest thing about zines. Come join us in this untamed new world. ■

Excerpt from *The World of Zines* by Mike Gunderloy and Cari Goldberg Janice (Viking Penguin, 1992) appears by permission of the authors.

Student Close-Up

Brooke Willmes, New York

A teen tells how she got into publishing her own zine.

Whenever I feel the urge to be heard, I know I can sit down at the nearest computer, and type something that I will eventually publish in my zine, *Cheese Log*. It's a privilege that I've gained over the three years I've been doing zines, trying to somehow express myself in a way that others can understand.

My zine is an outlet for all the things I felt needed to be said that couldn't be said in my high school newspaper or literary magazine. Anything too leftist, too politically incorrect, too "shocking" has its place in our culture, and I've made that place my zine. In a country "founded" upon free speech, I always felt strangely censored.

I learned about zines from a friend who had obtained one at a concert she had gone to and I decided to order some to learn more about them. I went to publications such as *Maximum Rock 'n' Roll*, a punk music collective magazine, *Action Girl*, a newsletter dedicated to listing zines done by women, and *Factsheet 5*, a magazine with a plethora of zines of all sorts. I learned that zines are much better than those underground newspapers that multiply in high schools across the U.S. Zines can be much more influential, and can be personal as well as political in the same space.

My best friend Emily and I started doing ours with little clue as to where or how we would get it copied, but first we concentrated on making it. We spent time on our own, writing about issues that were important to us like rape, abortion, and domestic violence, and it was a convenient way to document the great times we were having in high school. We wrote many articles about going to concerts, and hanging out. I included some poetry I had written, and people contributed artwork as well. The first issue came together in about two months, and we first used the copier at school to produce it (until we got caught). Then one of our friend's parents had access through work to get free copying. Now we use relatively cheap college copiers.

We just make sure that whoever does the copying clearly takes us seriously because it's not unusual to feel bad after the first person who sees the finished copy makes a joke of it. It must look strange to an outsider, spending all this time and money on something like a cut-and-paste-job, but it works. We started out making 80 copies an issue, but for our recent issue, #8, we made 200, all of which have sold. We are carried by several distributors like Blacklist Mailorder and Septophilia Records. I become friends with people who've ordered the zine. People from Canada, England, and Australia have ordered it, and among the hundreds of zines being made, people actually write back and order issue after issue.

I've realized through doing a zine that there is a world out there, and there is an arena that is receptive to the things I feel the need to say. Recently I've started an all-review zine called *Alice the Camel*, dedicated to spreading the news about zines, and now I'm getting piles of zines and records to review from all over. Before I got involved, it seemed literally impossible that I could get involved to this extent, but I have. And it takes time. It takes energy. It takes a considerable amount of money. Most of all it takes a kind of love and dedication that a lot of people aren't willing to give, but the rewards are immense. The great thing about doing a zine is you can start tomorrow. You don't need to take a class, or submit an essay, or pay a fee to anyone. You don't need to kiss up to anyone. You can set your own deadlines and rules, and you can say all you need to say. ■

Brooke Willmes.

Pictured above is a reproduction of the cover of *Cheese Log* #8, the "self-cover." This zine is made up of 12 sheets of paper printed on both sides and stapled. *Reprinted by permission of Brooke Willmes.*

Magazines are now available on-line. Above is a computer screen capture from America Online, which offers a "News Stand" from which you may select electronic magazines such as *Omni*. As an onl-line subscriber, you can select a magazine to read, bringing up articles, photos, and so on—choosing items from a menu. *Reprinted courtesy of America Online, Inc., Vienna, Virginia.*

MEDIA LAB   Profiling Magazines

- Go to the largest bookstore or newsstand in your area you can find with a magazine section and "scan." What are the most popular categories of magazines there? What do the variety of and types of magazines say about your community and pop culture in general? Examine various magazines. Who is being targeted for each one? Which magazines have the most ads? Which have the slickest visual design? Why?
- Your teacher may have each person or small groups in the class select different magazines to profile. To research for this assignment, refer to the *Writer's Market* or the Standard Rate and Data Service's *Consumer Magazine* in the library; you may seek the help of the reference librarian or media specialist for other information sources.
- In your profile, provide such information as the subscription rate, the frequency of publication, the intended audience, and so on.
- Now imagine you are launching your own magazine. Devise your profile along the lines of the actual magazine you researched and profiled in the activity above.
- Create a mock cover for your magazine.
- Create a "sales pitch" for your magazine.

Building Your Media Archive

Select and analyze a magazine of your choice. You will find varying amounts of text (low-C symbols) and graphics and/or photos (high-C symbols). Note that the amount of advertising in your magazine may vary quite a bit, depending on whether you're working with a mass-circulation magazine, such as *Rolling*

Stone, or a specialized magazine, such as *Picture Framers Monthly*. In addition to investigating the magazines in your archive according to the five stages of the Media Literacy Paradigm (Classification, Origin, Mediation, Consumption, and Impact), you may conduct the same inquiry of your magazine as you did in the Media Lab.

Create Your Own Media

As you can tell from reading the section on zines and from the Student Close-Up of Brooke Willmes, it doesn't require much money or equipment to publish a zine. The biggest task is deciding what you want to write about, then writing it. Zines can be produced on any size paper (though it should be easy to copy on a standard photocopy machine). Your zine can be stapled or folded (in either direction). Remember, don't just consume someone else's media products, dig into them. Understand them. Then create your own!

Career Bank

Following are just a few of the many careers available in the magazine publishing field:

- freelance writer
- literary/talent agent
- photographer
- graphic designer
- art director
- advertising sales associate
- editorial assistant/editor
- production coordinator
- circulation director
- publisher

Recap

Magazines are the most diverse of the mass media. The world of pop culture is reflected in over 10,000 magazines available in the United States alone.

Magazines have evolved through several stages to get to where they are now. From their political origins in the late eighteenth century through the Industrial Revolution, magazines grew steadily as a medium that reflected vibrant national growth. Television halted the trend toward mass-circulation magazines. In the second half of the twentieth century, the trend is for more specialized magazines.

Most magazines are written by a combination of staff writers and **freelance writers** who are paid by the length of the articles they submit. A few magazines, such as the major newsweeklies, are written entirely by staff writers.

Most traditional magazines rely on advertising for the majority of their revenues. Because most magazines target a specific audience, advertisers interested in selling to that audience are willing to pay substantial dollars for ad space.

Zines are magazines written and published by individuals (who rarely make any money doing so). Zine writers bring a distinctly alternative feel to their labors of love, the topics of which are as diverse as in the mainstream magazine industry.

Magazines in the future will continue to be printed on paper, but they will also be delivered electronically. On-line magazines and CD-ROM-based magazines offer the promise of interactivity, sound, and moving graphics.

Resources for Further Reading

Books

Draper, Robert. *Rolling Stone Magazine: The Uncensored History of the Greatest Rebel Journal.* New York: HarperCollins, 1990.

Gunderloy, Mike, and Cari Goldberg Janice. *The World of Zines: A Guide to the Independent Magazine Revolution.* New York: Penguin Books, 1992.

Wainwright, Loudon. *The Greatest American Magazine: An Inside History of LIFE.* New York: Knopf, 1986.

Industry Publications and Magazines

The Magazine Handbook (available from the Magazine Publishers of America, 575 Lexington Avenue, New York, NY 10022)

Magazine Industry Market Place (published annually by R. R. Bowker Publishing and found in most public library reference sections)

Key word database searches for library research on magazines:

Magazines, magazine publishing, electronic magazines, on-line magazines, freelance writing, magazine design

SEGUE

Magazines

Just as the traditional print magazine industry is evolving into new digital forms, radio is also facing many changes. Like magazines, radio stations rely on advertising for revenue. New digital radio, delivered by cable and satellite, is starting to compete with over-the-air broadcasts. For a subscriber fee, you can get 24 hours of CD-quality music with no commercials or DJs. How will this trend affect traditional radio? Like magazines, will radio become an increasingly specialized medium in the next decade?

CHAPTER ELEVEN

Radio

Learning Targets

After working through this chapter, you will be able to

- Summarize the early history of radio broadcasting;
- Explain the development of programming formats;
- Discuss the possible social impacts of talk radio; and
- Describe the main features of digital audio programming.

Checking In

- How might the growth of television have influenced the development of radio in the 1950s?
- How do you think radio stations decide what kind of music to play?
- Locate from a local newspaper a listing of radio stations in your area.
- How do you think radio would change if it played only music—no commercials and no DJs?

The First Electronic Mass Medium

The Beginnings

With the first experimental broadcast in 1910 by U.S. inventor Lee De Forest, radio began to shape the expectations of what an electronic mass medium could deliver. On November 2, 1920, radio station KDKA of East Pittsburgh, Pennsylvania, broadcast the first nonexperimental public program, announcing that Warren Harding had just been elected the twenty-ninth president of the United States. Only a few hundred people had the equipment necessary to hear KDKA in 1920, but radio as a mass medium had been born. KDKA exists today and is still owned and operated by Westinghouse Broadcasting.

Within a year radio became a national craze. Some called the invention a "wireless telephone," others "radio telephone" or simply "wireless." People bought crude receivers by the tens of

335

thousands. The earliest sets required headphones; only later did top-of-the-line models include loudspeakers that allowed an entire family to hear the broadcast. Reception was poor, static ever present, and programs were few and infrequent. Nevertheless, two years after the first KDKA broadcast, there were 1.5 million radios in the United States and more than 500 broadcast stations.

Many corporations and wealthy businesspeople quickly obtained federal licenses to broadcast. Some of the earliest license holders included Ford Motor Company and, of course, Westinghouse. By the end of 1922, 70 newspapers as well as an equal number of universities owned radio stations.

Early Radio Programming

Early programming was primitive by today's standards. There was much recorded music (often classical), many lectures, and some news. Early broadcasters had no guidelines as to what kinds of programs to air. While early television stations imitated previous radio successes, early radio was truly a frontier. Only a month after KDKA's broadcast, the Texas A&M University station broadcast the first college football game. A few months later KDKA broadcast the first church service, and the first radio debate on record came from WJH in Washington, D.C., on the argument that "The Daylight Saving is an Advantage." Early radio drama consisted mainly of dramatic readings. We take sound effects for granted in radio and television today, but the techniques had to be invented from scratch. Thunder was created by shaking a thin sheet of metal, and the sound of rain was created by rolling dried peas down a cardboard tube.

Music as the most popular type of programming on early radio, and it remains such today. Many radio pioneers believed radio would bring culture and art to the masses. Opera and classical music were quite common on 1920s radio compared to their very selective place today. Variety and comedy shows became popular around 1922.

The first linking of radio stations into a **chain** (now known as a network) was in January of 1923 to broadcast a concert both in New York and Boston. The music was played in New York and was broadcast by WEAF to New Yorkers. The show was also carried by long-distance telephone lines to Boston's WNAC, where it was aired for Bostonians.

Radio broadcasting and listening in the 1920s—a far cry from today's technology. *Photo on left: Broadcast from a radio-equipped yacht, 1925, the Bettmann Archive. Photo on right: The Danny Kramer Family, copyright 1924 by Underwood and Underwood, New York, the Bettmann Archive.*

Calvin Coolidge used a network of more than 20 radio stations to broadcast his words around the country. These first networks were small, however, and reached few households compared to today's total coverage of the country.

Radio succeeded in bringing music, both popular and classical, to thousands who had no access to live music. It also succeeded in creating a national interest in sports. Without mass media, sports events would have remained of only local interest. Radio (and later television) helped create national heroes out of sports stars and gave rise to fans who knew all about nationally famous teams.

Boxing was a popular sport in the 1920s, and the heavyweight championship fight between boxers Jack Dempsey and Georges

Carpentier on July 2, 1921, became a radio event. The ringside announcer telephoned his "blow-by-blow" account to the radio station. The radio announcer wrote down the account and relayed the description to an audience of thousands.

Early baseball games were covered by a play-by-play announcer reading a ticker-tape account of the game in a different city. Announcers tried to make the event sound live and appropriate sounds were added to give the "game" a live quality.

Financing Radio

Radio was exciting and filled with potential. How were radio stations to survive financially? How could music, sports, and talent be paid for? Entertainers agreed to perform on radio because of the publicity it generated; but as quickly as 1922, the members of the American Society of Composers, Authors and Publishers (ASCAP) demanded to be paid for the right to air their music. Stations were asked to pay annual fees from several hundred to several thousands dollars yearly. This basic system remains in effect today.

In 1925, however, radio was not as profitable a medium as it is now. A national debate raged over how to finance our radio system. Some favored the European method, which was to charge a tax on every radio sold. The tax would then be turned over to radio stations by the government. Others thought radio could be supported by subscriptions or membership. Radio pioneer David Sarnoff of the Radio Corporation of America (RCA) argued that the freedom of radio meant listeners should not have to pay fees. Who would pay the bills?

That question was answered by the discovery that businesses were willing to pay for time to advertise on radio. The first radio commercial was a long announcement by an apartment complex in New York aired on WEAF in August 1922. The fee for the commercial was $50. The idea caught on and stations that aired advertising were called "toll stations."

Businesses agreed to sponsor specific shows. Often the corporate name was attached to the show or the performers—the Eveready Hour, the RCA Victor Hour, the Goodrich Silver Chord Orchestra, or the Philco Playhouse.These variety shows thrived during the 1930s and 1940s, the time referred to as the golden years of radio. **Soap operas** such as "Helen Trent" became popular at the same time, so called because these daytime radio dramas were sponsored by soap manufacturers.

The Birth of the FCC

The rapid growth of radio caused problems. Frequencies overlapped and some channels were not usable because of interference from competing stations. Some sort of government regulation was needed to keep radio growing in an orderly way.

In 1922 Herbert Hoover, then secretary of commerce, called a series of radio conferences to act as arbitrator between conflicting interests hoping to exploit radio. Hoover played a major role in developing a radio system controlled by business yet closely watched and regulated by government. His efforts led to the Radio Law of 1927, which created the Federal Radio Commission (FRC). In 1934 the FRC was replaced by the Federal Communications Commission (FCC), which still exists today.

As explained in Chapter Eight, the Federal Communications Commission licenses radio stations and controls many of the technical aspects—transmitter power, wavelength, antenna height—of broadcasting. The FCC has other powers, but in recent years they have been downplayed in favor of industry self-regulation.

Programming Formats

After World War II, radio resembled today's television in many ways. People listened to specific programs, and radio was dominated by three major networks. The growth of television and the increasing number of radio stations changed the nature of radio, and various programming format developed.

With so many radio stations available, it was no longer possible for one station to deliver a large enough audience to make a network profitable. There were not enough advertising dollars to go around. In addition, the energies and the development dollars were being spent on the more glamorous medium of television. Radio lost network-supplied programs and became a local medium.

Local stations turned to phonograph records, disc jockeys, and broadcasts of "rip and read" news items from wire services to survive. Some stations tried talk shows, sports broadcasts, even all news. They needed inexpensive programs that would attract local

All-news radio is a popular format. Shown above is Felicia Middlebrooks, a broadcast journalist in Chicago. *Photo courtesy of WBBM, NEWS-RADIO 78.*

advertisers. The formula, still used today, worked and was later refined to what is sometimes called "narrowcasting." **Broadcasting** means sending out a signal to attract everyone; **narrowcasting** means carefully selecting music to attract a certain segment of the population to deliver to advertisers. For instance, a young audience today is gathered by playing alternative rock music, a somewhat older audience with middle-of-the-road programming, and the mature market with easy listening.

By the 1960s, radio revenues were at an all-time high, but no mass medium is immune to technological change. Change came about due to the introduction of a new kind of radio—FM (frequency modulation).

FM is a broadcasting method in which the frequency of sound carrier waves is changed to match variations in audio-frequency waves. FM broadcasting produces higher quality or **high-fidelity** (hi-fi) sound. First broadcast in 1939, up until 1960 FM was of interest only to hobbyists and classical music fans. There were few radios that could receive FM and even fewer FM radio stations. Many of those stations played only classical music.

In the mid-1960s, the FCC decided that AM stations that owned FM outlets should not be allowed to broadcast the same signal on both stations all the time. The FCC wanted to encourage a greater diversity of programming to serve the public. Limits were placed on the amount of time an AM station could simulcast. This ruling created a demand for a new type of programming, different from AM.

The programming void was filled by "underground rock" formats, by so-called "free-form" radio, and often by creative combinations of music, talk, interviews, and off-beat humor. Some stations narrowed their intended audience to certain sections of a large city instead of the whole metropolitan area. FM established itself as the forum for rock 'n' roll music and, during the 1970s, FM practically overwhelmed AM, much as television practically overwhelmed radio in the 1950s. AM radio countered this with the addition of stereo broadcasting in the 1980s, but FM has prevailed as the most popular "band" for music programming.

Current Radio Trends

The 1980s saw an explosion in the numbers of specialized program formats. The trend of narrowly targeting people with a particular taste in music continues into the 1990s. *Radio and Records,* a Los Angeles radio industry newspaper, keeps track of the songs played on stations in eight popular formats around the country.

Format	Artists Holding the Top 5 Songs in That Format (1994)
Urban Contemporary	Brandy, Boyz II Men, Anita Baker, Blackstreet, B.M.U.
Contemporary Hit Radio (Top 40)	Boyz II Men, Sheryl Crow, Madonna, Real McCoy, Babyface
Country	Allan Jackson, Sammy Kershaw, Tracy Lawrence, Collin Raye, Mary Chapin Carpenter
Rock	Stone Temple Pilots, Page and Plant, Eagles, R.E.M., Black Crows

A state-of-the-art stereo AM/FM radio. *Photo courtesy of Magnavox/Philips Consumer Electronics.*

Format	Artists Holding the Top 5 Songs in That Format (1994)
Adult Contemporary	Elton John, John Mellencamp, Madonna, Jon Secada, Amy Grant
New Adult Contemporary	Russ Freeman, Peter White, Anita Baker, Art Porter, Special EFX
Progressive	Eric Clapton, Lyle Lovett, Shawn Colvin, R.E.M., Tom Petty
Alternative	Cranberries, R.E.M., Nirvana, Stone Temple Pilots, Green Day

In addition to these formats, many radio stations further specialize their material. For example, many stations claim to play only "classic rock" (which falls in the rock format), and some further limit their playlists to "70s classic rock."

According to the *Radio and Records Fall Ratings Report*, in 1994 the following broadcast classifications were the seven most popular formats overall in the United States:

1. Country
2. Adult Contemporary
3. News/Talk Radio
4. Contemporary Hit Radio (Top 40)
5. Rock
6. Golden Oldies
7. Urban Contemporary

Note that the format of "oldies" stations (Golden Oldies)—that is, the broadcasting of popular music from past decades—is not one of the eight formats tracked by *Radio and Records*. This is because that format does not result in or reflect current sales of recordings.

Talk radio, the fastest growing format at this time, is built around a host/authority (sometimes self-proclaimed) and listeners who are invited to call in and participate in the broadcast. Doctors, psychologists, home and car service experts, media celebrities, and political commentators such as Rush Limbaugh are just some of the talk radio hosts who are on the air in the mid-1990s.

Future Watch: Radio in the Digital Age
Digital Audio Programming

The introduction of **digital audio programming,** in which CD-quality audio signals are transmitted to the home through cable TV wire, has already begun. Basic digital audio service typically offers 30 narrowly targeted music formats with no commercials or disc jockeys (DJs). Using a small receiver hooked up to your stereo and a wireless remote, you can instantly identify the title, artist, album title, and record label of the song you're listening to. Without commercials, providers of digital audio programming make all of their money through subscription costs, which average around $10 a month. You will read about how digital audio programming comes to the home later in this chapter.

As of November 1994, Digital Music Express, the largest provider of digital audio programming, is available through about 800 cable TV systems in 48 states. Out of the 17 million cable TV subscribers served by those 800 systems, however, only 325,000 have tried the new DMX service so far. That leaves a lot

Student Close-Up

Amanda Johnson, Indiana

Music director of her school's radio station, this teen describes what it's like to be a broadcaster at the control board.

Radio broadcasting allows me to express myself in a way that someone listening might relate to and enjoy. I like the way I can cast a certain mood or feeling just by changing the tone of my voice. I can paint pictures for my audience with the words I choose. If the enthusiasm I put behind my voice creates enthusiasm in my audience then the broadcast is successful.

I have always enjoyed drama and performing for an audience. Broadcasting is a lot like acting, except I get to play the part of myself and ad lib most of my own script. As a control board operator, I also get to do all the behind-the-scenes—technical work.

I am the music director at WRFT. I am in charge of all the music that goes over the air. During the school day we play light to medium rock format, alternating between new and old hits. It is important to have a format that attracts an audience. The more specific the for-

mat, the more concentrated the audience. WRFT's format during the day is geared to listeners who are at home or in their cars in our community. After school on-the-air personalities can pick their own formats and music. For instance, I host the "Monday Afterschool Show" and play my favorite tunes from the 1980s.

All my radio broadcasting experience comes from working at my high school's radio station, WRFT. I like getting hands-on training while earning credits toward my high school diploma. A school radio station is a great place to start if you plan a career in broadcasting. WRFT is a learning and relearning experience. If I make mistakes, I am taught how to correct them for the next time as opposed to losing my job!

I love to be on the air and know that I am reaching people who are listening intently to what I have to say. My experience at WRFT makes it easier for me to speak in public and in class. I hope to major in telecommunications in college and to pursue a career in broadcasting. ■

of room for growth, and industry forecasts predict rapid expansion of this new form of radio well into the next decade.

As the era of interactivity unfolds, many believe that it will be possible to purchase CDs through the wireless remote. If you hear

Amanda Johnson. *Photo courtesy of L. Schlabach, instructor, WRFT Radio, Franklin Central High School, Indianapolis.*

a song you like, you can punch in your credit information and the CD will arrive at your door three days later. Further into the future, it is possible that the CD you order will be transmitted electronically via cable or satellite; you will then record the temporarily stored data on a blank CD, the way you now record on cassette tape.

Digital audio programming is great for home, but what about the car? How will that work? The company profiled in the reading on page 348 is working to provide mobile digital programming for car radios.

Building Your Media Archive
Archive Analysis

Though you will be able to answer many of the questions in the Media Literacy Paradigm, some of the questions will be difficult

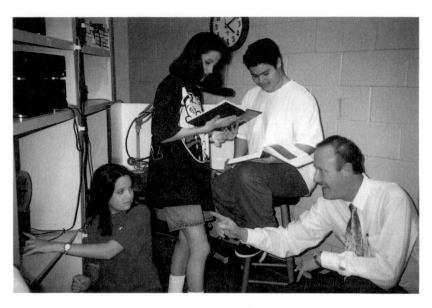

A school radio station can serve special needs of the school and community. Shown above is a team at the "Warrior Radio" station taping a dramatic reading for later broadcast to English classes. Sound effects are being added with a cue from the director. *Photo courtesy of Val Gause, instructor, Hodges Bend Middle School, Texas; photographer: Jessica Larson.*

 **Practice**

Consider digital audio programming in terms of the Media Literacy Paradigm. As you examine the following chart and the next reading on page 348, cover the five stages: Classification, Origin, Mediation, Consumption, and Impact of this media product.

because your half hour of radio—your media product—is probably a few dozen separate media products—each song, each ad, each station promotion could be analyzed by itself. Keep in mind that you are examining the entire 30 minutes as a whole.

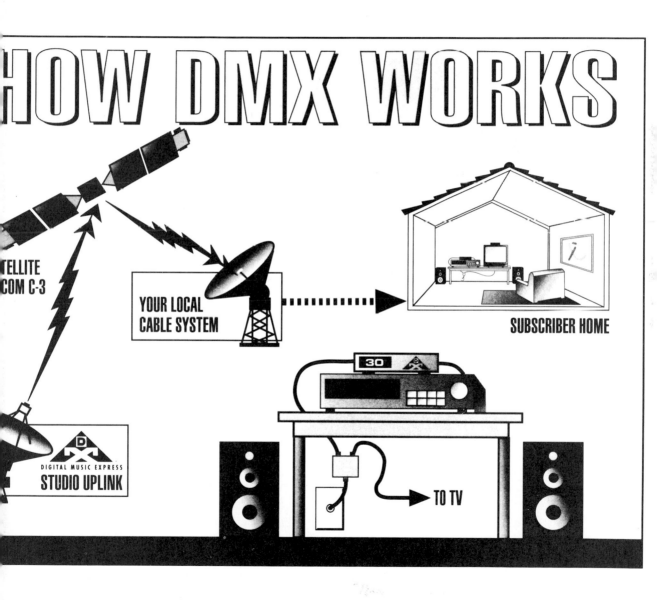

The Next Wave in Radio

Michael Wilke

On a recent afternoon in Arlington, Va., a black Lincoln Mark VIII left the parking lot of a small shopping strip and drove into radio's future. Picking up satellite signals on a silver-dollar-size disk antenna hidden in the car's roof, the radio, sonorous and static-free as a compact disk player, piped out a tune on channel 10. The driver punched a button and the radio's display printed the song, "Walk on the Ocean," and the band, Toad the Wet Sprocket.

Another punch of the button and channel 25 came up—the Alternative Rock format, the display screen indicated briefly before showing that the new song pulsing through the Lincoln was "Man on the Moon" by R.E.M. Another punch and the screen displayed the record company's CD catalogue number.

And so it went, driving and button-punching through 30 test channels of digital satellite radio as envisioned by the man in the car's back seat, David Margolese, chairman and chief executive of CD Radio Inc.

His privately held company, based in Washington, is one of four seeking permission from the Federal Communications Commission to launch satellites and blanket the nation with digital-radio programming.

As the first radio stations with truly national reach, these satellite channels would compete with local stations by pouring out as many as 30 channels of 24-hour formats, including jazz, children's programming and talk radio in a variety of languages.

The F.C.C. may take action on the applications next year. But even if the agency approves CD Radio's plan, it would take several more years and several hundred million dollars before Mr. Margolese's dream takes flight. (The signals picked up in the Lincoln, for example, did not come directly from the satellite borrowed for the test but from satellite-relay antennas perched on the roofs of buildings along the test-drive route.)

Still, as not just the first satellite radio applicant nearly four years ago, but with backing from the Loral Corporation and other investors, and as the developer of the first rudimentary system to be publicly demonstrated, Mr. Margolese evinces few doubts about satellite radio. "These things take a long time," he stressed. "We're actually moving along pretty quickly. We're in our final lap."

The F.C.C., which calls satellite radio Digital Audio Radio Service and has assigned it a swath of spectrum

The Next Wave in Radio *(continued)*

known as the S-band (2310 to 2360 megahertz), still must determine how many service providers can fit onto the band, and which proposals would best serve the public.

The F.C.C. is weighing competing applications from three other companies formed in pursuit of satellite radio: the American Mobile Radio Corporation, the Digital Satellite Broadcasting Corporation and Primosphere Limited Partnership. With estimated costs of the proposed systems ranging from CD Radio's $320 million to $622 million for Digital Satellite's plan, rich backers are a necessity.

American Mobile is a venture of the American Mobile Satellite Corporation of Washington, Hughes Aircraft's Space and Communications division and the nation's largest cellular telephone company. McCaw Cellular Communications (which itself is being acquired by A.T.&T.).

Digital Satellite's investors include Cleartel, a Washington-based long-distance carrier, and the Walter Group, a telecommunications consulting firm based in Seattle.

Primosphere is a venture of Q-Prime, the Manhattan-based holding company of the rock music impressarios Cliff Burnstein and Peter Mensch, who manage the heavy-metal bands Metallica and Def Leppard and who also own three radio stations in California.

Radio broadcasters have been lob-bying against the idea of satellite radio. John Abel, executive vice president of the National Association of Broadcasters, said in an interview that satellite radio was "the single greatest threat to the radio industry." The radio broadcasters, with plans of their own to convert to digital technology, fear that satellite radio would further threaten an industry already scrambling to compete with other media for audiences and advertisers.

USA Digital—a partnership of Gannett Broadcasting, CBS Radio and Westinghouse's "Group W" radio division—hopes to lead the way with its digital technology, which would bring computer precision to the signals of local AM and FM radio stations. If, as USA Digital hopes, the F.C.C. approves its technology within a year, local stations could be broadcasting with the clarity of digital sound well before the first satellite-radio spacecraft is launched.

But once those satellites go into service they will be able to send digital sound directly to any radio with the proper receiving equipment, making it possible to drive cross-country listening to the same channel without interruption, or sit in a cabin in Wyoming using a 1.9-inch disk antenna to pull down the same program being heard in Hollywood.

The cost of the receiving equipment has not been determined. The applicants say only that they are holding dis-

The Next Wave in Radio *(continued)*

cussions with manufacturers, which they decline to identify. If auto makers agree to offer satellite radios as factory-installed equipment in cars and trucks, this large guaranteed market could keep prices down. Eventually, consumers may have to choose what kind of radios they want for car and home, selecting among sets designed for satellite radio, local digital radio, AM-FM only, or combinations of each.

There are also uncertainties about who will provide the satellite service. Damon Ladson, an engineer in the F.C.C.'s Office of Engineering and Technology, said it was unlikely that all four applicants would fit into the available radio-frequency bandwidth, making consolidation likely. Thus far, all the applicants seem amenable to this possibility.

"Unless somebody is pursuing this as an art form, economics will prevail," said Ted Pierson, Digital Satellite's general counsel.

The high cost of the ventures stems from the need for a type of satellite unlike anything currently in orbit. "Believe me, if it could be done on a present satellite, we wouldn't have spent four years and millions of dollars," Mr. Margolese of CD Radio said. His company plans to launch two customized Loral FS-1300 Superbirds satellites, adapted models of spacecraft currently used by television programmers and long-distance telephone companies.

Some media analysts say they like the concept of satellite radio, but wonder about the details.

"The product itself is intriguing," said Ken Goldman, a media analyst formerly with Bear Stearns. "There is a potential symbiosis for CD sales, since there is no cost to sample formats you wouldn't normally listen to. The question is, what are people willing to pay per month?"

The applicants' plans vary in this regard. CD Radio, which would scramble its programming except to listeners who pay a subscription fee, expects to charge about $5 a month. Primosphere, which plans to makes its money from advertising, would charge nothing. The other companies may base their business plans on a mixture of listener fees and ads.

Of the applicants, Mr. Burnstein of Primosphere has been the only one willing to provide projected revenue figures for his plan. He estimates that after several years of operation Primosphere will be able to attract about 10 million households, or about 10 percent of the United States radio audience. That, he figures, would give Primosphere annual ad revenue of $160 million, against costs of $100 million a year, leaving a $60 million profit.

"Somewhere around the fifth year the business should turn cash-flow positive," he said. "You're positioned for the next 10 years to make high profits, and the next 20 can be wonderful."

The Next Wave in Radio *(continued)*

Before those two decades elapsed, of course, Mr. Burnstein would have to think about such niggling details as replacing his two satellites, which are expected to have a fuel supply that lasts just 12 to 15 years.

For all the applicants, there are other nagging questions, like how safe is it to read song titles, band names and music-catalogue numbers while motoring? "If you are not trying to do too much with it, it's O.K." Mr. Margolese of CD Radio said. "If you actually wanted to remember something, you might have to pull over and write it down.

"Of course," he continued, imagining a future above and beyond the streets of Arlington, "the radios could be equipped with a limited-scale memory. . . ." ■

Satellite radio is now being developed. Satellites will be used to beam CD-quality digital signals to radios—such as this one—in cars equipped with small specially-designed antennas. *Photo courtesy of CD Radio, Inc., Washington, D.C.*

MEDIA LAB   Radio

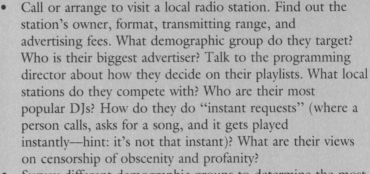

- Call or arrange to visit a local radio station. Find out the station's owner, format, transmitting range, and advertising fees. What demographic group do they target? Who is their biggest advertiser? Talk to the programming director about how they decide on their playlists. What local stations do they compete with? Who are their most popular DJs? How do they do "instant requests" (where a person calls, asks for a song, and it gets played instantly—hint: it's not that instant)? What are their views on censorship of obscenity and profanity?

- Survey different demographic groups to determine the most popular radio formats/stations in each group: junior high students, high school seniors, teachers, parents. How aware are members of each group of programming formats?

- Interview a local radio station executive on the subject of digital audio programming. Does he or she see it as a threat to the station? How will radio without ads and DJs cause commercial radio to change?

- Research the October 20, 1938, radio broadcast of "War of the Worlds." Based on the story by H. G. Wells, this radio play, performed by Orson Welles's Mercury Theatre Players, was so realistic (for its time) that thousands of listeners thought New Jersey had been invaded by Martians. Newspapers the following day reported mass confusion and even suicides resulting from the theatrical hoax. Though it's hard to believe that people were so easily fooled, many people argue that we would fall for a carefully planned hoax even more easily than people did in 1938. After reading about—and listening to—the broadcast, write a scenario describing how such a hoax could be played out today. What would have to happen for society to be thrown into a panic by a TV hoax? Your writing could take the form of a newspaper story in which you report on the previous evening's events.

Create Your Own Media

You can get an idea of the complexity of running a radio station 24 hours a day by creating a half-hour radio show. With little more than two cassette decks (one with the ability to record from a microphone), you can put together a radio show. Airing it on a real station may be another story, although a local college radio station might air it if your product is of high quality.

To create a half hour of radio programming, look back to your archive radio show. Using a stopwatch, log each element of the 30 minutes. How much time is spent on station identifications and promotions; on ads; on news, weather, and sports; and on music? In what order are these elements aired during the half hour? If you want to recreate a standard 30-minute block of FM station programming, you can write scripts for the promotions, ads, and news, weather, and sports segments and record them with background music or sound effects. Leave 10 seconds of blank tape between the items and use your tape deck's counter to log the location of each segment you record. Then select your songs and record them onto your master tape. Add your previously recorded ads, promotions, and news segments between song blocks.

Instead of replicating commercial radio, you might want to create a half-hour show focusing on a specific issue or idea. You could conduct and record interviews, write a script, and assemble them with songs relating to your topic, creating a unique media product. What is important to you? With whom do you want to share your views? What point do you want to get across to your listeners? What experience do you want them to have? You'll need to plan out your 30 minutes very carefully. What do you need to record? What equipment will you need? How will you edit your recording? Creating a homemade half-hour radio program is not that difficult to pull off technically, but, like all do-it-yourself media products, it requires thorough planning.

Career Bank

Following are just a few of the careers available in the radio industry:

- audio technician
- broadcaster/audio talent
- music director
- program director
- airtime/commercial sales association
- news reader
- disc jockey/combo-operator
- station manager

Recap

Radio was the first electronic mass medium, and it grew in popularity very quickly. Within two years of the first broadcast in 1920, there were over 1.5 million radios in the United States and millions of regular listeners.

From its start, radio carried sports, news, and musical programming, all of which remain today. Advertising has always been the main source of income for radio stations. The Federal Communications Commission (FCC) was born in 1934 to regulate the booming radio industry.

In the 1960s and 1970s, radio stations began restricting their programming to certain categories of music. Today, stations have even narrower formats—for example, playing only reggae or 1970s rock.

Several companies now provide digital audio programming in which CD-quality music is transmitted through the same wire that brings cable TV to the home. For an additional monthly fee, consumers can receive approximately 30 narrowly targeted music formats which play only music, with no DJs or commercials. Direct satellite reception of digital audio to the home and car will likely be available by the end of the year 2000.

Resources for Further Reading
Books

Keith, Michael. *The Radio Station*. Boston: Focal Press, 1989.
Ladd, Jim. *Radio Waves: Life and Revolution on the FM Dial*. New York: St. Martin's Press, 1991.

Sterling, Christopher. *Stay Tuned: A Concise History of American Broadcasting.* Belmont: Wadsworth, 1990.

Industry Publications and Magazines

Billboard Magazine, One Astor Plaza, 1515 Broadway, New York, NY 10036

Broadcasting and Cable: The Newsweekly of Television and Radio. 1705 Desales St., N.W., Washington, DC 20036

Radio and Records, 1930 Century Park West, Los Angeles, CA 90067

Key word database searches for library research on radio:

Radio, radio stations, programming formats, digital radio, talk radio, FCC, AM, FM

SEGUE

Radio

The United States had one generation's worth of experience with radio before television made its way into our living rooms. In that 30-year span, from 1920 to 1950, the country wrestled with many of the questions brought on by the growth of the first electronic mass medium—questions it would wrestle with all over again as TV swept the nation.

Who should control the new medium of TV? How should consumers pay for it? What content should be broadcast? What role should advertising play in its development? How would TV change living patterns? Answers to these questions are still being debated, and a new round of questions is just around the corner as TV moves into the interactive future.

CHAPTER TWELVE

Television and Video

Learning Targets

After working through this chapter, you will be able to

- Debate several issues regarding the impact of TV;
- Identify TV production techniques that MTV pioneered;
- Explain the basic structure of broadcast and cable TV;
- Describe the role of audience ratings in TV;
- Describe how videotape, the VCR, and the remote have changed TV; and
- Conduct research into the future of TV.

Checking In

- List some of the pros and cons of the role of TV in American society.
- Describe the effects of MTV, the VCR, and the remote control on TV viewing.
- Explain what you know about how TV channels come into your home.
- Describe the differences between broadcast (over-the-air) and cable TV.
- Write about TV ratings and their influence on which shows stay on the air.

Television's Impact: The Debate

The Ultimate in Popular Culture

More than any other medium, television is the medium of pop culture. Programming unique to TV, such as game shows, home shopping, and prime-time sitcoms (situation comedies), mirrors and promotes popular cultural values. Television also recycles or imitates pop culture from other media. For example, the pop culture churned out by the Hollywood film industry comes straight into our homes every time a feature film is aired. TV regularly duplicates the sensationalism of tabloid newspapers on its tabloid shows such as "Hard Copy" and "A Current Affair." The ads on TV present a virtual encyclopedia of our culture's needs, desires, and dreams.

    If for no other reason, the sheer amount of time we spend watching TV makes it an important indicator of our personal and cultural values. TV is the most popular medium for consuming popular culture. Is it an overstatement to claim that TV *is* pop culture?

The World of Television

You will spend nine years of your life watching shadowy images moving in a glass tube. These figures you invite daily into your home look like tiny people. They talk, dance, get into trouble, and even die. They live for 30 or 60 minutes a week, then disappear like the genie of Aladdin's famous lamp, waiting for your remote control to bring them to life again.

These patterns of dancing phosphors try to make you laugh or cry, or at least feel entertained. Sometimes they ask for your love, and often get it. You become attached to some of these images and invite them back more often than your closest relatives. You become best friends with some of these electronic genies and visit them often for years. These genies of the picture tube have the power to change lives. They tell stories, teach you how the world works, show wonders you would see only in picture books, and try to sell you what they say you need, from deodorant to fast cars. Of course, you don't think of them as ghosts or genies; you call them television personalities or celebrities.

These tiny creatures that live in every household were unleashed around 1939. No single person is credited with inventing television, but it was introduced to the masses at the New York World's Fair. Hundreds of curious people crowded around a television screen not much bigger than this page to view fuzzy black-and-white images. Most thought the invention a clever novelty. The newspapers dismissed the gadget as a toy the masses had little time to support.

These creatures, however, have changed the world. They have served well as messengers of news and have turned out to be wonderful storytellers. You often talk about them with your friends.

The stories they tell on the tube are the myths that shape our society. If Shakespeare lived today, he would probably write for television. If Beethoven were a contemporary composer, his themes might trumpet the network news.

However, as sometimes happens with a large group we invite home, some behave rudely. Some are violent. Others tell stories that may be embarrassing. Many speak incessantly of bodily functions and dentures and panty hose and various illnesses as they sell their wares; but we are patient in the face of their rudeness.

Television in the 1940s and television today. *Photos: left, Bettmann Archive; right, courtesy of Magnavox, Philips Consumer Electronics Company.*

Some say television is the greatest invention of the twentieth century, while others see it as a "vast wasteland" that steals time. Some blame television for teaching violence, while others claim TV turns viewers into couch potatoes. Still others see television as history's most effective educator, bringing knowledge of the universe to even the poorest citizens. Such education, they point out, was once available only to the wealthy who could afford to travel and to attend the best schools. Children today seem to know more about the world than their parents or grandparents did at the same age.

When asked for an opinion of television, some describe it as a harmless pastime that provides escape from the troubles of daily life. Others argue that it presents a dangerously unreal picture of the world. For every convincing statement about the dangers of television, there seems to be an equally compelling argument about its benefits. To watch or not to watch—that is the decision. Each time you make that decision, you reveal values.

Clearly, Americans have long since decided that watching television is an important activity. According to Nielsen Media Research, as of late 1994, 98 percent of homes in the United States have at least one TV. Of that number (94.2 million homes) over a third have two or more TVs. The average set is turned on 7 hours and 32 minutes each day. The typical young person will spend at least as much time in front of the TV as in school, which means those imaginary beings who live behind the glass may spend more time with you than your parents or friends. The reading on page 361 examines television's power to addict.

Why Is Television So Dangerous?

The second reading on page 363 was taken from the introductory newsletter of TV-Free America, an organization founded in 1994 to educate people about the dangers of TV. "TV-Free America" sums up the major issues surrounding the negative impacts of TV.

Practice

As you read the following two articles, keep the Impact stage of the Media Literacy Paradigm in mind. Do you agree or disagree with the messages stated in these readings regarding TV's effects on viewers?

On the Other Hand . . .

Whether or not you agree with the specific arguments presented in "TV-Free America," many things can be said in television's defense. First, in an increasingly diverse population, TV affords the country shared experiences. When the nation "comes together" by way of TV to view collective triumphs and tragedies, we share common ground. Whether we agree or disagree on a nationally consumed event, such as the Rodney King beatings and the riots that followed, we pretty much have the same *access* to the event. When so many of us watch our Olympic athletes, the country experiences the collective pride and enthusiasm of millions of individuals.

Are You Addicted to Television?

Jeffrey Schrank

For millions of regular viewers, television is no longer one choice among many to occupy a weekday night. The option has become which programs to watch, not if the set should be on. On any given weekday night, year after year, no matter what programs are presented, there is a fairly constant TV audience of one hundred million people.

People do not watch television because of certain shows they find exciting. If the show they claim to enjoy is not on, they watch some other show. Paul Klein, former vice-president for audience measurement at NBC, claims that viewer choice is based on the L.O.P. theory—the least objectionable program.

The L.O.P. theory states that people don't watch particular programs—they watch television. The set is turned on for the same reason people climb mountains—it's there. The program viewed at the time is the one that is considered least objectionable. To garner high ratings, all a show has to do is be less objectionable than its competition. A show does not have to be well written, well acted, or lavishly produced. Network programmers know that some well-received programs are stupid, but they also know that a program doesn't have to be good, it only has to be less objectionable.

Our language further supports Klein's L.O.P. theory in that we read THE newspaper, listen to THE radio, read A book or A magazine, but simply watch television. There is truth buried in this linguistic habit, for we do watch the medium of television, and that is significant no matter if the program is about culture or crooks.

Many people watch television simply because they are addicted to the tube. . . . Television's power to addict might spring from its ability to involve us emotionally.

We have all experienced deep emotions in front of TV screens; we have all learned about the world we will never visit in person or experience "live." We watch television in order to be manipulated into feeling. We want . . . those images on the screen to be frightening, to make us cry or howl with laughter, to help us feel vicarious thrills and excitement, to stimulate awe at the ability of others. Our nervous systems do not distinguish between the fear of a mugger lurking ahead on the deserted street at three in the morning or the fear aroused by the midnight creature feature. In both cases our heart throbs, the pulse quickens, and the

Are You Addicted to Television? *(continued)*

body sensations are real. The feelings are real, only the televised stimulus is lacking a third dimension.

People have always sought out games and theater to experience feelings normally missing from daily life. But when the seeking takes six to eight hours a day, it is a sign of an absence of a rich emotional life based on reality. The shadows become substitutes for reality. A Los Angeles soap opera addict explains: "Without these programs going on, I wonder if I would go on. People seem to forget me. . . . These people are my company. My real friends. I have it [TV] on because I feel people are talking to me."

This woman is an extreme case of TV-as-reality-substitute, but her symptoms are common to millions. By watching television, the feelings and sense of companionship can be enjoyed without responsibility, without the need to share these feelings with others or express them in public or even to "own" them as ours. These TV-generated feelings come from skilled writers and producers and not from within ourselves—they are safe and nonthreatening. Television encourages habitual viewers to avoid responsibility for their own recreation and feelings of aliveness. . . .

A professional polling organization conducted a survey of the attitude of readers of the *National Enquirer*. Of the respondents, 76 percent agreed that "TV makes me feel tired," 75 percent agreed that it "makes me eat more," and 56 percent claimed that TV causes them to "sleep more." Less than half rated entertainment programs as "satisfactory." Yet this box that shows mainly unsatisfactory programs and makes viewers hungry and sleepy is one of the few experiences we as a nation have in common.

The medium itself teaches values, regardless of the programs. Children who grow up on "Sesame Street" learn early to be regular consumers of TV programming. They also learn to accept as normal the fast cutting of "Sesame Street" and fail to learn the value of watching any one scene or visual for more than a few seconds. Television in general teaches the value of frequent change. Images change constantly, programs change, and there is always that remote control to change the channel.

Some psychologists believe TV may be partly to blame for the belief that life's problems can be solved by changing the channel. Los Angeles psychiatrist Dr. Lawrence Friedman explains one tendency of the channel-changing personality. "I'm convinced that at least fifty percent of all divorces in this country are unnecessary. And it's all because TV teaches us simple solutions to complex problems. People tell me, 'If only I could get rid of this marriage, everything would be all right.' " ■

Adapted from the original article by Jeffrey Schrank from *Understanding Mass Media*, Fourth Edition.

TV-Free America

Henry Labalme and Matt Pawa

How much television do people watch?

- The average American spends four hours a day watching television,
- The television set is on in the average household more than seven hours a day,
- Only work and sleep take up more time than TV watching for the average American,
- American children spend 900 hours a year in school and from 1200 to 1800 hours watching television,
- By age 20, the average American has seen 800,000 television commercials.

What are the effects of all this television-watching?

Television watching is causing a sharp decline in literacy. Children who watch the most television are the poorest readers while those who watch the least read the best. Advanced literacy skills, like the ability to construct a logical argument, are in sharp decline.

As young people have become less book-oriented and more TV-oriented, school has become less demanding and more simplistic: a twelfth-grade textbook of today is about as difficult as a fifth-grade textbook of a century ago.

In addition, one-third of adult Americans are illiterate or functionally illiterate. Of the remaining two-thirds, many are aliterate—they know how to read but don't. Reading time has fallen by a third since 1965.

Television-watching is interfering with healthy family life. TV is often used as a substitute babysitter or parent. One-third of four- and five-year-olds would rather spend time with their televisions than with their fathers. According to a Cornell developmental psychologist, "when the TV set is on, it freezes everybody. . . . Everything that used to go on between people—the games, the arguments, the emotional scenes out of which personality and ability develop—is stopped. So when you turn on the television, you turn off the process of making human beings human."

Excessive television watching is eroding the line between fact and fiction. On television, image is so much more important than substance that no clear line separates fact from fiction. News programs have begun fabricating footage. In 1993 NBC's "Dateline" used model rocket engines to rig the explosion of a G.M. truck. Newscasts, which now must compete with entertainment programs, have become entertainment themselves.

TV-Free America *(continued)*

Heavy television watchers tend to have a distorted view of the world. They overrate the crime problem and wildly overestimate the United States' portion of the world population. In a recent poll, half of viewers believed they are watching real-life violence even though a clear statement to the contrary appeared at the bottom of the screen.

Television watching is making serious political discourse impossible. The Lincoln-Douglas debates could not take place today because it would be impossible to gather a crowd at a county fair who could understand the complex oral prose of either Abraham Lincoln or Stephen Douglas. Nor could a book like Thomas Paine's *Common Sense* help start a revolution—for there aren't enough capable readers. The television demands a sound bite, an item whose average length has shrunk from 42 seconds in the 1968 presidential campaign to less than ten seconds in 1988. Fifty-four percent of Americans can name the judge on "The People's Court," but only nine percent can name the Chief Justice of the U.S. Supreme Court.

Even the "MacNeil-Lehrer News-Hour," which is substantive by TV standards, would, if transcribed, fit on one newspaper page. A newspaper can afford to print lengthy and detailed articles that might not interest everyone, but because every item of television news must have some appeal to everyone, TV news is greatly simplified.

American public opinion changes from day to day because too many of us get our information from a medium where image and brevity triumph over substance and depth. No political consensus can form when most people change their minds about important issues in response to the latest ad campaign.

Television relentlessly promotes the ideology of consumerism. Television commercials long ago ceased to be a means of communicating useful information. One study showed that of fourteen possible product characteristics that might be useful to consumers, more than half the commercials in a single night did not mention even one. Instead, television commercials—as well as programs—deliver a central message: that no matter what product you buy, happiness in life comes from buying products.

This message is harmful to both people and planet. Most of our environmental problems are tied to excessive resource use. Moreover, the very act of watching isolates people from the natural environment. ■

Reprinted from the July 11, 1994 newsletter by permission of TV-Free America, Washington, D.C.

ANIMAL CRACKERS is reprinted with permission of Tribune Media Service, Chicago, Illinois.

Defenders of television point out that it is educational. Public television series, such as "Nova," and entire cable channels, such as The Learning Channel, provide exposure to an amazingly wide range of topics, ideas, and events here and throughout the world. (You can learn how to cook some interesting dishes from some of those TV chefs.) C-SPAN, the network that broadcasts the complete proceedings of the U.S. House of Representatives and the U.S. Senate, lets Americans (and the rest of the world) keep tabs on our government in action.

The Violence Question

The most hotly debated topic regarding television is whether it causes us—as individuals and as a society—to be more violent than we would be without it. It is difficult to scientifically prove a *direct* cause-and-effect relationship between watching violent TV and acting violently. Yet there *seems* to be a large amount of research that *points* to a connection between heavy viewing of violent TV and heightened *aggressiveness*. Those who believe there is a connection often resort to common sense. How can watching thousands of murders *not* influence us in some way? Those who argue that television should not be blamed for personal and societal violence point to the hundreds of other variables that contribute to violence—poverty, stress, depression, availability of guns, gangs, and so on. The truth (if that's what it can be called) is probably found somewhere in the middle of the two sides. Again, we want what

TV gives us, and TV gives us what we want. Does TV violence make us violent, or do our already violent natures draw us to the tube? The following two readings present both sides of the question.

Practice

As you read "Imagebusters" and "Honey, I Warped the Kids," select a key passage from each to analyze and discuss in class. Analyze the passage in terms of one of the following stages of the Media Literacy Paradigm: Mediation (production), Consumption, or Impact of the media product—television violence.

Imagebusters: The Hollow Crusade against TV Violence

Todd Gitlin

I have denounced movie violence for more than two decades, all the way back to *The Wild Bunch* and *The Godfather*. I consider Hollywood's slashes, splatters, chain saws, and car crashes a disgrace, a degradation of culture, and a wound to the souls of producers and consumers alike.

But I also think liberals are making a serious mistake by pursuing their vigorous campaign against violence in the media. However morally and aesthetically reprehensible today's screen violence, the crusades of Senator Paul Simon and Attorney General Janet Reno against television violence are cheap shots. There are indeed reasons to attribute violence to the media, but the links are weaker than recent headlines would have one believe. The attempt to demonize the media distracts attention from the real causes of—and the serious remedies for—the epidemic of violence.

The sheer volume of alarm can't be explained by the actual violence generated by the media's awful images. Rather, Simon and Reno—not to mention Dan Quayle and the Reverend Donald Wildmon—have signed up for a traditional American pastime. The campaign against the devil's images threads through the history of middle-class reform movements. For a nation that styles itself practical, at least in technical pursuits, the United States has always been remarkably quick to become a playground of moral prohibitions and symbolic crusades.

If today's censorious forces smell smoke, it is not in the absence of fire. In recent years, market forces have driven screen violence to an amazing pitch. But the question the liberal crusaders fail to address is not whether these violent screen images are wholesome but just how much real-world violence can be blamed on the media. Assume, for the sake of argument, that *every* copycat crime reported in the media can be plausibly traced to television and movies. Let us make an exceedingly high estimate that the resulting carnage results in 100 deaths per year that would not otherwise have taken place. These would amount to 0.28 percent of the total of 36,000 murders, accidents, and suicides committed by gunshot in the United States in 1992.

That media violence contributes to a climate in which violence is legitimate—and there can be no doubt of this—does not make it an urgent social problem. Violence on the screens, however loathsome, does not make a significant contribution to violence on the

Imagebusters: The Hollow Crusade against TV Violence *(continued)*

streets. Images don't spill blood. Rage, equipped with guns, does. Desperation does. Revenge does. As liberals say, the drug trade does; poverty does; unemployment does. It seems likely that a given percent increase in decently paying jobs will save thousands of times more lives than the same percent decrease in media bang-bang.

Now, I also give conservative arguments about the sources of violence their due. A culture that despises and disrespects authority is disposed to aggression, so people look to violence to resolve conflict. The absence of legitimate parental authority also feeds a culture of aggression. But aggression per se, however unpleasant, is not the decisive murderous element. A child who shoves another child after watching a fistfight on television is not committing a drive-by shooting. Violence plays on big screens around the world without generating epidemics of carnage. The necessary condition permitting a culture of aggression to flare into a culture of violence is access to lethal weapons.

It's dark out there in the world of real violence, hopelessness, drugs, and guns. There is little political will for a war on poverty, guns, or family breakdown. Here, under the light, we are offered instead a crusade against media violence. This is largely a feel-good exercise, a moral panic substituting for practicality. It appeals to an American propensity that sociologist Philip Slater called the Toilet Assumption: Once the appearance of a social problem is swept out of sight, so is the problem. And the crusade costs nothing.

There is, for some liberals, an additional attraction. By campaigning against media violence, they hope to seize "family values" from conservatives. But the mantle of anti-violence they wrap themselves in is threadbare, and they are showing off new clothes that will not stop bullets.

The symbolic crusade against media violence is a confession of despair. Those who embrace it are saying, in effect, that they either do not know how, or do not dare, to do anything serious about American violence. They are tilting at images. If Janet Reno cites the American Psychological Association's recently published report, *Violence and Youth*, to indict television, she also should take note of the following statements within it: "Many social science disciplines, in addition to psychology, have firmly established that poverty and its contextual life circumstances are major determinants of violence. . . . It is very likely that socioeconomic inequality—not race—facilitates higher rates of violence among ethnic minority groups. . . . There is considerable evidence that the alarming rise in youth homicides is related to the availability of firearms." The phrase "major determinant" does not appear whenever the report turns to the subject of media violence.

Imagebusters: The Hollow Crusade against TV Violence *(continued)*

The question for reformers, then, is one of proportion and focus. If there were nothing else to do about deadly violence in America, then the passionate crusade against TV violence might be more justifiable, even though First Amendment absolutists would still have strong counterarguments. But the imagebusting campaign permits politicians to fulminate photogenically without having to take on the National Rifle Association or, for that matter, the drug epidemic, the crisis of the family, or the shortage of serious jobs.

So let a thousand criticisms bloom. Let reformers flood the networks and cable companies and, yes, advertisers, with protests against the gross overabundance of the stupid, the tawdry, and the ugly.

But not least, let the reformers not only turn off the set, but also criticize the form of life that has led so many to turn, and keep, it on. ■

Reprinted with permission from *The American Prospect* (Spring 1994) © New Prospect Inc.

Genres and Program Types

Television programs serve to gather an audience for the commercials. For this reason there has been surprisingly little change in programming since the beginning of television. Networks tend to stick with what has worked in the past.

When a certain type of program proves successful on one network, the others often rush to produce a similar one. This "success copying" accounts for the waves of popularity of certain types of shows from season to season. One season medical shows may be popular; the next, ethnic humor or dramas about rural families; the next, police stories or westerns.

Most commercial TV programming can be placed in one of the following categories:

News and documentaries
Sports
Movies
Music videos/Variety shows
Westerns
Police/Adventure series
Talk shows

Quiz and game shows
Daytime drama (soap operas)
Situation comedies
Dramatic series/Miniseries
Tabloids/"Reality" shows

Honey, I Warped the Kids

Carl M. Cannon

Tim Robbins and Susan Sarandon implore the nation to treat Haitians with AIDS more humanely. Robert Redford works for the environment. Harry Belafonte marches against the death penalty. Actors and producers seem to be constantly speaking out for noble causes far removed from their lives. But in the one area over which they have control—the excessive violence in the entertainment industry—Hollywood activists remain silent.

The first congressional hearings on the effects of TV violence took place in 1954. Although television was still relatively new, its extraordinary marketing power was already evident. The tube was teaching Americans what to buy and how to act, not only in advertisements, but in dramatic shows, too.

Everybody from Hollywood producers to Madison Avenue ad men would boast about this power—and seek to use it on dual tracks: to make money and to remake society along better lines.

Because it seemed ludicrous to assert that there was only one area—the depiction of violence—where television did not influence behavior, the TV industry came up with this theory: Watching violence is cathartic. A violent person might be sated by watching a murder.

The notion intrigued social scientists, and by 1956 they were studying it in earnest. Unfortunately, watching violence turned out to be anything but cathartic.

In the 1956 study, one dozen 4-year-olds watched a "Woody Woodpecker" cartoon that was full of violent images. Twelve other preschoolers watched "Little Red Hen," a peaceful cartoon. Afterward, the children who watched "Woody Woodpecker" were more likely to hit other children, verbally accost their classmates, break toys, be disruptive, and engage in destructive behavior during free play.

For the next 30 years, researchers in all walks of the social sciences studied the question of whether television causes violence. The results have been stunningly conclusive.

"There is more published research on this topic than on almost any other social issue of our time," University of Kansas Professor Aletha C. Huston, chair of the American Psychological Association's Task Force on Television and Society, told Congress in 1988. "Virtually all independent scholars agree that there is evidence that television can cause aggressive behavior."

There have been some 3,000 studies of this issue—85 of them major research

Honey, I Warped the Kids *(continued)*

efforts—and they all say the same thing. Of the 85 major studies, the only one that failed to find a causal relationship between TV violence and actual violence was paid for by NBC. When the study was subsequently reviewed by three independent social scientists, all three concluded that it actually did demonstrate a causal relationship.

Some highlights from the history of TV violence research:

•In 1973, when a town in mountainous western Canada was wired for TV signals, University of British Columbia researchers observed first- and second-graders. Within two years, the incidence of hitting, biting, and shoving increased 160 percent.

•Two Chicago doctors, Leonard Eron and Rowell Heusmann, followed the viewing habits of a group of children for 22 years. They found that watching violence on television is the single best predictor of violent or aggressive behavior later in life, ahead of such commonly accepted factors as parents' behavior, poverty, and race.

"Television violence affects youngsters of all ages, of both genders, at all socioeconomic levels and all levels of intelligence," they told Congress in 1992. "The effect is not limited to children who are already disposed to being aggressive and is not restricted to this country."

•In 1988, researchers Daniel G. Linz and Edward Donnerstein of the University of California, Santa Barbara, and Steven Penrod of the University of Wisconsin studied the effects on young men of horror movies and "slasher" films.

They found that depictions of violence, not sex, are what desensitizes people. They divided male students into four groups. One group watched no movies, a second watched nonviolent X-rated movies, a third watched teenage sexual-innuendo movies, and a fourth watched the slasher films *Texas Chainsaw Massacre, Friday the 13th, Part 2, Maniac,* and *Toolbox Murders.*

All the young men were placed on a mock jury panel and asked a series of questions designed to measure their empathy for an alleged female rape victim. Those in the fourth group measured lowest in empathy for the specific victim in the experiment—and for rape victims in general.

The anecdotal evidence is often more compelling than the scientific studies. Ask any homicide cop from London to Los Angeles to Bangkok if TV violence induces real-life violence and listen carefully to the cynical, knowing laugh.

Ask David McCarthy, police chief in Greenfield, Massachusetts, why 19-year-old Mark Branch killed himself after stabbing an 18-year-old female college student to death. When cops searched his room they found 90 horror movies, as well as a machete and a goalie mask like those used by Jason, the grisly star of *Friday the 13th.*

Honey, I Warped the Kids *(continued)*

Or ask Sergeant John O'Malley of the New York Police Department about a 9-year-old boy who sprayed a Bronx office building with gunfire. The boy explained to the astonished sergeant how he learned to load his Uzi-like firearm: "I watch a lot of TV."

Numerous groups have called, over the years, for curbing TV violence: the National Commission on the Causes and Prevention of Violence (1969), the U.S. Surgeon General (1972), the National Institute of Mental Health (1982), and the American Psychological Association (1992) among them.

During that time, cable television and movie rentals have made violence more readily available while at the same time pushing the envelope for network television. But even leaving aside cable and movie rentals, a study of TV programming from 1967 to 1989 showed only small ups and downs in violence, with the violent acts moving from one time slot to another but the overall violence rate remaining pretty steady—and pretty similar from network to network.

"The percent of prime-time programs using violence remains more than seven out of ten, as it has been for the entire 22-year period," researchers George Gerbner of the University of Pennsylvania Annenberg School of Communication and Nancy Signorielli of the University of Delaware wrote in 1990. For the past 22 years, they found,

adults and children have been entertained by about 16 violent acts, including two murders, in each evening's prime-time programming.

They also discovered that the rate of violence in children's programs is three times the rate in prime-time shows. By the age of 18, the average American child has witnessed at least 18,000 simulated murders on television.

But all of the scientific studies and reports, all of the wisdom of cops and grief of parents have run up against Congress' quite proper fear of censorship. For years, Democratic Congressman Peter Rodino of New Jersey chaired the House Judiciary Committee and looked at calls for some form of censorship with a jaundiced eye. At a hearing five years ago, Rodino told witnesses that Congress must be a "protector of commerce."

"Well, we have children that we need to protect," replied Frank M. Palumbo, a pediatrician at Georgetown University Hospital and a consultant to the American Academy of Pediatrics. "What we have here is a toxic substance in the environment that is harmful to children."

Arnold Fege of the national PTA added, "Clearly, this committee would not protect teachers who taught violence to children. Yet why would we condone children being exposed to a steady diet of TV violence year after year?" ■

Reprinted with permission from the July/August 1993 issue of *Mother Jones*, Boulder, Colorado.

"NYPD Blue" is a modern example of the police drama, one of the most popular TV program types. Pictured (left to right) are Sharon Lawrence, James McDaniel, Nicholas Turturro, Jimmy Smits, Dennis Franz, Gail O'Grady, and Gordon Clapp. *Photo © 1994, copyright Capital Cities/ ABC, Inc. All rights reserved.*

The Message of the Police Tale

Stuart Kaminsky and Mark Walker

Unlike other popular forms such as the western, the melodrama, or the horror story, police tales have a relatively brief history, with roots in the nineteenth century. For the most part the police did not exist as a separate profession until the nineteenth century. Those who apprehended criminals before this time were soldiers, as they still are in Italy and some other countries, or extensions of the judicial system, as in contemporary Soviet Russia. In England, a police force was established when the judges started to pay people—usually "reformed" criminals—out of their own budgets to go out and catch criminals.

Novels and stories about the police officer came slightly after the rise of the police force in nineteenth-century Europe. In France, such stories predated this slightly, because the police force was established as a separate entity from the army after the French Revolution. A transitional tale, Victor Hugo's *Les Misérables* (a public domain story that was the inspiration for one of the most successful series in television history, "The Fugitive"), began the pattern. Initially police tales—and many existed in the previous century—were presented as true-crime reports and not as fiction, in spite of the latitude authors often gave themselves. Alan Pinkerton, who founded the Pinkerton Detective Agency (which still exists), promoted his own exploits as true police tales in books and periodicals with great success.

Almost from the inception of storytelling in the medium, police tales became a staple of television. "Dragnet" may have been one of the first, but it was far from the only example ("Racket Squad," "M Squad," "Highway Patrol," and "Rocky King" are all early examples) of the genre in its half-hour format. Today's television police tales are all one hour long. . . . Critical attention to these and current police tales on television has tended to focus on whether or not the series or particular episodes are accurate in their depiction of police work and whether they are too violent.

The problem for the writer who gets caught up in the realist argument is that while viewers do want the illusion of reality, the same illusion we try to capture in dialogue, they probably do not want the actuality of police procedure and routine as regular weekly fare. A friend and I conceived a pilot for the most realistic police tale ever done. We were sure it would fail, and it did. The

The Message of the Police Tale *(continued)*

treatment for the first episode read as follows:

Real Police

Patrolman Watkins and Patrolwoman Ennis are in their car on a hot summer day. They cruise the streets of the city, listening to calls on their radio and looking out for suspicious characters or incidents. Generally, they talk about their families, financial problems, where they are going to take their coffee break and have lunch. They get two calls: a domestic disturbance that proves to be a false alarm and a possible breaking and entering that proves to be a window accidentally broken by kids playing baseball. They stop one driver, an old woman, for having a dragging muffler, and they are called upon to direct traffic at a busy intersection where the traffic light goes out. On the way in from their shift they see a suspicious-looking man hurrying into an alley. They follow and find that he is dumping a bag of garbage illegally. They decide to warn him instead of giving him a ticket. Back at the station they report that their patrol car needs some minor work.

There are some possibilities for mild comedy here, but when treated as pure realism, normal police work does not translate into exciting adventure. Police stories on television are more about the fantasy life of the audience than the experience of the police.

Several kinds of police tales have been shown on television: those that involve an individual investigator or pair of investigators, such as "Columbo" and "Hunter"; those that involve uniformed officers, and those that concentrate on an ensemble effort by the police, such as "Hill Street Blues" and "Crime Story."

Characteristics of Television Police

In plain clothes or uniform, the central character in a television police series has an inevitable commitment to the norm, to the status quo, to keeping things the way they are. Related to this is the convention that the police detective is not usually highly intelligent. He or she may not be a fool, but with rare exceptions intelligence is not a part of television's heroic definition of the police officer. "Columbo," obviously, was one of those exceptions. "Sledge Hammer" is a comic recognition of this element of the genre.

The virtue and possible defect of the television police detective is his commitment to the rule of law and the protection of the populace, which can often become obsessive. If, for example, the police officer has a family, the police officer's commitment to the job may threaten the family situation. That familial tension is often the basis for the second problem in an episode of a police series.

In some ways the police tale on television has become an urban substitute for the western, which is no longer a popular television form. As in the west-

The Message of the Police Tale *(continued)*

ern, the hero in early police shows was inevitably male. In recent years, police tales have offered female protagonists within what was once an exclusively male community. Potentially interesting series ideas and episodes exploring the differences between television's male and female police remain to be done.

Another characteristic of both uniformed and nonuniform police tales is the importance of partnership. One does not work alone. One is part of a social group. Again, this is quite different from the private forms. Private detectives may have, but usually do not need, partners. On television they traditionally work alone or with helpers who are not equal to them. "Simon and Simon," obviously, is an exception. The exploration of male/female relationships, a combining of comedy/romance/private-detective genres has been explored in such series as "Remington Steele" and "Moonlighting." Frequently, people supposedly helping the private detective prove to be more impediment than aid. But the police officer is dependent on other people. There is a primary relationship with a partner or team. The work situation becomes the primary social support for the television police officer. The police officer tends to live within his or her job.

Again, domestic tension becomes the basis for antagonism or even secondary plot. The neglected spouse who

says, "You spend more time with your partner than you do with me," is familiar in the police genre. It may, in fact, reflect at an exaggerated level the viewer's tension as a worker or spouse in terms of time spent on the job and at home.

Work in the television tale is a way of living. The partnership is established as one of dependent parts. The police tend to be successful only when they get along and work together. When one is removed or made vulnerable, the others are endangered.

Criminals

The officer's relationship to the police force seems to depend on the nature of the criminal. Much of the criticism of police tales on television has stressed that, with the exception of some uniformed-police tales, the shows do not deal with the real nature of most crime. The criticism is, in one sense, quite true. The overwhelming majority of criminal cases in actuality are domestic, people harming people they know. This, coupled with routine and petty crime, takes up most police time. However, the police tales we see on television are not about real crime and seldom have been. They present, instead, a mythology about crimes that are symbolically important to the viewer.

In television, the overwhelming majority of crimes fall into two categories that may be mythically important but exist only in small numbers in real-

The Message of the Police Tale *(continued)*

ity. The two kinds of criminals predominantly presented on television are individual lunatics and organized crime figures (Mafia, street gangs, drug gangs, terrorists). Organized crime and individual madness are opposites. Each represents something the police officers (and, obviously, the writer) must handle in a different way. When the television show defines the criminal as insane, the individual police officer assigned to the case tends to grow more and more alienated from his or her partner and other officers. The central detective becomes obsessed with catching the mad killer. Since the detective team represents a unified whole, the existence of the lunatic, who is a fragmented personality, mocks the existence of the team and the social response to the threat he or she poses. The hero, in dealing with a lunatic, comes more and more to see that lunatic as a disease to be wiped out and often as a reflection of the officer's own dark side. The hero is impelled to operate the way the lunatic operates and moves outside the law toward emotionalism and violence. . . .

On the other end of the spectrum, when the criminal is a member of organized crime, the police officer tends to work more closely with the members of his or her group. The criminal organization is presented as paralleling the police organization so that there are two institutionalized forces opposing each other. What usually leads to the downfall of organized crime in a police

tale is the criminal body's need for direction from above. If the police can get the key figure, the leader, the organization crumbles. That is not necessarily the way gangs or organized crime really work, but, mythically, it functions that way in television episodes because organized crime is presented as a patriarchy (and, rarely, as a matriarchy). We watch the crumbling of one family (criminal, distorted) in the face of another, the police family.

The police, in contrast to organized criminals on television, are well trained and can function without a hierarchy. The criminals are totally dependent on their rules, their parental figures. The police can be hampered by the rules of law, but unlike the criminals, they are not dependent on their hierarchy. There is no single person a criminal can "get" in the police force to stop an investigation. . . .

The Structure of the Police Show
While you do have the option of altering the pattern, the narrative pattern of police tales exists for a reason. It is familiar, fulfills the functions I have outlined, and provides the framework for the particular kind of moral tale that characterizes the police show.

The pattern which provides a model for treatments for a police episode, is as follows.

1. The tale begins with the *commission of a crime*. This immediately gives us information the police do not have,

The Message of the Police Tale *(continued)*

which places us in a position superior to the hero's.

2. An officer, *the hero, is assigned to the case by chance.* The cop has no personal ties to the case. Obviously, variations can be played in which there is an immediate personal tie, but these are rare. The second problem, usually involving the central figure's partner, is introduced. The problem often reflects the central figure's problem. For example, if Cagney is involved in trying to deal with a criminal who tried to kill her and who she fears will escape punishment in his trial, Lacey may be involved in what proves to be an unfounded fear of a recently released criminal who threatened her years earlier at his trial.

3. *The destruction widens.* The lunatic kills another apparently random victim, or organized criminals blow up one more Vietnamese restaurant. The villain always commits at least two crimes. Whatever the specific nature of the acts, the crimes become more personal to the hero. Perhaps the hero knows the random victim or a relative of the victim, or the random victim bears a painful resemblance to someone the hero knows, or in questioning a relative of the victim the hero begins to identify with the victim. As the crimes continue, they start happening to people who represent something particular and personal to the police officer. In a made-for-television movie or a miniseries and sometimes in an individual one-hour

episode, the officer will begin to neglect his or her personal life and relationships.

4. *The quest becomes more and more obsessive*, and the hero behaves less and less rationally.

5. *The hero meets the criminal.* Sometimes this takes place a bit earlier or later, but it is usually in step 5. Sometimes it is a chance meeting. The hero doesn't know the criminal is the one who committed the crime and, possibly, the criminal doesn't know the hero is the person pursuing him or her. Sometimes the police officer does know but does not have the evidence to hold the culprit. But there is some meeting, perhaps a confrontation, and then the criminal gets away. This usually involves a chase either immediately before the face-to-face confrontation or after it.

6. *The warning.* Someone—spouse, partner, superior—warns the police officer about obsession and the danger of loss of balance. The clichéd line, which exists because it is meaningful, is, "Don't lose your perspective. You're a cop. You have a responsibility to the law, the public." The warning is, of course, ignored.

7. *Following the trail.* The hero has to work his or her way through a cross-section of society in an attempt to find or retrieve the criminal. The rich, the poor, bartenders, taxi drivers, rooming-house owners, bums, and company presidents provide a chain of information that leads to . . . .

8. *The second confrontation.* A

The Message of the Police Tale *(continued)*

direct, open, physical confrontation between the hero and the villain takes place in a hostile or an unfamiliar environment.

9. *The police officer destroys or captures the villain.* The strong tendency in television is not to destroy, however, but to capture, contain, and control the symbol of evil.

10. *The epilogue.* The second prob-lem, that of the partner, is resolved. If the central problem is resolved violently, the secondary problem is usually resolved nonviolently. The resolution of the second problem can also take place during step 8. The criminal dealt with, the hero is either alone and shaken, or, more often, taking the first steps toward returning to the partnership and balance. ■

 Practice

Apply the Media Literacy Paradigm to the previous reading. How did the TV police show originate? How is it mediated (produced)? Who watches and what is the show's impact on the audience?

Popular Programs

No one knows before a television show is broadcast how many viewers it will attract. Very few series last more than three years;

many are cancelled during their first year. One dependable type of program is the daytime TV drama, popularly known as the soap opera because it originated on radio shows and soap companies were often sponsors. Another dependable type of program is the police tale or crime show.

The article on page 374 reveals much about television in its behind-the-scene examination of the world of the prime-time drama. It is revealing for the student of television to look at typical programming, and nothing is more typical than the police drama or "cop show." The reading details the history of this program type and tells how it has evolved.

The Emergence of a New Genre

A new kind of TV program that has recently been developed is the **reality show**. FOX TV's "Cops" and MTV's "Real World" are examples of this new genre. One cable network, Court TV, featured in the accompanying newspaper ad, devotes itself entirely to the reality show, using high-profile court trials as its programming material. Court trials have few production-related costs and live coverage of highly publicized trials delivers huge audiences, which in turn draws advertisers to the network.

Television and Stereotypes

Each person has a mental picture of what the world is like. For centuries this picture was shaped by personal experience and education. These two factors are still present in shaping mental pictures, but a third force assumes an ever-increasing importance. Today, mass media play a major role in teaching people what the world is like, and television sets the standard as electronic teacher.

By pushing aside the limitations of experience and schooling, TV has created a nation of people who have opinions on just about every subject and mental pictures of places never visited, people never encountered, and events experienced only as tiny images on a television screen. News and entertainment media distribute so much information about the world that many educators claim schools are no longer the main source of learning for most people. Television has taken over the role of forming our mental image of the world.

Reprinted courtesy of Court TV. Photographer: Cyndy Warwick.

Our mental map or picture of the world is in some areas quite detailed and well developed. Sometimes, however, our picture of the world is only a rough sketch with few details. Human psychology seems to demand that the sketch be filled in with details. Once the outline is formed we use what we are taught by our parents, schools, and mass media to fill in the details. Often what we are taught, though, is stereotype.

The application to an entire group of the qualities of a limited sample of that group is a **stereotype**. In themselves, stereotypes are a convenient mental device. They help us deal with the vast amount of reality that can never be known in detail. The problem is that most stereotypes contain only a kernel of truth and so are dangerous if taken to be the whole truth.

Stereotypes give people a feeling of security, a feeling that something complex is understood. They provide the illusion that we know our way around in what otherwise would be unknown territory. When the stereotypes we hold (and everyone believes *some* stereotypes) are attacked or challenged, we view this as a personal attack and often actively defend our stereotypes.

Clearly, stereotypes are not limited to the prejudiced or bigoted, to racial categories, or to the unschooled. Many stereotypes are strengthened by television, although at other times TV can replace a commonly held stereotype with a fuller picture. Because of the power of TV, some stereotypes are rather commonly accepted as the full truth.

Television often shows cardboard characters—people whose personalities are not developed in the plot. These cardboard characters—such as the jolly fat man, the dumb secretary, or the hard-boiled cop—are easily recognized by viewers and can be used for laughs or instant plot development. The constant repetition of such characters tends to condition viewers to expect fat people to be jolly, secretaries to be dumb, or cops to be hardboiled. People who belong to often-stereotyped groups find it difficult to overcome media-created expectations.

On television murder, assault, and armed robbery are the most common crimes. In reality burglaries, larcenies, unspectacular auto thefts, and drunkenness and driving under the influence of drugs and alcohol are the most common. Video detectives solve 90 percent of their cases; in reality, the figure is considerably lower. On television a small percentage of violence occurs between relatives, while this accounts for over 30 percent of real-life interpersonal violence, according to some studies.

Groups that are often stereotyped include the following:

Scandinavians	"Jocks"	Handicapped people
Poles	People on welfare	Wealthy persons
Women	Jews	Librarians
Texans	Teenagers	Radicals
New Yorkers	Models	Conservatives
Italians	People over 65	Liberals
French	Homemakers	Professors
African Americans	Intellectuals	Scientists
Mexicans	Construction workers	Overweight people
Artists	Professional athletes	Arabs
Punk rockers	Straight-A students	Politicians

MTV: A Video and Television Revolution

Television has already passed many milestones in its young life that altered the course of its evolution. These milestones include the 1960 Nixon-Kennedy debate, the coverage of Kennedy's assassination, the coverage of the Vietnam war, and the development of communication satellites, to name a few. MTV is another such milestone. It is not that TV aired no music programming before MTV. "American Bandstand," "Soul Train," and before them, "The Lawrence Welk Show" provided musical entertainment. What MTV (Music Television—a cable network) did—and continues to do—is to push the boundaries of the look and feel of TV. Created in 1981 as an all-music video channel for young audiences, MTV constantly strives to use the capabilities of video as a medium in new ways, such as a combination of special digital effects and mixed-media video editing for promotional spots. If the saying that "imitation is the sincerest form of flattery" is true, MTV has been amazingly successful. Production techniques pioneered by MTV are routinely adopted by other producers, networks, and advertisers.

Popularizing New Production Techniques

The rapid-fire editing found in countless videos and in MTV promotional spots is one example of new production techniques imitated by other producers. The pace is so fast that hundreds of shots can be found in a 15-second span. The handheld jerky camera movements that are so common in ads and on shows such as "NYPD Blue" were also introduced on a regular basis by MTV. Another important but rarely noticed production technique is the synchronizing of visual edits to the beat of music. In most music videos, if you tap your foot to the music, the shot will change in time with the beat. This is now standard practice in ads using music. More than any other network, MTV integrates digital production technologies in its programming. It is often the first network, for example, to air an interview with strobed or intentionally fuzzy special effects.

How Do They Think of That Stuff?

Why is it that the people who produce material for MTV are so conscious of experimenting with the acoustic and visual capabilities of the medium? One answer could be that they represent the first generation of Americans who grew up with TV. They grew up watching such programs as "Leave It To Beaver," "Bewitched," "Mod Squad," and the hundreds of other shows that defined TV in its first 25 years. The people who created those shows grew up on film and radio. Television was a new medium to them, and their shows reflected it. The plots of that first generation of TV were patterned after the structure of radio dramas, and the shows were shot using standard film techniques. The mediators of current TV took for granted what the first generation provided and have moved the art form of TV into new territory. Think of it: TV went from "Father Knows Best" to "Liquid Television" in one generation.

How Will You Change TV?

What will you, the first generation to grow up on MTV, create when you work at the production companies and networks in 10 to 15 years? If you take MTV for granted now, how will you push the boundaries out even farther when your generation is in charge? The coming of interactive digital media will allow you ample opportunity to be part of setting many new milestones.

How Television Works
Broadcast Television

According to the *Gale Directory of Publications and Broadcasting Media*, there are currently about 1,350 television stations in the United States, roughly equal to the number of daily newspapers. Television stations operate on channels 2–13 (VHF) and channels 14–83 (UHF). Adjacent VHF channels (2 and 3, or 7 and 8, for example) in the same city could interfere with each other and so are usually separated by an unused channel. This means that even large metropolitan areas have only about five **VHF** (**Very High Frequency**) stations. **UHF** (the **Ultrahigh Frequency**) has many more channels available. UHF stations have a smaller coverage area than VHF stations because of the higher frequencies on which they operate. Because they reach fewer people, such stations are not as attractive to advertisers. Currently they tend to be smaller stations with smaller audiences than VHF.

VHF stations operate on frequencies similar to those of FM radio stations (in fact, TV sound is FM) and can therefore reach only a area in a 50- to 100-mile radius from the transmitting tower. If you had a television set that could tune between channels 6 and 7, you could listen to local FM radio stations on the TV set; FM radio would be considered channel $6\frac{1}{2}$.

Television stations are privately owned businesses just like newspapers, radio stations, or publishing companies. Unlike these other communications industries, however, television stations are licensed by the Federal Communications Commission (FCC) to serve the "public interest." Every three years a station's license must be renewed, and, to keep its license, the station must prove that it has served the public.

According to court-supported decisions, the channels belong to the people. Television stations are licensed to use those channels only to serve the public in their viewing area. If any person or group can prove that a station has not served the viewing public, then that station could lose its license. In theory, a TV station that broadcasts only network shows and old movies could lose its license for failure to treat local issues. In practice, the FCC has refused license renewals only a few times since the beginning of television.

A television production studio. *Courtesy of CLTV News, Illinois.*

The logos of the four major broadcast television networks

Nearly 85 percent of all television stations are **affiliated** with (but not owned by) one of four major networks—Columbia Broadcasting System (CBS), American Broadcasting Company (ABC), National Broadcasting Company (NBC), and Fox Broadcasting Company (FOX). The most profitable stations are generally those affiliated with these commercial networks. A TV station that does not belong to a major network is either an independent or a member of the Public Broadcasting Service (PBS). Independent stations program movies, local sports, and syndicated TV shows (often reruns of TV series originally run on major networks). PBS stations, sometimes called educational TV, generally carry cultural and educational programming. PBS is supported by government grants (currently subject to possible budgetary cuts by Congress), donations from foundations and corporations, and contributions from individuals and groups. PBS is not as dependent on advertisers as commercial television networks are. However, PBS stations do present messages about their underwriters or supporters. Messages about businesses shown on PBS are intended to present corporate images; they do not sell specific products as commercials do on network television.

Networks and Local Stations

Networks are not television stations; they do not broadcast programs. They supply programs to the local television affiliate by using telephone lines or satellites. Each local TV station is ultimately responsible for its own programming. A station can choose not to broadcast a network-supplied program, but such refusals are rare. Networks supply local stations with morning news, game shows, "soap operas," evening news, and nighttime programs. Local stations must fill in with their own programming (usually movies, local news, or reruns) when the networks do not supply programming.

The networks provide programs free to the affiliates and are paid for the advertising time they can sell during the program. A 30-second "spot" commercial in network **prime time** (the desirable evening hours) sent to all the network affiliates in the country costs an advertiser $1,000 and up. A 30-second spot on the first TV showing of a major movie can cost well over $600,000. The exact cost depends on the popularity of the program: the more viewers, the higher the cost.

A small amount of time during each program is left for the local station to sell to local advertisers. This advertising constitutes the main source of income for local stations. Local stations also receive some of the money their network is paid for national commercials.

Networks obtain their programs either by making them (news and documentaries), by covering live events (special news events, sports), or by purchasing the programs from producers. Most prime-time programs and weekly programs are supplied to the networks by producers. The producers (or sponsors of an event such as the National Basketball Association or the National Football League) receive money from the networks; the networks receive money from national advertisers; local stations receive money from local advertisers.

Cable Television

Cable television began in the late 1940s as a simple solution to a problem in rural areas. In mountainous areas far from television stations, an enterprising businessperson would construct a huge master antenna on a mountaintop to capture TV signals from

Many schools have their own cable television studios and produce their own programs. *Photo: Jeff Ellis Photography, Chicago.*

stations 100 or more miles away. People in the area paid a fee to have their own set wired by a cable to the master antenna. People thus had good TV reception without the expense of an elaborate rooftop antenna. Any signal fed into the antenna could be relayed easily through the cables to the system's subscribers.

The next step in the development of cable television was the realization that, because everyone was hooked up by wire, it would be relatively easy and inexpensive to set up a small TV studio and feed original programs into the antenna. Some stations set up an automatic revolving camera that scanned a clock and a weather forecast and sent this service to subscribers on an otherwise unused channel.

From isolated rural areas cable television moved to large cities. There the problem of TV reception is also difficult because signals ricochet off tall buildings and airplanes, causing "ghosts" on home TV receivers. With TV sets connected directly to a tall master antenna, such problems were eliminated, so cable television moved to some cities. A few cable systems offered subscribers additional channels brought in from nearby cities as an added service.

TOP 20 CABLE NETWORKS
RANKED BY NUMBER OF SUBSCRIBERS

1. ESPN*
   Affiliates: 26,700   Subscribers: 63.0 million

11. MTV: MUSIC TELEVISION
   Affiliates: 8,730   Subscribers: 59.4 million

2. CNN (CABLE NEWS NETWORK)*
   Affiliates: 11,654†   Subscribers: 62.6 million

12. LIFETIME TELEVISION
   Affiliates: 5,800   Subscribers: 59.0 million

3. THE DISCOVERY CHANNEL
   Affiliates: 10,036   Subscribers: 62.0 million

NICKELODEON/NICK AT NITE
   Affiliates: 9,171   Subscribers: 59.0 million
   (NICK)
   Affiliates: 4,381
   (N@N)

USA NETWORK*
   Affiliates: 12,500   Subscribers: 62.0 million

14. THE WEATHER CHANNEL
   Affiliates: 5,550   Subscribers: 55.4 million

Weather You Can
Always Turn To™

5. TNN (THE NASHVILLE NETWORK)*
   Affiliates: 15,790   Subscribers: 61.3 million

15. HEADLINE NEWS
   Affiliates: 11,654   Subscribers: 54.47 million

C-SPAN
6. C-SPAN
   Affiliates: 4,599   Subscribers: 61.1 million

16. CNBC*
   Affiliates: 4,000   Subscribers: 52.0 million

7. THE FAMILY CHANNEL*
   Affiliates: 12,860   Subscribers: 60.2 million

17. AMC (AMERICAN MOVIE CLASSICS)
   Affiliates: NA   Subscribers: 51.0 million

8. TBS*
   Affiliates: 14,954   Subscribers: 60.03 million

18. VH1 (VIDEO HITS ONE)
   Affiliates: 5,304   Subscribers: 50.2 million

9. A&E NETWORK (A&E)
   Affiliates: 9,400   Subscribers: 60.0 million

19. QVC
   Affiliates: 4,977   Subscribers: 48.5 million

TNT (TURNER NETWORK TELEVISION)
   Affiliates: 8,731   Subscribers: 60.0 million

20. BET (BLACK ENTERTAINMENT TELEVISION)
   Affiliates: 2,622   Subscribers: 40.1 million

Reprinted by permission of the National Cable Television Association in Washington, D.C., from *Cable Television Developments*, Fall 1994.

The cables used to connect the TV antenna to the set can transmit hundreds, some say thousands, of channels of information. Cable television opens the possibility of more TV channels than are possible with broadcast television. The combination of this larger multichannel potential plus the perfect picture fed into every set could lead to cable television replacing broadcast television.

The greatest benefit of cable television is that it offers a large number of channels to everyone. With current television programming, millions of viewers are needed to make a program a lasting success. If only a few hundred thousand people are interested enough to watch, the program dies. This leaves many interests unsatisfied. With cable TV a local chess tournament that might attract only 2,000 viewers could easily be shown, as could the city council meeting, the stock market ticker, a wire service video teletype machine, and similar programs for other special interest groups. In addition, the Federal Communications Commission has required each cable operator to provide a channel for ordinary citizens to express their viewpoints—a **public access channel**. The cable operator is also charged with providing assistance with videotape equipment to interested parties who wish to make a tape to be used on the public access channel.

By 1994 about 60 cable networks had become available, ranging from all news programming to music video formats, such as MTV, and from all movie or sports channels to channels devoted to children or family entertainment, such as the Disney Channel. The top 20 cable networks as of 1994 are shown in the chart on page 389.

Some cable networks produce full-length movies strictly for cable channels. In the future, first-run movies may open at movie theaters and on cable television at the same time. If that happens, the future of movie theaters will be affected.

The most revolutionary aspect of cable television is that it can easily function as a two-way communication system. Because each house is connected by a cable, messages can be sent back to the central sending station. Just as with telephone wires, the video cable can carry video or audio messages in both directions. The technology for two-way cable television exists now on a limited basis. Two-way cable TV could easily become as common and essential as a telephone in the not-too-distant future.

With two-way cable and the necessary coding and message-sending boxes, subscribers can gain access to their savings and checking accounts to pay bills via TV; they can take part in school or special education classes from home; they can shop, vote, or express opinions on important public issues; or even call up research information from the local library computer.

Comparing Over-the-Air and Cable TV

Over-the-Air	**Cable**
Quality of signal varies with location of set and with weather.	Consistent high quality of transmission for everyone.
Number of channels available is limited. Even a large city such as Chicago has only 16 channels.	Over 60 cable networks available in addition to commercial networks.
Currently reaches about 98 percent of all households.	Currently reaches about 63 percent of all households with TV sets.
Requires a TV set and sometimes a rooftop antenna.	Requires that the house be wired to the cable operator. The hook-up charge ranges from nothing to $100.
Free. No monthly bills.	Those wired to the system pay an average monthly fee of $25.
One-way system.	Has the potential for two-way communication.
Needs many viewers to interest advertisers.	Needs far fewer viewers than over-the-air transmission to be economically workable.
Few individuals can obtain TV time to state their opinions.	Each cable franchise is required to have at least one channel for citizen access.

Viewing Options

A continuing trend is that the major broadcast TV networks are losing their monopoly on our viewing time. Cable television, satellite dishes, independent "superstations," and alternative networks mean the average household can now see almost 60 TV channels. Television networks now have more competition and find fewer viewers in prime time, especially on Friday and Saturday nights. In the 1970s major networks used to count on capturing 90 percent of all TV viewers; in the 1980s, that figure was closer to 75 percent.

Competition for viewers now comes from cable TV networks; independent superstations, such as Turner Broadcasting's WTBS in Atlanta, WOR-TV in New York, and Chicago's WGN; public television; Spanish-language television; home video software;

home shopping stations; radio networks; and pay-per-view or pre-mium cable movie channels such as HBO and Showtime.

Advertisers are spending more money on cable stations because they can deliver a more controlled audience. This reflects a move away from "bigger is better" in audiences to capturing the loyalty of defined segments of the public. Some network executives see television as having two levels. They view network television (which they call "free" TV) as being much like a basic car with no options. They see a second level controlled by cable networks that deliver first-run movies and sporting events. Of course, this second level is not free.

Television Ratings

A number of companies offer ratings services to television and radio. The largest and best-known company is Nielsen Media Research Company. The Nielsen ratings have been accused of reflecting only the habits of those who watch a lot of televi-sion—not the occasional viewer who seeks out a particular show. The networks, however, have found this system the best available and so the Nielsen ratings usually determine a program's future—or lack of it.

The ratings list on page 393 indicates the relative popularity of shows in October 1994. For example, on Monday, October 17, 16 million watched "Fresh Prince of Bel-Air," which earned it a rating of 10.7 (one ratings point represents 954,000 TV house-holds). This means that approximately 17 percent of all households with a television watched "Fresh Prince," which made it the 47th most popular show for the week.

(Although networks have lost viewers to their cable competitors, they still are the dominant delivery system of programming. By adding up the shares of the four broadcast networks in the 8:00 P.M. time slot, you come up with 69. That means that almost 70 percent of all the homes in America that were watching TV at that time were watching one of the four networks, while the other 30 percent were dividing their viewing among the dozens of other public, independent, and cable channels.)

Measurement Techniques

Nielsen Media Research compiles its ratings by installing devices called "people meters" in 4000 carefully chosen households. These

'Grace' leads ABC to tie with CBS

By Robin DeRosa
USA TODAY

ABC and CBS tied for first place in the ratings last week, with a 12.1 rating and a 20 share.

But ABC had the No. 1 show, *Grace Under Fire*, bumping *Home Improvement* into second place. This

NIELSEN RATINGS

marks the first time *Grace* has been the No. 1 show during the regular season.

Other ABC shows in the top 10: *Monday Night Football*, No. 4; *Roseanne*, No. 6; *Ellen*, No. 9; and *NYPD*

Blue, No. 10.

CBS' *60 Minutes* was No. 5 and *Murder, She Wrote* was No. 7. And the CBS Sunday movie, *Ghost*, at No. 12, beat NBC's *Danielle Steel's Family Album*, No. 15, and ABC's *Terminator 2: Judgment Day*, No. 25. CBS' new medical show, Thursday's *Chicago Hope*, was No. 31.

NBC is having success with its new medical drama, *ER*, which has steadily been climbing up the ratings chart to No. 3 last week.

And NBC's acclaimed police show *Homicide: Life on the Street* is still struggling in its Friday 10 p.m. ET/PT time slot, No. 75 for the week, losing to ABC's *20/20*, No. 23.

Using this chart

▶ Ratings information comes from Nielsen Media Research.

▶ A ratings point represents 954,000 TV households. shares are the percentage of sets in use; number of viewers is in millions.

▶ (*) indicates a Nielsen ratings tie.

▶ (r) indicates a repeat episode.

▶ (s) indicates a special broadcast

Top 10

1 Grace Under Fire (ABC)
2 Home Improvement (ABC)
3 ER (NBC)
4 Monday Night Football (ABC)
5 60 Minutes (CBS)
6 Roseanne (ABC)
7 Murder, She Wrote (CBS)
8 Seinfeld (NBC)
9 Ellen (ABC)
10 NYPD Blue (ABC)

Bottom 5

91 Empty Nest (NBC)
92 Party of Five (Fox)
93 Something Wilder (NBC)
94 Encounters (Fox)
95 M.A.N.T.I.S. (Fox)

Network ratings

For the week	Season to date
ABC: 12.1	ABC: 12.0
CBS: 12.1	CBS: 11.8
NBC: 11.4	NBC: 11.8
Fox: 7.7	Fox: 7.6

Evening news

For the week	Last week
ABC: 9.8	ABC: 9.8
CBS: 8.8	CBS: 8.6
NBC: 8.2	NBC: 8.5

Monday, October 17, 1994

	Viewers	Rating	Share	Rank
8:00 The Nanny (CBS)	18.2	13.0	20	*20
Coach (ABC)	15.9	11.1	18	*38
Fresh Prince of Bel-Air (NBC)	16.0	10.7	17	*47
Melrose Place (Fox)	13.2	9.5	14	61
8:30 Dave's World (CBS)	21.4	14.8	22	14
Blossom (NBC)	16.2	11.1	17	*38
Blue Skies (ABC)	11.1	7.8	12	*75
9:00 Monday Night Football (ABC)	25.5	18.7	32	4
Murphy Brown (CBS)	21.9	15.8	23	11
Moment of Truth (NBC)	16.4	12.7	20	*25
Party of Five (Fox)	7.7	5.6	8	92
9:30 Love & War (CBS)	18.7	13.9	21	17
10:00 Northern Exposure (CBS)	18.0	13.5	22	19

Tuesday, October 18, 1994

	Viewers	Rating	Share	Rank
8:00 Full House (ABC)	18.8	12.4	20	27
Wings (NBC)	18.2	12.3	20	28
Rescue 911 (CBS)	15.6	10.8	17	46
Stop or My Mom Will Shoot (Fox)	10.2	6.8	11	89
8:30 Me and the Boys (ABC)	19.7	12.8	20	*23
Wings (NBC) (r)	17.8	12.1	19	*29
9:00 Home Improvement (ABC)	33.2	20.4	00	2
Frasier (NBC)	21.0	14.9	22	13
Sleeping With the Enemy (CBS)	14.0	10.5	17	*50
9:30 Grace Under Fire (CBS)	31.6	20.5	31	1
John Larroquette Show (NBC)	15.1	10.9	17	*42
10:00 NYPD Blue (ABC)	22.1	16.1	27	10
Dateline (NBC)	14.4	10.9	18	*42

Wednesday, October 19, 1994

	Viewers	Rating	Share	Rank
8:00 Beverly Hills, 90210 (Fox)	15.5	11.1	18	*38
Cosby Mysteries (NBC)	14.7	10.9	18	*42
Thunder Alley (ABC)	15.1	9.8	17	*55
The Boys Are Back (CBS)	11.4	8.3	14	*71
8:30 All-American Girl (ABC)	16.3	10.7	17	*47
Dave's World (CBS) (r)	10.3	7.5	12	*79
9:00 Roseanne (ABC)	26.9	17.7	28	6
Dateline (NBC)	12.9	9.6	15	*59
Touched by an Angel (CBS)	12.4	9.0	14	68
Models, Inc. (Fox)	9.4	7.3	12	*84
9:30 Ellen (ABC)	24.2	16.3	26	9
10:00 Law & Order (NBC)	18.2	13.6	24	18
48 Hours (CBS)	14.8	11.2	19	*36
Turning Point (ABC)	12.9	9.8	17	*55

Thursday, October 20, 1994

	Viewers	Rating	Share	Rank
8:00 Mad About You (NBC)	20.0	14.0	23	16
Due South (CBS)	16.1	10.7	17	*47
Martin (Fox)	12.4	7.6	12	78
My So-Called Life (ABC)	9.3	6.7	11	90
8:30 Friends (NBC)	18.6	12.9	20	22
Living Single (Fox)	13.1	8.3	13	*71
9:00 Seinfeld (NBC) (r)	25.4	17.2	26	8
Chicago Hope (CBS)	16.3	12.0	18	*31
Matlock (ABC)	14.1	10.4	16	52
Cops I (Fox)	11.8	7.5	11	*79
9:30 Madman of the People (NBC)	18.8	13.0	20	*20
Cops II (Fox)	12.2	7.7	12	77
10:00 ER (NBC)	27.3	19.4	32	3
Eye to Eye/Connie Chung (CBS)	12.4	9.8	16	*55
PrimeTime Live (ABC)	9.7	7.1	12	*86

Friday, October 21, 1994

	Viewers	Rating	Share	Rank
8:00 Family Matters (ABC)	17.4	11.4	22	34
Diagnosis Murder (CBS)	13.6	10.1	19	53
Unsolved Mysteries (NBC)	12.7	9.1	17	*66
M.A.N.T.I.S. (Fox)	7.7	4.8	9	95
8:30 Boy Meets World (ABC)	19.0	11.6	21	33
9:00 In the Heat of the Night (CBS) (s)	16.7	12.0	21	*31
Step by Step (ABC)	18.0	11.0	19	41
Dateline (NBC)	13.1	9.7	16	58
X-Files (Fox)	15.5	9.6	16	*59
9:30 Hangin' With Mr. Cooper (ABC)	16.9	10.9	18	*42
10:00 20/20 (ABC)	18.1	12.8	23	*23
Homicide: Life on the Street (NBC)	10.9	7.8	14	*75

Saturday, October 22, 1994

	Viewers	Rating	Share	Rank
8:00 Dr. Quinn, Medicine Woman (CBS)	16.8	11.2	21	*36
Problem Child 2 (ABC)	14.8	8.7	16	70
Cops (Fox)	10.2	6.9	13	88
Empty Nest (NBC)	8.1	6.0	12	91
8:30 Cops 2 (Fox) (r)	10.9	7.4	14	*82
Something Wilder (NBC)	7.4	5.5	10	93
9:00 Five Mrs. Buchanans (CBS)	13.1	9.4	17	62
Sweet Justice (NBC)	11.3	8.3	15	*71
America's Most Wanted (Fox)	10.1	7.1	13	*86
9:30 Hearts Afire (CBS)	12.5	8.9	16	69
10:00 Walker, Texas Ranger (CBS)	18.6	12.1	23	*29
The Commish (ABC)	13.4	9.1	17	*66
Sisters (NBC)	10.9	8.2	15	*74

Sunday, October 23, 1994

	Viewers	Rating	Share	Rank
7:00 60 Minutes (CBS)	25.5	18.4	31	5
America's Funniest Home Videos (ABC)	15.0	9.3	16	*63
Unexplained: Witches (NBC) (s)	10.7	7.3	12	*84
7:10 Encounters (Fox)	7.5	5.2	9	94
7:30 On Our Own (ABC)	15.2	9.2	15	65
8:00 Murder, She Wrote (CBS)	23.9	17.4	27	7
seaQuest DSV (NBC)	18.7	11.3	17	35
Lois & Clark (ABC)	18.2	10.5	16	*50
The Simpsons (Fox) (r)	15.5	9.3	14	*63
8:30 Hardball (Fox)	11.8	7.5	11	*79
9:00 Ghost (CBS)	21.7	15.3	25	12
Danielle Steel's Family Album Pt. 1 (NBC)	19.9	14.5	23	15
Terminator 2: Judgment Day (ABC)	20.5	12.7	21	*25
Married ... With Children (Fox)	15.7	9.9	15	54
9:30 George Carlin Show (Fox)	11.6	7.4	11	*82

Reprinted by permission of USA Today.

selected "Nielsen households" are given small gifts for their help and assistance in paying for TV repairs. Households that have been in the sample for 24 months are replaced to increase the total number of households and prevent skewed or inaccurate measurements. Nielsen claims that the randomly selected group of households mirrors the interests and characteristics of the entire population. While this may seem unlikely, TV businesspeople accept it to be statistically true.

Nielsen households are equipped with a people meter, which is a small device containing a sophisticated microprocessor that sits atop the television set. Each household member's age, sex, and other demographic information is programmed into the Nielsen people meter. An accompanying remote-control device records who is viewing. Both have a series of buttons, one for each member of the household and guest viewers. Each household member pushes the assigned button when beginning to watch television.

Advertisers can thus determine if the members of a specific target audience—say men aged 25 to 54 who watch the first basketball game of the season—continue to watch through the finals. Nielsen is also developing an audience measurement system that is passive, meaning it requires no viewer button pushing. An infrared scanning system scans the viewing area in a room in seven seconds, detects and records heat generated by people, and processes the information. The passive scanner supplements the people meter to determine when someone enters or leaves the viewing area. Each day, Nielsen computers "call" the people meters at 3:00 A.M. to gather information. By 3:15 P.M. that same day Nielsen produces the daily ratings report, which is then available to its clients electronically.

The VCR and Videotape

The home VCR (videocassette recorder) is a relatively young electronic medium, who celebrates its twenty-first birthday as a consumer product in 1997. Back in 1976, when Sony introduced the first consumer version of a VCR, most thought it a toy for the wealthy. As recently as 1984, only 12 percent of households owned a VCR; today this rapidly maturing invention sits in nearly 80 percent of all American households, according to Nielsen Media Research. The videotape machine has changed our entertainment habits and is now changing the nature of commercial television.

The VCR introduced the concept of "time shifting," meaning

The latest in videocassette recorder technology. *Courtesy of Magnavox/ Philips Consumer Electronics.*

viewers could view what they want when they want. A VCR owner no longer has to turn down a social invitation just to be able to stay home and watch a favorite series or the final installment of a made-for-TV miniseries. No one knows how many prime time TV shows or sports events are taped and watched the next day, but millions of machines turn themselves on every night in obedience to preset directions.

Sports fans now enjoy the security of knowing they will be able to view Sunday's "big game" even if they are not at home when it's played. Of course, they also know how difficult it is to avoid hearing or reading about the final score until they watch the tape.

The VCR is threatening to TV network programming because it gives viewers some control over commercials. The millions who watch a network broadcast on tape often fast-forward right through the commercials. Should TV sponsors receive a rebate from the networks for all the lost commercial time? VCRs threaten the networks' schedules, carefully prepared to capture audiences.

Viewers using a VCR can watch shows aired simultaneously on competing networks. VCRs play havoc with television rating systems, making old concepts of "audience share" obsolete. Before 1976, using the TV set at night meant watching ABC, CBS, NBC, or public TV. Today a VCR and videocassette tapes can provide a whole week's TV viewing without a single program from a cable or broadcast network.

Without a doubt, VCRs have revolutionized the movie industry. Going out to the movies today means a social night out to see what's new. No theater can survive on reruns and old movies.

The latest in remote controls. *Photo courtesy of Magnavox/Philips Consumer Electronics.*

Older movies, in contrast, can live for years on the shelves of video stores instead of silently vanishing when their run in local theaters ends. People might go to the movie theater less often today than in years past, but they spend more time watching movies on television.

Consider how videotape has changed living patterns:

- Before 1976 no video stores existed. Today, video rental outlets are as commonplace as gas stations and fast-food franchises. Many supermarkets even rent videotapes right next to the bakery and produce departments.
- The camcorder has virtually replaced super-8 home movies as a way to document the life of a family. A family album is as likely to be on videocassettes as photographs.
- Disasters, such as tornadoes, plane crashes, and other news events often reported but rarely seen live, are now seen more often captured on a bystander's camcorder.
- Many high schools offer videotape versions alongside or instead of the school yearbook.
- Instructional videos, from aerobics to how to improve

your golf score or fix a leaky faucet, now teach difficult-to-explain subjects even to those not highly literate.

Flipping, Zapping, and Zipping

Another innocent-looking invention that changed television is the remote control. If you use remote control, you know it as a convenience. However, those who make TV schedules and keep a pulse on what the public watches know it has changed the way we use television. Remote control has created new types of viewers—the flippers, zappers, and zippers.

One-third of all TV viewers are "flippers." They change channels instead of watching a program from beginning to end. Younger viewers are more likely to be flippers. According to a J. Walter Thompson survey, over 50 percent of 18- to 24-year-old viewers are flippers. Only 9 percent are "zappers"—they zap out ads, changing the channel when one comes on. Zappers treat television the way some handle a pushbutton car radio, looking for music and avoiding ads. Nearly 20 percent of viewers are "zippers," who avoid commercials by fast-forwarding through them while watching on a VCR.

Why are flippers, zappers, and zippers a problem for television? Television depends on delivering a measured number of viewers to advertisers. Measurement systems have not yet caught up with those who graze from channel to channel instead of watching single programs when broadcast. These new viewing patterns suggest television is following the pattern of radio.

When radio was a young medium, people listened to entire programs from beginning to end. The shows were listed in radio guides and broadcast weekly much as television schedules are today. A radio schedule from the 1920s bears a surprising resemblance to today's evening TV schedules. However, television changed radio. Today, people listen to "the radio"; they rarely tune in specific programs at a set time. Radio is part of the electronic environment and is often listened to while doing other tasks. Television is becoming a constant part of the electronic environment—on all the time—serving sometimes as a background and other times as a foreground. Cable TV, VCRs, and increased program choices have changed the nature of television. Today, we watch MTV, the news, a sportscast, the weather forecast, or "Seinfeld," or some other favorite program. Increasingly, however, we just watch "the tube".

Future Watch: Television in the Interactive Age

HDTV (High-Definition Television)

Television in the 1990s has seen the most dramatic change since 1954, the year color TV was introduced. High-definition television (HDTV) promises a picture as clear as that on a movie screen with stereo sound matching that of the digital audiotape. HDTV is already operative in Japan, where the system was demonstrated with daily hour-long broadcasts on publicly placed HDTV screens.

HDTV's technology is digital—it has more in common with a computer than a traditional TV set. The implications of HDTV go far beyond merely bigger screens and clearer pictures. According to the American Electronics Association, HDTV means "an eventual merger of communications, computer, and entertainment into interrelated high-resolution digital technologies and markets. The resulting electronics-based industry may well underlie the world's economy and shape its political organization in the 21st century."

The prime obstacle to HDTV is that it is not compatible with our existing broadcast system. The FCC has ruled that HDTV must be compatible with existing sets, just as the first color transmissions had to be compatible with older black-and-white receivers. HDTV requires more than an improved TV set—it needs a whole new broadcast system. The current American broadcast system (called NTSC) scans a picture tube 525 times with a resolution of about 300 dots per line. Current European sets use a more advanced system and scan 625 lines per image. HDTV, in comparison, will feature over 1000 lines per image and 1000 dots per line.

Direct Broadcast Satellites

If you owned your own home satellite dish back in August 1989 you could have tuned to GE Satcom F2R, Transponder 13, at 71 degrees west longitude, 3960 megahertz, vertical polarity—and have seen the future. The future consisted of digital pictures transmitted from

Student Close-Up

Antoinette Bennett, New York

•••

A teenaged video producer tells how she uses the medium of videotape in terms of her communication goals.

My biggest rush as a young person producing my own video documentary is the power I feel: the power to communicate my personal ideas and opinions about any particular issue to a great mass of people who otherwise would have never heard of me or about my opinion. Our society always looks down on young people and treats them as if they don't have anything of importance to say. Young people have a different way of speaking and may go about getting things accomplished in an unconventional way. This in turn makes adults afraid of what they cannot understand, so their way of handling it is by not taking us seriously. Using video as a way of combating this problem has proven to be successful for me because now I'm dealing with society on a level that is understood by all.

Growing up, I was so busy working towards personal achievements, dancing and running track, I had no concern for others and the ills in our society. While in a New York City high school, I had to "wake up and smell the coffee." My peers' lives reflect many things considered problems in our society, from poverty to violence. After experiencing life through the eyes of my peers, I was transformed into a young black female with a mission. This mission is to make people aware of what's really going on with young people today. When introduced to producing using video, I decided that this would be the outlet for carrying out my mission.

My first video documentary is called *360 Degrees of Violence.* This video was produced during 1992–1993 at the Educational Video Center, a nonprofit organization in New York City, where I worked with eight other students from different high schools. It offers a more in-depth analysis of the overall problem of violence in New York City public high schools. Students, parents, and community leaders were looking critically at the use of metal detectors in the city high schools, weighing the pros and cons of other initiatives to deterring violence. We wanted to show what actually happens to students.

My experience as a teen video producer has given me a clear understanding of what I must do to accomplish my goal of becoming a professional video producer. Now, at age nineteen, I am employed at the Educational Video Center and am working on video documentaries on domestic and street violence. ∎

Antoinette Bennett. *Photo courtesy of Duane Cunningham.*

Voyager 2 during its flight past the planet Neptune and of live news conferences by Voyager scientists. The transmission by-passed TV networks and beamed the programs via satellite directly into the home of anyone with a correctly tuned backyard satellite dish.

The technology for receiving direct broadcast satellite (DBS) transmissions is now available to the consumer. Satellites are sending stronger signals; now homeowners can use smaller satellite dishes. DBS broadcasting has existed for some time in Europe, where there is economic incentive to overcome national borders. Now in Europe as well as the U.S., older satellite dishes the size of a house are being replaced with smaller dishes hardly more visible than the standard rooftop TV antenna. Another, more technical name for a home satellite dish is TVRO, which stands for TV Receive Only earth station. With the system described in the following illustration, the satellite dish or receiver is only 18 inches wide.

Looking to the Next Century

In addition to improvements in picture quality and variety of sources, such as satellites, cable TV, and on-line computer

RCA has recently introduced their 18" Digital Satellite System™ (DSS) for the consumer. Satellite transmissions are picked up by the 18" dish. With the receiver—similar to a cable box—and an interactive remote, an individual can choose from up to 150 channels of information and entertainment. *Photo courtesy of RCA/Thomson Consumer Electronics.*

programs, the biggest change to watch for in the future is in the area of interactivity. It is almost a sure thing that we will have giant, flat-screen, wall-hung HDTVs. Whether the programming displayed on them comes into our homes by phone line, cable, over-the-air broadcast, or satellite depends on several factors: the evolution of technology, government regulation, capitalistic competition, and consumer needs. The big question is how much control we'll have from our homes to send information back down the line (or through the air). Many media experts point to the efforts of cable, phone, and entertainment companies to create "video-on-demand" (VOD). They believe that the first major new service millions of us will be willing to pay for is the ability to instantly access a movie or show from a database of thousands of video products. Goodbye video stores?

Reflections

- Why do so many Americans watch so much TV? To what degree does the L.O.P. theory stated in the first reading explain your own TV viewing?
- In what ways can TV be compared to addictive drugs?
- One of the undeniable effects of TV is that it takes up a lot of time. If TV were to vanish, a lot of extra time would be available to do other things. How would you be different if you had this time to fill? How would you spend your time differently? How would society be different?
- Several countries have conducted experiments in which all TVs were removed from selected communities for periods ranging from a week to a year. In a typical experiment researchers in Germany found that after a few months, tensions and conflict increased among family members who had previously watched a lot of TV. Why do you think this happened? What are the ramifications of your conclusion?
- Obtain a weeknight program listing from *TV Guide* or your local newspaper and study it for what is on from 6:00 P.M. to midnight. Compose a piece of science fiction based on the following premise: You are a sociologist from another solar system far more socially and technologically advanced than ours. In advance of your first visit to Earth, you intercept one complete night of TV programming (from 6:00 to midnight) and watch it all. Use this programming as data to make predictions about life on Earth before you actually visit. What is the most important conclusion you draw from your data about what life is like on Earth? Remember, you will view all programming on all channels during that time, *including all the ads*. Remember, too, that you are drawing conclusions about life on Earth as a whole. Address issues of *content* (what is shown) as well as of *structure* (how do people experience TV? What do they do while watching it? What is the effect of interruptions for sales purposes?

Building Your Media Archive
Archive Analysis

Classifying your archive TV show should be fairly straightforward. Depending on how deeply you want to examine the origin of your show, you may wish to research the production company. As a group project, your class may write to the company for information on how the TV program was developed.

Analyzing your show's mediation is also quite straightforward. By answering the questions in the Mediation stage of the paradigm—especially the questions regarding conventions of presentation—you will be able to conduct a thorough analysis of your show.

As with examining the show's origin, you can do some extra research into how your show is consumed. If your show is a popular one, you can check the Nielsen ratings, which are published on a weekly basis in most major newspapers, to get some information on it. You may try writing the companies that advertise on the show and research advertising costs. First make some observations about whom the show seems targeted to based on the types of products advertised. Watch the program *and* commercials. Who does the advertiser want to reach by placing their ads on that show? How often do they advertise on that particular show?

One area to focus on as you investigate the consumption of your show is how personal background affects viewing perceptions. Write a personal response to a show, then interview and get the point of view of someone with a very different background. How do the two responses differ? The genre of your show will to some extent guide how you address its impact on the consumer and society. If the program is a nonfiction genre, such as a talk show or reality show, you could explore the issues of how society's standards of sexuality and violence evolve over time. If your show is of a fictional genre, such as a soap opera or sitcom, you might focus on the personal effects of watching shows like yours. (If you write the production company that created the show, ask them about international distribution. What other countries get the show? Is it broadcast in English? How popular is the show in other countries? From this information you can make educated guesses about the global impact of your show specifically, and about TV in general.)

MEDIA LAB

Analyzing Television

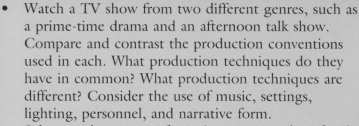

- Watch a TV show from two different genres, such as a prime-time drama and an afternoon talk show. Compare and contrast the production conventions used in each. What production techniques do they have in common? What production techniques are different? Consider the use of music, settings, lighting, personnel, and narrative form.
- Select a subcategory of a major genre, such as family sitcom or hospital drama. Identify and analyze stereotyped characters. How are they presented? In what situations? How do their attitudes, goals, values, and looks contribute to the stereotype?
- Compare and contrast the structure of a current cop show with the 10-point structure in the reading "The Message of the Police Tale."
- Debate whether TV causes real-life violence. Divide into teams and debate the following proposition: American society is more violent today because of TV than it was prior to TV. Regardless of which side you are responsible to argue, research the incidence of violence in several pre-television eras of human and American history. How violent was life during the American westward expansion of the 1900s, and for whom was it violent? How violent was life in the South for African-Americans before and after the Civil War? What was life like during the Middle Ages in Europe prior to all electronic mass media? Social studies teachers and local college professors are excellent sources of information on this topic. To debate your position successfully, practice arguing your opponent's point of view. What arguments and evidence are they likely to offer? By anticipating your opponent's arguments, you have a much better chance of countering them when they are presented.

Career Bank

Following are·just a few of the many careers in the television and video industry:

- production assistant
- script reader/writer.
- TV/video camera operator
- audio/lighting technician
- station engineer
- videotape editor
- set designer
- computer graphic artist
- actor
- TV journalist/news commentator
- technical director
- producer

Create Your Own Media

With a video camera and some planning you can create your own video. Use the five stages of the Media Literacy Paradigm to help focus the content and purpose of your video. Once you have decided on a genre (dramatic, documentary, music video, and so on) divide the project into the stages of preproduction, production, and postproduction. Chart what steps you will need to accomplish in each stage. You may use a script (storyboard) format described in Chapter Six or your instructor may supply a form. A word of caution: Keep your script short—no longer than 10 minutes—unless you are sure you have the time and equipment necessary for a longer production. As with the video you produced for the film chapter, if you have access to an editing machine you will have more flexibility in shooting than if you have to shoot each shot in sequence with no room for error. You can shoot a show this way, but it takes even more specific preproduction planning.

Recap

In its first 50 years TV has become the world's most powerful distributor of pop culture. Debates continue to rage over the impact of TV on individuals and society. One of the strongest charges against TV is that it is addictive. Hundreds of millions of people watch TV for a major percentage of their lifetimes, and they usually watch the least objectionable program (L.O.P.).

They don't watch shows—they simply watch TV. Television watching is often blamed for social ills: declining rates of literacy and academic performance, erosion of traditional family life and values, and the trivialization of the political process. The most popular charge against TV is that it promotes personal and social violence. Dozens of respected research studies have concluded that heavy viewing of violent programming leads to increased aggression, or at least the greater acceptance of aggression. Those opposing such conclusions argue that aggression and violence have much more complex origins, such as poverty, racism, and social injustice.

Television has several distinct genres, each with unique conventions of presentation, and the variety of genres and subgenres is growing. Tabloids and reality shows are among the more recent newcomers to the tried-and-true genres of sitcoms, soap operas, and dramas.

Stereotypes are everywhere on TV mainly because stereotypes are easily recognizable. A stereotyped character is predictable and therefore is easy to write lines for.

In addition to its launching a whole new genre (the music video), MTV is a powerful force in the evolution of TV because it sets production trends that are copied by other networks and producers.

American TV is basically made up of two systems, broadcast and cable. Broadcast TV is made up of local stations that send their programming through the air on specific frequencies called channels. Most of these stations are affiliated with one of the four major networks (CBS, ABC, NBC, or FOX). Cable TV transmits its programming through fiber optic and coaxial cable. Local cable TV companies devote channel space to local broadcast stations, cable and satellite networks, and public access programs. Cable TV systems offer the potential to provide interactive service.

Ratings are the name of the game for most American TV. The larger the audience for a show, the more that station or cable system that transmits it can charge advertisers. Rating companies determine how many people are watching a given show at a given time. The ratings information generated becomes the numbers used in "ratings wars."

The biggest changes in TV over the next decade are expected to involve interactivity and growth in the numbers of channels available.

Resources for Further Reading
Books

Barnouw, Erik. *Tube of Plenty: The Evolution of American Television*, 2nd Edition. New York: Oxford University Press, 1990.

Bianculli, David. *Teleliteracy: Taking Television Seriously*. New York: Simon and Schuster, 1992.

Brooks, Tim. *The Complete Directory to Prime Time Network TV Shows 1946–Present*, 5th Edition. New York: Ballantine Books, 1992.

Dennis, Christopher. *Favorite Families of TV*. New York: Citadel Press, 1992.

Doyle, Marc. *The Future of Television*. Lincolnwood, Ill.: NTC Business Books, 1992.

Geller, Matthew. *From Receiver to Remote Control: The TV Set*. New York: The New Museum of Contemporary Art, 1990.

Gilder, George. *Life After Television*. Knoxville, Tenn.: Whittle Direct Books, 1990.

Gitlin, Todd. *Inside Prime Time*. New York: Pantheon, 1985.

Hartwig, Robert. *Basic TV Technology*. Boston: Focal Press, 1993.

Hickman, Harold. *Television Directing*. New York: McGraw Hill, 1991.

Jones, Gerald. *Honey, I'm Home! Sitcoms: Selling the American Dream*. New York: St. Martin's Press, 1992.

Mander, Jerry. *Four Arguments for the Elimination of Television*. New York: Quill, 1978.

Miller, Mark Crispen. *Boxed In: The Culture of TV*. Evanston, Ill.: Northwestern University Press, 1988.

Parish, James. *Let's Talk: America's Favorite Talk Show Hosts*. Las Vegas: Pioneer Books, 1993.

Postman, Neil. *Amusing Ourselves to Death: Public Discourse in the Age of Show Business*. New York: Penguin Books, 1985.

Sackett, Susan. *Prime Time Hits: Television's Most Popular Network Programs 1950 to the Present*. New York: Billboard Books, 1993.

Savan, Leslie. *The Sponsored Life: Ads, TV, and American Culture*. Philadelphia: Temple University Press, 1994.

Selnow, Gary. *Society's Impact on Television: How the Viewing Public Shapes Television Programming*. Westport, Conn.: Praeger, 1993.

Weiner, Edward. *The TV Guide TV Book: 40 Years of the All-time Greatest Television—Facts, Fads, Hits, and History*. New York: Harper Perennial, 1992.

Industry Publications and Magazines

Billboard Magazine, One Astor Plaza, 1515 Broadway, New York, NY 10036

Broadcasting and Cable: The Newsweekly of Television and Radio, 1705 Desales St., N.W., Washington, DC 20036

Entertainment Weekly

Rolling Stone Magazine

Satellite TV Week, P.O. Box 308, Fortuna, CA 95540-0308

TV Guide

Variety, 5700 Wilshire Blvd., Suite 120, Los Angeles, CA 90036

Key word database searches for library research on TV

TV networks, TV stations, cable TV, MTV, censorship, interactive TV, Direct Broadcast Satellites (DBS), TV ratings, tabloid TV, TV violence, broadcasting, TV production, TV producers, home shopping, educational TV, reruns, syndication

TV, Video, and Films about TV

Being There (film)

Lawnmower Man (film)

Network (film)

"Television" (eight-part PBS special, rebroadcast periodically)

SEGUE

Television and Video

This chapter concludes Part Two, which examined each mass medium as a separate entity. Part Three looks at two institutions that are delivered to the public via several different media and have become central to America's identity: journalism and advertising. Like television, both are increasingly criticized as being harmful to American society. Are the criticisms fair?

PART THREE

Media-Based Institutions

© 1994 Tom Tomorrow. Reprinted by permission of Dan Perkins from *Greetings from This Modern World*, St. Martin's Press.

We Americans often take for granted the constitutional right to be informed by a free press, as well as the economic right to create and respond to advertising. But what happens when things are taken for granted? Many times people become blind to those very things, whether they are relationships, the environment, a fundamental idea such as democracy, or their media consumption.

Part Three examines how the press (the news media, including print and electronic media) and advertising work. These two American institutions help to create popular culture. Because we often take them for granted, we may fail to see their impact on us as citizens and consumers, and on our society in general.

Strange Bedfellows: The News Media and Advertising

As you begin this part, consider that more Americans get their news from television than any other medium, as "ABC's World News Tonight" proudly proclaims. An entire TV network, CNN (Cable News Network), was created in the early 1980s to provide nothing but "news." Many critics of nightly news programs broadcast on the major networks have written about the sometimes silly chitchat that goes on among the members of TV news teams. These same critics are nervous about lowered journalistic standards, describing the 22 minutes of actual nightly news coverage on many television stations as "infotainment." Some critics are also concerned about the interruption of news broadcasts by commercials.

February 1994 provided an example of how commercial interruptions of the nightly news have become so accepted that viewers don't think such "messages" are strange. That month, Americans watched in horror as scenes of massacre from across the world—from Bosnia and Israel's West Bank—were whisked in and out of their living rooms, neatly sandwiched between advertisements urging them to relieve the minor discomforts of everyday living. Many Americans did not think twice about this contrast, what media critic and writer Neil Postman describes as "conceptual discontinuity." On the news, profound human tragedy and relatively minor personal concerns, about such things as headaches and upset stomachs, are rolled into one neat package.

The fact that advertising does not seem out of place in television is understandable, some might say, because viewers essentially watch TV to get immediate gratification. We watch TV to be entertained by dramas, comedies, sports, and game shows. Even when we watch so-called educational programs, we still expect our

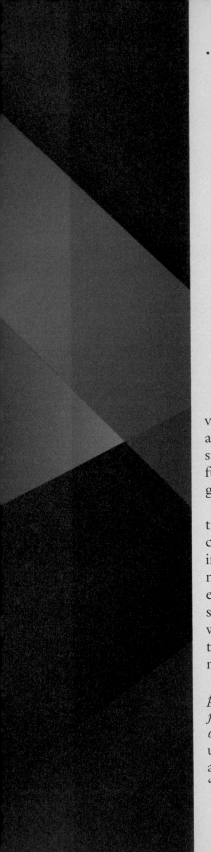

viewing to be satisfying and enjoyable. Often we watch TV to achieve the basic gratification of being distracted from life's pressures—to escape. Therefore, commercials that promise relief and fulfillment seem only natural. After all, the search for momentary gratification brings us to TV in the first place.

However, unlike most other categories of TV programming that are predicated on their entertainment value, news broadcasts claim to serve the nobler journalistic mission of creating an informed—and ultimately empowered—citizenry. Why don't more viewers find it just a little weird when our news—the supposedly "serious stuff"—is laced with appeals to buy products or services and fulfill our desires? Consider that the TV audience is wrapped in a **paradigm of consumption**, which constantly blends the presentation of problems and daily events (the news) with messages urging personal fulfillment.

The underlying message seems to be: *However significant the problems in our community, our individual problems and needs are just as important. However pressing a need there is for local, national, or global change, fulfilling our personal needs comes first.* Many of us accept this fact and that the TV news is, as veteran TV journalist and former "CBS News" anchorman Walter Cronkite used to say, "the way it is."

In the last two chapters of *Understanding Mass Media*, you will look at news media as a whole, the role that advertising plays in the media, and the nature of advertising in general.

CHAPTER THIRTEEN

The News Media

Learning Targets

After working through this chapter, you will be able to

- Identify the criteria of newsworthiness in newspaper and TV news stories;
- Chart the similarities and differences among various news media;
- Devise a public relations strategy for obtaining press coverage of an event;
- Identify a news anchor's presentation technique; and
- Explain ethics self-censorship in journalism.

Checking In

- What do you think news is? Compose a definition of the term *news*.
- List two strengths and two weaknesses of each of the following news media: TV news, newspapers, news-magazines, radio, and on-line news services.
- Describe the personalities and presentation styles of the anchorpeople from a local television newscast.
- Why do you think tabloid newspapers and tabloid or "magazine" TV shows are increasingly popular?

What Is News?

"Hey! What's goin' on?" You ask that question all the time in a variety of ways. You mostly ask it in relation to the particulars of your daily life—when you haven't seen a friend for a few weeks, when you're planning your weekend, when you're getting brought up-to-date by a cousin who moved out of state three months ago. In all these cases you find out "what's goin' on" directly from the people who were there.

When it comes to knowing about what's going on in the world, you rely on the press—that American institution that brings us news—news about local politics, global economic trends, natural disasters, celebrity escapades, and a million other things. But what exactly *is* news?

Why do so many people refer to *the* news? Think for a minute about all the things that go on in the world, the country, and your town in one single day that are not reported. Out of the

417

When a press conference is called, representatives of *all* the news media attend. *Photo courtesy of NASA.*

mind-boggling range of events, issues, people, and stories that could be presented, only 22 minutes' worth shows up on network news broadcasts (30 minutes minus 8 minutes of ads). In its advertising, CNN radio captures the spirit of slicing away most of the world's happenings: "You give us two minutes, we'll give you the world," and "A whole day's news, every half hour." The world in two minutes? That's an absurd abbreviation of the complexity and breadth of daily life. Yet that is how the world is mediated—constructed—for us by most of the press.

Defining News

The dictionary definitions of *news* are most unsatisfactory. For example, one dictionary's first meaning is "recent events and happenings, especially those that are unusual or notable." The fact that you ate cauliflower yesterday for the first time would fit this definition, but it would hardly make the morning paper or the evening newscast. The dictionary next describes *news* as "new information about anything previously unknown." When you walk into math class and learn for the first time how to factor a quadratic equation, that is new and previously unknown information to you. Again, your math class would not make the news. What is news? Can it be defined?

For you and me, the consumers of news, *news* might be defined as what newspapers and newscasters decide is newsworthy. The people who run the papers, write the stories, and edit the news have to decide what is news and what is not. They do this by following tradition and by making educated guesses about what the reading, viewing, or listening public wants to know.

If a person eats a fish, that is not news; but if a fish eats a person, that is news. If a fish eats someone in your town, it will certainly be news in your town. If a fish eats a celebrity or world leader, it will be news worldwide. News favors events that are unusual. The fact that thousands of airplanes land and take off safely every day is an amazing feat of technical competence and human expertise, but it is not news. However, if one airplane crashes, or even blows a tire while landing, it is news precisely because it is so uncommon.

Why All the Bad News?

The desire of journalists to report the unusual—a desire encouraged by their readers' attraction to the out of the ordinary and the bizarre—explains why so much news is "bad news." People often ask why newspapers and TV newscasts dwell on tragedies, accidents, crimes, and generally negative human events. Given that planes are safe, people are usually honest, buildings rarely burn, and criminals are only a small part of the population, such negative events are precisely what is *unusual.* It is normal for things to work fairly well and for people to lead their lives with a certain degree of contentment. A society in which the good news would be out of the ordinary would be a sorry place to live.

However, all that is unusual is not news (cleaning your room, for example), nor is all news unusual. There are other qualities that make items newsworthy.

Five Criteria of Newsworthiness
Timeliness

News should be new. There is no such thing as old news—only history. Instant news has become the standard.

Significance of the Event

This news value demands the most personal judgment on the part of the news editor. News events must be events that are important in some way to the audience.

Closeness to the Audience

A fire in the house next door would certainly be news in a neighborhood paper, or even a city paper. The fire would not be news on national television because it would not be close enough to most viewers. A national election in Austria might not even be mentioned in American papers, but the national election in America will fill several editions of most American papers.

Importance of the People Involved

If your next-door neighbor is famous, the fact that his or her house burned down might make national news. A speeding ticket is rarely a newsworthy event unless the person speeding is well known.

Drama or Human Interest

The news has to be interesting (some say entertaining) or the audience will not read or watch it. Some stories are included with the news because they are particularly dramatic or have human interest value; this news value can make an otherwise minor event into real news. If the fire in your neighbor's house happened on Thanksgiving Day, for instance, the human value in the story might make it national news.

Practice

- Examine each story in the first three pages of your local newspaper and decide which of the news criteria they contain. In doing this, you will answer the question, Why is this story news?
- Do the same analysis for the first three stories broadcast on a local television news show.

How Are the News Media Similar?

Freedom from Direct Government Control

The news media are united by their concern for reporting news and the need for an audience. News in the United States is a product that is sold to consumers. In some countries, news is whatever the government wants the people to believe. The fact that the U.S. government does not run the news media gives journalists a certain independence and a willingness to point out flaws and to criticize the government. This ability of the news media (both print and electronic) to criticize government and industry is essential to freedom of the press. It is common for governments to at least bend the truth they give out. Furthermore, it is the mission of the press to dig for the whole truth. For this reason many politicians, from mayors to presidents, can be antagonistic toward the press. If the press were subject to the government, it would do little but print whatever the government told it to. The Watergate scandal, which broke in 1973, would never have been uncovered (*Washington Post* newspaper reporters were the first to report it); mistakes made during the war in Vietnam would still remain hidden (*The New York Times* first published a secret government study, the *Pentagon Papers,* in 1971); and scores of dishonest politicians and businesses would still be in power preying on the ignorant and uninformed.

Dependence on Advertising

News media must pay a price for this freedom. Because news organizations are supported by taxpayers' money, the high cost of gathering and distributing the news is assumed by advertisers anxious to bring their messages to the news-consumers public.

Reliance on News Services

The third similarity among the news media is their reliance on news or wire services, such as Associated Press (AP) and Reuters. If you were to walk into the nerve center of news-gathering activity in any TV or radio station, newspaper, television network, or even newsmagazine, you would find computer-transmitted items coming from a news service on a 24-hour basis.

Look at the beginning of each story in a newspaper and see how many are supplied by news services. Such services collect information (stories and photos) and send it electronically.

Newspapers and news departments of broadcast stations subscribe to or join the wire service. Each subscriber pays a fee to the wire service and also agrees to supply it with coverage of local events that might have national interest. For example, AP reporters all over the world phone or send stories to the New York headquarters. From there the stories are sent to subscribers who can print them as news, rewrite them, use them as a research source, or ignore them. (*Wire* service originates from the time reports were sent by telegraph and, later, by teletype machines.)

The average newspaper contains more news from the wire services than from its own reporters; and the smaller the paper, the truer that is. Many small-town papers are little more than a collection of wire service reports and syndicated material. The average radio news broadcast is at least 90 percent wire service material. Edward Jay Epstein, in his five-year study of network (not local) TV news, concluded that the source for 70 percent of NBC-TV's "Nightly News" was wire service reports. Of course, most consumers don't know the source of a broadcast story.

Use of a Gatekeeper

The fourth similarity all news media share is the use of a gatekeeper. A news medium can be pictured as a funnel. Into the wide—and always open—mouth of the funnel flows a steady stream of news. As there are over 6 billion humans on earth, billions of potential news events happen every day. Someone has to make the decision as to what is worth presenting to the public and what belongs in the wastebasket or on the floor of the editing room. The person who performs this function has different titles in each news organization. In many places he or she is called the managing editor or simply the news editor or news director. Social scientists use the term *gatekeeper* to describe this person, because he or she acts as a kind of control for the news, deciding which items make the paper or the broadcast and which do not gain entry.

Although gatekeepers are extremely important to the news process, they are usually unknown to the general public. They do not get bylines in newspaper stories, nor do they read the news on television. The gatekeeper is a powerful ongoing influence, but when decisions are made on important stories, the publisher of the newspaper or the director of the TV or radio station may step in. However, the sheer volume of news that flows into news media headquarters and the limited amount that comes out means that the gatekeeper is the one person most influential in deciding what is and what is not news.

In newspapers the gatekeeper uses only about one in five stories that come in; in television and radio the number is probably closer to one in ten or twenty. On large city newspapers, news pours in so fast that only one in ten items scanned by the gatekeeper makes the paper. The gatekeeper is given a certain amount of airtime or magazine space or newspaper pages to fill. This number is determined by the amount of advertising available. A large amount of advertising means less news; less advertising gives the consumer more news. Because ad space has already been committed, it is figured first, and the news must fit in the space that is left over.

How Do the News Media Differ?

Each news medium may report the same news, but the words, the images, and their effect on the news consumer differ. Consider how the four major news media—TV, radio, newspapers, and newsmagazines—differ in their presentation of the news.

Television: Visuals Rule!

Television and, to some extent, radio use one or two individuals to present the news. The television viewer sees a person who is

News from around the world can be seen on television as it happens, thanks to broadcast via communication satellites such as this one. *Photo courtesy of NASA.*

regarded as trustworthy or hears a radio announcer with a voice that rings with authority. Newspapers and newsmagazines lack this element of personality and instead must depend on the printed word. Television news commentators are often highly paid public celebrities. Some TV newscasters are not reporters at all; they are announcers with a favorable public image. Newspaper editors are seldom recognized on the street and rarely become celebrities.

Television presents a strong visual image. A written news story about poverty will often make less of an impression on a reader than a powerfully filmed story of a starving family. A live telecast of some important happening is far more memorable and emotionally powerful than a series of printed words in the newspaper. Television news is at its best when it can show what is happening as it happens—cameras in outer space, congressional hearings, wars, disasters, and sports. National networks require events of great national interest before they will preempt regularly scheduled programs for a live telecast.

Another form of network news that is almost as powerful as a live telecast is the documentary. These network specials have included in-depth programs on topics such as poverty, AIDS, terrorism, racial conflict, pollution, drug abuse, and other topics of vital concern. Such documentaries are usually produced by a network for nationwide broadcast, but some are done by individual stations on topics of local concern. Documentaries are expensive to produce and invariably lose money for the networks. Although they do rather poorly in the ratings, they are still seen by millions of people and sometimes have a noticeable effect on governmental agencies and future legislation. In these documentaries television is at its best in providing in-depth news coverage. A one- or two-hour documentary can give the depth lacking in the evening news as well as present powerful visual images to influence opinions.

A television newscast permits less viewer selectivity than a newspaper gives its readers. A newspaper reader scans the headlines first and reads complete stories only if the headline promises a story of particular interest. Television news is usually watched in its entirety. The TV viewer is not as free to select which items he or she will watch. Some older Americans find TV news difficult because they were not subjected to regular newscasts until the 1950s, when networks began to broadcast nightly news programs. Before that, people, for the most part, read daily newspapers. If people didn't want to read about an ax murder, they didn't have to read about it. If they didn't want to read about world news, they didn't have to read about world news. Then came television, and in order to see any news you pretty much have to see it all. It's a very brutal way to get the news. You can either accept the news that comes from the tube or turn it off completely. You can't pick and choose.

The Effects of Being Televised

Another unique quality of television is that the presence of film or TV cameras at an event can change what happens there. In the presence of a camera, we all, in a sense, become actors; television news becomes a stage on which we can act out our viewpoint. When C-SPAN was first considered, some members of Congress objected to the idea of televising congressional hearings on the grounds that the presence of TV cameras would create a "circus" atmosphere. It seems the TV camera does have far more effect than a reporter with a notepad or a small tape recorder. For this reason many states still forbid cameras in courtrooms.

Yet another aspect of television news not shared by the other media is that a person who looks and sounds believable can influence viewers' opinions. The same person's statement in print might be far less convincing. However, the opposite can also be true. The fact is that the image a person can project over television has become an important factor in political campaigns.

Radio: The Headline Service

For the most up-to-the-minute, quickest, and most frequent news, no medium as a whole currently does better than radio. Many stations carry news every 30 minutes; most, every hour, and large cities are served by one or more "all news" stations. Radio is available anywhere in the country and by using a telephone, a radio station can present news almost as it happens. A newspaper has to wait at least until the next edition, and television has to wait (with the exception of special reports) until the next scheduled newscast. Radio serves the nation more as a headline service. Many radio news broadcasts are what is called "rip and read." The talent (sometimes called the disc jockey, announcer, or combo-operator) is given news reports, as they came in from a news service, to read for five minutes.

Large news-radio stations, usually in large cities, have news departments and reporters out looking for stories. However, radio news today functions best as a headline service, as a first alert for important news, and as the best source for current weather and local traffic information.

Newspapers and Newsmagazines: In-Depth Coverage

The ability of television to provide up-to-date evening newscasts has caused a decline in the number of evening edition newspapers. The decline began in 1977, and, during 1988 alone, 27 cities lost their daily evening newspaper. The physical problems associated with publishing a newspaper make the news at least a few hours old by the time the paper hits the street. Of all the news media, however, newspapers offer the reader the greatest variety and the greatest personal choice. Each newspaper reader is his or her own editor, selecting the news that he or she thinks is important and ignoring what is not. Newspapers have been in the news business far longer than any of the electronic media and have the most people working on gathering and writing the news.

Newspapers and newsmagazines provide the most in depth reporting, while radio and television (with the exception of documentaries) go into comparatively little detail. Newsmagazines often provide the most detail about national stories but are a few days or a week behind the newspaper in getting the news to the readers.

There are currently three national news weeklies with a large circulation— *Time*, with over $4\frac{1}{2}$ million readers; *Newsweek*, with over 3 million; and *U.S. News and World Report*, with over 2 million. Newsmagazines report the news with a more entertaining and lively writing style than do newspapers. They have more time to prepare in-depth stories because they are not under the pressure of putting out a daily publication. However, both *Time* and *Newsweek*, which are printed on a Sunday, can publish a story about an important event that happened on Saturday in time for the newsstand copies available Monday morning. *Time* is printed in a number of printing plants around the world and begins selling each edition on Sunday night and Monday morning in more than 150 countries.

The newsmagazines provide the most retrievable form of news. Radio and TV news is gone once the show has ended. A listener or viewer cannot easily go back and check what was said or find the text of the news broadcast at a public library. A newspaper is more retrievable, but its size and inexpensive paper make it hard to store without the inconvenience and expense of microfilm. However, back issues of newsmagazines are available in any library or even on the coffee table or stacked in piles in the basement of thousands of homes. A newsmagazine also is on sale for at least a week, while a newspaper disappears from newsstands within 12 hours. Due to this longer sales period and the relative permanence of the newsmagazine, magazines have developed a policy of stressing facts and checking their accuracy.

Newsmagazines (as well as other magazines that use factual articles) have full-time "checkers" whose only job is to verify the facts reporters mention in their stories. The checkers are also charged with filling in facts that reporters leave out. A story might come to a checker with a line such as "The 00-person Sudanese army. . . ." It is up to the checker to fill in the "00." Other news media are careful about reporting facts accurately, but none treat even the least important facts with the passion of newsmagazines. The presence of insignificant but often colorful facts is one of the aspects of newsmagazine writing that distinguishes it from newspapers. A newsmagazine story might begin: "Flowers were in bloom on the crumbling towers of St. Hilaron, and hawks turned soundlessly high above Kyrenia." A newspaper story, on the other hand, would begin simply by noting: "Strife-torn Cyprus was reported quiet today with only sporadic outbreaks of shooting."

Newsmagazines present the news in the form of dramatic stories. Unlike newspapers, they have no tradition of reporting unbiased news and restricting opinions to columns and editorials. They often present opinionated news and interpretations of events, sometimes in articles signed by the writer. Newsmagazines present their opinions as part of the news; newspapers keep opinion pieces separate; television editorials are clearly labeled on the local level, while interpretive documentaries are presented on the national level. The presentation of news in a TV documentary is somewhat similar to that in a newsmagazine.

TV News: The Art of Public Relations

Most of what appears on televised news is not really the "news"; it is people reacting to the news. How can you gain television time on the news other than by committing a crime or hitting a home run to win the World Series? Easy. Public Relations (P.R.). Just represent a special interest group such as a political party, corporation, or an entertainer—and stage an event or "pseudo-event" to which the news media are invited.

Once television time is gained, you either prepare a favorable statement or stage an event with visual interest that makes your point.

Joe Saltzman is a former journalist and a journalism professor and media consultant. The reading on page 430 gives some of his reflections on media control by major corporations and special interest groups and the fine art of controlling interviews.

Watching TV news critically is important to today's viewers. *Photo: Bradley Wilson.*

Making the Right Impression

When you think about it, local TV news gives you little information that you can do anything about. You are glad that the fire that left four families homeless struck someone else's house. You may be reminded to check the batteries in your smoke detectors. You catch sports scores and weather information, although that information is at your fingertips in other, more immediately available ways, such as the daily newspaper. Why do so many people watch local news so regularly? Could it be that we are drawn to news personalities—those reliable, consistently happy anchorpeople who chitchat so smoothly between segments? Media critic Neil Postman thinks so and explains the process in the second reading.

How to Manage TV News

Joe Saltzman

It is a blunt fact of life that the local television news we see every night—the only news source for more than 60 percent of the American people—has been staged for television by outside special interests.

Consider the following cases and use them as a guide when watching tonight's local news programs:

A politician wants to get publicity for legislation he is sponsoring. He calls a news conference. Reporters from every television station show up. Viewers will see the news conference on the evening news but probably little else. What they won't hear about is any political wheeling and dealing out of the glare of the television lights. . . .

A major company holds a news conference to issue its year-end report. The figures are glowing, the cameras are rolling, everyone is smiling. If the reporter works harder than most do, the viewers might hear figures questioned and policies doubted when the story gets on the air, but that kind of information can't be dug up in the course of a press conference. No one will call in cameras and reporters to reveal economic reverses, mishandling of funds, or worse. And if reporters find out something suspicious on their own, they probably won't even get to talk to the company president, much less record an interview with that person.

A picket line goes up around a market to protest higher prices. A spokesperson is there when the television reporters arrive. For the next hour or so, the cameras cover the staged event. The reporters thank the spokesperson and leave. Five minutes later, the picket line disappears.

The list is endless. Politicians, police, the military, entertainers, government agencies, corporations, businesspersons, individuals, and groups all stage news "events" for their own benefit. And those with money to hire a savvy public relations firm can get their news—and usually their version of the news—broadcast into living rooms with sports and the daily weather.

"Any sharp public relations person can get the story covered by television," says Robert Irvine, a former news director of the Eyewitness News team at KABC—TV in Los Angeles. "He knows how to schedule a story for maximum exposure, how to alert the news media and make sure they show up, how to get the inexperienced reporter to put his PR release on film, how to make sure it will get on the evening news. Most of what you see on television is stuff handed to . . . assignment

How to Manage TV News *(continued)*

desks who then feed it to reporters who are usually guided in their coverage by the public relations person involved. . . ."

A local television news reporter who has worked for 25 years for several stations shares Irvine's opinions. He says news executives like well-organized stories that don't leave unanswered questions. "Investigative reports or stories that take a lot of time and effort never look as smooth or polished as the simple PR story," he explains. "Nobody is very happy about partially finished, dull, or nonvisual stories. So eventually you either give up or keep fighting until you get fired or change jobs."

Thousands of stories from special interests make the air only slightly altered from their staged creation. It takes money to cover stories well and most local television stations don't have the funds. Assignment desks, faced with limited budgets and a handful of inexperienced personnel, look for stories they can film fast—and most of the time those are staged for the media by outside sources. ABC producer and former NBC reporter Mike Gavin explains: "Every demonstration, every scheduled interview, every news conference, every notification of a planned story, every time a person wants to get his or her point across—it's 'staged.' " . . .

Most editors and reporters insist that the bulk of these staged events is not inherently bad. They often provide information the public should have. The danger is that this is the *only* news the public usually gets while enterprising, investigative television reporting is becoming a thing of the past.

Couple that with television management that is entertainment-oriented and wants short, snappy stories with no loose ends, all packaged neatly into less than two minutes, and it is easy to see why most local news shows are filled with stories that are the easiest to get. . . . ■

Reprinted courtesy of Joe Saltzman.

Getting Them into the Electronic Tent

Neil Postman and Steve Powers

At carnival sideshows, the barkers used to shout intriguing things to attract an audience. "Step right up. For one thin dime, see what men have died for and others lusted after. The Dance of the Veils as only Tanya can do it."

The crowd would gather as lovely Tanya, wrapped in diaphanous garb, would wiggle a bit, and entice grown men who should have known better to part with their money for a ticket. . . .

———■———

In television news there is no Tanya we know of but there are plenty of Sonyas, Marias, Ricks, and Brads who have the job of getting you into the electronic tent. They come on the air and try to intrigue you with come-ons to get you to watch their show. "Step right up" becomes "Coming up at eleven o'clock." And, instead of veils, you get a glimpse of some videotape which may intrigue you enough to part with your time instead of a dime. It is no accident that in the television news industry, the short blurb aimed at getting you to watch a program is called a "tease." Sometimes it delivers what it advertises but often it hooks us into the electronic tent and keeps us there long enough that we don't remember why we were there in the first place.

The tease is designed to be very effective, very quickly. By definition, a tease lasts about ten seconds or less and the information it contains works like a headline. Its purpose is to grab your attention and keep you watching. In the blink of a tease you are enticed to stay tuned with promises of exclusive stories and tape, good-looking anchors, helicopters, team coverage, hidden cameras, uniform blazers, and even, yes, better journalism. It is all designed to stop you from using the remote-control button to switch channels. But the teasing doesn't stop there. During each news program, just before each commercial, you will see what are known as "bumpers"—teases that are aimed at keeping you in the tent, keeping you from straying to another channel where other wonders are being touted. And the electronic temptations do not even cease with the end of the program. When the news show is over, you are still being pleaded with "not to turn that dial" so that you can tune in the next day for an early-morning newscast, which in turn will suggest you watch the next news program and so on. If news programmers had it their way, you would watch a steady diet of news programs, one hooking you into the next with only slight moments of relief during station breaks.

Getting Them into the Electronic Tent *(continued)*

If you think you can beat the system by not watching teases, you'll need to think again. We are dealing here with serious professional hucksters. The game plan, aimed at getting you to watch the news, starts even before you have seen the first tease. It starts while you're watching the entertainment shows *before* the news. Whether you know it or not, we are programmed to watch the news, by programmers. They know that most of us tend to be lazy. Even with remote controls at our fingertips, we are likely to stay tuned to the channel we have been watching. So the United Couch Potatoes of America sit, and sit, and sit, and before they know it, Marsha and Rick have hooked us into their news program, promising "team coverage," no less, of today's latest disaster. In the textbook vernacular: the lead-in programs must leave a residual audience for the news shows which follow. To put it plainly, a station with a strong lineup of entertainment programs can attract a large audience to the news tent. High-rated shows such as "Oprah Winfrey," programmed just before the news, bring in a big audience and premium prices at the broadcast marketplace. This is why the best news program may not have ratings as high as a news program with a strong lead-in. It may not be fair but it is television.

Now, let us say all things are equal. Station A and station B both have excellent lead-ins. What news program will

you watch? Most people will say something like "I want the latest news, the best reporting with state-of-the-art technology presented by people I can trust and respect."

But while people might say they like the most experienced journalists presenting the news, many news consultants claim that no matter what they *say*, the audience prefers to watch good-looking, likable people it can relate to (perhaps of the same age group, race, etc.). News organizations spend a lot of time and money building up the reputations of their anchors, sending them to high-visibility stories that they hope will convince viewers that they are watching top-level journalists. Unfortunately, in some markets the top anchors are sometimes "hat racks" who read beautifully but who can barely type a sentence or two without the aid of a producer and writer. They may know how to anchor but many are strictly lightweights. In television, looking the part is better than being the real item, a situation you would rightly reject in other contexts. Imagine going to a doctor who hadn't studied medicine, but rather looks like a doctor—authoritative, kindly, understanding, and surrounded by formidable machinery. We assume you would reject such a professional fraud especially if he or she had majored in theater arts in college. But this kind of play-acting is perfectly acceptable in the world of television news and entertainment where actors who have played

Getting Them into the Electronic Tent *(continued)*

lawyers on a TV series frequently are called on to give speeches at lawyers' conventions and men who have played doctors are invited to speak at gatherings of medical professionals. If you can read news convincingly on television, you can have a successful career as an anchor, no journalism experience required. This is not to say there aren't bright men and women who are knowledgeable journalists and who can and do serve as anchors. But the problem is that it is almost impossible for the viewer to figure out which anchor knows his stuff and who's faking it. A good anchor is a good actor and with the lift of an eyebrow or with studied seriousness of visage, he or she can convince you that you are seeing the real thing, that is, a concerned, solid journalist.

You may wonder at this point, what difference does it make? Even if one cannot distinguish an experienced journalist from a good actor playing the part of an experienced journalist, wouldn't the news be the same? Not quite. An experienced journalist is likely to have a sense of what is particularly relevant about a story and insist on including certain facts and a perspective that the actor-anchor would have no knowledge of. Of course, it is true that often an experienced journalist, working behind the cameras, has prepared the script for the actor-anchor. But when the anchor is himself or herself a journalist, the story is likely to be given additional dimensions, especially if the journalist-anchor does his or her own script writing.

And there is one more point: even if there were no differences between the stories presented by actor-anchors and journalist-anchors, the fact that the audience is being deluded into thinking that an actor-anchor is a journalist contributes a note of fakery to the enterprise. It encourages producers and news directors to think about what they are doing as artifice, as a show in which truth-telling is less important than the appearance of truth-telling. One can hardly blame them. They know that everything depends on their winning the audience's favor, and the anchor is the key weapon in their arsenal.

If you are skeptical about the importance of the anchor in attracting the audience to the electronic tent, you must ask yourself why they are paid so much. Network anchors earn over a million dollars a year. Over two million dollars a year. Do we hear three? Yes, more than three million dollars a year in the case of Dan Rather at CBS. Is he worth it? From a financial point of view, certainly. He brings people into the tent because they perceive him to be an experienced, solid reporter, who has paid his dues and knows what's going on. And an experienced newsman such as Rather starts to look like a bargain when you think of local anchors being paid as much as 750,000 to a million dollars without serious journalistic cre-

Getting Them into the Electronic Tent *(continued)*

dentials. Anchors who work for network-affiliated stations in the top ten markets make an average of $139,447 a year. Nationwide, the average anchor, as of this writing, makes $52,284 a year, according to the National Association of Broadcasters.

So there you are ready to watch the news presented by a high-priced anchor and on comes the show, complete with a fancy opening, and music sounding as though it was composed for a Hollywood epic. The host appears—an anchor god or goddess sculpted on Mount Arbitron, at least the best of them. But even the worst looks authoritative. Of course, the anchor has had plenty of help from plenty of crafts people in creating the illusion of calm omniscience. After all, it's not all hair spray. That glittering, well-coiffed, Commanding Presence has been placed in a setting that has been designed, built, and painted to make him or her look as wonderful as possible. Consultants have been used to make sure the lights are fine-tuned to highlight the hair and to fill in wrinkles. Color experts have complemented the star's complexion with favorable background hues. Short anchors have their seats raised to look taller, with makeup applied to create just the right look, accenting cheekbones, covering baldness, enlarging small eyes, hiding blemishes, perhaps obscuring a double chin.

And of course there is camera magic. A low camera angle can make a slight anchor look imposing. Long and medium shots, rather than close-ups, can hide bags under the eyes. The anchor-star has probably had the benefit of a clothing allowance and the best hairdressers and consultants. It is cosmetic television at its finest.

The music fades and the parade of stories and the people reporting them begins. Whom you see depends sometimes on professional competence and journalistic ability. But it may also depend on the results of "focus groups," where ordinary viewers are shown videotapes and are then asked which anchors and reporters they prefer to watch and why. The group gives its opinion without the benefit of observing a performer over a period of time or knowledge of the reporter's background and experience. What is wanted is an immediate, largely emotional reaction. Performers are also evaluated by a service called "TV Q," which claims to rate television performers on the basis of who the public recognizes. The company, called Marketing Evaluations/TV Q, polls about six thousand Americans by mail, then sells the results to networks, advertising agencies, and anyone else willing to spend about a thousand dollars to find out someone's Q score.

Some news show consultants believe in forming a television news pseudo-family to attract audiences. After the "Today" show started to slide in the ratings, NBC brought back sportscaster

Getting Them into the Electronic Tent *(continued)*

Joe Garagiola to try to pep up the ratings. Garagiola had been on the program from 1969 to 1973. NBC had alienated its viewers by replacing popular coanchor Jane Pauley with Deborah Norville, who was supposed to be a hot ratings-getter. She wasn't. The show nosedived. Executives realized they needed something or somebody with pizazz. They reached for a person who, they hoped, could make the "Today" show cast a family again. Warm, affable Joe Garagiola. The return of the Prodigal Son. Exit Norville, now cast as the "other woman."

The "family" concept is at work at many local stations. The anchors probably will be a couple, male and female, both good-looking and in the same relative age category as husband-wife (although in our modern society with second marriages common, the male anchor may be twenty years older than his female counterpart). The other "family" members may be like Archie and Veronica to appeal to the younger set: Archie the sportscaster, who never tires of watching videotapes of highlights and bloopers, and Veronica the weather person. There is also Mr. or Ms. Breathless Showbiz who always feigns being thrilled to see the heart-throb or hottest rock group of the moment.

Whatever kind of television family is presented, it always has one thing in common. It is a happy family, where everybody gets along with everyone else (at least for thirty minutes) and knows his or her place. The viewer usually gets to see the whole "family" at the "top," or beginning, of the show. They will either be featured in a taped introduction or be sitting on the set, en masse, to create a sense of cohesion and stability. Throughout the program, members of the family will come on the set and do their turn, depending on their specialty. No newscast is complete without Archie the Sportscaster rattling off a list of clichés that he believes bond him to his fans. "Yes!" "In your face!" "Let's go to the videotape!" "Swish!"

Theoretically, sportscasters are supposed to be reporters, not fans. But depending on what they believe to be the roots of their popularity they might decide to bask in the glorious light of sports heroes and become cheerleaders. It is, in any event, the sportscaster's job to keep the audience excited, complete with taped highlights and interviews with the top players who often have nothing more to contribute than standard-brand sports-hero remarks: "It's not important how I played, as long as I can contribute to the team" or "I might have scored a few more touchdowns, but the real credit has to go to the front line who made it all possible." Picture and cliché blend to fill the eye with a sense of action and the nose with the macho smell of the locker room.

No newscast would be complete without a weather report that usually starts with a review of what already hap-

Getting Them into the Electronic Tent *(continued)*

pened that day. The report is supposedly made interesting by moving H's and L's, and by making clouds and isobars stalk across a map. Whatever the weather, the one thing you can always count on is a commercial break *before* tomorrow's weather forecast. You can also count on the peculiar tendency of anchors to endow the weather person with God-like meteorological power as in, "Well, Veronica, I hope you'll bring us some relief from this rain." To which the reply is something like "Oh, Chuck, I'm afraid we've got some more rain coming tomorrow, but wait till you see what I've got for you this weekend."

If you have ever wondered why all this fuss is made about the weather, the answer is that, for reasons no one knows, weather information is of almost universal interest. This means that it usually attracts an attentive audience, which in turn means it provides a good environment for commercials. The executive producer of the "CBS This Morning" show, Eric Sorensen, has remarked that research shows weather news is the most important reason why people watch TV in the morning. The weather segments also give the anchors a chance to banter with the weather people and lighten the proceedings. A pleasing personality is almost certainly more important to a weathercaster than a degree in meteorology. How significant a personality is can be gauged by what these people earn. Weather people in small markets earn an average of

$21,980 a year, according to the National Association of Broadcasters. Weathercasters make an average of $86,589 in the top ten markets, with some earning a half million dollars or more. Nonetheless, it should not surprise you to know that these people rarely prepare weather forecasts. There are staff meteorologists for that. The on-air weather person is expected to draw audiences, not weather maps.

Feature reporters usually ply their craft near the "back of the book," close by the weather. They keep the mood light, and try to leave the viewer with a smile. The subject matter of some feature vignettes is called "evergreen" because it is not supposed to wilt with the passage of time. It can be stored until needed. (Two of the best practitioners of "evergreen art" are Charles Kuralt and Andy Rooney.) Locally, you usually see "evergreen" reports on slow news days, when the editor has trouble filling the news budget (the newsworthy events of the day). But as entertaining news becomes more of a commodity, feature reports are being used more and more to attract and hold audiences through the news program.

No news "family" would be complete without a science reporter, a Doctor Wizard, who usually wears glasses, may have an advanced degree, and is certainly gray around the temples. These experts bring to the audience the latest in everything from cancer research to the designer disease of the year.

Getting Them into the Electronic Tent *(continued)*

Once the family has gathered, everyone in place, each with a specific role, the show is ready to begin. The anchor reads the lead story. If you are expecting to hear the most important news to you, on any given day, you will often be disappointed. Never forget that the producer of the program is trying to grab you before you zap away to another news show. Therefore, chances are you will hear a story such as Zsa Zsa's run-in with the law, Rob Lowe's home videos, Royal Family happenings, or news of a Michael Jackson tour. Those stories have glitter and glamour in today's journalism. And if glitter and glamour won't do the job, gore will. Body bags have become an important currency of TV news and a four-bagger is a grand slam.

If viewers have stayed through the lead story, they probably will be hooked for a while because the newscast is designed to keep their attention through the commercial breaks into the next "section," when the process starts again. Taped stories from reporters are peppered throughout the show to keep interest from flagging as anchors keep the show on track "eyeballing," or reading, stories on camera. When the news stories thin out, there are sports, features, and weather to fill up the time.

All this is presented with slick lighting and production values, moving along at a crisp pace. The tempo is usually fast since some programmers believe that fast-paced news programs attract younger audiences. Older audiences, they believe, are attracted to a slower-paced, quieter presentation. No matter how fast or slow the pace of the show, there is not much time to present anything but truncated information. After we have subtracted commercial time, about twenty-two minutes of editorial time are available in a half-hour broadcast. If we subtract, further, the time used for introductions, closings, sports, and the weather, we are left with about fifteen minutes. If there are five taped stories of two minutes each, that leaves five or six minutes to cover the rest of the world's events. And if more time is subtracted for "happy talk," chalk up another minute or so just for "schmoozing" on the set.

Giving the limited time and objectives of a television newscast, a viewer has to realize that he or she is not getting a full meal but rather a snack. And depending on the organization presenting the news, the meal may contain plenty of empty calories. ■

Reprinted from *How to Watch TV News* by Neil Postman with Steve Powers. Copyright © 1992 by Neil Postman and Steve Powers. Used by permission of Viking Penguin, a division of Penguin Books USA, Inc.

Practice

Analyze the content—the messages—of the previous readings in terms of the five steps of the Media Literacy Paradigm: Classify the product (TV news), examine its origin, analyze its mediation—how it is produced—investigate how it is consumed, and perceive its impact on you, the viewer.

News As Popular Culture
Information + Entertainment = Infotainment

"Tabloidization" is one of the hot media buzzwords of the 1990s. It refers to the trend in almost all journalism to spice up, dramatize, or otherwise make more entertaining the presentation of news. However, this trend not only affects the *presentation* of news, it changes the *content* of news as well. The news organizations covering the latest national scandals freely admit that they are providing entertaining information—that is, infotainment. It's not just the crop of "A Current Affair"–type programs on the bandwagon. The prime-time "newsmagazines" such as "20/20" are also getting into the act. They argue that they are only providing what millions of American consumers want. If we did not want to watch, read, and listen to this subgenre of news, they wouldn't give it to us. In the following article from *TV Guide*, Neil Gabler discusses why many of us were so powerfully drawn to the O. J. Simpson saga of the mid-nineties.

Practice

Using the Media Literacy Paradigm, analyze the following article and the O.J. Simpson "event" that unfolded in the news media—not just on television, but on radio, in newspapers, and in newsmagazines.

O.J.: The News As Miniseries

Neal Gabler

Let's face it. It was riveting, this O.J. Simpson stuff. It was addictive. During the pretrial hearing, I found myself staying up until 2 A.M., fastened on Court TV's umpteenth rehash of the day's O.J. events, and then picking up the tabloids each morning for my fix of the latest rumors. I even found myself, when sitting on the subway or strolling down the street, pricking up my ears to overhear conversations about O.J., which was all anyone was talking about anyway.

What was it about the Simpson affair that held us in its thrall, bumping everything else off the airwaves and front pages? Let me propose an answer so simple, so self-evident, and so incriminating of us all, when one stops to think of the two victims, that it is not likely to be seriously adduced anywhere else—namely, that this whole O.J. Simpson miniseries has been fabulously, deliriously, dizzying *entertaining*.

In sheer plot terms, it is one whale of a narrative—one of the great blockbusters. A beloved grid star allegedly kills his beautiful ex-wife after a tempestuous relationship. Then to the story itself is added a bizarre pursuit and a mesmerizing pretrial hearing with sensational plot elements like a bloody glove, a questionable alibi, and, of course, that mysterious envelope. It's been the news equivalent of a great beach read.

But the O.J. case has also got the sort of artful metaphors that one would find forced and false if one were to find them in fiction, not life. A man who came to fame by juking and outrunning his football opposition must now juke and outrun the legal system. A man whose job it is to act must now, guilty or innocent, give the greatest performance of his life. And for mordant comic relief, a man whose most memorable TV image is his dash through an airport may actually have had to dash through an airport to catch his redeye flight to Chicago the night of the murders. No wonder novelist Philip Roth once complained that fiction could no longer keep pace with the inventions of reality. Entertainment used to be an escape, a distraction from the news; during the Simpson hearings, the news became a distraction from entertainment—his soap opera preempting the networks'.

That the chief appeal of the Simpson case lay in its entertainment value may not be a very high-minded conclusion, but it seems inescapable in a time when entertainment has become the primary force in American life and especially in our media. For all the high-blown pala-

O.J.: The News As Miniseries *(continued)*

ver about the ribbon of information highway rolling our way, the media are no longer primarily purveyors of information; they are purveyors of drama. The tabloid, once journalism's reprobate for its preoccupation with the sensational, has become its model. What is the difference between *A Current Affair, Hard Copy*, or *Inside Edition* and the half-dozen network newsmagazines that have proliferated in the last year or so, save the latter's pretense of seriousness? What is the difference between *A Current Affair*'s Steve Dunleavy and *PrimeTime Live*'s Diane Sawyer, save that one is overtly smarmy, the other earnestly smarmy and gets invited to better parties?

The real sea change in American journalism over the last decade—and the one the Simpson coverage dramatically illustrated—has been the extent to which the story function in the news has eroded the information function. Where once the network evening news routinely reported items of national and international import and little else, sordid tales and feature stories now as often as not shoulder aside the hard news. And even in the grayest of newspapers, articles that once began tersely with who, what, where, and when now routinely begin with an eye-catching line or a vivid image as appropriate to fiction as to news.

In stressing the story function over the information function, most journalists, I imagine, would say that they are merely repackaging the same information in a more palatable form, not abandoning their traditional functions and obligations to the public. Frankly, they are not entirely wrong, but they underestimate the ways in which storytelling can distort both *what* news gets presented and *how* it gets presented. Journalists who stress the story are compelled to *find* stories whether these come equipped with information or not. We got a lot more about Tonya and Nancy than we ever got about the S&L scandal, which didn't lend itself to a melodramatic plotline.

More, the emphasis on story changes the forms of journalism and makes journalism seem much more like entertainment. Just a few years ago the TV news divisions were prestigious money-losers. Now the ubiquitous TV magazine programs have become huge profit centers for the networks, not because we've suddenly become more news-conscious, but because these shows structure events by the laws of fiction, of storytelling, and are almost undistinguishable from made-for-TV movies. (*60 Minutes* founder Don Hewitt once described his program's success in four words: "Tell me a story"). Court TV with its phalanx of commentators resembles nothing so much as *The NFL Today*. And watching Simpson's attorney, Robert Shapiro, orchestrate the appearance of a mysterious envelope at the pretrial hearing, which was after all a TV show, I couldn't help but think

O.J.: The News As Miniseries *(continued)*

of *Perry Mason*. I have a feeling Shapiro was thinking of old Perry, too.

Just as important as the way the emphasis on story changes the forms of journalism is the way it changes the audience's reaction to news events. As media analyst Neil Postman has said in his insightful screed against television, *Amusing Ourselves to Death*, when we see something that looks like entertainment, we are likely to respond as if it is entertainment.

Take Simpson's flight with Al Cowlings—a bang-up opening sequence, by the way, that Hollywood could not improve upon, whetting our appetite for action. When the white Bronco led that caravan down the freeway and onlookers cheered, I suspect they were reacting as much to the form of the event as to any personal feelings for O.J. It looked just like a movie—say, "Bonnie and Clyde"—where an outlaw eludes capture and the audience is made to feel some vicarious identification with him. Those much-maligned onlookers were merely playing their part in the show.

Because we all love a good show, we can't really blame the media for trying to satisfy our hunger by having given us O.J. morning, noon, and night. Plot sells—always has and always will. And good, juicy, real-life plots with terrific protagonists sell especially well in a crowded, competitive market with dozens of maws to feed.

But if great plot is what hooked us,

there are other forces that still insist on elevating the plot above trashy melodrama and on turning Simpson's tragedy into a festival of national reflection and self-criticism in which we all participate. It has become part of a new social ritual that articles like this one sift notorious cases for shards of revelation, assuming that in Amy and Joey, Lorena and John Wayne Bobbitt, and now in O.J. Simpson, we shall find hard truths about who we are and what we want.

Three weeks ago *The New Yorker* editorialized that this effort to tease meaning from the event and turn it into a parable was perhaps the most nauseating feature of the whole Simpson media circus. "To look for meaning where only sensation resides is to put an end to rationality," it said. But I suspect this attempt to find meaning has become part of the narrative process not just because the media need to assuage their guilt in shamelessly exploiting the Simpson case (poor Jane Pauley boasted an exclusive interview with Nicole Simpson's realtor!), but because we want them to analyze it as a way for us to understand our own ghoulish fascination with Simpson and to put some higher gloss on it.

In a world abundant with nonsense, O.J. Simpson is a screen onto which we can project almost anything we choose, and attempt to make sense of it, which is one of the functions of narrative art, if not of news. So O.J.'s life becomes a cautionary tale of a black man trying to

O.J.: The News As Miniseries (continued)

make it in a white society. Or an example of male brutality in a male-dominated society. Or of our deep denial when confronted by the misdeeds of famous people we like. (After all, many of us knew of his spousal abuse and liked him anyway.) Or of the way pampered individuals lose their moral bearings because they have always played by different rules than the rest of us. Whatever theme we select, the allegorical possibilities keep us listening and pondering.

My own armchair analysis is that the fall of Simpson may be the latest, most dramatic version of another, long-running American parable, one for which every celebrity is a potential symbol. This is the one that celebrates the American Dream, of which O.J. Simpson is certainly an outstanding example, and simultaneously questions it as a chimera in which success is more the product of media manipulation than merit. It is the one that pits our desire to believe against our skepticism that there is anything in which to believe.

As Harry Stein wrote in his *TV Guide* column a month ago, we make an "arrangement" with our celebrities. We agree to accept their personas—if they agree not to violate them. Some of us, like the fans who insist O.J. is being framed, buy the image. Some of us totally reject it. But most of us keep negotiating between the image and some deeper, less attractive truth, between the need to accept a celebrity's

role in the ongoing movie that is life and the need to deconstruct it, between our idolatry of them and our envy of them, between promise and reality. In breaking the arrangement, Simpson confirmed our skepticism. He turned his life into a parable of disillusion.

Whether he is found innocent or guilty, the old, lovable O.J., like the beloved silent-film comedian Fatty Arbuckle, who was accused of murder and lost his career, is gone forever, never to be repatriated with his new, darker image. He will always be, in his words, "this lost person," and the genre that has constituted his life since he entered the world of celebrity will no longer be that of exhilarating athletics on the gridiron or of self-deprecating comedy in the movies but of spellbinding whodunit with Simpson as the American Raskolnikov. The irony is that this whodunit has obviously focused more attention on Simpson, made him a bigger "star" than anything else he had done.

And that may be the final reason we all wait raptly for the latest O.J. reports. It takes a mighty big show to bind us, but for the last three weeks and presumably for many more when the trial opens, we have been galvanized to a degree I can't recall since John F. Kennedy's funeral—joined in the only way we seem to be able to come together now: as an *audience*. In this bizarre national mania with the Simpson case, we have found a common subject, if

■ O.J.: The News As Miniseries *(continued)*

not exactly common ground, as if we were all in the same theater watching the same movie at the same time, which, of course, we are. The theater is called America and this month the main feature has been "The Crime of O.J. Simpson." It's been a great, great show. ■

Reprinted with permission from *TV Guide* Magazine. Copyright © 1994 by News America Publications.

The Press and the Power of Advertising Dollars

One of the thorniest issues in journalism is the economic influence of advertisers on the content of news. Because much of American journalism relies heavily on advertising for revenue, journalists occasionally walk the fine line between reporting the truth and offending the businesses that pay their salaries. Many independent journalists argue that walking this line results in massive self-censorship.

For example, U.S. government studies have shown for at least two decades that more people die from taking over-the-counter and prescription drugs than from all illegal drugs combined. However, this issue is rarely presented on television news programs, which are funded in part by the pharmaceutical industry. (Watch how many ads for pain relievers appear during local and network news—headache, backache, sleeplessness, indigestion, stress, flu, and so on.)

The article by Jeff Cohen and Norman Solomon on the next page looks at the influence of tobacco industry advertisers on coverage of cigarette health risks.

Future Watch: News in the Interactive Age

The shifting style of news content (from straightforward to sensationalized) is not the only change afoot for the news industry. The future of news delivery is tied directly to the future of the media industries that carry the news. Just as the future of entertainment is expected to change with the technological convergence of various

Journalism Lost in Smoke

Jeff Cohen and Norman Solomon

Every once in a while, big media outlets criticize the cigarette industry. Then, like habitual puffers dashing out of smoke-free zones, they take evasive action.

The occasional media probes of tobacco are popgun assaults compared to the steady "war on drugs" barrage.

Cigarettes now kill 434,000 Americans each year, according to the federal Centers for Disease Control. Cocaine and crack claim 3,300 lives. But double standards pervade mass media.

A TV documentary, "48 Hours on Crack Street," inspired the weekly CBS program "48 Hours"—which returns regularly to the topic of illegal drugs. But out of the first 162 hour-long productions, only one dealt with cigarettes.

The Lorillard tobacco tycoon who owns CBS, Laurence Tisch, probably does not object to such priorities.

Tobacco interests maintain influence over broadcast media even without owning them. Federal law bars cigarette ads from the airwaves, but Philip Morris buys plenty of commercials for products like Miller Beer, Jell-O and Kool-Aid. As the country's third-largest advertiser on network TV, Philip Morris paid $390 million to ABC, CBS and NBC in 1991.

With its huge circulation—15 million copies per week—*TV Guide* could shine a bright light on network deference to a tobacco industry responsible for more than one in six American deaths. But the magazine won't touch the story with a ten-foot antenna.

As assistant managing editor Andrew Mills told us in 1989, "It wouldn't look good for *TV Guide* to go after the networks when *TV Guide* runs cigarette ads in every issue." In recent years the weekly has not printed a single article about television and tobacco.

Ironically, in a 1992 interview with us, *TV Guide* editor-in-chief Anthea Disney expressed concern about the impact of role models: "I wouldn't run a photo of a person smoking if I could help it." Yet *TV Guide* does so routinely—in colorful cigarette ads. And, the magazine brags to advertisers, more than 5 million teenagers thumb through its pages each week.

We've all seen fervent pleas by the Partnership for a Drug-Free America. Using ad space donated by mass media, the organization warns young people against marijuana, crack and cocaine—but never mentions cigarettes or alcohol. As it happens, the "Drug Free" partnership has some corporate funders that are anything but drug free, such as Philip Morris, Anheuser-Busch, and RJR Nabsico.

Journalism Lost in Smoke *(continued)*

While RJR Nabisco helps bankroll save-the-kids-from-drugs ads, its subsidiary R.J. Reynolds keeps ignoring pleas to cancel massive Old Joe Camel advertising campaigns that are hooking children.

In the wake of findings that 6-year-olds are as familiar with the Camel's Old Joe cartoon character as with Mickey Mouse, U.S. Surgeon General Antonia Novello and the American Medical Association denounced the ad campaign and urged a halt to it. With the nation's children already smoking 947 million packs of cigarettes annually, the stakes are high.

Women are also special targets. In 1991, a half-dozen women's magazines—*Cosmopolitan, Family Circle, Glamour, Harper's Bazaar, Mademoiselle* and *Self*—raked in $27 million from cigarette advertisers.

Every month 12,000 American women die as a result of cigarettes. But *Cosmopolitan* editor Helen Gurley Brown is unapologetic that her magazine collected $8.6 million from cigarette ads last year—while staying away from articles about smoking. "I can't be interviewed on the subject of cigarettes," she told us last week.

Brown, whose glossy magazine includes nine pages of cigarette ads in its April 1992 issue, seems to be standing by her 1985 statement: "Having come from the advertising world myself, I think 'Who needs somebody you're paying millions of dollars a year to come back and bite you on the ankle?' "

An exhaustive study—published in the Jan. 30, 1992 issue of the *New England Journal of Medicine*—found "strong statistical evidence that cigarette advertising in magazines is associated with diminished coverage of the hazards of smoking. This is particularly true for magazines directed to women." As a result of the scarcity of independent journalism, "Americans substantially underestimate the dangers of smoking as compared with other risks to health."

Tobacco companies spend $3.2 billion a year on advertising in the United States. They are not only promoting their deadly product. They are also buying media silence.

Full-color cigarette ads keep rolling off the presses. Respiratory illnesses, cancer, and heart disease will come later, mentioned in plain black ink on obituary pages. ∎

Reprinted with permission from *Adventures in Medialand* by Jeff Cohen and Norman Solomon. © 1993 by Common Courage Press, Monroe, Maine.

Practice

Discuss the previous reading in terms of advertising using the news media, and the news media using advertising. Select one passage from "Journalism Lost in Smoke" and analyze it in terms of the Media Literacy Paradigm (classification, origin, mediation, consumption, and impact). To which of those five stages or steps does your passage relate?

media, predictions about how we will receive our news center around new technologies. A central theme of the information superhighway vision of the future is that of individualization. With 500 TV channels, so the predictions go, we'll be able to watch whatever we want, whenever we want to. We will be able to dial up many electronic shopping catalogs and access various information services. This is where the future of news comes in.

Many scenarios are something like this: You'll come downstairs in the morning to your TV or your wireless laptop computer and, by pressing a button or speaking a command, you can watch a personalized newscast assembled and downloaded for you while you slept. First, you will receive your sports news—national, then local, and only the sports you're interested in. Then you'll check out the weather, complete with a personalized forecast for your town, and, if you're traveling that day, a separate one for your destination. Comics are next—only the ones you've pre-programmed for delivery, of course—followed by articles dealing with topics of personal interest, such as the entertainment business, technology, and world trade.

Thanks to all the new interactive technology coming down the pike, the really big twist in the future of news is that you will be able to produce and transmit your own news. It is being done in various cities already. As high-quality cameras and editing equipment continue to drop in price, more and more amateurs are playing the role of news director, reporter, technician, and broadcaster rolled into one. These often offbeat journalists use public access channels, lease increasingly affordable satellite time, and even digitize their video for transmission over the Internet. You won't just watch the news, you'll make the news!

Student Close-Up

Mark Brodie, Connecticut

A news director in the TV news program at his school, Mark Brodie tells what it's like to be part of a news team.

When I was four years old, I refused to go to bed until the end of the CBS Evening News. I knew all of the correspondents, but my favorite was Walter Cronkite. As he signed off to the country, I wished him a personal good night, as well. From that point on, I figured that I was somewhat destined to go into broadcast journalism. There is very little else that can match the excitement that covering a story does.

As a senior at Manchester High School in Manchester, Connecticut, I was the news director of the MHS TV News program, an award-winning production. My job was one of great responsibility, yet it was rarely tiresome. I was responsible for assigning reporters to stories and specific events, and making sure that what the reporters came back with was usable. I also edited most of the scripts that the anchors and reporters used. While all of this was enjoyable, and surely important, it was not the best part of the job. For me, nothing beats being on location, in front of a camera, reporting on something that affects a large number of people. There is a feeling of exhilaration that comes with the job, and it is a feeling that I will never get tired of. Whether it is reporting on the Board of Education's budget, or on the new lights for the football field, I always try to capture the spirit of the event, and I often find myself getting caught up in it, as well.

There is also the recognition factor of being an on-air personality. People often stop me and tell me what they thought of the last show. This is one of the rewards for all of the hard work. I hope to be able to pursue a career in broadcast journalism. I would like to be one of the few people who are able to do something they love to do for a living. ■

Building Your Media Archive
Archive Analysis

As you analyze your news product, make sure you are clear on what part of the product you are going to focus—the paper or broadcast as a whole, or on a particular section or story? If your product is locally produced, you can almost certainly get an inter-

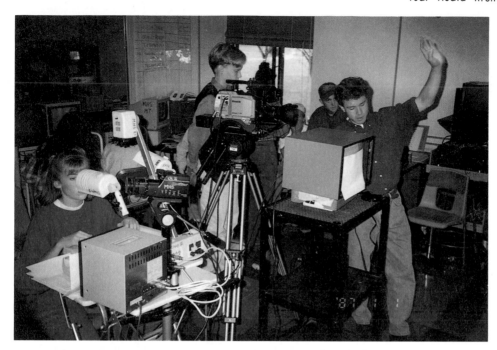

Mark Brodie with the news team. *Photo courtesy of Charles Lewis, Manchester High School, Connecticut.*

view with some of its mediators. The reporter, at least, will probably be willing to spend some time with you, so prepare written questions in advance. (You can use the Media Literacy Paradigm questions to start, because journalists are fairly aware of the ideas you are working with.)

What ads are present in your media product? (Even if you're focusing on a particular news story, look at the ads in the overall media product.) Why are they located where they are? Are the values they contain in keeping with, or in contrast to, the values contained in the news product you're analyzing? What do the ads tell you about the target audience for your news product?

Create Your Own Media

With whatever media you have to work with, you can create a news product. Using some of the story ideas from the list you read in Chapter Nine or better yet, your own ideas—you can practice the essence of journalism. You can research and interview,

File   Edit   Go To   Mail   Members   Windows   Fax

FAA Bans Commuter Plane In Icy C

FAA Bans Commuter Plane In Icy Conditions

   WASHINGTON (Reuter) - The Federal Aviation Administration said Friday it was grounding ATR aircraft during icy conditions after receiving new information following an American Eagle crash in which 68 people died.
   ``This decision is the result of new technical information that we receiv
confer
   The
ATR-7
The in
yet to
wings
  AMR

NEWSSTAND

Entertainment

Education

Today's News

TODAY'S NEWS

Clinton Fires Elders After Remark
Clinton Urges Hemispheric Partnership
Pentagon Buys V-22, Axes Stealth Missile
U.S. Determined To Avoid Bosnia Combat
FAA Bans Commuter Plane In Icy Conditions
Frigid Temperatures Move Into Midwest
Court Takes Major Voting Rights Case

Search News

US & World   Business   Entertainment   Sports   Weather

MAIN MENU   MEMBER SERVICES   INDEX   Keyword: News

Trash

A recently developed way of delivering the news is America Online. Pictured above is a screen capture—what you would see on your personal computer screen. *Reprinted courtesy of America Online, Inc., Vienna, Virginia.*

then publish or record a news story for an audience of your choice (your class, another class, or even an elementary school class).

   Another way to get the idea of putting together a news product is to "cut and paste" a new one out of old ones. Working in a team, obtain as many used newspapers and newsmagazines as possible, then cut out articles and ads. Assign team members particular responsibilities (for example, news editor, sports editor, ad manager, headline writer). Decide on rules for assembling the articles and ads back together into your own publication. Who is your main target audience? How will the answer to that question determine news items and ads that will appear in your product? What conventions of presentation will you follow? How will you resolve possible conflicts between news content and advertising (for example, when your

In the not-too-distant future, we will be able to receive the news electronically on a battery-powered audio- and video-equipped "tablet," also known as a portable information appliance. Roger Fidler, pictured on the left holding the tablet, is a pioneer in the field of electronic delivery of printed materials. Pictured on the right is the front page or "browsing" page of the prototype newspaper. By pressing on the tablet over a particular story, the tablet "jumps" to the full page of that story inside the newspaper. *Photo courtesy of Knight-Ridder Company, © 1994; photographer: Neil Hamberg.*

news editor wants to run a story on underage drinking that might offend one of your biggest alcohol advertisers)?

If you have access to desktop publishing, use your computer to design a prototype for a new school newspaper or newsletter. If you have access to a school broadcasting station, plan a program on an issue of interest to your class or to your school in general.

Reflections

- Compose a persuasive argument to convince local gatekeepers to place more emphasis on positive news and downplay "bad" news.
- How would news in the United States be different if it were controlled and funded by local or federal government? Select a socially controversial topic, such as military spending or school-based health clinics, and describe how public debate on the topic would be affected by such government control.
- Growing numbers of people are capturing events on video and sending them in to air on local news shows. CNN as well as many local stations encourage the practice. How does this trend fit in with the rise of tabloid journalism?
- How would you handle the following situation? As a reporter for your school TV news show or paper, you uncover an ongoing cheating scandal in which the senior star of your school's basketball team is paying another student to do all of his math homework and to create "cheat sheets" for his tests. You discover that many of the players know about the cheating and, furthermore, that the coach knows as well. You compile solid evidence, as students from other teams in the school (who were not given special treatment from their coaches) provide you with many leads. When you approach the coach and the student, they admit to the cheating, but ask you not to run the story. The star will be kicked off the team, which will surely lose the state championship as a result, and the player's college dreams will come to a screeching halt. They beg you to at least not run the story until after the season is over. Assume your no-censorship principal will let you run the story. Do you run the story right away? After the season? Never? Explain your answer.
- What is your opinion of your local TV news anchorpeople? Whom do you like or dislike the most? Why? What do their personalities seem to be like?
- Dr. George Gerbner, one of the nation's foremost researchers into the social effects of media, refers to the "mean world syndrome" in which people have a more negative view of the world as a mean and violent place than it really is as a result of the violence they are exposed to in the media. He points to the phrase often used to describe local TV newscasts: "if it bleeds, it leads" (meaning stories with violence usually start off the broadcast). How do you think repeated viewing of violent news stories affects society's perception of itself?

MEDIA LAB   The News

- List presentation conventions for each of the four news media. What do all newspapers have in common (for example, photo captions and larger headlines near the top of the page)? All TV news shows (theme music, anchor chitchat)? All radio news? All newsmagazines? What is the purpose of each convention you identify?

- Research the phenomenon known as the "sound bite," in which someone is presented in a TV or radio news story saying something for less than 20 seconds. Usually the person's remarks were originally spoken within a much longer context, such as a speech, press conference, or interview. Why are sound bites so common? What is the danger with taking someone out of context? What is the overall effect of a political campaign being waged as a series of orchestrated sound bites? How would campaigning and politics be different if the news was not allowed to air candidate sound bites?

- Record a typical evening's local news weather segment. Time the segment. How much of the piece provides information that you can use? How are the other several minutes spent? Why is so much emphasis placed on the weather segment? How do our attitudes about TV "meteorologists" carry over into the broader area of "news personality as expert"? Why do local news shows present food experts, health experts, financial experts, and animal experts? In what ways are these people experts?

- Obtain copies of the June 27, 1994, copies of *Newsweek* and *Time* magazines, both of which had a photo of O.J. Simpson on the cover. Your school and local library should have them, as well as subsequent articles dealing with the controversy surrounding the two covers. Here's the story: *Newsweek* published the original arrest "mugshot" of O.J. Simpson unaltered. *Time* published the same photo but had a computer artist alter the photo for artistic effect, blurring and darkening it in the process. Public opinion— particularly in the African-American community—was that the *Time* photo made Simpson look racially stereotypical, evil, and thus, guilty. In small print on an inside page, *Time* described the cover as a "photo-illustration" but did not clearly acknowledge that the photo had been altered. What are your impressions of the difference between the covers? What questions can you ask about *Time*'s alteration of the photo? What elements of the Media Literacy Paradigm apply to the controversy? If you locate articles about the *Time* cover, evaluate the responses of the *Time* editors who defended their decision.

Career Bank

Following are just a few of the many careers available in the news media industry:

- reporter
- photographer
- researcher
- press agent/public relations
- video producer
- news commentator
- newsteam member/anchorperson
- news director

Recap

Though a precise definition of *news* is impossible, there are five major criteria used for almost all news products: **timeliness, significance** of the event, **closeness** to the audience, **importance** of the people involved, and the **drama** of human interest.

The four major news media have three main similarities: They all depend on advertising for revenues; they all rely on wire services for a major portion of their news reports; and they all use a system of **gatekeepers** who make decisions about what gets included in the product.

Each news medium has its strengths as well. TV news, because it employs high-C symbols, is the most emotional and compelling (as a result it is the most popular and influential). Newspapers provide the widest traditional variety of daily news and strike the best balance between detail and timeliness. Newsmagazines, while not the most timely, provide the greatest depth and background of all news media. As a medium, radio news is the most up-to-date source of information on a daily basis. (CNN is a kind of visual news radio format.)

Most of what is presented as news is made up of staged events. Political appearances, press conferences, and other preplanned events are set up by public relations managers to receive coverage. Reporters are routinely given advance notice about local happenings; the unplanned stories are usually the tragedy stories or the human interest stories.

Tabloidization refers to the trend toward sensationalizing the news, making it more dramatic, more entertaining. Media critics have been warning about the slide into infotainment for more than a decade, but the 1990s have seen an all-out race among news organizations in the effort to attract consumers. Are news organizations covering sensationalistic stories because we, the consumers, want them, or have we learned to want what we're shown?

A fundamental issue facing the press in the United States is the influence of advertisers on news content. All news media walk a fine line between reporting the truth and not offending the advertisers who fund them. Stories about illegal or unethical business practices of large companies are often left unreported as a result of behind-the-scenes agreements between big advertisers and the news organizations they pay to run their ads.

Resources for Further Reading

Books

Bagdikian, Ben. *The Media Monopoly.* Boston: Beacon Press, 1992.

Bates, Stephen. *If No News, Send Rumors: Anecdotes of American Journalism.* New York: Owl Books, 1989.

Dobson, Christopher. *The Freelance Journalist: How to Survive, Succeed and Prosper.* Oxford: Butterworth-Heinemann, 1992.

Gans, Herbert J. *Deciding What's News: A Study of CBS, NBC, ABC, Newsweek, and Time.* New York: Vintage Books, 1979.

Koch, Tom. *Journalism for the 21st Century: Online Information, Electronic Databases, and the News.* Westport, Conn.: Prager, 1991.

Love, Robert. *The Best of Rolling Stone: 25 Years of Journalism on the Edge.* New York: Doubleday, 1993.

Postman, Neil. *Amusing Ourselves to Death: Public Discourse in the Age of Show Business.* New York: Penguin, 1985.

Postman, Neil and Steve Powers. *How to Watch TV News.* New York: Penguin USA, 1992.

Schulte, Henry. *Getting the Story: An Advanced Reporting Guide to Beats, Records and Sources.* New York: Macmillan, 1994.

Weaver, Paul. *News and the Culture of Lying: How Journalism Really Works.* New York: The Free Press, 1994.

Industry Publications, Magazines, and Associations

American Journalism Review, 9701 Adelphi Road, Adelphi, MD 20783

Columbia Scholarly Press Association, Box 11, Central Mail Room, Columbia University, New York, NY 10027-6969

Fairness and Accuracy in Reporting (FAIR), 130 W. 25th St., New York, NY 10001

National Press Photographer's Association, 3200 Craisaile Drive, Suite 306, Durham, NC 27705

Newspaper Association of America, 11600 Sunrise Valley Drive, Reston, VA 22091

Key word database searches for library research on the news media:

Journalism, journalist, tabloids, tabloidization, infotainment, press freedom, First Amendment, press bias, reporting, wire services, news coverage, TV news, newspapers, radio news, newsmagazines, local news, national news, political reporting, hard news, soft news

TV, Video, and Films about the News Media

Broadcast News (1988)
The China Syndrome (1979)
The Killing Fields (1984)
Network (1976)
The Paper (1993)
C-SPAN and Close Up Foundation Forums (current)

SEGUE

The News Media

If it is true that our perceptions—our paradigms—of the world around us are influenced by the news we consume, it is equally true that we are influenced by the advertising we consume. Many of the ideas we hold about progress, self-image, governance, and a thousand other realms reflect—and are reflected in—the popular culture of advertising. The final chapter of *Understanding Mass Media* zeroes in on this omnipresent part of our lives.

CHAPTER FOURTEEN

Advertising

Learning Targets

After working through this chapter, you will be able to:

- Summarize the evolution of U.S. advertising;
- Describe the three stages of film production as applied to the making of a TV commercial;
- Identify examples of advertising techniques found in current ads;
- Explain product placement as a new form of advertising; and
- Apply the Media Literacy Paradigm to the advertisement in your Media Archive.

Checking In

- What role does advertising play in your decisions to buy certain products?
- Identify your favorite magazine ads or TV commercials; explain why you like them.
- List radio, magazine, and newspaper ads and tell why you remember them.
- List as many advertising jingles/slogans as you can; why are the memorable?
- What kinds of information do you think advertisers know about you as an American teenager?

Why Advertising Exists

Advertising exists to solve a problem: the presence of more goods than are needed. In a society of scarcity, where there is not enough to go around, there is no need for ads. Everything that is grown or made is put to immediate use. Advertising requires a surplus of goods or services. It exists to create a demand. There is no need for advertising if the demand already exists far beyond the supply.

As long as goods were supplied locally, handmade as needed, there was little need for advertising beyond an occasional announcement or sign. A shoemaker would hang a sign outside his house (which was also his workshop), but had no need to advertise. All he could do was make a few pairs of shoes a week. Each shoe was custom made for a specific person—there was no back room filled with inventory; no surplus of shoes to be moved before the new fashions could be introduced.

Even if our humble shoemaker could hire workers to turn out a surplus of shoes, how would he advertise? The technology of printing was not a mass medium until the fifteenth century after the invention of the Gutenberg printing press. Only with printing could the shoemaker make handbills to pass around the village. Before printing he would have to rely on a town crier or perhaps a strolling minstrel to sing a jingle about his shoes.

Modern advertising had to wait for a surplus of goods. A surplus of goods came about only with machines that could turn out more than one item at a time—not until the Industrial Revolution. Only after the Industrial Revolution were there enough products and money to support mass advertising.

The Evolution of Advertising

Mass advertising thus required the technology of printing and the Industrial Revolution. There was a third requirement—literate customers. During the 1800s laws were passed both in England and the United States requiring children to attend school. These laws were important to advertising because they raised the literacy level of the general population to the point at which printed advertisements could be understood.

Printers were quick to see that handbills were a profitable source of business. By combining handbills with news, printers produced what would eventually become the modern newspaper and magazine. Printers realized they could make money both by selling their paper to readers and by charging merchants to print advertisements.

Printers soon found that they spent too much time soliciting ads from merchants, so they hired agents to sell advertising space. These agents were not paid a salary; they were paid a commission on each ad they sold. The size of the commission became standardized at 15 percent of the cost of the ad and often remains that today.

As more newspapers, newsletters, and magazines were printed, merchants were besieged by advertising agents. "Which publication is best for my goods?" each wondered. The agent knew the most about advertising and so became a kind of selling consultant. In 1870, two competing agents, J. Walter Thompson and N. W. Ayer, realized that they could best serve their clients by writing effective selling copy and by planning an advertising campaign. These agents created the age of modern advertising.

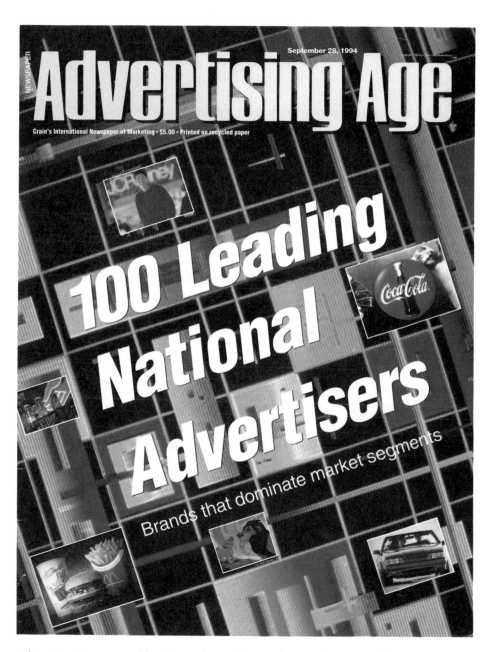

Advertising is generated by those who market products and services. This magazine keeps companies and advertising professionals up-to-date in the industry. © *1994 Crain Communications.*

Advertising changed as new media—color posters, radio, and television—became available. Advertisements transmitted via broadcast media are called commercials. The purpose of advertising, both print ads and commercials, changed as well. Advertising went through a series of refinements, each representing a new approach to selling. For instance, at first advertising was only information. Later, advertisers saw the value of capturing reader attention before presenting the information.

Consider the following eight stages that have emerged since the beginnings of advertising. Note that these stages did not necessarily follow in an orderly manner, nor—as time went on—did one stage completely replace the previous one. Indeed, an advertisement or commercial could include all eight. However, tracing these eight stages will give you a clear picture of how advertising has developed into the role it plays in today's world.

Information Stage

Before the nineteenth century most advertising was merely informative. It consisted of price lists, signs on walls, printed announcements, and even the calls of the town crier. Supply and demand were in balance and there was no need to produce new products. People bought what they needed and needed what they bought. There was limited competition among merchants.

Attention Stage

By the start of the nineteenth century, factories were turning out goods that needed public attention to sell. The goods had to be sold in markets away from the factory. Manufacturers found it necessary to use various devices to attract attention.

To call attention to the "advertisement," devices such as borders, headline type, and increased white space were used. Today, we take these devices for granted, but remember, the earliest ads were considered news. "A shipment of tea arrived by ship yesterday and is available for sale at dockside" is both news and an ad. In fact, the word *advertise* originally meant "to announce." Many early newspapers (and some today) were named the "Advertiser" not because they carried ads but because to advertise meant to announce.

Consider page one of Boston's *Daily Evening Transcript* of April 9, 1840, reproduced above. On its front page were three-line notices for Italian cravats, money to loan, potatoes, two teens who wanted work in a "Publik House," and shares of bank stock. The page was a solid mass of small type, broken only by a large capital letter here and there. Ads and news were not separated, nor were ads classified according to type of merchandise. Not until the late nineteenth century were large sizes of type and graphic design used to gain readers' attention.

Repetition Stage

Many influential large city newspapers objected to large-sized type for some announcements. They felt it would be unfair to others. The "agate rule" stated that all announcements had to be set in agate type. Following is a typical 1800s newspaper advertisement, announcing a cure for rickets—a disease once common in children, caused by a lack of vitamin D. Note that the ad is set according to the agate rule.

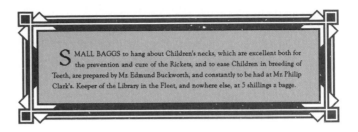

SMALL BAGGS to hang about Children's necks, which are excellent both for the prevention and cure of the Rickets, and to ease Children in breeding of Teeth, are prepared by Mr. Edmund Buckworth, and constantly to be had at Mr. Philip Clark's. Keeper of the Library in the Fleet, and nowhere else, at 5 shillings a bagge.

If the type could not be made larger, it could be repeated to attract attention. Repetition as an advertising device was created to get around the "agate rule." It is still used today as perhaps the most common of all persuasive devices.

Robert Bonner, an early publisher, took a whole page of the *New York Herald* in 1856 and repeated his message 600 times. P. T. Barnum was a master of the art of repetition. The ad below was run by Barnum in a newspaper in 1841, promoting his museum of Americana.

While Bonner and Barnum were practicing repetition, technology made it possible to sell food in glass containers or tin cans. Prior to this time, merchants scooped food from huge bins or barrels. There was little room for the development of a name brand. Cans and bottles made possible the sale of small quantities of food under a brand name. The method of repetition was ideally suited to making the public aware of brand names.

Repetition as a means of persuasion still thrives today. It received a boost from the scientific work of Ivan Pavlov and J. B. Watson

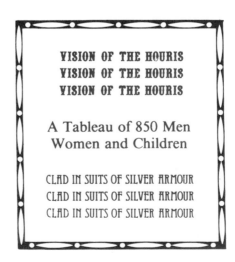

VISION OF THE HOURIS
VISION OF THE HOURIS
VISION OF THE HOURIS

A Tableau of 850 Men
Women and Children

CLAD IN SUITS OF SILVER ARMOUR
CLAD IN SUITS OF SILVER ARMOUR
CLAD IN SUITS OF SILVER ARMOUR

in the 1920s. Pavlov and Watson introduced the idea of the "conditioned reflex." The theory held that learning involved the association of a response with a stimulus. A response to the specific stimulus was learned if the stimulus was repeated often enough. Pavlov demonstrated that a dog learned to lift its paw at the sound of a bell if the dog was repeatedly rewarded for doing so.

J. B. Watson was hired by the J. Walter Thompson Advertising Agency to apply this theory to advertising. Advertising quickly learned to repeat often and to treat the purchase as a reward for the consumer's correct response.

By the 1930s repetition meant using a catchy phrase or jingle on the radio that was repeated over and over again. A classic example is the famous Pepsi jingle reproduced below. Pepsi Cola set this jingle to the tune of an old English hunting song and used it in their radio advertising for decades.

Pepsi-Cola hits the spot.
Twelve full ounces, that's a lot.
Twice as much for a nickel, too.
Pepsi-Cola is the drink for you!
Nickel, nickel, nickel, nickel,
Trickle, trickle, trickle, trickle,
Nickel, nickel, nickel, nickel.

The repetition approach thrives today—and not only for products. Celebrities also know that keeping a name before the public breeds familiarity and acceptance.

Association Stage

By the end of the nineteenth century, advertisers began to suspect that pure repetition was not enough. Advances in color printing and techniques developed by French poster artists led to the next phase in advertising—association.

Artists such as Aubrey Beardsley, Toulouse-Lautrec, and Edward Penfield showed that paintings of attractive people in poster ads created pleasant associations for the product. Even today, pleasing graphics and appealing pictures lead to favorable product associations.

Product-Benefit Stage

As products became more complex, advertisers found it necessary to explain what the products were and why the consumer would benefit from their use. In the 1950s, advertising executive Rosser Reeves developed the phrase "unique selling proposition" (USP) to show that every ad must present the product as unique. The USP had to be a product benefit that no other brand could offer.

Reeves' agency took Colgate toothpaste and coined the word *Gardol* for its decay-fighting ingredient. It didn't matter if the ingredient was unique to Colgate; it was sufficient that the name *Gardol* be unique. Colgate was unique because it alone had Gardol; and it alone had Gardol because its ad agency made up the word.

Motivation Stage

By the end of the 1930s, the fledgling science of motivational research was discovered by ad agencies. Products were seen to have psychological meanings. Advertisers realized that people bought goods not only because they needed them but also because of various and often hidden psychological needs.

During this time the work of Austrian neurologist Sigmund Freud, the founder of psychoanalysis, was recognized in the United States. Although few advertisers completely understood his theories, they realized that people often bought products for unconscious motives. In other words, before this time advertisers assumed that people bought a certain brand of soap because it cleaned best or cost less. From Freud's work they realized that a brand may be bought because the buyers feel the brand makes them more powerful, more loved, or more socially acceptable.

Motivational research showed, for example, that women would not pay more than a dollar for a bar of soap to make them clean; but they would pay many dollars for a "cream" that promised to make them beautiful. In other words, don't sell soap—sell dreams. Don't sell oranges—sell health and vitality. Don't sell automobiles—sell prestige and power.

Ernest Dichter became the leading proponent of motivational research, and his ideas still exert a strong influence on advertising. One of the most popular books on advertising, *The Hidden Persuaders* by Vance Packard, became a best-seller in the late 1950s. The book "exposed" motivational techniques, but they are still used today to create new products and repackage old products.

....

Why your wife buys 35 percent more in the supermarket
than she intends to.
Why your children like cereals that crackle and crunch.
Why men wouldn't give up shaving even if they could.

....

Entertainment Stage

In the middle of the 1950s, the Doyle Dane Bernbach agency
realized that advertising could also be entertaining. The history
of advertising so far assumed ads were to be informative. However,
the Doyle Dane Bernbach television commercials entertained.
Television commercials today take entertainment value for granted,
but keep in mind that the only good commercial is one that sells.

Behavioral Stage

By the 1980s consumers were more critical and better educated.
They were becoming increasingly skeptical about commercials.

Behavioral research studied consumer needs and buying patterns
to present a product image that would be seen as satisfying a real
consumer need. An example of the behavioral approach can be
seen in the long-running Virginia Slims ("You've Come a Long
Way, Baby") cigarette campaign. The campaign seemed to illustrate an understanding of the changing role of women in society
and presented a product that fit this changing self-image. Another
example of this approach is the ads for reduced-calorie, sugar-free
drinks, or wholesome natural foods for health-conscious, active
people.

During the 1990s, the behavioral approach to advertising was
refined and focused on a quantitative analysis of buying patterns.
Advertisers target their commercials and ads accordingly, in a more
"scientific" manner.

The Making of a TV Commercial

The process of making an important TV commercial—a mega-ad
or "super pitch"—is quite similar to the process of making a

feature film. The task is divided into three stages: preproduction, production, and postproduction. The reading on page 469 describes the creation of a commercial that was broadcast during the 1994 Super Bowl game.

Practice

Analyze the reading by Martha T. Moore on the making of McDonald's ad in terms of two states in the Media Literacy Pardigm: mediation (production) and impact on the viewer/consumer.

The Language of Advertising
The Fine Art of Deception Detection

By the time you are 60 years old, you will have seen and heard over 50 million advertising messages. Most will be ignored, some will help, but others will mislead.

Advertising can help you discover new products or show you where to buy goods at the lowest price. However, it can also mislead you into buying what you don't want or into believing a particular brand is better than it really is. To be able to tell the difference, you need to become a skilled reader of ads.

You must learn to determine exactly what facts are presented in an ad. You must also recognize how the ad strives to make the product appealing. These may seem two simple skills, but advertising experts spend millions to make the job difficult.

Looking for facts in ads and commercials requires the mind of a Sherlock Holmes and the logic of a computer. Almost every advertisement makes what is called a **product claim.** The claim is simply what the ad says about the product. For example, "Jumbo pens write longer than any other ballpoint pen" *claims* very clearly that the Jumbo pen writes longer than any other pen. That sounds simple, yet claims are rarely that plain.

There are two basic kinds of claims—one provides information useful in making a purchase decision, and one tells little or nothing factual.

Making a McDonald's Ad

Martha T. Moore

At 7 o'clock on a December morning, copywriter Jim Ferguson, rumpled and sleepy, walks into a hotel room in Arizona for a meeting to kick off a two-day shoot of McDonald's biggest commercial of the year. Inside a manila folder is a photocopied script and scene-by-scene drawing of the proposed ad, which stars three of the greatest names of basketball: Michael Jordan, Charles Barkley and Larry Bird. On the outside is written one sentence: "Can we use the word 'horse'?"

Such are the decisions that make a Super Bowl ad.

Since 1967, every year but one, McDonald's has advertised on the Super Bowl. This year, it spent more than $2.5 million to do so. The company calls these ads "reputation" spots, and that's just what's on the line. For Super Bowl XXVIII, its 60-second ad required four days of filming, 75 hours of special effects work, 140 hours of editing, 10 hours of sound mixing and the talents of about 80 people, including the best-known and most-expensive commercial director in the business. Ten days of technical work was crammed into a four-day session so intense that a special-effects artist started to faint over his computer. "We just wheeled him out and brought in another one," says Chris Rossiter, the producer.

And that was before the earthquake damaged the editing studio and the film had to be hastily flown to Chicago to be completed. It was still two days late.

The ad is a sequel to McDonald's 1993 Super Bowl ad, which paired Jordan and Bird in an ever-escalating game of horse and won the USA TODAY Super Bowl Ad Meter. This year, Jordan and Bird end up in even more outlandish situations—shooting baskets over the Grand Canyon, out of the hatch of a submarine and from outer space. The twist: '93 MVP Barkley is begging to join in and Jordan and Bird won't let him. In the 1994 Ad Meter, the ad scored 8.59 and tied for fifth place.

It didn't use the word horse.

Horse is the playground name for the game Jordan and Bird play—shoot till you miss. Then again, it's also a word that any fast-food restaurant selling inexpensive hamburgers might fear.

"I'll admit, years and years ago we were very sensitive about that," says Roy Bergold, McDonald's vice president of advertising. "We used to not allow horses in commercials, and stuff like that." The ban is over: In this ad Barkley makes his entrance on horseback. Still, Bergold decides that "one on one" is the preferred term.

Making a McDonald's Ad *(continued)*

At $900,000 per 30 seconds, running a commercial on the Super Bowl is one of the biggest advertising decisions a company can make. The dozen or so companies that do so regularly have ad budgets in the hundreds of millions. They want their names and images in front of the 135 million Americans who watch the game.

CHICAGO
Coming up with the concept

Before the cameras roll, before Jordan, Barkley and Bird show up on the set, before the sound can be mixed and remixed, there has to be the idea for the ad. Leo Burnett, the Chicago agency that does most of McDonald's ads, creates about 150 TV commercials a year for the chain. Ferguson, his partner Bob Shallcross and their boss, Cheryl Berman, create most of the big ads.

This year, the team had a tough act to follow: themselves. The 1993 Bird-Jordan showdown was a hit. So in September, when the creative team started planning for the Super Bowl, thoughts of a sequel "rose to the top right away," Shallcross says. What also surfaced were fears of a flop. For every Godfather, Part II, there's a Caddyshack II.

"We talked about it a lot and said, 'What if it's not good?' " Shallcross says. "But then we realized there was enough (new) stuff to do." The sequel would be even more absurd than the original: Bird and Jordan could be on an elephant. They could be at the North Pole in a whiteout. They could bounce the ball off the spout of a whale. "We kept going, 'We could do this (scene), we could do this,' " Shallcross says.

In November, McDonald's approved the idea of another Bird-Jordan shootout, with Barkley whining like an 8-year-old to be allowed to play. Joe Pytka, a top ad director known for his way with spokesjocks, his love of basketball and his fiery temperament, signed up. He had directed the original "Showdown." The budget was fixed at $700,000 for the ad and three shorter NBA promotions to run in March. That cost doesn't even include the price of three of the most expensive endorsers around.

Filming was scheduled for two days in December, outside Phoenix, where Barkley plays. By then, Jordan had announced his surprise retirement, and Barkley was the only one of the three stars with a day job.

"Now it just has to be good," Shallcross says the day before the shoot starts. "The pressure's not on—much."

CHICAGO
Fightin' words over the words

Artistic vision is one thing, advertising is another. The scenes may last just a second or two, the dialogue may be but a few phrases. But each word and each storyboard—drawings of each scene, like a comic strip—get scrutinized. This minimovie is supposed to somehow, indirectly, in some general

Making a McDonald's Ad *(continued)*

feel-good kind of way, sell burgers. And it's not supposed to cause any waves.

In a meeting the morning that filming begins, Bergold goes over the ad with Pytka and the creative team.

Trouble starts with the opening line. Bird is supposed to suggest that the stakes for the shootout—a Big Mac—be raised to "double or nothing." His agent doesn't want him to say the line; it sounds too much like gambling. But Jordan, who's had well-publicized gambling losses, certainly can't say it. "We need a new line," Bergold decides.

There's a beach scene. "No thongs," Bergold, keeper of the McDonald's advertising flame, says. "No extremely skimpy bathing suits."

Then Bergold spots the scene with Barkley floating in the ocean in an inflatable raft. "The safety issue. The life vest. We have to."

"Are you SERIOUS?" Pytka yells. It's 7:15 a.m. and suddenly, he is fully awake. He says he was once asked to make Michael Jackson wear a helmet on a ski jump in a Pepsi ad, "and THIS is DUMBER than THAT."

Bergold is completely unmoved. Some child somewhere is going to fall out of a raft and drown and McDonald's will be blamed. "He gets a life vest."

End of discussion.

PHOENIX
Rising tension on the set

The location is an airplane hangar-sized building in the desert. There,

Pytka's crew has built the sets: the interior of a submarine, two front doors with stoops and plants—one labeled "Bird's House" and the other, "The Jordans"—and on one wall hangs a huge green backdrop. For special effects, the actors are filmed in front of the "green screen." Backgrounds for the ad—Monument Valley, the wing of an airplane, the life raft, outer space—are superimposed digitally later. Outside is Pytka's traveling basketball hoop.

The ads are filmed in bits and pieces: the submarine scene, then a doorstep scene for the promotional ads, then Barkley on a horse for the opening of the Super Bowl ad, then the spacesuit scene.

When Barkley, who has already donned cowboy hat, goggles and life vest in the service of selling Big Macs, lumbers out in his puffy white spacesuit, he cracks, "I have no pride. 'Pay him enough and he'll wear anything.' " Jordan, equally stiff in the suit, says to Pytka, "So this is how you feel when you play."

The big excitement comes when Barkley has trouble with a scene where he's knocking on Bird's front door. Suddenly Pytka starts to blow up. He accuses Berman, the ad agency creative director, of "cackling" during a shot and tells Ferguson he's a pig. Pytka's rages are both famous and routine.

"You were waiting for this, weren't you?" he yells to Bird, who's standing

Making a McDonald's Ad *(continued)*

behind the set, waiting to open his front door. "Yes," Bird yells back. The door opens. "Now get your camera and let's go to work." Slam.

When work resumes, Pytka tells a couple of dirty jokes to get things going. Barkley nails his line.

But it's Bird who joins in Pytka's basketball game. When he fails to block a shot from this 55-year-old stocky former high-school football player, Bird stops and covers his eyes in shame.

CHICAGO
In the 'How Come' room

In early January, a "rough cut" of the ad, with only the green screen background, is shown to Paul Schrage, McDonald's top marketing executive. Then on Jan. 20, four days before the ad is due to the network, the final—well, almost final—version is taken to McDonald's Oak Brook, Ill., headquarters to be screened again, in a small auditorium that Ferguson calls the "How Come" room.

Schrage wants more fine-tuning. It's hard to understand Bird's Hoosier accent through his space helmet; the soundtrack has to be fixed. And he cuts one of the few references to McDonald's food—in a line added on the set, Jordan says to Bird, "I'll even buy you an Extra Value Meal."

It's very easy dialogue until you get there, and then it sounds like a commercial," Schrage says.

The ad goes back to the studio that afternoon. Everybody phones home to say they'll be late again.

NEW YORK
Making the deadline—barely

Two days after NBC's deadline, in the middle of the night, the ad is sent via satellite from Chicago to an editing house in New York. Two videotapes are made, two messengers are standing by—just to ensure that one of them makes it to NBC headquarters. The ad lands at 1 p.m. Thursday. On Sunday night, it's beamed into about 44 million homes. It rates fifth in the USA TODAY Super Bowl Ad Meter, where viewers rate the ads from 1 to 10. "I thought it looked great," McDonald's Bergold says the next day. "My mother-in-law poll rates it higher than USA TODAY did."

In advertising, a mother-in-law poll is as scientific as any other. After all the work, the money, the talent, the fiddling, an ad ultimately is—to use a phrase that Larry Bird wouldn't—a crapshoot.

Who knows if this ad, more than another, will sell Big Macs. "Does it contribute? Does it help? Sure," Schrage says. "Quantify it? I can't. It's just part of a whole mix that contributes to this thing called McDonald's." ■

Movie-making techniques are used during the filming of commercials, such as in this production of a Pepsi commercial shown above. *Photo: Shooting Star; photographer: Diana Lyn.*

In the following Practice activity, you will examine four examples of advertising claims similar to ones that have been used repeatedly on radio and television commercials and in print advertising.

··

Practice

Read the following fictional ad claims and then in your notebook write what you think each commercial claims about the product being promoted. Rate each claim as either (a) one that provides useful information or (b) one that gives little or no useful information. After you have done this with each of the four ads, go on and read the comments made by a skilled ad reader.

CLAIM 1
"Everbright toothpaste helps get your teeth whiter and cleaner. Its special ingredient XT-40 fights tooth decay."

CLAIM 2

"Brushing with Goodteeth toothpaste helps fight tooth decay. Nine out of ten dentists interviewed agreed that brushing with Goodteeth is effective in combating decay."

CLAIM 3

"New improved Blubbers bubble gum now has twice as many sticks of gum. New Green Blubbers is chewed by more professional football players than any other bubble gum. Look for Blubbers in the bright green package wherever good gum is sold."

CLAIM 4

"Strictly controlled scientific tests by an independent testing laboratory show that Imperial gasoline with PowerTane® outperforms any gasoline made without PowerTane. Get Imperial gasoline with PowerTane to help your car run quieter, smoother, and get more miles per gallon."

An Expert's Opinions

Now read the following comments made by advertising experts about the claims (the advertisements in quotation marks) you just analyzed. Compare your comments to the expert's.

Claim 1

"Everbright toothpaste helps get your teeth whiter and cleaner. Its special ingredient XT-40 fights tooth decay."

This ad contains no useful information. Many ads make use of comparative adjectives, such as *whiter, cleaner,* or *quieter,* without saying whiter or cleaner than what. Cleaner than if you used mustard as toothpaste? Whiter than if you used licorice paste? The ad doesn't say. Perhaps the ad means only that brushing teeth is better than not brushing. The claim invites the reader to supply the missing comparison by saying "cleaner and whiter than any other toothpaste." But the ad does not say this, and to believe it does is a misunderstanding. The ad can be misleading unless it is read very carefully.

Another claim made in the ad is that Everbright contains a special ingredient—XT-40—to fight tooth decay. What is XT-40? It could be something that has always been in the toothpaste; it could be something that all toothpastes contain.

The claim "fights tooth decay" is very carefully worded. It doesn't say "stops" tooth decay. If Everbright could stop tooth decay, the ad would say that. Brushing with water also "fights tooth decay"; so does using toothpicks.

Claim 2

The word *helps* is used constantly in advertising. Remember that "helps" does not mean "does"—it means "helps." It would be perfectly accurate to say that "a bucket of water helps fight forest fires." But that is not the same as saying that a bucket of water can put out a forest fire.

"Nine out of ten dentists" (or doctors, athletes, or whomever) means simply that the company was able to find nine who agreed. Note that dentists would agree that brushing with anything would help fight decay; brushing is more important than what is put on the brush. Dentists know that the proper brushing technique is more important than the brand of toothpaste. The statement doesn't say that Goodteeth itself stops or fights decay—it says that *brushing* with Goodteeth "helps" (remember that word) fight decay.

"Brushing with Goodteeth toothpaste helps fight tooth decay. Nine out of ten dentists interviewed agreed that brushing with Goodteeth is effective in combating decay."

Claim 3

The word *new* (or *revolutionary,* or *improved,* or *all new*) is another of the advertiser's favorites. "New" does not necessarily mean better—it simply means different.

The fact that Blubbers has twice as many sticks is not the same as saying twice as much gum. They simply may have cut up the same amount of gum into smaller pieces. If the amount of gum had doubled, the ad would probably state that very clearly.

The claim that pro football players chew Blubbers means little. Perhaps each player was mailed a case at the beginning of the season. It would be a very hard claim to either prove or disprove. Also, there is no real connection between chewing gum and playing football.

"New improved Blubbers bubble gum now has twice as many sticks of gum. New Green Blubbers is chewed by more professional football players than any other bubble gum. Look for Blubbers in the bright green package wherever good gum is sold."

Claim 4

Be careful with this claim. Begin with the knowledge that gasolines are all pretty much the same. The claim here sounds good, but if you read carefully you can see that you never find out exactly what PowerTane is (remember XT-40). If PowerTane is simply a trademark for some common ingredient, then it would certainly be honest to say that "Imperial gasoline outperforms any gasoline made without PowerTane." All gas has the same ingredient that Imperial calls PowerTane. But Imperial has registered the name

"Strictly controlled scientific tests by an independent testing laboratory show that Imperial gasoline with PowerTane® outperforms any gasoline made without PowerTane. Get Imperial gasoline with PowerTane to help your car run quieter, smoother, and get more miles per gallon."

"PowerTane" so no other company can use it—this is called a registered trademark. The claim amounts only to saying that "our car with wheels rides smoother than any car made without wheels."

The ad encourages the unskilled reader to think that Imperial outperforms any other gasoline. But the ad does not actually say that. If Imperial did indeed outperform all others, you can be sure the ad would say so very clearly. Notice that the ad never uses untruth. Also notice that the final sentence again contains comparisons without an ending. Quieter, smoother, and more miles per gallon than what?

Analyzing Techniques of Advertising

One basic rule to remember in analyzing ads is that if any product is truly superior, the ad will say so very clearly and will offer some kind of convincing evidence of its superiority. If an ad hedges at all about a product's superiority, you can suspect that it is not really superior. You will never hear Mobil (or any other brand) say "Mobil gasoline in your car gives you 4 miles per gallon more than any other brand." Mobil would love to make such a claim, but it simply isn't true. Various brands of gasoline are more alike than different. Although there were some clever and deceptive gasoline ads a few years ago, no one has yet made an outright claim that one brand of gasoline is better than any other.

To create the illusion of superiority, advertisers often resort to one or more of the following nine basic techniques. Each is common and easy to identify.

Examples:
"**Magnaflux gives you more.**" (More what?)
"**Supergloss does it with more color, more shine, more sizzle, more!**"
"**Twice as much of the pain reliever doctors recommend most.**" (Twice as much as what?)
"**You can be sure if it's Westinghouse.**"
"**Scott makes it better for you.**"
"**Turbo Glide—700% quieter.**"

The Unfinished Technique

This advertising technique is one in which the ad claims that the product is better or has more of something but does not finish the comparison.

The Weasel Word Technique

Weasel word is a modifier that makes what follows nearly meaningless. The term *weasel word* comes from the habit of weasels of sucking out the inside of a raw egg through a tiny hole. An unsuspecting person picks up what looks like a whole egg only to find it is empty. Weasel words sound convincing at first, but upon closer examination turn out to be empty.

The most common weasel words include *helps* (perhaps the most used), *virtual* or *virtually*, *like* (used in a comparative sense), *acts* or *works*, *can be*, *up to*, *as much as*, *refreshes*, *comforts*, *fights*, *the feel of* (also *the look of*), *tastes*, *fortified*, *enriched*, *strengthened*.

Examples:
"Helps control dandruff symptoms with regular use." This claim is an accurate statement about the product. A consumer would be wrong to think that the claim is the same as "cures dandruff."

"Leaves dishes virtually spotless." An unskilled ad reader will remember the claim as being spotless and not *almost* ("virtually") spotless. We hear so many weasel words that we tend to tune them out, which is exactly what advertisers want.

"Only half the price of many color sets." "Many" is the weasel here. The ad does not claim that this set is inexpensive, only that others cost twice as much.

"Made with wool." This phrase does not mean "made entirely out of wool" or "100% wool." It means only there is some wool in the garment.

"BINGO cereal is part of a nutritious breakfast." This phrase does not mean BINGO is nutritious. If you serve pure junk food with milk and fruit, you could still claim it is "part of" a nutritious meal.

A special weasel —"better" and "best"

The reason so many ads need to use weasel words and the other techniques described here is that they are *parity products*. A parity product is one in which most of the brands are nearly identical. Because no one superior product exists, advertising is used to create an illusion of superiority. The largest advertising budgets are devoted to such parity products as beer and soft drinks, cigarettes, soaps, and various drugstore pain remedies.

In parity claims, the words *better* and *best* take on unique meanings. In such claims, *better* means "best" and *best* means "as good as." Here's how this word game works: Let's say that in a given product category there are a number of brands that are alike. Legally this means that each can claim to be best—they are all "superior." Since they are all equal, they must all be best. So "best" means that the product is as good as all the other superior products in its category. If one orange juice says "the best there is," this means only that it is as good as (not better than) any other orange juice on the market.

On the other hand, the word *better* has been legally interpreted as being comparative and therefore becomes a clear claim of superiority. That orange juice ad could not legally have claimed "better than any other brand." The only times "better" can be used are (a) if the product is indeed better than anything else; (b) if "better" is actually used to compare the product with something else ("our orange juice is better than powdered drinks"); or (c) if "better" is part of an unfinished claim ("the better breakfast drink").

••

Examples of "better" and "best" weasels:
"Better Shopper brand cocoa is the very best."
"Tests confirm Fresh mouthwash is better against mouth odor."

••

The "We're Different and Unique" Technique

This technique states simply that there is nothing else quite like the product advertised. For example, if a lemonade manufacturer added blue food coloring to its product, it could advertise, "There's nothing like new blue Tarttaste." The uniqueness claim is supposed to be interpreted by readers as an indication of superiority.

Examples:

"There's no other mascara like it."

"Only Inca has this unique filter system."

"Panther is like nobody else's car."

"Either way, liquid or spray, there's nothing else like it."

"If it doesn't say Goodyear, it can't be Polyglas®."
"Polyglas" is a trade name that was copyrighted by Goodyear. Other tire manufacturers could make a tire identical to the Polyglas tire Goodyear marketed; yet they couldn't call it "Polyglas"—a registered trademark for fiberglass belts.

The "Water Is Wet" Technique

"Water is wet" ads say something about the product that is true for any brand in that product category, such as, "Smith's water is really wet." The claim is usually a statement of fact but not a real advantage over the competition though it is made to sound like one.

Examples:

"The Detergent Gasoline." True of any gas.

"Brasilia: The 100% Brazilian Coffee." Most American brands import coffee from Brazil.

"Super Lash greatly increases the diameter of every lash." Any mascara does.

"Friendly Persuasion Perfume smells differently on every one." As does all perfume.

The Vague Technique

This technique is simply not clear; this category often overlaps others. The key to the vague ad or commercial is the use of words that are colorful but meaningless as well as the use of subjective and emotional opinions that defy verification. Most of these ads contain weasels.

Examples:
"Lips have never looked so luscious." Can you imagine trying to either prove or disprove such a claim?
"Lipslicks are fun—they taste good, smell good, and feel good."
"Its deep rich lather makes hair feel new again."
"For skin like peaches and cream."
"For hair that attracts."
"Take a bite and you'll think you're eating on the Champs Elysees."

The Endorsement or Testimonial

This technique uses a celebrity or authority in an ad to lend his or her stellar qualities to the product. Sometimes the people actually claim to use the product, but sometimes they don't. Some agencies survive by providing "names" for testimonials.

Examples:
Model/Actress Cindy Crawford for Pepsi
Michael Jordan for Nike
Candice Bergen for Sprint

A variation on this technique is the "John or Jane Doe" testimonial, where an average person endorses a product.
This approach can be used to convince potential customers that people "just like them" use the product.

The Scientific or Statistical Technique

This kind of ad refers to some sort of scientific proof or experiments, to very specific numbers, or to an impressive-sounding mystery ingredient.

Examples:

"Bread helps build strong bodies 12 ways."
Even the weasel *helps* did not prevent the Federal Trade
Commission from demanding that this actual advertisement
be withdrawn. But note that the use of the number *12* makes
the claim far more believable than if it were replaced by—for
example—"many ways."

**"Mrs. Molly's Oven Cleaner has 33% more cleaning power
than another popular brand."**
"Another popular brand" translates simply as some other kind
of oven cleaner sold somewhere. What the claim probably means
is that Mrs. Molly's Oven Cleaner comes in a can $\frac{1}{3}$ larger than
the can used by another brand.

"Special Morning—33% more nutrition." Also an unfinished
claim.

"Certs contains a sparkling drop of Retsyn."

**"Sinarest. Created by a research scientist who actually gets
sinus headaches."**

The "Compliment the Consumer" Technique

This type of ad flatters the consumer.

Examples:

"You've come a long way, baby."
For the real man.
For the special person you are.

The Rhetorical Question

This technique demands a response from the audience. A question
is worded so that the viewer's or listener's answer affirms the
product's goodness.

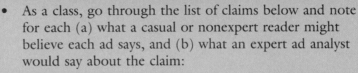

MEDIA LAB   Analyzing Advertising Language

- As a class, go through the list of claims below and note for each (a) what a casual or nonexpert reader might believe each ad says, and (b) what an expert ad analyst would say about the claim:

  "Built better, not cheaper."

  "You're not getting older. You're getting better."

  "The taste of extra freshness."

  "Five of these six top shipping pros are more than satisfied with the new Pony Express Shipping System."

  "New lemony Woodwright gives you the look of hand-rubbed wood beauty instantly."

  "Hair Beauty shampoo is enriched with protein and conditioners to make hair look healthy."

  "Custom Blend Coffee lets me be different."

  "If you care enough to serve the very best, you serve Crystal springs natural water."

  "Super-Clean works to eliminate unwanted odors. It words faster and smells fresh."

  "Give an acne pimple something to worry about. Use Wipeout medicated soap. Fortified with AR-2."

- Find examples of each of the nine advertising claims or techniques explained in this section. Write down or photocopy the ads from magazines or newspapers or quote directly from TV or radio commercials.

- Select one or more products and devise a way to compare the advertising claims made for that product with the product itself. Construct a test (or a series of tests) to verify or disprove the advertised claims.

- Rewrite vague ads you find, so that they change from ads presenting little or no information to ads that are genuinely helpful to consumers.

- Write copy for an advertisement that accurately describes a product you believe to be of high quality. Make your ad useful to consumers and completely honest—but at the same time make it one that will sell the product.

Examples:

"Plymouth—isn't that the kind of car America wants?"

"Shouldn't your family be drinking Hawaiian Punch?"

"What do you want most from coffee? That's what you get most from Hills."

"Touch of Sweden: Could your hands use a small miracle?"

"Wouldn't you really rather have a Buick?"

Advertising, Emotions, and Pop Culture

Understanding Emotional Appeal

Once you are able to evaluate ad claims so that they don't mislead, you are ready for the second important skill needed to deal with advertising. You need to see how the ads appeal to you, involve your feelings, wishes, and dreams. Ads attempt to make products look luxurious, sexy, grown-up, modern, happy, patriotic, or any of dozens of other desirable qualities.

Nearly every ad (except purely factual advertising, such as that of a grocery store listing its prices) attempts to give the impression that the product advertised will make the user one or more of the following: Popular, Powerful, Happy, Free, Successful, More Grown Up, Younger, A Real Woman, A Real Man, Important, Creative, WITH IT, or "in," SAFE, SECURE. The people who appear as the "stars" of our pop culture are all of these and more.

Of course, toothpaste, shampoo, soap, or deodorant will *not* make their users any of these things. However, the advertiser tries to say that the user will *feel* loved or popular or whatever if he or she uses the product.

Ads and commercials always have appealed to emotions, but researchers now find that even practical, everyday products are purchased more on emotion than on durability, ease of use, or other functional qualities. For example, a series of ads for cake mixes forgoes the traditional emphasis on ease of baking or superior results and instead shows that using the cake mix is an expression of love for one's family.

Esther Thorson, an advertising researcher, found that making viewers feel *both* sad and happy during a commercial is most effective. A commercial for Hallmark cards, for example, shows a soldier waiting in the rain to pick up a letter from home, thus combining the sadness of being away from family with the joy of getting a letter. Thorson finds that "making consumers feel something is much more important than convincing them that a product is better."

For example, researchers found that some teens feel a pimple can call a halt to their social lives. That research led to a commercial in which an active teenage boy walks down a street and glimpses at a pimple on his face in a store window reflection. The world stops at this discovery, but he applies Clearasil, the pimple recedes, and life continues at full speed.

Many ads appeal to feelings and emotions. Studies have shown that a person's choice of a specific product and brand is more often based on feelings than on specific product claims. Most ads have both a reasonable-sounding claim and an appeal to feelings. The careful viewer or listener should be able to see in any ad not only what claim is being made but also what emotional appeal is being used.

Here are some descriptions of scenes from six different commercials, shown on the next two pages. What do you think is the main emotional appeal of each?

APPEAL #1:
Automobile ad: the auto is parked in front of a huge mansion. A uniformed chauffeur stands nearby as a man in a tuxedo and woman in a formal gown exit the car.

APPEAL #2:
Ad for any one of many possible products: picture of a handsome man and a beautiful woman hugging each other while looking over a lush green valley.

APPEAL #3:
Razor ad: a football player in uniform holds a Quik Shave disposable shaver, saying, "If a Quik Shave disposable shaver can shave me close, it can shave anybody."

APPEAL #4:
Soap ad: picture of a beautiful rose with fresh dewdrops on its petals. The rose grows out of a sink filled with soapsuds. Somewhere on the ad are the words "For hands soft as roses use Rosebud."

#3

2

#4

#5

#6

APPEAL #5:

TV commercial: a man is unable to get a date with a woman he likes. A friend tells him that he has dandruff (any one of many other countless evils). He takes the advice of his friend, switches to the product advertised, and in the end he and the woman are together.

APPEAL #6:

TV commercial for a certain kind of videotape: a family is together at home. Mom is videotaping the happy family.

The Ad Reader's Comments

APPEAL #1:

In looking for the emotional or feeling hook in an ad, always notice the setting in which the product is placed. Placing the automobile by the mansion with a chauffeur and people in expensive-looking clothing says that this is a car for wealthy people: If you want to feel wealthy or be considered wealthy by others, buy this car. Such an ad never states directly, "Buy this car and people will think you're rich," but that is what the picture implies. Always look for the setting in which the product is placed for a clue to the feeling hook.

APPEAL #2:

This picture could be used for hundreds of different products. Probably the ad would show a bit of ad copy (written claims) at the bottom and a picture of the product. The picture suggests love, beautiful people, freedom, the beauty of nature, and even a certain "naturalness" and youth. The picture could be used in an ad for shampoo, deodorant, clothes, hair spray, or even cigarettes or jewelry. The emotional appeal of the ad is that, by using the product advertised, you will somehow be associated with the feelings the picture suggests. At the very least, the picture creates a good mood, so the reader will experience a pleasant feeling when seeing the product's name.

APPEAL #3:

Celebrities are paid huge sums to appear in advertisements holding, sitting in, or wearing, eating, or drinking certain products. If you view such ads carefully, you will see that the celebrity rarely says he or she uses the product all the time. Advertisers pay famous people to endorse their products. Theys elect according to the feeling the person communicates—a feeling the advertiser wants associated with the product. In the Quik Shave ad, the maker assumes that men like to think of themselves as rough and tough, and the football player is an excellent choice to suggest such a person.

The idea behind endorsements is that some of the heroics and fame of the star "rub off" on the product and on the users of that product. The ad suggests that you, too, can be like this famous person by using Quik Shave.

APPEAL #4:

The rose suggests softness, beauty, and delicacy. By placing the rose in the soapsuds, the ad suggests that your hands will feel as soft as rose petals if you use Rosebud. The picture says this far more appealingly than words could.

APPEAL #5:

This is a very common kind of commercial. It suggests that the product will make the user popular and will instantly solve a personal problem. The commercial appeals to people who feel left out or unpopular. People who are popular know that their popularity has nothing to do with which brands they use.

APPEAL #6:

This commercial creates good feelings by showing a happy family. The suggestion is that, by using the kind of videotape being advertised, you too can achieve such family joy.

 Reflections

Do we buy the products advertisers pitch to us because we want them, or do we want them because they are advertised? Many social critics argue that America's central value system is **consumerism** and that our need to consume is carefully engineered by corporate America. Advertising, these critics claim, is the major force by which our thirst for consumption is created and fueled. How are your values reflected in, or created by, the advertising you consume?

When is advertising not really advertising? When a product is displayed in a movie that you've paid to see. The growing trend of **product placement** in moviemaking started with the presence of Reese's Pieces candy in Spielberg's 1982 film *E.T.* Now the practice is quite common. The article on page 490 outlines the debate: Is product placement really advertising?

Practice

Select a passage from the reading beginning on page 490 and identify one of the stages of the Media Literacy Paradigm to which that passage relates. Be prepared to debate whether product placement is advertising. Cite your passage as evidence.

Consumer Research and Marketing: YOU Are a Big Target

Ads do not just magically appear in magazines or newspapers, on television, or on the radio. They are placed only after much planning and research by the products' company. **Demographics,** and its more recent offspring, **psychographics,** are two crucial fields in which advertisers invest huge amounts of money. Demographics is the statistical study of a large group of people. Demographic research provides profiles on the age, sex, race, education level, and income of a target group (for example, residents of a particular city). This information helps advertisers target their products and ads to specific locations.

Psychographics is a subfield of demographics that provides advertisers with a more specific profile of their target audience. Through marketing surveys this research yields information on the target audiences' values, lifestyles, emotional triggers, fears, and dreams. Advertisers, in turn, use this information to create the language and images we consume every day in media and on store shelves. Research takes place even before the ads or commercials reach us.

Products Compete for Roles in Feature Films

Harry Berkowitz

A magical mask, a speeding bus and a floating feather landing on Forrest Gump's shoe are not the only objects starring in this summer's biggest movies.

Also featured are more mundane products—such as Dr Pepper bottles, AT&T cellular phones and a pair of Nikes—that companies hope will advance not only the plots, but also their brand image and sales.

"It's like being selected to the all-star team," said Jim Ball, a vice president at Dr Pepper/7Up in Dallas, which provided old-fashioned bottles of Dr Pepper to Paramount for the surprise blockbuster "Forrest Gump." "It reinforces the qualities of the product."

Like doting stage parents, companies constantly vie for starring roles, or at least bit parts, for their products. Critics complain it is a deceptive and often distracting form of advertising. But companies and movie studios say that, as long as it's not overdone, brand-name product placement can make scenes look more natural and save studios money.

In most cases a company is satisfied if a movie just reminds consumers that its product exists. But once in a long while, someone hits the Hollywood jackpot.

Sales of Reese's Pieces soared after the product appeared in "E.T.," and sales of Red Stripe beer jumped when it showed up in "The Firm." Last year, "Jurassic Park" boosted sales of Ford Explorers, and "Risky Business" saved RayBan's Wayfarer sunglasses from extinction.

"It is relatively rare that you can see a direct relation between placement and sales increase," said Gary Mezzatesta, president of UPP Entertainment Marketing in North Hollywood, Calif., whose 70 corporate clients include Campbell Soup, Coors, Evian, IBM, McDonald's, Procter & Gamble and Quaker Oats.

Coca-Cola, Pepsi, Budweiser and Miller are among the most aggressive companies in trying to get into films, sometimes paying studios tens of thousands of dollars as a fee, industry executives say. Companies even hire specialized product placement agencies in California and New York, which scan more than 100 movie scripts each year looking for prime opportunities, and then negotiate placements with studios. Every major studio has opened a product placement department, replacing informal systems that in the past included under-the-table gifts to prop masters.

Companies sometimes pay studios

Products Compete for Roles in Feature Films *(continued)*

fees that range from $5,000 to $50,000 but have gone as high as $100,000. But many companies, including McDonald's and AT&T, prefer instead to provide their product or service: free food, sneakers, airline flights, cars, phone equipment, the use of airline terminals, other products or services, or big promotional tie-ins.

Dr Pepper did not pay to be in "Gump," since the original script included the bottles as a plot element. On a visit to the White House, Gump drinks so much Dr Pepper that he tells President John F. Kennedy he has to use the bathroom.

Nike says it never pays fees. It does provide specialized shoes—such as boots for Batman and futuristic, self-lacing shoes for Michael J. Fox in "Back to the Future II"—as well as sneakers and jackets for production crews and casts. In "Forrest Gump," the Tom Hanks character runs across the country wearing 1970s-style Nikes and gets a pair as a gift.

Of course, despite their efforts, companies aren't sure how prominently their products will be featured until the film is released. Several product brands, including a champagne, a perfume and a beer, agreed to pay fees to be in "True Lies," but their scenes were edited out. Kawasaki skimobiles, Canali tuxedos and Marriott, whose hotel was promi-

nent in a scene with Arnold Schwarzenegger dangling from a roof, made it in, although they didn't pay.

Many companies are reluctant to be in R-rated films, and most of them avoid unflattering scenes, such as murders. Still, a Toblerone chocolate bar can be seen on the desk of a mob boss in "The Client." AT&T, which is in 40 to 50 films a year, was excited that Billy Crystal used one of its cellular phones in "City Slickers 2," even though stampeding horses crushed it.

"Every time [product placement] is used, it's an abuse of moviegoers," said Michael Jacobson, cofounder of the Center for the Study of Commercialism in Washington, D.C., which unsuccessfully petitioned the Federal Trade Commission to force studios to identify products that paid to be in a film. "The whole practice is based on deception. People assume that what is in movies is there for artistic reasons, not commercial reasons."

Frank Devaney, senior vice president of product placement at Rogers & Cowan in Los Angeles and founder of a trade association for product placement, rejects that notion.

"It's not advertising," Devaney said. "In advertising you have control, and you place the product where you want it. We have no control." ■

Advertisers try to gauge the potential effectiveness of an ad or a product package using a variety of methods, such as **focus groups,** where carefully selected groups of people are surveyed for reactions.

One group of American consumers that is targeted in particular is the teenaged population. Teens are the ultimate consumers, according to marketing experts, including Teenage Research Unlimited (TRU), a market research group in Illinois. Research has shown that teenagers do a lot of spending. The 1995 TRU Teenage Marketing & Lifestyle Report states that boys spent an average of $68 a week, while girls spent an average of $65—totalling $99 billion in 1994, an increase of 11 percent from 1993. With the number of teenagers expected to grow considerably in the next decade, advertisers are seriously targeting this group of consumers—YOU!

Cross-Media Advertising

Following are the storyboard for a TV commercial and a print ad that appeared in magazines for a recent L'Oreal product promotion. Many advertising campaigns, such as this one, involve a multimedia or cross-media approach.

Practice

Which of the nine advertising techniques do you find in the commerical and the print ad on the following pages? Explain the specific words and images that illustrate the techniques you identified. How do they tap into emotion appeal? What message and mood are conveyed by the model? Describe as specifically as you can the target audience for these ads. List some magazines and TV shows you think they may have ran in.

McCANN-ERICKSON

Client: L'Oréal	Title: "Accentuate the Positive"	Art Director: David Dixon
Product: Colour Riche Lipcolour	Time: 30 Seconds	Writer: Alice Ericsson
Comml. No.: OMOC 3313	Date Aired: 10/11/93	Producer: Chuck Ryant

(MUSIC)

WOMAN: Accentuate the positive.

ANNCR (VO): New Accentuous

mascara from L'Oréal. It precisely

defines each lash for a very new

eye opening look.

WOMAN: Don't tolerate the negative.

ANNCR: New L'Oréal technology

gives you more impact

less clumping

WOMAN: Extend the possibilities.

ANNCR: A new sculpting brush lengthens,

defines,

accentuates each lash.

New Accentuous

mascara

from L'Oréal.

WOMAN: More definition by the lash.

ANNCR (V/O): More beautiful by design.

Reprinted by permission of L'Oreal/McCann-Erickson.

MEDIA LAB   Advertisements

- Select a common type of product (for example, a lawn mower or shampoo) and make up a name for a new brand and/or model of that product (for example, "GreenMaster" or "Jahzaz SalonSelect"). Create two magazine ads for your product. In the first ad use as many techniques as a real ad for that kind of product would; make the ad as realistic as possible. Then create a second version of the ad, but limit yourself to pure facts about the product. Use visuals and text in both versions, but in the second ad, refrain from using emotional appeal and visual associations.

- Locate examples of ads that are designed to make the viewer feel multiple or opposite emotions. How do the specific ads do this? What is the intended effect?

- Catalog as many ads for over-the-counter medications as possible. List the slogans and phrases used in the ads that encourage the consumer to use the product.

- One of the strongest collective values in the United States is that of progress. As a country we constantly talk of "moving forward" and "expanding our economy." However, progress is a complicated idea. For example, technological progress often carries with it unintended consequences, such as reduced employment and environmental impacts. Yet advertising is one of the greatest purveyors of "the myth of progress." Some common advertising words and phrases that encourage devotion to progress are: *new, better, faster, improved, cleaner, enhanced, brighter.* Create a poster listing all the "progress words" you can find in current ads.

- Select a medium and a genre of advertising, such as TV commercials for jeans, fast food, and cars. Tape five of those ads and study them to identify common conventions of presentation. How is music used? How are characters displayed? What are they doing? What dialogue do they speak? How are editing styles and camera angles similar? Do any of the ads ignore conventions by using radically different techniques? If so, what are they? How effective are they?

- Because advertising plays such an important role in our society, there are many more issues to investigate than those mentioned. Some additional research topics are: junk mail as a form of advertising; telemarketing as advertising; the portrayal of women in advertising; the portrayal of people of color in advertising; the portrayal of non-Americans in advertising; stereotyping in advertising; billboards as advertising; the use of popular music hits in advertising; political campaign advertising.

Student Close-Up

Clark Baker, Vermont

A computer artist, this student tells how he uses computer animation in the advertising field.

I began working with computer animation in the spring of my sophomore year in high school. Because this form of art was new to everyone in school, we all had to work together to learn from and teach each other. As I grew proficient through the use of tutorials and experimentation, I began to explore the many uses of computer animation in the area of advertising. Through school programs, I have spent many hours working on logos for organizations such as the Pepsi Cola Company, Saint Michael's University, the American Cancer Society, and Vermont Teddy Bear. The advantage computer animation has over traditional media is its ability to portray realistic or unrealistic situations in a believable manner. This is what appeals most to me about computer animation. I am able to create new worlds bounded only by my imagination rather than the limitations of reality.

For me, in my hobby of computer animation, the sacrifices are few and the rewards are plentiful. Even the long hours of brainstorming and the tedious work of modeling three-dimensional objects are enjoyed by imagining the final product as I work. When an uneducated viewer sees an animation or logo, they may like it, but they don't appreciate the hard work and dedication it takes to create something so complex. My longest completed animation took three months and another has been in the works for nearly one year. As more students get involved with computer animation at my school, my audience grows, as well as the appreciation for my work.

The hundreds of hours I have spent in the past two years gaining experience and skill have been well worth the effort. I have reached a level where I am able to earn money and respect for my skill. My learning will never end. In a field such as computer animation where technology and technique change constantly, I will have to work harder to increase my knowledge. I am well prepared to do this because of experience. ■

Clark Baker. Photo courtesy of South Burlington Schools AV; Bill Haulenbeck.

Future Watch: Advertising in the Interactive Age

As is true for the future of every medium discussed in this book, the future of advertising is linked to the future of communications technologies. Already the rise of cable and satellite TV has brought about a far more diverse spectrum of programming than existed only 15 year ago. This in turn has allowed advertisers to reach more narrowly targeted groups of consumers. For example, sporting goods, cooking-related products, and home-improvement-related products have all benefitted from being able to place ads on channels devoted to their fields. For that matter, Home Shopping Club and QVC can be considered pure advertising channels.

Beyond the inevitable trend toward narrowcasting of ads, the real change will involve interactivity. A typical scenario goes like this: Because you'll be able to watch whatever show you want whenever you want it, it won't make sense for advertisers to place ads in particular time slots on particular channels, as they do now. Furthermore, because technology is evolving to allow the viewer more control over blocking out ads, advertisers are going to have to make you *want* to watch their ad. How will they do this? By offering you incentives to watch. For example, if you choose to watch a highly entertaining four-minute interactive ad for a car, the advertiser may provide you with a 100-dollar rebate certificate to redeem at your local dealership if and when you purchase a car there. If you respond to the interactive buyer survey while you're watching, you might get a 200-dollar rebate.

Advertisers will be willing to offer incentives because they will be more confident that you are watching the ad because you want to.

Today, advertisers spend millions to present their ads to millions of people in the hope of grabbing the small percentage who are interested in their products. If they can target only the consumers who are already interested, they can focus their efforts—and their dollars. At any rate, even if the much-anticipated information highway does not materialize in its grandest form for several more decades, it is a sure bet that advertising and marketing will become increasingly target specific.

Building Your Media Archive

Select a print ad, a radio commercial, or a TV commercial. Analyze the language and images used and determine what consumer group is being targeted. What appeals are being used? You may try exploring the process used to create the ad by writing to the advertising agency, sometimes noted on the ad itself. If it appears the product manufacturer generated the ad, you may try writing the corporate headquarters for information. Research for company and agency addresses can be done by referring to business directories such as *Dun & Bradstreet's,* available at large public libraries.

Create Your Own Media

Create your own advertisement for a product or service, real or imaginary. Pick the medium you wish to use: a magazine ad, a radio or TV commercial, or a multimedia message campaign. You may refer to the Media Literacy Paradigm to guide your process: choosing your product, selecting your target audience, and determining your selling strategy. Present your ad or commercial to the class. You may wish to have class members evaluate it using a questionnaire you prepare.

Career Bank

Following are just a few of the many careers available in the advertising field, which incorporates all the mass media:

- copywriter
- graphic/computer artist

- designer/illustrator
- art director
- market researcher
- sales/account executive
- videotape producer
- camera operator
- actors/talent/including voice-over
- marketing specialist

Recap

Mass advertising only exists in cultures where the supply of goods and services is greater than the demand for them. This condition has only existed since the Industrial Revolution. Advertising has evolved through several stages, from presenting simple information to presenting images designed to influence the consumers' attitudes about themselves.

Ads use a variety of techniques to make their sales pitches. Most of these techniques allow an ad to create a favorable emotional impression of the product being sold without making statements about the product that could be proved false. Unfinished statements of comparison, vague words, and associative images are among the most common advertising techniques. Product placement in movies is a relatively new technique to create product awareness.

Advertisers study the people to whom they market their products. Market research includes demographic and psychographic consumer profiles, designed to help advertisers devise strategies aimed at getting the public to *want* to buy their products. Often the ads or commercials are tested before release to determine whether they are effective.

The future of advertising will change as evolving technologies develop into some version of the information highway. Ads are certain to become more narrowly targeted to specific groups of consumers; some may eventually be adapted for interactive transaction.

Resources for Further Reading

Books

Crispell, Diane. *The Insider's Guide to Demographic Know-how: Everything You Need to Find, Analyze, and Use Information About Your Customers.* Chicago: Probus, 1990.

Gay, Kathlyn. *Caution! This May Be an Advertisement: A Teen Guide to Advertising.* New York: Franklin Watts, 1992.

Hahn, Fred. *Do-It-Yourself Advertising: How to Produce Great Ads, Brochures, Catalogs, Direct Mail and Much More.* New York: John Wiley, 1993.

McNeal, James. *Kids as Consumers: A Handbook of Marketing to Children.* New York: Macmillan, 1992.

Ogilvy, David. *Ogilvy on Advertising.* New York: Vintage, 1983.

Rank, Hugh. *The Pitch: A Simple 1-2-3-4-5 Way to Understand the Basic Pattern of Persuasion in Advertising.* Park Forest, Ill.: Counter Propaganda Press, 1991.

Schudson, Michael. *Advertising, the Uneasy Persuasion: Its Dubious Impact on American Society.* New York: Basic Books, 1986.

Sutherlans, Max. *Advertising and the Mind of the Consumer: What Works, What Doesn't and Why.* St. Leonards, Mo.: Allen and Unwin, 1993.

Wiechmann, Jack. *NTC's Dictionary of Advertising.* Lincolnwood, Ill.: NTC Business Books, 1993.

Industry Publications and Magazines

AdBusters, The Media Foundation, 1243 W. 7th Ave., Vancouver, B.C. V6H 1B7 Canada

Advertising Age, 220 East 42nd Street, New York, NY 10017-5846

Advertising Research Foundation, 641 Lexington Avenue, New York, NY 10022

AdVice, Center for the Study of Commercialism, 1875 Connecticut Ave. NW, Suite 300, Washington, DC 20009

Adweek, BPI Communications, 1515 Broadway, New York, NY 10036

American Demographics, 127 West State Street, Ithaca, NY 14850

Keyword database searches for library research on advertising:

Advertising, marketing, demographics, psychographics, product placement, celebrity endorsements, truth-in-advertising, Federal Trade Commission (FTC), focus groups, target marketing, market research, copywriting, copywriters

TV, Video, and Films about Advertising

Crazy People (Film, 1990)
How To Get Ahead In Advertising (Film, 1988)
Still Killing Us Softly: Advertising's Image of Women (available from Cambridge Documentary Films, Box 385, Cambridge, MA 02139)

GLOSSARY

Affiliates: Radio or television broadcast stations in partnership with, but not owned by, a broadcast network.

AM: Amplitude modulation; type of radio transmission in which the sound wave modulates the height (or amplitude) of the carrier wave. AM is the original form of radio broadcasting; FM is a more recent system.

America Online: Computer service accessible from home computers using a modem; provides users with e-mail, chat rooms, electronic print material, home shopping, audiovisual material, and so on.

Animation: The film art of making drawings move. An animated film is often called a *cartoon*. All film cartoons are animated, but not all animations are cartoons.

ASCAP: American Society of Composers, Authors, and Publishers; collects fees from recording companies, radio and TV stations, and others who use the music of their members for profit. The fees are then distributed to the copyright owners. BMI (Broadcast Music, Inc.) performs a similar service.

Associated Press (AP): A news service (often called *wire service*) that supplies news and features to thousands of newspapers and TV and radio stations. Associated Press is a cooperative owned by its members.

Audio book: Books recorded on cassette tape; often abridged.

Broadcast: A word borrowed from agriculture originally meaning to cast seeds broadly. In media contexts, it refers to using airwaves to beam radio or television signals.

Cable television: A means of delivering television signals to homes via coaxial cables (usually buried underground) in contrast to broadcast TV, which delivers programs by airwaves. Cable systems charge monthly fees and transmit programming from a variety of sources, such as broadcast networks, cable networks, local broadcast stations, and independently produced programming.

CD: A compact disc storing digital information that is retrieved by a low-power laser beam; made of iridescent plastic.

CD-I: Similar to CD-ROM; *I* stands for "interactive," which implies that program content is more user-controllable than CD-ROM.

CD-ROM: A compact disk storing acoustic and visual information; used with personal computers; *ROM* stands for "read only memory."

Censorship: The intentional suppression of information to prevent it from being received by an audience; most mass media censorship in the United States stems from within the various media industries, not from the government.

Circulation: The average number of copies of a magazine or newspaper sold over a period of time.

Classified advertising: Advertising in a newspaper or magazine; arranged by subject (such as want ads, employment ads, rental ads, and so on).

Closure: The mental act of filling in missing information between two pieces of information—for example, between two panels of a comic book or two scenes in a film.

Communication: The act of making something known or exchanging information.

Communication behavior: Any behavior that initiates or receives communication.

Communication environment: All of the acts of communication that surround us moment by moment, from personal communication to mass communication.

Composition: In visual communications, how the parts of a picture are arranged.

Consumption: The fourth stage in the Media Literacy Paradigm that investigates how people consume media products.

Convention: The routines, traditions, and patterns of presentation that are common to media products of a particular genre.

Convergence: The trend of merging communications technologies that were previously separate; hastened by the rise in the digitization of information across media boundaries.

Copyright: Legal protection granted to the creator of literary works, graphics, music and lyrics, recordings, and audiovisual works. The law allows the creator or copyright owner to distribute and profit from the copyrighted work.

Cyberspace: The world of the Internet and online services and everything available online.

DAT: Digital audiotape; a recording medium that stores digital information.

DBS: Direct broadcast satellite; a satellite that broadcasts signals directly to an earth-based satellite dish.

Demographics: The study of an audience to determine its characteristics—for example, its age, wealth, education, and so on.

Deregulation: The process of reducing or eliminating government regulation of industry.

Desktop publishing: The use of personal computers to format text and graphics for publication.

Digital: Information reduced to a binary form of ones and zeroes or on/off. Once information is converted to a digital form, it can be manipulated, stored, and used by computers, as well as transmitted by a variety of media.

Digitization: The process of encoding previously formatted information such as video or sound into a digital medium.

Docudrama: A genre of TV show presenting a drama based on actual events.

Editorial: Opinions expressed by a news organization's management. These opinions are clearly labeled as opinions and are often found on the editorial page.

E-mail: Electronic mail; computers, telephone lines, and/or communication satellites are used to transmit messages between computers, rather than using the postal system to deliver paper-based messages.

Equal time: An FCC requirement that stations that sell time to one political candidate must sell or give equal time to all qualified candidates for the same office; the provision applies only to candidates for political office. News programs are not required to give equal time to each candidate.

Fax: Facsimile; machines that convert printed documents into signals carried by ordinary telephone lines.

Federal Communications Commission (FCC): Government agency charged with regulating broadcasting in the United States.

Federal Trade Commission (FTC): Government agency that regulates federal trade, including radio and television advertising.

Feedback: An act of communication from the receiver of a message to the sender of that message; the sender interprets the feedback to assess the impact of the original message.

Fiber optics: Thin strands of glass or plastic that can carry electronic data through pulses of laser light.

Fidelity: The sound quality of acoustic information;

digital technology allows music to be recorded and played at a higher fidelity than traditional tape technology.

First Amendment: Constitutional amendment guaranteeing freedom of speech, press, and religion. It states simply: "Congress shall make no law respecting an establishment of religion, or prohibiting the free exercise thereof; or abridging the freedom of speech, or of the press; or the right of the people peaceably to assemble, and to petition the government for a redress of grievances."

FM: Frequency modulation; a type of broadcast signal that contrasts to AM (amplitude modulation). FM sound is considered superior to AM, but the signal does not travel as far.

Foley: Adding sound to a movie scene already shot by recording sound to match the visual action.

Font: The style of lettering used for printing text.

Format: The basic programming style of a radio station, such as classic rock, urban contemporary, talk radio, and so on.

Freelancer: A self-employed journalist who gets paid for each article he or she gets published.

Gatekeeper: An individual or group that controls the flow of information or entertainment. The gatekeeper can block, add to, or change information. An example of a gatekeeper is a managing editor of a newspaper.

Genre: A category within a family of artistic forms or media products, such as novels, TV shows, or music; items within a genre share unique conventions of presentation.

Global village: Term used by Canadian media critic and philosopher Marshall McLuhan to describe the result of global telecommunications.

Graphic novel: A complete novel presented in comic book format.

Hard news: Fact-based accounts of actual events.

HDTV: High-definition TV; provides twice the visual resolution and a wider screen.

Impact: The fifth stage of the Media Literacy Paradigm that looks at the impact of consuming media products.

Infomercials: TV commercials, usually thirty minutes long, presented as informational programs.

Information: Any symbols, signals, or content contained in a media product; also, any content transmitted from a source (a sender) to a receiver.

Information Superhighway: General term referring to the communications infrastructure that has resulted from the convergence of previously separate media, such as TV, computer, and telephones.

Infotainment: The blending of informational and entertaining content.

Instant book: A book produced within days or weeks of an event to capitalize on public interest.

Interactivity: Blanket term used to describe the growing ability of communications technology to allow user control over, and interaction with, the source of the communication.

Internet: The global network of computer networks composed of commercial online services, university computer networks, and government computer networks; the infrastructure of cyberspace.

Interpersonal communication: Two-way communication between individuals or small groups of individuals, either in person or through personal communication media such as the telephone.

L.O.P. theory: A theory stating that we gravitate toward whichever program we find least offensive at that time (the least objectionable program).

Marketing: A broad term for activity in support of product sales and distribution.

Mass communication: One-way communication

from a central source to a mass of people simultaneously.

Mass medium: A communications medium capable of reaching a mass of people simultaneously.

Media literacy: The ability to think critically about media products and media industries and to create media products.

Media Literacy Paradigm: A five-stage framework for analyzing media products.

Media product: Any single item from a given medium, such as a book, a magazine, a TV show, a CD, and so on.

Mediation: The third stage in the Media Literacy Paradigm that examines how media products are mediated or constructed.

Medium: (plural: *media*) A channel or system of communication or expression. To a communication specialist, television is a medium; to an artist, chalk is a medium; to a sculptor, clay is a medium.

Microprocessor: A silicon chip with millions of microscopic transistors; the main brain of a home computer or other digital device.

Modem: A device that hooks a personal computer to a telephone line. Modems can transmit and receive computer files through telephone lines.

Monopoly: The control of a market or a commodity by a single owner, which restrains competition.

Motivational research: The study of what motivates consumers to buy or not buy certain products and brands. The focus in this kind of research is on the "why" of behavior.

Network: A media company that obtains and distributes programming to affiliated stations or cable systems for transmission to consumers.

News hole: The amount of space in a newspaper (measured in column inches) available for nonadvertising material.

Noise: Any interference that blocks or weakens communication between sender and receiver.

Online service: Commercial information service accessible by home computer and modem for which subscribers pay monthly or hourly fees; examples include America Online, Prodigy, and CompuServe.

Origin: The second stage in the Media Literacy Paradigm that examines the origin of a media product.

Paradigm: The complex mix of attitudes, beliefs, and experiences that cause a person to think about things in a particular way; our own paradigms are often difficult to perceive, but they are deeply influential in how we respond to the world around us.

Pay-per-view: Cable TV programming (such as movies or sporting events) that is paid for on a per-event basis.

Pay TV: A system in which a viewer pays either a monthly fee or a special charge for a specific program. HBO (Home Box Office) is an optional pay TV service for cable subscribers.

PC: Personal computer. Portable computers designed for use in an office, at home, or at school.

Perceptual filtering: The human tendency to filter out those elements that do not fit in our paradigms of how the world works. We tend to see what we want rather than to see what is.

Persistence of vision: The persistence of an image on the eye for a fraction of a second after the image is actually seen. This "eye slowness" enables us to see an illusion of movement when we see more than twenty-four images in a second.

Pop culture: The totality of widely popular media products such as contemporary music, mass market paperbacks, prime-time television shows, mass circulation magazines, and so on.

Postproduction: The stage in producing a media product after the main elements have been produced; involves editing, revision, marketing, and so on.

Preproduction: The stage in producing a media

product before actual physical production begins; involves planning, financing, and the like.

Press release: Prewritten "news story" released by a person or organization seeking media coverage; often written by public relations professionals.

Prime time: The times during which television has its largest audience: 8:00 to 11:00 P.M. Eastern or Pacific Time and 7:00 to 10:00 P.M. Central or Mountain Time, Monday through Saturday. Prime time starts an hour earlier on Sunday.

Product: The first stage in the Media Literacy Paradigm that classifies the media product being studied.

Product claim: The part of an advertisement that states or implies the value of the product being advertised.

Product placement: The growing trend of featuring products as props in films; advertisers usually contribute money to the film project in exchange for the promotion.

Production: The stage in producing a media product during which the basic product is produced.

Pseudo event: An event staged for the purpose of gaining time or space in mass media. Examples include press conferences, ribbon cuttings, press releases, surveys, demonstrations, awards and contests, and other staged events.

Public relations (PR): The practice of influencing the attitudes and opinions of people in the interest of promoting an idea, product, person, and so on.

Rating: The percentage of all TV households tuned to a particular program. A rating of 22 means that 22 percent of all TV households were tuned in.

Receiver: The person receiving information in the act of communication.

Referent: The object represented by its symbol.

Resolution: The visual quality of an image; the more crisp and defined the image, the higher its resolution.

Royalty: Payment made to a copyright holder for permission to duplicate or perform an original work.

Sampling: Digitizing actual portions of a recording and then using those samples in the production of a new recording.

Scene: In film, one or more shots unified by time and place.

Sender: The person or entity initiating an act of communication.

Sequence: In film, a group of shots joined by a common purpose or setting—for example, a chase sequence.

Share: The percentage of television sets that are in use at a given time and tuned to a particular program.

Shot: The basic building block of a film or video. A shot is what happens in front of the camera from the time action starts until it stops. A shot can be a fraction of a second or over an hour. Shots are further defined by the distance of the camera from the subject, the angle at which the shot is taken, and any movement of the camera.

Sitcom: A popular genre of television show; short for situation comedy.

Soft news: Feature stories and syndicated material of general interest; makes up most of the nonadvertising content of a newspaper.

Station: A radio or television facility that broadcasts on a particular channel in a particular area.

Stereotype: An oversimplified description based on limited experience. TV shows often use stereotyped characters who are instantly recognizable by viewers.

Storyboard: A series of drawings on a panel indicating the major steps or shots in a visual media product such as film, TV show, or magazine advertisement.

Superstation: A local TV station whose signal is delivered by satellite to cable and DBS systems across the country. Examples include TBS in Atlanta, NOR in New York, and WGN in Chicago.

Surfing: The act of rapidly switching between TV or radio stations in search of a desirable show (channel surfing); surfing also applies to cyberspace—for example, "surfing the Net."

Symbol: Something that stands for or represents something else; high-correspondence symbols, such as photographic images, bear a clear resemblance to their referents, while low-correspondence symbols, such as printed or spoken words, bear little resemblance to their referents.

Syndicates: Organizations that supply newspapers with material such as comics, advice columns, and commentary.

Tabloid newspaper: Any newspaper with a page size that is approximately 11" wide and 17" high; usually indicates sensationalistic publications, such as *The National Enquirer*, which are legally classified as magazines.

Tabloid television: Television shows such as "Hard Copy"; the equivalent of tabloid newspapers.

Talk radio: A programming format in which hosts discuss political and social issues with guests and listeners who call in.

Telecommunications: The umbrella term for all communications technologies that transmit information electronically over vast distances.

Trade book: A fiction or nonfiction book aimed at the general public (as distinct from a *textbook*).

Typography: The process of composing a printed page through the selection of paper, fonts, and layouts.

UHF: Ultra High Frequency; channels 14 and higher on TV sets. UHF signals do not travel as far as VHF.

VHF: Very High Frequency; channels 2 through 13 on TV sets.

VHS: Video Home System; VHS uses half-inch videotape in a cassette format.

Viewer fatigue: Information overload as applied to television commercials. Evidence suggest viewers are seeing more commercials but remembering fewer.

Virtual reality: Computer-based technology that allows users to experience simulated environments via head-mounted video displays and user-controlled interfaces such as gloves or body suits.

Wire service: News-gathering organization that provides stories to subscribing newspapers, radio stations, and television station; well-known services include the Associated Press and Reuters.

Zine: A small magazine, usually produced by a single person focusing on a single topic and using simple production techniques.

INDEX

A

Acoustics in communication, 8
Acting, 182
Advertising, 252, 458–500
  cross-media, 492–94
  emotional appeal in, 483–88
  evolution of, 460–67
  government regulation of, 260–61
  in the interactive age, 497–98
  language of, 468, 473–76
  making of TV commercial, 467–68
  and news media, 412–15, 421–22
  in newspapers, 275–76
  power of dollars, 253–54
  reasons for existence of, 459–60
  techniques of, 476–81, 483
  on television, 392, 444
Affiliated, 386
Alphabet, 26–27
Ambient sounds, 169
American Broadcasting Company (ABC), 386
The American Magazine, 314
American Society of Composers, Authors and
  Publishers (ASCAP), 338
America Online, 39, 136
AM stations, 341
Animation, 146
  careers in, 153–54
  future for, 149
  golden age of movie house, 146, 148
  production of, 149–53
  in television era, 148–49
Architectural Record, 319
Artistry, 224
Associated Press (AP), The, 422
Atlantic Monthly, 314
Audience share, 395
Audio copy machine, 212
Ayer, N. W., 460

B

Ballinger, Lee, 216, 218–20
Barnum, P. T., 464
Beardsley, Aubrey, 465
"Beavis and Butthead," 149
Bell, Alexander Graham, 29
Benton, Stephen, 44
Bergold, Roy, 469, 471
Berkowitz, Harry, 490–92
Berliner, Emile, 209–10
Berman, Cheryl, 470
Bernbach, Doyle Dane, agency, 467
Best-sellers, 95–96
Binary formatting, 43
Blume, Judy, 108
Bonner, Robert, 464
Books, 88–120
  application of Media Literacy Paradigm to,
  115
  censorship of, 106, 108–12
  desktop publishing of, 103, 106
  in the digital age, 112–15
  history of, 93–94
  judging by their covers, 98, 100–102

markets for, 94–98
  methods of reading, 89–90
  as permanent communication, 91–92
  and popular culture, 98–99, 102–3
  as portable communication, 92
  speed of producing, 106, 107
  for teenage market, 104–5
  as uniform communication, 90–91
Boom, 176
Boyz N the Hood, 189
Brain, symbols and your, 16–17
Bridge, 221
Britt, Donna, 283
Broadcasting, 340
Broadcast media, government regulation of,
  257–59
Broadcast standards, 262
Broadcast television, 384–86
Brodie, John, 162–64
Buys the rights, 160

C

Cable News Network (CNN) television, 412
Cable News Network (CNN) radio, 418
Cable television, 387–91, 391
Camcorders, 37–38
Cannon, Carl M., 370–72
Capitalism, 251
Captions, 96
Careers
  in books publishing industry, 117
  in comics and animated film industry,
  153–54
Cartoon Network, 149
Caruso, Denise, 41–42
Caruso, Enrico, 210
Cassettes, 211, 212
Castillo, Miguel, 147
Catcher in the Rye (Salinger), 108
CD, 23, 221
CD-I, 23, 73–74
CD-ROM, 73–74
CD-ROM-based books, 113
Censorship of books, 106, 108–12
Chain, 336
The Chocolate War (Cormier), 108, 109–12
Cinematography, 172–73, 183
Classified ads, 275
Close-up (CU), 174
Closure, 124
Cohen, Jeff, 444, 445–46
Colors, 189
Columbia Broadcasting Systems (CBS), 386
Comic book artist/publisher, profile of,
  143–44
Comic books, 125, 129
Comic Code Authority, 133
Comic industry, 136–42
Comics
  careers in, 153–54
  categories of, 125, 129
  closure in, 124–25
  conventions of presentation, 130–31
  in the digital age, 134, 136

genres in, 130
  history of in America, 131–33
  media of Media Literacy Paradigm to, 142,
  144
  as a medium, 123–25
  and popular culture, 133–34
  text and illustrations in, 124
Comic strip, 125
Communication
  acoustics in, 8
  behavior in, 8–10
  breakdowns in, 12
  definition of, 3
  environment of, 7–8
  "Five Ws and an H," 5
  human capabilities in, 4
  interactive, 40–44
  interpersonal, 4, 5
  mass, 4
  model of, 10–13
  noise in, 12–13
  symbols in, 13
Communication events log, 14
Communications technology, chronology of,
  23–25
Compact discs, 212–14
"Compliment the consumer" technique, in
  advertising, 481
Composition, 176–78
CompuServe, 39
Computer chips, advances in, 45–46
Conditioned reflex, 465
Consumer research and marketing, 489, 492
Context, 14
Convention, 223–24
Coolidge, Calvin, 337
Copyrighted, 68
Cormier, Robert, 108, 109–12
Cosmopolitan, 315
Court TV, 380
Crime coverage, 281
Cronkite, Walter, 414
Cross-media advertising, 492–94
C-SPAN, 365, 425–26

D

Dailies, 165, 167
Davis, Fred, 231–40
DBS, 23
DC, 133
DC Comics, 136
De Forest, Lee, 335
Demographics, 318, 489
Deregulation, 259–60
Desktop publishing, 103, 106, 115
Development phase, 160
Dialogue, 182
Digital age, 33–34
  books in, 112–15
  comics in, 134, 136
  film in, 193–94
  magazines in, 321
  music in, 224–25, 229–30
  newspapers in, 296–301

MIKE SMITH is a foreign correspondent for AFP news agency. He was AFP bureau chief for part of West Africa from 2010 to 2013 and has extensively covered the Boko Haram insurgency.

'There is certainly an urgent need for a comprehensive yet accessible account of Boko Haram about which much is written but yet little understood. The author is eminently well qualified, especially from his connection with AFP, who have been at the forefront of reportage on the situation of northern Nigeria, to tackle this subject. The book should find a ready readership among the policy and diplomatic community as well as academics and interested lay readers.'
– Richard Reid, Professor of the History of Africa,
SOAS, University of London

'I enjoyed [this book] very much – it's a good read. It's [...] the best account I have read and offers a real sense of place – and crisis. Mike Smith's book will be widely read and cited.'
– Murray Last, Emeritus Professor of Anthropology,
University College London

'Perceptive and fair-minded [...] eminently readable [...] Smith's achievement is to demonstrate how Boko Haram arose from the particular conditions of northern Nigeria, where brutal security forces, a corrupt and predatory state, and a long tradition of Islamist radicalism all combine to create a perfect breeding ground for terrorism.'
– David Blair, *The Telegraph*

'Mike Smith has written an unsparing study of both Boko Haram's cruelty and the failure of the Nigerian state to defeat the movement. In this timely book he tells a demoralising but necessary story, of the violence and negligence that is rapidly undermining the stability of sub-Saharan Africa's most important country.'
– Barnaby Phillips, author of *Another Man's War:
The Story of A Burma Boy in Britain's Forgotten African Army*

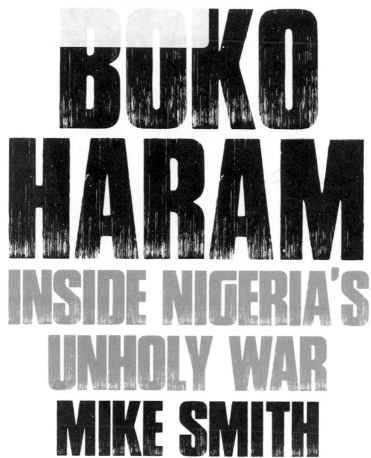

BOKO HARAM

INSIDE NIGERIA'S UNHOLY WAR

MIKE SMITH

I.B. TAURIS

LONDON · NEW YORK

Published in 2015 by I.B.Tauris & Co. Ltd. Reprinted 2015.
London • New York
www.ibtauris.com

ISBN: 9781784530747
eISBN: 9780857735775

A full CIP record for this book is available from the British Library
A full CIP record is available from the Library of Congress

Library of Congress Catalog Card Number: available

Typeset in Adobe Garamond

Printed and bound in the United States of America by Bookmasters

CONTENTS

When my companions passed, and my aims went awry
I was left behind among the remainder, the liars
Who say that which they do not do, and follow their own desires.
Abdullah Ibn Muhammad, brother of
Usman Dan Fodio, from the *Tazyin Al-Waraqat*

It is never easy to keep secrets in Nigeria; it is just that secrets,
when divulged, are tied up in many distractions.
Wole Soyinka, from *You Must Set Forth at Dawn*

LIST OF MAPS

ACKNOWLEDGEMENTS

This book would not have been possible without an enormous amount of help from many others. My colleagues at AFP's Lagos bureau deserve special recognition for their tireless efforts in covering a story that has only seemed to grow more horrifying by the day, and my knowledge of Nigeria and the forces underlying the insurgency was endlessly enriched by working alongside them.

Aminu Abubakar, AFP's northern Nigeria correspondent, has broken so many stories that I long ago lost count. His intelligence and insight have helped the rest of the world understand the terrible violence that has shaken his home region. He and I spent countless days and nights over bad phone lines trying to make sense out of the latest attack, and despite it all, he still managed to be the nicest guy you'll ever meet. I'm also proud to have worked with Nigerian journalists and AFP staffers Ade Obisesan, Tunde Agoi, Ola Awoniyi and photographer Pius Utomi Ekpei, along with the rest of the Lagos bureau, including our irreplaceable driver and all-around guide Hassan Jimoh, Patrick Chikwendu, Johnson Moses, Timothy Jamani, Dauda Ishola, Bola Meseda and Isaac Momoh.

Our coverage also would not have been possible without the talented non-Nigerian journalists I worked with in the bureau, including Susan Njanji, Sophie Mongalvy, Ben Simon and Cecile de Comarmond. I owe particular thanks to Sophie for reading through an earlier draft of this book and providing important feedback. I was also honoured to work alongside numerous colleagues from other news outlets, including Jon Gambrell, Sunday Alamba,

Lekan Oyekanmi, Christian Purefoy, Tom Burgis, Nick Tattersall, Joe Brock, Tim Cocks, Julie Vandal and Will Ross.

Wise Nigerians willing to share their thoughts on issues facing their country provided me with the kind of perspective any foreign correspondent needs to do his or her job properly. They include Chidi Odinkalu, an anti-corruption activist who is now the head of Nigeria's National Human Rights Commission; Clement Nwankwo, whose PLAC non-governmental organisation keeps an eye on Nigeria's corrupt politics; Kyari Mohammed of Modibbo Adama University of Technology, who has provided astute analysis of Boko Haram; and Catholic Bishop Matthew Kukah, who has for years served as an important voice of reason in Nigeria. I am also grateful to Murray Last for sharing his insight as well as for his important book, *The Sokoto Caliphate*.

I.B.Tauris provided me with support for this project, and I am especially grateful to Lester Crook, who commissioned the book and provided invaluable input, and Joanna Godfrey, who guided it towards publication. I would also like to express my gratitude to the Centre of African Studies at SOAS, University of London, for allowing me to work from its excellent library for the purposes of this project.

Finally, and most importantly, I want to also thank my family, especially my parents, who have supported my travels and my work while hoping that it would some day lead me back home.

While my name is on the cover, this book has in many ways been a team effort. Any and all errors, however, are completely my own.

A NOTE ON SOURCES AND THE 'BOKO HARAM' LABEL

Much of the information in this book is the result of my more than three years in Nigeria between 2010 and 2013, when I was based in Lagos as bureau chief for part of West Africa for Agence France-Presse news agency. I have cited instances where I have relied on reporting from colleagues or on the work of academics. My reporting on the insurgency has included four trips to Maiduguri and a number of other visits to various parts of northern Nigeria, including Kano, Sokoto, Kaduna and Zaria.

I have decided to use the term 'Boko Haram' throughout the text rather than the full name of the group (Jama'atu Ahlus Sunnah Lid Da'awati Wal Jihad, or People Committed to the Prophet's Teachings for Propagation and Jihad). I have done this because the world knows the group as Boko Haram, and Nigerians, including the security forces, continue to refer to it as such. In addition, as a result of the shadowy nature of the insurgency, several different groups or cells may in fact be operating beyond Abubakar Shekau's faction. Boko Haram serves as a catch-all phrase encompassing the entire insurgency.

The description of what happened on the day of the UN attack in Chapter 1 is mainly based on my phone interviews with UN staffers Geoffrey Njoku and Soji Adeniyi as well as a personal account written by Vinod Alkari that was distributed to his colleagues internally. He agreed to allow me to quote from it, and I have in some cases corrected minor typos or grammatical errors that would otherwise distract the reader. I also spoke in detail with

Alkari by phone. A separate, anonymous source who has seen the video surveillance footage of the attack described to me details from it, and I have also visited the site to see the layout.

I have included a select bibliography, but it is worth pointing out several books that were especially helpful. For my research for Chapter 1, the late Mervyn Hiskett's books on Islam in West Africa and the life of Usman Dan Fodio were invaluable. Murray Last's history of the Sokoto Caliphate also provided me with great insight on the period, and Toyin Falola and Matthew Heaton's *A History of Nigeria* served as a useful overview along with Michael Crowder's *The Story of Nigeria*. For the section on the British conquest of northern Nigeria, I relied heavily on Frederick Lugard's papers, archived at the Bodleian Library of Commonwealth and African Studies at Oxford, as well as his annual reports.

I have drawn from a wide range of sources to piece together Mohammed Yusuf's rise, as specified in the endnotes, but I am particularly grateful to an academic who has carried out an extensive analysis of the Boko Haram leader's recorded sermons and speeches. The academic, to whom I spoke by phone, has asked to remain anonymous out of fears for his own safety, and I agreed to abide by his wishes.

For translations of Boko Haram videos and statements from Hausa to English, I often relied on Aminu Abubakar, AFP's correspondent in northern Nigeria who in most cases was the first journalist for an international news agency to obtain them. Aminu translated many of the videos on deadline as we worked together to prepare stories on them for our news agency and I have stuck for the most part with those original translations. Professor Abubakar Aliyu Liman of Ahmadu Bello University in Nigeria worked on two translations at my request and specifically for this book: Yusuf's interrogation before his death and his 'tafsir' quoted in Chapter 2.

The vital work by Human Rights Watch, Amnesty International and Nigeria's National Human Rights Commission led by civil society activist Chidi Odinkalu, among others, documenting alleged abuses committed by the security forces has also served as an important source, as reflected in the endnotes.

As specified in the epilogue and prologue, I interviewed Wellington Asiayei in person both in the hospital in Kano after the 2012 attacks there as well as in Warri in 2013. I also spoke by phone with Wellington in addition to speaking with his wife, his brother, his son and his doctors in Kano, India and Warri.

I repeatedly requested interviews with Nigerian government and military officials to allow them to respond to allegations and criticisms. Requests made specifically in connection with this book were not granted; however, I did carry out interviews with officials as part of my work for AFP in Nigeria. I have included details from those interviews, such as the military's denials of abuses, and relied on public statements from officials when necessary.

A TIMELINE OF KEY EVENTS IN NORTHERN NIGERIAN HISTORY AND THE BOKO HARAM INSURGENCY

- *c.*1085   Kanem-Bornu Empire becomes officially Muslim under Mai Hummay.
- *c.*1349   Kano becomes first state in Hausaland to have a Muslim king.
- 1804   Usman Dan Fodio and followers of his Muslim reformist movement migrate to Gudu, marking the start of a jihad in Hausaland that would lead to the creation of the Sokoto Caliphate across much of what is today northern Nigeria and beyond.
- 1903   A military assault on Kano begins the final conquest of northern Nigeria and the Sokoto Caliphate for the British.
- 1914   Northern and southern Nigeria are amalgamated by the British into a single entity, creating the outlines of the nation that exists today.
- 1956   Nigeria strikes oil in commercial quantities in the Niger Delta in the south.
- 1960   Nigeria gains independence from Britain.
- 1967   Civil war begins after the south-east declares itself an independent Republic of Biafra.
- 1970   Civil war ends with the defeat of the Biafrans. Nigeria remains one nation, but deep divisions persist.

- **1980** Deadly riots break out in Kano involving members of a radical Islamist movement known as Maitatsine.

- **1999** Northern politicians push to institute sharia law for criminal cases. Some 12 northern states later adopt some form of sharia criminal law, though it is selectively enforced.

- **2003** The beginnings of Boko Haram begin to take shape when followers of radical cleric Mohammed Yusuf retreat to a remote area of Yobe state and clash with authorities.

- **2009** Boko Haram under Mohammed Yusuf launches an uprising in north-eastern Nigeria after a clash with authorities in Maiduguri. Around 800 people are killed in five days of violence. Yusuf is shot dead by police after being captured.

- **2010** Boko Haram re-emerges after more than a year in hiding with a series of assassinations and a prison raid under the leadership of Yusuf's deputy, Abubakar Shekau.

- **2011** Boko Haram claims responsibility for a suicide car bomb attack on United Nations headquarters in Abuja that killed 23 people.

- **2012** A series of coordinated assaults and bomb attacks leave at least 185 people dead in Kano, Nigeria's second-largest city. Shekau claims responsibility.

- **2013** Nigerian President Goodluck Jonathan declares an emergency in three north-eastern states after Boko Haram seizes territory in remote areas of the region.

- **2014** Boko Haram attackers raid the north-eastern town of Chibok and kidnap 276 girls from their dormitory, sparking global outrage.

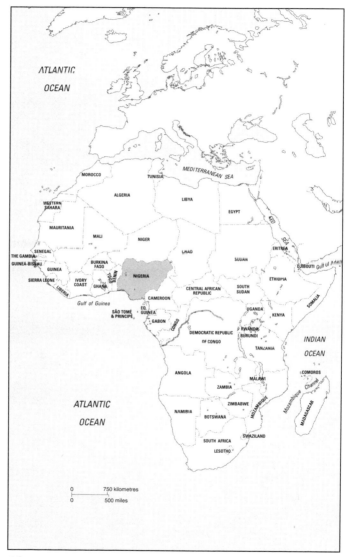

African states

Key cities in Nigeria

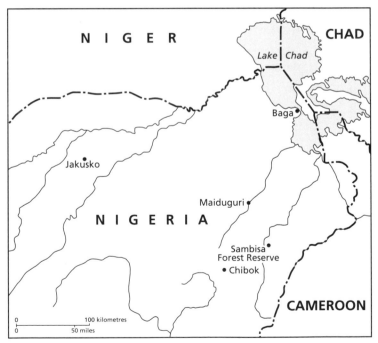

North-eastern Nigeria, including key sites of Boko Haram activity

PROLOGUE: 'I THINK THE WORST HAS HAPPENED'

The siege that would shake Nigeria seemed to unfold at shocking speed, young men blowing themselves up in bomb-laden cars, hurling drink cans packed with explosives and gunning down officers with AK-47s, all in the space of a few hours. But for Wellington Asiayei, the horror would play out in slow motion.

It was a Friday in Kano, the largest city in Nigeria's predominately Muslim north, and prayers at mosques had drawn to an end, worshippers in robes having earlier filed out into streets thick with dust in the midst of a dry season near the Sahara desert. Residents of the crowded and ancient metropolis were returning home, manoeuvring their way through traffic or climbing on to the rear of motorcycle taxis that would zip them through and around lines of cars. At police headquarters in a neighbourhood called Bompai, Wellington Asiayei wrapped up his work for the day and took the short walk back to his room at the barracks to begin preparing his dinner.

When the 48-year-old assistant police superintendent reached his room, he heard explosions. 'Everybody from the barracks was running for their dear lives', Asiayei would explain to me three days after the 20 January 2012 attacks. The barracks would soon be empty, but despite the confusion, it would still occur to him to lock the door to his room before fleeing. As he began to do so, he noticed a young man who looked to be in his twenties and dressed in a police uniform, an AK-47 rifle in his hands. Asiayei knew that members of a certain branch of the force were often assigned to work as guards at the barracks, and he assumed the young man was one of them. He yelled out to him, telling him that they should both run to headquarters. 'I saw him raising the rifle at me, and that was all I knew', he said.

The veteran policeman, still trying to piece together what was happening, felt what seemed to be a gunshot pierce his body. He fell to the ground and lay there face down, blood pooling underneath him. He did not know where the young man with the gun went next. He would remain face down on the floor for what he believed to be hours before a group of women making their way through the barracks spotted him and finally contacted his supervisor, who arranged for a rescue. Asiayei survived, and three days later he and other victims from the same set of attacks would be in a Kano hospital, his bed among lines of others in a sprawling room. The bullet had damaged his spine and lung. He could not walk.

By the time Asiayei was shot, an unprecedented siege of Nigeria's second-largest city was well underway, dozens or perhaps hundreds of young men, a number of them dressed as police officers, swarming neighbourhoods throughout Kano with no remorse for their victims. The first attack occurred at a regional police headquarters, a suicide bomber in a car blowing himself up outside, ripping off much of the roof. The number of explosions then became difficult to count, one after the other, the blasts echoing through the city. Residents said there were more than 20, and judging from the amount of unexploded homemade bombs that police later recovered, that may be a vast understatement. One doctor who helped treat the wounded said the force of some of the blasts caused at least one home to collapse. Witnesses and police said the attackers travelled on motorbikes, in cars and on foot. They included at least five suicide bombers. In one neighbourhood, they threw homemade bombs at a passport office and opened fire. They also attacked a nearby police station, completely destroying it: the building's tin roof collapsed, the inside burnt, cars outside blackened by fire. Gunshots crackled, corpses were piled on top of one another in the morgue of the city's main hospital and dead bodies were left in the streets to be picked up the next morning. The official toll was 185 people killed, but there was widespread speculation that it was at least 200. It was the deadliest attack yet attributed to the Islamist extremist group that had become known as Boko Haram.

This was long before the kidnapping of nearly 300 girls from their school in north-eastern Nigeria, an atrocity that would draw the world's attention to an insurgency that had by then left a trail of destruction and carnage so horrifying that some had questioned whether Nigeria was barrelling toward another civil war. To understand what led to the abductions, it is important to first know what occurred in Kano. To begin to wrap one's mind around what happened there – bodies lying in the streets and police helpless to stop a rampaging band of young men engaging in suicide bombings and wholesale slaughter – one must first look backward, not only at the formation of Boko Haram itself, but also at the complex history of Nigeria, Islam in West Africa and the deep corruption that has robbed the continent's biggest oil producer, largest economy and most populous nation of even basic development, keeping the majority of its people agonisingly poor. One must look at colonisation and cultural differences between Nigeria's north and south, the brutality of its security forces and the effects of oil on its economy. But before all of that, it is perhaps best to begin with a charismatic, baby-faced man named Mohammed Yusuf and an episode two and a half years before the attack in Kano.

In a video from 2009, Yusuf can be seen building his argument, the crowd before him off camera but roaring its approval. He describes a confrontation between security forces and his followers when they were on their way to a funeral, and soon he is lashing out at the soldiers and police, accusing them of shooting members of his sect. It is time to fight back, he says, and to continue fighting until the security task force he believed was set up to track them is withdrawn.

'It's better for the whole world to be destroyed than to spill the blood of a single Muslim', he says. 'The same way they gunned down our brothers on the way, they will one day come to our gathering and open fire if we allow this to go unchallenged.'[1]

Yusuf was thought to be 39 at the time and the leader of what had come to be known as Boko Haram. Some had considered him to be a reluctant fighter, content to continue expanding his sect through preaching, but the brutality of the security forces and pressure from his bloodthirsty deputy, Abubakar Shekau, who would later be known as the menacing, bearded man on video threatening to sell kidnapped girls on the market, pushed him toward violence. Not long after the video was recorded, Yusuf would be dead.

His call for his followers to rise up against Nigeria's corrupt government and security forces would lead them to do just that, beginning with attacks on police stations in the country's north. Nigeria's military, not known for its restraint, would soon respond. In July 2009, its armoured vehicles rolled through the streets of the north-eastern city of Maiduguri toward Boko Haram's mosque and headquarters, soldiers opening fire when they drew within range. What resulted was intense fighting that saw soldiers reduce the complex to shards of concrete, twisted metal and burnt cars spread across the site. Around 800 people died over those five days of violence, most of them Boko Haram members. Security forces claimed Yusuf's deputy, Shekau, was among those killed, but they would soon be proved wrong. Yusuf himself somehow survived the brutal assault, but was arrested while hiding in a barn and handed over to police. They shot him dead.

Years later, rubble remains at the former site of the mosque. Shekau has repeatedly shown up on YouTube or videos distributed to journalists to denounce the West and Nigeria's government and Boko Haram, once a Salafist sect based in Nigeria's north-east, has morphed into something far more deadly and ruthless: a hydra-headed monster further complicated by imitators and criminal gangs who commit violence under the guise of the group. Throughout years of renewed violence, it had been building toward a headline-grabbing assault that would shock the world, and it would do just that in April 2014 with the kidnappings of nearly 300 girls from a school in Chibok, deep in Nigeria's remote north-east. The abductions and response to them would lay bare for the world to see the viciousness of Boko Haram as well as the dysfunction of Nigeria's government and military. But for Nigerians, it was yet another atrocity in a long list of them.

Boko Haram had been dormant for more than a year after the 2009 military assault which killed Yusuf, with Shekau, believed to have been shot in the leg, said to have fled, possibly for Chad and Sudan. During that time, authorities in Maiduguri remained deeply suspicious and on the alert for any new uprising. Academics and others in the area with knowledge of the situation predicted a return to violence, saying underlying issues of deep poverty, corruption, a lack of proper education and few jobs left young people with very little hope for the future. Journalists, including myself, visiting Maiduguri one year after the 2009 uprising were made to understand they were not welcome, with secret police trailing our movements. The police commissioner for Borno state, of which Maiduguri is the capital, refused outright to discuss Boko Haram at the time and warned journalists they could be arrested for even uttering those words. Despite such restrictions, I and two other journalists were able to carry out a number of interviews, including with one man who claimed to be a Boko Haram member – a claim to be taken with a heavy dose of scepticism. Looking back now, I have serious doubts about whether he was indeed a Boko Haram follower, particularly since intelligence agents were monitoring us and would have likely questioned him if they suspected him of being one, but certain details of what he told us seemed to ring true in retrospect, whether by coincidence or otherwise.

Through a local contact, we arranged for the man to be brought to our hotel, a hulking building out of sync with its scrubby savannah surroundings. There were few other guests, and the hotel, the Maiduguri International, was badly in disrepair, with mouldy carpets and dirty sheets. Staff, including employees who said they had not been paid in months, refused to turn on the generator for much of the day, leaving the hotel without electricity, since Nigeria was, and remains, unable to produce anywhere near enough power for its burgeoning population. It felt as if we had taken up residence in an abandoned building.

The supposed Boko Haram member, dressed in the same type of caftan any average Maiduguri resident would wear, was led into one of our rooms and took a seat in a chair. I pulled up across from him and began asking him questions, a Nigerian correspondent who works for my news agency translating. The man, who spoke in Hausa, said he was 35 years old, and he claimed Boko Haram members had weapons hidden in various parts of the country with a plan of eventually striking again. Despite my repeated attempts to lead him into explaining in detail why one would willingly join such a violent group, he mostly spoke in generalities.

'We are ordained by Allah to be prepared and amass weapons in case the enemy attacks', he said. 'Anybody who doesn't like Islam, works against the establishment of an Islamic state, who is against the Prophet, is an enemy.'

At the time, we, like so many others, could see the elements that could spark another uprising, the deeply rooted problems that had led to such hopelessness, and we certainly felt that more violence was possible, if not likely. We would not have to wait long for a more definitive answer. Any sense of normalcy the police commissioner and others hoped to portray would soon be shattered. Boko Haram's deadliest and most symbolic attacks were yet to come.

*   *   *

In some ways, unrest seems inevitable in parts of northern Nigeria, a country thrown together by colonialists who combined vastly different cultures, traditions and ethnicities under one nation. This was the case for many African civilisations, but a number of factors would make Nigeria a particularly volatile example, and one must of course start with the oil.

Nigeria first struck oil in commercial quantities in 1956 among the vast and labyrinthine swamps of the Niger Delta in the country's south. Commercial production began in relatively small amounts at first, but new discoveries would soon come, offshore drilling would eventually take hold and Nigeria would become the biggest oil producer in Africa, gaining astounding amounts of money for its coffers – and a list of profound, even catastrophic, problems to go with it. So much of that money would be stolen and tragically misspent, leading to the entrenchment of what has been called a kleptocracy, assured of its vast oil reserves but with electricity blackouts multiple times per day and poorly paid policemen collecting bribes from drivers at roadblocks, to name two examples among many. Most telling is the fact that it must import most of its fuel despite its oil, with the country unable to build enough refineries or keep the ones it has functioning at capacity to process its crude oil on its own. On top of that, petrol imports are subsidised by the government through a system that has been alleged to be outrageously mismanaged and corrupt. In other words, Nigeria essentially buys back refined oil after selling it in crude form – and at an inflated cost thanks to the middlemen gaming the system.

All the while, Nigeria's population has been rapidly expanding. It is currently the most populous country in Africa with some 170 million people, including an exploding and restless youth population. It also recently overtook South Africa as the continent's biggest economy strictly in terms of GDP size, but its population is far larger, meaning the average Nigerian remains much poorer than the average South African. The title of Africa's biggest economy means little or nothing to most Nigerians, the majority of whom continue to live on less than $1 per day.

It is those Nigerians who are obliged to scrape whatever living they can in whichever way they can find it, while their leaders and corrupt business moguls force their way between traffic in SUVs with police escorts and seal themselves off inside walled complexes. The daily struggle to survive has led to all sorts of outlandish schemes that have, much to the chagrin of hard-working Nigerians, badly damaged the country's reputation. Emails from Nigerian 'princes' promising riches have become so common worldwide that they are now a punchline, but that is only one part of the problem. In Nigeria itself, many residents have taken to painting the words 'Beware 419: this house is not for sale' on the outside walls of houses in a bid to keep imposters claiming to be the owners from selling them when no one is there. The number 419 refers to a section of the criminal code, and all such forms of financial trickery have come to be known as 419 scams. Another infamous example involves the police. Newcomers learn quickly that being pulled over by a policeman can be a maddening experience. They have been known to jump into the passenger seat and refuse to exit until they are 'dashed', or bribed, even if the driver has done nothing wrong. The almighty dash is central to Nigerian life.

Because the oil has brought riches, there has been little incentive to develop other sectors of the economy. It would be wrong to say that Nigeria's mostly Christian south, where the oil is located, has done well for itself in these circumstances, but it is certainly true that it has fared better than the north. It is better educated, has more industry and jobs and less poverty. Oil-producing states are handed a significantly bigger chunk of government revenue. Despite that, the region has in no way been immune to violence. The deeply poor Niger Delta, badly polluted by years of oil spills, has seen militants and gangsters take up arms, carry out attacks on the petroleum industry and kidnap foreigners. Some of the worst of this violence occurred under the name the Movement for the Emancipation for the Niger Delta and continued until a 2009 amnesty deal drastically reduced the unrest.

The neglect of other aspects of the economy particularly hit Nigeria's north, which relies heavily on agriculture, despite northern leaders having run the country for much of its post-independence history. Its culture is vastly different from that of the south, with Islam having migrated along with trade across the Sahara and into the region's savannah lands around the Middle Ages. Much of present-day northern Nigeria, long ruled by Hausa kings, eventually fell under a caliphate in the early nineteenth century following an armed jihad led by a Fulani Islamic cleric, Usman Dan Fodio. Even today, Dan Fodio remains revered, but it is difficult to locate his reformist legacy in the region, where corrupt elites siphon off revenue at will and a huge population of young people roam with nothing much to do. Boko Haram figures may have occasionally paid lip service to Dan Fodio's caliphate, but the extremists' blood-thirsty slaughtering of innocents and lack of any practical plans for how to improve the lives of Nigerians reveal the insurgency to be far different.

As some have pointed out, many in northern Nigeria have come to see democracy as a system that keeps them poor and enriches undeserving, corrupt leaders. In Maiduguri, located near the borders of the neighbouring nations of Niger, Chad and Cameroon, the wealthy take up residence in heavily secured mansions while the poor fetch water from wells, and signs at roundabouts are written in Arabic, proclaiming 'Allah is the Provider'. It was amidst this atmosphere that Mohammed Yusuf began to lead his followers.

Boko Haram's re-emergence more than a year after the 2009 uprising and Yusuf's death began mysteriously, with men on motorcycles and armed with AK-47s carrying out drive-by shootings targeting community leaders and security forces. It was unclear at first whether these killings were indeed being committed by the same group, but whisperings of its return eventually grew louder, and attacks became more deadly. Police stations were once again bombed and burnt, and roadside explosions began to occur regularly. If Nigeria's southern president was willing to simply ignore it as long as this remained restricted to Nigeria's remote north-east, he would not be allowed to do so for long. Attacks would eventually spread into other parts of the north, then central Nigeria, then the capital itself.

An attack in June 2011 would signal what was soon to come. A man believed to be a suicide bomber in a car sought to penetrate national police headquarters in the capital Abuja, blowing himself up outside. While the death toll was relatively low, it was considered Boko Haram's first suicide attack. There would be more.

On the morning of 26 August 2011, a man driving a Honda Accord made his way through the streets of Abuja, his destination the United Nations headquarters for Nigeria. He managed to barrel his way through the exit side of the front gate, guards unable to stop him. He crashed into the front lobby and set off the explosives inside the car, the blast ripping into the building and gutting much of the inside. The attack killed 23 people and wounded dozens more.

It would only get worse, with churches later targeted, including on Christmas Day near the capital, and an office of one of the country's most prominent newspapers was hit. A British and an Italian hostage were killed in north-western Nigeria by what may or may not have been Ansaru, considered a splinter faction of Boko Haram and which would also be blamed for other kidnappings. Boko Haram members would overrun remote areas of north-eastern Nigeria and raise their own flags, part of the reason the president would eventually decide to declare a state of emergency. Seven members of a French family, including four children, would also be abducted in an incident claimed by Shekau, while dozens of students would be massacred in attacks on schools. Reports began to emerge in 2013 of girls being kidnapped and taken as wives by Boko Haram members. In April 2014, when attackers stormed the town of Chibok and abducted 276 girls from their school, Nigeria's military seemed to have barely put up a fight.

This has all led to intense speculation over what Boko Haram has become, including from Western nations deeply worried over the spread of what they call terrorism. The group's re-emergence, and its increasingly violent and sophisticated insurgency, would occur at a time of major change not only in Nigeria, but also among Islamist extremist groups globally. A decade after the 11 September 2001 (9/11) attacks, US President Barack Obama's administration was claiming to have decimated the core of Al-Qaeda's leadership, with the help of a campaign of drone strikes. The bulk of those assertions may have been attributed to Obama's strategy ahead of the 2012 elections, with the president eager to show he had succeeded in his earlier promise of bringing the war in Iraq to a close and refocusing on defeating his country's main enemy, Al-Qaeda.

Still, political rhetoric aside, there certainly seemed to be important shifts occurring in the landscape of 'global terrorism', as it was labelled by the Western world, and there were concerns that unstable African nations could become safe havens for Islamist extremist groups. US military officials in 2011 began warning of signs that the main extremist groups based in Africa – Al-Qaeda in the Islamic Maghreb (AQIM), Al-Shebab in Somalia and Boko Haram – were working toward closer cooperation through arms or financing. There had been evidence of Nigerian Islamists travelling to northern Mali since 2004 for training with extremists from what would later be known as Al-Qaeda in the Islamic Maghreb, but deeper ties remained an open question. Muammar Gaddafi's fall in Libya in 2011 led to fears that the region's black market would be flooded with looted weapons from depots in that country. A rebellion in Mali in 2012 that saw Tuareg and Islamist groups take over half of the country prompted further concern and fuelled speculation over whether Boko Haram members had gone there to fight – and what would happen after they returned home. France responded with a military assault to push out the rebels in Mali, and a US drone base was established in Niger with the aim of monitoring the Islamists who were responsible.

The US government has since labelled Boko Haram a 'global terrorist' group, but the move has not seemed to have had any major effect, and the debate over whether to designate it as such seemed to again heavily involve American politics. Shekau himself has been put on a US wanted list offering a reward of up to $7 million. After he was named a 'global terrorist' by the United States, allowing his assets there to be frozen, he mocked the designation in a video message. 'I know the United States exists, but I don't know which part of the world it is located in, whether in the west or the north, the south or the east', he said in a sarcastic tone, an AK-47 leaning against the wall next to him. 'I don't know where it is, not to talk of freezing my assets there.'

Mapping out the details of what Boko Haram is remains extremely difficult. Even the name Boko Haram is something of an illusion. Roughly translated to mean 'Western education is forbidden', it was given to the group by outsiders based on their understanding of the budding sect and its beliefs. The group itself, or at least Abubakar Shekau's faction of it, says it wants to be known as Jama'atu Ahlus Sunnah Lid Da'awati Wal Jihad, or People Committed to the Prophet's Teachings for Propagation and Jihad.[2] As for Shekau himself, little is known about him. The US government's wanted notice lists three different possible dates of birth, 1965, 1969 and 1975. His vicious rhetoric and bizarre behaviour in video messages, where he has said he likes to kill humans when commanded by God to do so in the same way he enjoys killing rams and chickens, has led some to label him a psychopath. He also strangely refers to long-dead Western leaders as his enemies, from Abraham Lincoln to Margaret Thatcher. But simply labelling him insane is inadequate, a conclusion based on guesswork that ignores the possibility that he may be trying to provoke by acting in that way. There is also the question of whether it is always the same person appearing in video messages over the last several years. The appearance of the man identified as Shekau in videos has been significantly different at times.

All of this becomes quite confusing very quickly, but overall outlines have emerged and a larger picture can be assembled. It is perhaps best to think of Boko Haram as an umbrella term for the insurgency and the violence that has come with it, with an unclear number of cells or factions carrying out attacks. Foot soldiers may be shared or recruited as needed, drawn from the massive population of desperate young men vulnerable to extremist ideas and perhaps attracted to the money and support the group can provide. Any kind of true organisation may exist only at the very top, with limited cooperation between the various cells. Their aims seem to vary greatly, from the sincere will to create an Islamic state to the desire to collect ransom money, with many other motivations in between. 'Do I think that the kids who abducted the girls in Chibok are the ones who set off the bombs in Jos? No', one Nigerian official who has closely followed the insurgency told me. It appears that they finance themselves mainly through illegal activity, including ransom kidnappings and bank robberies. They have stolen weapons from the Nigerian military, and likely would not find it difficult to buy arms on the region's black market. Explosives have also been stolen from private companies.

How much all of this involves politics has been continually debated. As elections scheduled for February 2015 began to draw near, new accusations of politicians financing elements of Boko Haram emerged – certainly a possibility, but if so, more likely on the margins. The overarching conspiracy theories repeatedly offered in Nigeria – northern elites seeking to bring down a southern president; southern power brokers seeking to discredit the north – do not hold up to scrutiny. There are simply too many varying interests, the range of targets too great, to be attributable to one sole purpose.

Concerning foreign links, as one well-versed observer put it to me in early 2014, it seems that a practical relationship has developed between certain Nigerian Islamists, particularly those identified with Ansaru, and the leadership of Al-Qaeda in the Islamic Maghreb or its offshoots. They seek out help when they need it, but otherwise act on their own. Another knowledgeable source, a Western diplomat with extensive experience in the region, told me in March 2014 that it appeared that cooperation involving training and weapons had been deepening over the last few years.

Shekau has pledged solidarity with jihadists globally, including ISIS in Syria and Iraq, but it has never been clear whether such feelings were mutual. For one, outside extremist groups would face the same problem that authorities and would-be peace negotiators have encountered when seeking to probe or communicate with Boko Haram: one never knows with whom one is dealing. Beyond that, Boko Haram's mindless violence may not fit with more recent Al-Qaeda strategy, with the group's leadership having expressed concerns over the indiscriminate killings of fellow Muslims and civilians by its regional affiliates.

Yet it is important to keep all of this in perspective. While links have formed with foreign groups and attacks have been carried out in neighbouring Cameroon, the various elements of the Boko Haram insurgency have remained Nigerian in their outlook. Though demands have ranged widely, they have to a large degree focused on local concerns. The insurgents have sometimes simply seemed bent on the destruction of the Nigerian state, seeking to tear everything down with no end goal in mind. In late 2014, the group again seized territory in parts of north-eastern Nigeria and declared it would be part of a caliphate, but it was not clear whether there were any true attempts at governing such areas.

'While there are links and there's procurement of weapons and there's communication and a whole range of ties between Boko Haram and AQIM and to a lesser extent al-Shebab, it really remains a domestically focused group in the sense that their enemy really is the Nigerian federal state and certain state officials', the same Western diplomat said. 'And I think that in an opportunistic manner they cooperate and have communications with transnational groups that may be committed to the global jihad like AQIM, but that's not their primary objective.'

It is a problem born and bred in Nigeria – and one that Nigerians must resolve amongst themselves. The conditions that have given rise to it must remain the focus of any potential solution.

Nigerian President Goodluck Jonathan, a Christian from the Niger Delta, has offered little beyond heavy-handed military raids that have led to accusations of widespread abuses against civilians – including shootings of innocent people, the burning of homes, torture and indiscriminate arrests. The government has engaged in doublespeak, at one point claiming to be involved in back-channel talks in a bid to halt the violence, but later dismissing this, with the president calling the Islamists 'ghosts' who refuse to show their faces. Shekau, whose whereabouts are unknown and who has often been rumoured to be dead, has repeatedly ruled out dialogue in videos.

While it is impossible to know for certain whether it is always the same man in Shekau's video messages, it would also not seem to matter much. Regardless of whether there have been Shekau look-alikes, attacks have continued and even worsened. 'If in fact he is dead, then it shows that we are in a much worse situation than we thought', the Nigerian official who has followed the situation closely told me. In other words, it showed he could easily be replaced without an interruption in the violence, while the decline of the Nigerian army, largely because of corruption, has left little hope that it can defeat the insurgency. Soldiers 'would rather go to the Niger Delta to make money', he said, referring to the allegations of members of the army being involved in the lucrative oil theft racket and other crimes in that region. 'Whoever is doing this knows they can get the Nigerian army involved in a war they cannot win.'

The lack of faith in both the government and the military has remained one of the most important reasons why the insurgency has not been stopped. 'I don't know that northern populations have a great affinity for Boko Haram or whatever they're advocating, and civilians and moderate Muslims have been the principal victims along with security forces of course', the Western diplomat said. 'But there's this sea of indifference in which they are able to operate because you just don't have a lot of loyalty or affinity for a central government which is seen as completely clueless and, more importantly, unresponsive to the legitimate needs and grievances of local populations.'

As for recruitment into Boko Haram, some see a cycle of poverty and lawlessness as a main cause. 'Religion is the basis of recruitment, so that's why they can get so many people, but the incentive for people to get into it and remain in it is the profit they make from it', Clement Nwankwo, a respected Nigerian civil society activist based in Abuja, told me in June 2014. 'So if there is money available and these people would ordinarily live a street life, where they don't know what they get for the day, but here somebody's paying their bills, somebody is feeding them, clothing them and giving them some little profit [...] And then there is really very little consequence for their actions. They can get away with it. The military hasn't been able to respond in a way that proves a disincentive for them to continue this path.'

In the meantime, the list of the dead only grows longer, each attack helping push the unrealised potential of such an important nation further out of reach. In the south, in the country's largest city of Lagos, steps have been taken in a bid to begin taming the famously chaotic former capital of some 15 million people, whose hours-long traffic jams and exhausting pace of life have become legendary, leaving even the most resilient souls gasping for air. Lagos, along with the rest of the south, has been mainly spared the violence, though there have been questions over whether an explosion in June 2014 claimed by Boko Haram signalled the end of the city's relative peace. If so, the insurgency would reach yet another, far more dangerous stage, and the shoots of progress that have taken root would be tragically ripped out.

There have of course been other bright spots, and recently Finance Minister Ngozi Okonjo-Iweala, a former World Bank managing director, and Central Bank Governor Lamido Sanusi have worked to bring about reforms where possible and reduce corruption. But the frequent refrain in Nigeria is that when one fights corruption, corruption fights back. When Sanusi began to publicly ask questions in 2014 about billions of dollars linked to the state oil firm missing from Nigeria's accounts, he was removed from office by the president. From an aristocratic family, he has since become the emir of Kano, one of the country's most highly respected traditional rulers. He has not entirely abandoned his criticism of government corruption.

*   *   *

By May 2012, Maiduguri, still considered the home base of Boko Haram, resembled something approaching a war zone. Entire neighbourhoods appeared deserted and security checkpoints kept the city on edge. Christians trying to attend church passed through metal detectors and razor wire, with women forced to leave their bags outside. It was by no means only Christians being targeted; Muslims were often the victims. Residents were caught between the incessant attacks and the heavy-handed response of soldiers, who had been accused of rounding up young men for arrest, burning homes and killing civilians.

The extremists had taken to burning schools, and yet classes were still being held in at least one of the damaged buildings. At that school, a teacher said parents insisted that it remain open, so students dressed neatly in yellow and green uniforms were there scampering among piles of broken glass and shards of cement. 'I'm not scared because I think the worst has happened', one 14-year-old girl said as she stood near scorched walls and collapsed tin sheets. 'There's nothing left for them to attack.'

How tragically wrong she would turn out to be. On the night of 14 April 2014, hordes of attackers would descend upon the town of Chibok and swarm the boarding school where several hundred girls were sleeping. They were dressed as soldiers and they told the girls not to worry, that they were there to protect them. They led them outside and towards waiting pick-up trucks, and it slowly began to dawn on the girls that these men were not members of the military. They fired their guns and shouted 'Allahu Akbar', and they forced the girls into the trucks before driving away towards a camp in the forest. Military reinforcements did not arrive. Parents, their daughters gone and the school burnt, set off towards the forest on motorcycles. They had no choice but to try to find the girls themselves.

1

'THEN YOU SHOULD WAIT FOR THE OUTCOME'

Geoffrey Njoku heard it, the sound of a bang and the screech of metal on metal, a distant crash somewhere outside. It was a Friday morning, and the 53-year-old was inside a Standard Chartered bank branch on the ground floor of United Nations headquarters in the Nigerian capital, Abuja. He had gone there to take care of some routine personal banking before returning to his work at UNICEF offices on the third floor. Besides the bank staff, there were only two customers inside, Njoku and another person, but other areas of the sprawling, four-storey UN building, spread out over three wings in the shape of a Y in the city's diplomatic district, were already buzzing with the day's activity. When the crash rang out around 10.20 a.m., Njoku said out loud in the bank, 'What's that sound?'

Up above on the first floor, at least two meetings were in progress. Soji Adeniyi, a UNICEF specialist in emergency planning walking with crutches at the time because of a broken leg, was leading one of them, attended by around 10 colleagues from various UN departments. It had started at around 9 a.m., more than an hour earlier, and was supposed to wrap up by 10 a.m., but it ran over, so they were all still there, in one section of an open-space work area cordoned off with movable partitions, a large table set out in the middle. Adeniyi, too, heard a sound, 'as if it were a crash through a door or something', and also did not know what to make of it.

Vinod Alkari, a UNICEF expert from India who had worked in post-invasion Iraq, had not heard anything. He was on the third floor speaking with his colleague Shalini Bahuguna, asking whether she had seen his email related to a water, sanitation and hygiene programme. She seemed distracted and did not respond, confusing Alkari, and instead asked him if he had 'heard something falling'.

Presumably sometime before that – perhaps days, perhaps weeks – a 27-year-old, softly spoken man in a polo-style shirt had stared into a video camera, his head wrapped in a turban, an AK-47 rifle in his hands and two others leaning against a wall on either side of him. Two gas cylinders, the type used to manufacture bombs, sat in front of him. He was thin, and the way he occasionally smiled made him appear meek. He spoke in Hausa, the predominant language in northern Nigeria, and seemed almost apologetic at times as he meandered through his speech. He was wearing something that looked like a suicide vest.[1]

As the young man explained what he was preparing to do, he said that he had no choice, that he must carry out Allah's bidding, and he asked his mother, father and wife to understand, while also hoping that his son would follow in his footsteps. At certain points, the sound of what seemed to be a child could be heard in the background along with the clanking of someone apparently tidying up or putting away dishes.

'I am going to shed my blood and I pray to Allah to make me steadfast', said the young man, later identified as an auto repair worker named Mohammed Abul Barra. 'May he take me there safely [...] My mother, my father and my wife, these three people, I call on you to be patient. I know you will be at great pains by losing me, especially you, my mother [...] It is the love of God that made me to be obedient to you and it is the same Allah that commanded me to go and carry out this mission. He even wonders if we prefer our parents, children or relations or the wealth we amassed, or a mansion you built. If you prefer this to Allah, his Prophet and jihad, then you should wait for the outcome.'

His described his belief that a suicide attack would lead him to paradise and hoped the same for his own son.

'Then my son, my son Barra, the son of Allah, may Allah nurture you on the path of the Prophet to make you useful to Islam, to make you follow my footsteps and do what I am about to do now, which is called suicide attack.'

Later in the video, a group of unidentified men took turns giving him hugs, presumably to bid him goodbye. He was then shown sitting in the driver's seat of a grey car and spoke again, this time offering a disjointed message to the US president. When he finished, a blurry and shaky sequence showed a car being driven down a road.

'I tell Obama and other world leaders they were created by Allah in the same way he created us', he said while seated in the driver's seat. 'So whoever rebels against Allah and goes against his dictates, whatever his status, especially Obama, who is their leader, if he does not repent and convert to Islam, if he dies, he's going to hell and live therein for ever. Obama and other infidels should know God knows about them and is only giving them a respite. And if he seizes them, they have no excuse.'

On the morning of 26 August 2011, as Njoku was banking, Adeniyi was conducting his meeting, Alkari was trying to sort out his sanitation project and many other UN staffers were going about their usual business, the driver of a Honda Accord would make his way into the diplomatic district of the Nigerian capital, a city newly built with petrodollars, its wide boulevards and concrete office buildings giving it an artificial feel in comparison to much of the rest of the country. The driver would pull on to the street leading to UN headquarters, where some 400 staff worked, before directing his car towards the exit gates of the compound and barrelling through.

In the building itself, the atrium and reception area were located where the three branches of the Y converged, facing out in the direction of the two angled arms, about 100 metres away from the gate. The driver moved towards it, crashing through the glass and entering the building. When he did this and burst into the reception area, shattering the glass front and colliding with a wall on the inside, a bizarre moment of uncertainty would occur. Those inside the building seemed unsure how to react, and one woman would walk towards the car. After a few moments, some would begin to run away, seemingly realising that this may not have been an accident. It would be more than 10 seconds before the bomb exploded, pulverising much of what surrounded it.[2] The force of the blast collapsed walls and shattered windows, raining down shards of glass in parts of the building as if it were a hail storm.

Njoku and others inside the bank on the same floor were thrown to the ground by the impact. Something heavy had fallen on his leg, but he did not notice the pain as panic set in and he and the others began figuring out what to do. They could not see the area where the bomber had crashed into the building from where they were, but it was by then obvious that something terrible had happened and they had to escape. The entrance to the bank had collapsed and was blocked, so they were forced to look for another way out. They made their way to a back door, Njoku somehow moving under his own steam despite his injury. When he and the others finally arrived at the back of the building where everyone was gathering, he collapsed on the grass and could not stand again, his leg now swelling. While waiting to be evacuated by an ambulance, he sent a text message to his wife, telling her 'we've been attacked and I'm injured, but I'm OK'. He was unable to make calls, possibly because of network congestion since so many people were trying to phone out, but the message had reached his wife, who tracked him down at a hospital in the area.

On the first floor where Adeniyi was holding a meeting, parts of the ceiling crashed in, windows shattered and the fire alarm rang out. Adeniyi, then 44, sensed it was a bomb and told colleagues to get under the table, worried there could be a second blast. He manoeuvred himself despite his broken leg as they all took cover.

As they did so, they could hear people wailing and crying for help from the room next door, the main auditorium, located just above where the car bomb detonated and the site of some of the worst suffering. They waited briefly under the table – Adeniyi estimates it was between three and five minutes – until they heard the sound of voices from UN security workers calling out from downstairs for everyone to evacuate to the back of the building. Adeniyi was able to get a signal on his phone, so before evacuating, he called the director of search and rescue from Nigeria's National Emergency Management Agency – someone he knew through his work – and spoke to him briefly. He was assured that the fire service was on its way. He and the others then began determining how they could get out. The partitions surrounding them had collapsed, and they had to clear one out of the way. A glass door was stuck, so Adeniyi used his crutches to break through it, and they made their way to the stairs past a gauntlet of debris. They arrived at the evacuation point at the rear of the building about 10 to 15 minutes after the explosion, everyone from Adeniyi's meeting having made it out alive. He repeatedly sent text messages to his entire contact list, telling everyone he was fine, and received calls for about an hour from those hoping to confirm with him, including his wife, before his phone battery died. He also went back into the building to try to help and document what had happened. He remembers people yelling; he took pictures and video and directed arriving rescue workers to where victims were trapped. He later found out that two of his close colleagues were among the dead on the ground floor, and he wondered what could have happened if his meeting had wrapped up earlier. 'It would have been more disastrous for us, because maybe by then some of us may have been in the lobby or in the lift', he said.

Alkari, further up on the third floor, described a surreal series of events, followed by tense moments where it had seemed more lives were at stake if help did not arrive. Windows along with their frames collapsed inside the room, scattering glass everywhere, and ceiling tiles fell. One of the frames crashed on to the table between him and his colleague, lightly scraping Alkari's head and drawing a small amount of blood. The lights went out, and then there was 'a sudden silence, the kind of silence one rarely encounters'.

'We both say "it is a bomb",' Alkari wrote later in a personal account of what happened that day. He said subsequently: 'The threats have come true.'[3]

Based on Alkari's experience in Iraq and Shalini's in Afghanistan, they decided, like Adeniyi, to take cover temporarily under the table – a procedure taught in emergency drills in case a second blast hits and to avoid being caught up in falling debris. They heard others scrambling to evacuate, but decided to wait a few minutes longer to be sure. While sitting there, Alkari managed to think to collect his laptop and his bag, and they then decided to leave, moving a window frame out of their way. Everyone from their division had already gone. When they arrived at the central atrium on the same floor, Alkari recalled that 'everything that was on the ceiling was now on the ground, as if the whole building was turned upside down [...] Lift doors were blown off and could not be seen anywhere. There were two big gaping holes where the lift doors used to be. The lift frame was twisted out of shape as if made of paper. At the central atrium level where the lift opens, every glass panel was blown out. A wall had collapsed.'

It was then that they heard cries for help. The collapsed wall had crashed into an area occupied by the UN Office on Drugs and Crime, trapping two staffers underneath tables. Two others who were not trapped were scrambling to move the collapsed part of the wall, but it was too heavy. Alkari could not be of much assistance, either, since he had suffered a slipped disk in his back, so they decided the best option was to seek help from elsewhere. It would not be so simple. Alkari moved to a window, its frame blown out, and shouted and waved repeatedly at those below. They noticed him, but seemed not to understand amid the chaos. Some waved back, signalling for him to come down. His urgent message not getting through, Alkari asked his colleague Shalini to go downstairs to find help, and in the meantime he continued to shout from the window as well as make phone calls to colleagues. Most did not answer their phones, but he reached one man, who told him he was on his way to the hospital. By this point, Alkari could see Shalini from his spot next to what used to be the window as she pleaded with people outside.

'They were dazed and confused to the point that nothing registered', Alkari wrote later. 'Finally I see Shalini waving at me saying no one is coming up. She is trying to tell me that there is fire on the ground floor. I am not able to get that message. She sends me an SMS but my mind is occupied with finding help. I did not look at my mobile.'

He then saw a man in the distance down a corridor on the same floor, but the nightmare would only continue. Alkari shouted, and when the man looked his way, he tried to signal to him that people were trapped and needed help. The man stared for a moment from about 20 metres away, and Alkari later wondered if he was debating in his head whether to put himself in further danger or simply get out while he still had the chance. 'He just turned and left', Alkari remembered. 'I do not blame him, but feel like a person left to fend for himself.'

Shalini returned with the bad news that no one had come with her, while the UNODC staffer leading the effort to dislodge the collapsed wall was growing angry and frustrated. Alkari decided he would go downstairs himself to recruit help, and it was while moving down the steps that he began to get a more complete picture of the devastation.

'Stairs are littered with broken glass, blown-off wood panels, light fixtures and electric wiring. From the second floor down, the stairs have blood stains everywhere. Ground floor was a complete mess. As I step on to the ground, I am in two inches of water. The sprinkler system seems to be working and most likely some water pipe had burst. And there was acrid smoke.'

An ATM machine had been thrown towards the door by the force of the blast, partially blocking Alkari's way, but he managed to slip past and make it outside, where he saw 'several people badly hurt, lying on ground crying for help. There is one ambulance taking in someone and another is entering the area to carry others. Some people were lying lifeless, soaked with blood, either dead or in shock. Sirens are wailing, adding to confusion [...] I approach the first person I see and ask him to come with me to the third floor. He is in another world. What I am saying does not make any sense to him.'

He eventually saw two people he knew and they agreed to follow him, along with a third 'Good Samaritan' he was not familiar with. The four of them went back into the building, squeezing past the ATM, but saw fire burning on the ground floor with flames Alkari said looked to be five feet high. They decided to push on towards the third floor anyway, Alkari reasoning that the blaze would not spread quickly because the water sprinklers were on, the building's electricity was off and the first floor was reasonably high up from the ground. As they reached the third floor, they joined one of the UNODC staffers and, finally, lifted the collapsed part of the wall. One of the two women who had been trapped had no injuries, but she seemed to be in shock, shaking and crying. Debris was cleared from a sofa so she could sit and Alkari ran to his office to grab tissues and water. The woman drank and began to calm down, but they realised she had somehow lost her shoes – a problem since broken glass covered the stairs. 'I suggest to Shalini that she clean up every step for the rescued lady to put her foot. A laborious task, but Shalini is up to it', Alkari wrote.

The condition of the second trapped woman was the complete inverse. She was calm, so much so that she was able to warn her rescuers before they moved her that her leg was broken. There was also another problem: a second piece of the wall was in situ and had to be moved to get her out, but it was too heavy even for the five people who remained. Finding help proved to be far less complicated this time. Alkari turned to look around and immediately saw two UNDP staffers who had come up from the second floor. They instantly agreed to assist, but even with seven people, it was a struggle to move the wall. They worked together with 'one, two, three – heave', and eventually succeeded. They lifted the woman out carefully, keeping in mind her broken leg, and carried her over to the sofa, allowing the team to catch their breath before bringing her downstairs. Alkari and one of the UNDP staffers decided to climb to the fourth floor to check if anyone else was there. They called out, but heard nothing in response, then headed back down to inspect other areas of the third floor. It was there that they would see Ingrid Midtgaard, a 30-year-old Norwegian lawyer who had been working for the UNODC, and Alkari described a heartbreaking scene, with the young woman 'sitting lifeless in a chair'.

'Her face is calm', Alkari wrote. 'The Good Samaritan climbs back and checks her pulse [...] She was gone. We are not sure if we should move her to the ground floor. We decide not to move her because by then we had seen several ambulances ferrying people to hospital. Paramedics had arrived. With heavy hearts we leave her behind. If you believe in God, then the God had taken her to be with him.'

Returning to the task of evacuating the woman with the broken leg, they began the journey downstairs. Arriving on the bottom floor, they were greeted by two inches of water, with the sprinklers still working, but no fire. They could not squeeze past the ATM while carrying the woman to use the same exit, so they decided to manoeuvre her through a broken window, rescue workers on the other side helping to make sure she was not cut on the remaining jagged glass. She was put in an ambulance and taken to a hospital, and Alkari then told a doctor on the scene about Midtgaard on the third floor.

As the day wore on, rescue workers pulled people out from the damaged front of the building with stretchers. The damaged front gate that the bomber drove through sat on the ground. At least 23 people were killed, including 13 UN staffers. Immediately, suspicion fell on the Islamist extremist group that had become known by the name Boko Haram, which would later claim responsibility for the attack in the suicide bomber video and through a spokesman. It was the first time the group had struck at a foreign or international target, setting off a scramble to determine who or what could be hit next. There was a problem, however: apart from the tense, bearded face of Abubakar Shekau, the group's new leader, who had appeared in videos with an AK-47, few knew what Boko Haram was.

*   *   *

One of history's most successful armed jihads occurred in what is today northern Nigeria. It was more than two centuries ago, when a revered Islamic cleric, the son of a learned preacher who had built a fast-expanding following, found himself on a collision course with the kings who ruled at the time. One of the many tales and legends surrounding his life describes a meeting at the palace of the sultan of Gobir, a former student of the cleric who now feared his authority was threatened by his growing influence. The cleric, an ethnic Fulani named Usman Dan Fodio, along with a group of other Muslim leaders, visited the palace after being summoned by the sultan, Yunfa, who had sent signals that he was interested in making peace with them. He had apparently changed his mind. Once there, the Shehu, or Sheikh, as the preacher would later be known, found himself confronted with a musket cradled by the sultan himself, apparently prepared to kill the man who had caused so much trouble for him and his court. As he pulled the trigger, however, the musket misfired and burnt Yunfa, though not fatally.[4] He lived long enough to see the tables turned, when the Shehu's army, after having routed their Hausa opponents in key battles, collecting their horses and weaponry, marched into the Gobir capital of Alkalawa. Yunfa and his men put up a final fight, but by then there was little hope for him and his court. The Muslim fighters killed him, and the Shehu and his allies across a wide expanse of what had been known as Hausaland were on their way to forging an Islamic empire. It would come to be known as the Sokoto Caliphate.

The Shehu would turn out to be one of Islam's greatest messengers in what we now call Nigeria, leaving a legacy of Muslim practice, thought and law still very much alive today, but he was by no means the first. Long before that, in the centuries after the Archangel Gabriel appeared to the Prophet Muhammad in a cave near Mecca and revealed to him words of the Qur'an, the Islamic faith had begun to filter across into sub-Saharan Africa. It would be a gradual process, sometimes involving conquest, though it was mainly the result of trade and the innumerable aspects of society that interact with and depend upon it. As camels began to replace donkeys for journeys in the Sahara from around the second century, making it easier to traverse the desert and its forbidding conditions, fleets of caravans began plying its routes, trading gold and salt, among other items, and, of course, slaves. A new world would slowly trudge across it, and the societies it came into contact with would be changed for ever.[5] Many of those societies were prepared to profit from the opportunities the increasingly busy trans-Saharan trade routes offered. In today's northern Nigeria, they included two separate regions in particular: one the Kanem-Bornu Empire, the other a collection of states led by kings in Hausaland.

Bornu would come to be centred mainly in today's north-eastern Nigeria near Lake Chad. It was not founded until the fourteenth century, but its roots lie much further back in Kanem, near Lake Chad's north-east. The Sefawa dynasty came to power there possibly as early as the ninth century or perhaps later, towards the end of the eleventh century, enduring war, societal upheaval and religious change, its power and influence at one point extending, as one historian wrote, from 'the Niger to the Nile'.[6] The dynasty would last until the nineteenth century.

It is difficult to pinpoint when Islam first arrived in Kanem, though some of the religion's initial messengers seemed to have been Ibadi gold traders.[7] Travelling Muslim scholars who sought lucrative jobs in the royal courts of the day would also play an important role in sub-Saharan Africa, with their advanced knowledge and literacy seen as particularly impressive. The kings of West Africa, including in Kanem, would have seen great benefits in cultivating links with their Muslim visitors as well as the states from where they came. Trade relationships with the Arab world and northern Africa brought considerable wealth and knowledge, not to mention useful allies.[8] It was through these initial contacts that the long, slow journey toward Islam began.

Islam's influence became official in Kanem by the late eleventh century, possibly in 1085, under a king, or mai, known as Hummay, who went on pilgrimage to Mecca perhaps twice or even more.[9] While Kanem was officially Muslim by then, much of the population remained pagan or animistic and would have known little about Islam. The new religion had been mainly confined to the elite, and even among those who did convert, a hybrid version of the faith developed, mixing Muslim and ancestral beliefs, as was the case throughout West Africa.[10] It was in the thirteenth century that Kanem would rise to become the most powerful state in the region and see its influence extend into the Arab world.

Civil wars would gradually intrude on Kanem's prosperity and force the Sefawa dynasty to flee. They moved south-west of Lake Chad and established a new capital at Ngazargamu in an area known as Bornu[11] – where Boko Haram would wreak havoc centuries later. The Kanuri people had come to dominate, and they are still the largest ethnic group in the area today. Both Muhammad Yusuf, the first Boko Haram leader, and Abubakar Shekau, his successor, are considered Kanuri. Bornu would establish a reputation by the eighteenth century as an important centre of Islamic learning.[12] Some 300 years later, Boko Haram would take root amid the remnants of that former empire, by then part of the nation of Nigeria.

* * *

The tale begins with the son of a king of Baghdad, or so one of the many different versions of the legend goes, who fought with his father and fled to Bornu before later arriving in Daura, located in today's north-central Nigeria. When a villager there told him he could only draw water from the well on Fridays because it was guarded by a snake, this wandering prince, named Bayajida, refused to listen. He went to the well anyway, and when the snake appeared, he cut off his head with his sword, freeing the people from the serpent's tyranny. The queen of Daura – it was ruled by a matriarchy at the time – was naturally impressed with this man's skill and bravery, and she decided to marry him. The queen and Bayajida had a boy, named Bawo, whose own sons would go on to found the seven states of Hausaland, which took shape west of Bornu. Another seven states, known as the Banza Bakwai, or Bastard Seven, would also be founded.[13]

The story is obviously a myth, rich in symbolism – a heroic man from Arab royal stock freeing Daura from its older, traditional ways. Some have pointed to the similarities with Islamic traditional stories and suggest it may have been a useful way of describing the arrival of North African newcomers, who mixed with the local residents and formed what we now call the Hausa people.[14] The Hausa were not a distinct ethnic group, with the label given to the combination of people who spoke the language and who gradually coalesced.[15] Today, Hausa is the lingua franca of northern Nigeria.

It seems Islam began to make headway in Hausaland around the time Wangara gold traders and Muslim missionaries from other parts of West Africa flowed into the area in the 1300s. The first state to have a Muslim king was Kano, when Yaji dan Tsamiya ruled from 1349 to 1385. Other Hausa states would eventually move toward Islam as well, and the kingdoms' wealth and trading power grew strong. They were blessed with natural resources, trading nuts and other produce as well as ivory and gold. Slave trading was also practised. Hausaland became known for its leather and textile production; by one account it was considered the workshop of West Africa for a time. Its reputation spread to such a degree that Italian-speaking merchants arrived in Kano likely via

Tripoli as early as the sixteenth century. Islamic learning deepened among the elites and literacy spread. Kano and Katsina battled it out – sometimes literally, as they were frequently at war – for the title of the most important trading centre in the region during the eighteenth century.[16] Today, Kano remains northern Nigeria's largest city, a bustling, crowded commercial centre. Its 'workshop of West Africa' glory faded, however, as the country's attention turned to oil. Some of the city's centuries-old textile dyeing pits remain in use as a reminder of its prosperous past.

While the Hausa had come to rule the kingdoms in the region, they were by no means the only people inhabiting them. On the margins of the main cities and towns in Hausaland, the Fulani were in certain ways divided between two worlds, living within the kingdom but with their own customs and ways of life, traditions dating back centuries. While certain Fulani clans were nomadic and cattle-herders, others were more stationary, tending to remain in one area for longer periods of time, forming their own communities that included subsistence farming. Some clans, including the Toronkawa, gravitated toward Islamic teaching and their members travelled as itinerant scholars. They were speakers and readers of classical Arabic and were respected for their knowledge. One family that emerged from that clan and eventually settled in the Hausa kingdom of Gobir was that of Usman Dan Fodio.[17]

The young Dan Fodio showed promise as a scholar and preacher. His father taught him how to read and write in addition to studies of the Qur'an, and the community at Degel, where the family had settled, believed him to have certain powers that allowed him to control supernatural spirits, or djinns, even as a boy. After his father, another of his early teachers was a Tuareg named Sheikh Jibril Umar, a controversial figure at the time thanks to his strict beliefs. Umar had been influenced by the Wahhabi school of Islam, which had begun in part as a reform movement advocating a return to a purer version of the faith. Despite disagreements early on between Umar and Dan Fodio, who was brought up in the

Sufi tradition, the learned and travelled scholar would have an important influence on the Shehu's life.[18]

Dan Fodio would begin preaching himself when he was 20 years old as a travelling holy man, which was common at the time. According to one biography, he deliberately lived an austere life, with 'only one pair of trousers, one turban, and one gown. He ate abstemiously and was uninterested in wealth and possessions, which he regarded as corrupting. He is said to have earned his food by twisting rope, an occupation he could carry on while reading or teaching.' He would also compose books and poems, both in Arabic and Fulfulde, the Fulani language. He would not, however, make it on pilgrimage to Mecca despite attempting when he was younger, when his father reeled him back.[19]

As the number of his followers expanded and a tide of Muslim reformers joined with him, Gobir's leaders would become increasingly worried. The balance between the Shehu's formal religious preachings and his sermons criticising the injustices of the day is difficult to determine, but both were part of his movement. It allowed the reformists to gain backers from those who were at the time still believers in the ancient religions, helping to usher in a profound change in the culture and history of what is today northern Nigeria. Dan Fodio also would have benefited from 'Mahdist' beliefs at the time – the idea among some Muslims that, when the end of the world is near, a messenger will appear, similar to Christian 'end times' beliefs. Many likely saw the Shehu as the 'Mahdi', though he never claimed to be. The turn of the Islamic century in 1200 (1785 in the Gregorian calendar) would have added to such speculation, since Mahdist prophecies have often been associated with the end of the century.[20]

Gobir's rulers would seek to crack down on the growing reform movement as they began to feel threatened by it. Around 1788, the sultan at the time, Bawa, hatched a plot to end the threat once and for all. He invited all of the Muslim reformists to his palace under the guise of a goodwill gesture to commemorate the Eid al-Adha holiday, but instead planned to kill them when they arrived. He thought better of it and abandoned the idea after seeing the large number of reformers who showed up – and instead offered the Shehu a gift. The Shehu, unbowed, refused the gift and used the occasion to demand better treatment for his followers.[21] Bawa, in a sign of the Shehu's growing power, would agree to five important concessions: the Shehu would be allowed to convert people; those who wished to convert would be allowed to do so; that 'any man with a turban' – a Muslim, that is – should not be harassed; prisoners should be freed; and Gobir residents should not be unfairly taxed.[22]

That was, however, by no means the end of the struggle. Sultan Nafata reversed Bawa's earlier commitments, issuing a number of proclamations aimed at cutting off the reform movement. They included outlawing anyone from preaching except the Shehu and the banning of turbans and veils. Sons would also not be allowed to abandon their father's faith, and converts were ordered to return to their ancestors' beliefs. Such blanket restrictions were unlikely to ever work in practice, and the laws were a failure, prompting an even harsher response from Nafata, who later had members of the Shehu's family detained.[23]

The Shehu would begin having what he described as mystic visions in 1789, when he was 36, and these experiences would have a major effect on him and his movement. As he wrote himself in his Wird, or Litany, the Shehu believed that the Prophet Muhammad had appeared to him along with Abd al-Qadir al-Jilani, the founder of the Sufi order to which he belonged, the Qadirriyi. A key vision would appear to him in 1794, when the Shehu would see al-Jilani handing him the *saif al-haqq* – the 'sword of truth' or 'sword of God'.[24]

When Yunfa came to the throne in Gobir, it would appear the Shehu would have an ally in him. He had by some accounts been his student, and the Shehu may have used his influence to help him become sultan. The turbulence of the day would, however, bring them into direct conflict despite the fact that both had initially seemed intent on avoiding war. The assassination attempt at Yunfa's palace involving the misfiring musket may be at least partly legend – at least two versions of the story exist, including one where the Shehu used magical powers to avoid death – but the fighting that would break out later shows that the situation had intensified to the point where a compromise may have no longer been possible.[25]

A confrontation would provide the spark for the jihad. There are once again varying interpretations on what exactly happened in the incident, but it seems to have started with a Gobir raid on a Muslim community in Kebbi. Yunfa then took the drastic step of ordering the Shehu and his family to leave Degel, which he initially refused to do. Instead, the Shehu decided that the time had come for 'hijra', an imitation of the Prophet Muhammad's migration with his followers from Mecca to Medina. The community packed the few supplies it had and left for Gudu in February 1804, the books belonging to the ever-scholarly Shehu transported on the back of a camel.[26] Their journey marked the start of a rebellion – an armed jihad, to the Shehu's followers.

War would result, and the Muslim reformers would use their knowledge of classical Arab battle manoeuvres, religious conviction, skilled archers and a motley collection of fighters willing to join the cause for various reasons – Fulani, Hausa and Tuareg – to defeat the Gobir army. The Shehu, who was 50 at the time the jihad began, would be in charge, but he did not participate directly in the fighting. His son Muhammad Bello and his brother, Abdullahi, would be commanders in the field. Those fighting would include a large number of Islamic scholars, an indication of the idealistic community the Shehu had fostered. As Murray Last points out in his book *The Sokoto Caliphate*, when 2,000 fighters from the Muslim side were killed in one battle, 200 were said to have known the Qur'an by heart.[27] Not all of those fighting were as well intentioned, though. At one point during the trying campaign, the Shehu's brother Abdullahi grew weary as many of his fighters abandoned the movement's ideals and engaged in outright plunder. He tried to leave for Mecca, but was talked into remaining. In his biography of the Shehu, Mervyn Hiskett quotes from one of Abdullahi's poems, where he laments their thievery and lack of morals:

> When my companions passed away and my aims went awry
> I was left behind among the remainder, the liars
> who say that which they do not do and follow their own desires.[28]

By October 1808, the Muslims, despite having begun the war under-equipped and with few supplies, would have the Gobir army on the run. A final assault would occur that month, when Yunfa's men were unable to stop an invasion of the capital, Alkalawa. Yunfa himself was among those killed.[29] The Shehu had encouraged Muslim leaders in other Hausa states to also rise up and fight for the cause, and many did, extending the jihad beyond what Dan Fodio's army could have accomplished on its own. What would result over the following years would be what we now call the Sokoto Caliphate. It would last nearly a century, at one point including much of today's northern Nigeria and beyond.[30] It would be wrong to think of it as a cohesive and united nation state; it was instead a very loose collection of allied 'emirates', with the caliph in Sokoto as the central power.

Sokoto's history should not be romanticised. The war that led to it was brutal, leaving behind destroyed villages and scores of dead. There has also been evidence of extreme, barbaric punishments during the time of the caliphate, including impaling prisoners or burying them alive. It is not clear how common such punishments were. Slavery and slave-raiding were also widespread and an integral part of society, and all of these practices must be factored into any judgement about the caliphate's place in history.

At the same time, its positive aspects must not be cast aside, either. It was a relatively stable society throughout its century-long existence, and in some ways could be considered a natural outgrowth of the region's history, or at least a more natural process than what was soon to follow. Its emphasis on education and literacy also stands in stark contrast to the nihilistic violence of Boko Haram, whose kidnappings of girls and slaughtering of boys in their school dormitories show it to be a very different and perverse movement – a betrayal of the Shehu's vision.

'As an example of state-building, it was truly remarkable', Murray Last, author of *The Sokoto Caliphate*, wrote recently, while also cautioning that its dark side must not be overlooked:

> It witnessed almost no rebellions or schisms, famines or epidemics, and it was economically successful as well, with trade and manufacturing in the region expanding as never before and merchants who travelled far and wide. Its reformist leaders wrote more than three hundred books.[31]

The late Mervyn Hiskett, who wrote extensively on Islam's advance into West Africa and particularly northern Nigeria, has written that the region's nineteenth-century jihads set in motion a wave of social change. 'Not only were they military and political victories for literates over non-literates, to a large extent; they also intensified literate activity in areas where Islam was already established and they introduced it into areas where it had never before existed.' Such an emphasis on literacy included education for women,[32] and Dan Fodio's daughter became a renowned poet and scholar, following in her father's learned footsteps.

Hiskett continued later: 'What the final result of this process of change might have been, if Africans had been left to work things out for themselves, can only be guessed at; but they were not left to do this.'[33]

*   *   *

The letter stood as a final set of instructions, and it involved a mission of such audacity that considering it now evokes both awe at its daringness and disgust at its intent. Sir George Taubman Goldie, an intense but private man who enjoyed reading and who was doggedly committed to extending the British Empire, was the letter's author. He wrote forthrightly and clearly, setting down the mission's goals and some of its dangers. The recipient of the letter was Frederick Lugard, then a 36-year-old who had served various roles in Afghanistan, India, Burma and East Africa. He had been hired by Goldie to lead an expedition to an area of West Africa known as Borgu, located in parts of today's Benin and Nigeria. In one section, Goldie favourably described one of the men who was to be travelling with Lugard and touched on the problem of drinking.

'You will find him docile and active, while his constitution is thoroughly acclimatized – an immense advantage in Western Africa', Goldie wrote. 'I believe him to be thoroughly sober, but there are few men in West Africa whom I should trust too far with the care of liquors; the depressing climate predisposing the best men to take stimulants unduly.'[34]

The mission set out in the letter, written on 24 July 1894, was to be on behalf of the Royal Niger Company, and Lugard was due to travel soon to West Africa aboard a steamer leaving from Liverpool. The Royal Niger Company by then was officially chartered by Britain and had worked to open up the interior of what is today Nigeria to trade. The French and Germans had been at the same game, penetrating into African territory as far as possible to cut out coastal middlemen and lock up new markets. Goldie was particularly concerned about the French, who, according to him, had been entering into dubious treaties with local chiefs who did not have the authority to do so. To counter this, he called on Lugard, a restless former military officer and explorer who had been lauded for his work in East Africa. In the letter, Goldie told Lugard that he was to arrive at the port of Akassa in the Niger Delta region, journey upriver 550 miles to Jebba, then head westward on land towards Borgu. In places where no treaties between the French and the local rulers existed, he was to do his best to obtain a declaration saying so and seek to sign his own. Goldie also warned Lugard 'to remember, above all, that diplomacy and not conquest is the object of your expedition westwards'.

> 'The French Press for the last six years have incessantly boasted that French officers and travellers, with (or even without) a single French companion and with very few native carriers and armed men, are able to cross new regions peacefully, and acquire valuable treaty rights where Englishmen can only make their way by force, leaving behind them a hatred and fear of Europeans. I do not for a moment admit the truth of this; but it is possible that, in regions where Europe has absolutely no military power, the gaiety, cajolery and sympathetic manner of the French have more effect in obtaining treaties than the sterner and colder manners of our countrymen.'

Goldie also told Lugard that he should try to collect as much information on the places he encountered as possible 'and to bring home for investigation any specimens of rock or sand which the natives assure you contain gold. The gradual lightening of your loads as you proceed will enable you to do this on a considerable scale.' He was also informed to be on the lookout for gum trees, shea butter trees and rubber vines.[35]

Lugard was a natural choice to lead such an expedition. He had made his name in Uganda with the Imperial British East Africa Company. A month before receiving his instructions from Goldie, he had written to his brother saying that he was 'pledged to W. Africa, and apart from W. Africa, my life is pledged to Africa. I would not chuck my life's work'.[36] One should not take that to mean he had a bleeding heart of altruistic intentions. He, too, was committed to the British Empire, and what he was mainly pledged to seems to have been his government's mission on the continent – though he would later call it the 'dual mandate', or advancing the British cause while also improving the lives of Africans.[37] At the same time, Lugard was also a complicated and curious man, and his life had up to that point taken drastic turns. His military career was derailed when he set off on a doomed pursuit of a woman, which left him distraught and in search of new adventures. As a result, he was to embark on his first of many missions into a region that would eventually come to define his life and legacy.[38] As Lugard would later write, he would travel to areas where no European was believed to have been. In the thick of the Borgu expedition, he wrote to a friend in England in October 1894 from Camp Kiama in the 'Niger Territories', frightened because he had been warned that he and his party were set to be attacked. Two weeks later, he wrote again, saying the attack did not happen and seeming to be embarrassed that he had panicked.

'I am very vexed with myself for having mentioned the matter', Lugard wrote. 'I had just been sent for by the king in the night, and naturally my mind was full of the matter, for I thoroughly believed in its truth. Suffice it to say that I am travelling in a part of Africa which does not bear a good name – that I find my way very full of difficulties. No European has been here before.'

More than two weeks after that, he would indeed be attacked, and Lugard himself was hit in the head with what may or may not have been a poisonous arrow. He set out the details in another letter to the same friend.

These people of Borgu are famed for their treachery, and I have had occasion to prove it. After welcoming me most hospitably, and exchanging presents, etc., they arranged a night attack on me. The old local chief of the town was not in the plot, and opposed it very strongly. Being helpless against the 'princes' who had hatched the design, he sent and warned me – but I already had the news. The hostile party then gave up the night surprise, and determined to attack us openly as we started on our march. Their object was to loot all our goods, and kill or drive us away. They got a severe lesson, but I was myself hit in the head by a poisoned arrow. The Borgus are celebrated through this part of Africa for their deadly poisons. The arrow penetrated the skull a good way, and was so firmly wedged in it that it required very great force to extract it. Fortunately it was not one of the common barbed ones, and was merely a straight spike. I ate all kinds of filth that was given me as antidotes against the poison, and whether amongst them I took a really effectual remedy I do not know. Anyway the wound has given me no trouble whatever, and is now healing rapidly.[39]

Lugard would succeed in the main goal of his journey and conclude a treaty with Nikki, the capital of Borgu, on 10 November, ahead of the French by 16 days. It would be dubbed a 'steeplechase', won by Lugard, though he would later say that those using that word would have chosen a different one if they were familiar with the trudging pace of the expedition's donkeys.[40] He would later head back south to Akassa before deciding to move north again after falling ill in the delta's humid climate and taking large amounts of quinine to avoid contracting malaria.[41] His Nigerian adventure was only beginning.

*　*　*

European interference in what is today Nigeria dates back centuries before Lugard's Borgu expedition. The Portuguese arrived in the kingdom of Benin in today's south-western Nigeria in the fifteenth century and began trading in pepper and slaves. The British arrived later, seeking to muscle in on Portugal's dominance of trade in the region.[42] By the mid-nineteenth century, Britain and other European countries had outlawed slavery, and changes were sweeping across not only their countries, where Enlightenment ideas were taking hold, but also West Africa, which was seeing trade patterns shift dramatically. Britain was seeking palm oil to help power the industrial revolution back home, and it wanted to penetrate into the interior of West Africa to cut out middlemen and trade directly. The so-called 'scramble for Africa' would also play out between European powers seeking to expand their footholds on the continent in search of new markets and vital resources. For the British, a focused and determined Goldie would take on the role of pushing further inland, first through his United Africa Company, which saw him bring together several trading outfits, and later with the Royal Niger Company, which would be chartered by the British government after initial reluctance to do so, with concerns of overextending in the region. The results of Goldie's pursuit of furthering the Empire would have far-reaching consequences, and some would later label him, with or without irony, 'the founder of modern Nigeria'.[43]

By the time Goldie turned to Lugard for the Borgu mission, the British had already established a fully fledged colony in Lagos and protectorates in the Niger Delta and parts of Yorubaland in the south-west. Christian missionaries had also been arriving in southern Nigeria, bringing with them new beliefs, Western forms of education and a desire to eradicate slavery. Despite reluctance among many in Britain for further colonial expansion because of the costs involved, among other reasons, a combination of factors moved the country gradually in that direction. First, as Goldie and others sought to open up more markets, security was a major problem. Fighting in Yorubaland disrupted trade, and African middlemen retaliated against British traders who sought to penetrate further inland and break their hold on the market. Disputes over pricing and other matters related to trade also broke out regularly.

Beyond that, there had also been a major effort to halt slave trading along the coast, with British ships pursuing and stopping slave ships leaving the region. The bid to stop slave trafficking was no doubt to a large degree altruistic, driven by Enlightenment ideas that were changing the world, but it also worked hand in hand with Britain's goal of expanding its own trade. If African traders could not deal in slaves, a more lucrative business, they would opt for palm oil, which Britain needed. British officials would also remove local leaders based on their involvement in the slave industry.[44]

Another important factor was that competition among European nations over African territory was intensifying. In 1884, negotiations began in Berlin among the major European powers – the so-called Berlin Conference – that would stretch into the next year and reach decisions on how to divvy up the continent among them. Judging from the results, one could mistakenly believe that the Europeans must not have realised that ancient, functioning societies existed in the locations that they were carving up on paper. They of course knew better.

Britain's punitive expeditions in today's Nigeria to end slavery as well as bring local chiefs and kingdoms in line with the Empire's will would have devastating consequences. Perhaps the worst example occurred in 1897, when an overwhelming British force of some 1,500 men was sent to the kingdom of Benin, centred in part of what is today's south-western Nigeria. A dispute had arisen over trade as well as the kingdom's continued use of human sacrifice and slavery. After a treaty was signed covering those three issues, a British party sought to visit the kingdom to ensure the treaty was being followed. When it drew near, the king's messengers informed them that it was not an appropriate time to visit and that they must turn back. Fighting erupted and resulted in a massacre on the British side, with six from the British party killed including the protectorate's acting consul-general along with most of the 200 or so African troops travelling with them. In response, the force of 1,500 was sent to Benin's capital, Gwato, and reduced it to ashes. As the historian Michael Crowder has noted, the punitive expedition 'marked the end of one of the greatest and most colourful of West African kingdoms'.[45] One legacy of the assault can be found today in far-away London. Many of the now-famous Benin brass plaques, produced by skilled artisans in the kingdom in the sixteenth century, were carted off. Some remain on display in the British Museum.

Despite the presence of the British, the Sokoto Caliphate founded by Usman Dan Fodio remained in power, but it would soon fall. Lugard would be the driving force, having been appointed high commissioner of the newly formed British protectorate of northern Nigeria in 1900. In one letter to his brother in February of that year, he talks of the beauty of the site of his house in Jebba on the River Niger. He was writing from Lokoja, at the confluence of the Niger and Benue rivers in central Nigeria, located south-east of Jebba, and the protectorate's administrative capital at the time. He expressed pride in the progress he had made so far in setting up an administration in the new protectorate despite battling through illness. He wrote to his brother Edward:

> Personally I have a house on a most exquisite site at Jebba – a superb view. I have had furniture sent out, enormous cases of writing tables, folding tables, sofas, armchairs, Almiras, wardrobes, marble wash-stands, chests of drawers, settees, & chairs of rosewood, &c, ice machines, huge sets of china (120 dinner plates &c), & of glass and electro-plate – carpets, utensils, every mortal thing, as furniture of Govt. House – had to have a small room enlarged to hold it – looks very well now, & I've dined 6 guests every Wednesday. So I really feel a start has been made even in so short a time.[46]

Lugard and Goldie, the two men who would be, for better or worse, largely responsible for the creation of modern-day Nigeria, had also become friends, and they exchanged letters about their struggles as well as more personal anecdotes. In one letter from July 1900, Goldie, who had struggled over the death of his wife two years earlier, seemed in better spirits, having just returned from a trip to China. His Royal Niger Company had been bought out by the British government at the start of the year in 1900 to make way for the new protectorates, and his work in West Africa would be all but done.[47] 'I believe I have reached a plane of stoicism (not hard heartedness) from which nothing can dislodge me', wrote a 54-year-old Goldie. 'I have a few friends (you among the chief) and I want no more.'[48]

As for Lugard, he had struck up a relationship with a well-regarded journalist named Flora Shaw. She had travelled extensively, and she suggested in her writings that Britain's territories along the River Niger in West Africa be given the name Nigeria.[49] In 1902, she and Lugard married.

Within a few years, Lugard's efforts to bring northern Nigeria – all of the Sokoto Caliphate as well as the remnants of the Bornu Empire – under one administration were coming to a head. He had been carrying out his version of 'indirect rule', the idea, also used elsewhere, that the British would govern through the local authorities, meaning the emirs and the existing structure of the caliphate, though they would have the final word on all matters. He had decided on such an arrangement mainly because the British did not have nearly enough people on the ground to even come close to effectively governing a region as large as northern Nigeria, though he also spoke of his desire not to interfere in religious beliefs and of instituting reforms gradually.[50]

While the caliphate's Islamic ideals may have been severely compromised in its final years, with its later leaders far less attached to the vision of the Shehu, the state itself appeared to remain in somewhat functioning order.[51] Lugard would, however, argue otherwise when he later pushed for a military assault in his correspondence with the Colonial Office in London. He also acted with a firm hand when he believed it was necessary, replacing non-compliant emirs from a combination of humanitarian concerns and hard-nosed practicality. The humanitarian aspect involved the continued use of slave raiding and attacks on other communities by certain emirs, which Lugard insisted must end. But those reasons often seemed to mix with a more simple desire to install someone willing to cooperate with Lugard on his terms.

By 1902, much of the region had been subdued, but the main leaders of the caliphate had no intention of giving up control to the Christians. A series of controversial letters between Lugard and the caliph showed the dicey diplomacy being engaged in by both sides. One in particular would become the subject of debate in later years, with doubts since raised over whether it had been badly misinterpreted or misrepresented – a vital point, since Lugard used it when arguing in favour of the raid that would lead to the caliphate's downfall.[52] It was said to have come from the caliph at the time, Abdurrahman, who had earlier been informed in letters from Lugard that he was replacing the emirs of Bida and Kontagora, which were part of the caliphate.

'From us to you. I do not consent that any one from you should ever dwell with us', read a British translation from its original Arabic into English of the letter received in May 1902. 'I will never agree with you. I will have nothing ever to do with you. Between us and you there are no dealings except as between Mussulmans and Unbelievers ("Kafiri") War, as God Almighty has enjoined on us. There is no power or strength save in God on high. This with salutations.'[53]

Later that year, in October 1902, the murder of a British officer named Captain Moloney in Keffi set off a final chain of events leading to an assault on Kano. The murderer was the Magaji – a high-ranking official there – though the circumstances of what happened have been in dispute. The Magaji then took refuge in Kano, where the emir welcomed him, all but inviting a firm response from the British. In convincing the British government of the need for military action, Lugard quoted from the caliph's hostile letter as a way of responding 'to the strong feeling which you inform me exists in England that Military Operations should if possible be avoided, and the desirability of conciliatory measures'. After quoting the letter, he wrote that 'to send a messenger to Kano would probably be tantamount to condemning him to death and courting insult myself'. Lugard then wrote in striking language of what he clearly saw as the righteousness of the British campaign, literally labelling it a mission ordained by God, and spoke of the noble goal of wiping out slavery and barbaric punishments. He also argued that the Fulani rulers of the caliphate had come to be seen as oppressors by Hausa commoners and brutal slave masters.

> The advocates of conciliation at any price who protest against Military Operations in Northern Nigeria appear to forget that their nation has assumed before God and the civilised world the responsibility of maintaining peace and good order in the area declared as a British Protectorate and that the towns of Kano and Sokoto are ruled by an alien race who buy and sell the people of the country in large public slave markets daily, these being now – thanks to the British rule – the last remaining centres of this traffic. That methods of cruelty involving a complete disregard for human suffering are daily practised. Underground dungeons in which men are placed and left to starve, public mutilation in the market places, bribery in the so-called Courts, oppression and extortion in the whole scheme of rule. The Military Operations so much deprecated have, in the great cities of Bida, of Kontagora, of Yola, of Bautshi, of Illorin, of Zaria and elsewhere led to the suppression of these things, while the Fulani caste, though aliens, have been re-instated and treated with honour and consideration. The bulk of the population is on our side, those who oppose us are their oppressors. The task upon which I am employed is one of prevention of the daily bloodshed which has already denuded this country of probably half its population and even the suppression of the forces of tyranny and unrest has been achieved with almost no bloodshed at all.[54]

Lugard laid out his strategy ahead of the assault, telling the Colonial Office that he did not expect significant resistance in Kano and would not need further troops. After taking Kano, the soldiers were then to travel through Katsina on their way to Sokoto. The plan was to send a letter to Katsina ahead of the deployment's arrival which was, according to Lugard, 'conciliatory in tone'. It would, however, state that the emir had been uncooperative and 'the time has come when Government must declare its Sovereignty and assert its right to send Officials without molestation to any place within the Protectorate'. A similar letter would be sent to Sokoto, but would also state that the late caliph – who had recently died – had ignored the treaty made with the Royal Niger Company. 'Both letters contain strong assurances that it is not my intention to interfere in any way whatever with the Mohammedan religion or the position of the Sultan of Sokoto as the Head of the Faith', Lugard wrote. He then again wrote of the Fulani rulers as brutal dictators and returned to his insistence that the British mission was just and noble.

> The Fulani race are aliens to the country whose population they have oppressed. Their power has become effete and their rule has degenerated in most places into a tyranny. They recognise themselves that their day is past [...] At this crucial moment the task of setting up the Pax Britannica in the country was assigned to me. My policy has been to retain the Fulani as a ruling caste, but to transfer to the Government the Suzerainty which they claimed by right of conquest involving as it does the ultimate right to the Land and Minerals of Nigeria.[55]

The stage was then set for the British deployment under Colonel T.L.N. Morland, whose expedition left Zaria for Kano on 29 January 1903. It included nearly 800 troops from the West African Frontier Force – African soldiers led by British officers – as well as four Maxims, the machine guns that gave the British such an advantage in firepower.[56] They would not face much resistance. On the way to Kano, the company would have to fight its way through the town of Bebeji, blasting through the gate and leaving the king, two chiefs and some 30 others dead. When they reached Kano, they encountered earthen walls and fortifications surrounding the city so imposing that Lugard would later write that he had 'never seen, nor even imagined, anything like it in Africa'. Parts of it were 30 to 50 feet high and 40 feet thick. The walls themselves were testimony to the ancient civilisation in Kano, with construction having begun on them in the eleventh century.[57] Morland was not able to enter at the so-called Zaria gate, so he moved to the next one, which his men blasted through, then stormed the town, killing about 300 of the emir's soldiers. The emir himself was said to have fled to Sokoto about a month earlier. A letter was sent to the caliph in Sokoto from Morland seeking to explain the reasons for the British expedition, but stating bluntly that they were there to stay.

> After salutations know that the cause of our fighting with Aliu [the emir of Kano] is that Aliu received with honour Magaji, the murderer of a white man, when he came to Kano, and that he also sought war between us. For those two reasons we fought him and are now sitting in his house.
>
> We are coming to Sokoto and from this time and for ever a white man and soldiers will sit down in the Sokoto country. We have prepared for war because Abdu Sarikin Muslimin [the late caliph] said there was nothing between us but war. But we do not want war unless you yourself seek war. If you receive us in peace, we will not enter your house, we will not harm you or any of your people.
>
> If you desire to become our friend you must not receive the Magaji. More, we desire you to seek him with your utmost endeavour and place him in our hands.
>
> If you are loyal to us, you will remain in your position as Sarikin Muslimin, fear not.

If you desire to be loyal to us, it is advisable for you that
you should send your big messenger to meet us at Kaura (or
on whatever road we follow). Then he will return to you with
all our words.

My present to you is five pieces of brocade.[58]

The caliph responded with his own letter saying he would
have to discuss the situation with his councillors. Lugard felt the
response to be 'evasive', and the expedition, some of whose soldiers
were by then suffering from lung sickness as a result of the dusty
Harmattan wind, moved toward Sokoto, joining up with another
party of about 200 troops along the way in Argungu. When they
arrived, they were met by around 4,500 Sokoto fighters, including
some 1,500 on horseback. Lugard wrote later that 'the Sokoto army
contained many fanatics, who charged our square in ones and twos,
and courted certain death, but except for these the resistance shown
was feeble, and the whole army was soon in full flight, pursued by
our mounted infantry'. He put the Sokoto army's death toll at 70
dead and 200 wounded, while the British side had one killed and
one wounded.[59]

The conquest of the proud Sokoto Caliphate was at hand, and
Lugard would arrive in the city on 19 March 1903. The caliph had
fled and intended to make it to Mecca, with thousands eventually
following him on his journey. A British force caught up with him
at Burmi near the River Gongola and, according to Lugard, 'was
opposed (on July 27th) with great determination and fanaticism.
The town was taken after a fight which lasted till dusk, and about
700 of the enemy were killed, including the ex-sultan and most
of the chiefs.' The man who had murdered Captain Moloney, the
Magaji, also died there. The ex-emir of Kano, Aliyu, had travelled
north 'disguised as a salt merchant', but was captured by the local
authorities in Gobir. He was sent further south, where he was given
a place to live and an allowance.[60]

Lugard addressed the remaining elders in Sokoto on 20 March 1903, instructing them to decide on a recommendation for who would be the new sultan. He told them 'there will be no interference with your religion'. The following day, he spoke plainly about the British now being in charge, saying 'the treaty was killed by you yourselves and not by me'. Lugard said:

> The Fulani in old times under Dan Fodio conquered this country. They took the right to rule over it, to levy taxes, to depose kings and to create kings. They in turn have by defeat lost their rule which has come into the hands of the British. All these things which I have said the Fulani by conquest took the right to do now pass to the British. Every Sultan and Emir and the principal officers of State will be appointed by the High Commissioner throughout all this country.[61]

It was not the end of the resistance the British would face in northern Nigeria, with a number of uprisings occurring in later years led by Muslim Mahdists, who believed the world would soon end and that it would be preceded by the coming of a redeemer, or the Mahdi. The uprisings, however, sometimes had little to do with religion and saw criminals or runaway slaves take advantage of such beliefs to whip up anti-establishment sentiment. That was the case in Satiru near Sokoto in 1906, the site of a particularly brutal uprising against the British. A man named Dan Makafo, described by Lugard as 'an outlaw from French territory', seems to have persuaded the son of a leader of a previous such movement to become head of a new uprising. When the acting British Resident for Sokoto received word of what was occurring, he rode to the village with a mounted infantry company. According to Lugard, the mission was aimed at negotiating a peaceful solution, but 'a series of mistakes were made, which ended in a complete disaster'.

Upon reaching Satiru, the Resident moved ahead of the rest of the company and shouted that he had come in peace, but the commander of the troops became concerned and rode forward to catch up. The movement prompted those gathered at Satiru to charge against the company while the resident and his entourage remained unprotected. 'The horses took fright, and a general melee ensued', Lugard wrote. The acting resident was killed along with the assistant resident and the commander of the troops and 25 soldiers. The medical officer on the mission later provided a detailed description of what they had encountered after they had arrived on a ridge and the village with a 'good number of huts' came into view. After the confusion and the charge by those in the village, hand-to-hand fighting broke out.

'I managed to catch a horse and was going to mount when some men ran at me', read an account provided by the medical officer, Martin F. Ellis:

> One killed my horse with a spear, and a second one I shot with my revolver. The third lunged at me with a spear and stuck it in my right shoulder. A trooper Moma Wurrikin then came up and shot the man who wounded me and then caught me a horse and lifted me into the saddle. The same trooper then rushed cross to [assistant resident] Mr. Scott who had got free from the enemy for a few moments but could not catch his horse which had broken loose, caught the horse and gave him it and then mounted his own. On Mr. Scott trying to mount, a man thrust at him and knocked him back off the horse, and he was then attacked by several men on the ground. Sergeant Gosling then came up from the right and helped me to keep in my saddle assisted by Private Arzika Sokoto and afterwards put on a tourniquet and stop the artery bleeding. As I was quite unable to mount Moma Wurrikin undoubtedly saved my life and tried his best to save Mr. Scott's, shooting at the enemy as he went to and fro.[62]

The incident left the British stunned, and Lugard would leave little doubt about how he intended to deal with such violence. He sent a company of troops to wipe out the uprising.

'The enemy made several brave charges, and resisted the troops hand to hand in the village', wrote Lugard, but they were no match for the British forces. 'The village of Satiru was razed to the ground, and the Serikin Muslimin (sultan of Sokoto) pronounced a curse upon anyone who should again rebuild it or till its fields.'

The local authorities, including the sultan of Sokoto, had remained loyal to the British throughout. 'It is permissible to call these people "rebels", for they were fighting not merely against the British suzerainty, but against the native Administration, and the Sultan of Sokoto was at one time in great fear lest his own city might be carried away by the infection', Lugard wrote in his annual report.[63] More than a century later, when Boko Haram would target Nigeria's traditional rulers as part of its insurgency – including an assassination attempt on the revered emir of Kano – Lugard's description would echo in a familiar way.

*   *   *

The Satiru uprising would be among the last challenges Lugard would face before leaving Nigeria, a dozen years after embarking on the Borgu expedition for Goldie's Royal Nigeria Company, but he was to return. After a stint in Hong Kong, Lugard was reassigned to Nigeria in 1912 to oversee the amalgamation of the northern and southern protectorates – creating the outline of the country that exists today. The amalgamation officially occurred on New Year's Day 1914, with Lugard as governor-general.

Lugard, like the colonial era itself, can now be judged in the light of history. When writing on the administration of northern Nigeria, he displayed his sweeping intelligence and understanding of the Sokoto Caliphate and the history that led to it. 'We are here the inheritors of a civilization, which ranked high in the world when the British Isles were in a state of barbarism, – a civilization which later, through the Moors, placed Spain in the foremost rank of culture and progress', he wrote in 1905.

> The races of Hausaland have from time immemorial been accustomed to taxation on the lines adopted by modern nations, graduated taxes on property, death duties, ad valorem dues and the like. They have for ages lived under a system of rule through graduated offices and specialised functions in each department of State. The Fulani rulers of today are educated gentlemen, who are fully able to appreciate our ideas of progress, their judges are deeply versed in Mohammedan law and are imbued with the fundamental principle of its impartiality.[64]

Yet, despite such understanding, he was a man of his era, and the profoundly unjust views that led to colonialism could perhaps be summed up by a brief passage in another letter Lugard wrote in 1908 to a successor in Nigeria. After being informed that one of the colonial officers there 'apparently affects native dress and has married a native', he responded indignantly:

> Webster, you say, has married a black woman! He ought to be cleared out *at once.*[65]

2

'HIS PREACHINGS WERE THINGS THAT PEOPLE COULD IDENTIFY WITH'

It had been nearly a week of violence in July 2009 and Mohammed Yusuf stood shirtless, a bandage on his left arm, a soldier to his right wearing camouflage and a chin-strapped army helmet. Others in the room held up their mobile phones as someone off-camera put questions to him, recording the inglorious end to his violent, short-lived uprising. The most wanted man in Nigeria had been captured, found in his father-in-law's barn. His mosque now sat in ruins.

Yusuf responded calmly and matter-of-factly, though he looked far more haggard than he had only days before, when he sat before a crowd at his mosque, dressed in a white robe and fez-like cap, and denounced the same security forces now surrounding him, stirring the anger of his followers, who shouted 'Allahu Akbar!' in response. He perhaps could have predicted that he would not make it through the day alive, but he gave no hint of it while answering his interrogator's questions.

'We went to your house yesterday. We saw lots of domestic animals; we saw medical facilities; we saw materials [another voice mentions materials for making bombs] that you assemble. What are you going to do with these things?', Yusuf was asked in Hausa.

'As I said, I use these things to protect myself', Yusuf responds.

'To protect yourself – is there no constituted authority to protect you? Is there no constituted authority to protect you?'

'It is the constituted authority that is fighting me.'

'What have you done to warrant authorities going after you?'

'I don't know what I have done. It is because I propagate Islam.'

When the questioner tells Yusuf that he, too, is a Muslim, Yusuf says, 'I don't know the reason why you reject my own Islam.'

'You have said Western education is forbidden?'

'Yes, Western education is forbidden.'[1]

Yusuf had by then become something of a folk hero to his followers and a marked man for the security forces. He was 39 and had been repeatedly arrested, but always found himself later released, welcomed back to his neighbourhood in Maiduguri by adoring crowds. Some described him as a reluctant fighter, content to continue to build his movement by preaching the evils of Western influence, condemning evolution and denying that the Earth is a sphere. Whether or not he had truly been pushed toward violence earlier than he would have liked, he was certainly convinced by the time of his capture, with Maiduguri having been shaken in the days before by gun battles in the streets and a relentlessly brutal military assault in response. Terrified residents fled like refugees. There would be no question of Yusuf's release this time. Amid a crowd of soldiers in a drab room, the interrogator continued his line of questioning. He sought to force Yusuf to explain his opposition to Western education while at the same time embracing other elements of Western culture.

'How is it forbidden? What about the (Western-style) trousers you are wearing?'

'There are several reasons why Western education is forbidden. The trouser is cotton, and cotton is the property of Allah', Yusuf said.

It was the kind of logic that Yusuf had been preaching for years and what brought him increasingly into conflict with his early mentors. For all its obvious flaws, his philosophy and sometimes odd interpretations of the Qur'an appealed to young men in Maiduguri, a city once known as a crossroads and major market as the capital of Borno state, whose reputation for Islamic learning had been widespread. It was now seen as a place whose restless, unemployed youth, corrupt politics and unforgiving poverty had helped induce a violent uprising by a seemingly bizarre religious sect led by Yusuf. His interrogator pushed ahead on the same line of questioning.

'You know Allah urges us to acquire knowledge. There is even the chapter of the Qur'an that makes that clear', he told Yusuf.

'But not the type of knowledge that goes against Islam. Any type of knowledge that contradicts Islam, Allah does not allow you to acquire it. Take magic. Allah has created its knowledge, but He does not allow you to practise it. The path of godlessness is based on knowledge, but Allah has disapproved of that type of knowledge. Astronomy[2] is knowledge; again, Allah has prohibited such knowledge.'

'When they went to your house, they saw computers, other equipment and hospital facilities. Are these things not products of knowledge?'

'These are technological products. Western education is different. Western education is Westernisation.'

'How is it you are eating good food – see how you are looking very healthy. You drive fine cars, you eat good food, you wear fine clothes, but you direct your followers to wear these things [referring to ragged clothing], and then you give them only water and dates, then you tell them to go and sell their property?'

'No, no. It is not like that. Everybody lives according to his means; everybody has his means in his hands. Even you are all of different means. Everybody lives according to his means. Anybody living in affluence, driving a fine car, must have the means to do so.

The other person that does not have those things, he simply does not have the means.'

Yusuf could have simply refused to answer, declined to participate in a debate with a man from the Nigerian security forces, whose members had just gunned down his followers and destroyed his mosque. He instead responded in detail, seeking to convince his doubters. It is worth asking whether Yusuf assumed the recording of his interrogation would one day become public.

'Why did you leave the premises of your mosque?'

'The reason is because you have come and dispersed the people staying in the place.'

'You have sent people to fight. As their commander you should have stayed with them.'

'My followers have left.'

'Where did they go to when they left?'

'They have left.'

After more back and forth on where his followers escaped to and questions about the location of his headquarters, Yusuf was asked who was 'assisting' him.

'It is said that you have soldiers, you also have police, you have everything, and you are organised?'

'No, that is not true.'

Asked who his assistant was, he named Abubakar Shekau and added that he did not know where he was.

'You have all run away together with your followers. Where are the remaining people? How many people ran away?'

'It is not everybody who runs.'

'Who are the people who are assisting you internally and externally in the jihad you have declared?'

'There is nobody from outside.'

'No, no.'

'By Allah, I will not lie to you. By Allah, I will not lie to you.'

He was asked whether he had a farm and admitted that he did, then the interrogators questioned him on the violence.

'Now you have caused the death of innocent people because of your views in the community.'

'The people who died are those that you have killed yourselves.'

'What about the killings done by your followers?'

'My followers did not kill people.'

'All those that have been killed?'

'It is my followers who have been killed.'

'Yes?'

'All those who killed them are the real offenders.'

*   *   *

The rise of a man like Mohammed Yusuf in north-eastern Nigeria might seem predictable. The once-proud region and centre of Islamic learning, home to the ancient Kanem-Bornu Empire east of the Sokoto Caliphate that had long ago dominated West Africa, its power resonating into the Arab world, has fallen on hard times more recently. As Nigeria's oil economy led to the neglect of other industries and corruption flourished, the north-east struggled. The region, for so long a crossroads of ideas and trade in the scrubby savannah near Lake Chad and the Sahara desert, trailed much of the rest of the country in education and wealth by the time Yusuf began building his movement. In 2000–1, the north-east had the smallest number of students admitted to Nigerian universities – 4 per cent of the country's total.[3]

The poor state of education in the north has resulted from an array of causes. It is rooted in history, including suspicions over Western education and its purpose, as well as access to proper schools and families unable to afford to send their children to classes. The British colonial administration did manage to establish a certain number of quality schools, but the Christian missionaries who promoted Western education throughout the south during the colonial era were largely denied access to the north. Reasons included resistance from northern Nigerian leaders themselves as well as from Lugard, who argued that the region's culture and religion should be left intact to as great a degree as possible. Qur'anic and Islamic education remain an important part of the culture, and in many cases they can be of high quality, though there have been accusations of fly-by-night schools also existing, provoking concern over whether they are simply churning out roadside beggars and potential extremists. In any case, the dilemma facing northern Nigeria is clear: the days of the region's trade and interests being orientated toward the Arab world have long since passed, and failing to adapt to the reality of today's Nigeria holds obvious dangers. Even now, the outlines of a feudal culture remain in place, with emirs living behind palace walls while hangers-on gather outside. The emirs' power is mainly ceremonial, but in a country where patronage and traditional links play an integral role, they wield important influence. Such influence can be quite positive, with traditional rulers working to mediate conflict and serve as voices of reason, such as efforts toward Muslim–Christian dialogue by the sultan of Sokoto, for example. But the approach of each of the emirs varies, and the potential for abuse of power is evident. They, too, would become targets for Boko Haram, viewed as part of the same elite lacking true Islamic values and which has robbed the country of its riches for so long.

While cultural and historical factors have certainly played a part, it is Nigeria's legendary corruption and mismanagement that have been most responsible for the current condition of the north-east and the country as a whole. Nigerians of all ethnicities and origins have lost any faith they may have once had in their government, justice system and security forces. The bright light of the country's vast potential has been snuffed out by thieves disguised as businessmen, military generals and politicians. It is worth asking whether even the best intentioned leaders could have overcome the daunting challenge left behind by colonialism: a country in name only, with ancient societies and hundreds of different ethnic groups thrown together under one nation state. But that original sin has only been compounded by graft on a scale so enormous it baffles the mind. Consider a few infamous examples among many: 1990s military dictator Sani Abacha, himself a northerner, along with his family looted hundreds of millions of dollars from the Central Bank, even by the truckload, according to one informed account;[4] James Ibori, once the influential governor of the oil-rich Delta state in southern Nigeria, was found to have embezzled possibly more than $250 million, while also allegedly trying to bribe his way out of being investigated with a sack stuffed with $15 million;[5] the theft of Nigerian oil has been estimated at $6 billion per year, with suspicions of involvement by members of the military and high-profile figures.

The list goes on, and all the while tens of millions of Nigerians live in deep poverty, often with little access to electricity or decent roads. The poverty rate stood at around 28 per cent in 1980, but shot up to 66 per cent by 1996, when Abacha was leader.[6] The percentage of the population living in poverty has decreased from the dark days of the Abacha regime, but a World Bank calculation using data from 2009–10 showed 63 per cent of Nigerians were still living on less than $1 per day.[7] Meanwhile, the population has been booming at an incredible rate, with Nigeria projected to grow from its current 170 million people – the highest in Africa – to around 400 million by 2050.[8] One does not need to be a fortune-teller to predict the potential trouble ahead. A World Bank study found that as many as 50 million young people in Nigeria may be unemployed or underemployed, a situation the bank's lead economist for the country told me was 'a time bomb' if not addressed.[9] The Boko Haram insurgency shows the clock is ticking and time is running short.

Nigerian history since independence in 1960 has been replete with struggle and tragedy, while at the same time producing some of the world's most revered artists, including the late writer Chinua Achebe and Africa's first Nobel laureate for literature, Wole Soyinka, as well as the afrobeat musician Fela Kuti. All three stridently criticised Nigerian mismanagement, and Achebe's often-quoted first lines of his 1983 essay *The Trouble with Nigeria* remain true today: 'The trouble with Nigeria is simply and squarely a failure of leadership. There is nothing basically wrong with the Nigerian character.'[10]

The British decision to throw north and south together to create an amalgamated Nigeria in 1914 would set it on a path of becoming the potential giant of Africa, both in terms of its economy and its population. The problem was that it would also lay the groundwork for ethnic, regional and religious divisions that would tie the nation up in power struggles and spark violence, with the question of whether the country should call it quits and break up continually being posed. It is an option that Nigeria's leaders have always ruled out, but the debate roils on nonetheless, renewed regularly by eruptions of the country's many crises.

Nigeria's colonial rulers can certainly be blamed for much of this. Britain's policies toward Nigeria often seemed to exacerbate divisions rather than bring its people together. The north's culture had to a large degree been preserved, while the south was being transformed through Western education, the spread of Christianity and trade along the coast. At first, Lugard sought to extend his version of indirect rule in the north throughout the rest of Nigeria, where it often did not fit. In the Igbo areas of the south-east, for instance, Lugard's blueprint for how indirect rule should work was completely at odds with the local, decentralised form of governance.[11]

At the same time, there were projects put in place to connect the country, particularly through infrastructure. Railways and roads were constructed, allowing people and goods to circulate far more easily, while waterways were dredged to make way for ships. Such infrastructural improvements were built out of self-interest, since they made it easier to ship goods in and out of the country, allowing European companies to take full advantage.[12] But it would also help lead to an economic inter-dependence among various ethnic groups. As the years passed, Igbos from the south-east set up as market-sellers in the north; northern Fulanis and Hausas raised livestock and produce sent to the south. Those are just two examples, and such links have only deepened over time. Nigeria's largest cities, particularly Lagos, are now melting pots of all of the country's ethnic groups, who flock there in search of work. Arguments on behalf of breaking up the country become far more knotty when considered from that perspective. What does a Hausa businessman born in Kano but living in Lagos do if the two cities become capitals of separate nations? The same goes for the Igbo trader from south-eastern Enugu living in Maiduguri in the north-east.

The social, political and economic patterns that would later define modern Nigeria slowly began to take shape after 1914. A lack of Western education in the north caused problems early on. Unlike in Lagos, which had long been a fully fledged colony and where an elite section of the population schooled abroad had begun to develop, or in the south-east, where missionary-established schools dotted the humid landscape, only a relatively small number of northerners had been European-educated. This led to southerners being sent north to work as civil servants, which would feed into fears among northerners that their region would be trampled upon by rival ethnic groups.[13] Such fears would greatly intensify as Nigeria tumbled toward independence, and not only among northerners, though they were more apprehensive than others.

The drive toward independence was led mainly by educated elites from Lagos, including Herbert Macaulay, as early as the 1920s, followed by the Nigerian Youth Movement. It came at a time when other African colonies were also seeking to break away from their colonial masters and with global opinion turning against imperialism, pushing Britain to cooperate.[14] Economic factors also played a role, among a list of other reasons, with the cost of maintaining the British Empire becoming too heavy a burden to justify.

It is impossible to understand modern-day Nigeria without considering its ethnic and regional divisions. Seeing the potential trouble ahead, much of the debate in formulating the Nigerian state in the run-up to independence and afterwards has centred on how to divide power. In the years before independence, models were put forward that ranged from being strongly centralised to a collection of regions. Those in favour of a more centralised government argued that citizens should first consider themselves Nigerians instead of Igbos, Yorubas, Hausas or Fulanis, and the state must reflect that goal. Others said such a goal was unrealistic and the vast differences between the regions must be taken into account and accommodated.[15] A form of that debate continues today, with those who believe the presidency must be rotated between regions every couple of terms and others who believe the country has moved beyond ethnic politics, that the best candidate should win, regardless of background.

In the north, trepidation over how it would fare under an independent Nigeria could be seen in its reluctant embrace of self-rule. The final version of the constitution just before Nigeria's independence locked in place a federal system with three regions: west, east and north. The east and west were more eager to break away from the British and run their own affairs, and both regions opted for self-rule in 1957. The north, however, delayed the move until 1959, a year before fully fledged independence for Nigeria.[16]

The British withdrawal left behind a newly independent nation in 1960 with the same federal system of government. Traditional rulers remained in place, including the emirs in the north, and though they had no formal powers, they continued to wield influence in all manner of decisions, from appointments and the distribution of public money to behind-the-scenes negotiations to settle disputes. They also served as living links to Nigeria's pre-colonial past and continue to do so today. The sultan of Sokoto remains Nigeria's highest Muslim spiritual figure, and emirs are symbols of the region's Islamic traditions, but the Sufi traditionalism and established authority they represent would put them at odds with more radical, anti-

Western clerics who would begin to emerge in the 1970s, often aligned with Wahhabi-Salafi thought, with financing from Saudi Arabia promoting its spread globally.[17] For Boko Haram decades later, the emirs would come to be seen as enemies and betrayers of the extremists' version of the Islamic faith. Some would be targeted in assassination attempts.

Ahmadu Bello, the great-great grandson of Usman Dan Fodio and a vigilant protector of northern interests, was the northern region's first premier, taking office in 1954. He argued forcefully that the emirs must be maintained and given important roles in the north, contending that they would act in accordance with local government and not as overlords. 'To remove or endanger this prestige in any way, or even to remove any of their traditional trappings, would be to set the country back for years, and indeed, were such changes to be drastic, it might well need another Lugard to pull things together again', Bello wrote in his autobiography published in 1962. 'We must get away from the idea that they are effete, conservative, and die-hard obstructionists: nothing could be farther from the truth.'[18]

The north was given the most seats in the federal parliament of the three regions, thanks to both its size and population, and elections before independence in 1959 set the stage for Nigeria's post-independence politics. Ahmadu Bello's Northern People's Congress won the greatest number of seats and formed a coalition with the main eastern party, the Igbo-dominated National Council of Nigerian Citizens, which lent the new government at least some semblance of north–south unity.[19] The first prime minister was Tafawa Balewa, a northerner, and he and Bello worked to improve conditions in the north through quotas in the military and government projects aimed at benefiting the region, among other moves. Such programmes added to tensions, angering southerners, who felt cheated.[20] There was also a fledgling oil industry following its discovery in commercial quantities in the Niger Delta in the south in 1956, and it would soon come to dominate the country's economy while also further exacerbating ethnic divisions as a result of disagreements over how to share the wealth.[21]

With those fault lines in place, the run-up to Nigeria's devastating civil war began soon after independence. In 1966, a group of military officers, mainly from the Igbo ethnic group dominant in eastern Nigeria, would attempt a coup and assassinate Prime Minister Balewa. Ahmadu Bello, as well as the premier of the Western region, Samuel Akintola, would also be killed. An army general, Johnson Aguiyi-Ironsi, was installed as leader, but he too was an Igbo and the entire affair came to be seen in the Hausa-Fulani north as a power play by Igbos. A counter-coup would result.

The counter-coup sparked by anger from northern officers occurred about six months later and brought to power Lieutenant-Colonel Yakubu Gowon, a Christian from ethnically mixed central Nigeria. The country remained on edge, however, and the bitterness resulted in massacres of Igbos living in the north. As a result of such killings and other factors, south-eastern Nigeria decided on 30 May 1967 to secede from the country and form the new Republic of Biafra, named for the bight off the West African coast. It was led by Odumegwu Ojukwu, an Oxford-educated army officer who would become a hero to many in the south-east, his thick beard and intense eyes giving him the air of a revolutionary. The country's government led by Gowon would not accept such a move, especially considering control of vast oil reserves was at stake, and war began in 1967. The rest of the world's attention was gradually drawn to Biafra as images of starving children haunted TV screens and the pages of newspapers. Many died from starvation as a result of a blockade, prompting harsh criticism against the Nigerian side, but also of Ojukwu over his refusal to surrender even when defeat became apparent, a position he defended by saying that an attempted 'genocide' of Igbos was underway and he had to do all he could to stop it. In 1970, with the Nigerian military charging ahead and the Biafran cause essentially lost, Ojukwu was forced to flee to Ivory Coast. Gowon declared a policy of 'no victor, no vanquished' and Nigeria would remain one nation, but in reality the country was deeply divided. By the end of the so-called Biafran war, an estimated 1–3 million people had died.[22]

In an interview 30 years after the war with journalist Peter Cunliffe-Jones, Ojukwu, who died in 2011, defended his actions, saying 'the war was a tragedy, but it was inevitable, unavoidable'. He said that 'the Igbos had no choice. It was a fight for the survival of the Igbo people against plans to wipe out a generation. That was the issue that we faced: genocide.'[23] The tragedy of the war was poignantly depicted decades later by the Nigerian writer Chimamanda Ngozi Adichie in her novel *Half of a Yellow Sun*, while Chinua Achebe would also write of his experience at the time in his memoir *There Was a Country*.

Gowon would lead the country into the 1970s, a period that would give rise to many of the afflictions that have kept Nigeria from realising its enormous potential. While corruption had certainly existed in Nigeria previously, an explosion in oil revenue in the early part of the decade greatly raised the stakes, caused inflation to skyrocket and led industry not linked to petroleum to be ignored.[24] Gowon also dragged his feet on returning the country to civilian rule, and by 1975, some members of the military had had enough. Their response was perhaps unsurprising: another coup. General Murtala Mohammed, from Kano in the north, was installed as head of state and pledged reforms – only to be assassinated about six months later. His deputy, the civil war general and future two-term president Olusegun Obasanjo, a Yoruba from the south-west but with close links to his northern military colleagues and politicians, would take over until elections could be organised.

Obasanjo oversaw a transition to civilian government, with 1979 elections won by a former finance minister from the north named Shehu Shagari. A new constitution was put in place ahead of the elections changing Nigeria's system of governance over to a US-style democracy, with a president, vice president and national assembly, and renewed efforts were made to develop political parties that were broad-based instead of representing only one region or ethnic group.[25] But Shagari became president with the country still wallowing in severe economic troubles, and the situation was only to become worse. When the bottom fell out of the petroleum industry with the so-called oil glut of the 1980s, Nigeria was left utterly unprepared. The country had badly overextended itself in terms of spending, and Shagari's government splurged on projects that benefited cronies.[26]

Civilian rule under Shagari would last a mere four years. On New Year's Eve 1983, Muhammadu Buhari, a military officer with rigid ideas about how to run his country, would come to power with yet another coup. He, too, would seek to reform Nigeria, but his approach was short-sighted. He sought to instil a sense of discipline in Nigerians, as if the frantic scramble to survive in the country was a cause and not an effect of mismanagement at the top. He labelled this effort the War on Indiscipline, and it ranged from petty concerns, such as forcing Nigerians to stand in line properly, to more serious measures, including public executions for alleged criminals. The infamous tale of Umaru Dikko, transport minister under the Shagari regime before the coup, served as an illustration of the approach by the Buhari administration. Suspected of major corruption, he fled to London, where Nigeria's government tracked him with the help of Israeli agents. He was drugged and stuffed in a crate for shipment back to Nigeria to face corruption charges, but the British authorities discovered the plan and stopped it from being carried out to completion. The box was opened at the airport, and inside was an unconscious Dikko with the doctor who had drugged him.[27]

Patience ran thin with Buhari and his narrow-minded authoritarianism, and another power-hungry military officer would see to it that his days as Nigeria's leader were numbered. This time, however, the officer who would lead the coup and later the nation, Ibrahim Babangida, was a far more sophisticated politician, and he would manoeuvre to remain as head of state for eight years, from 1985 to 1993. He was a civil war veteran and one of the plotters of the coup that ousted Gowon, and would oversee the final transition of the nation's capital from Lagos to Abuja, along with the lucrative contracts that went with it.[28] He would gain the nickname 'Maradona', with Nigerians comparing his shifty political and survival instincts to the great Argentine footballer's nimble play. Wole Soyinka, the Nobel prize-winning Nigerian writer who personally knew Babangida but kept him at an arm's distance, wrote of him:

> Nettled by a seemingly consensual and persistent view in the media that he was evil at heart and in intent, he finally retorted that if he was indeed evil, he was at least an evil genius [...] Suave, calculating, a persuasive listener and conciliator but with sheathed claws at the ready – ever ready to cultivate potential allies, he had a reputation for meticulous planning.[29]

Unfortunately for Babangida, even his formidable skills at outsmarting his opponents were no match for the circumstances in which Nigeria found itself. With the economy in tatters and the country drowning in debt, he had little choice but to submit Nigeria to a rigorous regime of cuts and financial policies. The plan, the Structural Adjustment Programme, allowed Nigeria to reschedule its debt, but it was deeply unpopular, leading to cuts in government jobs and increases in fuel prices, to name two examples.[30]

Other issues added to public anger toward Babangida. The 1986 assassination of journalist Dele Giwa by letter bomb led to suspicions that his regime may have been involved – he has firmly denied it – while the transition to new elections and a planned return to democracy was tortuous and repeatedly delayed. After banning all 13 political parties that applied to participate, claiming they were not 'national' enough amid other concerns, Babangida's regime eventually created two artificial groupings, the Social Democratic Party and the National Republican Convention, that would be the only ones eligible.[31] It was a discouraging start to what was supposed to have been Nigeria's new era of democracy, but the election itself in 1993 would turn out to be far more promising. Election day exceeded expectations, and even today Nigerians speak of the polls as the cleanest in their country's history. Moshood Abiola, a wealthy Yoruba businessman from the south-west, appeared set to be the next president of Nigeria. While he had been pilloried years earlier in a song by Fela Kuti, there was little doubt that he had won the vote and was the choice of the people. The problem would come afterwards, when Babangida would overplay his hand. He decided to annul the vote for a list of reasons that few took seriously, denying Abiola the presidency. His move sparked outrage, particularly in Lagos, where street protests broke out and mobs set up roadblocks.[32] Babangida was finally forced to yield, and he installed a transitional government under the direction of his ally Ernest Shonekan. It would turn out to be a move that would have disastrous consequences for the years ahead.

Less than three months later, a military officer who had served as Babangida's deputy took advantage of the weak Shonekan and ousted him from power, installing himself as leader and beginning perhaps the most despicable period of Nigeria's post-independence history. Sani Abacha, a northerner from Kano, set about enriching himself and his family by looting hundreds of millions of dollars from the treasury, trampling on the basic rights of the population and overseeing a brutal military and police force. Nigerians suffered daily from his rule, and Wole Soyinka, who has described Abacha as a 'psychopath', was forced to flee into exile out of fears for his life.[33] Moshood Abiola, the winner of the 1993 election, was jailed a year after the annulled vote after declaring himself president.[34] The regime's execution in 1995 of the Niger Delta activist Ken Saro-Wiwa along with eight others put Abacha's outrageous behaviour in the international spotlight. Leaders worldwide, including the revered Nelson Mandela, condemned the executions and the Commonwealth suspended Nigeria's membership. Nevertheless, Nigeria would have to live with Abacha for another three years. He died in 1998 in suspicious circumstances, supposedly having had a heart attack. Rumours swirled and continue to do so today, including whether he was in the company of Indian prostitutes at the time he died.[35] In Lagos, there were celebrations to mark his death.

With Abacha gone, years of military rule and turmoil would finally draw to a close. All three military rulers since Buhari's New Year's Eve 1983 coup had come from the country's north, but it had meant little in terms of progress for the average northern Nigerian, not to mention the country as a whole. The nation's elite were siphoning off vast amounts of oil money and leaving the poor and working class to scrap for what remained. Nuhu Ribadu, who would later serve as head of the country's anti-graft agency, estimated in 2006 that more than $380 billion had been stolen or wasted since independence – an amount greater than the total gross domestic product of a long list of countries, including Colombia, Iran, South Africa and Denmark.[36]

A transition to civilian rule was on the way, and this time it would not be annulled. That did not mean, however, that Nigeria was on the cusp of a new era of true democracy. There would be elections, but they would be marred by fraud and violence, and the corruption that had become so entrenched would continue to strangle hopes of progress. The 1999 vote led to a return of Olusegun Obasanjo, the former general and one-time military ruler from south-western Nigeria with extensive connections in the north. Election day was largely peaceful, but observers reported serious allegations of fraud, including ballot-box stuffing and altered results.[37] Obasanjo had run as the candidate of the newly created Peoples Democratic Party, which would become an all-encompassing, nationwide behemoth with a multitude of competing interests. The party would essentially develop into a coalition of influential politicians, kingmakers and regional strongmen agreeing to line up under one banner to control power, with the understanding that the presidency would be rotated between north and south.

Obasanjo would be re-elected to a second term in 2003, again amid voter fraud allegations from observers,[38] and his two terms delivered decidedly uneven results, with significant economic improvements, but a failure to tackle many of the problems plaguing Nigeria's development. The prospect of a return to the bad old days of strongman rule was also raised with a push for a constitutional change that would have allowed him to seek a third term of office.[39] The bid was denied by members of parliament, and Obasanjo stepped down after his two terms, clearing the way for a third straight election – at the time, the longest period of uninterrupted civilian rule since independence.

Meanwhile, the government had been collecting billions in oil revenue, prompting deep resentment in the Niger Delta region in the south, the heart of the country's petroleum industry. Obasanjo would face a militancy in the Niger Delta that would eventually cut deeply into revenue from the nation's prized resource.

The Delta had seen unrest before, particularly when protests and violence in the Ogoni community had led the oil giant Shell to abandon production there in 1993. The region remained desperately poor despite its natural resources, while its creeks and rivers had also been badly polluted by years of spills, often without any repercussions for the companies responsible. The Ogoni movement in the 1990s for a fairer distribution of resources had to a large degree been led by the activist and writer Ken Saro-Wiwa, whose execution by the Abacha regime drew global condemnation. Shell would be accused of collaborating with the regime in the executions of Saro-Wiwa and his fellow protest leaders, an allegation it has always denied. It agreed to pay some $15.5 million in compensation in a lawsuit related to the executions and Ogoniland unrest in 2009, but did not admit guilt.[40]

When frustrations again boiled over in the Delta in the late 1990s and 2000s, the militancy would develop into a mix of many interests, including gang leaders seeking a slice of industry revenue, jobless youths and genuine activists. Pipelines were regularly blown up and foreign oil workers were kidnapped for ransom, resulting in a sharp reduction in Nigeria's oil production. An umbrella group took shape named MEND – the Movement for the Emancipation of the Niger Delta – that claimed responsibility for attacks and advocated for the region in statements emailed to journalists. Military raids had little permanent effect on the worsening militancy, and Obasanjo would leave behind a festering crisis in the Delta. With so much oil revenue at stake, it would be up to his successor, Umaru Yar'Adua, to find a solution.

In 2009, an amnesty programme was launched for Delta militants, offering stipends and job training to those who agreed to give up their arms. All of the major gang leaders and thousands of their followers participated, leading to a steep reduction in violence and allowing production to rise to previous levels of around 2 million barrels per day. But while the amnesty succeeded in its goal of boosting oil production, conditions in the delta have not changed and the possibility of a return to violence once payments to gang leaders are reduced or stopped altogether remains a serious concern. Indeed, certain gang leaders are reputed to have been made extremely wealthy by the amnesty and related deals, having not only collected stipends from the programme, but also lucrative contracts for 'pipeline surveillance' or 'waterways security'. It has also reinforced the idea that those who create problems in Nigeria can be paid to stop, providing an incentive for people with little hope of otherwise finding their way out of poverty.

Nevertheless, because it has calmed the violence, the Niger Delta amnesty programme has been cited by some as an example of what could be done in the north-east to bring at least a temporary end to Boko Haram's insurgency and halt the horrific attacks that have killed thousands. Unfortunately, the problem is far more complicated.

*   *   *

Mohammed Yusuf is believed to have been born in 1970 in Jakusko in Yobe state in north-eastern Nigeria, where the savannah begins to fade into desert. His family origins are something of a mystery, though those who were familiar with him and others who have investigated his movements say his parents seemed to have been poor, perhaps subsistence farmers. He eventually found his way to Maiduguri, the capital of Borno state and the most important city in the region.[41]

It was in Maiduguri where an influential trader, Baba Fugu Mohammed, would act as something of a foster parent to Yusuf. They were from the same ethnic background – they were Kanuris, the largest ethnic group in Borno state – and Mohammed had a reputation for taking people in at his large compound. He had amassed his wealth mainly through dealings in agricultural products such as gum arabic and beans.[42] He engaged in regular legal battles with the authorities and others over land rights when they sought to encroach on his property, and his lawyer, Anayo Adibe, said some of his cases were among those taught at his law school.

Yusuf, according to his own account, did not have any formal Western education.[43] He eventually married one of Mohammed's daughters, who was one of several wives and, by some accounts, the most prominent since she was the daughter of his foster-father. He would worship at Maiduguri's Indimi mosque, an impressive structure with stained glass, marble tiling and two minarets, situated in a relatively upscale district of the city and named for the wealthy businessman who financed it. It was at Indimi where Yusuf is believed to have encountered a cleric in the Wahhabi-Salafist tradition named Ja'far Mahmud Adam, who was widely known as Sheikh Ja'far.

The cleric was based in Kano several hundred miles away, but sometimes visited Maiduguri and Indimi to preach. His strong critique of Nigeria's establishment Sufi Muslims gained him a following in the north. The bespectacled cleric was well versed in Islamic studies, a graduate of the Islamic University in Medina, but was not averse to Western-style education and attended secular schools while growing up. He was influenced by Nigeria's Izala[44] Islamic reform movement, an organisation that grew out of the teachings of another cleric, Abubakar Gumi, in the 1960s and 1970s. It would become powerful and attract a number of highly educated Muslims, but the emergence of a new generation and various ideological disputes eventually led it to fracture. Adam was one of several bright, younger figures to strike out on their own.[45]

Amid such turbulent change in northern Nigeria, a populist movement in the 1970s and 1980s that was far less intellectually driven would also emerge, led by an itinerant preacher originally from Cameroon but based in Kano. It would spark deadly riots and serve as a prelude to the later rise of Boko Haram. It became known as the Maitatsine movement, the Hausa name given to its leader, Muhammadu Marwa, and which translates roughly to 'The Anathematiser' or 'the one who damns'.[46] He had declared himself a prophet and interpreted the Qur'an in odd ways, and the movement was driven in part by class and ethnicity, with Marwa a non-Hausa in an area where Hausas dominated. Those factors combined with the hangover from an oil boom in the 1970s, which brought about an economy utterly dominated by the petroleum industry and the corruption that came with it. Initial riots broke out in 1980 in Kano and killed more than 4,000 people, with Marwa also left dead. Rioting in other locations in subsequent years would kill several thousand more.[47]

Debates over Islamic sharia law also occurred when a new constitution was being debated in the late 1970s. There were already local sharia courts dealing with civil matters and personal status law, but a push from some in the north sought the creation of a federal sharia appeals court and led to a bitter dispute between Christians and Muslims hashing out the new constitution.[48] The issue arose again after the 1999 return to civilian rule, with northern states moving to incorporate sharia criminal law. It was a combination of political opportunism on the part of local politicians as well as sincere campaigning by Islamic reformers. Today, sharia law is official policy across most of northern Nigeria at varying levels, though it is selectively enforced. While a number of people have been sentenced to death by stoning for crimes including adultery, it seems such sentences have all been overturned or reduced later. At least two amputations have been carried out, with a man convicted of stealing a cow having his hand cut off in 2000 and another for the theft of bicycles.[49] More recently, after Nigeria's federal government enacted a law outlawing homosexuality in 2014, sharia authorities in the north carried out a witch-hunt, resulting in a number of people being flogged for being gay, with some protesters demanding that they be stoned to death.[50] Both the new law and the action by the sharia courts have drawn international outrage.

In a sign of the tensions that had been building by the early 2000s, a comment in a newspaper column helped lead to rioting in the northern city of Kaduna that killed around 250 people. The column had suggested that the Prophet Muhammad would have been happy to have selected a wife from a Miss World pageant that was to be held in Nigeria. Many saw the column as blasphemous, exacerbating already existing ethnic and religious divisions in Kaduna.[51]

Mohammed Yusuf came of age within this ferment. Crudely educated but evidently curious, he would become a student of the more learned and disciplined Sheikh Ja'far, who was about a decade older. Some have called him his 'intern' or protégé, and one imam has said that Adam had labelled him the 'leader of young people'.[52] It seems, however, that their master–student relationship was always doomed. Adam, at least publicly, was a much more practical man, advocating for Muslims to work within the system to bring change. Rather than opposing Western-style education, he instead argued that Muslims must be equipped with such knowledge in order to be in a better position to face their opponents and transform society. He also did not believe Muslims should refuse to accept positions within a secular government since doing so would leave them powerless and dominated by non-believers.[53] Yusuf would turn out to be far more radical on both of those points, plus a range of others, and that would set the two men on a collision course. They seemed to have split by around 2003, and the beginnings of what would later become known as Boko Haram were emerging.

It was that year when another radical named Mohammed Ali, said to be a Borno native who may have studied in Saudi Arabia, led a group of young people who had been followers of Yusuf on an imitation of the Prophet Mohammad's withdrawal to Medina, or hijra.[54] Ali and Yusuf had fallen out for unclear reasons. The group set up a camp in a remote part of Yobe called Kanamma, and by one account, it included 50 to 60 members who lived in tents and mud huts. Other accounts put the number at as many as 200. As described in a US diplomatic cable, they were said to have initially been unarmed, trading peacefully with local residents, but a dispute erupted when a local chief insisted they pay for fishing rights at a pond. Locals then demanded that the group leave the area, and the police were said to have arrested some of them on 20 December 2003. Less than two weeks later, on 31 December, the group launched a series of attacks on police stations, stealing weapons along the way, including at least five AK-47s from police in Kanamma.[55] The wave of violence lasted four days, and Ali was said to have been among those killed in the unrest. More attacks would occur in September 2004 in Borno state, leading to a clash with soldiers near the border with Cameroon. It was also around this time when a certain number of Nigerian extremists would seek training in northern Mali with the group that would later become known as Al-Qaeda in the Islamic Maghreb.

It is unclear whether Yusuf played any role in the violence at
the time and he would later deny it. In any case, he was already
known to the authorities through his preaching in Maiduguri and
was suspected of being involved. In a 2006 interview with two
of my AFP colleagues, Yusuf said that he had not advocated the
2003–4 violence. 'These youths studied the Qur'an with me and
with others', Yusuf would say, referring to the group that left for
Kanamma:

> Afterwards, they wanted to leave the town, which they
> thought impure, and head for the bush, believing that
> Muslims who do not share their ideology are infidels [...]
> I think that an Islamic system of government should be
> established in Nigeria, and if possible all over the world, but
> through dialogue.[56]

The group began to be known as the Nigerian Taliban around
the time of the 2003–4 attacks. There were claims that the name
was given to them by local officials because they had called their
camp in Kanamma 'Afghanistan', though that story has been
disputed and different versions have been offered.

Yusuf would again perform the hajj in Mecca in 2004; he would
himself say that he travelled to Saudi Arabia for pilgrimage in 2000,
2002, 2003 and 2004.[57] His return home this time, however, was
delayed because he was wanted back home over the Nigerian
Taliban violence. A negotiation would be required to allow him to
fly back, and the then deputy governor of Borno state would step
in to mediate. The deputy governor, Adamu Dibal, would say later
that Yusuf approached him in Saudi Arabia, where Dibal had been
leading a pilgrimage, and asked for assistance in getting home,
telling him that he was non-violent and had been wrongly accused.
Dibal reasoned that intelligence officers could gain important
information from Yusuf if he were back in Nigeria.

'Through my discussions with him [...] and through my contacts with the security agencies, he was allowed back in', Dibal said in a 2009 interview with Reuters news agency.[58] 'It is true he was brilliant. He had this kind of monopoly in convincing the youth about the Holy Qur'an and Islam.'

It was apparently not the only meeting Yusuf would have during his extended stay in Saudi Arabia. Another important discussion would occur in which Yusuf would be confronted by his old master. Sheikh Ja'far Adam and several others met with Yusuf to try to convince him to renounce his radical beliefs. During the meeting in Saudi Arabia, Yusuf is said to have promised to change his ways and tell his followers he had been wrong. He would return home in 2005, but would not keep his promise to Adam.[59]

Back in Nigeria, Yusuf had become isolated from more mainstream Muslim leaders, having been kicked out of Indimi mosque after angering its hierarchy. Members of Indimi were reluctant to speak in detail about Yusuf during my two visits there out of fear of retaliation by Boko Haram, as well as not wanting to be associated with the notorious sect leader, though they have provided a general idea of what led to his expulsion. In October 2013, I spoke to a small group of men gathered in a room at the back of the mosque, including one who identified himself as an imam. Dressed in loose-fitting robes and wearing no shoes in accordance with Muslim tradition as they sat casually on the floor, they recalled that Yusuf had been there around 2002 and 2003.

'He was trying to mislead people', said one of the men, adding that he attended the mosque at the time and remembered seeing Yusuf. 'He was saying that, automatically, people must leave Western education. He was emphasising that anything in government is bad, that any uniformed man should not be accepted.'

During a brief visit three years earlier in 2010, a security worker at the mosque told me that elders there had tried to convince Yusuf to follow a different path. 'We did all we could', the 65-year-old said. 'Muslim clerics had spoken with him [about his views].'

* * *

Yusuf started his own mosque by at first preaching in a makeshift set-up outside his home before using his father-in-law's land to build his own complex nearby in the Maiduguri neighbourhood known as Railway Quarters.[60] While it was widely known simply as the Markaz – Arabic for centre – Yusuf named it after Ibn Taymiyyah, the Islamic cleric born in the thirteenth century in Mesopotamia, in an area that is today part of Turkey. Ibn Taymiyyah's movement sought a more austere form of Islam, as it existed at the time of the Prophet, and his ideas would later have a major influence on Wahabbism and Salafism.[61]

Yusuf's group gradually came to be known as 'Boko Haram', not necessarily by its members, but by local residents and the news media who picked up on the idea that its leader was opposed to Western education. The most commonly accepted translation of the Hausa-language phrase is 'Western education is forbidden', though it can have wider meanings as well.[62] The group would eventually refer to itself as Jama'atu Ahlus Sunnah Lid Da'awati Wal Jihad, or People Committed to the Prophet's Teachings for Propagation and Jihad.

While Yusuf became notorious for opposing Western education, his underlying beliefs and the reasons why he attracted followers were somewhat more nuanced. His knowledge of the Qur'an and Islamic learning were believed to be sufficient, and he certainly knew enough to win over and preach convincingly to a small army of recruits. He felt that British colonialism and the creation of Nigeria had imposed an un-Islamic way of life on Muslims through all the various layers of a modern state – Western schools, a Western legal system, Western democracy, and on and on. He advocated the development of an Islamic state where Muslim principles and sharia law would be obeyed, and denounced northern Nigeria's traditional leaders, including the sultan of Sokoto, the country's highest Muslim spiritual figure.[63] He is said to have expressed similar such ideas in a book he wrote, apparently all in Arabic.[64]

Whether he specifically emulated Usman Dan Fodio, the nineteenth-century jihad leader in what is today northern Nigeria, is up for debate. One Nigerian journalist who knew him contends that he did, saying Yusuf spoke of returning the lands of Dan Fodio's Sokoto Caliphate to what he perceived as their former Islamic glory. Others are not so sure, saying Dan Fodio did not seem to feature prominently in his sermons. Some also point to ethnic differences, since Dan Fodio was Fulani while Yusuf was Kanuri. It is clear, however, that Yusuf admired a number of hardline clerics from elsewhere, as his decision to name his mosque for Ibn Taymiyyah and his references to various texts showed. His teachings were in line with Salafist thought, and those who have studied him label him as such.

He was a fundamentalist in the strictest sense of the word, believing very literally in all of what he took away from the Qur'an. He seems to have lacked, if not the capacity, then at least the will for metaphorical understanding and a practical approach to his beliefs. Like many other extremist leaders, he took verses of the Qur'an and the teachings of the Prophet out of context and bent them to fit his arguments. Describing Yusuf's thoughts on education according to his sermons, an academic who analysed his rhetoric, based on dozens of recorded sermons, wrote:

> Following the common understanding of the Hausa word 'boko', Yusuf understood it to mean modern secular education brought to Nigeria by the British colonial administration, including agriculture, biology, chemistry, engineering, geography, medicine, physics, and the English language. For Yusuf it was haram for Muslims to acquire, accept, learn, or believe any aspects of these subjects that contradicted the Qur'an and Sunna, while all other aspects that supported or did not contradict the Qur'an and Sunna were halal

(i.e., religiously permissible) for Muslims. In addition, Yusuf condemned the Nigerian educational system as ḥaram because it mixed men and women in the same classrooms.

His theories outside of education included an insistence that the world was flat.

Yusuf argued that the geographical conception of how rains occur contradicts Qur'an 23:18, where Allah says: 'And we sent down water from the sky according to (due) measure, and we caused it to soak into the soil; and we certainly are able to drain it off (with ease)'. He also quoted a Hadith that says that whenever it rained the Prophet Muhammad would go outside and touch the rain because it was fresh – i.e., created anew by God. He stated that the geographical idea that the earth is spherical is a mere research finding that is void because it contradicts the clear text (naṣṣ) of the Qur'an – but without mentioning chapter and verse.[65]

Yusuf would espouse similar views during a 2009 interview with the BBC, whose Hausa-language broadcasts are widely listened to across northern Nigeria. In the interview, he would also dispute the theory of evolution.

'There are prominent Islamic preachers who have seen and understood that the present Western-style education is mixed with issues that run contrary to our beliefs in Islam', he was quoted as saying. 'Like rain. We believe it is a creation of God rather than an evaporation caused by the sun that condenses and becomes rain. Like saying the world is a sphere. If it runs contrary to the teachings of Allah, we reject it. We also reject the theory of Darwinism.'[66]

Yusuf may have lacked the learning of Sheikh Ja'far and other Nigerian Muslim leaders, but his charisma and ability to win over followers was not in doubt. Judged from videos of him, his chubby face and inviting speaking style gave him the air of a kind older brother who knew something you did not and was willing to help you by sharing it. He was able to attract followers both through his charisma and because hopelessness among the region's young men made them open to hearing his call. He painted an image of his followers standing firm in the midst of an evil world, with him as the enlightened leader – a cult of personality in many ways. While he may not have always directly spoken about government corruption, he was certainly anti-establishment and his attacks on Nigeria's secular and traditional authorities were set against the backdrop of crushing poverty that were the everyday reality of his followers. Strict sharia law may seem like a promising option to those in such circumstances.

Even some non-Muslims found themselves agreeing with what they interpreted as Yusuf's anti-government rhetoric. Anayo Adibe, the lawyer for Yusuf's father-in-law Baba Fugu Mohammed and a Christian born in Lagos, was living in Maiduguri at the time, running his law practice. He would meet regularly with Mohammed at his home and would sometimes cross paths with Yusuf, though he said they did not know each other and never had conversations. He was, however, familiar with some of his preachings, or at least second-hand versions of it, with talk of his rise having spread throughout Maiduguri. He said he understood Yusuf's anti-government sentiment since corruption was, and remains, maddening, though he stressed he did not support his decision to pursue violence.

'Even myself, I agreed with him – completely', the 41-year-old Adibe, thin and bald-headed with a grey-flecked goatee, told me one afternoon at his bare-bones law office in Abuja, where he moved after the situation became too tense in Maiduguri. As we spoke, there was no electricity in his office thanks to another of Nigeria's repeated power cuts. The windows were open and the sound of horns bleating outside on Abuja's roads occasionally echoed into the building. Adibe, his voice calm but insistent, explained further: 'Because his preachings were usually against the ruling class, and you don't need any special kind of education, or even come close to him, to agree with him, particularly when you consider the level of poverty in the land at that time. His preachings were [...] things that people could identify with.'

Kyari Mohammed, who has closely followed Boko Haram as head of the Centre for Peace and Security Studies at Modibbo Adama University in Nigeria, held a similar view. For him, Yusuf's crusade against Western influence resonated in Maiduguri and elsewhere because all many young people in north-eastern Nigeria know of Western-style democracy is what they have been subjected to: elites filling their pockets while the masses of poor struggle to survive.

There were of course other factors that helped feed Yusuf's movement. One was political thuggery, with politicians in the north-east, like their counterparts in the Niger Delta in the south, using local gangs to intimidate opponents and rig elections. Once elections ended and politicians stopped paying them off, the 'militias', bitter over being abandoned, were said to have joined with Yusuf. One politician who has come under particular scrutiny over the issue is Ali Modu Sheriff, the former governor of Borno state. Ahead of the 2003 elections, he was a member of the Senate, becoming Borno governor after the April 2003 polls and serving for two terms. Sheriff has been accused of using and abandoning thugs who went by the name ECOMOG – co-opting the name of a West African military force – and as a result contributing to the development of Boko Haram. He has repeatedly denied the allegations. A Nigerian government committee appointed to look into the Boko Haram crisis described the problem in detail, as highlighted in a White Paper produced from its findings.

'The report traced the origin of private militias in Borno state in particular, of which Boko Haram is an offshoot, to politicians who set them up in the run-up to the 2003 general elections', the White Paper drafted by a panel headed by Interior Minister Abba Moro said, according to an account by Nigeria's *Sunday Trust* newspaper.

The militias were allegedly armed and used extensively as political thugs. After the elections and having achieved their primary purpose, the politicians left the militias to their fate since they could not continue funding and keeping them employed. With no visible means of sustenance, some of the militias gravitated towards religious extremism, the type offered by Mohammed Yusuf.[67]

There have also been allegations that Sheriff promised he would institute strict sharia law in order to gain the backing of Boko Haram followers in the 2003 vote before later reneging.[68] In 2014, with elections months away, the ex-governor would again be accused of financing elements of Boko Haram by an Australian mediator seeking the release of more than 200 kidnapped schoolgirls. The mediator, Stephen Davis, also accused a former army chief of staff of sponsoring the insurgents. Both men forcefully denied the accusations.[69]

Another factor some argue helped supply Yusuf with followers involved the young Qur'anic students known as almajiris, who travel from rural areas to study under Islamic teachers in cities and towns, including Maiduguri. The system has long been in existence and has been described as producing promising students in line with tradition – Usman Dan Fodio was himself a travelling scholar, for example. But it has been criticised more recently as unadapted to the modern world, without enough supervision of schools and their teachers. There have been allegations of families in northern Nigeria too poor to care for their children on their own sending them to live at schools that sometimes amount to little more than shacks, with the students then sent begging on the streets for alms. However, many caution against blaming almajiris for the rise of Boko Haram, and they are correct in saying that no one is sure whether they constituted a significant number of Yusuf's followers. Nevertheless, the government panel on Boko Haram called for the almajiri schooling system to be modernised since it may be producing young people susceptible to becoming extremists.[70]

The number of followers Yusuf had has never been authoritatively determined, though a military estimate said there were 4,000 in 2009 at the time of his uprising.[71] The government White Paper said most members were poor and aimless young people, though the military has claimed that earlier on it included educated adherents such as university professors and civil servants. Borders in the north-east are porous, and it is certainly not out of the question that young men from Chad, Niger or Cameroon were also part of the movement, but attempts by some to blame the problem on foreigners have never been backed up with proof.

'The sect draws the bulk of its membership from [motorcycle taxi drivers] and the vast army of unemployed youths, school drop-outs, and drug addicts that abound in the affected areas', the government White Paper said. It added that 'the federal, state and local governments should as a matter of priority, initiate and design appropriate measures for mass economic empowerment. To this end, the federal and state governments should immediately address the issue of unemployment in the face of the large number of jobless youths in northeast zone.'[72]

While there were more than enough rudderless young men in Maiduguri and its surroundings for Boko Haram to draw from, Yusuf's movement required more than just members. He also needed money, and determining where he received it from has long been one of Nigeria's great parlour games and the impetus for grand conspiracy theories, including from those who suspected Yusuf of acting on behalf of powerful politicians. It is important to distinguish between Boko Haram under Yusuf and its re-emergence after his death, when such questions would become far more complicated and suspicions over links to foreign groups would deepen.

First, a significant amount of its financing under Yusuf is believed to have come from members themselves, including those encouraged to sell their goods and property and commit to the cause. It is not unreasonable to suggest that the group also provided some form of welfare assistance to its particularly impoverished members, with the Nigerian state failing to supply any basic level of social programmes or safety net, and that this could have strengthened Yusuf's standing among the poor.[73]

One specific instance that has given rise to conspiracy theories involved a high-profile member named Buji Foi, a former Borno state commissioner for religious affairs under Sheriff who later became a Boko Haram member. Foi was suspected of financing the group, and some have sought to link Sheriff, the former Borno governor, to Boko Haram through him, alleging that the governor funnelled money to Yusuf through his commissioner.[74] Sheriff, again, has always denied this, and Foi was killed in 2009 following the uprising. A shaky video purportedly showing police summarily executing him was posted online.[75] 'Buji Foi was a politician [...] And he was out of my cabinet two years before the Boko Haram crisis and, if I would be held responsible for anything done by anybody who served in my cabinet, then nobody can govern any state in Nigeria', Sheriff told local journalists in 2011.[76]

Beyond Nigeria, there have been claims of Osama bin Laden supplying seed money to Boko Haram in its early years through intermediaries. It should be stressed, however, that such claims are questionable and no proof has ever been offered for them.[77] Bin Laden, however, did in 2003 name Nigeria as one of several countries ready for 'liberation'.[78]

In 2012, allegations also emerged in Britain and Nigeria that Boko Haram had benefited from money from a London-based Islamic charity named as the Al-Muntada Trust Fund. An inquiry by Britain's Charity Commission found no organisation by that name, but it did locate an Al Muntada Al-Islami Trust. The commission turned up no evidence of such activity, and the Trust has strongly denied it.[79]

With or without prominent backing, Yusuf was able to build a formidable movement, with recordings of his sermons being sold in the markets and circulated among sympathisers. The police repeatedly arrested him, but he does not appear to have ever been convicted of a crime. The government White Paper noted two occasions when a court in Abuja discharged him and followers welcomed him home in celebration. It said that 'the reception accorded him upon his return to Maiduguri attracted a mammoth crowd that temporarily undermined state authority, and served as an avenue for him to attract additional membership into the sect'.[80] He also participated in debates where he defended his beliefs and interpretations of the Qur'an. The academic who studied his recorded sermons quoted him as saying in one such debate: 'The system of modern education that the Europeans brought to Nigeria contradicts Islamic faith. I am not the first to say so for earlier scholars like Ibn Taymiyyah as well as modern scholars of Islam have also said so.' The academic then paraphrased Yusuf: 'When asked whether he had studied in schools, he responded that he never even attended primary school, and that he obtained his information about modern subjects from the British encyclopedia.'[81]

Adam became increasingly frustrated with Yusuf and publicly questioned his teachings, seeking to point out what he saw as his former student's hypocrisy. In particularly scathing comments, Adam sought to portray Yusuf as a dilettante misleading his followers with potentially dangerous consequences. He said:

> You are not a prophet. You have not yet proven your faith or moral character to your neighbours. If it took Prophet Muhammad 23 years preaching Islam, for how many years have you preached before you decided to judge Muslims as unbelievers because they have Western education or because they work for the government? You did not have sufficient religious knowledge, or even enough general knowledge. You only know your little town. What do you know about the history of various struggles for Islam?

[...] Nearer to home, how many battles did Usman Dan Fodio fight? Apart from Fodio's name, what do you know about his battles? In how many battles did he participate in the fighting? [...] Above all, right now, what plans do you have?

Adam would also paint Yusuf as a hypocrite.

He has an international passport to travel. Does the passport contain quotations from the Qur'an or Hadith? Does it open, 'In Name of God, the merciful and compassionate?' Does it have God's Greatest Name? Or does it say Federal Republic of Nigeria, and bear the image of Nigeria's coat of arms? Who gave him the passport? Was it not the authorities of the Nigerian government? Why did he accept it? Does that not indicate his acceptance of the government? He could have said, 'I do not accept Nigerian government. It is worthless and any paper it issues is equally worthless'. He could have travelled to Saudi Arabia without his Nigerian passport. When asked, 'Where is your passport? Where is your visa?' He could have said, 'Saudi Arabia is a Muslim country. I am a Muslim. I believe there is no god but Allah and Prophet Muhammad is his Messenger' [...] He took his wife to a government hospital [...] and he rides on a road constructed by the government with revenues from usury, taxes collected from alcohol manufacturers and from petroleum, mixed all together to pay for road construction. Still, he uses water and electricity produced by government agencies. So he refused to enter the government through the door but gets in through the window.[82]

Worries grew over the intentions of Yusuf and his followers, and the intelligence and security agencies would say later that they were keeping an eye on them. A well-known Salafist cleric in Nigeria,

Sheikh Muhammad Awwal Adam Albani, claimed he met with Yusuf to counsel him on his misguided beliefs, while Adam was said to have had a series of meetings with him for the same purpose in addition to their encounter in Saudi Arabia.

'I was one of those who constantly talked to him about the ideology of Boko Haram', Albani told Nigeria's *Sunday Trust* newspaper in an interview published in January 2012.

> On some occasions, I sat with him with his students, and [on] other occasions, only two of us sat. The essence was to convince him that Islam doesn't accept the ideology of Boko Haram. I tried to convince him that since he claimed to be the follower of Sunna, therefore Sunna has its teachings and principles, and the idea of Boko Haram is contrary to those teachings. All our efforts, because I know other scholars like late Sheikh Ja'far also engaged him on such issues, fell on deaf ears. He proffered some defenses, which are not authentic in the jurisprudence of Islam.[83]

In 2007, as Adam led dawn prayers in Kano, gunmen stormed the Dorayi Juma'at Mosque and shot him dead. Suspicions have remained that Yusuf acted against his former master and was behind the murder of the man who once mentored him. There have also been allegations of political motives for the killing as the murder occurred a day before governorship elections, with presidential polls set for the following week. Albani, too, would be murdered along with his wife and son years later in February 2014, with Boko Haram members also suspected.

* * *

The march towards a violent uprising by Yusuf and his followers moved ahead, and a number of his recorded lectures and sermons reflecting his militant rhetoric can still be found on the Internet and elsewhere. In one of his sermons, he portrays himself and his followers as in a struggle together against the evil of the world and the Nigerian state. He tells them to be ready for when the authorities come to abuse them based on their Islamic beliefs and says 'do not leave your weapons behind'.[84]

The date of the recording is not clear, though Yusuf references both the Abu Ghraib detainee controversy in Iraq, which became public in 2004, as well as the Prophet Muhammad cartoons published in September 2005 that led to protests across the Arab world. During the speech, Yusuf is dressed in a white robe and traditional cap with followers seated on the floor around him. A scroll with phone numbers runs across the bottom of the screen as well as a notice advertising video and audio.

'Instilling fear in you, arresting you, beating you, killing you or killing someone else, torching the whole lot of you ablaze, tear-gassing you, whatever they will do to you, should not make you abandon your religion', Yusuf says in the Hausa language.

> I swear to Allah it is important to know, for instance, one day out of the sheer hatred they have for you, they will be throwing tear gas at you, because there is the opportunity to do that to you, because they know that you can't do anything. They will round you up and throw tear gas at you together with your children. The children will be coughing. They will do that to even the tiny kids that pass by here, including the toddlers who are strapped on the back of their mothers. I swear to Allah they will do that to you. That is what they are doing in all other countries.

He continues later: 'One day you will see your leader placed on the table being tortured. They will be hitting him with a club and he will be falling and rising up as a result. We know this is going to happen to us. We also know this will not be considered as humiliation, but as a test from Allah. This is the nature of Islamic path. If this is not done, people will not wake up.' At that point, the audience chants 'Allahu Akbar'.

Towards the end of his speech, after referring to the Prophet Muhammad cartoons, he broadens his argument and encourages violence against those who 'insult' Islam. He also, however, tells his followers that they should not burn churches, since the buildings can be used for other purposes 'after the jihad'. Chants of 'Allahu Akbar' also break out a couple times during this part of his speech.

> Once Islam is insulted, just go and fish out the leader of those people and slaughter him. All the individuals involved in the insult should be killed. Why is it so? It is because they are not trustworthy. Allah said if you do that they will desist from the act. Allah used a definitive term in the Qur'an here. If you kill even a few from among their leaders, they will stop the insult. I hope it is understood? You should not even bother yourself with burning and destruction of churches because the person who builds the church is still around. You have not done anything by burning churches. That is why it is counterproductive to do things without planning, by just waking up and going to burn a church. No, no! This is not what Islam is teaching. Everything requires careful planning, organisation, leadership, doing the right thing. You must know that when you start moving forward there is no turning back. I hope it is understood? Don't just go and burn churches. After the jihad it can be turned into a storage space. Remove the leaders of unbelievers because they are not trustworthy if you want them to stop insulting your religion.

An incident on 11 June 2009 in the Gwange area of Maiduguri would set off the uprising. It would occur after Boko Haram followers were killed in a traffic accident, with members of the group travelling to the cemetery for the funeral. In one of several different versions of what happened that day, a government committee of inquiry found that Yusuf's followers spotted another Boko Haram member being 'disciplined' by security forces from Operation Flush II task force, originally formed to combat armed robberies and other such crimes. Police often force those they deem guilty of minor infractions to perform frog-jumps on the roadside or other humiliations. Various reports said the run-in occurred when police sought to enforce a new law requiring motorcycle riders to wear helmets. According to the government committee's report, which was obtained by the anonymous scholar who studied Yusuf's sermons, Boko Haram members then tried to 'rescue' the man being detained and steal the police officers' guns, prompting them to open fire. The police officers said they shot only at the legs and did not try to kill them, and the report said 17 Boko Haram members were wounded.[85]

In what would amount to a call for armed jihad, a deeply angered Yusuf would provide a sharply different version. He would appear before his followers and deliver a passionate and fiery speech labelled an 'open letter' to the government. He would lash out at Nigeria's security forces and stir the audience with his forceful denunciations. The crowd repeatedly responded with either jeers at the mention of the Borno state governor's name and others they deemed enemies or loud shouts of 'Allahu Akbar', and Yusuf would stoke their anger. He began calmly, but his voice built at various moments as he pointed and gestured forcefully with his hands. He said that on the previous Thursday, several Boko Haram members were taking four corpses for burial at Gwange cemetery.[86]

'They ran into some Nigerian army members along with mobile policemen belonging to Operation Flush under the leadership of Ali Modu Sheriff, the governor of Borno state', Yusuf said. He continued:

> They opened fire on the procession, and at the moment 18 brothers are in hospital receiving treatment. One was shot in the back. Two bullets were removed in an operation. There

was one who was shot in the groin. A bullet brushed someone close to the eye. If it had moved an inch, he would have been killed. Another one had both his legs battered. Somebody was shot in the thigh [...].

We said that we would not rely on rumours and stories reaching us, which was why we refused to comment yesterday until we went and saw for ourselves. We went and saw them drenched in their blood. They did nothing; they did not insult anyone; they did not commit any crime. But simply out of sheer aggression, which is the hallmark of the government of Borno state, which was the reason why they formed the Operation Flush unit, with the sole aim of creating obstacles to our movement and harassing other residents.

We've been saying that this unit was formed purposely against us and it has now become evident. The blood of a Muslim is precious [...] It's better for the whole world to be destroyed than to spill the blood of a single Muslim. The same way they gunned down our brothers on the way, they will one day come to our gathering and open fire if we allow this to go unchallenged. The way they did this, they will commit terrorist acts against women if they are allowed. We'd rather die than to wait for them to commit aggression against our women or to come to our gathering and humiliate us. You should know we would never keep silent and allow anyone to humiliate us. It's not possible for someone to come and shoot our brothers. We take them to hospital and bear the medical bills while [the shooter] goes home, without giving a damn. It's not possible [...] Mad soldiers. As long as they are not withdrawn from the city, there will be no peace.

The first strike would occur on 26 July in the city of Bauchi, located south of Yusuf's home state of Yobe. An estimated 70 Boko Haram members, armed with guns and grenades, descended on two locations: a police station and a mosque belonging to Izala.

According to one account, police on duty at the station fled, but a larger deployment returned later and managed to keep the attackers from breaking into the armoury. A police raid in response on a shanty town where the Boko Haram members in Bauchi were believed to have lived then set off a gun battle. The death toll was put at 55, with as many as 200 people arrested.[87]

It was only the beginning. After the Bauchi clashes, Yusuf told a reporter by phone that 'we are ready to die together with our brothers'. He called a person killed in Maiduguri in an accidental bomb blast a martyr who was building a weapon in self-defence.

> What I said previously, that we are going to be attacked by the authorities, has manifested itself in Bauchi, where about 40 of our brothers were killed, their mosque and homes burnt down completely, and several others were injured and about a hundred are presently in detention. Therefore, we will not agree with this kind of humiliation. We are ready to die together with our brothers and we would never concede to non-belief in Allah [...].
>
> I will not give myself up. If Allah wishes, they will arrest me. If Allah does not wish, they will never arrest me. But I will never give up myself, not after 37 of my followers are killed in Bauchi. Is it right to kill them? Is it right to shoot human beings? To surrender myself means what they did is right. Therefore, we are ready to fight to die.
>
> The end of this crisis is: kafirci (apostasy) and the kind of harassment my people are facing must stop. Democracy and the current system of education must be changed otherwise this war that is yet to start would continue for long.[88]

Over the course of the next day, police stations in Potiskum in Yusuf's home state of Yobe and in an area of Kano state called Wudil were attacked, while the worst would occur in Maiduguri, where a series of assaults targeted state police headquarters, police training facilities, a prison and two other police stations.[89] Street battles broke out between Boko Haram fighters and police there, with residents taking cover, leaving roads deserted. The attacks, while using mostly basic weapons, nevertheless revealed a level of coordination and capacity that the authorities seem to have underestimated, with violence in four states: Kano, Bauchi, Yobe and Borno.

My AFP colleague Aminu Abubakar, who was in Maiduguri at the time, compared the situation to war. Anayo Adibe, the Maiduguri lawyer for Baba Fugu Mohammed, said it was like being in 'hell'. On the first night, Adibe took cover inside his house with his wife, his seven-year-old daughter and his three-year-old son. The gunfire quieted early the next morning, and when he saw soldiers had taken up positions on the streets, he thought calm had been restored and decided to go into his office.

'While in the office, fighting broke out again', Adibe told me. 'Bomb fire, right at the roundabout. Two policemen were killed by close range, so there was a lot of pandemonium immediately. So I had to close the office.'

He and others from the building waited until the fighting stopped just outside, then he ran for his car and rushed home. He decided he would take refuge at the army barracks, where many Christians living in Maiduguri were relocating out of fear that the extremists would target them. Most were simply setting up makeshift camps outside on the grounds of the barracks, but Adibe had friends in the army and they allowed him and his family to stay with them inside as gunfire echoed through the city.

The fighting roiling the streets of Maiduguri was sporadic, and the breaks in the violence left residents unsure of what was occurring. Adibe and his family remained at the barracks for a couple of days. Conditions began to worsen there since many people did not have adequate food or water, so families began deciding to risk it and return home. Adibe and his family were among them. If you were going to die, 'it was better to die at home', he said. Besides, rumours were circulating that the situation was in fact finally being brought under control. Was it, I asked him? 'No, at that time it wasn't', he said.

Despite the mayhem, there had not appeared at the time to be attacks specifically targeting Christians, with the extremists focusing on retaliating against symbols of the Nigerian state. However, claims have emerged since indicating Christians may have in some instances been killed after being threatened with death and told to convert to Islam. Human Rights Watch, in an October 2012 report, quoted several witnesses who said Christians were abducted and killed, including one woman who told the organisation the attackers slit her husband's throat after he refused to 'do the Muslim prayer'. It is not clear how widespread such killings were and I have not personally come across such accounts in my reporting.[90]

On Tuesday 28 July, the third day of the uprising, the security forces would seek to crush it once and for all – though President Umaru Yar'Adua would stick to his schedule and fly off on a visit to Brazil. Troop reinforcements from the central city of Jos would prepare for a brutal raid on Boko Haram's mosque and headquarters. After gathering at a military barracks, they flooded into the Railway Quarters neighbourhood, arriving, according to one report, in 'six armoured tanks and five military trucks loaded with troops'.[91] Piles of dead bodies and wholesale destruction would result.

The troops would raid Yusuf's mosque and reduce it to rubble, with journalists who were there at the time saying it appeared the military used mortar fire. In the wake of that clash, authorities would also be accused of rounding up young men they suspected of being Boko Haram members, forcing them to kneel down or lie on the ground, then shooting them. In a particularly stomach-churning video, alleged security forces shoot dead a number of young men in that way. Such footage would later be used in Boko Haram propaganda, including in the UN suicide bomber 'martyr' video. One man identified as a Sufi activist, speaking to

US embassy officials at the time, spoke of 'excessive use of force by security agents who alleged[ly] shot motorists and pedestrians "just because they have a beard". "As a result", he said, "residents are shaving their beards and changing the style of their dress to avoid being targeted."'[92] In another video, a man identified as Buji Foi, the former religious affairs commissioner for Borno state and prominent Boko Haram member, can be seen being forced to walk before being shot dead.

Calm finally began to return by Thursday, but by then the toll was shocking. More than 800 people had been killed since Sunday across four states. Yet, somehow, Mohammed Yusuf had managed to survive and escape from his mosque. Soldiers were on his trail though, and they arrested him on 30 July apparently having located him in a barn on his father-in-law's property not far away from the mosque. Before handing him over to police – alive – he would be interrogated as he stood shirtless, defending his beliefs.

Later that day, images of what appeared to be Yusuf's dead body were shown to journalists. They showed a man lifeless in the dirt, his torso riddled with bullet holes. In the hours after Yusuf's death, Nigerian police officials offered at least two different versions of what happened: one claimed that he was shot while he had been trying to escape, another that he was killed in a shoot-out between Boko Haram members and security forces. However, witnesses said that police had carried out a summary execution on the grounds of state police headquarters. Human Rights Watch interviewed a 24-year-old woman who described seeing Yusuf handcuffed and sitting on the ground, saying that they should pray for him, when three enraged policemen opened fire.

'They first shot him in the chest and stomach and another came and shot him in the back of his head', the woman told the rights group on condition of anonymity. 'I was afraid and started running. When I came back, he was dead.'[93]

The US State Department's Country Reports on Terrorism for 2009 provided this account:

The Nigerian military captured Maiduguri-based Boko Haram spiritual leader Mohammed Yusuf alive after a siege of his compound, and turned him over to Maiduguri police, whose colleagues had been killed by the group. A local policeman summarily executed Yusuf in front of the station in full view of onlookers, after parading him before television cameras.

For Yusuf's father-in-law, Baba Fugu Mohammed, the nightmare was not yet over. On Friday morning, 31 July, the day after Yusuf was killed, he contacted his lawyer, Adibe, to say the police had summoned him, asking how he should respond.

'He just said the police were looking for him, so I told him that if the police were looking for him, that he should answer them [...] That was the last time I heard from him', Adibe told me. He said he did not expect that his client's life would be in danger.

At some point later, the old man, believed to be in his seventies, rode to the police station – on the back of a motorcycle taxi, according to what Adibe was told – and never returned. His dead body was later taken to a morgue, a gunshot to his head. His son, Babakura Fugu, went to Adibe's office and showed him a photo of his dead father.

'The morgue attendants recognised his father when they brought his corpse, so with their phone they snapped photographs of the body, which they now gave to the family', Adibe said. 'Everybody was upset, even myself. I was very upset. How could such a thing happen, for a man as old as that? [...] He was almost 80 at the time [...] Just because he was an in-law.'

Without a trial, it was impossible to know if he had ever been guilty of any wrongdoing. The body was never released to the family, likely buried in a mass grave with many others killed over the course of those five days, with no known records saying where. In 2012, his family would be given a measure of justice when the government, after refusing for nearly two years, would finally decide to obey a court ruling ordering it to pay damages for the unlawful death of Baba Fugu Mohammed. They were given a payment of 100 million naira, or about $625,000. His son Babakura would also participate in an attempt at peace talks with Boko Haram. That, too, would end tragically. He would be assassinated over it.

3

'I WILL NOT TOLERATE A BRAWL'

It had been a tumultuous few months in Nigeria, for reasons that had nothing to do with Boko Haram, and the man being asked to lead the country seemed unsure of many things. In his defence, he was by no means the only one. On a Friday in February 2010, as he met with the US ambassador, the fedora-wearing zoologist recently named acting president of Africa's most populous country, Goodluck Jonathan, according to an account in a diplomatic cable, would make a few startling admissions.

The main subject of the meeting was the condition of Umaru Yar'Adua, who, at least on paper, remained Jonathan's boss and the president of the country. He had fallen ill with pericarditis, a heart condition, and had long struggled with a kidney ailment,[1] his weight loss and increasing frailty having become evident despite efforts by his aides to hide his condition from the public. As his illness gradually took hold, he continued to try to carry out his duties, but on a limited schedule. Finally, in November 2009, the president would become so sick that urgent treatment was required, and he was flown abroad to Saudi Arabia.

As the weeks passed, his aides said little about the details of his condition, and Nigeria found itself with essentially no true leader, drifting off in an unpredictable direction, an unsettling state of affairs in a country with a history of military coups. Those surrounding Yar'Adua manoeuvred to keep Jonathan, vice president at the time, from being made head of state. Regional and ethnic politics, as always, played a major role, with politicians from the north, where Yar'Adua was from, reluctant to see the power of the highest office in the land – and the astonishing levels of patronage that go with it – shift to the south, Jonathan's native area. But the longer Yar'Adua remained out of sight and in another country, the more difficult it became for his camp to defend their position. Speculation was rampant. The respected *Next* newspaper reported in January 2010 that he was 'seriously brain damaged' and could no longer carry out his duties.[2] In a bid to refute such reports, the president's advisers arranged a phone call with a BBC reporter in which a man claiming to be Yar'Adua spoke briefly.[3] It resolved nothing, and with the leadership of the country increasingly adrift, Nigeria's parliament finally made Jonathan acting president on 9 February 2010.

The move at least gave the government the illusion of clarity, though it would be short-lived. Two weeks later, on 24 February and about three months after being taken to Saudi Arabia, Yar'Adua would be flown back home, again muddling the picture of who was in charge, though he was kept out of the public eye. It was amid those circumstances that then US Ambassador Robin Sanders met acting president Goodluck Jonathan at his official residence in Abuja.

An account of the meeting in a US diplomatic cable portrayed Jonathan as a man trying to do his best, but struggling to figure out how.[4] He was said to have told her that '"everyone's confused" about who is in charge of Nigeria'. He was described as being upset that the first government statement after Yar'Adua's return home referred to Jonathan as the vice president rather than acting president. He added, according to the cable, that a second statement was issued the next day after the presidency 'received a lot of pressure to correct this error so that the lines of leadership and executive direction were clear'. He was said to have spoken of his belief that 'this terrible situation in the country today has been created by four people', naming Yar'Adua's wife, his chief security officer, his aide-de-camp and his chief economic adviser, implying that they were running the show behind the scenes and refusing to relinquish any power. According to the account in the cable made public by Wikileaks, Jonathan said 'he does not know their motives, but expected it was likely for nefarious purposes'. When Jonathan met with Yar'Adua's chief security officer, Yusuf Mohammed Tilde, and his aide-de-camp, Colonel Mustapha Onoedieva, he was said to have told them that 'the best thing is to stop the charade' since he believed Yar'Adua was semi-comatose and did not understand what was happening. He visited Yar'Adua's wife, Turai, to express his sympathies, but, reflecting the deep mistrust at the highest level of government, 'under no circumstances did he want Turai to come to his official residence'.

Jonathan was described as saying that he and others would seek to persuade those close to Yar'Adua that the best course for the country would be for him to resign. In the meantime, military chiefs were seeking to ensure politicians were not plotting with soldiers in the barracks, considering the risk of a coup. The confusion could even be seen in cabinet meetings, with Jonathan explaining, according to the cable, that the last one before Sanders's visit 'was disastrous and included yelling and screaming', declaring it 'totally dysfunctional'.

'He said he is "not a politician" and had very limited experience as an administrator, but concluded, "I will not tolerate a brawl"', the cable said. He was said to have indicated he planned to dissolve the cabinet and appoint a new one once he felt the public was comfortable with him as acting president.

It had already been a remarkably accidental political career for Jonathan, the son of a canoe maker born in the village of Otuoke in the swampy Niger Delta. He was a slow-moving man who could seem uncomfortable speaking in public, uttering generalities and occasionally fumbling his words. Seeking to portray himself as an everyman in a country where so many live in poverty, he spoke of having no shoes or electricity when he was a boy. He would attend university and study zoology, eventually earning a PhD in the subject, before beginning a career in politics that would seem as fortuitous as his first name. While deputy governor in his home state of Bayelsa, his boss, Diepreye Alamieyeseigha, would become entangled in a corruption probe that led to him fleeing to Britain, allegedly dressed as a woman.[5] Alamieyeseigha denied doing any such thing and refuted the accusations against him, but in any case, he was impeached and forced out of office back home, ushering in Jonathan.

Fortune would soon favour Jonathan again. When Yar'Adua prepared his run for president in the 2007 elections, he would search for a running mate from the Niger Delta, where oil militants had been wreaking havoc on the country's cash cow industry. Jonathan, to his credit, was not blind to this. During his meeting with the US ambassador, he was described as saying that he understood that he was picked to be vice president because he 'represented the Niger Delta'.

'I was not chosen to be vice president because I had good political experience', the diplomatic cable quoted him as saying. 'I did not. There were a lot more qualified people around to be vice president, but that does not mean I am not my own man.'[6]

The world was about to find out. With Yar'Adua dying in May 2010, Goodluck Jonathan, ready or not, would become Nigeria's leader at a crucial time in the country's history. Elections were approaching, the youthful population was becoming more engaged and Islamist extremists in the country's north would re-emerge under his watch with their most violent and sophisticated attacks yet.

* * *

It had been almost a year since the dark days of July 2009, and the insurgents from what everyone now called Boko Haram, at least those who had survived, had gone underground. Mohammed Yusuf's mosque still lay in ruins, an uncleared pile of rubble guarded by policemen who kept people from lingering in the area and refused to allow photos to be taken without prior permission from the authorities. The neighbourhood surrounding it, set back from Maiduguri's main roads, was quiet and calm, almost bucolic. Goats crossed the unused railway tracks that led to an abandoned nearby station. Women and children pedalled bicycles along dusty paths or rode on the backs of motorcycle taxis, the low hum of their engines among the only sounds.

A walk among the rubble of the former mosque provided glimpses of the catastrophe that had occurred there, and in some ways what lay ahead. Concrete had been smashed into jagged chunks and two IV bags hung from a tree, presumably where Boko Haram members sought to treat their wounds. Cars and motorcycles were burnt, and clothes, pots and pans were strewn across the site. It all just sat there as an eerie, macabre reminder of what had happened a year before. No one had bothered to clear it.

The Nigerian security forces stationed in Maiduguri remained on high alert. The local police commissioner finally agreed to meet me and three colleagues in his office during a visit to the city in July 2010, but he refused to say anything during our brief, tense encounter. He warned that even uttering the words 'Boko Haram' was illegal and declined to answer any questions on the subject, making it clear he preferred that we simply leave – both his office and the city. Operatives from the country's main intelligence agency trailed us, at one point telling me and my colleagues we were 'invited' to visit his boss, the euphemism used by Nigerian security forces to summon someone for questioning. It is an invitation one is not allowed to decline. We did as we were told and, after arriving, were asked to sit in a small waiting room. We were nervous since we had no idea what they had planned for us, and the appearance of red splotches on the wall in the room we were waiting in only added to the discomfort – very likely not blood, but, given our mindset at the time, who knew? There were some initial tense moments after we were called in to meet with the local director, but he turned out to be a reasonable man after he learned that we lived in Nigeria and were not parachuting in on a quick visit to the country. We explained that we aimed to do stories on what was happening in Maiduguri one year after the uprising, and we were able to reach an understanding. He allowed us to continue working, albeit under the close scrutiny of his men, and did not object to us taking photos and making video recordings at the site of Yusuf's destroyed mosque. We were followed so frequently by intelligence officers that it became almost farcical. They eventually began speaking casually to us, in a friendly manner. I asked one for a suggestion of where to eat, and he mentioned a place in a nearby shopping centre. I believe I had the chicken and rice. It wasn't bad.

Most officials, much like the police commissioner, declined to say anything at all on the record during that visit, but we did manage to arrange an interview with Borno state's information commissioner at the time, Isa Sanda Beneshiekh. He told us Boko Haram had been defeated and a new requirement that all religious groups must register with the government would help prevent future unrest. 'We are assuring our people [...] and the whole world, that such a situation will never happen again', Beneshiekh said.

Even before the first anniversary of the 2009 uprising and military assault, there were signs that whatever peace had been obtained through the military's brutal crackdown would only be temporary. In the weeks before the anniversary date, video and audio clips began to circulate in northern Nigeria purporting to feature Abubakar Shekau, Yusuf's deputy during the 2009 uprising and its presumed new leader. The police called the footage faked, clinging to their story that Shekau had been killed in the previous year's assault, though they offered no proof and there was no way of knowing the truth at the time.

Mysterious indications later led to suggestions that Boko Haram had restarted its violent campaign, though with a different strategy. The first signs were assassinations of local clerics or members of the security forces, usually involving two men on motorcycles and armed with AK-47s carrying out hit-and-run attacks. It was at first difficult to know what to make of these incidents. While it was reasonable to think that Boko Haram had indeed returned, gangland-style killings could also occur for all sorts of reasons, from shady business dealings to political score settling. There was the real possibility that criminals were taking advantage of the fears stoked by the Islamists as cover to carry out retribution against their rivals since they knew Boko Haram would likely be blamed. This uncertainty would later turn out to be another element of the complex threat posed by a new and stealthier Boko Haram.

An incident in September 2010 served to put aside further doubts that Boko Haram was re-emerging. It occurred in the city of Bauchi, where Yusuf and his followers began their short-lived uprising more than a year before. On a Tuesday evening just before the end of the Muslim holy month of Ramadan, a group of men, heavily armed with AK-47s and what seemed to have been homemade bombs, descended on a prison, chanting 'Allahu Akbar'. They shot at the prison gate and forced their way inside, freeing more than 700 inmates, including about 150 alleged Boko Haram members.[7] It was then clear to many that Boko Haram was back, no matter what the authorities wanted the country to believe.

The pattern of assassinations of local officials, police and clerics that had emerged would continue over the next several months, leaving dozens of people dead. There would also be bank robberies that the group was suspected of using to finance their operations. However, as disturbing as the situation was becoming, the trouble mostly remained concentrated in north-eastern Nigeria, far away from the seat of power in Abuja and a world apart from the bustling and chaotic economic nerve centre of Lagos in the south-west. There were indications that some of the president's political backers in the south saw the insurgency not as an awful symptom of severe poverty, neglect and the absence of faith in government in northern Nigeria, but as a conspiracy. Power brokers from the Niger Delta region would question whether the violence was being sponsored by northern politicians intent on discrediting the president.[8] In making such a case, they were also expressing what some average Nigerians in the south believed. In some ways, it was understandable. Nigeria's do-or-die politics, with so much corrupt money at stake, had led certain politicians over the years to govern as if they were running an organised crime racket. Nigerians may have seemed prepared to explain much of what was happening in their country with conspiracy theories for a simple reason: they often turned out to be true.

This was different, however. It certainly could not be ruled out that some northern politicians had played a role on the margins, as had been alleged with Ali Modu Sheriff, who was governor of Borno state from 2003 to 2011, but Boko Haram was in the process of growing into something far more complex, beyond the control of any politician or traditional ruler. Blaming northern elites for the violence could give the president and his team a convenient excuse for failing to stop it, but it would do nothing to get to the heart of the problem and in fact obscure the root causes, suffocating hopes that the government would act to address them. Such conspiracy arguments would become even harder to defend as the situation spiralled further out of control and Boko Haram's targets widened. Even the northern emirs – meant to be upholders of Muslim tradition in the region – were not spared. One of Boko Haram's most high-profile attacks was an assassination attempt against the emir of Kano, when gunmen opened fire on his convoy in January 2013. He was not hurt, but two of his sons were wounded and at least three people were killed.[9]

Another awful line would be crossed on Christmas Eve 2010, showing how bad the threat was becoming and how much worse it could get. It would demonstrate that Boko Haram had evolved into a more lethal, sophisticated and diffuse force, likely with various cells that operated independently and for their own reasons.

It had been a busy day in Abuja. President Jonathan had hosted a summit of West African leaders to discuss responses to a dangerous political standoff in Ivory Coast, with Laurent Gbagbo at the time refusing to cede power after losing the presidential election to his rival Alassane Ouattara. When it finally broke up and the region's presidents made their way back to their home countries, Nigerians were beginning to celebrate, popping off fireworks as night descended to commemorate Christmas and the upcoming New Year.

In Jos, a major city in Nigeria's ethnically and religiously divided central region, many Christians headed to church, and markets were crowded with shoppers stocking up for the holiday. The city and surrounding region had been deeply torn in recent years by unrest not linked to Boko Haram. It had often been described as religious violence because it opposed Christians and Muslims, though the disputes were really ethnic in nature, sparked by local power struggles, land disputes or cattle theft. Such violence often saw residents shot or hacked to death with machetes and houses set on fire, sparking cycles of attacks and retribution. The last serious outbursts in the region had occurred early that year, in January as well as in March 2010, leaving hundreds dead.[10] The violence on Christmas Eve would, however, involve explosives.

Seven bombs planted at various spots ripped through the city, including at a market busy with Christmas shoppers, killing at least 32 people.[11] On the same evening in Maiduguri, hundreds of miles away, extremists attacked three churches and killed six people. In Jos, where even the slightest spark is capable of setting off ethnic tensions, rioting broke out in the days following, killing dozens more. It was unclear if the attacks in the two different cities were planned together, but the simple fact that they occurred at all were startling enough. Bombs had never before been used in Jos, and churches had not been previously singled out for attacks.

On 28 December, a statement appeared on a website believed to be from Boko Haram claiming credit for both the Jos bombings and the church attacks in Maiduguri. A video was also posted of a man believed to be Abubakar Shekau, Boko Haram's new leader, calling the attacks part of a 'religious war'. In the video he said:

We are the ones who carried out the attack on [...] Jos. We
are the Jama'atu Ahlus-Sunnah Lidda'Awati Wal Jihad that
have been maliciously branded Boko Haram [...] Everybody
knows about the gruesome murders of Muslims in different
parts of Nigeria [...] Jos is a testimony to the gruesome
killings of our Muslim brethren and the abductions of our
women and children whose whereabouts are still unknown
[...] My message to my Muslim brethren is that they should
know that this war is a war between Muslims and infidels.
This is a religious war.[12]

The bombings marked the group's first move out of the north
and into the tinderbox known as the middle belt, as central Nigeria
was often referred to, threatening to inflame the ethnic and religious
tensions that had long haunted the region. It was exactly the kind
of provocation that had so worried those afraid that Nigeria could
again go to war with itself, as it had more than forty years earlier.
Nigeria had repeatedly defied such doomsday predictions, somehow
surviving repeated catastrophes and remaining together as one
nation, however fragile, but escalating the conflict in the middle
belt posed new, unpredictable risks.

There was at first widespread scepticism about whether Boko
Haram was indeed responsible for the Jos bombings. In some ways
it seemed more likely that those involved in the ethnic conflict
in the middle belt would carry out such an attack in Jos, even
though bombs had not been previously used there. The middle-
belt conflict had gradually worsened over the years, from the use
of rudimentary weapons such as sticks and arrows to guns, and
it was certainly plausible that bombs could be the next stage in
the crisis. Another factor that was especially important was that
election season was approaching, and it had long seemed that local
power brokers had exploited the region's tensions and stoked some
of the violence for political gain. In the face of all of that, however,

as time passed and Boko Haram was blamed for more violence in central Nigeria, the group's claim seemed to ring true.

Speculation over the Jos attack would quickly be interrupted. The next bombing would be yet another escalation, not in terms of casualties or scale, but location. It would occur in Abuja, the nation's capital, on New Year's Eve night as crowds gathered in an area known as Abacha Barracks, where an outdoor market and bar were located. Though it was next to a military barracks, it was a popular place for civilians, similar to many other spots across Nigeria where people go to relax, sip Star and Gulder beer and eat grilled fish at tables set up under the stars. The bomb would go off early in the evening, killing at least four people and wounding around 12 others.[13] Nigeria's president spoke of the bombing at a church service the following day, referring to whoever carried it out as 'criminals' being used by 'demons' and employing biblical language to describe the country's struggles. He seemed to hint at political links with elections approaching and politicians from northern Nigeria opposing his candidacy, but his remarks were too vague to interpret.

'Some people say they are politicians, some say they are religious fanatics, but to me they are pure criminals', Jonathan said. He continued:

> They are ones demons are using these days, not only in Nigeria. For those of you who have time to listen to world news on Al-Jazeera or CNN, you will see that terrorism is criss-crossing the whole world. Today, there are two things that are so important and so noticeable – technological developments. Countries, nations, are developing technologically. The next that is pushing these countries backward is terrorism. But I will tell Nigerians, be calm, be stable. If you look at the journey of the Israelites to go to the promised land it was tortuous. A number of them even died along the way [...] These explosives and explosions are part of the road

bumps that are being placed, but God will see us through. They will never stop Nigeria from where we are going to [...] God will help us as a nation that we will get to the root of this matter. I urge Christians to continue to pray that some of these people will even confess to Nigerians, that at the appropriate time they will tell us that they are behind this. But for now, the security people are on it and they will get to the root of this matter.[14]

*   *   *

The election campaign ground ahead. Despite having earlier signalled that he may not run, leaving open the possibility that the north could regain the presidency, Jonathan eventually launched himself into the campaign with the strong backing of his southern political benefactors. This had led to a rift within the Peoples Democratic Party, with northern politicians plotting a way to win the primary and deny Jonathan the nomination for the office he already held. Prominent northerners announced their candidacies, including former military dictator Ibrahim Babangida, the so-called Maradona and evil genius of Nigerian politics. Babangida, who had remained influential despite having left office in 1993, was remembered by much of the country, however, particularly in the south-west, for his cancellation of the 1993 elections. After Babangida announced he was running, posters went up in Abuja with 'June 12, 1993' written on them, reminding everyone of the annulled vote. Other northerners to announce their candidacies for the PDP primary were Atiku Abubakar, who was vice president under Obasanjo and a wealthy ex-customs official invested in sectors ranging from telecommunications to oil; Aliyu Gusau, a former national security adviser and intelligence expert known for his ample connections and behind-the-scenes influence; and Bukola Saraki, the then-governor of Kwara state and scion of an influential family.

The campaign for the nomination largely amounted to a series of negotiations, not to mention the distribution of cash-stuffed envelopes as the 12 January primary drew near.[15] In the end, the party would have to decide whether it would maintain what it called 'zoning', a policy of rotating the presidency between the north and south every two terms, or if it was prepared to abandon it and hand the nomination to Jonathan. As the weeks passed, it became increasingly clear that Jonathan's team was having some success in building support for his case that the country was better off without 'zoning', that such a power-sharing agreement was no longer needed to hold the vast and complex country together, that it had moved beyond ethnic politics. Among the electorate, he seemed to inspire a certain amount of hope – somewhat ironically given his sleepy persona. His unlikely rise and calm demeanour led to the impression that he may be different from the country's dominant politicians who had robbed Nigeria of so much of its wealth over the years. His campaign managers seized on this and sought to capitalise on it, using Jonathan's Facebook page to announce his candidacy and emphasising his family's humble roots. Despite his sometimes fumbling speech and arguments from his opponents that he was ill-prepared, there was a feeling among many in the country that Nigeria had tried strongmen, military men and slick dealmakers, only to be left disappointed. Perhaps it was time for something else.

Meanwhile, as this feeling gained momentum, the northerners who had announced their candidacies and other elite politicians from the region forged ahead with discussions on how to proceed. All of the major northern PDP candidates eventually agreed on a united strategy, though perhaps for their own reasons. Babangida, Gusau and Saraki announced that they would drop out of the race in support of a single northern candidate, Atiku Abubakar, setting up a showdown between him and the president at the party's primary, where thousands of delegates would line up at Eagle Square parade ground in the capital and drop ballots in clear boxes live on national television. Their votes were counted aloud immediately afterwards as the cameras rolled, a process that would not finish until the early hours of the next morning. As the count droned on, it became clear that Jonathan had managed to lock up more than enough delegates, and he would go on to dominate the primary vote.

In a sense, Nigerian history had been made. The PDP had cast aside its rotation policy and nominated a southerner when it was supposed to be the north's turn. Beyond that, Jonathan could also become the first elected president from the oil-producing and impoverished Niger Delta region, and since he was an Ijaw by ethnicity, the first not to be a Yoruba, Hausa-Fulani or Igbo, Nigeria's main ethnic groups. His journey was not yet complete, however. The general election awaited, and it posed a potentially significant challenge to the PDP's grip on the presidency, which the party had controlled since Nigeria ended military rule in 1999. His main opponent, the ex-military dictator Muhammadu Buhari, was a northerner with populist support, based largely on the impression that he was tough on corruption, even though his regime in the 1980s had been accused of major rights abuses.

As election day approached, there was intense focus on preparations and whether or not the polls would be fair this time around. There were high hopes for the academic now heading the electoral commission, Attahiru Jega, a respected intellectual viewed as relatively independent. The presidential election was to be the second of three votes staggered over three weeks, with the parliamentary polls set to be first on 2 April, the presidential vote on 9 April and the state governors' ballot on 16 April. It was going to be a marathon, and with so many uncertainties, there was a feeling of both hope and trepidation in the country. Could Nigeria finally get it right and set itself on a course that would allow it to fulfil its great potential? Or would the election descend into chaos and violence like others before it? The potential for both could be seen during the voter registration process in the weeks leading up to the election. Young and earnest election workers, intent on seeing their country improve, diligently sought to enlist

Nigeria's huge population using an electronic registration system. At the same time, registration centres lacked electricity, sometimes causing them to borrow or rent small generators from residents. When generators were not available, there were delays, and crowds waiting to register grew frustrated. Yet, despite such challenges, the electoral commission announced at the end of the process that 73.5 million people had been registered, and there was reason to see progress in the perseverance showed by both election workers and the public.

But as the first of the three elections opened, Jega ran into trouble straight away. A few hours after the start of the parliamentary election, he was forced to appear on national television and announce what in many countries would have been unthinkable: he was calling it off and suspending the vote by one week because voting materials had failed to arrive at a long list of locations throughout the country. The rumoured and official reasons offered for why the materials had been delayed ranged from sabotage to a simple contractor's error. Whatever the true explanation, Nigeria's bid at holding respectable elections had stumbled badly out of the gate, and Jega would be forced to quickly recover as the nation waited impatiently. There was an initial backlash against him, with many people questioning how he could allow such a disastrous misstep. But as the furore died down and many of those criticising Jega acknowledged the near-impossible task before him, support once again swayed behind him. Election observers and anti-corruption groups expressed their faith in him and judged that he had made the right decision, that an election in such questionable circumstances could never have been called free and fair.

The following week, however, would bring worse news. The Boko Haram violence that had been ignored for so long would strike at the heart of what was hopeful about the election. In the city of Suleija, about 45 miles from Abuja in the country's centre, far away from the restive north-east, a bomb would explode as poll workers gathered at an electoral office on the night before the vote, including young university graduates from the National Youth Service Corps. Thirteen people were killed and dozens of others were wounded.[16] Blame fell on Boko Haram, with security forces later saying a cell of the group based in the area was responsible.

The parliamentary vote would nevertheless go forward as planned, though not in Suleija, where another postponement would occur. There would also be two other, less deadly bomb attacks in Maiduguri on election day, but overall there was a sense of progress, with residents appearing determined to cast their vote.

The following week's presidential election was the main event, and in many ways, the conduct of the vote was being seen as equally important as the actual outcome. Jonathan's government had been promising a free and fair ballot for months, and Western diplomats and good-government groups had also been urging the country's leaders to stick to that commitment. Holding a reasonably fair election would in itself be a major accomplishment for Nigeria and could serve as an example for other African nations given the country's status as the continent's most populous.

Election day opened smoothly in most of the country, but the unrelenting Boko Haram violence would again hit the north, with two explosions in Maiduguri, including one the night before, and one in the city of Kaduna. Casualties were said to be minimal. Sadly, the country had almost come to expect such incidents, and the explosions had no effect on the conduct of the vote in the rest of Nigeria. There were other isolated instances of violence and irregularities, but positive signs emerged as the day progressed. Locally based observer groups deployed motivated young Nigerians, who used mobile phones and social media to record and relay what they saw. Nigerians seemed committed to making a statement, peacefully queuing up and casting their ballots. As polling places closed and counting began, one could not help but feel encouraged by the scenes that unfolded: Nigerians stood by, sometimes in the rain, and recorded the counting process with their phones. That does not mean there were no problems;

there were many. There had been instances of underage voting, intimidation and violence, not to mention allegations of figures being doctored in some areas. What would happen after the ballots were taken away to collating centres would also be another matter, and one that observers would later raise serious concerns over.[17] But despite that, there was the sense that such incidents were far fewer than in previous years. As a result, election day produced a feeling of positivity for many, who felt that finally, after years of chaotic, violent and fraudulent polls, Nigeria had taken a step toward true democracy.

Unfortunately, the positive vibes would not last. As early results began to come in the morning after the vote, a potentially dangerous trend emerged. Initial figures revealed a sharp divide in the electorate between the north and south. As more results were reported, giving Jonathan a clear lead, the violence began. Rioting would break out in neighbourhoods across the north, eventually spreading to 12 of the country's 36 states. It spiralled completely out of control, with communities turning on one another and mobs targeting northern politicians they believed cooperated with Jonathan and his allies. In the city of Kano, mobs stopped cars and searched for southerners and Christians while fighting running battles with the police. They charged into the luxurious home of a former speaker of the House of Representatives, ransacking the inside. The worst violence occurred in southern Kaduna state, part of the middle belt between the country's north and south, where Christian communities turned on Muslim residents, burning homes, hacking people to death with machetes and gunning people down. One official, trying to find words to describe what had happened there, told me, 'I wouldn't like to use the term massacre [...] some places it was terrible'. Despite his reticence to use the word, what occurred in the southern Kaduna communities of Zonkwa and Kafanchan was certainly a massacre. Over the course of three days, an estimated 800 people were killed in the violence across the north, the vast majority in southern Kaduna state. Another 65,000 were displaced.[18]

The following month, I visited the city of Kaduna, the state capital further north and where thousands of displaced had taken refuge in a camp. One woman from Zonkwa, 67-year-old Talle Musa, spoke of hiding in a neighbour's house and her husband being murdered. 'He said whatever happened we should not go out, that we should just be patient', she said. 'We didn't know it was like his farewell to us.' She became faint and backed away, declining to speak further. Others at the camp talked of people being burnt, hacked or shot. One man said he managed to escape by hiding in a well.

Various theories were offered for why the violence occurred and what set it off. Some said rumours of rigging were to blame, while others claimed that the initial incident was the result of a simple dispute over money, with ruling party operatives failing to pay neighbourhood thugs who rounded up votes on their behalf. Whatever the initial cause, it quickly built on itself and became a general expression of frustration on various levels – anger over corruption, the north's loss of the presidency, long-festering communal disputes, to name a few. Nigeria had been once again shown to be a deeply divided country, and the riots led to rising calls for someone – anyone – to stop the violence before it was too late. Jonathan went on national television and made a frightening comparison. 'If anything at all, these acts of mayhem are sad reminders of the events which plunged our country into 30 months of an unfortunate civil war', the president said, evoking the Biafran conflict more than four decades earlier.

At the time of the speech, calm was returning, a large military deployment helping to restore order, but the underlying tensions remained. Jonathan would be sworn in for his first elected term as president amid deep bitterness and resentment in much of the country's north. While election observers called the polls a significant improvement over previous years despite major problems and said they believed Jonathan to be the legitimate winner, many in the north still felt the vote had been stolen.

Some academics and politicians from the north said they were seeing signs of a class war develop since rioters in cities such as Kano went after not only perceived political enemies, but also those believed to be wealthy or corrupt. Tanko Yakasai, a veteran northern politician and power broker, told me in the living room of his home in Kano that he feared something akin to a mass revolt if poverty and unemployment were not addressed. 'People will come to destroy my house', he said. 'Those unemployed youths will just vent out their anger regardless of the consequences, and they will attack anybody who appears to be a well-to-do person.'

The rioting was not caused by the Boko Haram insurgency, but it further exposed the insecurity confronting an inexperienced president and the country he had come to lead through various turns of fate. He would have another reminder after being sworn in for his first elected term under heavy security in Eagle Square in Abuja more than a month after the rioting. In the hours following Jonathan's inauguration, bomb blasts blamed on Boko Haram went off in four separate cities, killing about 20 people.[19]

* * *

It was a common refrain before 2011: Nigerians would never blow themselves up for any cause. They were too individualistic. The country can often feel like a brutally cut-throat place – every man for himself, with extremely difficult, if not impossible, odds for the millions of desperately poor. President Jonathan had apparently also subscribed to a version of this view. Back in February 2010, as ex-US president George W. Bush visited Nigeria, he and former secretary of state Condoleezza Rice met with Jonathan, with part of the discussion touching on the case of the so-called underwear bomber, a Nigerian named Umar Farouk Abdulmutallab, and his attempted bombing on Christmas Day two months earlier, when he sought to set off explosives on a flight into Detroit in the United States. The case had shaken Nigerians, but Abdulmutallab had travelled to Yemen and was believed to have been recruited into

Al-Qaeda in the Arabian Peninsula, so many people back home viewed him as an aberration.

'Jonathan joked that "Nigerians don't want to die" and that suicide bombers like Abdulmutallab possessed "traits alien to the nation", which were usually inculcated from abroad', according to a US diplomatic cable describing the meeting with Jonathan, who was then still acting president. 'He observed that most extremists since September 11 2001, have not come from economically disadvantaged backgrounds and "had stayed in some of the best cities in the world, but received some bad influences while they were there."'[20]

The analysis ignored the deep frustration, desperation and hopelessness among young people in his country, not to mention Nigerians' fervent religious beliefs. Such frustration, coupled with the chance for families to benefit financially and the promise of a better life achieved through martyrdom, would prove to be a recipe for disaster in Nigeria, as it has elsewhere.[21]

So much would change in 2011, when low-grade, homemade explosives and gun battles would give way to a frightening new reality that the Nigerian authorities were utterly unprepared to confront. The insurgents would use new weapons and strategies, selecting targets that seemed meant to deliberately inflame religious and ethnic tensions. There would be signs of an emerging new offshoot that included members with ties to Al-Qaeda's arm in northern Africa and which would seek to imitate foreign jihadist groups. But perhaps worst of all, Boko Haram would begin to use suicide bombers with devastating results.

A first glimpse of what lay ahead occurred in June 2011. In photographs and video later distributed to journalists by purported Boko Haram members and posted to a website which was later taken down, a smiling man holding an AK-47 waved from the driver's seat of a car. He was identified as Mohammed Manga, a 35-year-old with five children who had been a follower of Mohammed Yusuf when the Boko Haram leader was still alive.[22] According to those who distributed the images, he was also Nigeria's first suicide bomber, and the pictures showing him waving goodbye were taken just before his attack.

On 16 June 2011, Manga manoeuvred his car on to the grounds of police headquarters after a convoy that included the national police chief at the time, Hafiz Ringim. It was late morning, about 11 a.m., the building crowded, the car park filled with vehicles. A police warden was said to have intercepted Manga's car and directed it into an area of the car park to undergo an inspection.[23] It was there that the blast would occur, killing Manga, the officer and at least one other person, while destroying rows of cars and leaving a fire blazing in the car park. The police chief's convoy was not hit, and it was not clear why the bomber had not sought to reach the building or whether the explosives had gone off prematurely. There were also suggestions that the bomber had sought to get out of the car before the blast, raising questions over whether it was intended to be a suicide attack. An initial police statement, however, flatly called it a suicide bombing – Nigeria's first – and it has since been generally accepted as being such.

A message had been sent. It seemed Boko Haram was now ready to employ suicide attacks, and one of its 'martyrs' had barely missed either blowing up Nigeria's police headquarters or killing the country's police chief. A man claiming to be a Boko Haram spokesman said the group was ready to deploy more bombers and that the explosives had been brought in from abroad – a possibility, though homemade bombs, even powerful ones, do not require much expertise and explosives are readily available in Nigeria. In a story written by Nigerian journalist Ahmad Salkida, known for having sources within Boko Haram, the spokesman who identified himself as Abu Zaid said Manga acted as something of a runner for Boko Haram when Yusuf was still alive, travelling to neighbouring Benin and also Dubai while helping with an 'arms build-up'. It was not clear if Zaid meant he purchased arms in those places.

'Abu Zaid also confided in this newspaper that Manga left a will of over four million naira [$24,000 dollars] to his two daughters and three sons and urged fellow believers to sacrifice their lives for the sake of Allah', Salkida wrote in his story. 'This, the group said, is evident in the last-minute pictures of Manga, believed to have been taken at a camp somewhere in Borno state.'[24]

The extremists were now threatening to take their fight directly into the heart of the Nigerian state. The response from the authorities was, however, little more than the same pattern that would become so familiar and frustrating: condemnation, empty promises about bringing those responsible to justice and then little else. In the days after the attack, Jonathan issued a statement similar to other government responses. The president said, 'the explosion was an act of terror, which had become a global trend, but assured that the administration was taking steps to ensure the safety of all Nigerians, adding that no incident should be overlooked, no matter the circumstances or location of its occurrence.'[25]

Two months later, a suicide bomber would seek to drive into police headquarters in Maiduguri in the north-east during screening of potential new recruits, with about 1,500 on site at the time. He would be stopped, police shooting him dead before he set off his explosives and as he tried to drive into the complex.[26]

The attack on the UN building in Abuja would occur less than two weeks later, instantly transforming the image of Boko Haram, making it a dangerous new threat with unclear aims. It showed how far the extremists had advanced their planning and bomb-making abilities. A source who has seen the security video from the day of the attack said it seemed that advance surveillance had been done on the location by the attackers since the bomber knew to drive his car through the exit gate, which was less closely guarded than the entrance side. An investigation that included FBI agents from the United States also found that the bomb had been manufactured as a 'shaped charge', intensifying the force of the blast, and included 125 kilograms of explosives, according to Reuters news agency, which saw a copy of the classified report. It was made with both TATP and PETN, common for both military and commercial purposes, and regularly used by extremists worldwide to carry out attacks.[27]

Nigeria's intelligence service said the mastermind of the attack was a man named Mamman Nur, who was by some accounts Boko Haram's third-in-command at the time of the 2009 uprising, behind Yusuf and Shekau. His nationality has been debated, with some claiming he was from Chad or perhaps born in Maiduguri to Chadian parents, while others said he was Cameroonian. He was believed to be among the Boko Haram figures who formed links with AQIM and Al-Shebab, having recently returned from Somalia before the UN attack.[28]

Nigerian authorities said they received intelligence six days before the bombing that 'Boko Haram elements were on a mission to attack unspecified targets in Abuja' and arrested two suspects on 21 August named Babagana Ismail Kwaljima and Babagana Mali. They did not say, however, why they were unable to stop the attack.[29]

Vinod Alkari, the UNICEF official caught up in the bombing who struggled to help rescue others who were trapped, questioned why more was not done to secure the building ahead of time given the vague warnings. Alkari said that, during UN security meetings he attended, intelligence from the Nigerian government indicating attacks may be in the works against unspecified high-profile targets was discussed. He was not aware of any specific changes put in place on the ground to further guard against such a possibility. UN officials in Abuja did not respond to my requests to discuss the attack, and a spokeswoman at the secretary-general's office in New York declined to comment on security matters.

Boko Haram would claim credit for the attack. In the alleged bomber's 'martyr' video, a recorded message, purported to be Shekau's voice, played over an image of him, bearded and wearing a red-and-white keffiyeh and white robe. An AK-47 leaned against

the wall behind him, tape wrapped around its magazine. He said
that one of the group's main goals was establishing true sharia law,
and that his followers were prepared to die for it.

> My Muslim brethren, you should be happy with this
> incident in Abuja, which is a forum of all the global evil
> called the UN. May the wrath of God be on them. This
> forum is better called the United Nonsense, as we've been
> calling it even before we went to war, because this is a centre
> of Judeo-Christian plots. My Muslim brethren, you should
> obey Allah. Allah has in many places in the Qur'an forbade
> Muslims from cooperating with the Jews. And Allah has told
> us that any Muslim who goes into partnership with the Jews
> and the Christians is one of them [...].
>
> We feel the agony of what is happening to us year after
> year, month after month, in many towns. How many years
> has it taken when our brethren are being killed in many places
> and everybody knows this is being carried out by Christians?
> Besides, our mosque was demolished, our brothers killed and
> we were chased out. We had to leave the city. We raised up
> and picked up arms to defend ourselves and our religion. In
> this regard under the pretext of fighting us, they are killing
> you on all fronts. If you can understand under the pretext of
> fighting us and naming us Boko Haram, how many people
> have been killed? [...]
>
> [P]eople should understand that we are not after worldly
> things. Our main concern is the way the country is being
> run under the constitution and democracy, where Christians
> are given the opportunity to demean us. We are out to
> achieve two aims: one is seeking Allah's help to establish
> sharia so that Muslims will have peace to practise their reli-
> gion, and the second mission, even if we don't achieve this,
> there is a higher goal than this; may God cause all of us to
> be killed, to be wiped off the earth, instead of being alive

while Allah's laws are not adhered to. Don't take pride in killing us. To us, killing us is a source of pride. What we seek is martyrdom.[30]

* * *

When a helicopter landed in Maiduguri in September 2011 carrying former Nigerian president Olusegun Obasanjo, there would be a fleeting moment of hope. With the UN building blown up, hundreds killed across northern and central Nigeria, and the violence showing no signs of abating, it became obvious to many that some form of negotiation would be needed as part of any serious bid to end the insurgency. Obasanjo had flown to Maiduguri for that reason, and after meeting other organisers at the air force base in the city reeling from months of bombings and shoot-outs, he drove with them to the ruins of the mosque where Mohammed Yusuf once preached. A meeting had been arranged and it was to include an audience of about 60 people, a mat spread out under a tree at the site of the destroyed mosque for this purpose. According to an organiser of the meeting, northern-based rights activist Shehu Sani, those in attendance included relatives of the late Boko Haram leader and those identified as insurgents. The main speaker apart from Obasanjo would be Babakura Fugu, Yusuf's brother-in-law and the son of Baba Fugu Mohammed, the elderly man killed by security forces at the conclusion of the 2009 uprising. Despite a court ruling awarding Mohammed's family some $600,000 in damages over his death, the government still at that point had not paid.

'We sat down and had a frank talk', Sani told me one afternoon a couple years later at a cafe in the Hilton hotel in Abuja, where he had gone for meetings. 'President Obasanjo told them that he is here on a peace mission [...] and he is passionate about peace and he wants an end to this violence, and he wants to hear their grievances. And now it was then that they came out with a list of their – the "crime", in quotes, that was committed against them by the state.'

They showed him pictures of supposed Boko Haram members they said had been killed by the security agencies during the crackdown in 2009 as well as documents related to their case against the government.

'They didn't ask for court money, but they showed how even a secular order from a secular court could not even be obeyed by even the president himself, by the government', Sani said. Other points they raised included 'the need to release some members of the Boko Haram group and also to stop the raiding of houses and arresting of people, and then to look at the possibility of rebuilding the mosque, schools and homes that were [...] demolished by security agencies, and to end the harassment of their wives and children'.

The meeting lasted around four hours, according to Sani. He said he sought to have Obasanjo act as mediator for a few specific reasons, including the fact that he was a Christian from the south, making him less vulnerable to accusations of 'sponsoring' the violence, as some northern politicians had been accused of doing. Sani said he also chose him because Obasanjo remained highly influential in Nigerian politics and could speak directly with the president. On top of that, Obasanjo and Sani knew each other, having both been held in the same prison under the regime of Sani Abacha in the 1990s.

Obasanjo, whose commanding presence stands in sharp contrast to Jonathan, accepted the documents and photos presented to him and told them he would speak with the president. Others in the audience took turns speaking, including some who 'said clearly that they will not stop fighting until justice is done to them', Sani said. The ex-president listened, but also told them the violence had been counterproductive.

'He was saying they should stop killings, that it is destroying the image of Nigeria – it is destroying democracy – and that he has listened to their grievances and he will do something about it', Sani said. 'He said it is demonising the north as a region, it's demonising the country, it's giving us a bad name, and they should stop all these killings.'

There were doubts then, and there continue to be, over whether those Obasanjo met with had any real influence over the Boko Haram that had re-emerged after Yusuf's death. Babakura Fugu was a relative of Yusuf's, but it was not clear by any means whether he still had any contact with the group. In any case, Sani said he believed those at the meeting, based on their own assurances, could have exerted influence over Boko Haram as well as arranged contact with Abubakar Shekau.

After the meeting, Obasanjo and Sani travelled back to Abuja. According to Sani, Obasanjo met personally with his one-time protégé, President Jonathan, and presented him with the documents while describing the meeting. After that, it seems the government did nothing, and Sani said Obasanjo made no secret of his anger over his efforts having gone to waste.

'What he told me is that he is not happy with the way the president has not taken seriously what he has done', said Sani, relaying what he says Obasanjo told him. 'From my own thinking, the security chiefs at that time were those who were putting pressure on the president not to agree to the documents which president Obasanjo brought that may help in ending the insurgency.'

It may not have mattered anyway. Two days later, Babakura Fugu was shot dead in Maiduguri. There were suspicions over whether a faction of the insurgents opposed to negotiations was responsible, while others questioned whether the security forces may have been behind it. A man believed at the time to be a spokesman for Boko Haram's main faction denied they were responsible, while the military and police also said they had nothing to do with it.

Another short-lived attempt at negotiations would occur several months later in March 2012, this time with an Islamic cleric acting as mediator. When word leaked to journalists that talks were moving ahead, the mediator, Ibrahim Datti Ahmad, quit, issuing a statement questioning the government's sincerity.

Some had accused those within the government who were opposed to negotiations of leaking the story to sabotage the talks.

'To our shock and dismay, no sooner had we started this dialogue, Nigerian newspapers came out with a lot of the details of the meeting held', Ahmad said in his statement. 'This development has embarrassed us very much and has created strong doubts in our minds about the sincerity of the government's side in our discussion as the discussion is supposed to be very confidential to achieve any success. In view of this unfortunate and unhelpful development, we have no option but to withdraw from these early discussions. We sincerely regret that an opportunity to negotiate and terminate this cycle of violence is being missed.'

Asked why members of the security forces and government would want to sabotage a legitimate attempt at ending the insurgency, Sani, the organiser of Obasanjo's visit, repeated what many others have also said. He named pride among members of the security forces who continue to believe the insurgency can be defeated militarily, but also a factor that comes into play far too often in Nigeria: money. The national security budget would rise to some $6 billion by 2013, or about 20 per cent of the country's total spending, providing many opportunities for corruption. No one could ever prove whether anyone would go so far as to prefer violence over peace because of the financial benefits, but the way in which that perception spread was telling in itself of how little trust Nigerians placed in those who were supposed to be protecting them.

4

'THAT IS HOW COMPLEX THE SITUATION IS'

The president, apparently attempting to comfort the nation, would end up doing something else entirely. It was January 2012, at the end of a Christmas season that had been so bloody it had led some to again question whether Nigeria was careening toward a second civil war. Boko Haram insurgents had changed tactics and targeted churches in an onslaught of bombings on Christmas Day. In the worst of the attacks, a suicide bomber drove up outside a Catholic church in Madalla, near the capital Abuja, as Christmas morning mass was ending and set off his explosives near the entrance. The force of the blast ripped through the crowd, a combination of churchgoers making their way outside, motorcycle taxi drivers and passersby, killing 44 people. Some who were badly injured ran to the priest for a final blessing. 'It was really terrible', Father Christopher Barde told my AFP colleague Ola Awoniyi. 'People ran towards me, [saying] "Father anoint me."'[1]

After at first issuing statements with the usual condemnations and promises to track down the masterminds, President Jonathan made two speeches on New Year's Eve that would be his most forceful yet related to the insurgency. The first came as he visited the church in Madalla where the bomb attack had occurred. While there, he said Boko Haram 'started as a harmless group [...] They have now grown cancerous. And Nigeria, being the body, they want to kill it. But nobody will allow them to do that.'[2]

On the heels of that visit, Jonathan would later in the day give a nationally televised address to announce he was declaring a state of emergency in areas hit particularly hard by the violence. 'While the search for lasting solutions is ongoing, it has become imperative to take some decisive measures necessary to restore normalcy in the country especially within the affected communities', he said.[3] He provided few details on what exactly the declaration would mean on the ground, and as the days wore on, it seemed that little had actually changed. However, while the announcement may have been light on substance, it provided some relief in the country, since the government seemed to finally acknowledge the dangerous situation it was facing.

That relief would give way to more confusion only a few days later. On 8 January, Jonathan would give a speech that would have been extremely alarming had it not been so baffling. It occurred on Armed Forces Remembrance Day at the National Christian Centre, a cathedral-like structure in the capital Abuja, near the national mosque. It generated little interest beforehand, seeming to be one of the many functions and events a president shows up for, says a few words and departs. Jonathan seemed to speak off-the-cuff, ranging from the recent attacks on churches to corruption, but it was his comments about Boko Haram that were so startling. He suggested that the group had infiltrated the government and security forces, but in such vague terms no one knew what to make of it. 'The situation we have in our hands is even worse than the civil war that we fought', Jonathan said. The speech continued:

> During the civil war, we knew and we could even predict where the enemy was coming from. You can even know the route they are coming from; you can even know what calibre of weapon they will use and so on. But the challenge we have today is more complicated [...] Somebody said that the

situation is bad, that even if one's son is a member, one will not even know. That means that if the person will plant a bomb behind your house, you won't know.

Some of them are in the executive arm of government, some of them are in the parliamentary-legislative arm of government, while some of them are even in the judiciary. Some are also in the armed forces, the police and other security agencies. Some continue to dip their hands and eat with you and you won't even know the person who will point a gun at you or plant a bomb behind your house. That is how complex the situation is.[4]

The comments were so stunning that when they were sent to me by a journalist who occasionally worked for us in Abuja, I immediately questioned whether they were accurate, even though I knew him to be a solid reporter. I called him to stress the importance of the story and the need to quote the president with absolute precision, telling him that the comments were surely going to cause a stir. He assured me that it would withstand the scrutiny and told me that he had a recording of the remarks which he had double-checked. Satisfied with his assurances, I began trying to write a story that would shed some light on what the president had said. I was not particularly successful. I was flummoxed, and so were my editors in Paris, who were asking me to interpret these remarks against some coherent context. Was he saying the insurgency was political? Did he mean it was a conspiracy by his enemies? Was he simply trying to make exaggerated excuses for why his government had been unable to stop the violence? What could possibly be made of such pronouncements? Above all, and perhaps most frustratingly, they posed a simple question: if Boko Haram members were in the security forces, judiciary and government and the president was aware of it, why had they not been arrested? That question would never be answered, and Jonathan would give no further explanation. Whatever he meant, an attack less than two weeks later would show that Jonathan was at least right to be concerned about the threat Boko Haram now posed.

It seemed clear from the start that the attack on 20 January was going to be like no other Boko Haram violence before it. It occurred in Kano, the largest city in northern Nigeria, an important commercial centre dating back to the Middle Ages and where Frederick Lugard's men had begun their final conquest of the region for the British. The bomb blasts began to tear through the Friday afternoon bustle and simply kept exploding, one after another, so many that residents lost count. Gunfire rang out and residents in the city of about 3 million people rushed to take cover. Wellington Asiayei, the police officer shot and paralysed at his barracks whom I met in the hospital, was the victim of one of the cruellest individual assaults, the trigger pulled by a man dressed as one of his colleagues, but his story was one of many.

The assault may have been set in motion the month before, in December 2011, when a message purported to be from Boko Haram leader Abubakar Shekau was addressed to the Kano state government. It claimed that Boko Haram members had been arrested over the previous five months following allegations that they were armed robbers. 'We are therefore compelled to write this letter to inform Kano residents of this development so that when we launch attacks in the city as we have been doing in Maiduguri, they should not blame us', it said.

Kano Governor Rabiu Musa Kwankwaso would later acknowledge having seen the 'open letter', but sought to distance himself from any arrests, saying that the state had no policing powers, with the police force a federal agency.[5] The police commissioner in Kano state at the time, Ibrahim Idris, would say later that a number of people had been arrested ahead of the January attacks, but he declined to provide any further details, calling it 'sensitive'.[6] Kano up to that point had mostly escaped the kind of serious attacks that had so badly hit Maiduguri and other cities.

The first blast would occur at around five in the afternoon at a regional police administrative office, where a suicide bomber sought to crash into the building. His vehicle exploded outside, ripping off a chunk of the roof. A police corporal who was stationed at the building at the time tried to explain to me what had happened from his hospital bed before trailing off, unable to speak. Corporal Muazzam Aminu, a 37-year-old father of one, his wife seated next to him, spoke briefly in clipped phrases, saying he saw a motorcycle enter the compound first. There was shooting, then an explosion. He was unable to continue any further. According to police, three suicide bombers drove a car on to the grounds of that building, called a zonal headquarters, and detonated a bomb. As security forces arrived to assess the damage, it began to become clear that they were facing an assault far larger than that attack.

'We rushed there, and based on the assessment we made we discovered that it was a sort of a suicide bomber that drove into that compound', Idris, the police commissioner, told me and a group of other journalists at Kano police headquarters in the days after the attacks. 'It was there then that we heard of another two attacks on two of our police stations.'

Even that was an underestimate. In fact, dozens, possibly hundreds, of attackers were swarming through the streets in an incredibly coordinated set of assaults. Many were on motorcycles, while others drove cars loaded with explosives. Their weapons included AK-47 rifles, drink cans transformed into tiny bombs, larger powdered-milk tins also designed to explode and powerful IEDs built with 350-kilogram drums. They would run amok, hitting an immigration office, a nearby police station where detainees were set free, a girls' secondary school, Kano police headquarters and several others. Part of their strategy included throwing the drink-can bombs at the buildings they were targeting, then opening fire on those who ran away.

'That's what started the fire, and the whole place went up in flames', Idris said of the drink-can bombs. 'And as people are running helter-skelter, they now come – you know, these terrorists attack now with weapons, and they're just killing'.

Some wore uniforms resembling those of police or military divisions, and they would approach officers and civilians on the streets and gun them down.

'Some of our police officers who saw them on the streets, they thought they are their colleagues, and that's how they now identified them to be police officers, and that's how they shot – they just shot them in cold blood', said Idris. 'And it's true, we have some of the incidents like that in some locations in the city where [...] they were wearing uniforms resembling that of the mobile police and the military. They used that to deceive the members of the public, and in the process shot some of these civilians and some of our police officers. In fact, like I said, most of the casualties of the police are not killed at the police stations, but they are killed on the street where they saw them.'

At state police headquarters, a bomber who sought to enter crashed into one of the drums used as a security measure outside the gate and his explosives went off, killing at least one policeman on guard and four civilians at shops along the road. Several of the market stalls that line the street outside the headquarters were reduced to piles of splinters. While the bomber was not able to make it past the gates, others penetrated inside and roamed freely, which is what led to Assistant Superintendent Asiayei being shot and paralysed as he sought to lock the door to his room in the barracks before fleeing.

One 29-year-old man who was shot in the leg while on his way home from his job at a tannery told me the four friends who were with him at the time were all killed. He said they had been driving near the Palm Centre police station, one of those targeted by the attackers, and after hearing a bomb explode, everyone began to run.

'I'm the only one who survived', Monday Joseph said from his hospital bed. 'We heard a bomb, but what I felt in my body was a gun [...] Once I'm shot, I'm just down flat.' He said a friend arrived about 30 minutes later and brought him to the hospital.

The morgue at the city's largest hospital, Murtala Mohammed Specialist Hospital, filled with bodies piled on top of one another. My colleague Aminu Abubakar was allowed inside and counted at least 80 before stopping.[7] At the smaller Aminu Kano Teaching Hospital, the morgue would also fill to capacity. Dr Aminu Zakari Mohammed, chief medical director at Aminu Kano, told me that he went to notify the emergency room when he heard about the first attack.

'Even before I finished, already I heard another explosion [...] then a second and a third one', Mohammed said. 'I felt this was something out of the ordinary. I kept hearing the explosions.' He and his staff worked until 2 a.m. to treat the victims being brought in. He said one family arrived later in the night after their house collapsed from the force of the blasts.

There were at least five suicide bombers, according to police. The authorities put the death toll at 185, but many people suspected it was higher. Bodies were scattered on roads the next morning, particularly near state police headquarters. Police said they discovered 10 cars with unexploded IEDs along with about 300 drink cans, eight powdered milk tins and eight 350-kilogram drums – all loaded with explosives. Some of my colleagues and I were allowed to see what the police had seized and taken back to headquarters, and the cans and various bomb-making materials were spread out across the floor of a storage room. There was even at least one meant to be a time bomb wired to a conventional wall clock, the kind you might see in a kitchen.

A mobile-phone seller near the immigration office that was attacked, 35-year-old Abdulrazak Murtala, told me, 'we just heard a bomb blast and people started running. Some people are just shooting, shooting guns [...] Some are on bikes, some are inside cars.' He was unsure what to make of the people who carried out the attack. 'We don't even know what they want', he said. 'I don't think these people are fighting for religion. I just think they are fighting for their own selfish interest.'

Abubakar Shekau would deliver a message posted on YouTube a week later, claiming responsibility for the violence and threatening further attacks. He said security forces were to blame, alleging Boko Haram members had been arrested and tortured, while women and children had also been detained. Perhaps sensing that the group had taken the violence too far, he also falsely claimed that civilians had not been targeted.

'We attacked the security formations because our members were arrested and tortured', Shekau said in the audio message played over a picture of him.

> Our women and children have also been arrested [...] They should know that they also have wives and children. We can also abduct them. It is not beyond our powers [...] Soldiers raided an Islamic seminary in Maiduguri and desecrated the Qur'an. They should bear in mind that they also have primary and secondary schools and universities, and we can also attack them [...] After we finished our war, policemen stuck around and started killing civilians and later blamed us. We are not fighting civilians, but security forces. We only kill soldiers, policemen and their collaborators.[8]

The message was posted as the situation spiralled even further out of control. Another police station in Kano was attacked a few days after the 20 January wave of violence, while a couple of days after that, gunmen kidnapped a German engineer working for a construction firm on the outskirts of the city. The kidnapping signalled that earlier abductions of a Briton and an Italian from Kebbi in north-western Nigeria were not isolated incidents, with yet another new and different phase of the insurgency ahead. In the case of the German, Al-Qaeda in the Islamic Maghreb would at one point claim to be holding him and demand the release of the wife of an Islamist leader in exchange for his freedom, signalling murky links between AQIM and kidnappers in northern Nigeria. He would eventually be killed by his abductors during a raid to free him in Kano.[9] There were also more bombings over the following months, including a suicide attack on the Abuja office of one of Nigeria's most prominent newspapers in April 2012.

* * *

Blood covered the floor of the bathroom in the unguarded and now empty house, its walls pocked with bullet holes, children from the neighbourhood entering and exiting at will. Crowds were still gathering outside on the morning of 9 March 2012, intrigued by what had happened the previous day in the quiet residential neighbourhood of unpaved roads and modest houses in the city of Sokoto, the home of Nigeria's highest-ranking Muslim spiritual leader and the former capital of Usman Dan Fodio's caliphate. They spoke of a chaotic raid that sparked a shoot-out, with the men inside refusing to surrender and around 100 Nigerian soldiers, who had been supported by British special forces, surrounding the house. The soldiers were pursuing them because they had been holding two Western hostages, Franco Lamolinara, a 48-year-old Italian, and Chris McManus, who was British and 28. The two men were kidnapped almost a year earlier, in May 2011, while working on a construction project in Kebbi state in north-western Nigeria, near the border with Niger. At one point during the intense gun battle at the house in Sokoto, according to some of the residents, Nigerian soldiers asked people in the neighbourhood to bring them old tyres. When they did, the soldiers set them alight and tossed them over the wall of the complex, a single-storey series of structures with a zinc roof and a courtyard. They wanted to smoke the kidnappers out.[10]

Unlike AQIM, which had collected millions of dollars in ransom payments by abducting Westerners, Boko Haram had not yet used kidnapping as a tactic. Abductions were in general rare in northern Nigeria, unlike in parts of the south, where ransom kidnappings had become big business. That began to change when a group of Boko Haram members seemed to break off and create their own faction, called Jama'atu Ansarul Muslimina Fi Biladis Sudan, or Vanguard for the Aid of Muslims in Black Africa.[11] It would later come to be known simply as Ansaru, and it would be blamed for the kidnappings of the British and Italian engineers and a number of other abductions.

Several theories were offered as to why they had split, with some arguing that they had grown frustrated with the killing of civilians and particularly fellow Muslims by Shekau's Boko Haram. Others reasoned that the dissidents wanted to more forcefully pursue an international agenda, in line with Al-Qaeda affiliates in northern Africa and elsewhere. A third reason put forth was more opportunistic: those in Ansaru had the connections and the will to try to create a kidnapping market in northern Nigeria and wanted to profit from it as their extremist colleagues elsewhere had done. It is certainly possible that the true story was a combination of all of those factors. Some experts said Ansaru's leader, or one of them, may have been Khalid al-Barnawi, long a Boko Haram figure who may have run a training camp with AQIM in Algeria and had some form of relationship with the Algerian extremist Mokhtar Belmokhtar.[12] The US government would later label al-Barnawi a 'global terrorist' along with two other Nigerian extremists: Shekau and Abubakar Adam Kambar, who was also said to be linked to AQIM. Nigeria's military claimed Kambar was Boko Haram's main link with Al-Qaeda and Al-Shebab in Somalia.[13] How separate Boko Haram and Ansaru truly are has been heavily debated, and it seems the two overlap, particularly when it comes to their foot soldiers. It has been described by some as an umbrella-like arrangement that includes both Boko Haram and Ansaru.

After the May 2011 abductions of the Briton and Italian, there had been no word from the kidnappers or the victims for months, fuelling speculation that they had been carried out by Islamist extremists whose agenda was more complicated than simply collecting a ransom. Abductions in the Niger Delta in the south had tended to follow a pattern, with a ransom demanded shortly after the kidnapping and victims usually released unharmed after it was paid, often following negotiations to lower the price. The silence surrounding McManus and Lamolinara would be broken in August 2011, when a video emerged showing the two men blindfolded and on their knees. They were forced to read a statement in which they said their abductors were from Al-Qaeda and that their governments should meet the kidnappers' demands. The demands were, however, not listed – a clear set of demands would in fact never be issued, according to the British government – and after the appearance of the video, there was another long period of silence with no word on the victims' health, where they may be located and what exactly their kidnappers wanted. A second video emerged in December 2011 in which gunmen threatened to execute McManus.[14]

Britain's participation in a potential rescue operation had taken root when Prime Minister David Cameron visited Nigeria and held talks with President Jonathan in July 2011. The two men discussed the hostages during the visit, 'and as a result agreed a package of UK support for Nigeria's counter-terrorism efforts', Britain's defence secretary, Philip Hammond, would tell the UK House of Commons. 'As part of that package, a sustained operation was conducted to identify members of the group responsible for the kidnapping.'[15]

By March 2012, after the arrest of three people accused of having conducted surveillance on the victims before their abduction, authorities had discovered that the man behind the plot was someone named Abu Mohammed. Nigeria's Department of State Services (DSS), a secret police and intelligence unit, described Mohammed as the leader of a faction of Boko Haram.[16] A Nigerian security source told a reporter for my news agency that Mohammed had links to both Boko Haram and AQIM and had masterminded the kidnapping with the aim of collecting ransom money, which would be used to finance more operations.[17]

Nigerian authorities learned that Mohammed's hideout was located in the city of Zaria in north-central Nigeria, several hundred miles away from Birnin Kebbi, the site of the kidnapping. On 7 March, the authorities launched a raid on the hideout. The DSS said the raid was carried out while Mohammed and his faction were holding a meeting of its 'shura council', or consultative body, but that description may imply a more sophisticated level of organisation than the group actually had. During the raid, a number of gang members were believed to be killed, while five were arrested, including Mohammed, who had been shot and injured in the gunfight. A soldier had his throat slit. Those who were arrested, according to the DSS, then began providing information to the authorities that would lead to the raid in Sokoto. The information was said to include a warning: Those keeping watch over the two hostages had been instructed to kill them 'in the event of any envisaged threat'. The British government would decide a rescue attempt was not only necessary, but that it also required the backing of its special forces, who would participate in the operation.

'After months of not knowing where they were being held, we received credible information about their location', Cameron said later in a televised address. 'A window of opportunity arose to secure their release. We also had reason to believe that their lives were under imminent and growing danger.'

The British government has never said publicly how many members of its elite Special Boat Service were dispatched for the raid, though reports in the British media put the number at around a dozen and perhaps as many as 20. There were also reports of the commandos being stationed in Nigeria for up to a couple weeks before the operation, and British intelligence operatives at one point may have managed to begin listening in on the kidnap gang's phone calls.[18]

On the night of 7 March, one of those arrested – the man who killed the soldier, according to Nigerian authorities – led security forces to Sokoto, but any element of surprise may have been sabotaged by the military itself. Before the security team's arrival the next morning, Nigeria's military decided it would have to search and cordon off the neighbourhood where the hostages were believed to be held to make sure the kidnappers could not escape ahead of time.[19] Residents also said they saw two helicopters hovering overhead in the morning, which would obviously raise suspicions as well.

British forces became concerned that the Nigerian soldiers deployed throughout the neighbourhood had tipped the kidnappers off and decided they could wait no longer. It seems that, before that time, a final decision had not been made to go ahead with the raid since the Italian government had not been notified. The raid would begin shortly before noon, with the British government having given its final approval at 11.15 a.m.[20]

British commandos were among those who entered the walled-in compound and would be faced with gunfire from someone with an AK-47. They would spot and kill one of the gang members almost immediately after entering, but could hear more gunshots, except now they were muffled and seemed to come from inside a room. Two men then escaped, climbing a ladder over the wall. This all happened within six minutes after the start of the raid.

The soldiers then searched the premises, and after arriving in one section covered by tarpaulin, they went inside. When they entered a room with two beds, they spotted a Manchester United shirt that resembled the one Chris McManus wore in videos released by the kidnappers.

'They called out for Franco and Chris but received no reply', Detective Chief Inspector Grant Mallon said when reporting the findings of a British inquest into the death of McManus. 'To the right there was a metal door to a toilet and they noticed there were bullet holes to it, and the team noticed there were 7.62mm munitions and cases on the floor. The door was partially open and when the soldiers looked inside they could see two white males on the floor and they immediately recognised them as Chris and

Franco. Chris was lying to the left of the toilet. Both men had visible gunshot wounds. It appears they were killed fairly quickly into the engagement.'

The inquest found that the two men could not have been hit by the rescue team's bullets because those that killed them were a different type. McManus had been shot a total of six times, but died from a single gunshot wound to the head, while Lamolinara was hit four times and also died from a bullet to the head.[21]

They were eventually able to carry out the bodies, but the operation was far from over, however. At some point, a fierce firefight broke out between Nigerian soldiers and the kidnappers who remained. Residents said the gunfire lasted up to seven hours, though Britain's defence secretary said it was 90 minutes. According to residents I spoke to in the neighbourhood the day after the raid, there were about 100 Nigerian troops as well as a tank. As the gun battle raged, soldiers asked residents for the old tyres that they set on fire and tossed over the wall. A huge hole could be seen in one of the walls the next day, and residents said the tank had fired a shell into it. Three members of the gang were killed and 'none were taken alive', according to Defence Secretary Hammond.[22] Nigerian authorities said the wife of one of the gang members was wounded by a bullet and treated at hospital.

Every resident I spoke to claimed they did not know who occupied the house or that the hostages were being held there. The local chief of the Mabera neighbourhood, Umar Bello, told me the same and added that he did not believe the kidnappers were members of Boko Haram. 'It is just kidnappers. It's about money', he said. 'Their major priority is money, and once they don't get the money, they have nothing to lose.'

On the day after the raid, with dozens of people circulating through the compound, by then picked clean by looters, and viewing the blood-splattered bathroom where the men were killed, Nigerian authorities had apparently had enough. Three truckloads of agents, including those wearing DSS helmets, arrived in the afternoon and began firing their guns into the air, forcing the crowd to scatter.

The kidnappings would have repercussions beyond Nigeria. It would spark a diplomatic dispute between Britain and Italy, with Italian President Giorgio Napolitano saying that 'the behaviour of the British government, which did not inform or consult with Italy on the operation that it was planning, really is inexplicable'.[23] Britain said there had not been time, since there was a need to act urgently. Underlying the dispute may have been differences in how each country handled such situations. Britain refuses to pay ransoms, while Italy has been willing to do so.[24]

Beyond that, it would lead to Britain saying that Ansaru was likely responsible for the kidnapping, listing it as a banned terrorist group and proclaiming it as 'broadly aligned with Al-Qaeda'.[25] The supposed kidnapping ringleader, Abu Mohammed, would, however, not be able to answer questions on the group. He died in Nigerian custody a day after the operation from, according to the DSS, 'severe bullet wounds' he suffered during the previous raid that led to his arrest in Zaria.[26]

In the following months, Ansaru would be blamed for a series of other kidnappings as well as attacks, with the new group's methods becoming more ruthless and its rhetoric increasingly taking on an international tone. It would claim credit for a raid on a police unit in the capital Abuja in November 2012 where a number of Islamists were believed to have been detained in a jail known as the abattoir because it was inside a warehouse formerly used for slaughtering cattle, chains still hanging from the ceiling.[27]

An attack on a planned contingent of Nigerian troops expected to be deployed to Mali occurred in January 2013, with a homemade bomb exploding as the soldiers' convoy passed near Okene in Kogi state, located in central Nigeria and where a number of extremists tied to Boko Haram were said to be from. The attack killed two of the soldiers to be deployed to Mali, where a French-led offensive had begun targeting Islamists who had taken control of a huge swathe of the nearby country. Ansaru claimed the attack, and in doing so said it was targeting troops who aimed to 'demolish the Islamic empire of Mali'.[28]

One particularly audacious raid in February 2013 saw abductors storm a construction site in the northern city of Bauchi, blow a hole in the gate with explosives, kill a security guard and kidnap seven foreigners, including one Briton, one Greek, an Italian, two Lebanese and two Syrians. An email to journalists purported to be from Ansaru, written in English, said that the attack occurred because of 'the transgressions and atrocities done to the religion of Allah [...] by the European countries in many places such as Afghanistan and Mali'. It seemed doubtful those were the true motives behind the kidnappings, with ransom money often the ultimate goal, but the statement again showed that the group was seeking to take a more international stance, at least in its rhetoric.[29]

The following month, on 9 March, another statement would be issued, in both Arabic and English, claiming that the seven hostages taken in Bauchi had been killed. It was accompanied by images of some of the hostages appearing to be dead, and had been distributed by an arm of the Sinam al-Islam Network, which runs an online jihadist forum.[30] The process by which the statement was distributed again indicated Ansaru had cultivated some form of relationship with foreign jihadi groups. In the statement, it said it killed the hostages because of attempts to rescue them. It provided a link to an obscure website that carried a story on whether British planes had landed in Nigeria to attempt a rescue, with aircraft having been spotted in Abuja. According to the British government, the planes that were spotted were there to help airlift troops and equipment to Mali and had nothing to do with a rescue bid.[31]

A shocking kidnapping would occur in February 2013, when a French family of seven were abducted while visiting a national park in northern Cameroon, near the Nigerian border. The victims included the mother and father as well as four children, aged between 5 and 12, and their uncle. The French government said it was believed the victims were taken across the border into Nigeria after the abduction, and a video emerged later in which Abubakar Shekau claimed responsibility for the kidnappings on behalf of Boko Haram. The video also showed images of the family and included the father, Tanguy Moulin-Fournier, reading a statement for the camera. Shekau and the family were never shown in the same frame and it was unclear if they were ever in the same location.[32]

It marked the first time Shekau's Boko Haram had taken credit for a kidnapping. In the video, Shekau demanded the release of Boko Haram prisoners in both Nigeria and Cameroon, though there were suspicions all along that what the extremists were really after was money. It was never clear whether criminals had kidnapped the family and sold them on to Boko Haram, whether it was a planned action or if members of the extremist group simply came across them by chance and decided to carry out the abduction. The border with Cameroon in north-eastern Nigeria is porous, and Boko Haram members – like many average residents – are believed to circulate back and forth.

France insisted throughout the ordeal that it would not pay a ransom, though it was an open secret that it had done so to free captives repeatedly in the past in other countries, drawing criticism since the money would obviously provide financing to extremist groups. In the end, someone paid. A Nigerian security source told me the payment was made through the Cameroon government, though the family had been held in Nigeria, but he said he did not know the amount. French news channel iTele reported that 16 detained Boko Haram members were released and $7 million was paid to free the family.[33] Another report from Reuters, citing a confidential Nigerian government document, put the ransom figure at some $3.15 million.[34] It was never clear who paid the money, whatever the final amount was. The family was released in April after being held for two months through an arrangement that saw them arrive back in Cameroon. They appeared thin and scraggly, but seemed to be in good health considering the circumstances.

The first half of 2013 felt depressingly brutal. Shekau, wearing a knee-length green caftan with an AK-47 dangling from a strap around his neck, appeared in one video denying rumours of a ceasefire deal that had been circulating. The camera then cut to another shot where a man identified as an informer was pinned to the ground by others who slit his throat. They beheaded him later in the video.[35]

In Kano, gunmen opened fire on two clinics where polio vaccination workers had gathered, killing 10 people.[36] The attack came after a radio programme revived old conspiracy theories that had previously circulated in northern Nigeria about polio vaccines being a Western plot against Muslims. It was never clear whether the attacks were directly linked to Boko Haram, but they added to the nightmare of death and destruction in parts of northern Nigeria.

The situation was also becoming murkier. A US official who spoke to me in February 2013 on condition of anonymity talked of how little was known of the Nigerian extremists and their intentions. 'Even in painting a picture of where the lines are between these different groups, and how much of the criminal overlaps into it, all of this stuff is very difficult to determine', he said.

Beyond the mayhem in Nigeria, there were reports of Boko Haram members showing up in Gao and elsewhere in Mali to fight with the Islamist extremists who had taken control of the northern half of the country there. There were doubts over whether they were truly Boko Haram members, and such doubts continue to exist for some, but a Western diplomat told me in March 2014 that he believed they were.

'I think they were probably Boko Haram or Ansaru guys, which wouldn't be all that surprising because we've known since the early 2000s that you have Nigerian extremists travelling in ones and twos and fives and sixes up to northern Mali to train with, first, the

GSPC [Algeria's Salafist Group for Preaching and Combat], and then when it morphed into AQIM.'

The US official I spoke with in 2013 pointed out that foreign jihadists are often attracted to like-minded struggles elsewhere, while also raising an issue that would become salient in later months. 'You will also probably see a certain number of people go, and a certain number of people come back', he said. 'A concern is when they do come back, because they can come back with a greater skill set than when they left.' In other words, they would be better fighters.

From his work in previous assignments, the US official was familiar with Algeria's GSPC, and he saw certain similarities in what was then occurring in Nigeria. The GSPC had broken away from the Armed Islamic Group in the 1990s after growing frustrated with the widespread killing of civilians in its insurgency against the government. Later, GSPC declared its allegiance to Al-Qaeda and became known as Al-Qaeda in the Islamic Maghreb, taking on a more international and especially anti-Western stance. Criminality and Islamist extremism also blended with GSPC and AQIM, with its leaders believed to have made fortunes through various forms of smuggling in addition to kidnappings. Speaking of Ansaru, the US official said that 'they do seem to have a sort of different approach than (Boko Haram) writ large tactically [...] Kind of reminds me in some ways of how the GSPC originally broke out in Algiers because they didn't want to see so much broad targeting of Muslims, wanted to go in a different direction. So these things are not unprecedented in this region.'

* * *

Dependable information from the Nigerian security forces was in short supply, and by that time, the allegations against them of outrageous abuses were piling up. On a road near the Borno state government compound, a group of women were gathering regularly in 2013 in hopes that the governor would hear their pleas. They had lost their husbands or sons or other family members and, beyond the sorrow of their loved ones turning up dead, had in many cases also been robbed of their household's main breadwinner. When I was there in October 2013, there were about two dozen women gathered under neem trees along the roadside, and when I began speaking to one, others quickly crowded around, raising their voices and demanding that I interview them as well in the hope that I could somehow help. One woman I spoke with said her husband and son were killed by Boko Haram, but others I talked to in detail as the crowd pressed against me and a colleague, who translated from Hausa for me, blamed the military.

One 30-year-old woman said her husband had been arrested in the restive Gwange neighbourhood of Maiduguri about 15 months earlier during a military sweep. About a week later, the military returned his dead body to her for burial, informing her that he had died in detention. According to her, he had been shot. She denied he was a member of Boko Haram and accused soldiers of killing him. 'He was taken away, then later they killed him', she said, describing him as a 40-year-old taxi driver. She and her 12-year-old son had since moved back to her parents' home. Another 20-year-old woman said her husband went out to 'look for daily bread' in 2012 when soldiers arrested him along with others suspected of being members of Boko Haram, later returning his dead body to her, leaving her to look after her two-year-old daughter alone. Those I spoke with denied that their family members were connected to Boko Haram and said their pleas for assistance had been ignored by the government and security forces.[37]

Their accusations were not a surprise since similar ones had been made repeatedly. Many of the alleged cases tended to follow a pattern: a roadside bomb would explode near a military post or convoy and soldiers would respond ruthlessly, rounding up men from the neighbourhood and setting homes, market stalls and other buildings alight. According to accounts provided to journalists and human rights groups, the soldiers would accuse residents of cooperating with the insurgents.

Beyond the destruction itself, the allegations would limit the kinds of military training Nigeria's foreign allies could provide. The United States was prevented by law from providing training to soldiers whose units were suspected of serious rights abuses. Any soldier who rotated through Nigeria's so-called Joint Task Force operating in the north-east could be barred, no matter if they themselves were guilty or not.

A powerful report from Human Rights Watch released in October 2012 set out a long list of alleged abuses by Boko Haram as well as members of Nigeria's security forces, questioning whether both were guilty of crimes against humanity.[38] A few weeks later, Amnesty International issued a report with similar accusations, alleging widespread extrajudicial killings and torture by the security forces, among other abuses.[39] Nigeria's National Human Rights Commission would report in June 2013 that it had 'received several credibly attested allegations of gross violations by officials of the [military task force], including allegations of summary executions, torture, arbitrary detention amounting to internment and outrages against the dignity of civilians, as well as rape'.[40]

A Nigerian official who has followed the situation closely estimated, when I spoke with him in May 2014 on condition of anonymity, that the number of 'Boko Haram' detainees was 'in the low thousands [...] about 3,000 or so detainees'. He said that appalling detention practices may be radicalising some prisoners who may not otherwise have turned to extremism, with 'lots and lots being held in ratholes'. Many of the abuses of detainees were said to have occurred at the notorious Giwa military barracks in Maiduguri, as described in the Human Rights Watch report:

> During raids in communities, often in the aftermath of Boko Haram attacks, members of the security forces have executed men in front of their families; arbitrarily arrested or beaten members of the community; burned houses, shops, and cars; stolen money while searching homes; and, in at

least one case documented by Human Rights Watch, raped a woman. Government security agencies routinely hold suspects incommunicado without charge or trial in secret detention facilities and have subjected detainees to torture or other physical abuse.[41]

Untold numbers of young men seemed to have simply disappeared, with no indication of whether they had been killed or if they were being held somewhere by Nigeria's security forces. Since there had been no judicial process, there was no way of knowing whether any of them had anything to do with the insurgency. Human Rights Watch interviewed one former detainee who said he saw other prisoners tortured or killed. His descriptions of what happened to them were stomach-churning:

> For example, he said that while he was being interrogated by security agents in an office at the barracks he saw soldiers at another table torture a detainee by pulling on his genitals with a pair of pliers. He also described seeing soldiers try to 'peel the skin' off a detainee with a razor and kill another detainee while he was suspended from a tree at the barracks.[42]

Perhaps the worst single incident of soldiers being accused of rampaging would occur in April 2013 in the town of Baga, located on the edge of Lake Chad in Nigeria's far north-east. On the evening of 16 April, attackers believed to be from Boko Haram shot dead a soldier serving under a task force in the region, apparently the latest in a string of incidents blamed on Boko Haram in Baga. Reinforcements from the task force arrived in Baga later the same night and, according to residents and a police incident report, unleashed fury on the town. The soldiers 'started shooting indiscriminately at anybody in sight including domestic animals. This reaction resulted to [sic] loss of lives and massive destruction of properties', the police incident report quoted by

Nigeria's National Human Rights Commission said. Residents also accused the soldiers of setting entire neighbourhoods ablaze in revenge, and the police report said the troops 'completely razed down' at least five wards in Baga.[43] According to the Red Cross, 187 people were killed. A local senator put the death toll at 228. The military bitterly disputed those numbers as well as the assertions that soldiers set buildings alight, arguing that the fires would have been caused by insurgents. According to the military, 37 people were killed, including 30 insurgents, six civilians and a soldier.[44]

News of the violence was slow to emerge from the remote town, and when it did, access to the area was restricted by the military. My colleague Aminu Abubakar managed to enter Baga with a military escort more than two weeks after. One resident told him that the area where he lived 'was burnt the following morning in broad daylight by soldiers who went door-to-door setting fire to homes and everybody saw them'.[45]

As the military continued to deny abuse allegations, Human Rights Watch published satellite photos appearing to show wide swathes of the town destroyed by fire. It said that, according to its analysis, it had counted 2,275 destroyed buildings, 'the vast majority likely residences, with another 125 severely damaged', and that the destruction was spread over about 80,000 square metres – roughly the area of 11 football pitches.[46] Nigeria's space research agency conducted its own analysis and disputed Human Rights Watch's findings, saying that the area affected was 54,000 square metres and the 'active zone of destruction' was 11,000 square metres. It also argued that the area analysed was not large enough to fit the 2,400 buildings mentioned by Human Rights Watch.[47]

While the multiplying allegations could lead one to believe that Nigeria had developed its own form of the old colonial-era punitive expedition, but against its own people, the military has maintained its denial of using excessive force. When I interviewed the defence spokesman Brigadier-General Chris Olukolade in May 2013, he firmly defended the military's actions. He also argued that insurgents wearing camouflage have confused residents and led them to believe that soldiers were carrying out violence. As for indiscriminate arrests, Olukolade said anyone detained would have been accused of being directly involved in the insurgency.

'Our position is every troop operating in this mission has been sufficiently briefed of the need to respect the rights of citizens, the need never to engage in extrajudicial killings, the need to observe all the laws of armed conflict, and not to execute anybody for whatever reason', Olukolade said. 'So they are very much aware – the briefing is going on every day as a routine – and so every troop in this mission knows the implication of such. If we have such allegation and it is credible, it will be investigated and proper trial would go on. But so far, there is no indication apart from allegations that are evidently meant to be propaganda.'

Specifically regarding Baga, he said that 'if I take you to Baga now, all along the route between Maiduguri and Baga is full of burnt villages. It is a pattern [...] In that same Baga, the whole burning that people are referring to did not take place during this encounter. It is accumulating. Every house that was identified by Boko Haram as not supporting, because they had invaded the community, they burn down the house. And they were doing this not in one day. It has accumulated for years.'

Later, the defence spokesman said accusations against the military had been made unfairly, either for propaganda purposes or simply because residents had been duped.

'It's not unlikely you get people who will testify that it is done by soldiers [...] Sympathies vary, for whatever reason, and it depends on who is giving you testimony. It will reflect his sympathies.' He said insurgents have worn camouflage, sometimes of a different type from that worn by the Nigerian military. 'They found some camo that are not Nigerian camo – there is Chadian camo, there is Niger camo. But for civilians just seeing camo, what does he see? Soldiers.'

Olukolade told me during the interview that 'I have not confirmed that soldiers did the burning in Maiduguri or anywhere. No soldier will do that now. They know the implication. I can tell you no soldier is involved in any form of arson.'

5

'I DON'T KNOW. THEY'RE IN THE BUSH'

The dead bodies lay under a scorching sun, at least 26 of them, some contorted and twisted, others seeming to have been set out, if not neatly, then at least in something resembling a row. One man's head was tilted up toward the sky, his mouth open as if he were yelling. The smell was putrid, familiar to anyone who has smelled death before, but worsened by the intense heat, and yet somehow the workers in nearby medical units carried on, moving about the hospital grounds while occasionally covering their noses with their shirts or gowns. They seemed as if they had grown accustomed to it. One explained that the bodies had come from an area about 45 miles away called Benisheik and had been dumped either by security forces or residents who had recovered a corpse along the roadside. If relatives did not come soon to collect the bodies, the corpses would be buried in a mass grave like others before them. The hospital worker said that both victims of insurgent attacks and the insurgents themselves, or at least those labelled as such, were regularly dumped there in that manner, though dead soldiers were usually taken out of view inside the mortuary, steps away. Asked why all the bodies were not placed inside instead of on the dirt outdoors, she reasoned that the lack of steady electricity would cause them to rot even faster there. She said there was an electricity generator for the mortuary, but it didn't always work properly. In any case, the mortuary was locked up tight on this Friday afternoon since the workers there had gone to pray. It closes at other times because the attendants are often ill, according to the hospital worker. The conditions apparently make them sick.

This was at a time when, if the military was to be believed, things were getting better. The truth was far more complicated, and the reason the bodies were rotting in the dirt at the back of Borno State Specialist Hospital complex in Maiduguri would attest to that. Another state of emergency had been declared in the region more than four months earlier, in May 2013, with President Jonathan having decided after years of attacks and mayhem that something dramatic must be done. Additional troops were deployed into the region, tasked with taking back villages that the president said the insurgents had occupied. He told the nation in a televised speech that the extremists from Boko Haram had replaced the Nigerian flag with their own in certain remote border areas. Some estimates put the number of districts under Boko Haram control at 21 and described it as a gradual process, beginning around January 2013. Since Boko Haram had not been previously known to seek to take territory and had focused solely on insurgent attacks, the development would mean a sharp change in tactics. It came at a time when the world had been focused on a different Islamist extremist advance in nearby northern Mali, where rebels had taken control of around half the country, sparking a French military assault to chase them out. Jonathan's declaration led to worry over whether Nigerian extremists had gone to Mali and returned home battle-hardened, ready to emulate the strategy there, or whether insurgents who never left had simply taken inspiration from it.

Within hours of the president's emergency declaration, the military assault began, and it became clear almost instantly that determining what was really happening on the ground was going to be next to impossible. One of the army's first moves was to cut mobile phone lines in the north-east, ostensibly because the insurgents used them to coordinate attacks. Satellite phones would also be banned later for the same reason. Since landlines are virtually non-existent in Nigeria, this meant the region was cut off from the rest of the world. On top of that, visiting remote areas without a military escort was considered too dangerous – because of the insurgents, certainly, but also thanks to the presence of soldiers with ruthless reputations. Nonetheless, through a combination of military statements, limited visits to the region, accounts from local residents and, perhaps above all, the emergence of a new pattern of attacks, details began to filter through and a picture, however incomplete, gradually took shape.

Early on in the offensive, the military claimed to have cleared out insurgents from camps, often in forests or on the outskirts of villages. It said it had done this with aircraft providing cover for ground troops. How many insurgents were involved, how many died, how many were arrested and where those who fled escaped to were questions the military was refusing to answer in any coherent fashion. The lack of publicly known information also led to concerns that soldiers were again killing civilians whom they accused of cooperating with Boko Haram or simply to instil fear.

There were also doubts about what exactly the offensive was achieving. Sporadic military statements made grandiose claims of having taken over almost all of Boko Haram's remote camps, but no one knew for sure who had really been there or what the soldiers had done. Besides that, while the number of insurgent attacks seemed to have diminished since the start of the offensive, they had by no means stopped altogether. Shekau, dressed in camouflage, appeared in a video that surfaced at the end of May, claiming that Nigerian troops were retreating and being killed in the fight against Boko Haram, while also showing weapons and vehicles he said were taken from the military.

A couple of weeks in, with the military under pressure to give some account of what it claimed to be achieving, it arranged a tour for journalists into an area of the north-east said to have been taken over by insurgents before soldiers chased them out.

A first attempt was a disappointment. Defence officials invited a mix of local and foreign journalists on the tour a day and a half before it was due to occur, and we scrambled to arrange to be there. We were told to meet in the capital Abuja, where we would take an air force transport plane to Maiduguri, but further details were unclear. Our photographer and I, like other journalists, flew from Lagos to Abuja ready for any possibility, as we had no idea what to expect once we arrived in the north-east. I had not visited the region for about a year by that point, long before the president declared his state of emergency. When our flight landed in Abuja the night before we were to meet the soldiers and I turned my phone back on, I saw that a text message had come through from the army officer who had been arranging logistics. The trip was cancelled, he said. He later assured me by phone that there would be another one scheduled soon.

The trip was indeed rescheduled about a week later, so we again packed our bags and headed to Abuja, all the while doubting whether it would actually go ahead. This time it would, and along with the other journalists we piled into a military transport plane at an airbase in the capital Abuja and took off for Maiduguri. I had visited Maiduguri twice before, and as the insurgency intensified, it had become a city under lockdown. My previous trip there had been in May 2012, and certain neighbourhoods had eerily seemed like ghost towns, with burnt-out buildings, the carcasses of torched cars and bullet-pocked walls. Schools had been hit by arson, but children were still attending classes in what remained of at least one of them, scampering around the rubble in green and yellow uniforms, one of the teachers telling me that parents insisted that learning continue. A night-time curfew caused a scramble to get home and off the streets toward the end of the day or face the wrath of soldiers. Shop owners and traders said they could no longer support their families. While most Maiduguri residents were Muslim, it was also home to a substantial Christian population, whose churches had been attacked so many times that they were forced to erect large concrete walls topped with razor wire. Some were protected by small military posts, where soldiers with AK-47s stood behind sandbags near the church entrance. Worshippers attending Sunday mass were scanned with metal detectors and women were forced to leave their handbags outside. On the roads throughout the city, there were regular military checkpoints, causing excruciating traffic jams that left drivers waiting in fear over whether yet another homemade bomb targeting soldiers in the area would explode or a gun battle would break out. I visited retired army general Mohammed Shuwa, known for his role in Nigeria's civil war, at his home in the city and he showed me the Beretta handgun he carried because he feared that even he could one day be targeted. He was right. Later that year, gunmen shot him dead.

After we landed in Maiduguri for the military tour in June 2013, it was difficult to draw any firm conclusions about whether the situation in the city had significantly changed, with soldiers keeping us on a tight leash. We were corralled on a military base and an erratic form of show-and-tell began, with military officers making presentations that were haphazard and contradictory. Inside a meeting room, they first showed us slides that explained characteristics of the region as well as aspects of Boko Haram. We were then rushed around to different areas of the base so soldiers could present weapons to us supposedly seized from insurgents. They included rudimentary weapons such as daggers and bows and arrows, but also AK-47s, rocket-propelled grenades and machine guns to be mounted on 4×4s that one military official called anti-aircraft guns. Asked repeatedly where the insurgents were obtaining these weapons, military officials informed us that they did not know, but said most of the arms seemed to have been of the type that would typically come from the former Soviet bloc. There had also been concern that the fall of Muammar Gaddafi in Libya in 2011 and resulting chaos had led to looted weapons being sold across the region, helping further arm extremist groups.

Boko Haram elements may have benefited. A Nigerian military arms depot at a barracks in the town of Monguno had been raided as well.

We were hurried along, limiting the number of questions that could be asked but assured there would be time for further discussion later, then told to board buses for the drive deeper into the north-east towards the villages of Marte and Kirenowa, the area where insurgents were said to have set up a camp later cleared out by soldiers. The road would pass through increasingly remote territory as we travelled in the direction of Lake Chad, and we were soon moving through flat, semi-desert landscape, only acacia trees, shrub and occasional patches of grass breaking up the dull, grey sand for long stretches at a time. A tiny village sometimes made of thatched huts, others with homes of concrete or brick, would periodically come into view. It felt in some ways as if we were travelling back in time. The silent, wide-open savannah can seem like a separate country altogether compared to a place like Lagos, the heaving economic capital in Nigeria's south-west, or even nearby Maiduguri. As we moved closer to Lake Chad, the patches of grass became more frequent, the trees more prevalent. The rainy season had not yet fully begun, though it would soon come and would alter the landscape.

During the journey, the military asked that we wear flak jackets as a precaution, but, to our surprise, the route seemed to pose little risk. We reached a military base after driving for a few hours, the road having become so eroded in one stretch that we veered off to the side and rumbled across the sand, dust billowing around our convoy. When we entered the base, Lieutenant-Colonel Gabriel Olufemi Olorunyomi stood before maps and a large, hand-drawn diagram, then launched into a choppy explanation of how the army had retaken control of the area from Boko Haram. According to the narrative he laid out, Boko Haram members arrived in the area and preached to the local people that 'everything that has to do with government is haram' and forced girls to marry them. Later they sought to forcefully take control of areas of Marte, burning a local government secretariat, the governor's lodge and a church, while also destroying a hospital and looting drugs from it. He said they even raised their own flag in place of Nigeria's – an echo of one of the points made by the president in his state of emergency declaration. The lieutenant-colonel was unsteady when pressed for details, however. He could not say what the flag looked like, and his description of the military assault that reclaimed the area left many details open to interpretation. He did not want to say how many extremists had been arrested or killed. He said that some had scattered when soldiers cleared out a camp they had used. Asked where they had run to, he said, 'I don't know. They're in the bush.' The day would continue in this manner.

We were hurried back onto the buses to be driven to a second base, but along the way stopped in an area known as New Marte so we could be shown the blackened cement walls of a bare-bones church. There was only time for a few pictures before the soldiers began ordering us to board the buses again, saying it would be dark before we knew it and we must move quickly. We grudgingly followed the orders, aware that we were being made part of a ham-fisted attempt at public relations, but also understanding that even a glimpse of villages such as this one was worth the trip. We made another stop at a spot which military officials said would usually be planted with crops, but Boko Haram had caused farmers to flee.

At the next base, we were given another presentation, this one declaring how the villagers of Kirenowa had been rescued from Boko Haram and the nearby Islamist camp had been cleared. However, it seemed again that the military was cobbling together details that were contradictory. We held out hope that the next stop on our tour, a visit to Kirenowa itself, would shed some light.

We rode in military trucks and our convoy manoeuvred closer towards Lake Chad before crossing a canal, then into the village itself. We piled out of trucks and followed fast-walking military officials across the dusty ground broken up by patches of dry scrub.

The soldiers provided varying explanations of what had happened and why as they led us back to what they said had been the Boko Haram camp. Whatever had been there, it seemed that it had not been much.

Set within a clearing between trees and tangled scrub, we were shown burnt-out cars, empty food containers and abandoned clothes. Soldiers told us the insurgents had burnt the vehicles before they fled because they did not want the military to recover them, but the explanation did not seem to add up: why would they bother? They seemed to be just cars. Under the shade of a stand of trees, we were shown empty boxes of medicines and medical supplies such as surgical gloves, apparently looted from the hospital in Marte. There were also condoms – a reminder of a military statement several days earlier proclaiming that 'more of the dirty sides of the insurgents' lifestyle are being revealed as troops continue to stumble on strange and bizarre objects such as several used and unused condoms'. Needless to say, we were sceptical, and not only about the condoms.

We were led back to the village, where a gathering awaited us in the heart of Kirenowa. A local chief, wearing sunglasses and a light-green traditional robe, praised the soldiers for their work as hundreds of residents looked on and applauded. The chief told us that residents had been forced to flee when Boko Haram members arrived and took up residence nearby. Where they had gone or when they returned was not clear. Some residents told local journalists that girls in the village had been forced to marry Boko Haram members and that the insurgents had stolen from them.[1]

Such details were to be treated with caution, as with almost all aspects of the day's tour, since residents could have been coached on what to say before our arrival, but they were certainly worth noting and seemed plausible. As the brief gathering ended, we were again hurried aboard the trucks, taken to the nearby military base, then driven back to Maiduguri aboard buses, many of us left pondering what to make of it all. We would not be given much help from the military. The next morning, after repeatedly asking military officials to allow us the chance to ask questions for clarification, they finally relented, so we gathered in a circle around Brigadier-General Chris Olukolade,[2] the defence spokesman, as he stood in a car park, powered on our recorders and video cameras, and sought answers. They were not exactly forthcoming. Asked why the offensive was different from what occurred in 2009, when the military insisted Boko Haram had been wiped out before the group re-emerged, Olukolade said it 'involved not just the military but the security agencies of the country. The network this time is perfect, I mean near-perfect, in the sense that the operation was planned to ensure their bases were dislocated – not just dislocated but completely wiped out.' Pressed on how many Boko Haram members had been arrested, he said, 'I can just tell you that hundreds of them.' How many Boko Haram members had been charged or sentenced? 'Well, several of them.'

Sporadic bursts of information and disinformation from the military would continue in a similar manner in the weeks following the tour. It began to feel like a repeat of previous military operations: a flurry of activity, scattering the insurgents and temporarily reducing the number of attacks, only for the Islamists to return to fight another day. An unexpected development would, however, soon cast the crisis in a different light, one that offered a degree of hope, but which also presented severe dangers.

In mid-June 2013, word began to filter out that vigilante groups had formed in Maiduguri to fight the insurgents. One of the early signs came in the form of road checkpoints. Maiduguri residents had long become accustomed to security roadblocks as their city descended into violence, but the new checkpoints that began to materialise were different. They were now being manned by the vigilantes, a motley collection of mainly young men carrying homemade bows and arrows, swords, sticks, pipes and charms they said were powerful enough to stop bullets. They would peer into cars as drivers moved slowly past, stopping those they deemed suspicious, or wait for orders from the military that they were needed for a raid aimed at arresting Boko Haram members. Some of the vigilantes admitted that they sometimes killed people during these raids – though specifying only when they had to – and handed over those they arrested to the region's Joint Task Force, a security deployment run by the military. The task force was known across Nigeria by its initials JTF, and the vigilantes adopted this name, calling themselves the 'Civilian JTF'. The military encouraged the groups' formation, assisted them and spurred them along, apparently fed up with seeing their own men killed in a conflict that seemed to have no end. Military officials also reasoned that because the vigilantes were members of the community, they would know who were Boko Haram members and who were not. Rumours spread that some of the vigilantes were in fact also former insurgents. They at first denied being paid anything, insisting they were only a volunteer force interested in peace after years of upheaval, but it was widely believed that either the security forces or state government, or perhaps both, were somehow financing them. Later, the state government would seek to normalise the unwieldy force, providing training, light-blue uniforms and regular payments for a number of them.[3]

Several weeks into the formation of the vigilantes, there were signs of improvement. Attacks in Maiduguri itself were becoming increasingly rare, a stark turnaround considering the city had been wracked by incessant violence for much of the previous four years, causing thousands to flee, shutting down businesses and killing hundreds. Residents also seemed to be welcoming the vigilantes, relieved that they could venture outside again, reopen their market stalls and even send their children to schools with less worry. The phones were still cut, but there did not appear to be a major uproar over it in Maiduguri itself as many residents saw it as a legitimate sacrifice for peace.

The insurgents' response to the military offensive and formation of vigilante groups appeared to be to largely abandon the city of Maiduguri. They were said to have fled to border areas near Cameroon, Chad or Niger, particularly in the region's Gwoza hills. The border with Cameroon was considered especially porous, and local residents spoke of Boko Haram members crossing back and forth, sometimes carrying out robberies and attacks on the Nigerian side, occasionally slitting the throats of their victims in a show of force. Unconfirmed rumours spread over whether Shekau had been killed, while the military later claimed he 'may have died' after being shot in a clash with troops and taken over the border into Cameroon for treatment, but provided no proof. Shekau had been rumoured or declared to be dead several times before, only to later appear in video and audio messages. A man who seemed to be Shekau would repeatedly appear in more videos after the military statement on his supposed death. Yet another resurrection had occurred, it seemed.

Earlier hints of a new pattern of attacks would later prove to be true, with a terrifying series of civilian massacres beginning to unfold. It was widely believed such attacks were partly in revenge for the formation of the vigilante groups and for residents' cooperation with them in reporting insurgents' movements. Two attacks on schools in June saw gunmen shoot dead 16 students and 2 teachers.[4] They were similar to an attack the previous March in Maiduguri at the Sanda Kyarimi Senior Secondary School. Months later, a security guard walked the school grounds at Sanda Kyarimi with me and explained how it occurred.

According to the security guard, 35-year-old Ahmed Jidda, he and the school disciplinarian were at the school's front gate on a Monday morning trying to usher in stragglers who were arriving late when two people with AK-47s forced their way in and began shooting sporadically. He said the attackers looked like teenagers, guessing they were between 15 and 18 years old. They were not wearing masks. They made their way across the large open yard ringed by single-storey buildings housing classrooms on the school grounds, at one point throwing a homemade bomb that did not explode. Students and teachers panicked, taking cover or running to find a way out, as the attackers continued to fire their weapons. At one classroom, they shot inside at a teacher, killing him. Jidda showed me the classroom, and on the day I visited there were lessons on the English alphabet written neatly on the blackboard, with classes having since resumed at the school after a temporary closure. Jidda said he had managed to climb over a part of the wall surrounding the school, then run to a nearby military outpost to alert the soldiers. By then it was too late. The gunmen left after their brief flurry of violence. Besides the teacher they killed, four girls who were students were wounded, one of whom later died.

By July 2013, Nigerians had seen several such school attacks, but one that would occur in the town of Mamudo in Yobe state would lead to widespread disgust. The attackers stormed a secondary boarding school in the town, opening fire and throwing explosives inside a dormitory, burning students to death. A total of 42 people were killed, mostly students. President Jonathan's spokesman would break from the usual condemnations and promises of action, saying those responsible 'will certainly go to hell'.[5]

It began to seem that nothing was off limits to the attackers any more. As if to prove the point, the following month in the town of Konduga, gunmen stormed a mosque and killed 44 people.[6] That, too, was thought to be revenge for the actions of the vigilante groups.

Up to that point, the deadliest of the so-called revenge attacks would occur in an area known as Benisheik, a town on the road between Maiduguri and the city of Damaturu. On 17 September 2013, a group of insurgents dressed as soldiers, well-armed with AK-47s, homemade bombs and other weapons, stopped cars and buses, singled out residents of Borno state and shot them dead. They burned vehicles and set buildings on fire in the area. The military was slow to arrive – possibly because of the lack of a phone network, possibly for more ominous reasons, such as a reluctance to confront the killers. When soldiers did show up, according to some reports, they were overpowered and ran out of ammunition trying to fight the attackers.

When it was finally all over, bodies were strewn across the road. Travellers along the same route in the days that followed reported seeing surreal scenes as they passed through, their horrifying descriptions almost too gory to be believed, the capacity to inflict so much violence and death in such a cold, calculated manner hard to comprehend. State workers said they had counted at least 142 bodies.[7] Some of those apparently ended up at the Borno State Specialist Hospital in Maiduguri, among the bodies dumped on the ground at the back of the sprawling complex outside the morgue. This is where I stood about three weeks after the attack, covering my nose with my shirt to block the intense odour of rotting human flesh.

The hospital had been known for its overcrowded morgue. Neighbours had reportedly complained about the smell. Even before the start of the military offensive in May 2013, there were reports of sometimes dozens of corpses arriving daily, feeding fears that the military was simply resorting to extrajudicial executions for those suspected of being Boko Haram members, though such accusations have always been strongly denied by the security forces.[8] As I followed the covered concrete walkway back to where the morgue was located, a security guard with choppy English who saw me looking at the bodies on the ground said, 'Boko Harams', seeming to indicate they were dead insurgents. When I asked whether they were Boko Haram members, she seemed to say yes, but it was not clear if she understood my question. A medical worker then appeared from a nearby ward and began to speak to me calmly in English as we stood on the sidewalk near the bodies. We eventually moved slightly further away, since the smell was so strong. She told me that the bodies were in fact those of civilians killed in Benisheik and brought here, either by soldiers or by residents. After we spoke a few minutes more, I thanked her, then made my way back to the front of the hospital grounds, where a colleague I was working with waited.

Later that day as I reflected on what I had seen, I began to think that I needed to return. I had admittedly not moved off the sidewalk into the dirt to get a closer look at the bodies. From where I stood, I could not tell what types of wounds had been inflicted on them. I had been reluctant for a combination of reasons, including the smell, the fear of being kicked off the property or even arrested, not to mention the disturbing thought of walking between scattered corpses and studying them up close. I had not been able to speak with morgue attendants, either, since no one was there. As awful as it may be, I had to at least attempt to find out how these people died.

The next morning, a Saturday, our first stop was back at the hospital. My Nigerian colleague who was helping out as my guide and translator during my stay in Maiduguri parked his car out front and said he would wait there, unwilling to participate in the gruesome task ahead. I understood, of course, and began walking straight back toward the morgue, not wanting to waste any time and hoping not to be stopped. As the morgue came within view, I could make out some of the bodies, still lying on the ground, and I pushed on reluctantly towards them. I would not, however, get much further. A yell 'hey!' – punctured the air and I knew it was for me. At first I tried to ignore it and keep walking, but I heard it again a couple seconds later and decided I should turn and see who it was. As I spun around, I saw a guard holding his rifle – a soldier not in full uniform, I believe – angrily yelling at me to stop as he moved toward me. I now had no choice.

I had learned through experience in such situations that it is best to seek to defuse the tension rather than appear confrontational, and I tried to do just that. When the guard, a young man who actually appeared more nervous than angry when we met face to face, asked me where I was going, I told him in a conciliatory voice that I was a journalist and wanted to speak with the morgue workers. When he asked why, I said that I was hoping to get information about what happened in Benisheik. The explanation was reasonably truthful, as I had been told that the bodies were from there and I did want to speak with morgue workers, though I was of course also wondering if some of the dead had been killed by the military. He relaxed almost instantly, possibly because it was the insurgents who were accused of horrific acts in Benisheik and not the military, then told me calmly that the morgue attendants were not there today. As we spoke, however, a middle-aged man in civilian clothes approached with a stern look, unhappy about my presence. He too asked me what I was doing, then told me I had to leave. He said I was not allowed to simply show up at the hospital and wander around. 'Can you do that in your own country?', he asked. He said that if I wanted any information, I had to speak with the state commissioner of health. I asked whether there was anyone at the hospital I could speak with, and he said no. Out of options, I turned and walked back to the car.[9]

The sight of the corpses symbolised so much of the Boko Haram conflict for me – bodies brutally dumped, nameless people dead for unclear reasons, the lack of even a working morgue to store them in. It was not only the sight of the bodies themselves that was so troubling, but also the grim combination of circumstances that led to them being there and the question of whether such a spiral of killing and neglect could ever be brought to an end.

Yet at the same time, it was certainly true that Maiduguri itself had changed. With the sharp decrease in attacks inside the city after the deployment of additional soldiers and the formation of vigilante groups, life had begun to regain some semblance of normality. Markets that had been burnt down – either by soldiers or insurgents – were being rebuilt and reopened. The roads were busy, and the curfew had been relaxed.

It was tempting to see all of this as a ray of hope, and to a certain degree it was, but there was also the feeling that it was a mirage. There were regular instances of mayhem not far outside the city gates, while in Maiduguri, reminders of the conflict were everywhere. Rubble remained amid the overgrown weeds at the site of Mohammed Yusuf's former mosque, destroyed by the military more than four years earlier. Burnt cars and buildings could still be seen in neighbourhoods badly hit by insurgent attacks and the military's heavy-handed raids.

There were also members of the 'Civilian JTF', the vigilantes who gathered along the roadsides near military posts or who set up checkpoints, sometimes wearing masks. One young man who positioned himself in the middle of a busy street as two-way traffic meandered past him wore a gold-coloured carnival-type mask covering the area around the eyes. They were dressed in street clothes – mainly jeans and T-shirts. Some looked especially young, but vigilantes themselves insisted they recruited no one under 18. I cannot say I was convinced. They could be rowdy and menacing at times, peering into cars as they passed while holding pipes or bows and arrows fashioned from scrap wood and metal. At one point around the middle of the day during my stay in October 2013, a group gave chase on to the grounds of a courthouse in pursuit of someone they wanted to arrest as a crowd gathered around them. The commotion eventually subsided, the man apparently being taken to the military.

One group of around 20 vigilantes waited near a military post, saying they were to be taken for a raid into 'the bush' around the town of Damboa because they had been told that Boko Haram members were hiding out there, causing trouble for the farmers. When a convoy of cars pulled up later, apparently returning from such a raid, the crowd that had been waiting began to cheer them and ran toward the vehicles. Some followed them on foot as they pulled into the security post guarded out front by soldiers. One man told me that sometimes they kill their suspects if they have to, at other times they capture them. It was easy to see how the vigilantes' raids could end up turning community against community, unleashing a new demon in a region with too many. The same pattern continued in the months after my visit to Maiduguri. There was another school massacre, and an attack on the infamous Giwa military barracks led to allegations of vigilantes helping round up hundreds of escaped detainees who were then executed by the military.[10]

One young man I met in October 2013, a raggedly dressed 21-year-old named Umar Mustapha, described himself as chairman of one 'sector' of the Civilian JTF. He held a sword that was about waist-high in length and showed me small leather amulets he said were given to him by the chief imam of Borno state. The amulets had supernatural powers and would protect him from injury, he insisted. They would stop weapons from firing. 'Any AK-47 or any gun, you will not use it', he said. 'They want to shoot us and the gun refuses to work.'

6

'OUR GIRLS WERE KIDNAPPED AND THEY DID NOT DO ANYTHING'

The man dressed in a pearly white outfit wanted to speak with me. I knew this because one of his hangers-on insistently sought to direct me toward him, as if I were being summoned. His card, with a green and white background, Nigeria's national colours, provided his name as 'Hon. Amb. Jude Tabai'. The abbreviations stood for honourable ambassador, a title he said had been granted to him by the first lady.[1] Underneath his name was written 'director' and 'strategic team', while in the top left corner of the card was a picture of President Goodluck Jonathan's face.

'So you're working for the president, his team?', I asked him.

'Yeah, yeah, yeah, yeah', he said.

'So what do you do for them, for him?'

'Well, that's undercover actually. So more like security [...]'.

We had met nearby just a few minutes earlier, across from Nigeria's Unity Fountain in the capital Abuja, where a counter-protest was gathering for a second day. The counter-protest had drawn heavy criticism because it appeared to have been a paid-for crowd designed to disrupt another peaceful demonstration being held in the same location. The original protests had been occurring daily for nearly a month, demanding that the government and military take action over an issue that had suddenly brought Nigeria into the world spotlight: the abduction of nearly 300 girls from their school in the north-eastern town of Chibok. The original protests were not large – dozens of people – but it seemed that the government, or at least supporters of the government, were rattled by them. The campaign under the banner of Bring Back Our Girls had by then gained traction globally, helped along by social media. Moral support had come from a long list of famous names, including Michelle Obama, the American first lady, who tweeted a sad-faced picture of herself while holding a sign with the #BringBackOurGirls hashtag.

When I first met Tabai earlier, he had been seated among organisers of the counter-protest, the one in support of the government. We were now standing in the afternoon heat next to a car parked in the grass, a handful of young men next to us. He told me that he was not an organiser of the counter-protest and had simply been passing by, saw the crowd and decided to stop. 'If I am involved, I will tell you', he said, 'I am not in that business.' At one point while we were speaking, one of the young men said something to someone else, and Tabai turned on him, telling him sharply, 'my friend, keep your mouth shut'. The young man listened, a shamed look on his face. Besides claiming to hold some unspecified 'security' role for the president, Tabai, who looked to be in his fifties, also explained to me that he held the title of king of the youths in the Niger Delta, President Jonathan's home region.[2] There were many people like him in Nigeria who laid claim to such titles. The local media had also at times referred to him in that way, though his true influence would remain a mystery to me. He had also worked as an adviser in Bayelsa, President Jonathan's home state.

'But this protest, it seems sponsored, to be honest', I said, referring to the counter-demonstrators.

'That's what you think?' he asked me.

'It looks that way, yes.'

'OK, if you say "seems sponsored", I don't know from what angle, because these protests have been going on for like two, three weeks now', Tabai said, apparently hoping that I would not know the difference between the two separate demonstrations. He spoke clearly and articulately.

'Well, it's been the other people who've been protesting', I said.

He had taken his chance and failed, but he was undaunted. He changed tack and moved on to other arguments. It would turn out to be a lengthy conversation, filled with the kind of conspiracy theories one hears often in Nigeria. The gist of Tabai's argument was that the Boko Haram insurgency was political, backed by Jonathan's enemies and geared toward 2015 elections. But he did not stop there.

'As I speak to you, those girls have been released', he declared about midway through our conversation, referring to the students kidnapped in Chibok.

'You think they've been released?'

'Yes.'

'By who?'

'Their collaborators and co-sponsors have released those girls. Ask me why.'

＊　＊　＊

Stories have varied and a precise account of what happened will probably never be unravelled, but there are common threads that run through the descriptions provided by parents, school officials and girls who escaped. They have described an attack that began like many others before it. At close to midnight, deep in the savannah scrubland of north-eastern Nigeria, dozens of armed men, at least some in military uniforms, arrived in pick-up trucks and motorcycles and opened fire, battling a handful of overwhelmed soldiers and targeting government buildings. As gunfire crackled and fires set by the attackers raged, residents fled through the darkness and took cover in the scrubland surrounding the town of Chibok. Armed men then stormed their way toward a boarding school, where several hundred teenage girls had turned in for the night. 'We are sleeping', an 18-year-old girl who was there at the time told me. 'We hear when they shoot their guns in Chibok. We thought they were playing with guns.' Over the next several weeks, what had started as the kind of insurgent raid Nigerians had sadly grown accustomed to hearing about would set the world on edge.

In the north-east of Nigeria, where Islam is by far the dominant faith, Chibok stands out as an anomaly.[3] It is mostly Christian, though it includes a large number of Muslims as well. Its Christian heritage involves missionaries from the Church of the Brethren, a Protestant denomination, who began arriving in Nigeria in 1923.[4] Its population is largely people from the Kibaku ethnic group, separate from their rivals the Kanuris, who dominate the region. Gerald Neher, an American who lived in Chibok as a missionary between 1954 and 1957, in 1959–60, then again in 1968, remembered the town being isolated at the time, its dirt roads leading to the outside world cut off by streams in the rainy season. He worked with farmers using oxen and ploughs, while his wife taught, her students writing in the dirt with sticks. Religious education and conversion were of course part of the missionaries' activities as well, and many Chibok residents slowly embraced Christianity in place of their ancient beliefs – on the surface, anyway, since the two would likely have existed side by side. Such conversions would strike many today as objectionable given the paternalism it implies, but Neher, now in his eighties, makes no apologies for it. He told me he firmly believes he helped improve lives in Chibok and remains proud of his work, including its religious aspect. Travelling Muslim teachers also made their way to Chibok and sought to convert residents, gathering students under trees to teach the Qur'an, Neher remembered. Girls did not go to school at the thatched mud-brick classrooms when Neher was first there in the 1950s, but when he returned a decade later, some had begun attending. Today, its people are mainly farmers, its population estimated at around 70,000.[5]

In March 2014, about a month before the students were awakened by gunfire coming from outside their dormitory, Borno state, where Chibok is located, announced that it would be forced to close its secondary schools until further notice after repeated attacks.[6] The assaults that prompted the closures were far more deadly than what would occur later in Chibok, but they had not received sustained attention from the outside world. They included two massacres of dozens of boys at boarding schools in neighbouring Yobe state. School officials in Chibok would suggest later that their institution had simply closed for vacation, but they appear to have been telling only part of the story. As one government official I interviewed, as well as parents, explained, the closure was a forced vacation since no one wanted to see any other students killed.

While the reason for the closures may have been noble, the decision nonetheless drew concerns. Education is badly lacking in north-eastern Nigeria, and the situation is even worse for girls. About one in ten females aged six and older are considered literate in Borno state. That compares to a nationwide rate of 47.7 per cent and a rate in Lagos of 92 per cent. Shutting down schools would obviously threaten any progress made toward addressing the problem.[7] The school where the girls were taken had previously been called Government Girls Secondary School Chibok, and it was run by the Borno state government. Its name had recently changed, dropping the word 'girls' after it began accepting boys. The boys, originally from around Chibok, had been relocated from their schools in particularly dangerous areas of Borno state. They attended school in Chibok during the day and were not boarding students, unlike the girls. A total of 530 students were enrolled, 135 boys and 395 girls, according to the principal, Asabe Kwambula.

Though the schools had been closed in March, administrators and government officials faced a dilemma about what to do with the students in their final year, who were set to take their examinations and move on. According to a government official I spoke with, discussions were held with the Nigerian ministry of education and the West African Examinations Council, which administers the final exams, about how to proceed. The official told me that it was decided through the discussions that a number of schools in Borno state would be allowed to serve as examination centres, including the secondary school in Chibok, and that they would call back final-year students to complete the tests. Before that could be done, however, officials were to petition the authorities to provide proper security for the schools to ensure they would be as safe as possible. The story from that point on becomes increasingly murky.

Borno state and school officials say they met with the police and delivered a letter to the state police commissioner requesting additional security for the examinations period. Afterwards, according to one school official, four policemen were sent, but they were only to be on duty during daytime hours, when the exams were being taken. There would be no additional security at night. The military presence in the town itself was also light, with a contingent of 17 soldiers said to have been stationed there.[8] It would not be nearly enough, and the debate over whose fault it was that more security was not provided would later become an intense, politically charged dispute. There were also allegations that the students should not have been called back at all given the potential danger. The federal government blamed state officials in Borno, which is run by an opposition party, while the state said the opposite. It should be noted, however, that while the state-run school and Borno's government should have taken far more precautions, both the police and the military are federal institutions beyond their direct control. 'This thing happened due to the lack of proper security', the school official who did not want to be named to avoid antagonising the federal government told me. 'If there is proper security, I think this thing would not happen. But, you know, the security is not in the hands of the school.' There were also allegations, however, that the state had refused requests to relocate the exams to Maiduguri and that it had guaranteed that adequate security would be provided.[9]

According to the principal, a night-watchman was on duty at the time of the attack, but apart from that, there did not appear to be any adult supervision at the dormitory where the girls slept, such as a monitor to oversee them. The secretary to the Borno state government, Baba Ahmed Jidda, told a Nigerian news channel of the girls, who were generally between 16 and 18 years old, that 'literally, they were on their own because it was night and the principal and teachers live outside the dormitories of the students'.[10] There were initial reports that the principal was there and had been duped by the attackers since they were wearing military uniforms. She told me she was far away, however. She said she had gone to the state capital, Maiduguri, to see her doctor, who had been treating her for diabetes.[11] At least one vice principal remained in Chibok.

Boko Haram had been blamed previously for abducting girls, forcing them to convert to Islam, marrying them and making them work as slaves.[12] Human Rights Watch in November 2013 quoted a commander of one of the vigilante groups targeting Boko Haram as saying that the extremists had left their wives behind when they were forced to flee Maiduguri because of increased security. As a result, they began kidnapping girls to take with them. In addition to that, suspected members of the group had for some time been kidnapping wealthy Nigerians in and around Maiduguri in order to earn money from ransoms.[13] Such abductions received little attention, as the families preferred to quietly handle ransom negotiations on their own to best ensure safe release. One particularly high-profile victim was a 92-year-old former petroleum minister, Shettima Ali Monguno, who was released a few days later. Those abductions were of course in addition to the kidnappings of foreigners Ansaru and Boko Haram had been involved in throughout the previous months, either executing their victims or releasing them for vast sums of cash.

Despite the insecurity, Nigeria was in preparations to host the World Economic Forum on Africa in May 2014, a gathering of global heavyweights that the government hoped would showcase the country's potential as an investment destination. It had recently announced the results of a long overdue rebasing of its gross domestic product, which pushed its overall GDP figure above South Africa's, making Nigeria the continent's biggest economy. Finance Minister Ngozi Okonjo-Iweala had been seeking to promote her country as a solid place to do business despite all of its challenges, often repeating to potential investors what had in some ways become her catchphrase: 'If you're not in Nigeria, you're not in Africa.' On paper, she was right. Nigeria now boasted three distinctions: Africa's biggest economy, its largest population and its mightiest oil industry. Unfortunately, anyone familiar with the country knew that those three titles meant little for average Nigerians, whose troubles included contending with the violence that would intrude on preparations for the global gathering.

In a further sign of how out of control the insurgency had become, the Chibok assault that took place on 14 April 2014 was not the only horrific attack that day. During the morning rush hour, a bomb tore through a bus station on the outskirts of Abuja and killed at least 75 people.[14] That, too, was a shocking attack, the deadliest yet in the capital and occurring only weeks before Abuja was to host the World Economic Forum event. However, the death and destruction left behind by the bomb would soon be overshadowed by concern over the fate of the Chibok girls.

According to some accounts, word began to spread that a band of attackers were on their way to Chibok. Amnesty International, citing local officials and two senior military officers, said warnings started to filter in shortly after 7 p.m., more than four hours before the attack.[15] According to the rights group, vigilantes in the nearby village of Gagilam alerted authorities 'when a large group of unidentified armed men entered their village on motorbikes and said they were headed to Chibok'. Nigeria's under-equipped and demoralised soldiers were apparently unable to respond effectively. One of the military officers told the group that 'the commander was unable to mobilise reinforcements'. Amnesty quoted the officer as saying: 'There's a lot of frustration, exhaustion and fatigue among officers and [troops] based in the hotspots [...] many soldiers are afraid to go to the battle fronts.'

A government official familiar with details of the investigation into the incident provided a similar account to me, saying local residents had relayed word of an impending attack far in advance. 'They were told three to four hours before the attack', the official said of the military, adding that the response was hampered by 'capacity problems'. Nevertheless, the military has strongly denied the claims. Defence spokesman Major-General Chris Olukolade said troops in the state capital, Maiduguri, were not given advance warning and were instead notified of 'an ongoing attack on Chibok community' by troops in the town who fought the attackers and needed reinforcements. 'As the troops on reinforcement traversed the over 120-kilometre rugged and tortuous road from Maiduguri to Chibok, they ran into an ambush by terrorists who engaged them in [a] fierce firefight and a number of soldiers lost their lives', the defence spokesman wrote in a statement. 'Another set of soldiers also mobilised for the mission arrived after the terrorists had escaped due to a series of misleading information that slowed down the pursuit.'

Sometime between 11.30 and 11.45 that night, dozens of the attackers driving motorbikes and pick-up trucks stormed the town. The soldiers stationed there were no match for them and fled, and the Boko Haram members burned down houses and buildings. Enoch Mark, a pastor at a church in Chibok who had two daughters – one by birth, the other adopted – sleeping in the school dormitory, said he could hear the explosions and gunfire from his house. He decided to flee along with his other children. 'Unfortunately, I have some little children at home. I tried to grab the little ones and rush with them to the bush', he said. Another Chibok resident, Lawan Zanna, who had one daughter sleeping in the dormitory, said that 'we heard gunshots and bomb blasts [...] Some people are going out and leaving their houses.' Zanna told

me he could not say how many attackers had arrived in the town
that night, though the government official said estimates had put
it at around 100.

Either all or some of the Boko Haram members – no one
seems sure – set their sights on the school where the girls were
sleeping. When they arrived, they at first used deception to gather
the students. 'They are saying to us, "Don't worry, don't worry,
come. We are security, we are soldiers, nothing can happen to you.
We are here"', the 18-year-old girl, whose father did not want her
name used, told me by phone. When the men began shooting and
shouting 'Allahu Akbar', they realised that they were not soldiers.
By then it was too late for most, though a school official told
me some of the girls managed to slip away. The girls were told
to follow them to a spot less than a mile outside the school and
were forced aboard pick-up trucks – estimates of how many vary
between around 10 and 20 – while the extremists burnt down the
school buildings, though by some accounts, they first sought to
raid the food supplies. They were also said to have spoken in the
Kanuri language, more common in other parts of Borno state.[16]
The 18-year-old's father said his daughter told him they spoke in
various languages, including Kanuri, Hausa and Kibaku. The girls
were then driven away from the town and toward the Sambisa
forest. According to Chibok residents, the extremists remained
in the town until around 4 a.m., possibly later, but military
reinforcements were still nowhere to be found. One of them told
me on condition of anonymity: 'These people, they are coming
around 11.40-something. They were still in Chibok up to 4 [a.m.]
[...] So I think if the security men are serious, they would have sent
security men to come and stop them.'

On the road out of Chibok, some of the girls decided to risk an
escape and jump out of the trucks. The 16-year-old niece of Dauda
Iliya, who lives in Abuja but whose family roots are in the Chibok
area, was among them. 'One of the trucks actually stalled, got into
trouble, engine trouble, stalled, and when they tried to get it to

move, it wouldn't. So they abandoned it', Iliya told me. 'So the convoy had to slow down and [...] turn away from that disabled truck.' When it did, the truck in which his niece was riding passed beneath a tree. 'She held on to a tree branch and the truck drove off, and that was how she made her miraculous escape. She told me this', he said. He said she and others hid until they felt it was safe enough to walk back toward Chibok. His niece hurt her ankles during the escape, but has since recovered. Other girls escaped in a similar manner. Two of them told a *New York Times* reporter that they were among several who jumped out and ran through the bush when a truck of guards at the end of the convoy slowed down and fell behind.[17]

Either because they did not see the girls who escaped or because they did not care, the attackers pushed on, directing the convoy toward their camp inside what some of the girls and their parents believed was the Sambisa forest, a patch of about 200 square miles – some nine times the area of Manhattan – originally set aside as a game reserve by the British. Boko Haram had been using the forest, about 50 miles away from Chibok, as a hideout for some time along with the nearby Gwoza hills, which are close to the Cameroon border. After the government's state of emergency declaration in 2013, the military claimed to have cleared out extremist camps in the Sambisa reserve with the help of air power, though it was never clear whether soldiers had dropped bombs or fired machine guns from helicopters. Like much of the region's scrubby savannah, the reserve is not heavily forested or jungle-like, though it becomes more dense in its southern half, especially in the rainy season. At the time the girls were taken, it was the end of the dry season. As for wildlife, there is not much left there. A 2006 survey found no elephants and only a smattering of antelopes and warthogs, while noting that there was 'extensive clearing of the reserve for farmland and charcoal burning'.[18]

The convoy drove on for some seven hours before reaching the camp, and after arriving there the Boko Haram members ordered the girls to prepare their food for them. A few of the girls then thought they could slip away. Over a terrible phone line, the 18-year-old sought to explain to me how she escaped, but only some of her words came through. 'I run, I run, I run', she said. 'I run far [...] We are running, we are running, we are running in that bush.' Her father said she had been at the camp about two hours when the opportunity for an escape arose. 'When the other students were chopping that food, that is how she escaped', he said, using a common Nigerian term for eating. He said she told them she was going to the bathroom and made a run for it. After running for some time, she encountered locals from the Fulani ethnic group who agreed to help her. 'She said, "I am asking to show me the way to Chibok. They said OK."' She travelled with them on motorcycles, arriving back home on Wednesday following the Monday night kidnapping. 'I was very, very surprised how she escaped [...] She looked very very well', her father said. She was not alone on her journey; at least two girls, possibly more, managed to escape in that way.[19]

At daybreak, parents rushed to the school to check on their daughters and found burnt buildings. One mother described her anguish when she arrived and realised her 16-year-old daughter had been taken along with the others. 'After reaching the school, I was scared. I was shaking', said the mother, who also asked that her name not be used out of fears for both her and her daughter's safety. 'This school is our hope. This school is our hope [...] After reaching the hostel, I was shocked [...] I just burst out crying. I said, "Lord, why? Lord, why?"' Almost two months after the kidnapping, with no sign of her daughter, she lashed out at the government and military. 'It is real', she said, referring to the conspiracy theories floating around the country. 'Our girls were kidnapped and they did not do anything at all.'

Some of the parents decided to take matters into their own hands. On the day after the abductions, 15 April, they sought to follow what they believed were the girls' footsteps, but did not make it far before they were persuaded to turn around and seek a security escort because it was considered too dangerous. Two days later, there still seemed to be little help, so they either hired motorcycles or used their own vehicles and sped off in the same direction again in search of the girls. This time, it was an estimated 300 parents, relatives and sympathisers on their trail. They made it to a village near the Sambisa forest, and it was there that vigilantes and others told them to turn around, that they were no match for the insurgents. 'They told us it's better for us to go back', said Lawan Zanna, a 45-year-old Arabic teacher in a primary school whose 18-year-old daughter Aisha was taken in the raid. 'We don't have anything to face these people. They have sophisticated weapons. They will gun us down.'

The parents returned home, their daughters lost somewhere in the savannah, held captive by gunmen and with no sign that Nigeria's military was prepared to find them. A range of reasons existed for why the kidnappings had occurred. Boko Haram was opposed to Western education in general, and Shekau would later claim that he believed he was justified in taking slaves. He would also say girls should 'go and get married', and that he would marry them off as young as the age of nine. But there were also strategic reasons since the abductions would serve to embarrass the government, while a hefty ransom could also be demanded for the girls' release.

It seemed that the abductions at first barely registered on the world's radar. Part of the reason may have been confusion over what exactly had happened. School officials initially could not even say how many girls had been kidnapped. An early estimate of the total number of girls taken was 129, and school officials would say later that it took several days for them to establish a reliable count of the missing and confirm it with parents. The absence of a clear explanation left a vacuum that was to a large degree filled by conspiracy theories. Some were spread by President Jonathan's supporters, who said that the kidnappings were a hoax perpetrated by his northern opponents, designed to embarrass the president and perhaps force him to decline to seek re-election in polls less than a year away, in February 2015. As for the military, it claimed to be searching for the girls, but parents and activists said there was little evidence that soldiers were doing much at all.

An incident two days after the abductions would cut even further into the military's credibility. Despite the confusion and lack of verifiable information, the defence spokesman, Major-General Chris Olukolade, issued a statement on 16 April that claimed a major breakthrough. Unfortunately, anyone familiar with Nigerian military statements knew to treat it with caution. The statement said that, somehow, all but 8 of the 129 girls taken had been freed or had escaped, citing the school principal as a source. There were no details about how that may have happened, and it is worth asking whether military officials bargained that they could swiftly silence the embarrassing story emanating from an extremely remote area of north-eastern Nigeria by making such a claim. If so, the plan backfired. The principal immediately denied it, leaving the military brass with few options but to backtrack. The following day, Olukolade was forced to issue another statement in which he withdrew his earlier claim and essentially threw his hands in the air.

The statement sought to explain how the military had come to announce the girls' release, saying that 'a report was filed in from the field indicating that a major breakthrough had been recorded in the search. There was no reason to doubt this official channel, hence the information was released to the public immediately. Surprisingly, however, the school principal, one of the sources quoted in the report has denied all that was attributed to her for whatever reasons. This is an unfortunate development indeed, yet the Defence Headquarters would not want to join issues with anyone.'

It bizarrely added later that 'the number of those still missing is not the issue now as the life of every Nigerian is very precious', before completely disowning the earlier claim. 'In the light of the denial by the principal of the school', it said, 'the Defence Headquarters wishes to defer to the school principal and governor's statement on the number of students still missing and retract that aspect of the earlier statement while the search continues.'

The principal, Asabe Kwambula, had called what seemed to have been the military's bluff, but she, too, was coming under increasing criticism for different, competing explanations being attributed to her for how the kidnappings occurred. At least, finally, after more than two weeks, authorities managed to establish what they said was a precise count of the number of girls taken, arriving at a figure of 276. Of those, 57 girls managed to escape in one way or another, bringing the number missing to 219.[20] In other words, nearly 300 girls were taken from a school in north-eastern Nigeria and there was little understanding of how it had happened.

More than two weeks passed before much of the rest of the world took notice. A social media campaign would help spread the word, with the #BringBackOurGirls hashtag gaining traction among Nigerians. According to one version of the story, the hashtag began after a speech by Oby Ezekwesili, an anti-corruption activist, former World Bank vice president for Africa and ex-education minister. During an appearance in the southern Nigeria oil hub of Port Harcourt, Ezekwesili spoke of bringing back the girls, prompting one man who heard her to tweet it as a hashtag.[21] It gradually took off from there, and Nigeria's government was set to be hit by a tidal wave of criticism.

With authorities under growing pressure to act, President Goodluck Jonathan and Patience Jonathan, Nigeria's first lady, sought to show that they were engaged and that something was being done to find the girls. On 4 May, Patience Jonathan held a meeting with the Chibok principal and others, a part of which would be shown on a Nigerian news channel. The first lady, an evangelical Christian like her husband, at one point broke down in tears during an odd discourse that saw her repeatedly declare a phrase that would be mocked relentlessly by Nigerians online. She punctuated it with the 'o' common when speaking in pidgin English in Nigeria. 'There is God ooo!' she said. 'There is God oooo!'[22] If nothing else, it provided Nigerians with some comic relief amid the sadness.

The following day, Patience Jonathan was accused of ordering the arrest of at least one woman who had been protesting to call for the government to take action to free the girls. The woman had been accused of pretending she was one of the mothers of the girls during a meeting with the first lady and was arrested at the presidential villa, according to protesters, who said she was only representing mothers who could not attend the meeting.[23]

From there, the story gathered momentum globally. On 5 May, the first claim of responsibility for the kidnappings arrived in the form of a video purportedly featuring Boko Haram leader Abubakar Shekau.[24] Over the course of the 57-minute recording, the man identified as Shekau justified the taking of 'slaves' and made the shocking threat to sell the girls on the market – a claim to be treated with scepticism, however, since he would clearly be able to demand much more in ransom money in exchange for their freedom.

The first images of Shekau, or whoever this man was, showed him holding a rifle, his other hand raised in the air, exhorting his followers – a more ruthless, blood-thirsty and battle-scarred version of his predecessor, Mohammed Yusuf. As with Yusuf, they responded to him with shouts of 'Allahu Akbar', and he fired his gun into the air as if to punctuate his speech. The video then cut to another shot of Shekau, now standing on the ground, repeatedly firing his rifle as if he were engaging in target practice. He later spoke, reading from a piece of paper, while standing in front of two armoured vehicles and a truck, six men with their faces covered on either side of him.

'My brethren, you should cut off the necks of infidels. My brethren, you should seize slaves', he said in the video.

I abducted a girl at a Western education school and you are disturbed. I said Western education should end. Western education should end. Girls, you should go and get married [...] I abducted your girls. I will sell them in the market, by Allah. There is a market for selling humans. Allah says I should sell. He commands me to sell. I will sell women. I sell women.

He sought to justify his group's actions, saying:

You arrested and threw people in prison. What is your justification? You do yours but you are saying we should not follow Allah's command [...] Jonathan, I will sell you when I seize you. Obama, I will sell you. Bush, I will sell you. I will put you [up] for sale. Your price will be low. Don't think I'm joking.[25]

Later, speaking in broken English, Shekau repeated his bizarre habit of naming dead world leaders as his enemies, and this time he travelled far back in history:

In every nation, in every region, now has the decision to make. Either you are with us – I mean real Muslims [...] or you are with the Obama, François Hollande, George Bush, Bush, Clinton. I forgot not Abraham Lincoln. Ban Ki-moon and his people generally, and any unbeliever. Death, death, death, death [...] This world is against Christians. I mean Christians generally.

Shekau's threat to sell the girls in the market led to horror globally and began a brief period when the tragedy commanded the world's attention. The #BringBackOurGirls hashtag was used by celebrities and politicians intending to show concern, and Western nations faced pressure from their own citizens to act, particularly in the United States. Given the awfulness of the crime, it was understandable that the world wanted to help, but options were always going to be limited given the state of Nigeria's armed forces. Areas where nations with advanced military equipment and expertise could potentially assist included deploying drones for surveillance along with hostage negotiators. But comments from some in the United States were at times ridiculously jingoistic. Senator John McCain, declaring that he would send US Special Forces into Nigeria with or without approval from the country's government if the girls were located, said, 'I wouldn't be waiting for some kind of permission from some guy named Goodluck Jonathan.'[26]

The main problem with providing military assistance to Nigeria related to the country's mismanagement and the behaviour of its armed forces. Working closely with a military accused of such horrible human rights abuses could signal approval of its tactics, while bailing the Nigerian government out of a problem to a large degree of its own making would remove pressure on it to act on its own and look harder at the causes and potential solutions to the insurgency. Beyond that, even if Western nations could help, Nigeria's government must accept the assistance. Nigerians are suspicious of US military intentions and would not want to see their country turned into another battleground in the 'war on terror'. 'It does seem that Nigerians are caught in the difficult position of having to welcome the help and be deeply wary of it', Nigerian journalist Tolu Ogunlesi wrote in an opinion piece on CNN's website.

> On the one hand we know, from the evident helplessness of our government, that we're at the point where we cannot make any progress without the skills and knowledge and technology that Western countries will bring to this battle. On the other hand, there are questions (running the gamut of conspiracy theory to reasonable concern) about America's motivations, and its track record.[27]

It was also a question of pride. Nigeria sees itself as a regional power in its own right that can handle its own affairs. In this case, it is also worth asking whether Nigeria's government was reluctant to let the world in because it hoped the story would simply fade from public view.

The complications were on display in hearings before the US Senate's foreign relations committee. A senior official from the US Defense Department said allegations of rights abuses had made it extremely difficult for the US military to find Nigerian soldiers it could train without violating American law. A US law prohibits foreign military assistance for units suspected of serious human rights violations. Beyond that, the United States was careful about the kind of intelligence it shared with Nigeria out of fears that it could be used against civilians. It did not end there. The official, Alice Friend, acknowledged there were concerns over whether Boko Haram sympathisers had infiltrated Nigeria's military, but the larger issue involved something more basic.

'I'd say an even greater concern is the incapacity of the Nigerian military and the Nigerian government's failure to provide leadership to the military in a way that changes these tactics', Friend, the defense department's principal director for African affairs, told the committee. 'The division in the north that mainly is engaging with Boko Haram, the 7th Division, has recently shown signs of real fear.[28] They do not have the capabilities, the training or the equipping that Boko Haram does. And Boko Haram is exceptionally brutal and indiscriminate in their attacks. And so, as heavy-handed as the forces on the Nigerian side have been, Boko Haram has been even more brutal.'

She later spoke of corruption contributing to the decline of the Nigerian military. 'Another concern [...] is that the Nigerian military has the same challenges with corruption that every other institution in Nigeria does. Much of the funding that goes to the Nigerian military is skimmed off the top, if you will.'[29]

In the end, Nigeria accepted assistance from a handful of countries, including Britain, the United States, France, Israel and China, which essentially sent advisers, such as hostage negotiators and intelligence experts, and surveillance planes or drones. The US response was perhaps the most significant given its potential long-term implications. It deployed drones and manned aircraft to conduct surveillance, while stationing some 80 personnel in the neighbouring nation of Chad.[30] The choice was intriguing given the United States had recently opened a drone base in Niger, which also borders Nigeria, as part of efforts to battle Islamist extremists in Mali. It was never made clear why Washington did not simply use the same base or whether it intends to keep the base in Chad open over the long term, further expanding its drone programme on the continent.[31] Nigeria also had its own drones purchased years earlier from an Israeli firm – but they went unused. They had apparently not been maintained and were not operational.[32]

In any case, the hunt for the girls was now an international effort, at least in name, though foreign nations would stick to an arm's-length approach. It would not be wise to engage in on-the-ground operations with Nigeria's military given how badly such moves could end. Its reputation for ruthlessness was well known, and no nation would want the blood of hundreds of girls on its hands. Foreign forces would also face a lack of knowledge not only of the terrain, but also of the identities of those involved in the insurgency were they to become more directly involved. In Nigeria, things are very often not what they seem.

The first proof that at least dozens of the girls were still alive would occur on 12 May, nearly a month after they were kidnapped. Another video was distributed, and this one purported to show the students themselves. They were dressed in drab grey or black hijab-like outfits and sat in a tight group on the ground while others stood behind, including two who held a black jihadi flag. They all recited part of the Qur'an in Arabic together, as if it were a school lesson, and two of the girls said on camera that they were Christians who had been converted to Islam. A third girl interviewed on camera said that she was Muslim.[33] Shekau also spoke on the video, declaring that the girls had been liberated because they were now Muslim, and that they would never be released as long as Nigerian authorities were holding Boko Haram members. 'I will sell them. I repeat again. And by Allah you will never get them until the day you release our brethren you arrested [...] And the women you humiliate. There is a woman you held and her infant is still with you but you released her.'

Shekau also again claimed there was justification in the Qur'an for taking slaves. 'I will seize a slave. The only person who is not a slave is he who believes in "there is no God but Allah and Muhammad is His Prophet" and accepts faith and lives by all its dictates. This one is not a slave.'[34]

The video set off shockwaves and made it far more difficult for supporters of the government to make the claim that the abductions were a hoax or a conspiracy. However, it would by no means dispel such talk completely. For one, Shekau never appeared in the same frame as the girls.

On the day after the video became public, Borno state governor Kashim Shettima arranged for a group of parents and relatives, as well as some of the students who escaped, to travel to Maiduguri with the aim of having them watch it and identify the girls. They gathered in a room in a state government compound and went about the grim task, and by the end, 77 girls had been identified.[35] 'We went to Maiduguri and they showed us on a projector', Lawan Zanna, who was able to identify his daughter, told me, his voice sorrowful over the phone. 'She's not OK. She looks so sad [...] I was not happy when I saw her.' There were allegations later that some of the girls in the video could not have been students as they seemed to be much older. Shettima, however, told journalists that all of those in the video were students from the school, though it was unclear how he could know since only 77 of the more than 100 shown were identified. In any case, with many of the girls now identified, a clear claim of responsibility and foreign nations assisting with intelligence gathering, it would have seemed that the government and military would be poised to finally move quickly. If they did, there was little sign of it, and certainly there were no results to point to. The world would inevitably begin to lose hope and interest.

Indeed, international attention toward the kidnappings seemed to already be waning by the following weekend, when France organised a summit of leaders from Nigeria and its neighbours to discuss battling Boko Haram. The gathering was mocked by many who saw it as too reminiscent of the colonial era, with a European power summoning African leaders to discuss a problem that concerned Europe. At the same time, the reality was that France continued to hold strong sway over its former colonies in the region, including Cameroon, Niger and Chad, all of which bordered north-eastern Nigeria and were contending with Boko Haram members who navigated back and forth across the frontier. The aim of the summit was to encourage the countries to share intelligence and cooperate on defeating Boko Haram, and there would notably be an intensification of military raids targeting extremists in north-western Cameroon afterwards. However, the summit also resulted in a certain amount of overblown rhetoric, including President Goodluck Jonathan's claim that Boko Haram had transformed into 'Al-Qaeda in West and Central Africa' – an assertion many who were familiar with the situation did not take seriously. Portraying the problem as global rather than a local one that Nigeria had failed to address would allow it to duck blame. In fact, it was Nigeria's inability to tackle the insurgency and gain the trust of its people that had allowed Boko Haram to grow into something larger, albeit no Al-Qaeda for West and Central Africa. 'Boko Haram is no longer the local terror group with some religious sentiment that started in Nigeria in 2002 to 2009', Jonathan said.

From 2009 to date, it has changed and it is operating clearly as an Al-Qaeda organisation. It can better be described as Al-Qaeda in West and Central Africa. It's no longer the Boko Haram that came with the sentiments that Western education is prohibited and that women must not go to school – nobody should attend a formal institution based on Western education.

He also sought to portray Nigeria as doing all it could to find the missing girls:

We are totally committed to ensuring that these girls are found wherever they are, and make sure that they join their families. We will do all our best. Presently Nigeria has 20,000 troops in this part of the country, the northern part of the country, the north eastern part of the country, where we have these terrorists. We've been scanning the areas with surveillance aircrafts and of course also using local intelligence sources.[36]

But as the days passed following the summit, there were still no results, and the government seemed to lose patience with the criticism it was facing. Meanwhile, as the fate of the kidnapped girls dominated coverage of the insurgency, more deadly attacks were occurring, including in areas near Chibok.

* * *

What appeared to have been a coordinated effort to strike back began in late May. The problem was that the target was not Boko Haram, but those demanding action from the government. Daily protests of around 100 or so people wearing red had been occurring in Abuja, organised by civil society activists and others, including some with links to the opposition. The demonstrations had been peaceful and restrained, mainly led by Oby Ezekwesili, the former World Bank official and ex-minister whose speech in April was said to have led to the #BringBackOurGirls hashtag. At each of the gatherings, Ezekwesili would marshal the crowd with a single-minded set of call-and-response chants:

Ezekwesili: 'What are we demanding?'
Protesters: 'Bring back our girls, now and alive.'
Ezekwesili: 'What are we asking?'
Protesters: 'The truth. Nothing but the truth.'

It all appeared well-meaning, but seemed unlikely to start a mass movement among Nigerians. Nevertheless, on 26 May, they would begin to be targeted, and whoever was pulling the strings seemed to be following the crudest and most unsophisticated dirty-tricks playbook. A new group of 'protesters' would appear, a rowdy collection of young men and women driven to their meeting point aboard buses.[37] Many people instantly saw it for what it almost surely was: a paid-for crowd designed to provoke, intimidate and sow confusion. On the first day of their protest, they marched holding placards in support of the military and were greeted by a delegation that included the country's chief of defence staff, Air Marshal Alex Badeh, who used the occasion to make an extraordinary claim. He told a handful of journalists present that he knew where the abducted girls were located, then seemed to indicate that the government would negotiate a deal to free them, contradicting earlier statements that it would not bargain with Boko Haram. 'The good news for the girls is that we know where they are, but we cannot tell you, OK. We cannot come and tell you military secrets here. Just leave us alone. We are working. We will get the girls back', Badeh said. After referring to the kinds of weapons being seized from the Islamists that he said could not have come from Nigeria's armed forces, he hinted at conspiracies and agreed with President Jonathan's assessment that Boko Haram had become Al-Qaeda in West Africa. 'There are people from outside fuelling this thing. That's why when Mr President said we have Al-Qaeda in West Africa, I believe it 100 per cent, because I know that people from outside Nigeria are in this war. They are fighting us. They want to destabilise our country, and some people in this country are standing with the forces of darkness.'[38]

Addressing the crowd, he said that using force to rescue the girls would put their lives in danger, and the 'protesters' responded in support of him.

'We want our girls back. But I can tell you we can do it [...] But where they are held, can we go with force?' Badeh asked. 'No', the protesters said in response.

'If we go with force, what will happen?', Badeh asked. On cue, the crowd responded: 'They will die.'

'So nobody should come and say the Nigerian military does not know what it is doing', Badeh explained. 'We can't go and kill our girls in the name of trying to get them back.'

The comments were obviously intended to deflect criticism from the military, but days later, news emerged that an Australian negotiator who had previously helped mediate in the conflict in the Niger Delta was in Nigeria and seeking to broker a deal to free the girls. Stephen Davis told journalists that he had arrived in the country around the beginning of May at President Jonathan's request and had travelled to the north-east. In comments in early June, Davis said he believed that most of the girls had been taken over the border into Cameroon, Chad or Niger and separated into three different groups. He told Britain's Channel 4 that he had come close to negotiating a deal three times, but that 'vested interests' sabotaged the talks. He did not provide details on whom he meant, and it was also not clear which Boko Haram 'commanders' Davis had been in touch with.[39] Attempting to talk to Boko Haram would be a formidable challenge for anyone. It has never been clear whether anyone can truly represent the group and speak on its behalf given its lack of a clear structure. Davis may have indeed been speaking with someone, but whether they were truly Boko Haram 'commanders' was another question.

The original Bring Back Our Girls protesters led by Oby Ezekwesili and others pushed ahead with their campaign. However, the counter-protesters and their backers, whoever they were, began to target them specifically. The site of the protests were the country's Unity Fountain, a monument celebrating the coming together of such a diverse nation. Tellingly, however, the fountain, a series of white columns with Nigeria's states listed on them, did not function, its black hoses strewn across an empty pool. One of Abuja's major centres of power was located just across the street, the heavily secured Transcorp Hilton hotel, where politicians and businessmen hammered out deals in suites on the posh ninth and tenth floors and dined at a private restaurant whose windows overlooked the newly built city below.

The counter-protesters setting up at the Unity Fountain wore red shirts that mimicked the Bring Back Our Girls demonstrators, though with a slight change. The slogan written on the shirts was 'Release Our Girls' instead of 'Bring Back Our Girls' – in other words, they were not demanding that the government act; they were directing their plea to Boko Haram or, for the conspiracy-minded among them, to the northern politicians they believed were holding the girls as part of an anti-Jonathan plot. At first, the legitimate protesters sought to continue their rallies at the same location despite the rowdy crowd gathering nearby. One of the protest organisers, a civil society activist and professor named Jibrin Ibrahim, claimed the counter-demonstrators had been paid 3,000 naira ($20) each to attend and questioned who was responsible.[40] A counter-protest leader, Abduljalal Dauda, said the demonstration was independent of the government, though he added that participants may have been given 1,000 naira or so by organisers to cover their transport since they lived outside Abuja.

The Bring Back Our Girls leaders urged their followers not to respond to the provocations, remain calm and ignore them as much as possible. It worked at first, but the counter-demonstrators were not going to go away easily, and some of their leaders were spouting badly misinformed conspiracy theories, hinting at a vaguely defined international plot against Nigeria. Dauda made reference to a widely believed rumour in Nigeria: that the United States predicted the country's break-up by 2015.[41]

'The truth of the matter is that even the same people in the United States of America said that Nigeria would disintegrate in 2015', Dauda, chairman of a Nigerian youth council who said the young men at the protests were his 'constituents', told me. Felicia Sani, head of an organisation of market women, chimed in at that point. I had earlier told her I was American. 'As we didn't disintegrate, you are trying to disintegrate us', she said. A short while later, Dauda sought to explain in more detail, though I had difficulty following his logic.

'So what I am trying to tell you is this', he said as we sat in chairs in the grass near the Unity Fountain surrounded by counter-protesters he was supervising:

> There is international conspiracy. Not only in Nigeria. There is international conspiracy. I'm not saying opposition is doing it. Opposition cannot destroy our country. Some people are interested in destroying this country. It happens in Arab Spring. It started with youths. We have seen it clearly. It is social media. Now the issue of Bring Back Our Girls – it has gone viral in the world. Why it has gone viral? Because you post it. But if you didn't give somebody anything, why would you ask somebody to bring it back to you? We said release. That is why we changed the language from bring to release. These people, we didn't give them these girls. You abduct them, and now we are asking to please release the girls healthy and alive. We have suffered enough. As a young person in this country, I would never want what I passed through [for] my children to go and pass through it. We have gone in a harsh situation [...] We have generals in the north, they are not saying anything. We have to come out and say something because the destiny of this country lies in their hands [...] You see these youths? We brought them, with the

different ideology and different thinking. Our agenda is Save
Nigeria Campaign. We are not interested in 2015 [elections]
[...] What we are saying is this: we need our country in the
safe hands, so we need the country to be united. That is my
point only.

I first met Jude Tabai, the man who presented himself as
working in an unspecified security role for the president's team,
while speaking with Abduljalal Dauda and Felicia Sani. It was a
short time later, after one of his underlings insistently told me that
Tabai wanted to speak with me, that we discussed the situation in
more detail. We stood about 20 metres away from the counter-
protest organisers, and the more we spoke, the more he seemed to
relish explaining to me the sinister forces at work trying to bring
down President Jonathan.

'Why and where are they?', I asked him after he claimed that the
girls had been released by 'collaborators and co-sponsors'. 'Good',
he said, his voice climbing, pleased with the chance to tell the story.
'Because, you know why they have been released? Because of the
force the international community came with. Do you know that
all those who never spoke against Boko Haram – the heavyweights,
the religious leaders, the emirs who never spoke – all got up and
start speaking now, that Boko Haram is this, Boko Haram is that,
Boko Haram is this, Boko Haram is that. So it is like, why now?
Because they now know the gravity of international community
taking over this battle.'

His argument as far as I could tell was that the northern elites
pulling the strings had got more than they had bargained for and
must now find a way out before the plot is uncovered:

And basically their only bait to avoid that is to tell the
people to push out those girls. And that is why you see them
quickly saying that, 'Give us this and take your girls.' I'm a

psychologist and I'm a security expert. No militant can tell you that, 'take your girls and just give me one person' [...] That is a big loss to them, you understand? They will never. If they are actually firm in what they are doing, they will say that 'give us our prisoners'. They know that nobody will release their prisoners. But they are asking for soft bargaining so that it will just be easy for them to just release those girls. And they believe that once they release those girls, that pressure on them, on both the northerners and all those things, will calm down, and then they can continue the other phase of the battle. But they will never go kidnapping on this level again because that has exposed a lot of things. And they know that if they don't do it and this thing gets out of this level, it's going to expose everybody.

We spoke for about 30 minutes before I left him to talk to the original Bring Back Our Girls protesters. They were outnumbered by the counter-demonstrators, who were about 300 in total compared to the original rally's several dozen. Hadiza Bala Usman, one of the organisers for the Bring Back Our Girls rally, took the high road and sought to keep the focus on the Chibok girls when I asked whether she believed the counter-protesters were sponsored by the government. 'Well, I'm not aware because I haven't engaged them in any discussion. It's just interesting to note that people are coming out after – this is our twenty-eighth day of protesting, twenty-eighth day of sustained protests, and it is important to know that the girls have been abducted for 47 days now', said Usman, who has been aligned with the opposition in Nigeria and whose late father was a revered northern intellectual. 'So for people to start protesting two days, 45 days after the abduction of the girls, is quite an interesting thing to note. But I don't know who they are. I don't know where they're coming from. I hear them mentioning the fact that they are protesting for the release of the girls from the abductors.'

She continued as she kept an eye on the Bring Back Our Girls protesters assembling nearby since she was due to start the rally soon:

> It's interesting to note that we are citizens that have a social contract with our leader, and we believe our leader, based on our constitution, is mandated to provide security for the lives of every Nigerian, and in the event that security is not provided, citizens would go up to the leader and demand for him to have decisive and concise effort towards providing that mandate given to him [...] We believe in a state; we believe in a nation; we believe in the institution of the federal republic of Nigeria, and we shall continue demanding for our federal government to do everything possible to rescue and return the Chibok girls.

The rally began shortly after we finished speaking, civil society activists, students, Chibok elders and sympathisers dressed in red, some bearing slogans such as 'We are all from Chibok' and 'Bring Back Our Girls'. They chanted Ezekwesili's call-and-response and listened as others addressed them on the latest news regarding the kidnappings. All remained peaceful, but there was an ominous sign later. The counter-protesters eventually moved toward the rally, trotting in a line, clapping and chanting. They circled the Bring Back Our Girls demonstrators, clearly attempting to provoke them, but no one took the bait. The counter-protesters gave up and returned to their spot on the other side of the Unity Fountain, but it was easy to see how the situation could degenerate if they were allowed to continue to gather there.

They were allowed to continue, of course, and what played out the next day was inane and brutal – simple thuggery designed to end a peaceful protest of dozens of people who were only asking what any citizen should expect of their government. According to journalists and others present at the time, young men who were among the counter-protest rushed over, sought to grab cameras journalists were holding and smash them, broke plastic chairs being used by the rally and hit some of the demonstrators with sticks and bars. Then they were allowed to walk away. Some of those present at the time told me that the police briefly detained a couple of the youths, but later let them go. When I arrived at the rally after the madness had subsided, the pile of broken chairs was still there and the Bring Back Our Girls leaders were shaken. They had earlier warned the police that they were concerned about their safety given the thugs assembling near them and had delivered a letter to the authorities saying so. They explained this to a police officer at the scene and showed him a copy of the letter, but he seemed uninterested. He misunderstood and said he would deliver the letter for them, and they told him again that it had already been delivered. Rumours began to spread that more thugs were on their way, and Bring Back Our Girls demonstrators began warning that everyone should leave. I did not see Tabai, Sani and Abduljalal – the three government supporters I spoke with a day earlier – and cannot say if they were there when the violence broke out.

The same officer who misunderstood the protest leaders was later standing next to a police truck along with several of his colleagues. I walked over and asked him why they had not arrested those who attacked the demonstrators. He told me he did not know who was responsible. I suggested he could talk to witnesses to find out. 'I didn't ask them', he said. It was clear that he had no plans to do so, that he was helpless. There would be no benefit for this man dressed in the uniform of a Nigerian police officer to protect his fellow citizens from harm.

EPILOGUE: 'THEY SHOULD NOT ALLOW ME TO DIE IN THIS CONDITION'

It was drizzling rain on a Thursday in September 2013 as I landed in Warri, a hub for the oil industry in Nigeria's Delta state in the south, where gas-burning petroleum flares spew into the thick, tropical air. Along the bustling banks of the River Warri, flat-bottomed boats with outboard engines load passengers, food and supplies before winding their way deep into the creeks, past soot-covered makeshift oil refineries fed with stolen crude, where fuel is illegally produced for sale or survival. During a previous trip a couple years before, I had taken a boat and visited the village of Gbekebor, where I sat in a tiny community hall with a chief. He told me proudly that the plastic chairs there stamped with the words 'Donated by Niger Delta Freedom Fighters', along with goats and rice, were given to them by a prominent ex-gang leader who had participated in the oil militancy of the 2000s. A company believed to be controlled by that same ex-gang leader was later reported to be earning massive amounts of money through a government contract worth more than $100 million, ostensibly to provide security for waterways.[1] It was another reminder that the sleazy dealings with money belonging to the Nigerian people seemed to know no bounds.

I thought of that trip after I boarded a taxi at the airport and rode past an overgrown expanse of green brush and vines, dishevelled palm trees extending skyward like upside-down mops. Ramshackle hotels and storefronts stretched down the roadside along with shipping containers transformed into market kiosks. As we pushed our way through traffic, a billboard came into view wishing the former state governor, James Ibori, a happy fifty-fifth birthday. It called him 'The Living Legend of Resource Control', a phrase meaning he fought for Delta state to keep more of the revenue earned from crude oil pumped there. In fact, he has been accused of pocketing much of the money – or more precisely, using it to pay for an opulent mansion and luxury cars, among other properties – according to prosecutors.[2] He is currently serving time in Britain for money laundering and fraud, having been tried there after a Nigerian court acquitted him of 170 different charges.[3]

I was not in Warri this time to explore the creeks or look into illicit profits being raked in by corrupt overlords, however. I was there to see Wellington Asiayei, the police officer shot and paralysed outside his barracks room during the Kano attacks in January 2012. It would be the first time we would meet since the days after he was shot, when he spoke to me from his hospital bed, still overcome by what had occurred. I had been given a rough set of directions by his brother, and my taxi driver pushed on through the sopping-wet streets, a tassel dangling from his rear-view mirror with an emblem reading 'Doctor Jesus' and music on the radio declaring, 'up, up Jesus'. I eventually arrived at a dirt road off a larger paved street in Wellington's neighbourhood and walked with his brother to the front door. We entered the flat inside a fading yellow and white building, and I was led to a room at the back, where I found Wellington, lying on a mattress on the floor, unable to stand.

I knew before my trip that he had not been in good condition, having spoken by phone to his doctor and his wife, as well as Wellington himself. Still, it was jarring to see him there that way, an assistant police superintendent helpless on the floor of his aunt's spartan home, appearing much weaker and withered than when we had met some 19 months earlier. I knew he had agreed to speak with me because he hoped I would get the word out about his condition since his repeated pleas to the government and the police force for further assistance had gone unanswered. I didn't blame him, though neither did I have much hope. When I telephoned a police spokesman several weeks before with the aim of tracking him down, the spokesman told me they had been trying to contact him as well so they could figure out when he could come back to work.

I took a seat in a chair next to his mattress, and Wellington, slowly but deliberately, took me through the odyssey he had endured since our last discussion, from road journeys across Nigeria to stem-cell treatments in India, followed by a desperate resort to herbal remedies back in Warri. 'They should not allow me to die in this condition', he said.

He had remained in Aminu Kano Teaching Hospital, where I first met him, for six months, when his doctors advised him that he should seek treatment abroad since they had done all they could there. At one point during his stay at Aminu Kano, the national police chief, Mohammed Abubakar, visited those wounded in the attacks. According to Wellington, he promised the force would urgently look into his case. He did not hear back from the police force, but he was also not completely without help. The country's National Emergency Management Agency had covered the bills for his stay at Aminu Kano, and the Kano state government would later contribute 2 million naira, or about $12,000, to his expenses for seeking treatment abroad. He would also continue to receive his salary from the police force. It would not be enough, though, as further complications arose.

I should say clearly that the Nigerian police have a terrible reputation. Poorly paid, low-level cops find themselves reduced to shaking down drivers for bribes, while pay-offs are often required for investigations to move ahead. There have also been more serious allegations against police involving torture or rape. I could never know all the details of Wellington's life and his career; I do not know if he would have been considered a good cop or bad cop or something in between. But his path from his birthplace in a village in the creeks near Warri to his promotion through the ranks of the police, followed by his struggle to find adequate medical help, seemed to me typical of many in a country where the odds of succeeding are long.

He was born on 2 May 1964 in his grandfather's village of Asiayei Gbene. According to Wellington, his father had many wives and he does not know how many brothers and sisters he has. His father, an Ijaw by ethnicity, was in the army and moved regularly, so Wellington attended primary and secondary school in Ogun state in south-western Nigeria, where he was stationed at the time, many miles away from their home in the creeks of the Niger Delta. He said his father fought on the Nigerian side in the 1967– 70 civil war, though Wellington did not seem to remember much from that period. When his father retired from the army in 1977, Wellington returned to the Niger Delta and finished his secondary education in the town of Ayakoromo, also located within the creeks near Warri. In 1982, while living with his uncle in nearby Rivers state, he heard an announcement on the radio that the police were recruiting, so he went to headquarters and signed up. After passing a test to join, he was sent for training at Oji River, slightly further north, and became a recruit constable on 1 September 1983, when he was 19 years old.

'I have this respect for uniformed personnel because they command respect', he said when I asked him why he wanted to become a policeman. 'Wherever uniformed men – police, army, air force, navy – wherever they go, people respect them a lot.'

Later in the conversation, I asked him if that would have come from his father.

'Yes, yes.'

After some time on the force, Wellington began to realise he
needed to do more if he wanted to continue to advance through
the ranks. He decided to go back to school, and in 1999 he was
admitted into Ambrose Alli University in Edo state to study public
administration. He said he continued to work as a policeman
during that time and was placed on night duty to allow him to
attend classes. He graduated in 2004, and five years later he was
accepted into the police staff college. After completing the course,
he was posted to Kano. He had mainly been in the investigations
department throughout his career, and he remained there in his
new posting. Before his injury, he said he had never been shot
at and the toughest situation he had dealt with involved armed
robbers.

At around 6 p.m. on 20 January 2012, Wellington finished for
the day at state police headquarters in Kano and took the walk back
to the barracks. He had only a one-room flat since his wife was
not there with him. She had remained in Kaduna, where he had
been posted before attending officers' college. Back in the barracks
that evening, he intended to prepare food for his dinner, but was
interrupted by yelling and the sound of gunfire and explosions.
When he walked out, he saw a man dressed in the green beret,
black shirt and green trousers worn by the mobile police branch of
the service, estimating he was between 15 and 30 metres away. He
was thinking that both of them could run back to headquarters, or
if that was not possible, to a church located inside the barracks to
take cover.

'With the gunshots going everywhere, I just came out, and I
wanted to lock my door, and as I turned to lock my door, I saw
somebody in a mobile uniform from head to toe', said Wellington,
still lying on his back on the mattress on the floor. 'I was thinking
it was my colleague – the mobile men that are being posted to man
the barracks gate and the armoury in the barracks. And I was trying
to beckon on him so that we could all run to safety, and before I

could say Jack Robinson, I didn't know myself again. I was already on the ground.'

'He is the one who shot?' I asked.

'He is the one that shot.'

'You thought he was police, but he was one of the —'

'One of the Boko Haram members. I thought he was my colleague, and if he was my colleague, we would have run to safety. And maybe he would've shielded me while we were running. But I never knew he was an enemy. They have invaded the barracks. They have taken over the whole barracks [...] The one I saw was carrying [an] AK-47, because I saw him very vividly, very clearly, before he shot at me. I never knew that he was going to shoot at me. In fact, I didn't even think in that direction. I did not.'

Later, as I asked him further questions on the details of what happened that day, he pleaded for me not to go on. 'I don't want to recall this incident, honestly speaking', he said, his voice sorrowful. 'I don't want to recall this incident [...] In this condition today, it's very traumatic, very, very traumatic. I know what I'm passing through. I know what I'm passing through. I know what I've suffered.'

After his six months at Aminu Kano Teaching Hospital, he decided to return to Warri and begin looking into how he could travel to receive treatment. He had bought a wheelchair for himself, and he chartered a vehicle to drive south from Kano, reclining the front seat so he could lie back for the 11-hour journey, enduring the rough ride over Nigeria's poor roads. Once back home, his brother went on the Internet to research Fortis Hospital in India, which his doctors had recommended. He exchanged emails with doctors there who told him the cost of his treatment would be in the area of $10,000. With that in mind, Wellington calculated that he would have to come up with about $16,000. Including the money donated by Kano's state government, he was about $4,000 short. He said his family went to work trying to pull together that amount and was eventually able to do so, and he began planning the specifics of his trip to India.

In November 2012, he took an Etihad flight from Lagos, and was able to sit in business class so he could be in a reclining seat. After a stop in Abu Dhabi, he and his wife landed in New Delhi, some 15 hours after leaving Nigeria. The hospital sent a van to pick him up at the airport, and once at the hospital, his consultant began a series of tests. The results were not good.

'So finally, he now came out with this report and said that I have only one option now, that I did not come to Fortis in good time', Wellington said. The spinal injury had apparently worsened, and the doctors informed him that the only option was stem-cell therapy, an experimental procedure. Plastic surgery was also needed to repair a worsening bedsore. The stem-cell procedure came first, lasting about three hours, though Wellington said he felt no pain, thanks to the anaesthesia. Several days later, he underwent plastic surgery for the bedsore. He said doctors told him that if he did not begin to feel sensation in his lower limbs in six months or less, he should return for another round of treatments. After a period of recovery, Wellington flew out of India on 31 January 2013, hopeful that he would eventually be back on his feet.

There was more trouble just after he landed back in Nigeria. His wife, while tending to him at his brother-in-law's house in Lagos, noticed that the plastic surgery for the bedsore had ruptured. He had also begun to develop new sores since he had been lying in different positions to allow the surgery to heal. They returned to Warri, again by road, and he decided to enter a health clinic in hopes that they could deal with the sores. He remained there for six months, receiving antibiotic injections and with nurses cleaning and dressing the wounds, before leaving in July. He paid a bill of 650,000 naira, or about $4,000, but the sores had not healed.

'The wounds were infected, so they were giving me antibiotics, but the truth of the whole thing is that the doctor said that I need to get to a specialist hospital where they can handle the matter. They cannot handle it', Wellington said after having a relative assist him in showing me the worst of the bedsores as he lay on his mattress. 'I was spending money and I was not getting anything. I was spending my salary on treatment and drugs, and a few individuals, my friends, assisted me with money.'

He had also not regained any sensation in his legs and decided he should try to return to India, but to do so, he would have to raise thousands more dollars. While he was still in the clinic, a delegation from the ministry of health visited on a routine tour of private hospitals and were taken to meet Wellington. After hearing his story, they introduced him to newspaper journalists, who wrote stories on his plight. Features appeared in June 2013, including in two of Nigeria's largest newspapers, along with his contact information in hopes of donations. They ran pictures of him lying in his hospital bed alongside an older photo of him dressed sharply and standing proudly in his ceremonial uniform, taken at the police college in Jos in 2009. A headline in Nigeria's *Guardian* paper bluntly declared 'Boko Haram victim, ASP Wellington, dying gradually', while another in *ThisDay* newspaper said he was 'Dying to save Nigeria'. According to Wellington, police officials again looked into his case after the stories appeared, contacting him by phone and paying him a visit, but he did not see any results. He was still receiving his monthly police salary, but he told me he was unable to access any insurance money.

Back at home in Warri, he sought herbal treatments for his bedsores, but they did not seem to do much good. He couldn't remember exactly what herbs were used when I asked him. Family members were caring for him when I got back in touch with him in September 2013. His wife was not there, and he declined to discuss why. I found out later that he and his wife had split, with different reasons offered by her and Wellington's brother. There was also an odd discrepancy in the number of children I was told he had, and he had begged off when I asked him about his kids in Warri. I had noted when speaking to him in the hospital after the attack that he said he had five children, but his brother and wife told me later he had one son.[4]

After visiting with him in Warri and returning to Lagos, where I was based at the time, I began making phone calls to try to find out if his case was being attended to by someone in government. I exchanged text messages with the minister for special duties, who was in charge of organising help for Boko Haram victims, providing him with Wellington's details. I spoke to someone in the health ministry, who told me that the National Emergency Management Agency (NEMA) had been put in charge of victims' assistance. I called that agency's spokesman and explained the situation, and he informed me that Wellington would have to submit an application. As a result, I asked Wellington's brother to send me a letter explaining the circumstances. He did so and also emailed a letter from Aminu Kano Teaching Hospital, where he was first treated, and a copy of one of the newspaper articles on him. I then forwarded the documents to a colleague in Abuja, who agreed to deliver the paperwork in person to the NEMA spokesman. The spokesman later confirmed to me he had received the documents and would look into it.

Months passed and there was no response. Wellington's brother contacted me a number of times to find out if I had made any progress. In February 2014, I called the NEMA spokesman and asked about the file. He remembered me, as well as our previous exchange, and told me he was unable to find out anything about Wellington. I told him I did not understand his response since the reason for providing him with the documents was to initiate action. He said he would look into it again and get back to me. He never did.

'Even if the government is going to spend 10 million on me, am I not worth more than 10 million naira [$60,000]?', Wellington asked me that day in Warri in exasperation. 'Let's assume the government is going to spend 10 million on me to rehabilitate me so that I will get back on my feet. Am I not much more than

10 million naira? Is a life of a Nigerian citizen not more than 10 million naira?'

After not being in touch for some time, I sent Wellington's brother an email in February 2014 telling him he should also try to contact NEMA to see if he could get a response. I did not hear back, which I found to be strange since he had always responded before. The following month, I tried to call Wellington on both of his phone numbers but could not reach him. I then called his brother, who did answer. He told me he had received my email, but had some terrible news. Wellington had died in December. He was 50 years old.

The debate about Boko Haram, its international links and jihadi ambitions will and should go on, but for those faced with the everyday realties of the violence, it is almost beside the point. The problem is nothing less than the current state of Nigeria and the way it is being robbed daily – certainly of its riches, but more importantly, of its dignity.

GLOSSARY

Ansaru: a splinter faction of Boko Haram that has kidnapped foreigners and with rhetoric more in line with global jihadist groups. Its full name is Jama'atu Ansarul Muslimina Fi Biladis Sudan, or Vanguard for the Aid of Muslims in Black Africa. Another possible translation is Support Group for Muslims in Black Africa. Whether Ansaru remains truly separate from Boko Haram has been debated and it appears they may work together in an umbrella-like arrangement.

Boko Haram: the Hausa-language phrase given to the Islamist insurgency in Nigeria. The most commonly accepted translation is 'Western education is forbidden', though it could have a wider meaning since 'boko' may also be interpreted as 'Western deception'. The name was given to the insurgents by outsiders and not by the Islamists themselves, and Nigerian authorities as well as the news media continue to refer to it as such. The insurgency has morphed into an umbrella-like structure in recent years with various cells that may or may not work together, and 'Boko Haram' has come to stand as a catch-all phrase to describe it.

Caliphate: a territory ruled according to Islamic principles, with a caliph as head. Usman Dan Fodio's nineteenth-century jihad in what is today northern Nigeria led to what has come to be known as the Sokoto Caliphate.

Civilian JTF: vigilante groups formed in north-eastern Nigeria to help soldiers root out insurgents. The name is a reference to the military's Joint Task Force, which was the main deployment assigned to battle Boko Haram before it was replaced by the 7th Division.

Emir: a Muslim ruler, sometimes within a larger caliphate. Also referred to as shehu or sultan in northern Nigeria. Various emirs ruled over areas of the Sokoto Caliphate and the title has been preserved and passed on to the present day. Today's emirs of northern Nigeria officially have only ceremonial powers, though they retain substantial influence. The sultan of Sokoto remains Nigeria's highest Muslim spiritual and traditional authority.

Jama'atu Ahlus-Sunnah Lidda'Awati Wal Jihad: Abubakar Shekau's faction of Boko Haram says it wants to be known by this Arabic-language name, which translates to People Committed to the Prophet's Teachings for Propagation and Jihad. Another possible translation is the Sunni Group for Proselytisation and Jihad.

JTF: Joint Task Force. Military-led security deployments assigned to contend with unrest in parts of Nigeria. The JTF in north-eastern Nigeria had been the main force assigned to battle Boko Haram and had been accused of major human rights abuses before it was replaced by the 7th Division in 2013.

Salafism: a strict, fundamentalist interpretation of Islam that advocates a return to a purer form of the faith. Boko Haram's original leader, Mohammed Yusuf, was a Salafist. Boko Haram under his leadership before his death in 2009 was a Salafist-like sect based at his mosque in Maiduguri.

Sufism: a mystical version of Islam. Usman Dan Fodio, the nineteenth-century jihad leader in what is today northern Nigeria, was a Sufi. Nigeria's Muslim establishment today remains mainly made up of Sufis in line with Sunni tradition. Opposition to Nigeria's Sufi establishment developed in the 1970s through dissident clerics who had embraced Wahhabi-Salafist or Shiite beliefs. Such clerics retain substantial followings today.

NOTES

PROLOGUE

1 Translation by Aminu Abubakar.
2 Another possible translation for the name is 'Sunni Group for Proselytisation and Jihad'. Translation provided by Professor M.A.S. Abdel Haleem of SOAS, University of London.

1 'THEN YOU SHOULD WAIT FOR THE OUTCOME'

1 The 'martyr' video was originally obtained by AFP northern Nigeria correspondent Aminu Abubakar, who also translated it from Hausa to English. Some details from the video were included in a story he and I worked on together in September 2011 (Aminu Abubakar and M.J. Smith, 'Nigerian "bomber" videos emerge as Islamist fears mount', Agence France-Presse, 18 September 2011).
2 The details of the delay before the bomb went off were first reported by *Time* magazine (Alex Perry, 'Threat level rising: how African terrorist groups inspired by Al-Qaeda are gaining strength', 19 December 2011) and Reuters (Joe Brock, 'Special report: Boko Haram – between rebellion and jihad', 31 January 2012). I later confirmed these details and others with a source who has seen the surveillance video from the day of the attack.
3 There had been vague warnings in the weeks leading up to the bombing which are discussed in Chapter 3.
4 Mervyn Hiskett, *The Sword of Truth* (Evanston, 1994), pp. 70–1, 96.
5 Mervyn Hiskett, *The Development of Islam in West Africa* (New York, 1984), p. 2.
6 S.J. Hogben, *An Introduction to the History of the Islamic States of Northern Nigeria* (Ibadan, 1967), pp. 162–5.
7 Hiskett, *Development*, p. 59.
8 Toyin Falola and Matthew M. Heaton, *A History of Nigeria* (Cambridge, 2009), p. 30.
9 Hiskett, *Development*, pp. 59–60.
10 Falola and Heaton, *History*, p. 32.
11 Hogben, *Introduction*, pp. 165–7.
12 Hiskett, *Development*, p. 67.
13 Falola and Heaton, *History*, p. 28; Hogben, *Introduction*, pp. 73–5. It should be emphasised that there are many different versions of the Bayajida myth.

14 Hogben, *Introduction*, pp. 73–4; Hiskett, *Development*, pp. 69–71.
15 Hogben, *Introduction*, pp. 73–4; Hiskett, *Development*, pp. 69–70.
16 Hiskett, *Development*, pp. 73–96.
17 Hiskett, *Sword*, pp. 15–21.
18 Hiskett, *Sword*, pp. 17, 40–1.
19 Hiskett, *Sword*, pp. 23–4, 31.
20 Murray Last, *The Sokoto Caliphate* (Bristol, 1967), p. 10.
21 Hiskett, *Sword*, pp. 44–5.
22 Last, *Sokoto*, pp. 7–8.
23 Hiskett, *Sword*, pp. 47–9.
24 Hiskett, *Sword*, pp. 66.
25 Hiskett, *Sword*, pp. 70–1.
26 Last, *Sokoto*, pp. 15–16; Falola and Heaton, *History*, p. 64.
27 Last, *Sokoto*, p. 20.
28 Hiskett, *Sword*, p. 97.
29 Last, *Sokoto*, p. 39.
30 The Bornu Empire would lose some of its territory to the caliphate, but would ultimately remain independent, though far less powerful than Sokoto.
31 Murray Last, 'Contradictions in Creating a Jihadi Capital: Sokoto in the Nineteenth Century and Its Legacy', *African Studies Review*, 56(2) (September 2013), pp. 1–20, on pp. 2–4.
32 Muhammad S. Umar, 'Education and Islamic Trends in Northern Nigeria: 1970s–1990s', *Africa Today*, 48(2) (Summer 2001), pp. 127–50, on p. 136.
33 Hiskett, *Development*, pp. 242–3.
34 Papers of Baron Lugard of Abinger, 1858–1945, MSS Brit. Emp. s.58, f. 6.
35 Lugard Papers, MSS Brit. Emp. s.58, ff. 9–10.
36 Lugard Papers, MSS Brit. Emp. s.57, f. 106.
37 Sir F.D. Lugard, *The Dual Mandate in British Tropical Africa* (Edinburgh and London, 1922), p. 617.
38 A.H.M. Kirk-Greene, 'Lugard, Frederick John Dealtry, Baron Lugard (1858–1945)', Oxford Dictionary of National Biography, Oxford University Press, 2004; online edn, October 2008, http://www.oxforddnb.com/view/article/34628.
39 Lugard Papers, MSS Brit. Emp. s.57, ff. 180–1.
40 F.D. Lugard, 'An Expedition to Borgu, on the Niger', *Geographical Journal*, 6(3) (September 1895), pp. 205–25.
41 Lugard Papers, MSS Brit. Emp. s.57, f. 182.
42 Michael Crowder, *The Story of Nigeria* (London, 1978), pp. 48–53.
43 Crowder, *Story*, p. 149.
44 Crowder, *Story*, pp. 133–5, 147–8, 151.
45 Crowder, *Story*, p. 164.
46 Lugard Papers, MSS Brit. Emp. s.62, f. 8b.
47 Scarbrough, 'Goldie, Sir George Dashwood Taubman (1846–1925)', rev. John Flint, Oxford Dictionary of National Biography, Oxford University Press, 2004; online edn, September 2013, http://www.oxforddnb.com/view/article/33441.
48 Lugard Papers, MSS Brit. Emp. s.57, f. 94.
49 Peter Cunliffe-Jones, *My Nigeria: Five Decades of Independence* (New York, 2010), p. 73.
50 Lugard, *Dual Mandate*, pp. 222–9.
51 Crowder, *Story*, pp. 173, 179.
52 D.J.M. Muffett, *Concerning Brave Captains* (London, 1964), pp. 43–51; Hogben, *Introduction*, pp. 212–14.

53 H.F. Backwell, *The Occupation of Hausaland: 1900–1904* (Lagos, 1927), pp. 13–14.
54 Lugard Papers, MSS Brit. Emp. s.62, ff. 26–8.
55 Lugard Papers, MSS Brit. Emp. s.62, ff. 31–8.
56 *Colonial Reports – Annual, N. Nigeria: 1900–1911* (London, HMSO), p. 85.
57 UNESCO, 'Ancient Kano City Walls and Associated Sites', http://whc.unesco.org/en/tentativelists/5171/.
58 *Colonial Reports*, pp. 159–60.
59 *Colonial Reports*, p. 38.
60 *Colonial Reports*, pp. 91, 178.
61 *Colonial Reports*, p. 164.
62 Lugard Papers, MSS Brit. Emp. s.62, ff. 107–11.
63 *Colonial Reports*, pp. 365–74.
64 Lugard Papers, MSS Brit. Emp. s.65, ff. 27–8.
65 Lugard Papers, MSS Brit. Emp. s.63, ff. 156, 177.

2 'HIS PREACHINGS WERE THINGS THAT PEOPLE COULD IDENTIFY WITH'

1 The interrogation has been posted online at https://www.youtube.com/watch?v=ePpUvfTXY7w. Translation from Hausa to English was provided by Professor Abubakar Aliyu Liman of Ahmadu Bello University in Nigeria. Professor Liman felt the best translation of 'boko' in this instance was 'Western education', though others may have a wider interpretation of the word, such as Western deception.
2 Professor Liman felt Yusuf may have misspoken here and meant to use the word 'astrology', which has often been labelled un-Islamic.
3 Abdul Raufu Mustapha, 'Ethnic Structure, Inequality and Governance of the Public Sector in Nigeria', United Nations Research Institute for Social Development, Democracy, Governance and Human Rights Programme Paper No. 24, November 2006, p. 12.
4 Enrico Monfrini, 'The Abacha Case', in M. Pieth (ed.), *Recovering Stolen Assets* (Berne, 2008), pp. 41–2.
5 Mark Tran, 'Former Nigeria state governor James Ibori receives 13-year sentence', *Guardian* (UK), 17 April 2012; Estelle Shirbon, 'Nigerian governor gave $15 million cash bribe in bag, court hears', Reuters, 19 September 2013; 'Nigeria: UK conviction a blow against corruption', Human Rights Watch, 17 April 2012.
6 World Bank, 'The World Bank in Nigeria 1998–2007: Nigeria Country Assistance Evaluation', p. 69.
7 The World Bank report cited above said poverty had fallen to 54 per cent by 2004; the same report said 'wide, long-standing regional disparities result in a poverty range from about 34 per cent in the southeast to about 67 per cent in the northeast'. World Bank calculations using data from 2009–10 put the poverty rate at 46 per cent based on evaluations of the cost of supplying basic needs for a household, according to information provided to me by the bank's lead economist for Nigeria. Rapid population expansion, however, means that reductions in the poverty rate do not always translate into fewer people overall living in poverty.

8 Population Division of the Department of Economic and Social Affairs of the United Nations Secretariat, 'World Population Prospects: The 2012 Revision', http://esa.un.org/unpd/wpp/index.htm.

9 M.J. Smith, 'Lagos at centre of Africa's population boom', Agence France-Presse, 30 October 2011.

10 Chinua Achebe, *The Trouble with Nigeria* (Essex, 1984), p. 1.

11 Toyin Falola and Matthew M. Heaton, *A History of Nigeria* (Cambridge, 2009), pp. 112–13.

12 Falola and Heaton, *History*, pp. 119–21.

13 Falola and Heaton, *History*, p. 150.

14 Michael Crowder, *The Story of Nigeria* (London, 1978), p. 271.

15 Crowder, *Story*, p. 277.

16 Falola and Heaton, *History*, pp. 153–4.

17 Independent Task Force on Terrorist Financing Sponsored by the Council on Foreign Relations, 'Update on the Global Campaign against Terrorist Financing', 15 June 2004, pp. 20–2.

18 Sir Ahmadu Bello, *My Life*, p. 229.

19 Crowder, *Story*, p. 298.

20 Falola and Heaton, *History*, p. 166.

21 Falola and Heaton, *History*, p. 181.

22 Falola and Heaton, *History*, p. 180.

23 Peter Cunliffe-Jones, *My Nigeria: Five Decades of Independence* (New York, 2010), p. 101.

24 Falola and Heaton, *History*, pp. 183–5.

25 Falola and Heaton, *History*, p. 198.

26 Falola and Heaton, *History*, p. 202.

27 Max Siollun, 'Umaru Dikko, the man who was nearly spirited away in a diplomatic bag', *Independent* (UK), 20 August 2012.

28 Karl Maier, *This House Has Fallen: Nigeria in Crisis* (London, 2000), pp. 47, 55.

29 Wole Soyinka, *You Must Set Forth at Dawn* (New York, 2006), p. 222.

30 Falola and Heaton, *History*, pp. 217–20.

31 Falola and Heaton, *History*, p. 225.

32 Soyinka, *Dawn*, pp. 354–5.

33 Soyinka, *Dawn*, pp. 383–4.

34 Abiola died in 1998 while still imprisoned in what some deemed to be suspicious circumstances.

35 'General Sani Abacha', Africa Confidential, http://www.africa-confidential.com/whos-who-profile/id/2651/Sani_Abacha.

36 'Nigerian leaders "stole" $380 bn', BBC, 20 October 2006, http://news.bbc.co.uk/2/hi/africa/6069230.stm; GDP examples are based on World Bank data from 2013 (http://databank.worldbank.org/data/download/GDP.pdf).

37 The Carter Center, 'Postelection Statement on Nigeria Elections, March 1, 1999', http://www.cartercenter.org/news/documents/doc891.html.

38 European Union Election Observer Mission Nigeria 2003, 'Final Report on the National Assembly, Presidential, Gubernatorial and State Houses of Assembly Elections', 2003.

39 John Ameh, Josiah Oluwole, Ozioma Ubabukoh and Leke Baiyewu, 'Obasanjo is a joker, liar, he was behind third term – Nnamani, others', *Punch*, 8 April 2012.

40 Ed Pilkington, 'Shell pays out $15.5m over Saro-Wiwa killing', *Guardian* (UK), 8 June 2009.

41 These biographical details are based on various sources, mainly interviews conducted by me with those who have closely studied the group. Particular insight was provided by Kyari Mohammed, head of the Centre for Peace and Security Studies at Nigeria's Modibbo Adama University of Technology, as well as by an academic who has carried out an extensive analysis of Yusuf's recorded sermons. Because of the sensitivity of the situation, I agreed to abide by the academic's request that he remain anonymous.

42 Interview with Anayo Adibe, lawyer for Baba Fugu Mohammed.

43 Anonymous, 'The Popular Discourses of Salafi Radicalism and Salafi Counter-radicalism in Nigeria: A Case Study of Boko Haram', *Journal of Religion in Africa*, 42(2) (2012), pp. 118–44, on p. 126.

44 It is widely known as Izala, but its full name is Jamāʿ at ʿizālat al-bidʿa wa iqāmat al-sunna, or the Group for Removing Religious Innovation and Establishing Sunna, according to the study by Anonymous cited above.

45 Anonymous, 'Discourses', pp. 121–2, 131–2 and Roman Loimeier, 'Boko Haram: The Development of a Militant Religious Movement in Nigeria', *Africa Spectrum*, 47(2–3) (2012), pp. 137–55, on p. 147.

46 Mervyn Hiskett, 'The Maitatsine Riots in Kano, 1980: An Assessment', *Journal of Religion in Africa*, 17(3) (1987), p. 209, and Abimbola O. Adesoji, 'Between Maitatsine and Boko Haram: Islamic Fundamentalism and the Response of the Nigerian State', *Africa Today*, 57(4) (Summer 2011), pp. 209–33, on p. 101.

47 Elizabeth Isichei, 'The Maitatsine Risings in Nigeria 1980–85: A Revolt of the Disinherited', *Journal of Religion in Africa*, 17(3) (1987), pp. 194–208, on p. 194, and Hiskett, 'Maitatsine', pp. 214–15.

48 Falola and Heaton, *History*, pp. 205–6.

49 Sam Olukoya, 'Eyewitness: Nigeria's sharia amputees', BBC, 19 December 2002, http://news.bbc.co.uk/2/hi/africa/2587039.stm.

50 BBC, 'Nigeria gays: 20 lashes for "homosexual offences"', 6 March 2014, http://www.bbc.com/news/world-africa-26469501.

51 Human Rights Watch, 'The "Miss World Riots": continued impunity for killings in Kaduna', July 2003, p. 2.

52 Wikileaks, 'Borno state residents not yet recovered from Boko Haram violence', 4 November 2009.

53 Anonymous, 'Discourses', pp. 133–4.

54 These details come from various sources, including a Nigerian military briefing and interviews with Kyari Mohammed (cited above).

55 Wikileaks, 'Nigerian Taliban attacks most likely not tied to Taliban nor Al-Qaida', 6 February 2004.

56 Emmanuel Goujon and Aminu Abubakar, 'Nigeria's Taliban plot comeback from hideouts', Agence France-Presse via *Mail & Guardian* (South Africa), 11 January 2006.

57 Yusuf says this during his interrogation after his arrest, https://www.youtube.com/watch?v=ePpUvfTXY7w. Translation from Hausa to English was provided by Professor Abubakar Aliyu Liman of Ahmadu Bello University in Nigeria.

58 Nick Tattersall, 'Nigerian sect planned bomb attack during Ramadan', Reuters, 4 August 2009.

59 Anonymous, 'Discourses', p. 138.

60 Shehu Sani, 'Boko Haram: history, ideas and revolt', *Vanguard*, 4 July 2011, http://www.vanguardngr.com/2011/07/boko-haram-history-ideas-and-revolt-3/.

61 Henri Laoust, 'Ibn Taymiyyah', 23 June 2014, in *Encyclopaedia Britannica*; retrieved from http://www.britannica.com/EBchecked/topic/280847/Ibn-Taymiyyah.

62 For a detailed look at the phrase, see: Paul Newman, 'The Etymology of Hausa boko', Mega-Chad Research Network, 2013, retrieved from http://www.megatchad.net/publications/Newman-2013-Etymology-of-Hausa-boko.pdf.

63 Anonymous, 'Discourses', pp. 125–6.

64 Marc-Antoine Perouse de Montclos, 'Nigeria's Interminable Insurgency? Addressing the Boko Haram Crisis', Chatham House Research Paper, September 2014, pp. 7–8; Perouse de Montclos told me the book was written in Arabic. I have not seen it myself.

65 Anonymous, 'Discourses', pp. 124–5.

66 Joe Boyle, 'Nigeria's Taliban enigma', BBC, 31 July 2009, http://news.bbc.co.uk/1/hi/8172270.stm.

67 Theophilus Abbah, 'Inside the pages of White Paper on Boko Haram', Sunday Trust (Nigeria), 3 June 2012.

68 Perouse de Montclos, 'Nigeria's Interminable Insurgency?', p. 9.

69 Goddy Egene and Zacheaus Somorin, 'Australian negotiator names Ihejirika, Sheriff as sponsors of Boko Haram', ThisDay (Nigeria), 29 August 2014. Audio from Davis's interview with Arise News can be found here: http://www.arise.tv/headline/arise-news-now-uk-28-08-8043.

70 Yemi Ajayi, 'Boko Haram: fed govt report rejects compensation for victims', ThisDay (Nigeria), 2 April 2013.

71 Ikechukwu Nnochiri, 'Boko Haram: Yusuf had only 4,000 followers in 2009, Army tells court', Vanguard, 8 December 2011, http://www.vanguardngr.com/2011/12/boko-haram-yusuf-had-only-4000-followers-in-2009-army-tells-court/.

72 Theophilus Abbah, 'Inside the pages of White Paper on Boko Haram', Sunday Trust (Nigeria), 3 June 2012.

73 Walker, Andrew, 'What is Boko Haram?', United States Institute of Peace, Special Report 308, June 2012.

74 'How politicians help insurgents', Africa Confidential, 30 November 2012.

75 A representative for Sheriff I spoke to on the phone asked me to send a list of questions by email. He did not respond to the questions.

76 Juliana Taiwo, 'I'm not the brain behind Boko Haram', Sun (Nigeria), 14 July 2011.

77 One such claim can be found here: International Crisis Group, 'Curbing Violence in Nigeria (II): The Boko Haram Insurgency', 3 April 2014, p. 23.

78 'Transcript of Osama bin Laden tape', 12 February 2003, Associated Press via Sydney Morning Herald.

79 The Charity Commission informed me of its findings by email in response to my questions.

80 Abbah, 'White Paper'.

81 Anonymous, 'Discourses', p. 126.

82 Anonymous, 'Discourses', pp. 136–8.

83 Isa Sa'idu, 'My encounter with Mohammed Yusuf over Boko Haram', Sunday Trust (Nigeria), 1 January 2012.

84 Yusuf's 'tafsir' or interpretation, of chapter 9, verses 8–12 of the Qur'an. Translation from Hausa to English by Professor Abubakar Aliyu Liman of Ahmadu Bello University. Video can be found at http://www.youtube.com/watch?v=Y33rL_D_6pw and http://www.youtube.com/watch?v=R3NcgQv-LVM.

85 Anonymous, 'Discourses', p. 128. The committee's report was not released publicly and I have not seen it, but it was obtained by the anonymous academic cited and I am quoting from his account. I have discussed it with him and find what he has written to be trustworthy.

86 A recording of the speech is included as part of the 'martyr' video for the UN suicide bomber, which was obtained by AFP's northern Nigeria correspondent Aminu Abubakar, who translated it from Hausa to English when we initially worked together on the story. I have also watched the video.

87 Wikileaks, 'Nigerian Islamist extremists launch attacks in 4 towns', 28 July 2009; Country Reports on Terrorism 2009, US State Department.

88 Ahmad Salkida, 'Nigeria: sect leader vows revenge', *Daily Trust* (Nigeria), 27 July 2009, http://wwrn.org/articles/31419/?&place=nigeria.

89 Wikileaks, 'Nigeria: extremist attacks continue into night', 28 July 2009.

90 Human Rights Watch, 'Spiraling violence: Boko Haram attacks and security force abuses in Nigeria', October 2012.

91 Wikileaks, 'Nigerian government quashes extremists, but not the root of the problem', 29 July 2009.

92 Wikileaks, 'Nigerian military combing for extremists, Boko Haram deputy arrested', 30 July 2009.

93 Human Rights Watch, 'Spiraling violence', p. 35.

3 'I WILL NOT TOLERATE A BRAWL'

1 'Nigeria President Umaru Yar'Adua "has heart problem"', BBC, 26 November 2009.

2 *Next* has since gone out of business, but summaries of the story can be found at various sites and in other newspapers, including here: Mike Pflanz, 'Nigeria in crisis after president left "seriously brain-damaged"', *Telegraph* (UK), 11 January 2010, http://www.telegraph.co.uk/news/worldnews/africaandindianocean/nigeria/6962983/Nigeria-in-crisis-after-president-left-seriously-brain-damaged.html.

3 'Nigeria's ailing President Yar'Adua breaks silence', BBC, 12 January 2010.

4 Wikileaks, 'Goodluck Jonathan remains acting President of Nigeria', 26 February 2010. Nigeria's presidency dismissed the contents of the diplomatic cable as 'largely inaccurate'.

5 'Nigeria governor to be impeached', BBC, 23 November 2005.

6 Sanders declined to comment for this book.

7 Aminu Abubakar, 'Islamists free hundreds of inmates in Nigerian jail attack', Agence France-Presse, 8 September 2010.

8 Henry Umoru, 'Boko Haram: arrest Ciroma, Lawal Kaita – Clark', *Vanguard*, 9 August 2012, http://www.vanguardngr.com/2012/08/boko-haram-arrest-ciroma-lawal-kaita-clark/.

9 Aminu Abubakar, 'Gunmen kill three in Nigerian Muslim emir's convoy', Agence France-Presse, 19 January 2013.

10 Human Rights Watch, 'Leave everything to God: accountability for inter-communal violence in Plateau and Kaduna states, Nigeria', December 2013, pp. 48–65.

11 Taye Obateru and Daniel Idonor, 'Jos Xmas Eve Blast: 32 people confirmed dead, 74 hospitalised', *Vanguard*, 26 December 2010, http://www.vanguardngr.com/2010/12/jos-xmas-eve-blast-32-people-confirmed-dead-74-hospitalised/.

12 Translation from Hausa by Aminu Abubakar.

13 Ola Awoniyi, 'Bomb attack on Nigerian military barracks kills four', Agence France-Presse, 1 January 2011.

14 Quotations from Jonathan noted at the time by my AFP colleague Ola Awoniyi. Used here with his permission.

15 Several stories reported this, including: Sule Lazarus, '2011: inside Nigeria's expensive presidential primary elections', *Sunday Trust* (Nigeria), 23 January 2011, http://sundaytrust.com.ng/index.php/news/10548-2011-inside-nigerias-expensive-presidential-primary-elections.

16 Aisha Wakaso, 'Bomb targeting Nigerian election shatters young lives', Agence France-Presse, 9 April 2011.

17 Nigeria Civil Society Election Situation Room, 'Final Statement on the Presidential Election', 19 April 2011, http://electionsituationroom.wordpress. com/2011/04/19/civil-society-election-situation-room-final-statement-on-the-presidential-election-tuesday-april-192011/.

18 Human Rights Watch, 'Nigeria: post-election violence killed 800', 17 May 2011.

19 Aminu Abubakar, 'Nigeria probes deadly blasts after president's inauguration', Agence France-Presse, 30 May 2011.

20 Wikileaks, 'Jonathan tells former president his plans for new INEC commissioners', 23 February 2010.

21 Boko Haram is believed to have some form of welfare operation that provides financing to the families of 'martyrs', but I have not confirmed further details.

22 Ahmad Salkida, 'The story of Nigeria's first suicide bomber', *BluePrint* magazine via Sahara Reporters, http://saharareporters.com/news-page/story-nigerias-first-suicide-bomber-blueprint-magazine.

23 'Nigeria Islamists claim suicide bombing', Agence France-Presse, 17 June 2011.

24 Salkida, 'Story'.

25 Quotations from a Nigerian Presidency press release, 20 June 2011.

26 Aminu Abubakar, 'Police kill "would-be suicide bomber" in Maiduguri', Agence France-Presse via *Vanguard* (Nigeria), 15 August 2011.

27 Joe Brock, 'Special report: Boko Haram – between rebellion and jihad', Reuters, 31 January 2012.

28 'Mamman Nur: "mastermind" of UN attack in Nigeria', Agence France-Presse, 31 August 2011; Jacob Zenn, 'Leadership Analysis of Boko Haram and Ansaru in Nigeria', *CTC Sentinel* (US), February 2014.

29 Nigerian Department of State Services press release, 31 August 2011.

30 Translated from Hausa to English by my AFP colleague Aminu Abubakar, who obtained the video through sources. Some of the quotations were included in our story from 18 September 2011 (Aminu Abubakar and M.J. Smith, 'Nigerian "bomber" videos emerge as Islamist fears mount', Agence France-Presse, 18 September 2011).

4   'THAT IS HOW COMPLEX THE SITUATION IS'

1 Ola Awoniyi, 'Bomb at Nigerian church sparks dying pleas for blessings', Agence France-Presse, 25 December 2011.

2 'Jonathan visits Madalla, says "cancerous" Boko Haram wants to kill Nigeria', Agence France-Presse via *Vanguard*, 31 December 2011, http://www.vanguardngr. com/2011/12/cancerous-islamist-sect-wants-to-kill-nigeria-jonathan/#sthash. J7QK8jMK.dpuf.

3 Ola Awoniyi, 'Nigeria declares state of emergency', Agence France-Presse, 31 December 2011.

4 These quotations were reported to me by a journalist who covered Jonathan's speech for my news agency. Some of the quotes were used in our story (Wole Oyetunji, 'Nigeria unrest "worse than 1960s civil war": president', Agence France-Presse, 8 January 2012). Used here with his permission.

5 'We are open to dialogue with Boko Haram – Kwankwaso', Agence France-Presse via *Vanguard*, 27 January 2012, http://www.vanguardngr.com/2012/01/we-are-open-to-dialogue-with-boko-haram-kwankwaso/#sthash.lKfbWEpD.dpuf.

6 Press briefing by Idris after the attacks, which I attended.

7 Aminu Abubakar, '"At least 80 bodies in morgue" after Nigeria attacks', Agence France-Presse, 21 January 2012.

8 Translation from Hausa to English by Aminu Abubakar.

9 Aminu Abubakar, 'German hostage killed in Nigeria during rescue bid', Agence France-Presse, 31 May 2012.

10 This is taken from my own reporting in Sokoto the day after the raid.

11 The phrase could also be translated as 'Support Group for Muslims in Black Africa', according to Professor M.A.S. Abdel Haleem of SOAS, University of London.

12 Sources who closely follow the group mentioned some of this to me, but also see: 'Kambar, Barnawi: Qaeda-linked militants with Boko Haram ties', Agence France-Presse, 21 June 2012 and Jacob Zenn, 'Leadership analysis of Boko Haram and Ansaru in Nigeria', *CTC Sentinel*, February 2014.

13 According to the Nigerian military, Kambar was killed in March 2012, even before the USA designated him a global terrorist. The US government has never confirmed this.

14 'Video shows British, Italian hostages "held by Al-Qaeda"', Agence France-Presse, 3 August 2011; 'British, Italian hostages killed amid Nigerian rescue bid', Agence France-Presse, 8 March 2012.

15 House of Commons Official Report, Parliament Debates (Hansard), 13 March 2012, p. 142.

16 Press release from Nigeria's Department of State Services, 14 March 2012.

17 'SSS detains 5 with "Al Qaeda-links" over German kidnap', Agence France-Presse via *Vanguard* (Nigeria), http://www.vanguardngr.com/2012/03/sss-detains-5-with-al-qaeda-links-over-german-kidnap/#sthash.jVLHl2a3.dpuf.

18 Robert Winnett and Thomas Harding, 'British hostage killed in failed SBS rescue bid', *Telegraph* (UK), 8 March 2012.

19 Press release from DSS.

20 House of Commons, p. 142, and 'Chris McManus killed by kidnappers minutes after rescue mission began', Press Association via *Guardian* (UK), 17 May 2013.

21 Press Association, 'McManus'.

22 House of Commons, p. 142.

23 Aminu Abubakar, 'Nigeria grills kidnappers of slain European hostages', Agence France-Presse, 10 March 2012.

24 For a detailed look at European governments paying ransoms, see: Rukmini Callimachi, 'Paying ransoms, Europe bankrolls Qaeda terror', *New York Times*, 29 July 2014.

25 UK Foreign & Commonwealth Office, Nigeria Travel Advice, https://www.gov.uk/foreign-travel-advice/nigeria/terrorism.

26 DSS press release.

27 Amnesty International, 'Nigeria: trapped in the cycle of violence', November 2012.

28 Aminu Abubakar, 'Islamists claim attack that killed 2 Mali-bound Nigerian troops', Agence France-Presse, 20 January 2013.

29 Aminu Abubakar, 'Ansaru claims kidnap of 7 foreigners in Nigeria', Agence France-Presse, 18 February 2013.

30 SITE Intelligence Group, 'Ansar al-Muslimeen announces execution of foreign hostages', 9 March 2013.

31 Robert Booth, 'William Hague says British hostage "likely to have been killed" in Nigeria', *Guardian* (UK), 10 March 2013.

32 Aminu Abubakar, 'Boko Haram video of kidnapped French family emerges', Agence France-Presse, 21 March 2013.

33 'Otages au Cameroun: l'hypothèse d'une rançon se confirme', iTele, 25 April 2013, http://www.itele.fr/monde/video/otages-au-cameroun-lhypothese-dune-rancon-se-confirme-46925.

34 Tim Cocks, 'Nigerian Islamists got $3.15 million to free French hostages: document', Reuters, 26 April 2013.

35 Video special effects or trickery cannot be ruled out with this footage and others, but the beheading certainly looked gruesomely real.

36 Aminu Abubakar, 'Gunmen kill 10 in attacks on Nigeria polio clinics', Agence France-Presse via dawn.com, 9 February 2013.

37 Those quoted provided me with their names and agreed that I could use them, but I have withheld them out of fears for their safety.

38 Human Rights Watch, 'Spiraling violence: Boko Haram attacks and security force abuses in Nigeria', October 2012.

39 Amnesty, 'Trapped'.

40 National Human Rights Commission, 'The Baga Incident and the Situation in North-East Nigeria: An Interim Assessment and Report', Abuja, June 2013.

41 Human Rights Watch, 'Violence', p. 58.

42 Human Rights Watch, 'Violence', p. 72.

43 National Human Rights Commission, 'Baga', pp. 18–19.

44 Aminu Abubakar, 'Nigeria fishing town paralysed by fear after slaughter', Agence France-Presse, 1 May 2013.

45 Abubakar, 'Nigeria fishing town'.

46 Human Rights Watch, 'Nigeria: Massive Destruction, Deaths from Military Raid', 1 May 2013.

47 National Human Rights Commission, 'Baga', p. 19.

5 'I DON'T KNOW. THEY'RE IN THE BUSH'

1 'Channels TV visits liberated Boko Haram's camp in Borno', Channels Television, 7 June 2013, http://www.channelstv.com/home/2013/06/07/channels-tv-visits-liberated-boko-harams-camp-in-borno/.

2 Olukolade was later promoted to major-general.

3 Hamza Idris, 'Who are Borno's "Civilian JTF"?', *Weekly Trust*, 29 March 2014; Heather Murdock, 'Civilian security on front lines to fight Nigeria's Boko Haram', Voice of America, 9 December 2013.

4 M.J. Smith, 'Nigeria insurgents targeting schools for mayhem', Agence France-Presse, 8 July 2013.

5 Smith, 'Insurgents'.

6 Aminu Abubakar, 'Nigeria mosque attack raises questions over army offensive', Agence France-Presse, 13 August 2013.

7 'Death toll in northeast Nigeria attack "at least 142"', Agence France-Presse, 22 September 2013; 'Nigeria reinforces town after Boko Haram massacre', Agence France-Presse, 20 September 2013; 'Nigeria: Boko Haram Abducts Women, Recruits Children', Human Rights Watch, 29 November 2013.

8 Adam Nossiter, 'Bodies pour in as Nigeria hunts for Islamists', *New York Times*, 7 May 2013.

9 I later sought to contact the commissioner, who sent me a message saying I should call the hospital's chief medical director and provided me with a number. No one answered and I received no response to a text message sent to it. This was, of course, after mobile phone service was reconnected in Maiduguri.

10 Amnesty International, 'Nigeria: war crimes and crimes against humanity as violence escalates in north-east', 31 March 2014.

6 'OUR GIRLS WERE KIDNAPPED AND THEY DID NOT DO ANYTHING'

1 He said he was appointed as a 'peace ambassador'. He has never worked as a Nigerian ambassador in another country.

2 When I asked him in a later phone call what exactly his 'security' role was, he told me that he was in fact working for an NGO that aims to bring together the country's north and south.

3 I should stress that I have not visited Chibok myself and have relied on interviews with residents and others, as well as a history of the Chibok people written by Gerald Neher, the missionary I quote who lived there in the 1950s and 1960s. I sought to visit Chibok when I returned to Nigeria in late May and early June 2014 after the attack on the town, but decided against travelling by road because of security concerns.

4 Church of the Brethren's website: http://www.brethren.org/partners/nigeria/history/.

5 Nigeria's official 2006 census put the population at more than 66,000.

6 'Boko Haram: Borno schools closed indefinitely', 22 March 2014, Agence France-Presse via Nigeria's *Vanguard* newspaper.

7 'National Literacy Action Plan for 2012–2015', High-Level International Round Table on Literacy, UNESCO, Paris, 6–7 September 2012 (http://www.unesco.org/new/fileadmin/MULTIMEDIA/HQ/ED/pdf/Nigeria.pdf).

8 'Nigerian authorities failed to act on warnings about Boko Haram raid on school', Amnesty International, 9 May 2014; a school official in an interview with me estimated there had been about 15 soldiers, though he admitted he was not sure.

9 Talatu Usman, 'How Borno Governor caused kidnap of Chibok schoolgirls – WAEC', *Premium Times*, 3 May 2014.

10 Footage from Channels TV interview with Jidda can be found on YouTube in several parts. The first is: https://www.youtube.com/watch?v=YGmzexqk8xs. Links are provided in the video window for each subsequent part.

11 The principal told me that she never said she was there on the night of the kidnappings and that she was misquoted if reports said otherwise.

12 Joe Brock, 'Boko Haram, taking to hills, seize slave "brides"', Reuters, 13 November 2013; and Human Rights Watch, 'Nigeria: Boko Haram abducts women, recruits children', 29 November 2013.

13 A Nigerian security source spoke to me about this on condition of anonymity in October 2013.

14 Aminu Abubakar, 'Boko Haram leader claims Nigeria capital bombing in new video', Agence France-Presse, 19 April 2014.

15 'Nigerian authorities failed to act'.

16 Adam Nossiter, 'Tales of escapees in Nigeria add to worries about other kidnapped girls', *New York Times*, 14 May 2014.

17 Nossiter, 'Tales of escapees'.

18 Details on the forest come mainly from two papers: P. Omondi, R. Mayienda, J.S. Mamza and M.S. Massalatchi, 'Total Aerial Count of Elephants and other Wildlife Species in Sambisa Game Reserve in Borno State, Nigeria', Convention on International Trade in Endangered Species of Wild Fauna and Flora, July 2006 (available at http://www.cites.org/common/prog/mike/survey/0607_FW_AT_Survey_Sambisa_big.pdf); Y.P. Mbaya, and H. Malgwi, 'Species List and Status of Mammals and Birds in Sambisa Game Reserve, Borno State, Nigeria', *Journal of Research in Forestry, Wildlife and Environment*, 2(1) (March 2010), pp. 135–40.

19 The father I spoke with was only aware of two, but there have been reports of others.

20 These numbers were as of 26 July 2014.

21 '#BBCtrending: The creator of #BringBackOurGirls', BBC, 7 May 2014, http://www.bbc.com/news/blogs-trending-27315124.

22 Video from the meeting can be found at: https://www.youtube.com/watch?v=oMwIkuoAMj0.

23 'Nigeria arrests woman protesting for schoolgirls' release: activist', Agence France-Presse, 5 May 2014. Other reports said two people were arrested.

24 The man in the video resembled past images identified as being of Shekau and appeared to be authentic, but it is impossible to know for certain whether it was him, as with all such videos.

25 Translation by Aminu Abubakar, who was also the first journalist for a foreign news organisation (AFP) to obtain the video. The full video can be found at: https://www.youtube.com/watch?v=wrfWS_vL0D4.

26 Josh Rogin, 'McCain: send U.S. special forces to rescue Nigerian girls', The Daily Beast, 13 May 2014, http://www.thedailybeast.com/articles/2014/05/13/mccain-send-u-s-special-forces-to-rescue-nigerian-girls.html.

27 Tolu Ogunlesi, 'Opinion: Nigerians right to be wary of U.S. intentions', 13 May 2014, CNN Opinion, http://www.cnn.com/2014/05/13/opinion/nigeria-us-military-ogunlesi/.

28 The Joint Task Force (JTF) was later replaced by the 7th Division of the Nigerian military.

29 Video of Friend's testimony can be found at: http://www.foreign.senate.gov/hearings/bringbackourgirls-addressing-the-threat-of-boko-haram/051514.

30 US Defence Department press release, http://www.defense.gov/news/newsarticle.aspx?id=122310.

31 The US Department of Defense did not respond to my requests for comment.

32 Dan Williams and Tim Cocks, 'Nigeria's neglected Israeli drones won't help find girls', Reuters, 20 May 2014.

33 The video was first obtained by Aminu Abubakar of AFP news agency (Agence France-Presse, 'New Boko Haram video claims to show missing Nigerian schoolgirls', 12 May 2014). The full video is also available at: http://saharareporters.com/videos/full-video-boko-haram-video-showing-kidnapped-school-girls.

34 Translation provided by Aminu Abubakar.

35 Adam Nossiter, 'Small comfort as parents identify kidnapped Nigerian girls on video', *New York Times*, 13 May 2013.

36 Video footage of Jonathan's comments is available on the BBC's website: http://www.bbc.com/news/world-africa-27451966.

37 'Fake #BringBackOurGirls protesters surface in Abuja', Sahara Reporters, 26 May 2014, http://saharareporters.com/2014/05/26/photonews-fake-bringbackourgirls-protesters-surface-abuja.

38 Video of Badeh's comments is available online, including at: https://www.youtube.com/watch?v=Ooss0CEGtic and http://www.cbsnews.com/news/nigeria-defense-chief-we-know-where-the-girls-are/.

39 Jonathan Miller, 'Freeing Nigerian schoolgirls now "a very messy affair"', Channel 4 News, 2 June 2014, http://www.channel4.com/news/nigerian-schoolgirls-kidnapped-release-freeing-messy-affair; Miles Amoore and Dipesh Gadher, 'Welby aide in talks to free Nigerian girls', *Sunday Times*, 1 June 2014; Sarah Dean, Emily Crane, and Barbara Jones, '"We must not endanger their lives any further", says Australian man desperately trying to free Nigerian schoolgirls kidnapped by Boko Haram', *Daily Mail*, 1 June 2014; Patrick Begley, 'How amateur peacemaker Stephen Davis rescued kidnapped girls from Boko Haram', *Sydney Morning Herald*, 29 August 2014.

40 Jibrin Ibrahim, 'Rent a crowd and miss the message', 27 May 2014, originally published by Sahara Reporters, but no longer accessible there. It can still be found on other websites, including at: http://elotitv.com/entry/rent-a-crowd-and-miss-the-message-by-jibrin-ibrahim.

41 According to some accounts, the rumour began thanks to a US National Intelligence Council discussion paper that looked at possible scenarios in sub-Saharan Africa. For an overview of the issue, see: John Campbell, 'U.S. government never predicted Nigeria break up in 2015', Council on Foreign Relations Africa in Transition blog, 16 May 2012, http://blogs.cfr.org/campbell/2012/05/16/u-s-government-never-predicted-nigeria-break-up-in-2015/.

EPILOGUE

1 Shehu Abubakar, 'N16bn maritime security deal raises questions', *Sunday Trust*, 13 May 2012; Jon Gambrell, 'Nigeria ex-militant linked to bid', Associated Press, 29 March 2012.

2 Estelle Shirbon, 'UK court sees jailed Nigerian ex-governor's opulent palace', Reuters, 18 September 2013.

3 'Nigeria: UK conviction a blow against corruption', Human Rights Watch, 17 April 2012.

4 His son Rawlings later told me that he indeed had only one son, but had cared for other children who were not biologically his.

SELECT BIBLIOGRAPHY

BOOKS

Abdel Haleem, M.A.S., *The Qur'an: A New Translation* (Oxford, 2010)

Achebe, Chinua, *The Trouble with Nigeria* (Essex, 1984)

Adichie, Chimamanda Ngozi, *Half of a Yellow Sun* (New York, 2006)

Backwell, H.F., *The Occupation of Hausaland: 1900–1904* (Lagos, 1927)

Bello, Sir Ahmadu, *My Life* (Cambridge, 1962)

Crowder, Michael, *The Story of Nigeria* (London, 1978)

Cunliffe-Jones, Peter, *My Nigeria: Five Decades of Independence* (New York, 2010)

Falola, Toyin and Heaton, Matthew M., *A History of Nigeria* (Cambridge, 2009)

Hiskett, Mervyn, *The Development of Islam in West Africa* (New York, 1984)

——*The Sword of Truth* (Evanston, 1994)

Hogben, S.J., *An Introduction to the History of the Islamic States of Northern Nigeria* (Ibadan, 1967)

Last, Murray, *The Sokoto Caliphate* (Bristol, 1967)

Lugard, Sir F.D., *The Dual Mandate in British Tropical Africa* (Edinburgh and London, 1922)

Maier, Karl, *This House Has Fallen: Nigeria in Crisis* (London, 2000)

Muffett, D.J.M., *Concerning Brave Captains* (London, 1964)

Muhammad, Abdullah Ibn, *Tazyin Al-Waraqat*, trans. Mervyn Hiskett (Ibadan, 1963)

Neher, Gerald A. with Neher, Lois R., *Life Among the Chibok of Nigeria* (Kansas, 2011)

Perham, Margery, *Lugard: The Years of Authority 1898–1945* (London, 1961)

Pieth, M. (ed.), *Recovering Stolen Assets* (Berne, 2008)

Soyinka, Wole, *You Must Set Forth at Dawn* (New York, 2006)

Umar, Muhammad S., *Islam and Colonialism: Intellectual Responses of Muslims of Northern Nigeria to British Colonial Rule* (Leiden, 2006)

JOURNALS

Anonymous, 'The Popular Discourses of Salafi Radicalism and Salafi Counter-radicalism in Nigeria: A Case Study of Boko Haram', *Journal of Religion in Africa*, 42(2) (2012), pp. 118–144

Higazi, Adam, 'The Origins and Transformation of the Boko Haram Insurgency in Northern Nigeria'. Published in French translation as 'Les origines et la

transformation de l'insurrection de Boko Haram dans le nord du Nigeria',
Politique Africaine, 130 (2013), pp. 137–64

Hiskett, Mervyn, 'The Maitatsine Riots in Kano, 1980: An Assessment', *Journal of Religion in Africa*, 17(3) (1987), pp. 209–33

Isichei, Elizabeth, 'The Maitatsine Risings in Nigeria 1980–85: A Revolt of the Disinherited', *Journal of Religion in Africa*, 17(3) (1987), pp. 194–208

Last, Murray, 'Contradictions in Creating a Jihadi Capital: Sokoto in the Nineteenth Century and Its Legacy', *African Studies Review*, 56(2) (September 2013), pp. 1–20

Loimeier, Roman, 'Boko Haram: The Development of a Militant Religious Movement in Nigeria', *Africa Spectrum*, 47(2–3) (2012), pp. 137–55

Umar, Muhammad S., 'Education and Islamic Trends in Northern Nigeria: 1970s–1990s', *Africa Today*, 48(2) (Summer 2001), pp. 127–50

MISCELLANEOUS

Amnesty International, 'Nigeria: trapped in the cycle of violence', November 2012

Colonial Reports – Annual, N. Nigeria, 1900–11 (London, HMSO)

Human Rights Watch, 'Spiraling violence: Boko Haram attacks and security force abuses in Nigeria', October 2012

Mustapha, Abdul Raufu, 'Ethnic Structure, Inequality and Governance of the Public Sector in Nigeria', Democracy, Governance and Human Rights Programme, Paper No. 24, November 2006, United Nations Research Institute for Social Development

Papers of Baron Lugard of Abinger, 1858–1945, Bodleian Library of Commonwealth and African Studies, Oxford

Perouse de Montclos, Marc-Antoine, 'Nigeria's Interminable Insurgency? Addressing the Boko Haram Crisis', Chatham House Research Paper, September 2014

INDEX